M000236478

The Liability Maze

The Liability Maze

The Impact of Liability Law
on Safety and Innovation

Peter W. Huber and
Robert E. Litan

editors

The Brookings Institution
Washington, D.C.

Copyright © 1991 by
THE BROOKINGS INSTITUTION
1775 Massachusetts Avenue, N.W., Washington, D.C. 20036

Library of Congress Cataloging-in-Publication data:

The liability maze: the impact of liability law on safety and
innovation / Peter W. Huber and Robert E. Litan, eds.
  p.   cm
  Includes bibliographical references and index.
  ISBN 0-8157-3760-2 (cloth)—ISBN 0-8157-3761-0
  (paper)
  1. Liability (Law)—Economic aspects—United States.
  2. Products liability—Economic aspects—United States.
  3. Tort liability of corporations—United States. 4. New
  products—United States. 5. Product safety—United States.
  6. Technological innovations—United States. I. Huber,
  Peter W. (Peter William), 1952– . II. Litan, Robert E.,
  1950– .
  KF1251.C64   1991
  346.7303′8—dc20
  [347.30638]   91-9387
                                                       CIP

9 8 7 6 5 4 3 2 1

The paper used in this publication meets the minimum
requirements of the American National Standard for
Information Sciences—Permanence of paper for Printed
Library Materials, ANSI Z39.48-1984.

₿ THE BROOKINGS INSTITUTION

The Brookings Institution is an independent organization devoted to nonpartisan research, education, and publication in economics, government, foreign policy, and the social sciences generally. Its principal purposes are to aid in the development of sound public policies and to promote public understanding of issues of national importance.

The Institution was founded on December 8, 1927, to merge the activities of the Institute for Government Research, founded in 1916, the Institute of Economics, founded in 1922, and the Robert Brookings Graduate School of Economics and Government, founded in 1924.

The Board of Trustees is responsible for the general administration of the Institution, while the immediate direction of the policies, program, and staff is vested in the President, assisted by an advisory committee of the officers and staff. The by-laws of the Institution state: ''It is the function of the Trustees to make possible the conduct of scientific research, and publication, under the most favorable conditions, and to safeguard the independence of the research staff in the pursuit of their studies and in the publication of the results of such studies. It is not a part of their function to determine, control, or influence the conduct of particular investigations or the conclusions reached.''

The President bears final responsibility for the decision to publish a manuscript as a Brookings book. In reaching his judgment on the competence, accuracy, and objectivity of each study, the President is advised by the director of the appropriate research program and weighs the views of a panel of expert outside readers who report to him in confidence on the quality of the work. Publication of a work signifies that it is deemed a competent treatment worthy of public consideration but does not imply endorsement of conclusions or recommendations.

The Institution maintains its position of neutrality on issues of public policy in order to safeguard the intellectual freedom of the staff. Hence interpretations or conclusions in Brookings publications should be understood to be solely those of the authors and should not be attributed to the Institution, to its trustees, officers, or other staff members, or to the organizations that support its research.

Board of Trustees

Louis W. Cabot
Chairman

Ralph S. Saul
Vice Chairman

Ronald J. Arnault
Elizabeth E. Bailey
Rex J. Bates
Yvonne Brathwaite Burke
A. W. Clausen
William T. Coleman, Jr.
Kenneth W. Dam

D. Ronald Daniel
Charles W. Duncan, Jr.
Walter Y. Elisha
Robert F. Erburu
Stephen Friedman
Robert D. Haas
Pamela C. Harriman
Vernon E. Jordan, Jr.
James A. Joseph
Nannerl O. Keohane
Martin J. Koldyke
Thomas G. Labrecque
Donald F. McHenry

Bruce K. MacLaury
Samuel Pisar
James D. Robinson III
David Rockefeller, Jr.
Howard D. Samuel
B. Francis Saul II
Henry B. Schacht
Donna E. Shalala
Robert H. Smith
Howard R. Swearer
Morris Tanenbaum
John C. Whitehead
Ezra K. Zilkha

Honorary Trustees

Vincent M. Barnett, Jr.
Barton M. Biggs
Robert D. Calkins
Edward W. Carter
Frank T. Cary
Lloyd N. Cutler
Bruce B. Dayton
Douglas Dillon
Huntington Harris

Andrew Heiskell
Roger W. Heyns
John E. Lockwood
James T. Lynn
William McC. Martin, Jr.
Robert S. McNamara
Mary Patterson McPherson
Arjay Miller

Donald S. Perkins
J. Woodward Redmond
Charles W. Robinson
Robert V. Roosa
Gerard C. Smith
Robert Brookings Smith
Sydney Stein, Jr.
Phyllis A. Wallace
James D. Wolfensohn

Foreword

Aʟᴛʜᴏᴜɢʜ the "liability insurance crisis" of the mid-1980s has passed, the debate over the direction and impact of U.S. tort law continues. Critics of current tort law doctrines contend that they have discouraged innovation and thereby contributed to the slowdown of U.S. productivity growth. Defenders of the liability system disagree, responding that tort law has enhanced the safety of products sold and services delivered to consumers.

To date, little empirical research has been conducted to sort out these conflicting claims. The stakes are important. More than $100 billion a year is channeled through the U.S. tort system from manufacturers and service providers to lawyers and claimants.

In this book Peter W. Huber and Robert E. Litan, joined by a team of scientists, engineers, physicians, and attorneys, provide the first comprehensive look at the impacts of U.S. liability law on safety and innovation. The authors focus on five key sectors of the economy where liability appears to have had the greatest effects: the automobile, chemical, general aviation, and pharmaceutical industries and the delivery of medical services.

They find that the impact of liability trends has been highly uneven across those sectors. In some, such as general aviation, liability trends seem to have had devastating effects on innovation. In others, such as chemicals, tort litigation seems to have had little influence on innovation, though arguably it may also have failed to provide sufficient incentives for safety. The other sectors fall in the middle, with some examples in which the publicity generated by adverse liability verdicts has enhanced safety by reducing the demand for dangerous products, and other examples in which just the threat of tort litigation may have dampened research and innovation.

Despite the diversity of the findings, the project coeditors suggest that policy conclusions are warranted. Among other things, they point to the need for more certainty in liability doctrines, positive rather than negative incentives in the tort law for private actors to improve safety, and more systematic efforts to weigh the costs and benefits of liability doctrines themselves before they are unleashed on the private sector.

Peter W. Huber is a senior fellow at the Manhattan Institute for Policy Research in New York and counsel to Mayer, Brown & Platt in Washington, D.C. Robert E. Litan is a senior fellow in the Economic Studies program at Brookings, where he is also the director of the Center for Economic Progress and Employment.

The papers in this book were presented in draft form to a conference at the Brookings Institution in June 1990, which was attended by approximately 150 representatives of the corporate, public interest, and legal communities and by staff from the congressional and executive branches of the federal government. The authors of the papers incorporated responses to comments made at this conference where appropriate.

Caroline Lalire and Theresa Walker edited the manuscript, Pamela Plehn and Dawn Senecal verified its factual content, and Susan L. Woollen prepared it for typesetting. Jacquelyn Sanks, Kathleen M. Bucholz, Carolyn J. Hill, Elizabeth E. McKenney, David J. Rossetti, Evelyn M. E. Taylor, Anita G. Whitlock, and Kathleen Elliott Yinug provided valuable secretarial assistance. The index was prepared by Ward and Silvan.

Funding for this project was provided by the A. V. Starr Foundation, the Sloan Foundation, and the Center for Economic Progress and Employment, whose supporters comprise Donald S. Perkins, American Express, AT&T, Chase Manhattan Bank, Cummins Engine, Ford Motor Company, Hewlett-Packard, Morgan Stanley, Motorola, Springs Industries, Union Carbide, Warner-Lambert, Xerox Corporation, Aetna Foundation, Ford Foundation, General Electric Foundation, Prudential Foundation, Sloan Foundation, Smith Richardson Foundation, Institute for International Economics, and Alex C. Walker Education and Charitable Trust.

The views expressed here are those of the authors and should not be attributed to the trustees, officers, or staff members of the Brookings Institution.

BRUCE K. MACLAURY
President

April 1991
Washington, D.C.

Contents

Figures

Contributors

NICHOLAS A. ASHFORD
*Massachusetts Institute of
Technology*

RANDALL R. BOVBJERG
Urban Institute

ANDREW CRAIG
Wichita State University

ROBERT W. CRANDALL
Brookings Institution

HENRY GRABOWSKI
Duke University

JOHN D. GRAHAM
Harvard University

PETER W. HUBER
*Manhattan Institute for Policy
Research*

ROLLIN B. JOHNSON
Harvard University

LOUIS LASAGNA
Tufts University

ROBERT E. LITAN
Brookings Institution

MURRAY MACKAY
University of Birmingham, U.K.

ROBERT MARTIN
*Martin, Pringle, Oliver, Wallace
& Schwartz*

MICHAEL J. MOORE
Duke University

DOROTHY NELKIN
New York University

STANLEY JOEL REISER
University of Texas

GARY T. SCHWARTZ
UCLA School of Law

ROBERT F. STONE
*Massachusetts Institute of
Technology*

JUDITH P. SWAZEY
Acadia Institute

LAURENCE TANCREDI
University of Texas

W. KIP VISCUSI
Duke University

JOHN W. WILLIAMS, JR.
*Embry-Riddle Aeronautical
University*

CHAPTER ONE

Overview

Peter W. Huber and Robert E. Litan

WE KNOW much more about how the liability system works than about what it achieves. The legal rules can be described with some precision and the lawsuits they decide can be counted with reasonable accuracy. The financial value of the much larger number of settlements that are never put to judge or jury can also be estimated, though less precisely, by reference to insurance company data on claims settlements. Even some ancillary social costs, such as those entailed by litigants themselves in pursuing lawsuits or those entailed by society at large in operating the court system, have been estimated with some measure of confidence.

But in the legal system the ease with which variables can be measured or described seems to vary inversely with their social importance. Narrow legal rules can be described easily and accurately, but in themselves they tell us little about the social consequences of the legal system. Cases that go to trial can be counted, and jury verdicts can be tabulated; however, most cases are settled, and the settlements, which are much more difficult to monitor and aggregate than verdicts, are far more numerous and consequential overall. The larger social impact of the law is found far downstream from the case report or the legal treatise, precisely where the effects of the law are most difficult to measure.

In recent decades it has been widely assumed that liability rules promote safety. The logic is straightforward. Accurately targeted liability law that imposes properly calibrated costs will raise the price of negligence, product defects, and accident to efficient levels, and thus reduce their frequency from levels that would otherwise be inefficiently high. Such reasoning has been embraced by many modern legal academics and is frequently invoked to justify expanded liability principles, especially so-called strict liability under which defendants can be held liable even without proof of their negligence.[1]

More recently, others—including one of the editors of this volume—have suggested that the broad and unpredictable sweep of U.S. liability law deters innovation.[2] The logic here has been equally straightforward: when the legal costs of certain kinds of accidents are prohibitively high and unpredictable, entire sectors of enterprise shut down. Liability law will not promote anything systematically if it is imposed capriciously, if it imposes costs on superior options, or if it assesses damages that swing wildly. Such reasoning has been invoked more often in recent years to justify legislative or common law limits on liability.

Given the ubiquity and scope of the U.S. liability system, it is surprising that there is little empirical research to back up either assertion. Whichever side of this debate one is inclined to favor, the debate is surely important. The U.S. liability system is clearly a major force in the ordering of our affairs. A 1989 study by Tillinghast, a leading insurance industry consulting firm, estimates gross U.S. liability expenditures at $117 billion in 1987.

Of course, these gross figures do not represent *net* costs; some fraction of tort expenditures are returned to consumers. And insofar as the liability system does have positive effects on safety, it yields some offsetting benefits. Defenders of the current liability system may even argue that the safety benefits more than outweigh any gross costs, suggesting that the system yields net social benefits rather than costs. Some may also argue that liability awards contribute to a more just distribution of income or wealth.

Regardless of its net overall effects, the tort system may still be inefficient. Different studies have shown that roughly half of total awards and settlements are paid to attorneys and insurers for administering the claims settlement process.[3] In contrast, according to the Tillinghast study, transaction costs consume 30 percent of the costs of the workers' compensation system, 15 percent of health insurance, and just 1 percent of the social security system.[4] The differential in costs between the tort system, which has both deterrence and compensation functions, and these latter programs, which are devoted only to compensation, provides a

1. Calabresi 1970; Posner 1972, 69–97.
2. Huber 1989.
3. Kakalik and Pace 1986; Schotter and Ordover 1986.
4. Tillinghast 1989, 16.

rough measure of the proportional cost of deterrence: anywhere between 20 and 50 percent of the average claim dollar.

Whether or not this money is well spent, by most accounts the gross costs of the U.S. tort system have been rising steadily. The Tillinghast study reports that U.S. tort costs "are escalating at a pace far faster than in any other modern, competitive economy."[5] One recent, widely publicized study suggests that the legal winds have recently begun to shift in favor of defendants.[6] But another analysis of the same data reaches diametrically opposite conclusions.[7] In any event, regardless of the trends in tort verdicts, most studies in this area have concluded that, after adjusting for inflation and population, liability costs have risen sharply in the last thirty years, and most especially in the last decade.[8]

Any effects the liability system may have on safety or innovation should have been growing more apparent as the scope of liability doctrines has expanded, the number of suits has increased, and the average size of awards has escalated. The analytical task, however, is not so straightforward. As we discuss later, an array of forces independent of the liability system exert constant pressure for improvements in both safety and innovation. Distenglanging the effects of liability from these other effects is fraught with complications. Nonetheless, the size, pervasiveness, and economic importance of the U.S. liability system require that some attempt be made to gauge its practical impact, particularly since the expansion of that system has been justified in large part on the assumption that the net effect would be beneficial.

This book represents such an effort. It brings together the views of a broad panel of experts on five sectors of the economy where the liability system seems to have had the greatest effects, whether positive or negative: the private aircraft, automobile, chemical, and pharmaceutical industries, and the medical profession. Ten chapters deal with those sectors; they appear in pairs. One author of each pair was invited to look primarily at the safety effects of liability, the other primarily at the innovation effects, but both were free to pursue their inquiry wherever it might lead. As an introduction to those sector-specific papers, two chapters provide important overview material. Gary Schwartz examines the key legal developments that have contributed to the differences between the U.S. liability

5. Tillinghast 1989, 12.
6. Henderson and Eisenberg 1990.
7. Havenner 1990.
8. See, for example, U.S. Department of Justice 1986; Priest 1987; and Peterson 1987.

system and tort law in Western Europe and Japan. Michael Moore and Kip Viscusi provide data to help assess the impact of liability costs on innovation in a broad array of U.S. industries.

We recognize that in certain respects the safety-innovation dichotomy that lies at the heart of the organization of this book may be oversimplified. In some cases, it is conceivable that the liability system can encourage both safety *and* innovation. Indeed, Nicholas Ashford and Robert Stone argue that this can and should be the case for the chemical industry. Other authors, however, present evidence for the contrary proposition: that liability has both detracted from safety and discouraged innovation.

The sector-specific analyses presented here, in the aggregate, constitute what we believe is the most detailed, yet comprehensive, study to date of the actual impact of U.S. liability law. The authors of these chapters were selected according to a few simple and, in our view, even-handed criteria. We looked, of course, for authors knowledgeable about particular industries. We sought (though not always successfully) to select non-lawyers who were nevertheless capable of assessing the effects of legal developments on these sectors. The authors gathered raw material for their inquiries from interviews (mostly confidential), searches of the preexisting legal and technical literature, and, when possible, comparative analyses of safety and innovation trends in countries with different liability systems. The authors presented their preliminary findings at a conference held at Brookings in June 1990, attended by approximately 150 representatives from the private and public sectors knowledgeable about the U.S. liability system and the specific industries studied. The authors have incorporated suggestions and responded to comments advanced at that conference.

Unsurprisingly, given the differences between the sectors examined and the number of authors involved in the project, the chapters do not converge on any single, solid consensus about the total impact of the U.S. tort system on American living standards. Instead, the chapters highlight the dangers of generalizing in this area. The effects of liability on both safety and innovation seem to vary greatly among different parts of the U.S. economy and society. Where the dollar costs of liability have been the largest, so too, apparently, have been the effects. The challenge for future researchers will be both to deepen the analysis of the impact of liability in the sectors analyzed here and to extend that analysis more broadly throughout the U.S. economy.

Still, in our view, the evidence offered here justifies several changes in tort doctrine designed to make the law more predictable and less inhospitable to efforts by firms and individuals to innovate and enhance safety. We discuss these suggestions in more detail later.

What Was Known Before

The current literature addressing the broader social impacts of the liability system is abundant, but mostly theoretical and speculative. The best-known writings that deal with the effect of that system on safety chronicle various mass disasters, or the mass exposures to certain substances or products, and their legal aftermath: Agent Orange, the Dalkon Shield, and asbestos being the most prominent.[9] There are, of course, many other accounts of unsafe products or practices that have been attacked, successfully or otherwise, in court. Those accounts, however, are not always careful about documenting whether liability really did precede the remedial measures it is said to have precipitated, or alternatively whether these remedial measures in fact corrected real problems. Similarly, while Eads and Reuter find from their interviews of corporate managers that product liability exerts a strong "pro-safety" effect on product design, they also confess that current liability law sends an "extremely vague signal," since it does not indicate "*how* to be careful, or more important, *how* careful to be."[10]

In perhaps the only statistical analysis of the safety side of this debate, George Priest has found little evidence that liability expansion has enhanced safety.[11] His analysis shows that though the annual numbers of tort suits and liability insurance premiums rose sharply during the 1980s, injury rates for consumers and workers, death rates from medical procedures, and aviation accident rates declined no faster than they had been declining in the 1970s, when premium costs and the volume of tort suits were much lower. In addition, Priest points out, in areas of product liability, general aviation, and medical malpractice, accident rates have been declining steadily over exactly the same period during which claims and claims dollars have been increasing sharply; if courts had been attaching liability on grounds of accident prevention, then claims and claims payouts would have mirrored the accident rate.[12] Elsewhere, Priest has

9. See Schuck 1987 for a history of the litigation over Agent Orange; Brodeur 1985 for a history of the asbestos litigation and controversy.
10. Eads and Reuter 1983, ix.
11. Priest 1988; 1989b.
12. Priest 1989b, 187–94.

argued that "data on deaths and injuries cast great doubt on the proposition that the liability crisis derives from an increase in underlying accident rates."[13] He concludes that "the achievement of the risk control objectives of our modern legal system is more difficult than has been imagined. . . . There is little chance that our judges will retreat from the objective of risk control but substantial need for them to learn how better to achieve it."[14] Priest's work is obviously exploratory, and he does not pretend to have proved conclusively that tort law does not matter. In particular, his statistical work does not distinguish other factors that might have affected injury and death rates. Perhaps more consumers and workers would have suffered harm had tort suits been less numerous and compensation less generous. But Priest's simple juxtaposition of recent liability and injury trends at least raises serious doubts that the benefits from expanded liability have been large.

Although defenders of recent liability trends dispute the conclusion implied by Priest's work, they might also suggest that too little liability explains the absence of any demonstrable relationship between liability and safety. A recent compilation by Richard Abel, for example, highlights underclaiming for injuries from medical malpractice, occupational causes, and traffic accidents.[15] Abel, as well as Ashford and Stone in this volume (in the context of the chemical industry), argues that underclaiming leads to underdeterrence, which may explain why the safety effects of liability have been as insubstantial as studies like Priest's suggest or why an increase in claims and a simple lag structure could have produced the results Priest observes.

The literature on the innovation side of the debate is more limited still, though evolving. The most comprehensive and perhaps most widely publicized survey was conducted by the Conference Board, a well-known business research organization, which in 1986 asked 500 chief executive officers of large U.S. corporations about the impact of the tort system on their companies.[16] Among other things, the study reported that roughly one-third of all firms surveyed, and nearly half of those claiming "major impacts," had decided against introducing new products because of liability fears. And 58 percent of those who had experienced a major impact from liability had discontinued some of their products for the same reason.

13. Priest 1988, 203.
14. Priest 1990, 226–27.
15. Abel 1987.
16. Weber 1989.

Anecdotes about products said to have been withdrawn from the market because of liability concerns provide a second, though indirect, form of evidence. In this book, for example, Louis Lasagna cites the case of Bendectin (once widely used to alleviate pregnancy-induced nausea among women), while Robert Martin highlights the disappearance of small aircraft. Similar examples are cited in other studies. A study by the American Medical Association (AMA) on the development of new medical technologies found:

Innovative new products are not being developed or are being withheld from the market because of liability concerns or inability to obtain adequate insurance. Certain older technologies have been removed from the market, not because of sound scientific evidence indicating lack of safety or efficacy, but because product liability suits have exposed manufacturers to unacceptable financial risks.[17]

On the specific subject of contraceptives, the AMA notes:

In the early 1970's, there were 13 pharmaceutical companies actively pursuing research in contraception and fertility. Now, only one U.S. company conducts conctraceptive and fertility research. Unless the liability laws are drastically altered, it is very unlikely that pharmaceutical companies will aggressively pursue research in this area.[18]

An expert advisory panel of the Food and Drug Administration (FDA), the American Academy of Pediatrics, and the Institute of Medicine have made similar statements about vaccines.[19] Two other observers claim that "the distortions introduced by 'skyrocketing' punitive damage claims and awards have deprived patients of significant existing therapies and have inhibited research and development concerning new therapies."[20]

Michael Porter recently completed a large study, *The Competitive Advantage of Nations*, based on a survey of more than 100 industries

17. Weaver 1988, 1.
18. Weaver 1988, 9.
19. Advisory Panel on Review of Bacterial Vaccines and Toxoids 1985; Smith 1986, 115; Institute of Medicine 1985, 11.
20. Kuhlik and Kingham 1990, 698. For other studies that have found products or services withdrawn because of liability, see Institute of Medicine 1985 (for vaccines); Djerassi 1989 (contraceptives); Weaver 1988 (medicine); Rostow and Bulger 1989 (obstetrics).

in the major industrial nations. One of his conclusions is specifically addressed to liability. In the United States, Porter states, "product liability is so extreme and uncertain as to retard innovation"; it "places firms in constant jeopardy of costly and, as importantly, lengthy product liability suits." Porter finds the "risk of lawsuits is so great, and the consequences so potentially disastrous, that the inevitable result is for more caution in product innovation than [there is] in other advanced nations."[21] He recommends a systematic overhaul of the U.S. product liability system.[22]

The schismatic character of the current liability debate was sharply displayed by a pair of reports by the Conference Board. The initial study, relying largely on a poll of corporate risk managers, reported that the liability system generally encourages safer practices.[23] As already noted, however, the follow-up study polled the views of top corporate executives in many of the same firms and reported that liability was adversely affecting innovation and the introduction of new products.[24] It is possible, of course, that survey data of this kind reveal nothing but the biases of those surveyed, with risk managers prone to conclude that they are working effectively in response to outside pressures like liability, while corporate executives conclude that those same pressures are harming their businesses.

Both survey and anecdotal evidence are subject to criticism, however. Survey respondents, especially top-level corporate officials, can be quick to blame external forces for problems arising elsewhere. Anecdotes suffer from a similar drawback, since they too usually surface only through corporate complaints. Litan has recently attempted to examine more closely the available statistical data on links between liability and innovation, finding some but by no means conclusive evidence that liability has had negative effects.[25] Viscusi and Moore supply further evidence of the same effects in this book.

Donald Elliott has suggested a useful structure for analyzing how laws that aim to deter may have fundamentally different effects depending on the details of just how the laws operate.[26] Elliott distinguishes between

21. Porter 1990, 649.

22. Other views on the impact of liability law on innovation, emanating from agencies, research organizations, trade associations, academia, and businesses, can be found in the sources cited in a recent, broad-ranging review of the subject by Cortese and Blaner (1990).

23. McGuire 1988.

24. Weber 1989.

25. Litan (forthcoming).

26. Elliott 1989a.

"general" predictability (for example, planes sometimes crash) and "specific" predictability (this flight will go down), a distinction that he believes many discussions of deterrence have ignored. Elliott goes on to develop a point central to the debate in this book: "A person who knows that engaging in a class of activity will increase the risk of an adverse consequence may choose to restrict her participation in the activity, but *how* one conducts the activity is unlikely to be affected unless she also has information bearing on specific predictability."[27]

Thus if tort law is sufficiently (and predictably) specific, one may expect safety benefits without across-the-board industry deterrence. If the law succeeds in deterring only generally, one may expect to see broad declines in levels of investment and innovation in those activities generally deterred. As Elliott goes on to argue:

> If a company is engaged in the pharmaceutical business it can predict generally that it will probably be subjected to some punitive damage awards. It may even be able to predict roughly what the anticipated range of punitive damages awards will be over time. General predictability may lead to restricting participation in the pharmaceutical business (or to raising prices, thereby restricting the level of pharmaceuticals available to customers). In the absence of information about the liability consequences of specific predictability, however, it is unlikely that practices or modes of operation are going to be affected much. . . . Information going to general predictability may deter a general class of activities; only information about the liability consequences of specific practices or modes of engaging in the activity is likely to enhance specific predictability and thereby shape the way that the activity is conducted.[28]

Elliott has his own views about how well the U.S. tort system is currently performing as regards general and specific predictability. He notes that "the empirical support is surprisingly weak for the economic deterrence theory on which so much of the new tort law is predicated; it is hardly the stuff on which one would feel comfortable constructing a multibillion dollar change in public policy in any other area. Currently,

27. Elliott 1989a, 1058.
28. Elliott 1989a, 1058.

the theory that tort law has a significant effect in regulating risk-creating behavior in the intended way is just that: a theory."[29]

Dogs That Don't Bark

The biggest problem in making any empirical assessment of the effects of U.S. liability law lies in the nature of what must be measured. The entire debate—on both sides of the issue—revolves around things that *don't* happen. Many states have faced a similar question in connection with Good Samaritan laws, which limit liability for volunteers, rescuers, and the like. Those who oppose Good Samaritan liability limits point out that there are few cases on record of rescuers being sued. Supporters point out that the paucity of suits may simply reflect a paucity of volunteers and rescuers—the very problem that Good Samaritan laws are intended to redress. As another pair of commentators has noted, "Indirect costs . . . often defy quantification because they . . . are most frequently manifested by the absence of action. Identifying, categorizing and counting the *absence* of action in an objective, statistically valid survey clearly is not feasible using current methodologies."[30] The challenge, in effect, is to count the dogs that don't bark in the night.

On the safety side of the debate, the important question is how many accidents are successfully deterred. The Dalkon Shield, for example, represents a failure of deterrence—the shield was widely marketed despite the liability system in effect at the time, and it was withdrawn from the market long before any serious litigation had materialized. The key question is to what extent the liability example set in the aftermath of that disaster has made for safer contraceptive options in the future. To answer that question, however, one must somehow measure injuries successfully deterred by the prospective threat of liability.

A similar census of things that don't happen is required on the innovation side of the debate. One must somehow find ways to count valuable patents not sought, safe products not marketed, and needed services not supplied out of fear of liability.

Both inquiries are complicated by the fact that the baseline is constantly shifting. Whatever the liability system may achieve, safety is also affected by technological innovation, market demand, and regulatory pressure.

29. Elliott 1989b, 16.
30. Cortese and Blaner 1990, 171.

Technology provides a first strong impetus for both safety improvement and innovation; indeed, innovation and safety are often strongly linked. Aviation technology, for example, improves year by year, and much of the progress simply reflects advances in electronics, guidance systems, composite materials, and airfoil design. Planes that are bigger, faster, more durable, and cheaper to operate have usually proved to be safer as well.

Market demand provides a second impetus for innovation and safety; consumers are by no means oblivious to safety considerations and, other things being equal, will normally favor safer options. Finally, agencies like the FDA, the Environmental Protection Agency, and the National Highway Traffic Safety Administration (NHTSA) screen out some products and practices before they are brought to market, and monitor others thereafter.

In short, many forces independent of liability spur innovation and safety. Isolating the particular and unique effects of liability can therefore be difficult. For example, safety in the United States improved steadily in the first half of this century, when a much more limited liability system was in effect. And safety trends in Europe have usually paralleled those in the United States, though European countries rely less on liability to induce safety than on direct regulation.

The difficulty of discerning the connection between liability and accidents that do not happen, or innovation that does not occur, is compounded by the reticence of those most immediately involved. Providers of goods and services have little incentive to be forthcoming about the issues. Even if liability does encourage safer practices, no obstetrician or car company will wish to spend much time advertising the connection. Nor will providers care to dwell at length on the fact that they no longer sell a life-saving vaccine, or have decided not to market a safe substitute for asbestos. To concede positive safety effects resulting from liability is to invite more liability; to protest adverse effects on innovation is to identify a company with static or obsolete technology.

Finally, the inquiry is further complicated by the difficulty of interpreting trends that can be observed. A decline in the number of general practitioners willing to provide obstetrical services, for example, may reflect a loss of needed, safety-enhancing services. Or it may reflect inevitable and desirable specialization, which centralizes complex services in urban centers where they can be provided by the most experienced practitioners with the best available technology. The collapse of the general aviation industry almost certainly makes life more dangerous for those who continue flying in aging planes, but the overall impact on safety must also take into account those who stop flying altogether.

Findings in This Book

Expressly or by implication, most of the authors in this volume agree that the effects of the liability system, whatever they may be, depend on much more than the narrow question of whether liability is imposed, or on the still narrower question of what legal standard (like "negligence" or "strict liability") is applied. The authors all recognize that jury trials, contingency fees, long-tail liability, the sheer size of awards, and the stigmatizing effect of punitive damages, along with adverse publicity, market forces, and regulation are at least equally important.

Common "Safety" Themes

Most of the authors addressing the safety side of the debate found little direct or statistical evidence that specific liability verdicts have led to the development and introduction of substantially safer products. Judith Swazey's comment is typical: "From the sketchy and insubstantial information that is available, it seems reasonable to conclude that product liability law and litigation have had only a marginal impact on the development of safer drugs . . . as one factor in decisions not to bring new agents to the market or to withdraw marketed drugs." To be sure, several authors, notably John Graham and Swazey, agree that liability has on occasion impelled expansion or modification of warnings. Considerably less clear is whether these changes have had any positive effect on safety.

The dearth of evidence regarding product design does not mean, however, that the authors found that liability has no safety effects. A number concluded that tort verdicts adverse to defendants enhance safety indirectly by reducing the demand for the affected products and services. Many providers are acutely concerned about loss of reputation in the aftermath of widely publicized accidents or product defects. As several of the authors suggest, the publicity often precedes rather than follows the litigation. But tort victories for plaintiffs can help sustain or amplify adverse publicity and its impact on consumer demand.

For example, after reviewing five major safety controversies affecting the automobile industry, Graham concludes that the "indirect effect of liability on consumer demand—operating through adverse publicity about a product's safety and a manufacturer's reputation—is often the most significant contribution of liability to safety." In his study of private aircraft, Andrew Craig likewise concludes that liability may play some useful role in disseminating the results of investigation attendant on a lawsuit "through consumer advocate publications or traditional media."

When the tort system makes mistakes, of course, the publicity it generates can be positively harmful. In his chapter on the medical profession, Stanley Reiser argues that physicians' fear of being *wrongly* attacked in court has adversely affected the delivery of health care by eroding the trust once inherent in the doctor-patient relationship. The spillover of negative publicity from the Dalkon Shield litigation (which unquestionably was directed at an inferior product) all but eliminated intrauterine devices, though many such products remained generally desirable contraceptive options. Similarly, the adverse publicity about childhood vaccines generated through litigation may have deterred immunization that would have provided considerably more benefit, overall, than harm.

Whatever the net impact that the tort law has on safety, most of the authors who examined the issue concluded that factors *outside* the liability system provide the more important safety impetus. Reiser finds that the medical profession's standards of responsibility are the dominant influence for safe practice by physicians. Regulation is likewise the most important governmental factor in ensuring safety of pharmaceuticals and aircraft. Both Graham and Murray Mackay conclude that, at least in its early years, the NHTSA had an equally strong impact on car safety. One clear exception was the failure of the Consumer Product Safety Commission to regulate adequately all-terrain vehicles (ATVs); Graham describes regulatory response here as modest, weak, and belated.

Andrew Craig, writing on the subject of general aviation, describes the synergistic effects of liability and regulation in one case study but emphasizes the dominant role of the Federal Aviation Administation (FAA) and the National Transportation Safety Board (NTSB) in several others. He finds that "no firm conclusions can be reached about the relative influence of . . . liability and . . . regulation . . . in improving the safety record of general aviation. . . . In general, it appears that . . . liability . . . has acted more as a constraint than as a function for producing safety."

The authors also found evidence supporting the view expressed by

Eads and Reuter that the liability system sends confusing signals regarding safety, largely because courts and regulators often reach markedly different conclusions about how accidents are caused. Lasagna notes the dramatic difference between the FDA's pronouncements on Bendectin and various vaccines and the far more negative effect the legal system has had on these same products. Martin describes a sharp divergence between the post-accident findings of the NTSB and FAA and those implicit in patterns of litigation in the courts. "Accident investigators dispatched by the government agency charged by Congress with finding the probable cause of aircraft accidents find that a design or manufacturing defect in the airplanes caused none of the accidents [over 200]. Yet plaintiffs and their lawyers file lawsuits claiming that design or manufacturing defects caused 100 percent of the same accidents." Reiser likewise concludes that the incentives created by the liability system are often at odds with those that the professional medical associations have deemed to be best adapted for improving the quality of medical care.

Graham concludes that the uncertainty inherent in the tort system explains why it appears to have had so little effect on product design. He reports that "many auto engineers in the industry believe the legal process offers them limited information about how to improve the safety of their product." He further finds that the effect of liability on the safety of passenger cars is not detectable in aggregate fatality trends. Indeed, he concludes that there is "no evidence that expanded liability . . . has been a significant cause of the passanger safety improvements witnessed since World War II."

In fact, several authors claim that the current liability system may even have adverse effects on the safety of long-lived products. Aircraft are built to last for decades, and cars are often on the road for many years. Yet litigation often arrives years after designs have been changed and improved; in the meantime, regulators or manufacturers often identify possibilities for improvement in such products before the legal system makes any pronouncement. In such a context, liability may be counterproductive.

For example, Graham notes in one of his case studies that Ford officials feared that a design change could easily be interpreted by juries in future liability actions as an admission that the prior design was defective. More generally, sometimes vehicle manufacturers have delayed for years making decisions on feasible designs to improve safety. Graham also concludes that liability considerations probably did contribute to the decisions of manufacturers to phase out tension relievers on seat belts. Slack seat belts are less safe than snug ones, but safer than seat belts that aren't buckled, and studies show that comfort (enhanced by tension relievers) increases the use of belts.

Thus, Graham continues, the safety effect of eliminating tension relievers is far from clear.

Martin delivers a much more negative verdict on the safety impact of tort law in the private aircraft industry, by showing that the rate of safety improvement in general aviation has actually *slowed* as liability has expanded. He reports a "sharp downward trend [in the accident rate] for the twenty years [from 1950 to 1970] that were free of the influence of strict liability, in contrast to a significantly flatter downward trend in the accident rate over the twenty years after the intervention of strict liability and the litigation it has spawned." From these data he concludes that "strict liability has demonstrated no tendency to promote the safety of flight and, indeed, may have retarded it."

One chapter, however, expresses a much different view of the safety effects of liability law. Ashford and Stone argue that in fact the U.S. liability system vastly underdeters, at least with respect to the chemical industry. The reason, they find, is that except for such "signature diseases" as asbestosis and mesothelioma, which are clearly attributable to exposure to asbestos, it can be extremely difficult for juries and courts to link specific chemical agents with particular adverse health outcomes. In addition, the victims of harmful chemicals are often workers, whose compensation is strictly limited under workers' compensation. As a result, Ashford and Stone argue, chemical producers have yet to be confronted with proper incentives for making safer products. At the same time, they also conclude from their analysis of innovation theory that the uncertainties created by liability in the chemicals industry may actually promote the innovation of safer chemicals that reduce the uncertainties of liability exposures for chemical producers.

On balance, however, the documented direct linkages between liability and safety thus far are weak. In most of the sectors examined, other factors—primarily regulation and bad publicity—seem in the aggregate to provide much more important incentives to providers to improve the safety of products and services. Liability may, however, play an indirect role in amplifying the safety-enhancing effects of both reputational concerns and regulation; in the first instance, by promoting dissemination of safety-related information, and in the second, by helping regulators identify potentially unsafe products and encouraging them to take remedial action. And in certain sectors—notably chemicals—the safety effects of liability may appear insubstantial because in fact the current system underdeters and thus fails to provide sufficient incentives for safety.

Common "Innovation" Themes

Like the safety authors, the authors of the innovation chapters also looked to a combination of anecdotal and historical evidence to assess the impact of liability in specific industries and sectors. Viscusi and Moore also performed a statistical analysis of a newly compiled data series on insurance losses for various sectors of the economy for the period 1980–84, or the years when the so-called liability crisis of the 1980s first came to public attention. They attempted to determine whether differences in liability costs across industries were related to differences in various measures of innovation. They found that for industries with relatively low liability costs the liability system appeared, if anything, to enhance innovation. But in industries such as general aviation, in which liability costs rose sharply during the early 1980s and became a significant share of total costs, liability does seem to have dampened innovation.

Expressly, or by implication, the authors of the innovation case studies generally agreed with Viscusi and Moore. All the authors focused primarily on design, rather than manufacturing, defects. Martin, for example, notes that virtually all aviation product liability cases have involved claims of defective design. Similarly, in his discussion of vaccine litigation, Lasagna notes that in the 1950s and 1960s litigation over defective vaccine designs was more common than over defective batches of particular vaccines. Few of the authors offer much comment on manufacturing defect cases, from which one may perhaps surmise that these are much less problematic.

The case studies identify some concrete instances of the liability system's negative impact on innovation. General aviation appears to have suffered broad systemic effects; some segments of the industry have almost folded, apparently in large part because of the pressure of liability. In several industries—most notably some types of pharmaceuticals and small aircraft—the combined effects of uncertainty and high awards seem to have discouraged the research, development, and marketing of entire categories of products. Laurence Tancredi and Dorothy Nelkin suggest that fear of malpractice liability has in certain areas curtailed the use of innovative medical procedures, while stimulating in other areas (especially obstetrics, with a major increase in Ceasarean sections) excessive "defensive" medicine.

Several authors also discern an active, marketwide, liability-driven retreat from such things as obstetrics and the marketing of vaccines. Reiser argues that, the effects of informed consent aside, liability has transformed medical practice in ways that are fundamentally inimical to better health care. Mackay discusses various examples of auto design in which European manufacturers and consumers have either initiated or been the first to gain access to innovative design improvements. Martin presents figures on the declining rate of introduction of new light aircraft in the decades between 1950 and 1990, suggesting that this decline is a direct effect of expanding liability.

Lasagna concludes that at least for a few identifiable classes of products, liability has had a demonstrably depressive effect on innovation. On the basis of the Bendectin experience, he writes, "it seems safe to predict that never again will a manufacturer petition the FDA to approve for marketing a new prescription drug for nausea and vomiting during pregnancy." In one especially interesting case study, Lasagna revisits thalidomide, takes note of the "fascinating medical uses discovered for the drug in the years since 1961" (such as the treatment of leprosy and a dozen other rare diseases), and then briefly examines the difficulties that have been encountered in marketing the drug even for desirable uses. Tancredi and Nelkin point out how the depressive effect of liability on innovation of medical technologies, vaccines, and drugs may be reducing the quality of medical care.

Several authors observe that while manufacturers may win the great (sometimes overwhelming) majority of some kinds of cases tried, litigation costs may still be prohibitive. Martin notes that aviation manufacturers successfully prove that "in more than 80 percent of the cases brought to trial . . . there was no defect in design or manufacture which caused the accident." Lasagna notes that Merrell Dow has "won the great majority" of Bendectin claims. Nonetheless, both authors go on to describe the withdrawal of the products in question, because manufacturers concluded that even the costs of successful litigation were too high or unpredictable to shoulder.

In a similar vein, several authors emphasize the uncertainty of the legal system. Swazey comments: "For the present and the foreseeable future . . . pharmaceutical manufacturers must live not only with the indeterminacy surrounding the pharmacology and therapeutics of their drugs but also with the problems of uncertainty surrounding potential liability for the design of those drugs." Lasagna emphasizes the "unpredictability of litigation," liability "risks that are almost impossible to quantify," but that include the possibility of "financial catastrophe" for pharmaceutical companies. Martin quotes an aviation underwriter at Lloyd's as saying,

"We are quite prepared to insure the risks of aviation, but not the risks of the American legal system."

Few of the authors have ventured specific estimates on what liability is adding to the costs of the specific goods and services they address. Martin is an exception, providing estimates that liability costs in 1987 added "from $70,000 to $100,000 per [light airplane] built and shipped during the year." Mackay estimates that the costs of the U.S. product liability system for U.S. manufacturers "runs into hundreds of dollars per car sold."

Rollin Johnson's chapter on the effects of liability in the chemical industry is a notable exception to the other innovation papers. Using various standard quantitative indicators of innovation—R&D expenditures and patents granted, for example—Johnson finds that innovative activity seems to be alive and well in this industry. He sees little evidence that it has been dampened by liability litigation thus far, though he warns that future litigation over the effects of toxic substances eventually could chill innovation by chemicals firms.

International Aspects

As Schwartz emphasizes throughout his paper, and as other authors often note, many aspects of the U.S. liability system are still all but unique. Many relate to legal process rather than substantive standards—such as jury trials, broad discovery, contingency fees, and noneconomic and punitive damages—that appear to make the U.S. liability system more unpredictable and costly than legal regimes elsewhere. Schwartz notes that while the laws of other countries sometimes contain language similar to that used in U.S. liability doctrine, the practical application of these laws is demonstrably—and dramatically—different.

Predictability aside, we do know that the U.S. liability system is uniquely ambitious and pervasive. To judge from Schwartz's data, the per capita rate of tort suits in the United States is about four times as high as in England, and the gross per capita cost about ten times as high. Medical malpractice insurance premiums per physician in England are one-tenth of the cost for a U.S. doctor. The experience of other European countries is apparently comparable to England's. Mackay observes that "among industrialized nations no parallel can be found to the product liability industry in the United States." According to the Tillinghast study, U.S. tort costs now "range between three and eight times the relative cost of tort systems in major European countries as well as in Australia and Japan."[31]

Regrettably, none of the safety and innovation chapters include comprehensive international comparisons; systematic comparisons of that kind are clearly needed. Martin points out that foreign manufacturers of small planes appear to have gained some competitive edge as a result of the long-tail liability costs faced by U.S. manufacturers. Lasagna briefly compares international approaches to product liability, but offers little comparative data on the development or marketing of innovative drugs under the different regimes he describes.

The limited comparisons that are available nevertheless suggest that whatever positive effects the unique aspects of the U.S. liability system may be having on safety, those effects are not evident in comparative health and safety statistics. It may be that that modest positive effects do exist but are masked by other factors like demographics and regulation. Or it may be that the safety effects of liability rules and procedures peculiar to the United States are negligible or worse. But it is at least noteworthy that our safety authors generally did not find any significant correlations between more stringent liability demands in the United States and demonstrably higher levels of safety.

The same must be said for the innovation authors. They do document some instances of new products or design improvements (in cars, for example) introduced abroad before they were introduced in the United States. But again, systematic comparisons have proved difficult.

One important difference between the safety and innovation inquiries, however, may lie in what is being assessed. One would expect important safety benefits to show up in accident, morbidity, and mortality rates, and these statistics are readily available. Innovation is immediately more difficult to measure quantitatively, and systematic comparisons are therefore inherently more difficult.

With several exceptions, the limited evidence surveyed here suggests that the U.S. tort system has probably reduced innovation, though the magnitude of the negative effect is far from clear. It is not known whether the adverse effects on innovation are large enough to tip the overall cost-benefit verdict on the liability system from positive to negative, or just to make the net negative effects even worse.

31. Tillinghast 1989, 12.

Policy Recommendations

The large uncertainty that remains about the effects of liability in the United States may suggest to some that no policy conclusions are possible, and that therefore no policies should be formulated. There are "vitually no solid data," Swazey notes in her discussion of the effect of liability law on drug safety, and "it is interesting to wonder how policy is made in their absence."

Interesting indeed, but the one issue beyond dispute is that legal rules are policy, and policy *will* be made, in courts if not in legislatures, with or without data. Some will suggest that the absence of solid empirical data argues for leaving the legal system alone. Others will quickly respond that the absence of empirical data on efficacy argues equally well for curtailing a system that churns more than $100 billion through the U.S. economy, entailing transactions costs of perhaps half that amount, without demonstrable benefit and with some real risk of harm.

The debate between these two views will undoubtedly continue. Nevertheless, we believe several potentially useful and important policy recommendations do emerge from the discussion in this volume. Given the clear division of views of many of the authors, we stress that these recommendations are our own, though based on the analysis and conclusions of the various chapters.

First, those who formulate tort policy should perhaps learn from the well-established tenet in the field of psychology that rewards tend to be more effective in influencing behavior than punishments. Both liability law and regulation try to induce safety-enhancing behavior by punishing or curtailing the activities of firms and individuals. Graham suggests that it is time to try rewards instead, by offering positive legal incentives to manufacturers that promptly correct design defects and experiment with safety innovations. Along these lines, judges and legislators might consider allowing manufacturers partial, if not total, defenses against liability claims if they can prove they have behaved in that fashion.[32] At a minimum, such behavior ought to shield manufacturers from punitive damages.

Rules of evidence are also relevant in this regard. Both negligence and strict liability doctrines recognize that designing products and providing services are multifaceted undertakings, with many trade-offs among considerations of price, safety, and utility. Innovation can be a benefit in

---

32. See also Hoffman and Zuckerman 1987.

and of itself, for the individual consumer and society at large. The cutting-edge new drug or surgical procedure may offer the gravely ill patient a chance that cannot be found otherwise; society may also realize important benefits from its use even if the individual consumer does not. The legal system should be prepared to recognize such benefits, intangible though they are, and to give them serious consideration and weight in any analysis of liability in any particular case. Trying new things is always somewhat risky, but *not* trying them carries risks too. Legal rules, jury instructions, and evidentiary standards can all be crafted to give more equal weight to these symmetric considerations.

Second, a major theme that emerges from most of the chapters is that the uncertainty of the tort system is its greatest vice, magnifying risks of liability while disconnecting them from unduly risky conduct. To a large extent, of course, uncertainty is created by factors not directly related to liability doctrines, such as wide variations in jury awards. Doctrine is nevertheless important. One we would single out relates to the ability of plaintiffs to recover for product-related injuries decades after products have been on the market and previously not been held liable for injury. The prospect that liability may nevertheless be imposed in such circumstances clearly raises the risks for manufacturers seeking to introduce new products. At the same time, such retrospective liability can have no material effects on safety. A case exists for statutes of repose, at least for nontoxic products. A similarly strong case exists for shielding manufacturers from punitive damages where it is shown that product designs meet all applicable regulatory standards.

Third, legal scholars and jurists must become more willing to apply the same cost-benefit standards to the liability system that the liability system applies to doctors, drug companies, and the manufacturers of planes, chemicals, and cars. The risk-utility calculus so often applied *by* the tort law must also be applied *to* the tort law. It is of course true that engineers and pharmacologists sometimes settle on inferior designs, deliver imperfect services, or arrive at methods and procedures that could be considerably improved. Lawyers and jurists, however, are capable of making similar mistakes with the legal process itself. Without doubt, accidents outside the courtroom are socially costly. But accidents inside most assuredly can be too, in that they misallocate costs and discourage the wrong kinds of activities.

We need not resolve here whether the tort system has grown unduly fast in recent decades or whether it has just grown in step with technology and the advent of new risks. By any measures, the U.S. tort system today is a large instrument of government and social policy, certainly as expensive and far-reaching as any major government agency. Government institutions of this size and scope, whether centralized in Washington or dispersed in courthouses across the country, deserve systematic scrutiny. Even the watchdogs need to be watched; even the guardians need guarding. The difficulty of assessing the costs and benefits of the tort system cannot be a sufficient excuse for simply ignoring them, or refusing to undertake any systematic inquiry at all. Certainly there *are* costs and benefits of some sort, and the entries on both sides of the ledger are potentially as large as the system itself. It is the challenge for pundits and academics to determine whether the litigation industry is delivering, all in all, a social profit or loss.

Finally, it is important to recognize, as many of the authors point out, that the principal impetus for developing and producing safe products in the United States comes not from the fear of liability but from concern by firms for reputation, from demands by consumers for safe products and services, and from regulatory agencies. All these nonliability factors, however, require accurate and timely information. Accordingly, for those who remain concerned that the current levels of safety among products and services are inadequate, more attention and resources should be given to the production and provision of safety-related information. Graham, for example, urges the federal government to develop a new safety-rating system for automobiles, supplemented with additional resources for the NHTSA to initiate research and standards on a broader array of safety problems. Similar suggestions could be made for other industries.

We recognize that there are limits to the effects that doctrinal changes in tort law can have on both safety and innovation. As Schwartz describes, the tort laws of the United States, Europe, and Japan seem superficially quite similar. All countries purport to apply verbally identical standards of "negligence" to services (like medical practice), and most claim to apply "strict liability" of some sort to product defects. There are, nevertheless, profound differences in the practical operation of these various legal system. The U.S. system encourages many more suits and yields much higher awards and settlements.

It is impossible to say what accounts for these differences, but some possible factors have been noted. The United States, alone in the world, still relies on juries to decide most cases. The United States and Japan allow contingent attorneys' fees, but most other countries do not. The United States, almost alone in the world, does not require the losing party to pay the winning party's costs and legal fees. U.S. courts administer much more liberal rules of discovery, and are much more prone to award damages for emotional distress and for punishment. Some of these unique features of U.S. law might readily be changed, but not others. What is clear is that it might require more than modifying tort doctrine itself to significantly increase the safety benefits and lower the anti-innovation costs of the system as it now operates.

Research Needed

No academic study can end without a call for further research. But given the importance of the issues raised here, we are not embarrassed to suggest the need for more research in at least three areas.

First, tort scholars should systematically gather and analyze comparative data on safety and innovation in the United States and abroad. The safety data should be the easiest to assemble, since mortality and morbidity statistics should be available for different sectors and activities. If U.S. consumer, medical, and aviation injury rates, for example, turn out to be little different from those in other industrialized countries where tort costs are lower, this would suggest that the higher tort costs in the United States are not matched by offsetting safety benefits. Conversely, notably lower injury rates in the United States could support claims that the more costly liability system here confers additional benefits not available abroad.

Similar analysis might be possible for specific services or products. For example, U.S. obstetricians are sued far more often than their counterparts in Europe or Japan. Is it possible to separate other factors (like differences in demographics) to determine whether U.S. obstetricians provide safer delivery as a result?

Of course, even statistical evidence of this kind would not be conclusive unless the analysis controls for other factors that might contribute to differences in mortality and morbidity between countries; for example, differences in the intensity and type of regulation, and quality of the infrastructure (notably highways for automobiles). But at the very least, if it turns out that the United States does not rank especially well compared with other countries in these measures of safety, one would be hard pressed to argue that the current liability system is doing a good job of providing valuable incentives.

An international comparative analysis of the potential effects of liability on innovation is necessarily more difficult because of the problems of measuring innovation. Nevertheless, certain sector-specific analyses might be useful here too. For example, in this book Mackay compares the dates of introduction into Europe and the United States of such features as antilock brakes and seat belts with tension relievers for automobiles. Similar types of analysis might be possible for other products.

A second area of potentially fruitful inquiry concerns the effects of the U.S. liability system over time. Can we compare, more systematically, the relevant safety and innovation data from two different liability regimes—say, before and after 1960, when standards for product manufacturers shifted from negligence to strict liability. Both Martin in his study of private aircraft here and Priest in his work on consumer products generally have attempted analyses of this kind. But the work so far has been exploratory; more rigorous analysis should be possible and could be very illuminating.

A third field where more work could prove useful would develop comparisons among different states. This approach has already been taken, for example, in assessing the effects of different no-fault laws on auto insurance rates. A similar study recently found that various state tort reforms—notably caps on damage awards (for noneconomic damages) and reductions of liability under the "joint and several doctrine"—have in fact lowered both insurance claims and rates.[33] Following this line of analysis and controlling for other variables, one might be able to ascertain whether such interstate differences in liability doctrines have led to differences in safety. Interstate comparisons of liability law would be less useful, however, for identifying effects on innovation, at least in the provision of products rather than services, since most products are distributed nationwide.

Finally, we believe it is useful to extend and refine the statistical work of Viscusi and Moore on the relationship between liability costs and innovation. How would their conclusions be modified by data after 1984, the last year they were able to analyze? Could their data base, which currently includes only liability costs reported to insurers, be supplemented with liability costs borne directly or by captive insurers? Can their statistical analysis be used to determine whether differences in liability costs across industries have noticeably affected

---

33. Blackmon and Zeckhauser 1991. The joint and several liability doctrine holds that when more than one defendant is held liable for an injury, each one of them is responsible for the full award if the others cannot pay their share.

objective indicators of safety, such as product and workplace injuries and fatalities?

The difficulty of arriving at solid answers about the social effects of the liability system is not a sufficient reason to abandon the quest. For better or worse, the liability system is a very large presence in the United States. In its scope and ubiquity, the U.S. system remains unique in the world. Its costs and benefits accordingly deserve serious, searching, and continuing scrutiny.

References

Abel, R. L. 1987. "The Real Tort Crisis—Too Few Claims." *Ohio State Law Journal* 48:443–67.

Advisory Panel on Review of Bacterial Vaccines and Toxoids. 1985. 50 *Fed. Reg.* 51002–06, Dec. 13.

Blackmon, G., and Zeckhauser, R. 1991. "State Tort Reform Legislation: Assessing Our Control of Risks." In *Tort Law and the Public Interest: Competition, Innovation, and Consumer Welfare,* edited by P. H. Schuck. Norton.

Brodeur, P. 1985. *Outrageous Misconduct: The Asbestos Industry on Trial.* 1st ed. Pantheon.

Calabresi, G. 1970. *The Costs of Accidents: A Legal and Economic Analysis.* Yale University Press.

Cortese, A. W., and K. L. Blaner. 1990. "The Anti-Competitive Impact of U.S. Product Liability Laws: Are Foreign Businesses Beating Us at Our Own Game?" *University of Pittsburgh Journal of Law and Commerce* 9, issue 2: 167–205.

Djerassi, C. 1989. "The Bitter Pill." *Science* 245:356–61.

Eads, G., and P. Reuter. 1983. *Designing Safer Products: Corporate Responses to Product Liability Law and Regulation.* R-3022-ICJ. Santa Monica, Calif., Rand Corporation.

Elliott, E. D. 1989a. "Why Punitive Damages Don't Deter Corporate Misconduct Effectively." *Alabama Law Review* 40:1053–72.

———. 1989b. "Re-Inventing Defenses/Enforcing Standards: The Next Stage of the Tort Revolution." Pfizer Distinguished Lecture in Tort Law, Rutgers University Law School, Nov. 29–30.

Havenner, A. 1990. "Not Quite a Revolution in Products Liability." Manhattan Institute Judicial Studies Program White Paper.

Henderson, J. A., and T. Eisenberg. 1990. "The Quiet Revolution in Products Liability: An Empirical Study of Legal Change." *UCLA Law Review.* 37: 479–53.

Hoffman, J. A., and G. D. Zuckerman. 1987. "Tort Reform and Rules of Ev-

idence: Saving the Rule Excluding Evidence of Subsequent Remedial Actions."
Tort and Insurance Law Journal 22:497–510.

Huber, P. W. 1989. *Liability: The Legal Revolution and Its Consequences.* Basic
Books.

Institute of Medicine. 1985. *Vaccine Supply and Innovation.* Washington: National Academy Press.

———. 1989. *Medical Professional Liability and the Delivery of Obstetrical Care,*
vol. 1. Washington: National Academy Press.

Kakalik, J. S., and N. M. Pace. 1986. *Costs and Compensation Paid in Tort
Litigation.* R-3391-ICJ. Santa Monica, Calif.: Rand Corporation.

Kuhlik, B. N., and R. F. Kingham. 1990. "The Adverse Effects of Standardless
Punitive Damage Awards on Pharmaceutical Development and Availability."
Food Drug Cosmetic Law Journal 45:693–708.

Litan, R. E. [Forthcoming]. "The Liability Explosion and American Trade Performance: Myths and Realities." In *Tort Law and the Public Interest: Competition, Innovation, and Consumer Welfare,* edited by P. Schuck. Norton.

Mahoney, R. J., and S. E. Littlejohn. 1988. "Innovation on Trial: Punitive Damages Versus New Products." *Science* 246:1395–99.

McGuire, E. P. 1988. *The Impact of Product Liability.* Research Report 908.
New York: The Conference Board.

Peterson, M. A. 1987. *Civil Juries in the 1980s: Trends in Jury Trials and Verdicts
in California and Cook County, Illinois.* R-3466-ICJ. Santa Monica, Calif.:
Rand Corporation.

Porter, M. E. 1990. *The Competitive Advantage of Nations.* Free Press.

Posner, R. A. 1972. *Economic Analysis of Law.* Little, Brown.

Priest, G. L. 1987. "The Current Insurance Crisis and Modern Tort Law." *Yale
Law Journal* 96:1521–90.

———. 1988. "Understanding the Liability Crisis." In *New Directions in Liability Law,* edited by W. Olson, 196–211. New York: Academy of Political
Science.

———. 1989a. "The Continuing Crisis in Liability." *Products Liability Law
Journal* 1:243–50.

———. 1989b. "Products Liability Law and the Accident Rate." In *Liability:
Perspectives and Policy,* edited by R. E. Litan and C. Winston, 184–222.
Brookings.

———. 1990. "The New Legal Structure of Risk Control." *Daedalus,* Fall,
207–27.

Schotter, A., and J. Ordover. 1986. "The Cost of the Tort System." New York
University, C. V. Starr Center for Applied Economics.

Schuck, P. H. 1987. *Agent Orange on Trial: Mass Toxic Disaster in the Courts.*
Cambridge, Mass.: Belknap Press.

Smith, M. H. 1985. Statement before the Subcommittee on Health and the Environment of the House Committee on Energy and Commerce. In *Vaccine Injury Compensation*, 98 Cong. 2 sess. Government Printing Office.

Tillinghast. 1989. *Tort Cost Trends: An International Perspective*. Simsbury, Conn.

U.S. Department of Justice. 1986. *Report of the Tort Policy Working Group on the Causes, Extent and Policy Implications of the Current Crisis in Insurance Availability and Affordability.*

Weaver, R. H. 1988. *Impact of Product Liability on the Development of New Medical Technologies*. Chicago: American Medical Association.

Weber, N. 1989 *Product Liability: The Corporate Response*. Research Report 893. New York: The Conference Board.

CHAPTER TWO

Product Liability and Medical Malpractice in Comparative Context

Gary T. Schwartz

T HE CHAPTERS in this volume describe how modern American tort law—especially product liability and medical malpractice—casts its influence on safety and innovation in various industries. This introductory chapter provides the general reader with relevant background by delineating those modern American tort doctrines that the later chapters take for granted, and by showing how those doctrines have emerged over time within the American legal system. But there is a broader project that this chapter undertakes. Discussions of modern American tort law often tend to assume that this law is a uniquely American phenomenon, that our own tort doctrines are vastly out of line with those accepted by foreign legal systems. To test this assumption, the chapter describes those tort doctrines in the fields of product liability and malpractice that prevail in England, Germany, France, and Japan.[1] What I find, contrary to the common assumption, is that foreign tort doctrine is reasonably close to American doctrine. I also discover, however, that the rates of litigation and the costs of liability in those countries are only a small fraction of what they are here.

Since the differences in formal doctrine can account for no more than a limited part of these great differentials in tort costs, the effort to explain the latter must turn to features of the tort system other than doctrine itself. In providing this explanation, I consider, first, several ways in which American civil procedure differs from the procedures used elsewhere: here the focus is on pre-trial discovery, trial by jury, and the role played by counsel in preparing and examining witnesses. Next, I consider,

---

1. Occasionally I refer to the experience in other countries, where it seems germane to the questions under consideration.

in comparative context, the American system of remunerating lawyers, a system that includes both the so-called American rule and the contingent fee. I then turn to the rules and practices relied on in measuring and calculating damages. Finally, I look briefly at social welfare programs in effect in other countries, to ascertain how they might influence either the size of eventual damage awards or the more general motives for bringing suit. All these are factors that seem to be relevant to the burden of liability not only individually but in combination. What I find, in essence, is that the American tort system includes several distinctive features that interact with each other in a synergistic way. To be sure, the line that I generally draw between substantive doctrine on the one hand and procedural (and remedial) features on the other does not always hold up: at times, it is the interaction between substance and procedure that seems responsible for America's high levels of product and malpractice litigation.

Product Liability

This section examines product liability in terms of both comparative doctrine and comparative patterns of litigation. The review of doctrine pays special attention to a recent European Community Directive that will structure liability doctrine in Europe during the coming decades.

United States

Considering American tort law in a comparative context has led me to more fully appreciate one peculiar feature that tends to complicate the exposition of American tort doctrine. In England, Germany, France, and Japan, tort law is *national* law—law set forth in an ultimately unitary way by the judicial hierarchy within the national government. In the United States, by contrast, tort law remains *federalized*: the judiciary of each of the fifty states makes up its own mind about the proper content of tort doctrine. To be sure, American judges are all involved in a common legal culture, which tends to minimize differences in the content of the law from state to state. Moreover, at the more formal level of doctrinal transmission, one state's courts are willing to regard rulings from other states as relevant by way of analogy. Still, possibilities remain for diversity and multistate confusion in American tort law that do not exist in the other legal systems here under consideration.

Even conceding, however, the somewhat disorderly nature of American tort law, it remains possible briefly to trace the development of product liability doctrine in this country.[2] Before about 1920, American manufacturers were largely free of liability for harms resulting from hazards in their products. Between 1920 and the early 1960s manufacturers bore liability for defective products if, but only if, the defect could be traced back to some negligence on the manufacturer's part. Beginning in the early 1960s manufacturers became subject to a rule of strict liability for defective products. Recently, at least a few scholars have proposed that manufacturers should bear strict liability for *all* harms resulting from product use, regardless of whether the product contains any defect;[3] so far, however, American courts have shown no interest in pushing the strict liability doctrine in such a direction.

By the 1950s it had come to be realized that negligence cases could be grouped under three headings. In one set of cases, manufacturers were sued because of some assembly-line flaw in the individual product. In such cases, American courts were increasingly allowing plaintiffs to rely on the doctrine of "res ipsa loquitur" in order to call into play an inference or a presumption of negligence on the part of the manufacturer. (What this latinized formulation signifies is that the defect in the original product is a "thing" that "speaks for itself" on the issue of manufacturer negligence.) In other cases, manufacturers were being sued for having designed their products in negligent ways. In the abstract, a negligent design is one whose foreseeable risks outbalance its foreseeable benefits; but despite this broad concept, when plantiffs prevailed in negligent design cases before 1960, it was often because the manufacturer's design produced a hidden danger while the product was being used in ordinary ways. In a third set of cases, manufacturers were found negligent for not having supplied appropriate warnings to accompany their products. In many of these cases in which plaintiffs secured verdicts, the inadequacy of the manufacturer's warning seemed hard to deny.

Beginning in 1963 American jurisdictions began adopting a rule rendering manufacturers strictly liable for defective products. By the late 1960s, courts—in essence relying on the lessons of the earlier negligence era—were recognizing that products could be defective in any of three ways. The defect might be a manufacturing flaw in the individual product, it might relate to the poor design of an entire line of products, or it might

2. My account of American law relies here primarily on Schwartz 1983, 796–811.
3. For example, Latin 1985.

concern some inadequacy in the warnings or instructions that accompany the product.

In cases involving a claim of manufacturing defect, the criterion for ascertaining defectiveness has proved easy to identify: a product is defective if it deviates from the norm of the manufacturer's other products. In these cases, liability is meaningfully strict, in the sense that no inquiry needs to be conducted into the issue of manufacturer negligence. Here, however, courts have sometimes defended strict liability in a modest way. They have pointed out that even under a negligence regime, a plaintiff, having shown a manufacturing defect, usually can eventually secure a finding of negligence from the jury by invoking the cumbersome doctrine of res ipsa loquitur; one function of strict liability, then, is to streamline the process of litigation—to economize on litigation costs—without greatly changing the pattern of litigation results. In any event, whatever its rationale, the modern doctrine of strict liability for manufacturing defects has not proved controversial within the United States. What is, perhaps, controversial is the frequent willingness of courts to permit a jury to infer that a product was originally defective when the evidence shows only that the product malfunctioned at some much later time. In one case, for example, the plaintiff was injured when the steering mechanism of a two-year-old truck that had been driven more than 100,000 miles "froze"; even though the plaintiff was unable to identify any specific defect in the original truck that might have occasioned this later malfunction, his verdict against the manufacturer was affirmed.[4] Cases of that sort exemplify the aggressiveness with which American courts have gone about the business of applying modern product liability doctrine.[5]

In modern strict liability cases that concern product design, courts have struggled to develop a definition for the concept of defect. In many states, courts have ruled that a design is defective if it fails to comply with "ordinary consumer expectations" of the product's likely safety. But the nebulousness of this consumer expectation standard has resulted over time in a decline in its judicial popularity. Currently, the primary theme in design cases is that a design is defective if the risks associated with that design exceed all its benefits. (To render this criterion operational, the plaintiff usually needs to show some design alternative that

4. *Farmer* v. *International Harvester Co.*, 97 Idaho 742, 553 P.2d 1306 (1976); see Schwartz 1983, 836–38.

5. In the last few years there have been some signs that this aggressiveness is abating. See Henderson and Eisenberg 1990.

would be not only safer but all things considered a good idea.) Such a balancing approach considerably resembles the approach that American courts had previously taken in considering the negligence of a product's design.[6] Indeed, in comparing manufacturers' design liability in 1990 with their liability in 1960, the key difference does not really relate to the supposed distinction between strict liability and negligence; rather, it concerns the willingness of contemporary courts to apply the traditional negligence balancing in a free-wheeling and aggressive way. Thus modern juries regularly review, case by case, the basic design features of complicated products like automobiles; if a jury determines that the hazards of a design outweigh its benefits, it can find that design defective even though the hazards are "open and obvious" to the product user and even though the hazards can be avoided altogether if the product is used in normal ways. That is, under modern law, manufacturers can be held liable for not having properly designed the product with respect to "misuses" of the product that the jury might regard as "foreseeable"; for example, car manufacturers are now liable if they fail to design cars in ways that minimize the "second-collision" effects of highway accidents. In modern design defect actions, some courts refuse to allow the manufacturer to even introduce evidence showing that its design is in compliance with industry custom; some courts allow the plaintiff to introduce evidence of a subsequent design change rendered by the manufacturer; and all courts agree that the manufacturer's compliance with relevant public regulations is at best some evidence of the nondefectiveness of its design.[7]

In modern failure-to-warn cases, once again the most distinctive feature of post-1960 decisions relates not so much to the standard of strict liability itself but to the willingness of courts in many cases to aggressively scru-

6. In modern strict liability actions, courts focus on the appropriateness of the product's design. In pre-1960 negligent design cases, the ultimate issue was technically the reasonableness of the manufacturer's design decision. But in those cases courts had typically focused on the adequacy of the design itself, allowing an inadequate design to serve as a proxy for a negligent design choice. Schwartz 1979, 462–63. To this extent, strict liability for design defects indeed coincides with design liability under the negligence standard. It is true, however, that in a negligence case the manufacturer can attempt to impress the jury by introducing evidence on the conscientiousness of its design decisionmaking. This evidence would ordinarily be inadmissible in a strict liability action.

7. In a traditional negligence action, compliance with custom is admissible as evidence of nonnegligence, while evidence of post-accident improvements by the defendant is inadmissible. The idea that complying with regulation does not defeat a tort claim goes back to the nineteenth century. Schwartz 1989, 669. Still, this idea has been given dramatic application in modern product cases.

tinize product warnings to determine whether their *substance* is sufficiently complete and also whether their *style* is sufficiently effective in conveying that substance to the product user. (At times this aggressiveness seems to reach the point of nit-picking.) Moreover, in the abstract a plaintiff in a failure-to-warn case must show that the inadequate warning is causal; that is, that a better warning would have resulted in his using the product more carefully or his declining to buy the product in the first place. On this causation issue, however, modern courts have often hesitated to affirm such a burden of proof. Rather, courts have allowed juries to infer causation on the basis of little or no evidence, or they have ruled that a showing of an inadequate warning justifies a presumption that a proper warning would have been causally effective.

In design defect and failure-to-warn cases, what results do courts reach when the manufacturer neither knew nor should have known of the hazard in the product at the time it was originally distributed? In such cases a negligence standard clearly would not justify the imposition of liability. The distinctive feature of strict liability, then, might be that it would render irrelevant the manufacturer's actual and reasonable ignorance; indeed, mid-1960s discussions of the new strict liability rule suggested that strict liability took effect exactly by "imputing" all knowledge of product hazards to the product manufacturer. In 1982 the New Jersey Supreme Court followed through on this strict liability logic in *Beshada* v. *Johns-Manville Products Corp.*[8] But the *Beshada* opinion encountered a storm of criticism; and a year later, in *Feldman* v. *Lederle Laboratories*,[9] the New Jersey Court limited *Beshada* to asbestos cases and ruled that manufacturers of other products (such as drugs) can escape liability if they can show that at the time of product sale they had no reason to know of the product's hazards. Such a ruling—recognizing a "state-of-the-art" limitation on liability—moves modern product liability doctrine back toward the negligence standard; indeed, many recent courts have been willing to explicitly acknowledge that in design and warning cases negligence remains the actual standard of the manufacturer's liability.

Other Countries

While the multistate variety of American tort law makes that law somewhat difficult to summarize, the effort to understand the law of non-

8. 90 N.J. 191, 447 A.2d 539 (1982).
9. 97 N.J. 429, 479 A.2d 374 (1984).

English-speaking countries discomforts the analyst by requiring him to rely on a limited number of secondary sources. Moreover, describing product liability doctrine in foreign legal systems turns out to be an especially daunting task. Product liability jurisprudence, though primarily tort law, tends also to include elements of contract law and sales law. The analyst can be confident that he has an insider's understanding of how this combination works within his own legal system; but as an outsider, he should be humble in making statements about what such a combination adds up to in a foreign system.[10] Mindful of this need for humility, I set forth the following evaluations.

The practice of manufacturer "no liability" that prevailed in the United States until about 1920 survived for an additional decade or so in England. In a leading 1932 case, however, English law concluded that manufacturers can be held generally liable for their negligence;[11] yet even after that decision English plaintiffs may have encountered difficulties in trying to prove manufacturer negligence.[12] Before 1960, French law primarily adhered to the idea that manufacturers could be liable for fault or negligence; however, negligence could be sufficiently difficult to establish so as sometimes to provide French manufacturers with an immunity from tort liability.[13] In Germany a practice of no liability survived until 1968. One special feature of German tort law is that it has never fully accepted the doctrine of respondeat superior (the doctrine that renders an employer automatically liable for any negligence in its employee's conduct).[14] So, as late as the mid-1960s, even if the German consumer injured by a product defect could show that this defect was due to the negligence of the manufacturer's employee, the consumer could not recover unless there was reason to believe that the manufacturer was guilty of some negligence in either hiring or supervising the employee.

By 1980, however, all three of these legal systems had lightened the plaintiff's burden of proof in cases involving manufacturing defects. Eng-

10. This chapter somewhat eases its burden by focusing on the liability of manufacturers rather than that of retailers. It is retailers who are most frequently sued under contract-law and sales-law theories.

11. *Donoghue* v. *Stevenson* [1932] A.C. 562, 580, 599.

12. Compare *Donoghue* v. *Stevenson* [1932] A.C. 562, 622 (MacMillan, L.) (res ipsa loquitur has no role in products cases) with *Grant* v. *Australia Knitting Mills* [1936] A.C. 85, 101 (rebuttable inference of negligence can sometimes be derived from defect in product). See also *Daniels and Daniels* v. *R. White & Sons, Ltd.* [1938] 4 All E.R. 258 (denying manufacturer liability in circumstances where liability would almost certainly be affirmed today).

13. Viney 1986, 74–75.

14. Markesinis 1986, 349–64.

lish law now allows plaintiffs who sue because of manufacturing defects to take advantage of "the doctrine of res ipsa loquitur or its practical equivalents";[15] as a result, under English law the manufacturer is now "virtually an insurer against manufacturing defects."[16] As a formal caption for a legal doctrine, "res ipsa loquitur" seems unique to American and English law. Yet Germany and France, though deprived of the res ipsa caption, have reached results that are about as strong as England's. In Germany a leading 1968 case shifted the burden of proof to the manufacturer, requiring the manufacturer to explain the defect in an exonerating way in order to defeat liability;[17] given the difficulty of discharging this burden, in manufacturing defect cases German law "greatly approximates . . . strict tort liability."[18] In France, at least so long as the flaw in the product is "hidden," there is now a presumption of negligence running against the manufacturer that is almost conclusive;[19] in this way French law likewise "approximate[s] strict liability."[20] The French legal position is in part derived from a civil code section imposing liability on a person "for the injury [caused] by the act of . . . things that he has under his guard": French courts now conclude that the manufacturer has a continuing "guard" over the internal structure of the products it sells.[21]

In defective product cases, practices in Japan provide for the possibility of two sorts of sanctions that are nearly unheard of in the United States and Europe. Social customs associated with the Japanese tort system sometimes require company officials to deliver personal apologies to victims and their families.[22] Moreover, under Japanese law a company official who departs from the duty to avoid the sale of defective products can be subjected to criminal prosecution; apparently, however, such prosecutions are initiated only when the official's conduct seems seriously irresponsible and only if the hazardous line of products turns out to injure large numbers of consumers.[23]

Turning now to the more conventional remedy of tort compensation, one can note that Japanese law—unlike that of America and Europe—evidently never harbored any rule or practice of no liability. Currently

15. Albanese and Del Duca 1987, 203.
16. Fleming 1987, 469.
17. The case is translated in Markesinis 1986, 245–56.
18. Markesinis 1986, 60.
19. Viney 1986, 76.
20. Liebman 1986, 803; see also Sarrailhé 1981, 2.
21. Tebbens 1979, 92–93.
22. Wagatsuma and Rosett 1986, 487.
23. Fujita 1987, 45.

Japanese courts apply a negligence standard in product cases. It is, moreover, a broad version of that standard: manufacturers bear a "very high duty of care."[24] Accordingly, a manufacturing defect in a product justifies an inference of fault on the part of the manufacturer. This inference is described as moving Japanese law "very close" to strict liability;[25] the rule likewise renders Japanese law equivalent to the law in European countries.

How do these legal systems deal with the manufacturer's possible liability for inadequate product design? One 1982 House of Lords case makes clear that English manufacturers can incur liability for negligent design.[26] In a 1986 case the defendant, in assembling a specialized sports car, incorporated an engine marketed by the Ford Motor Company. That engine included a design feature that entailed a small risk of a carburetor fire. Although acknowledging that the chance of a harmful incident was "quite . . . small," an English court perceived that the harm that could ensue from such an incident would be quite serious; accordingly, the court found the design inadequate. The court also rejected the defendant's claim that it had behaved reasonably in accepting an engine marketed and recommended by an industry leader like Ford. Rather, the court reasoned, the defendant, though apparently a small-scale concern, had an obligation to conduct its own engineering review of the adequacy of the Ford design.[27]

This case apart, English law is thin in providing helpful clarification of the meaning of the negligence concept in its application to product design issues. But there have been interesting rulings on design liability in Canada, a country whose courts take seriously the precedent of English common-law doctrine. One Canadian court has ruled that car manufacturers can be found negligent (and hence held liable) for having failed to design automobiles in an appropriate "crashworthy" way.[28] Another Canadian court, in discussing the obligation of a manufacturer to adopt a safer alternative design when it is "available" and sufficiently "reasonable," has said that "it is not material that [this alternative design] may have been more costly";[29] moreover, the court made clear that the manufacturer cannot relieve itself of its obligation to adopt such a design by

24. Fujita 1987, 47.
25. Fujita 1987, 25–26.
26. *Lexmead (Basingstoke) Ltd.* v. *Lewis* [1982] A.C. 225.
27. *Winward* v. *T.V.R. Engineering Ltd.* [1986] B.T.L.C. 366 (C.A.).
28. *Gallant* v. *Beitz* (1983) 148 D.L.R. (3d) 522.
29. *Nicholson* v. *John Deere Ltd.* (1986) 34 D.L.R. (4th) 542, 547, 549.

warning the consumer of the danger in the existing design. In light of these rulings, this case goes about as far as any American case in suggesting the breadth of manufacturers' design liability.

Claims of negligent design have clearly been permitted by German law; the plaintiff must identify a feasible alternative design that suggests that the manufacturer's chosen design poses an unreasonable risk of injury.[30] French law likewise approves of the theory of negligent design.[31] It is hard to figure out, however, what the criteria are for ascertaining negligence in these design cases; in particular, it is uncertain what emphasis French law places on "hidden" hazards in negligent design cases. Claims of negligent design are also viable under Japanese law. In one case involving a Mitsubishi automobile, a Japanese court ruled that since the manufacturer operates under a "high duty of care," it can be found negligent even if its design complies with both public regulation and industry practice;[32] in this respect, Japanese law is in harmony with modern American legal norms. (French and German law also reject the defense of regulatory compliance.)[33] In Japan the courts, in ruling that the approval of a drug by the Japanese equivalent of the Food and Drug Administration does not afford the drug manufacturer a tort defense, extend their aggressiveness by rejecting any doctrine of governmental immunity and hence holding the government liable along with the drug manufacturers on a joint-and-several basis.[34] (To be sure, by calling for a sharing of liability between manufacturer and government, Japanese law reduces the liability the manufacturer would otherwise bear on its own.)

A manufacturer's negligent failure to warn has also produced liability under these countries' legal systems. In Japan drug manufacturers have been held responsible for side effects that they were evidently unaware of when they sold the drugs, but that they could have learned of had they done a more extensive job of premarketing testing.[35] In France courts has been described as engaging in a "strict" and "stringent" review of the adequacy of product warnings.[36] A 1983 case concerned an adhesive product sold in a package that contained warning labels identifying the

30. Markesinis 1986, 61–62.
31. Tebbens 1979, 85.
32. Fujita 1987, 55.
33. Viney 1986, 78; Will 1988, 136.
34. "Terms of Settlement" 1979, 111–14.
35. Ottley and Ottley 1984, 50.
36. Viney 1986, 79; Sarrailhé 1981, 26.

product as "highly flammable"; despite these labels, the court found the manufacturer liable for a failure to provide explicit instructions on how to use the product safely.[37] In Germany a 1972 case perceived that the warning obligations borne by drug manufacturers were "especially strict."[38] In addition, German law has obliged the manufacturer to provide warnings about product hazards that relate to "the intended product use in its broadest sense"; accordingly, manufacturers, while not required to warn about clear instances of misuse, must nevertheless provide warnings that relate to a considerable range of "foreseeable misapplications."[39] In this regard, German law has moved much of the way in the American direction. In one case a German court ruled that Honda (and its importer) had failed to warn existing owners of Honda motorcycles about the dangers of attaching to that motorcycle a windshield that another company had recently begun to market.[40] By imposing on manufacturers (and importers) a duty to warn that continues long after the original product sale and by combining that duty with a requirement that manufacturers conduct tests on accessories produced by independent companies, this case in its own way goes further than any American failure-to-warn opinion. In England a leading failure-to-warn case is *Wright* v. *Dunlop Rubber Company.*[41] *Wright* can be interestingly compared with *Borel* v. *Fibreboard Paper Products Corp.,*[42] the 1973 American opinion that has provided the framework for American asbestos litigation. *Borel* holds that when a manufacturer sells a product to an employer, the manufacturer has an obligation to warn of the extent to which the workers' exposure to that product might induce instances of occupational disease. In England the year before, the *Wright* court had reached the same conclusion. To be sure, *Borel* goes further than *Wright* in specifying that the warning needs to run directly to workers; *Wright* seems to assume that a warning to the employer is sufficient. In another respect, however, *Wright* may go further than *Borel*. *Borel* authorizes liability whenever the manufacturer "knows or should know" of the hazard in the product it sells. Under *Wright*, however, once the manufacturer merely acquires "suspicions" of the product's hazard, the obligation to warn attaches.

In design and warning cases, English courts have thus been capable of

---

37. Will 1988, 145.
38. The case is translated in Markesinis 1986, 256–62.
39. Will 1988, 137.
40. Will 1988, 139–40.
41. [1972] 13 K.I.R. 255.
42. 493 F.2d 1076 (5th Cir. 1973), *cert. denied*, 419 U.S. 869 (1974).

applying the negligence standard in an aggressive way. Nevertheless, negligence rather than strict liability has been the formal standard of liability. Accordingly—and leaving aside certain very recent developments, of which more below—English courts (and European courts gennerally) would agree with the American view that manufacturers are not liable in design or warning cases for hazards that were not reasonably knowable at the time of original product sale.[43] However, in both Germany and Japan statutes have been adopted that provide remedies for patients injured by the possibly unexpected side effects of drugs.

The German statute, adopted in 1976, imposes liability on the manufacturers of prescription drugs in circumstances in which

(1) the drug has harmful effects in the course of its prescribed use which objectively exceed acceptable limits in the light of medical scientific knowledge and whose cause lies in the field of development or manufacturing or (2) the detriment has occurred as a consequence of a label, disclosure for experts or disclosure for users not in accordance with medical scientific knowledge.[44]

Apparently, the meaning of this language has not yet been fleshed out by any major judicial opinions.[45] German scholars tend to assume that the statute imposes strict liability. Yet the statute's emphasis on "medical scientific knowledge" raises doubt about exactly how strict its liability rule really is.[46] Whatever the extent of this strictness, liability under the German statute is a limited liability: the drug manufacturer does not bear liability for the victim's pain and suffering, no one plaintiff can recover more that DM 500,000 (now about $325,000), and the cap on liability for any one drug is subject to a limit of DM 200 million ($134 million).

The Japanese statute, enacted in 1979, undeniably provides benefits

43. Fleming 1982, 308; Fleming 1987, 469; Will 1988, 140.

44. Part of the translation is set forth in Fleming 1982, 300. The rest was provided to me by the UCLA Law School Library.

45. No opinions are mentioned in Markesinis 1986, 63. John Fleming tells me that almost all claims under the statute have been resolved without resort to litigation.

46. The "acceptable limits" concept in the statute may well preclude compensation when the adverse consequence seems like the more-or-less normal or at least highly predictable by-product of taking the medication itself. An easy example would be the side effects induced by chemotherapy as administered to a cancer patient. Oddly, then, given its "acceptable limits" and "medical scientific knowledge" clauses, the statute can be read as denying liability *both* when the side effects of medication are very foreseeable *and* when they are unforeseeable.

on a no-fault basis; like the German statute, it excludes compensation for pain and suffering and places limits on the individual victim's recovery.[47] The fund is financed partly by government contributions but primarily by levies imposed on drug manufacturers and importers according to a formula that relies largely on each manufacturer's sales proceeds; unlike the German statute, the Japanese statute does not impose actual liability on the particular manufacturer. But this manufacturer does not avoid all responsibility. For one thing, the formula for the levy takes into account the number of claims involving the manufacturer's products during the previous year. In addition, if the manufacturer is guilty of negligence in the individual case, the victim can ignore the fund and sue the manufacturer directly for full damages under a negligence theory. Or, the victim having recovered from the fund, the fund can then secure indemnification from the negligent manufacturer.

Recent Law Reform

The multinational law I have described is law that was largely in place by 1980. There are also recent law-reform efforts in Japan and Europe that need to be examined. In 1975 a number of Japanese legal scholars organized themselves and prepared a draft of a model product liability law.[48] In many respects, this model law was designed to codify and clarify what already were Japanese product liability practices; in other respects, the model was designed to set forth new legal standards. In particular, the model law would shift the formal standard of liability from negligence to strict liability—strict liability, that is, once the plaintiff has established some "defect" in the product itself. The draft model law goes on to define "defect" as "any flaw in a product which causes an inordinate danger to life, to the person, or to property during ordinarily foreseeable use." Also, "when determining the existence of a defect, any statements or warnings concerning the product shall be taken into account." The Japanese Ministry of Justice has withheld its support for the draft model law; largely for that reason, the model has not yet even come close to legislative enactment. Also, there apparently is "resistance" to the strict liability idea within the Japanese business community, although in one survey "a majority of firms admit, though reluctantly, the necessity for

47. Fleming 1982, 303–04; Fujita 1987, 3; Ramseyer 1990.
48. Fujita 1987, 88–92.

such legislation."[49] The basis for the Ministry of Justice's position evidently is that the negligence standard which characterizes current law is flexible enough to produce appropriate results in most cases. Since the draft model law has never been adopted, the uncertainties in its definition of "defect" have never received judicial consideration.

In January 1977 the Council of Europe's "Convention on Product Liability" was opened for signatures.[50] In that year the Convention was signed by Belgium, France, Austria, and Luxembourg. However, no signatures have been obtained since 1977, largely because European countries were aware that the European Community (EC) had begun working on the draft of a directive on product liability. Moreover, even the states that signed the Convention never went on to formally ratify it; for lack of the requisite number of ratifications, the Convention has never gone into effect. Meanwhile the EC Directive, after years of discussion, was finally adopted on July 25, 1985, and then "notified" on July 30, 1985. Such directives are not generally self-enforcing; the Product Liability Directive calls on all member states to adopt implementing legislation by July 30, 1988. England complied with its obligation by adopting a Consumer Protection Act in 1987. Germany approved its implementing statute in late 1989; the statute went into effect on January 1, 1990. Implementing legislation is currently under consideration in France.[51]

What are the legal doctrines that the Directive endorses?[52] Under article 1 of the Directive, "the producer shall be liable for damage caused by a defect in his product." Since there is no mention of negligence here, the producer's liability is implicitly strict liability. Of course, to say that a

---

49. Hamada, Ishida, and Murakami 1986, 92–93.

50. The following draws on Albanese and Del Duca 1986, which reproduces the EC Directive on pp. 237–45.

51. For discussion of what happens when a member state does not comply with obligations imposed on it by a directive, see Thieffry, Van Doorn, and Lowe 1989, 82–84.

52. A separate question concerns the philosophy on which the Directive relies. In the United States, certain early product liability opinions included rhetoric indicating that strict liability plays an important role in achieving the societal goal of loss spreading and also in providing manufacturers with lavish safety incentives. Modern scholars have differed in assessing the significance of this rhetoric. Although some understand it as expressing the soul of modern American tort law (for example, Priest 1985), others interpret it as somewhat loose talk that is largely unnecessary in understanding the actual liability rules that American courts have adopted (for example, Schwartz 1979).

In light of this controversy, it is useful to note that rhetoric of this sort is absent from the preamble to the EC Directive. In explaining the background for the Directive, the preamble tends to refer, in a rather understated way, to the criteria of "the protection of the consumer" and "a fair apportionment of risk between the injured person and the producer."

producer is strictly liable for a product "defect" is to spotlight the importance of the definition of "defect." According to article 6, "a product is defective when it does not provide the safety which a person is entitled to expect, taking all circumstances into account, indicating the presentation of the product." This is without doubt a weak definition. Indeed, it runs the risk of being viciously circular, since one is "entitled" to expect that level of safety which the law itself requires. Moreover, by requiring that "all circumstances [be taken] into account" in identifying defects, the Directive emphasizes how unstructured and open-ended its criterion of defect seems to be. The Directive's definition also makes no effort to take advantage of the American experience with the defect concept: it does not distinguish between manufacturing defects, design defects, and warning defects, nor does it establish criteria that would enable courts to identify any of those defects. The language of "the safety which a person is entitled to expect" seems to resemble the "ordinary consumer expectations" theme that once was popular in American product liability law. In America, however, that theme has declined in popularity, as judges and scholars have come to appreciate the nebulousness of the "consumer expectations" notion. American law, of course, refers to "consumer expectations," while the Directive refers to the expectations of "a person." Apparently, controversy is already raging within the Community about whether the article 6 concept of "a person" should be interpreted as including "producing persons" as well as "consumer persons."[53]

The Directive makes clear that a product "shall not be considered defective for the *sole reason* that a better product is subsequently put into circulation" (emphasis added). This does not entail, however, the rejection of any pro-plaintiff position that an American court might adopt: the most that such a court might hold is that a later, better product is *some evidence* of the earlier product's defectiveness. The Directive also says that a manufacturer is not liable if "the defect is due to compliance . . . with mandatory regulations issued by the public authorities." This language falls short of establishing that compliance with regulations is a full defense. Rather, its point seems to be that a design that is *compelled* by public regulation cannot be regarded as defective and actionable. (Only if a design has been so compelled can it be said that the defect is "due to" the manufacturer's compliance with the regulation.)[54] One American

53. Will 1988, 131–32.
54. Whitaker 1986, 257; Wright 1989, 58.

court has indeed ruled in favor of liability in such a case;[55] however, that ruling seems like something of a fluke.

On one key point concerning the standard of liability, the Directive seems unintentionally ambiguous; on another key point, the Directive intentionally avoids taking a definitive position. The ambiguity relates to the Directive's attitude toward the American doctrine of "foreseeable misuse." The Directive refers to the manufacturer's obligation to take precautions against "the use to which it could reasonably be expected that the product would be put." By referring to "reasonably expected" uses rather than "reasonable" uses, the language of the Directive can be read as sympathizing with the American doctrine. The preamble to the Directive disputes that doctrine, however, by indicating that the manufacturer should bear no liability in the event of consumer "misuses" of its product that are "not reasonable."

The issue on which the Directive withholds final judgment concerns the manufacturer's liability for product hazards that were not reasonably knowable at the time of original product sale. Recall that most American jurisdictions recognize a state-of-the-art limitation on liability, primarily in design and warning cases. What Americans talk about in "state-of-the-art" terms is what Europeans discuss in the language of "development risk." How to handle development risks was the most controversial issue the Community faced in preparing its Directive. In the Directive the EC Council of Ministers left this controversy unresolved. Under article 7(e) of the Directive, the producer bears no liability if the defect in the product could not have been "discovered" at the time the product was originally placed in circulation, on account of "the state of scientific and technical knowledge at the time." However, article 15.1(b) says that member states, in passing legislation to implement the Directive, have the option of dispensing with this "unknowability" defense. Options like this obviously reduce the extent to which the Directive can achieve its stated goal of Community-wide uniformity. Acknowledging this difficulty, article 15 goes on to provide that in 1995 the Council of Ministers will reconsider the matter and make a recommendation on whether the article 7(e) defense should be repealed. Both the English and the German statutes, implementing the Directive, have incorporated the article 7(e) unknowability limitation on liability;[56] so far, the only member state to

---

55. *Ferebee* v. *Chevron Chemical Co.*, 736 F.2d 1529 (D.C. Cir.), *cert. denied*, 469 U.S. 1062 (1984).

56. For a close reading of the English provision, see Newdick 1988.

exclude this limitation is Luxembourg. Disagreement about the limitation is apparently the prime reason that no implementing statute has yet been passed in France.[57]

As for affirmative defenses in product liability cases, the Directive sets forth rules that do not much differ from those in effect in the United States. For example, disclaimers of liability are ineffective, and something like comparative negligence is the primary doctrinal response to issues of faulty behavior by the victim. In three other respects, however, the Directive comes across as distinctly conservative by American standards. The Directive, first of all, includes not only a conventional statute of limitations but also a statute of repose: all liabilities called for by the Directive are extinguished ten years after the date at which the product is put into circulation. Repose statutes have been adopted by American legislatures—but only in a minority of states, most of them with relatively small populations. Moreover, American repose statutes typically include important exceptions: for example, an exception for drugs that produce diseases only after long latency periods. The Directive's statute of repose is, by contrast, without exceptions; it would thus go a long way, for example, toward eliminating the liability of asbestos manufacturers and companies that make products like DES.

The Directive's damage provisions can likewise be regarded as conservative. The Directive gives countries the option of incorporating a ceiling on liability for all damages resulting from a particular product line; this ceiling "may not be less than 70 million ECU."[58] (At the time the Directive was adopted, this sum was equivalent to $51 million; currently, it is worth more than $70 million.) As with the development risk option, the whole matter is to be reconsidered by the Council of Ministers in 1995. No American jurisdiction currently provides any aggregate on liability of the sort the Directive authorizes. England, however, has declined the Directive's option; its 1987 implementing statute does not include any ceiling on liability. But the new German statute does incorporate a liability cap of DM 160 million (approximately $106 million).[59] In endorsing a cap, Germany was undoubtedly drawing on the "precedent" of its earlier drug statute.

The third conservative feature in the Directive is one that needs to be carefully described. Article 9 states that the Directive, standing alone,

57. Thieffry, Van Doorn, and Lowe 1989, 77–81.
58. There is one further option that the Directive explicitly confers on member states: whether to bring agricultural products within the scope of the directive's liability rules.
59. Ponzanelli (forthcoming).

does not provide for the award of "non-material damage"—that is, damages for pain and suffering. Article 9 then goes on to say, however, that "this Article shall be without prejudice to national provisions relating to non-material damage." In pondering the meaning of article 9, one should consider article 13, which says that the Directive "shall not affect any rights which an injured person" has under his own nation's laws "at the moment when" the Directive was notified—July 30, 1985. This article is a key part of the Directive; under its auspices, for example, plaintiffs, by relying on negligence theories endorsed by their member states in 1985, can assert claims that otherwise would be wiped out by the Directive's statute of repose or precluded by the ceiling on liability the Directive authorizes. As for article 9, it can be interpreted as deriving its meaning from article 13;[60] under this interpretation, the plaintiff, in order to collect pain-and-suffering damages, needs to invoke article 13 and assert a claim that relies on his member state's 1985 version of negligence law.

Article 9 is, however, ambiguous.[61] It might mean—quite independently of article 13—that the ability of the plaintiff who asserts his strict liability claim (as implemented by his member state's statute) to collect pain-and-suffering damages depends on whether those damages are recoverable in analogous circumstances under his member state's own tort law. This is the interpretation of article 9 that is supported by the EC official who has been most closely involved in the Directive's evolution.[62] Under this interpretation, pain-and-suffering damages *can* be recovered in a strict liability action filed in England, since English tort doctrine usually allows for the recovery of pain-and-suffering damages.[63] However, the plaintiff who files a strict liability claim under the German implementing statute would not be able to recover those damages, given the German tradition of withholding recovery for pain and suffering in the context of strict liability.[64] But the German plaintiff, by invoking

60. This is the interpretation of article 9 supported by Will 1988, 129. See also Orban 1978, 390.

61. The ambiguity is noted in Thieffry, Van Doorn, and Lowe 1989, 73.

62. Interview with Hans Claudius Taschner, July 10, 1990.

63. French law, like English law, provides for the award of pain-and-suffering damages in ordinary personal injury cases; under Italian law, however, those damages tend to be available only when the defendant has engaged in behavior that can be classified as criminal. Stoll 1986, 43–44.

64. There is perhaps a third reading of article 9: under this reading, whether pain-and-suffering damages are compensable depends on what specific provisions member states choose to include in their implementing statutes. Interpreted in that way, article 9 provides member states with yet another option in approving implementing statutes. Nothing in the English or German statute, however, speaks to this damage question.

article 13, can allege negligence under 1985 German doctrine and thereby seek compensation for his pain and suffering.

Under the first interpretation of article 9, plaintiffs throughout the European Community, wanting to maximize their chances of recovering for their economic losses, will file an EC-oriented strict liability claim; however, wanting to create the possibility of recovering for pain and suffering, those same plaintiffs will also file a claim under their member states' 1985 negligence doctrines. Under article 9's second interpretation, the English plaintiff can recover all damages by suing under EC-oriented strict liability; the German plaintiff, however, will find it necessary to join an EC-oriented strict liability claim with a claim under the 1985 German version of the negligence doctrine. These patterns of claims that the Directive can be expected to produce run the risk of turning the Directive into something of a debacle. One objective commonly associated with strict liability is the simplification of litigation. Given, however, the way in which the Directive, under either interpretation, will frequently require plaintiffs to join quite different theories, one of its consequences will be to render litigation much more complex. Indeed, a major early round of litigation will be needed merely to resolve the basic ambiguity in article 9 itself; and however that ambiguity is resolved, many plaintiffs' rights to recover for pain and suffering will depend, for the indefinite future, on the fortuity of exactly what form their own member state's negligence doctrine had assumed on one magic moment in 1985. I use vivid language like this because these 1985 doctrines do seem somewhat frozen in place. It seems clear enough that they cannot be enlarged in a pro-plaintiff way by any action taken by a member state's legislature or judiciary. (Such an enlargement would lead to a greater degree of nonuniformity within the EC than is tolerated by article 13.) Moreover, given the "shall not affect any rights" language of article 13, it is at least arguable that these lawmaking bodies are not permitted to diminish plaintiffs' mid-1985 rights either.

Patterns of Litigation and Costs of Liability

UNITED STATES: THEN AND NOW. I have described above the expansion of American product liability doctrine over the last thirty years. I can now report that during that thirty-year period the number of product liability claims has increased dramatically. As it happens, claim levels seem to have remained relatively stable in the 1960s. From 1970 through the mid-1980s, however, claims rose dramatically. Indeed, between 1974 and 1986 the number of annual product liability filings in federal court increased from 1,600 to 12,500.[65] Obviously, the expansion of doctrine in large part explains this growth in claims. But there are other explanations as well. One explanatory point is that lawyers have taken effective advantage of the opportunities afforded them by modern doctrine: they have become skillful in uncovering and proving the facts of a complicated product case. Another point—one which suggests that current claim levels might be artificially high—is that in recent years a limited number of products that have proved exceptionally hazardous (including asbestos and the Dalkon Shield) have generated a large number of claims. A third point concerns the quantum of damages. Studies undertaken by the Rand Institute for Civil Justice show that the average personal injury verdict in cases involving serious personal injury at least tripled in after-inflation dollars between the early 1960s and the early 1980s;[66] moreover, for reasons that are not yet well understood, there now seems to be an additional "premium" in the verdicts in product liability cases (and malpractice cases as well).[67] Undoubtedly, this surge towards much larger recoveries in product liability cases has been one factor encouraging the filing of product liability claims.

OTHER COUNTRIES. What can be said, however, about the level of product litigation in the United States compared with the levels in other countries? A recent article by P. S. Atiyah compares liability in England and the United States. According to his calculations, the lawsuit-per-capita rate for all of tort law in the United States is about four times what it is in England; moreover, the per-capita cost of torts in this country is, in his estimate, perhaps ten times the English cost.[68] His product liability numbers are even more one-sided: there are 70,000 product liability lawsuits in the United States annually, and only 200 in the United Kingdom. To be sure, the 350-to-1 ratio these numbers provide may be misleading. For one thing, as Atiyah makes clear, "claims" may lead to "lawsuits" more frequently in this country than they do in England; the American-English claims ratio might therefore be much less than the lawsuit ratio. Additionally, in England, as in the United States, there are large numbers of employees who have suffered disease on account of exposure to asbestos. In America tort suits resulting from these diseases are brought against manufacturers (since employers are shielded from tort liability by

65. Dungworth and Pace 1990, 14.
66. Peterson 1987, 37.
67. Hensler 1987, 490–91.
68. Atiyah 1987, 1009–14.

the exclusivity doctrine in workers' compensation). In England, however, an employee injured on the job not only has a workers' compensation–type claim (which he enforces against a government compensation fund) but also a possible tort action against his employer. Moreover, an English statute imposing on employers a near strict liability to keep job sites free of asbestos makes these tort actions against employers especially easy to win.[69] Accordingly, asbestos victims in England usually sue their employers in tort and make no effort to bring much more complicated actions against product manufacturers. A high volume of asbestos litigation thus exists in England, but it focuses on employer defendants and so does not swell the number of product liability claims against manufacturers (as it does in the United States).

Because of factors such as these, the notion of a 350-to-1 American-English product liability relationship is not meaningful. Still, without a doubt product liability is thriving in the United States in a way that it is not in England. This point can be confirmed by two simple observations. As of 1988 no product liability verdict had ever been entered against a drug manufacturer;[70] and until the 1986 specialty sports-car case described earlier, no auto manufacturer had ever been held liable under a theory of negligent design.[71] Furthermore, there is reason to believe that the huge difference between the level of product liability in the United States and its level in England is matched by similar differences between the United States and other countries. John Fleming's 1982 article described the German strict liability drug statute enacted in 1976. Between 1976 and 1982 not a single claim had been filed under the statute.[72] Five years later the liability costs that drug companies were incurring because of the statute equaled less than one-half of one percent of those companies' sales revenues.[73] A Canadian product liability defense lawyer recently discussed one product that was widely distributed both in the United States and Canada. In the United States there were a thousand claims against the manufacturer because of that product; in Canada, only eight.[74] One study of product liability in the Netherlands reported that in the past fifty years only five cases by injured consumers against the manufacturers

69. The English asbestos litigation is described in Felstiner and Dingwall 1987.

70. Fleming 1988, 15. The Opren cases, for example, settled before trial, and for a comparatively meager amount.

71. Atiyah and Cane 1987, 55–56.

72. Fleming 1982, 301.

73. Albanese and Del Duca 1987, 230.

74. Thomas 1989, 32–33.

of allegedly defective products resulted in published judicial opinions.[75] The 1985 EC Directive has occasioned a spate of law review articles written (or coauthored) by European scholars. None of these articles suggest significant pre-Directive differences in the litigation patterns from one member state to another, and several articles indicate that the litigation rate in the country under study is no more than a fraction of what the rate is perceived to be in the United States.[76]

Nor is there much indication that complying with the EC Directive will sharply increase the scope of liability within EC member states. The important limitations (and ambiguities) in the Directive have already been described. Acknowledging these limitations, one recent article concludes that the Directive "will bring hardly any change in the pattern of products liability decisions" in Germany, and that throughout the EC "the Directive will not bring about much change in the failure to warn area."[77] Another article perceives that "the Directive does not markedly advance the substantive law of a country like the Netherlands."[78] Insurance companies are now confirming these scholarly assessments; I am advised that when Germany's implementing statute went into effect on January 1, 1990, product liability insurers in Germany did not see fit to increase their premiums.

As described earlier in this chapter, the product liability rules applied in the United States differ in certain ways from those applied in other legal systems. These differences, however, are limited rather than extreme; hence they are not capable of providing more than a portion of the explanation for the order-of-magnitude discrepancies between levels of litigation in various legal systems. It follows, then, that much of the explanation for these discrepancies must come from elements of the legal system that extend beyond product liability doctrine itself. What these elements are is a question considered in a later section.

To be sure, the discussion so far has concerned Europe rather than Japan. As far as Japan is concerned, it is often pointed out that the number of trials and lawsuits in Japan (both for personal injury and for other kinds of losses) is quite low. One explanation commonly offered for this is that the Japanese legal system is costly and inefficient in a way that

---

75. Mann and Rodrigues 1988, 409. There were twenty other opinions in suits brought by "employers, insurers, and professional users."

76. For example, Albanese and Del Duca 1987, 228–29.

77. Will 1988, 149.

78. Mann and Rodrigues 1988, 407.

discourages the presenting of claims. A second common explanation is that Japanese cultural attitudes inhibit victims from even considering bringing lawsuits. However, a recent article coauthored by Mark Ramseyer, which focuses on auto accidents in Japan, offers a different description.[79] Although Ramseyer agrees that the number of Japanese auto accident cases that are finally tried in court is low, he thinks the legal system functions effectively—providing parties with such clear signals on the likely judicial results that the parties can (and do) settle claims for appropriate values without coming near the courthouse. Claims centers set up by liability insurance companies often facilitate these settlements. A small number of auto accident trials in Japan is thus compatible with a large number of claims and appropriate resolutions.

Ramseyer's account of the auto accident situation in Japan seems convincing.[80] His evidence, however, is limited to auto cases and does not profess to relate to the situation in other areas of tort law, such as product liability and medical malpractice. As far as the former is concerned, in Japan formal litigation against manufacturers is indeed uncommon. According to one survey of 194 major Japanese manufacturers, only 24 had been sued in Japan under product liability doctrines, and only 7 of these 24 had actually been subjected to judgments requiring compensation.[81]

Apparently, however, these Japanese litigation rates are as low as they are in part because of the availability of alternative procedures for the resolution of disputes. During a two-year period, for example, local consumer centers negotiated the outcome in more than 109 cases; personal injury damages were awarded in at least 34, with the largest award being about $20,000. The Japanese drug statute has been described above. Between 1980 and mid-1984, 270 claims were filed against the fund that this statute creates. Of these claims, 141 resulted in payments, averaging about $7,000. In addition, 54 products in Japan choose to carry an SG Seal. (The SG stands for Safety Goods; the 54 products are an odd assortment that includes baby carriages, swimming face-masks, mailboxes, bicycle helmets, and toilet-paper holders.) If a product marked with such a seal turns out to contain an injury-producing defect, the consumer can file a

79. Ramseyer and Nakazato 1989.
80. Of the systemic factors relied on below to explain the differentials between the levels of product and medical liability in the United States and the levels in other countries, some do apply—but many others do not—to the resolution of routine auto claims.
81. This and the next paragraph rely on Ramseyer 1990; on Hamada, Ishida, and Munakami 1986, 85–88; and on a memorandum prepared by Tadashi Yamanaka, deputy vice president of the Zurich Insurance Company.

claim against the SG Association; if the claim is accepted, the largest allowable award is about $165,000. To cover the cost of all awards, the association buys product liability insurance with the help of fees it collects from the manufacturers who elect to use its seal.[82] This voluntary program was authorized by 1973 consumer legislation.[83] As it happens, that legislation can be read as indicating that the association should bear liability only under Japan's ordinary negligence principles. Nevertheless, for whatever reason the association has chosen to neglect its defense of no negligence and accept liability whenever the labeled product is demonstrably defective. Between 1973 and early 1986, 132 claims—more than half of all claims filed—resulted in payments to victims by the association.

Auto manufacturers are not covered by any special program of this sort. Curious about the liability exposure of Japan's auto industry, I have been able to secure data from one of Japan's major manufacturers. This company has twice as many cars on the road in Japan as it has in the United States. Its American operations lead to about 250 product liability claims against the company each year. By contrast, in Japan the number of annual product liability filings averages about two. In a limited number of additional cases—in some years, no more than two—the company, having learned of the circumstances of a serious injury through its network of dealers, itself contacts the victim and makes what it regards as an appropriate voluntary payment.

In all, there are many ways in which Japanese manufacturers can end up encountering liability. Given this variety, one should avoid excessively confident statements about the exact level of liability in Japan. Still, the available data relating to the number of claims and the size of awards do make product liability in Japan generally appear quite modest.

Medical Malpractice Liability

This section first discusses in a comparative way the rules of liability that apply in malpractice cases. It then gathers available evidence on the incidence of litigation and the costs of liability in several legal systems.

82. It is unclear to what extent the fees paid by manufacturers are experience-rated to take the manufacturers' individual safety records into account.

83. For discussion of a scheme in Sweden that somewhat resembles this Japanese program, see Oldertz 1986. In Japan, there are also seal systems for children's toys and for construction materials; the latter system includes a liability insurance component.

Liability Rules

In responding to the adverse results of medical treatment, legal systems could adopt any of at least three basic legal positions. First, a legal system could hold that doctors should bear no liability for these adverse results. Second, a legal system could conclude that doctors should be subject to strict or automatic liability. Third, doctors could be held liable if (but only if) the results are due to some negligence or malpractice on the part of the doctor.

Given these doctrinal possibilities, it is revealing to realize that negligence—rather than no liability or strict liability—is just about the *universal* liability standard in suits against doctors.[84] That is, negligence seems to be the liability criterion currently relied on by almost every tort system. Moreover, at least within Anglo-American law, in medical cases negligence is just about the *eternal* liability standard as well—the standard that can be traced back to the first of the reported cases involving doctors, in late-fourteenth-century England. Some legal systems now conceptualize suits against doctors as a branch of tort law, while other systems regard that liability as arising out of the contract between doctor and patient. Yet no matter which way the doctor's liability is classified, negligence is the pertinent liability criterion. (In a contract-oriented jurisdiction, the contract between doctor and patient is understood to contain the doctor's implied promise to provide nonnegligent care.)

In other sectors of tort law, strict liability doctrines may well have made large strides during the last thirty years; medical liability law, by contrast, remains committed to the negligence standard. Of course, to say that negligence is the pervasive standard in medical cases leaves open the question of how leniently or stringently that standard is characterized in different legal systems. Negligence is often explained in the terms of "reasonableness" or "reasonable care." Japanese law, however, sets forth the idea that the doctor must comply with "a high duty of care," an obligation of the "utmost care."[85] Within negligence law, the reasonableness of a defendant's conduct is commonly determined by a balancing process that takes account of both the magnitude of the risk and the burden of risk avoidance. In using its "high duty of care" locution, Japanese law is probably expressing the point that since patient life and basic health are at stake in medical treatment, the negligence standard

84. I draw here on Grossen and Guillod 1983, 4–6; Zepos and Christodoulou 1983, 3–11, 14.

85. Fujita 1987, 16.

should place strong obligations on doctors.[86] Interpreted in this way, the Japanese locution is an elaboration on, rather than a departure from, the negligence standard. Still, it is a particular elaboration that one does not find in American malpractice opinions; and it is an elaboration that suggests that Japanese courts tend to be rigorous in how they apply the negligence concept to doctors.

A similar sternness can be found in German law: German courts are said to apply negligence principles to doctors in a manner that tends to be "severe."[87] Meanwhile, French law contains "a somewhat confusing array of apparently inconsistent opinions." At times, French courts seem to say that a doctor is liable for "any fault, even the slightest"; on other occasions, however, French courts indicate that even if a doctor is guilty of "imprudence, inattention or negligence," he should bear liability only if his conduct reveals "a positive ignorance of [the doctor's] duties." This latter language suggests that the French doctor is liable only for quite plain negligence, only (perhaps) for gross negligence. That, indeed, seems to be the situation in Switzerland, where a doctor is liable only for "obvious mistakes" and not for "the bare mistakes which are to some extent inherent in the practice of medicine."

In England, the malpractice standard was dealt with in *Whitehouse* v. *Jordan*. When *Whitehouse* was considered by the Court of Appeals, Lord Denning set forth his view that "in a professional man, an error of judgment is not negligent."[88] (In expressing this view, Lord Denning was explicit about his eagerness to see England avoid what he regarded as the excesses of malpractice liability in the United States.) On appeal to the House of Lords, the Denning formulation was found to be too broad. According to Lord Edmund-Davies, "while some such errors may be completely consistent with the due exercise of professional skill, other acts or omissions in the course of exercising 'clinical judgment' may be so below proper standards as to make a finding of negligence inevitable";[89] in Lord Fraser's view, "if [the error of clinical judgment] is one that would not have been made by a reasonably competent professional man . . . acting with ordinary care, then it is negligent."[90] The decentralized nature of American tort law makes it difficult to state what the American view is on the *Whitehouse* issue.

86. Ramseyer 1990.
87. This paragraph draws on Grossen and Guillod 1983, 7–9.
88. [1980] All. E.R. 650, 658.
89. [1981] 1 W.L.R. 246, 257–68.
90. [1981] 1 W.L.R. at 263.

Perhaps a half-dozen states have suggested that a doctor is not guilty of malpractice if he merely makes "an honest mistake of judgment"— at least where "the proper course [of treatment] is open to reasonable doubt."[91] Several other states, however, have rejected such a formulation, finding it either inaccurate or confusing; the most recent cases come out on both sides of this division in the law.[92]

In any event, all tort systems would apparently agree with one point suggested by Lord Fraser's *Whitehouse* formulation: that a doctor can be found guilty of malpractice if he departs from the custom of care established by other medical professionals. What is, however, the exact effect in a malpractice action of the doctor's proof that his treatment has *complied* with the treatment customarily provided by other doctors? As a general matter, in *non*malpractice tort cases, proof that the defendant has adhered to a custom within the relevant industry is evidence tending to suggest a lack of negligence on the defendant's part.[93] But this evidence is not conclusive on the issue of nonnegligence: the fact-finder remains free to find that an entire industry has lagged behind the standards of reasonable conduct required by the negligence test. In medical malpractice cases, however, custom often plays a more forceful role: a doctor is often said to be automatically nonnegligent if he has complied with medical custom.

To be sure, a minority of American courts have used language suggesting that evidence of custom compliance is not conclusive regarding the doctor's lack of malpractice. This minority position was given dramatic expression by a Washington court in *Helling* v. *Carey* in 1974.[94] In this case the court found an ophthalmologist guilty of malpractice as a matter of law for not having given a glaucoma pressure test to a patient under the age of forty, even though the court seemed to believe that not giving such a test was the common practice among the state's ophthalmologists. When the Washington opinion was first distributed, its bold approach was seen by many (including me) as a harbinger of judicial things to come. In retrospect, however, *Helling* has turned out to be an isolated case. Its reasoning has been rejected (or ignored) by other state courts; and even in Washington the *Helling* rule has been largely limited to its "unusual" facts by a later Wash-

91. Prosser and Keeton 1984, 186.
92. Prosser and Keeton 1984 (Supplement 1988, 29).
93. Recall, however, a special rule adopted by some state courts that regards evidence of compliance with industry custom as inadmissible in product liability actions.
94. 83 Wash. 2d 514, 519 P.2d 981 (1974).

ington opinion[95] (and also called into question by a somewhat awkwardly drafted Washington statute).[96]

English law clearly agrees with the majority American position: the doctor who complies with medical custom cannot be found guilty of malpractice. In France, Germany, and Japan, however, judicial opinions indicate that while medical custom should be given substantial respect, a doctor's proof of custom compliance does not entirely rule out a finding of malpractice.[97] Even so, in these countries it is difficult to find actual cases in which a doctor's custom-complying conduct has been found to be negligent; in this sense, while custom compliance is not in form conclusive, it may well be just about conclusive as a matter of fact.

Frequently, of course, the medical community is somewhat divided about what is the best course of treatment. That is, there may be several schools of thought concerning proper treatment, each of which can be considered respectable. What results, then, do courts reach on the malpractice question if the doctor has complied with the standards of one such school but if the plaintiff presents expert witnesses who express their views that the position of a competing school is superior? In England the law seems clear that a doctor cannot be found negligent so long as he has complied with the standard of practice set by "one respectable body of professional opinion."[98] In America a strong majority of states adhere to the same position;[99] one recent Texas opinion, however, can be read as indicating that there is at least some leeway for the jury to make up its own mind about which of the competing schools is "reasonable and prudent."[100]

In the nineteenth century, American tort law, in designating those standards or customs that should be considered in a specific malpractice case, limited itself to the standards that prevailed within the "locality" in which the doctor-defendant practiced. By 1960 most states had liberalized the law somewhat, to the point of focusing on doctors in the same "or similar" localities. In the last thirty years, however, the locality

95. *Gates* v. *Jensen*, 92 Wash. 2d 246, 252, 595 P.2d 919, 923 (1979).
96. Washington Revised Code §4.24.290.
97. Grossen and Guillod 1983, 8; Zepos and Christodoulou 1981, 18; Ramseyer 1990.
98. *Maynard* v. *West Redlands Regional Health Authority* (1983) W.L.R. 634, 639.
99. Note here the sharp contrast between malpractice and product liability. A malpractice claim is conclusively refuted if the doctor can show that he complied with the custom that prevails among one portion of the medical community; in product cases, evidence that the defendant complied with the custom of the entire industry is regarded by some state courts as a complete irrelevance.
100. *Hood* v. *Phillips*, 554 S.W.2d 160, 165 (Tex. 1977).

doctrine has been increasingly discarded by American courts. Those courts now measure the performance of specialists in accordance with national standards; in considering the conduct of general practitioners, many courts have abandoned the formal locality doctrine—even though they have shown a continuing willingness to take "locality" into account as one circumstance that is at least relevant in determinations of malpractice. In arriving at these positions, American law seems now to comply with the law prevailing in most of the rest of the world. The locality doctrine had been an invention of the American judiciary; it had never been accepted in England,[101] nor is there much sign of its invocation in other legal systems.[102] In Japan and elsewhere, however, courts are undoubtedly willing to consider locality as a fact of some relevance in individual cases.[103]

In a malpractice case—as in tort actions generally—the burden of proof on the negligence issue rests on the plaintiff-victim. In the United States, however, the plaintiff's burden is sometimes lightened by resort to the doctrine of res ipsa loquitur. To say that res ipsa applies is to indicate that the fact-finder—simply by considering the general circumstances of the patient's injury—can infer or presume that there must have been negligence on the part of the doctor. In fact, English courts themselves rely on the res ipsa doctrine in a limited number of malpractice cases, and the basic idea behind that doctrine also seems to be accepted by other legal systems—though they use other terminology.[104] For example, German law says that a trial judge, by relying on general "experience," can sometimes regard the nature of the patient's injury as providing "prima facie evidence" of the doctor's negligence.[105] French courts, meanwhile, refer to situations in which the doctor is presumed negligent—situations in which the doctor "must have made a mistake," in which there is "virtual negligence" on the doctor's part.[106]

Yet while the basic idea behind res ipsa is widely accepted in the medical context, the American tort system may well apply that idea to a considerably broader range of malpractice cases than tort systems do elsewhere.

101. Fleming 1959, 640–41.

102. It is not mentioned, for example, in Zepos and Christodoulou 1983. The doctrine is recognized, however, in Canada. Linden 1977, 114–15. Perhaps Canada borrowed the doctrine from its neighbor, the United States; perhaps the vast geography of both Canada and the United States makes the doctrine more attractive in these two countries than it is in compact European nations.

103. For Japan, see Ramseyer 1990.

104. Zepos and Christodoulou 1983, 26–31.

105. Markesinis 1986, 312–17.

106. Grossen and Guillod 1983, 12.

In Europe the idea seems to be relied on only in cases that are factually extreme: for example, a sponge left in a patient after surgery, or a patient who suffers a "remote injury"—one that is well outside the area of the surgery itself. But during the last twenty-five years many American courts have allowed res ipsa to be applied more liberally: it can be invoked whenever the plaintiff's expert witness testifies that in his view the adverse outcome would not ordinarily happen in the absence of physician negligence.[107] Moreover, in America res ipsa can be asserted against *all* members of a surgical team once the evidence shows that the patient has suffered an injury that was probably due to the negligence of one member of that team.[108] This entails a grouplike application of the res ipsa doctrine that European countries would not be willing to accept.[109]

One noticeable area of growth in American malpractice law during the last twenty years concerns the doctrine of informed consent. In a typical informed consent case, the doctor performs surgery in a competent way, but the patient nevertheless suffers injury because of one of the inherent risks of the surgery itself. Even though the doctor has secured the patient's advance consent for the surgery, the plaintiff can claim that the doctor failed to provide the patient with the relevant information on those inherent risks that would have better enabled the plaintiff to give his "informed consent." Although it has long been part of American law, the informed consent doctrine traditionally required the plaintiff to show that the doctor's failure to disclose certain information departed from the disclosure standards customary in the profession. However, in a leading 1972 decision, one American court rejected this doctor-oriented disclosure standard in favor of one that is overtly patient-oriented: the doctor must disclose all the information that a typical plaintiff would regard as relevant in making up his own mind about whether to undergo surgery.[110] Since many doctors apparently believe they should themselves make the key decisions bearing on their patients' health, a patient-oriented informed consent standard seems to be much more favorable to plaintiffs than the doctor-oriented standard. Several American courts have now followed this 1972 initiative. Apparently, however, most American states—either by judicial decision or by recent legislation—continue to accept the older doctor-oriented approach.

107. For example, *Quintal* v. *Laurel Grove Hospital*, 397 P.2d 161, 41 Cal. Rptr. 577 (1964).

108. *Ybarra* v. *Spangard*, 154 P.2d 687 (1944).

109. Zepos and Christodoulou 1983, 29. See also Linden 1977, 248–49.

110. *Canterbury* v. *Spence*, 464 F.2d 772 (1972).

The general doctrine of informed consent is by no means an American idiosyncrasy; it appears in many tort systems. In England the doctrine was reviewed by the House of Lords in a 1985 case. While one Lord wanted to adopt the patient-oriented disclosure standard found in recent American opinions, the majority of Lords voted to retain a reasonable-doctor standard of disclosure.[111] As Lord Bridge put it, the disclosure of inherent risks to patients should be "primarily . . . a matter of [the doctor's] clinical judgment." Indeed, Lord Bridge further said that a doctor discharges his informed consent obligations so long as he acts in accordance with a practice accepted at the time as proper "by a reasonable body of neuro-surgical opinion," even though other neurosurgeons might well have provided disclosure. Lord Bridge acknowledged, however, that there might be extreme cases in which the disclosure of a risk to a patient might be "so obviously necessary to [the patient's] informed choice" that the court could insist on disclosure even in the face of a practice of nondisclosure by many or most physicians.

Elsewhere in Europe, however, the view of informed consent seems to be more in line with the recent American initiative. In these legal systems it is said that the patient should be given "all necessary information" that is "likely to influence" the patient's decision.[112] As early as 1958 a German court gave informed consent a strong application in the case of a psychiatric patient who suffered injury from the administration of electric shock therapy.[113] Emphasizing that the relationship between doctor and patient is "much more than a contractual relationship" and is indeed "a human relationship, in which the doctor comes to the aid of the patient," the court seemingly placed on doctors the obligation to provide patients (or their guardians) with all the information they need to exercise "the right . . . to self-determination" meaningfully. The boldness of this 1959 German opinion can be compared with modern American opinions, which tend to be equivocal when applying the informed consent doctrine in psychiatric cases.

In completing this survey of malpractice law, I can briefly mention three areas in which there have been some recent signs of liability development. First, consider the patient who reveals to his psychotherapist

---

111. *Sidaway* v. *Bethlem Royal Hospital* [1985] 1 A.C. 871, 900, 901. For discussion, see Schwartz and Grubb 1985.

112. Zepos and Christodoulou 1983, 34. To be sure, these commentators waffle a bit. But a multinational trend toward a patient-oriented standard is described in Giesen 1988, 294–97.

113. Giesen 1988, 268–69; Markesinis 1986, 227–36.

an intent to commit a deadly assault on another person. Many American courts now follow the lead of a 1976 California opinion that effectively requires such a psychotherapist to provide the potential victim with a warning;[114] this, however, is an "affirmative duty" that has not yet been recognized in tort systems outside the United States. Second, consider the doctor who negligently fails to make a proper diagnosis of a disease such as cancer; had he made the diagnosis at the proper time, the patient would have enjoyed a 30 percent chance of recovery—but no more than that. In such a case, the patient cannot show that it is more likely than not that he would have recovered had the doctor diagnosed him non-negligently; given this inability, under conventional doctrine the patient would be unable to sue. In these cases, however, French courts are now willing to recognize that the patient has at least lost a *chance* of a recovery and hence to grant damages to such a patient in a way that takes that lost chance into account.[115] In England one 1987 case denied a recovery for such a lost chance;[116] in America recent court rulings are divided on this issue. Third, consider the doctor whose negligence results in the "wrongful birth" of a child to parents who had intended to remain childless. (The doctor, for example, may have done a bad job in giving the father a vasectomy.) Consider also the doctor whose negligence results in the "wrongful life" of a deformed child. (The doctor, for example, may have negligently failed to diagnose the deformity at a time during pregnancy when the mother could easily have aborted. For such a child, the non-negligent alternative to a deformed life would be no life at all.) Courts in the United States, Germany, and England have all recently grappled with the conundrums these cases raise.[117] While current American liability rules may well be somewhat more generous than those in Germany and England, what should be emphasized here is the extent to which all jurisdictions have striven to achieve sensible intermediate results. None of the legal systems have adopted the rule that medical professionals are never liable in cases of this sort, and no jurisdiction has allowed the disabled child in a wrongful life case to recover for all the emotional pain that accompanies his disability.

114. *Tarasoff* v. *Regents of the University of California*, 17 Cal. 3d 425, 551 P.2d 334, 131 Cal. Rptr. 14 (1976).

115. Grossen and Guillod 1983, 12.

116. *Hotson* v. *East Berkshire Area Health Authority* [1987] A.C. 750 (C.A., H.L.), [1987] 2 All. E.R. 909 (H.L.), [1987] 1 All. E.R. 210 (C.A.), as discussed in Fleming 1989, 672–75.

117. See Giesen 1988, 242–51; Markesinis 1986, 99–112.

Patterns of Litigation and Costs of Liability

UNITED STATES: The discussion above of American malpractice law permits us to compare the law now to what it was in 1960. Over these thirty years malpractice liability rules have expanded in certain respects. The locality doctrine has been scaled down, and the doctrines of informed consent and res ipsa loquitur have broadened somewhat. An additional point, not mentioned earlier, is that many courts have relaxed the statute of limitations that applies in malpractice cases, holding that the statute does not begin to run until the plaintiff has a reasonable opportunity to discover the adverse consequences of the doctor's treatment.[118]

These are the doctrinal changes that have taken place over thirty years. Especially in the aggregate, they are by no means insignificant. All the same, they are hardly overwhelming—especially since they have occurred during an extended period in which tort law has been in general turmoil and in which many areas of public policy nationwide have been in continuing ferment. Indeed, on balance, what may well be impressive about American malpractice doctrine is how relatively stable it has been over an extended period. Whatever the relevance of strict liability in modern American product liability law, the law of malpractice remains committed to a negligence standard, as elaborated on in a generally traditional way.

What is known, however, about changes in the rates of suits and costs of liability during this period? As of the early 1960s, there was about one malpractice claim filed each year for every sixty-five doctors.[119] By 1988 that ratio has risen to almost one in seven; moreover, doctors' malpractice insurance premiums now average about $16,000.[120] The various changes in malpractice doctrine are of course relevant to this increase in claim levels. Clearly, however, these moderate changes in doctrine can provide only a limited part of the explanation for the enormous increase in the level of claims. Moreover, the doctrinal shifts had largely been completed by the mid-1970s; doctrinal expansion is therefore especially ineffective

118. Statutes of limitation are not ordinarily regarded as falling under the heading of "tort doctrine." The liability of hospitals has been expanded by the abrogation of doctrines of governmental and charitable immunity and by the broadening of the hospital's vicarious liability for the malpractice of physicians with hospital privileges. Expanded hospital liability might enhance doctor liability by enabling plaintiffs to sue both doctor and hospital in circumstances in which the hospital might then have a motive to offer evidence that inculpates the doctor. Expanded hospital liability might, however, reduce doctor liability by effectively diverting claims from doctors to hospitals.

119. Danzon 1985, 59.

120. Weiler (forthcoming).

in explaining the continuing rise in claims between 1975 and 1985. Alternative explanations are, of course, available. The Rand studies, as described earlier, found a huge increase in the after-inflation jury verdicts in malpractice cases, and it is likely that the availability of much larger awards has functioned to encourage claims. Also, malpractice lawyers, like product lawyers, have over the years acquired a greater sophistication in developing the facts of a difficult case. It may well be that a deterioration in the relationship of trust between patient and doctor has facilitated claims. In addition, in light of one 1974 study showing that only about 10 percent of all incidents of malpractice were giving rise to malpractice claims, the growth in claims since then can plausibly be seen as part of a catch-up process.[121]

OTHER COUNTRIES: A sharp increase in the number of malpractice claims is by no means unique to the United States. Patricia Danzon reports that "claim frequency" has recently been rising rapidly in England, Canada, and Australia.[122] Her data show that in England, for example, there were 1,000 claims in 1983, but more than 2,000 in 1987. Yet even though England resembles the United States in having experienced a sharp increase in the number of malpractice claims, England continues to differ sharply from the United States in total claim levels. Atiyah reports that whereas there were 40,000 malpractice claims filed in the United States in 1983, in 1985 there were only 2,000 claims filed in England.[123] Since the population of the United States is four times that of England, the per capita claims ratio is five to one.[124]

The cost of malpractice insurance is a datum that may conveniently sum up the number of malpractice claims, the liability cost per claim, and the cost of defending against claims (be they weak or strong). In 1985 the standard malpractice premium paid by English doctors was about $500; by 1987 the average premium had risen to just over $1,000.[125] By 1988, Danzon reports, that premium had increased further to $1,700.[126]

---

121. California Medical Association 1977 (based on 1974 data). This study, like the Harvard Medical Practice Study (1990), reports that about 1 percent of all hospital patients end up as victims of malpractice, and that only about 10-to-12 percent of these victims eventually bring suit. Something, however, must be wrong with one of these sets of data. For taken together, they imply that the number of malpractice claims has remained steady (on a per-patient basis) since 1974; and this implication is drastically false.

122. Danzon 1990, 50–51.

123. Atiyah 1987, 1014.

124. Actually, the ratio may well be higher than this, since the number of malpractice claims in the United States was apparently increasing rapidly during 1983–85.

125. Atiyah 1987, 1014.

126. Danzon 1990, 51.

This is about one-ninth of the cost of malpractice insurance in America. That is, the per-physician cost of malpractice in the United States is nine times what it is in England. This number can be compared (and contrasted) with an estimate developed by Atiyah: that the entire per capita cost of the malpractice system in the United States is perhaps thirty times what it is in England.[127]

What data are available for other countries suggest that their experience is at an order of magnitude that resembles England's. (To be sure, the English and American experience of rising claim frequency shows that one must be cautious in interpreting the current significance of claims data that are more than a few years old.) The annual number of malpractice claims in France in the late 1970s was about 1,500;[128] in Switzerland as of 1979 the number was less than 200. In France in 1978 the malpractice insurance premium for a general practitioner was $100; for a surgeon, $1,400. In Switzerland a year later a general practitioner's premium was $215; a surgeon's premium, $1,025. Given the vastly higher cost of malpractice premiums in the United States, one is hardly surprised to learn that the medical profession in England "is almost paranoic" in its fear of American malpractice patterns,[129] and that many Europeans who comment on malpractice are "quite frightened" by what they know of the American system.[130] As for Japan, I have recently been able to consult three Japanese physicians (two of them surgeons). What they tell me is that their annual malpractice premiums are close to 50,000 yen (about $320);[131] moreover, these premiums have remained steady over the last several years. If insurance premiums do fairly reflect the overall cost of malpractice liability in Japan, then malpractice seems to be an area of Japanese tort practice that is extremely modest by American standards.[132]

In sum, the malpractice system in the United States clearly operates at a level of intensity unknown in malpractice systems in European countries or Japan. Nothing, however, in the comparison of formal malpractice doctrine is able to account for these order-of-magnitude discrepancies.

127. Atiyah 1987, 1014–15.
128. The European numbers in this paragraph come from Grossen and Guillod 1983, 17–18.
129. Atiyah 1987, 1002.
130. Grossen and Guillod 1983, 21.
131. The insurance policies are issued by national and local medical associations.
132. Granted, in comparing American and Japanese insurance premiums, one should acknowledge Ramseyer's suggestion that the Japanese tort system is sometimes able to resolve disputes in a low-cost way. The lower overhead for litigation will of course reduce insurance rates.

Here too, then, one must focus on nondoctrinal features of the tort system.

Systemic Differences

To identify those elements of the tort system that might explain the differences in liability patterns among countries, this section begins by considering ways in which civil procedures employed in American tort cases differ from the procedures relied on by other legal systems. I then look at how the American tort system provides for the remuneration of lawyers representing plaintiffs and defendants. Finally, I consider differences among countries in the calculation of damages in tort cases once liability has been affirmed.

Civil Procedure

A distinctive feature of American procedure is the availability of pretrial discovery. In American tort actions the plaintiff, seeking to acquire information that will support his case, can depose any potential witness and can subject the defendant to a series of written interrogatories. These are discovery techniques that are largely unavailable in European legal systems and in Japan as well.[133] Discovery in its American form clearly makes it enormously more feasible for the plaintiff's lawyer to develop the facts of a complicated tort case. And claims in medical malpractice and product liability are usually complex. Indeed, an experienced Japanese lawyer is emphatic that the lack of discovery places the Japanese product liability plaintiff in a "very weak and difficult position."[134]

Several writers, in comparing the American tort process to those in effect elsewhere, have focused on the availability of class actions under American law. This is, however, a feature of American civil procedure that impresses me as not being very important. For one thing, while the class action device is not available in most of Europe, "group lawsuits" *are* allowable under Japanese law,[135] and several of the early major cases involving product liability in Japan were group actions resulting from mass torts. Furthermore, even though a country like England does not

133. Fujita 1987, 40–41; Genn 1987, 32; Mann and Rodrigues 1988, 411–12; Thieffry, Van Doorn, and Lowe 1989, 88–89.
134. Fujita 1987, 41.
135. Fujita 1987, 20, 73.

allow for class actions, when there are a large number of tort claims against particular defendants, the English legal system seems to arrange itself so as to provide a test case or "test action"—the results of which will be binding, in a somewhat de facto way, on other tort claims.[136] In addition, even in the United States actions have been attempted in only a limited number of cases (for example, Agent Orange, and the Hyatt hotel disaster in Kansas City). And in those cases the results for plaintiffs have been sufficiently unfavorable to make it unlikely that personal injury victims (and their lawyers) will be enthusiastic about launching class actions in the future.

One distinctive feature of American procedure that clearly does make a major difference relates to the identity of the trier-of-fact. In the United States, tort cases are heard by a jury (under the supervision, to be sure, of a trial judge). But juries in tort cases are unknown in civil law countries like France and Germany;[137] nor are juries now provided for in tort actions in Japan.[138] In England personal injury cases were commonly heard by juries until 1883, when new rules of procedure were adopted that gave the trial judge the discretion to rule whether a jury trial is appropriate. The trial judge's discretion was reemphasized by a 1933 statute. However, judicial opinions subsequently interpreting that statute have declared that in personal injury cases jury trials should be ordered (if at all) only in exceptional circumstances.[139] The situation in Canada offers an intermediate position between the practice in America and the practice elsewhere in the world. Under Canadian law a jury is available in a tort action in the first instance. But on the motion of either party the judge can determine that the particular case is complex in a way that makes its consideration by a jury unsatisfactory.[140] In product and malpractice cases, defendants frequently move that the jury be dismissed— and judges frequently grant these motions and then hear the cases themselves.

What significance should be attached to the fact that in Europe and Japan malpractice and product cases are regularly considered by judges rather than juries? The widespread view among American trial lawyers is that juries tend to be sympathetic to plaintiffs: that is, they rule in

---

136. Atiyah 1987, 1016; *Wright* v. *Dunlop Rubber Co.* [1972] 13 K.I.R. 255.
137. Albanese and Del Duca 1987, 229.
138. Fujita 1987, 40. The court that decides tort cases usually consists of a three-judge panel.
139. Jolowicz 1986 55–56.
140. Picard 1978, 218–19; Thomas 1989, 33.

favor of plaintiffs more frequently than a fair assessment of the evidence would warrant. As it happens, empirical confirmation for this widespread belief is somewhat hard to come by; but if the data do not confirm the belief, they do not refute it either. Without such a refutation, it seems appropriate to accept the view of experienced trial lawyers and to agree that trial by jury inclines American tort trials toward pro-plaintiff results.[141] In malpractice cases English judges seem to be especially reluctant to second-guess doctors and hence rule in favor of liability.[142] This reluctance is said to be most obvious when the plaintiff merely alleges that the doctor failed to make an appropriate diagnosis or recommend a proper treatment.[143]

One particular mechanism by which trial by jury might affect the results of cases can be identified here. Malpractice and product cases frequently turn on the weight to be given to the testimony of expert witnesses. (Indeed, these cases frequently turn out to entail a battle of experts.) Professional judges are likely to be skilled in their ability to assess the quality of expert testimony; partisan testimony that can easily impress an American jury might if anything antagonize an English judge. Moreover, when an expert testifies in a jury case, his bedside manner may play an important role in influencing how the jury responds to his testimony. (Indeed, a top expert can exude a self-confidence that the jury might regard as off-puttingly arrogant.) Accordingly, the American practice of trial by jury may facilitate a situation in which what some call "junk science" plays an unfortunate role in determining the outcome of cases.

As for the battle of experts in product and malpractice cases, such battles are most likely in the United States and England, given the adversary system that is associated with the common law. By contrast, the civil law system that prevails in continental Europe assigns a far greater range of responsibilities to the judge. In the trial itself,[144] it is the judge

---

141. Note, however, that trial by jury takes much longer than trial by judge. Accordingly, a jury regime adds to the costs of litigation and increases the duration of pretrial delay. In these respects, such a regime may serve as a disincentive to victims who are thinking about filing suit.

142. Atiyah 1987, 1021. See, for example, the House of Lords' review of the evidence in *Whitehouse* v. *Jordan,* as commented on by Robertson 1981.

143. Quam, Dingwall, and Fenn 1988, 457.

144. Indeed, in civil law countries the very notion of a unitary "trial" is itself inapt. Rather, the legal proceedings consist of a series of sessions before the judge, with much of the information considered by the judge coming in by way of written statements, rather than live testimony. Kaplan, von Mehren, and Schaefer 1958, 1471–72.

who will probably examine the expert;[145] for that matter, the judge may well be the person who designates those experts who will testify. (For example, the Dutch judge hearing a product case involving the sleeping medication Halcion resolved to decide the case by arranging for a committee of three experts.)[146] And even when a party is allowed to select his own expert, for that party's lawyer to interview the expert before trial might be regarded as an impropriety.[147] For an American lawyer not to "prepare" the important witnesses in his case would be all but unthinkable; in civil law countries such preparation, far from being obligatory, is frequently just about forbidden.

What I have here claimed is that distinctive American procedures such as trial by jury and pretrial discovery probably play a significant role in explaining the difference between the size of the tort system here and its size elsewhere in the world. To be sure, these procedures have been part of American law at least since the 1940s, whereas the overall tort differential became as conspicuous as it now is only in the 1970s. For all we know, however, there might have been significant differences in earlier decades, even though they were not then frequently commented on. Moreover, at least in product cases the discrepancy in timing can be explained by referring to the interaction between the procedures themselves and the development of underlying rules of tort liability. Only in the 1970s, for example, did product liability law begin to allow plaintiffs to engage in a rather free-wheeling process of challenging the appropriateness of particular product designs. Such expansions in formal liability doctrine have thus greatly magnified the significance of the discretion the American jury possesses, and likewise have enlarged the advantage American plaintiffs can achieve by subjecting defendants to extensive discovery.

Financing Lawyers' Fees

This country's legal system differs considerably from legal systems elsewhere in how plaintiffs' lawyers and defendants' lawyers receive their compensation. As for the plaintiff's lawyer, in the United States the personal injury plaintiff routinely enters into a contingent fee arrangement with his lawyer pursuant to which the lawyer retains perhaps one-third of whatever recovery is eventually received but receives nothing if the

---

145. Thieffry, Van Doorn, and Lowe 1989, 89.
146. Mann and Rodrigues 1988, 398–99.
147. Kaplan, von Mehren, and Schaefer 1958, 1200–01; Langbein 1985, 835–41.

claim is disposed of without any payment by the defendant. Contingent fee arrangements are regarded as unethical, however, by the legal systems in England and other European countries.[148] In those legal systems, therefore, the middle-income victim who is thinking of filing a claim realizes that if his claim finally proves unsuccessful, he will be required to pay his own lawyer's fee. As for the fee of the defense counsel, the "American rule" specifies that, regardless of who finally wins the case, each side should bear its own legal costs. By contrast, the so-called English rule—which is also in effect in other European legal systems—specifies that the losing party must reimburse the prevailing party for the latter's attorney's fees. That is, the plaintiff who loses his case is required to pay not only his own lawyer's fee but also the fee of the defendant's lawyer.

Many of the scholarly articles that have considered the incentive effects of the American rule have given only limited attention to the contingent fee; moreover, articles looking at the incentive effects of the contingent fee have tended to accept the American rule as a given. In all, then, not many scholars have treated each of these practices as variables and have then assessed what their combined effects might be. Indeed, there do seem to be certain important litigation patterns for which this combination is responsible. Consider the plaintiff who is thinking of bringing a claim against the defendant and who realizes that he is an "underdog," that his chances of prevailing—while more than trivial—are still less than 50 percent. Assume, more specifically, that he has a 20 percent chance of prevailing and that his damages if he does prevail will be $100,000. Under American arrangements, so long as the plaintiff can find a lawyer who is willing to take his case, he can authorize the lawyer to proceed with the case without worrying about the expenses of litigation. His lawyer, moreover, will appreciate that the case has a settlement value of perhaps $20,000; he therefore may well agree to accept the case under a contingent fee arrangement. By contrast, in European legal systems the underdog plaintiff will need to take into account the fact that if the case goes to trial, there is a more than 50 percent possibility that he not only will receive no award but will also incur an obligation to pay both his own lawyer's bills and those of the defendant's lawyer. As compared, then, with the European alternative, the American incentive system almost certainly encourages the bringing of underdog claims.[149]

148. Fleming 1988, 19.
149. Legal actions that are brought with the law-reform hope of persuading appellate courts to break new doctrinal ground are generally long shots or underdogs. Accordingly, these are actions that the American system comparatively encourages. Prichard 1988.

An additional point is that the American rule may influence not only the bringing of suits but also the way in which those suits are structured. In this country a plaintiff filing suit will often find strategic value in bringing in a large number of defendants, many of whom are seemingly "peripheral"; that is, defendants whose relationship to the plaintiff's injury is questionable. By expanding his suit in this way, the plaintiff can encourage the defendants to quarrel among themselves in a manner that might eventually redound to the plaintiff's benefit. Under the English rule, however, whenever the plaintiff's claim against a peripheral defendant is dismissed, the plaintiff incurs an obligation to reimburse that defendant for its attorney's fees.[150] That rule thus discourages plaintiffs from expanding the scope of litigation in the way that has become common in this country.

In several respects, however, the account given here of the English system needs to be rendered somewhat more complex. Under that system the solicitor's fees the loser is required to pay are those that are "reasonably incurred."[151] Yet the full bill the defendant's solicitor runs up can easily be well in excess of what a trial judge would regard as the "reasonably incurred" figure. Accordingly, the obligation that the English rule places on the losing plaintiff is merely an obligation to pay a substantial fraction of the defendant's litigation costs. Moreover, in England there are informal practices that somewhat diminish the force of the formal rules themselves. For example, when a plaintiff of modest wealth sues in tort and loses, his solicitor is likely to "forget" the fee that he is technically owed;[152] similarly, the defendant may well allow his right to reimbursement from such a plaintiff to go unenforced.[153] Also, England makes available a legal aid program to low-income victims who might want to assert a tort claim. If the legal aid committee agrees to fund the victim's case, then the plaintiff is free of any compensation obligation to his solicitor;[154] moreover, under the rules pertaining to legal aid, the acceptance of the plaintiff by the legal aid committee usually releases the plaintiff from the obligation to reimburse the defendant for its legal fees if the plaintiff fails at trial.[155]

150. Felstiner and Dingwall 1987, 7.
151. Fleming 1988, 187.
152. Atiyah reports that the contract between solicitor and client often makes clear that the former's fee will ordinarily be paid from the recovery that the latter receives. Atiyah 1987, 1017.
153. Felstiner and Dingwall 1987, 17.
154. If the plaintiff has some assets, legal aid can require him to make some contribution to legal costs. Genn 1987, 85.
155. Genn 1987, 89.

A legal aid committee, however, will accept a tort case only if it assesses the case as having "reasonable grounds," a "reasonable chance of success."[156] Consider the $100,000 claim with a 20 percent chance of success. As noted, an American lawyer, operating under the contingent fee, might accept the case, perceiving that it has a settlement value of perhaps $20,000. In England, however, the legal aid committee might well conclude that the case's prospects for success were something less than "reasonable"; if so, it would decline to provide the victim with representation.

Of course, within the United States, to say that a $100,000 claim has a 20 percent chance of success may well mean that the evidence in support of the claim is objectively weak, but that it is nevertheless foreseeable that a jury, sympathizing with a badly injured plaintiff, might resolve all doubts in the plaintiff's favor. When this is the explanation for the 20 percent possibility of success, then the same lawsuit, if brought in juryless England, might have no more than a 5 percent chance of success. The American combination, then, of trial by jury and lawyers'-fee practices may *both* lower the odds against the underdog plaintiff *and* increase the likelihood that a plaintiff, facing such odds, will be able to find a lawyer who will provide him with representation.

American opponents of the contingent fee often claim that it encourages the bringing of "frivolous" cases. At one level, the arithmetic of this claim seems itself frivolous: one-third of nothing is nothing.[157] Consider, however, the $100,000 malpractice claim that has only a 20 percent chance of success and assume as well that most of this chance is due to the possibility of unbalanced jury decisionmaking. The economist would say that this claim is far from frivolous, in the sense that it has a clear and significant expected value. It is understandable, however, that doctors, faced with the possibility of such malpractice suits, would be inclined to deride those suits as frivolous.

In acknowledging, however, the incentives for litigation afforded by American attorneys'-fee practices, one should also note that Japanese practices seem on balance even more favorable to plaintiffs.[158] Japanese law does not prohibit, first of all, the contingent fee. What happens in Japan is that at the outset of a case the plaintiff pays his lawyer a "retainer" that corresponds to the lawyer's likely out-of-pocket expenses, along with moderate

156. Atiyah and Cane 1987, 260; Fleming 1988, 198; Genn 1987, 88.
157. See Bebchuk 1988, however, for an interesting discussion of how a plaintiff might find it advantageous to submit a nuisance claim—a claim that stands no chance of prevailing at trial.
158. Kojima and Taniguchi 1978, 704–05. The legal-aid plaintiff in England is in a somewhat similar position.

compensation for the lawyer's time. But a larger figure—called the success fee—is paid by the plaintiff to the lawyer only if the plaintiff's claim leads to a payment from the defendant. Moreover, at least in exceptional situations, Japanese lawyers apparently waive their right to the original retainer; in these cases, therefore, the plaintiff's lawyer's fee is completely contingent. Furthermore, as far as the defendant's lawyer's fees are concerned, Japanese law has developed a special practice of one-way fee shifting that applies only in personal injury cases. Under this practice a losing plaintiff is never liable to the defendant for the defendant's attorney's fees; nevertheless, if the plaintiff prevails at trial, one element of damages for which the plaintiff is entitled to compensation is a reasonable amount for his attorney's fees. In sum, Japanese plaintiffs receive the benefit of the English rule when they win and the protection of the American rule when they lose. It should be noted, by the way, that the Japanese practice of one-way fee shifting does not wipe out the significance of the Japanese practices relating to the quasi-contingent fee. For one thing, the reasonable attorney's fee for which the winning plaintiff secures compensation may well be less than the "success fee" previously agreed on by the plaintiff and his lawyer. Also, when Japanese cases are settled, it may be difficult to identify the plaintiff as an unambiguous winner; consider, for example, the $80,000 claim, with a 50 percent chance of prevailing at trial, that settles for $40,000. Since Japanese practices might not call for fee shifting in a case of this sort, the success fee might remain relevant.

Damages

The American plaintiff who prevails on the issue of liability is likely—for a combination of reasons spelled out below—to receive a much larger damage award than the plaintiff in Europe or Japan who is similarly successful.[159] In the American tort system, personal injury awards as large

159. But see a recent report on asbestos litigation in England indicating that the average asbestos award in that country is no more than one-third lower than the average award in the United States. Felstiner and Dingwall 1987, 23–24. This finding applies, however, only to the compensatory feature of the award, not to punitive damages, which are uniquely available to the American plaintiff. Moreover, since the study was primarily concerned with the benefits provided to plaintiffs rather than with the liabilities borne by defendants, in comparing awards the study tended to ignore the medical damages that the American plaintiff recovers (since the English plaintiff receives medical services without charge from the National Health Service). Also, in a recent conversation Felstiner has confirmed that his finding of relatively equal awards applies only to asbestosis cases, and not to lung cancer cases, where awards are both much larger and undoubtedly much more unequal.

as $15 million are by no means unknown.[160] In Japan, however, even the high-income professional who is totally disabled because of a defendant's clear negligence is able to recover no more than about $1,400,000.[161] And Japanese awards are high relative to awards in Europe. In 1989 the largest personal injury award in France was about $700,000.[162] As of the early 1980s the largest medical malpractice award in England was $775,000.[163] Danzon has more recently reported that the mean payment for malpractice claims in England is currently only one-fourth of the mean payment for such claims in the United States.[164]

Larger awards affect the burden that tort defendants bear in two obvious ways. First, even if the number of claims and verdicts is held constant, larger awards obviously result in a larger overall magnitude of liability. Second, the prospect of larger awards can be expected to increase significantly the number of suits filed in the first instance. Consider two tort claims each of which has, say, a 50 percent chance of succeeding. Claim 1, brought in the United States, will if it succeeds lead to a verdict of $100,000. Claim B, brought in Europe, will if it succeeds produce a verdict of only $40,000. As plaintiffs (and their lawyers) think about the advisability of filing suit, the American plaintiff is far more likely than his European counterpart to file, since the expected value of the American claim (50 percent times $100,000) is so much higher than that of the European claim (50 percent of $40,000).

In some respects larger damage awards in the United States are due to distinctive attributes of the American economy. For example, since real American wages remain higher than real wages elsewhere, American awards for income losses will be higher than similar awards in other parts of the world. In other respects our larger damage awards are due to distinctive features in the American law of damages. For example, American wrongful death statutes, as interpreted by American judges, provide for a mea-

160. One such award, affirmed on appeal, is in *Firestone* v. *Crown Center Redevelopment Corp.*, 693 S.W.2d 99 (Mo. 1985). A product liability case in California has recently been settled for $31 million, payable immediately. See *Los Angeles Times*, October 14, 1990, p. A20. Malpractice jury verdicts in excess of $50 million are reported in Weiler (forthcoming). It is possible that these verdicts were reduced by the trial judge or on appeal.

161. Fujita 1987, 71. Professor Koichi Bai has advised me, however, of a very recent malpractice award exceeding $2 million.

162. I rely here on a table of verdicts circulated on a periodic basis as part of the Juris-Classeurs series.

163. Grossen and Guillod 1983, 18.

164. Danzon 1990, 51. Danzon acknowledges that her data are limited. These data concern both verdicts and settlements. Cases are presumably settled with their verdict potential in mind.

sure of recovery in wrongful death actions that often greatly surpasses the damages available in such actions in countries like England.[165] Also, English damages for income losses are measured on an after-tax basis; most American courts, by contrast, are willing to afford compensation for pretax losses.[166] Moreover, in Germany, France, and Japan, punitive damages are understood to be simply unavailable in tort actions for personal injuries.[167] In the United States, however, punitive damages can properly be requested in personal injury cases. They are in fact awarded in only a small proportion of product and malpractice cases. Yet this proportion has grown considerably in recent years, as courts have confirmed relatively broad interpretations of the relevant criteria for the award of punitive damages. Also, when punitive damages *are* allowed here, they are increasingly awarded in large amounts. Accordingly, by including a prayer for punitive damages in his complaint, the plaintiff may be able to increase the settlement value of his suit significantly.

I should point out, however, one special feature of German law that somewhat reduces the contrast between America and Germany. Although German law does not allow personal injury plaintiffs to recover punitive damages, it does authorize in negligence cases the award of damages for pain and suffering. Furthermore, German law adopts the position that one function of pain-and-suffering damages is to provide "satisfaction" to the injured plaintiff. Having accepted this view, German law next concludes that the wealthier the defendant, the larger the pain-and-suffering award needs to be to provide the appropriate level of "satisfaction."[168] Since, in America, the wealth of the defendant is taken into account in calculating punitive damages, one feature of the American practice of punitive damages is that it enlarges the liability exposure of wealthier defendants. In Germany, even though punitive damages are

165. Atiyah 1987, 1022; Fleming 1988, 228–29.
166. Atiyah 1987, 1025; Fleming 1988, 212.
167. Markesinis 1986, 537; Albanese and Del Duca 1987, 229; Fujita, 1987, 19. In England, under the guidelines of *Rookes* v. *Bernard* [1964] A.C. 1192, punitive damages are almost never available in personal injury cases. Atiyah 1987, 1024.
168. See Markesinis 1986, 535–37, 558–71. Similarly, German courts have ruled that the defendant who is covered by a liability insurance policy should be subjected to a larger liability for pain and suffering, so as to better achieve the goal of providing the plaintiff with adequate "satisfaction." This ruling seems strange to me, partly because the relationship between insurance and satisfaction is hard to discern. See Schwartz 1990, 332–35. The primary problem with the ruling, however, lies in the burden it places on the market for liability insurance. Defendants buy this insurance to protect themselves from the burden of liability. Yet under the German practice the defendant who buys insurance increases the liability to which he and his insurer are exposed.

unavailable, a similar enlargement of liability exposure is achieved by the way in which the law handles pain and suffering.

Indeed, at this juncture in my analysis, pain-and-suffering awards need to be given a more general consideration. These awards seem much higher in the United Sates than they are elsewhere in the world.[169] To a limited extent, this difference results from the operation of formal legal rules. German law, for example, typically does not allow recovery of pain-and-suffering damages when the plaintiff sues the defendant under some doctrine of strict liability;[170] as noted earlier, the EC Directive on product liability similarly combines strict liability with a nonrecognition of pain-and-suffering damages. In Canada the Supreme Court, exercising its own judicial authority, has set a cap on pain-and-suffering awards that (adjusted for inflation) now equals about $200,000.[171]

Most of the difference in pain-and-suffering awards, however, probably results from the American practice of trial by jury. In this country every jury is invited to provide, on an ad hoc basis, what the jury may regard as maximum justice in the individual case. Studies reveal that in cases involving serious personal injury, jury awards for pain and suffering have increased even more rapidly than awards for economic losses.[172] This has happened even though the legal criteria for calculating pain-and-suffering awards have not undergone significant change.[173]

By contrast, in a country like England calculations of pain-and-suffering damages are rendered by judges. Any particular judge knows what awards he has issued in the past; moreover, given the close-knit society of English judges, that judge also knows about the awards his judicial colleagues have the practice of granting.[174] As a result, in England an informal "tariff" is in effect that essentially regulates the award of pain-and-suffering damages.[175] Indeed, the desire to standardize pain-and-

169. Fleming 1988, 224.

170. Stoll 1986, 45. More specifically, German law withholds pain-and-suffering damages unless they are specifically authorized; a statute *does* authorize such damages when the plaintiff can prove the defendant's negligence. By remaining silent on pain-and-suffering damages, the German drug statute implicitly denies their awardability.

171. *Lewis* v. *Todd* [1980] 2 S.C.R. 694.

172. Danzon 1990, 49.

173. In recent years, however, many American states, as a part of tort reform, have placed caps on pain-and-suffering damages. A surprising number of state courts have held such caps unconstitutional.

174. Indeed, awards are reported in the cumulative supplements to the leading English damage treatise. The current edition of this treatise is Kemp 1990.

175. Atiyah and Cane 1987, 186–87.

suffering awards apparently played a major role in persuading English jurists to displace the jury in personal injury cases.[176] In Japan pain-and-suffering damages are similarly standardized (and moderated) by the Japanese process of trial by judge; indeed, trial judges in Japan have published guidelines for the awards they can be expected to grant for various kinds of physical injuries.[177] As of 1987, the highest pain-and-suffering award available in England—and also in Japan—was about $175,000.[178] In Germany as of the mid-1980s, about the most any plaintiff could recover for pain and suffering was $100,000;[179] in France in 1989, $200,000 was the largest single award for any one victim's pain and suffering.[180]

There is another legal rule whose effect on tort damage awards is often great. Consider a tort action resulting from a fatal accident, and assume that the victim at the time of his death was covered by a large life insurance policy. American tort law recognizes the collateral source rule, a rule that specifies that a tort award should not be diminished by any payments which the plaintiff may have received from "collateral sources." In such a case American courts would thus award full wrongful death damages, with no offset to acknowledge the proceeds of the life insurance policy. The collateral source rule is by no means unique to the United States; it is recognized in other legal systems, whose courts would likewise ignore the life insurance policy in calculating damages.[181] Yet while the collateral source rule itself has been widely affirmed, the American version of that rule is far more categorical and comprehensive than the versions in effect in other countries.[182] Consider, for example, the American plaintiff who—unable to work because of an accident—receives income-replacement payments from employer sick leave or from the federal social security disability program. Consider, at the same time, the English victim who receives payments from his own employer or from his country's public disability program. Given the strong American version of the collateral source rule, the plaintiff's damages would *not* be reduced by the amount of the benefits he receives. The more modest version of the rule in operation in England, however,

176. Jolowicz 1986, 56. However, variations among judges do have some effect on the size of individual damage awards. See Genn 1987, 77–78.
177. Fujita 1987, 3.
178. Atiyah 1987, 1023; Fujita 1987, 19–20.
179. Lousanoff and Moessle 1988, 683.
180. See note 162.
181. Fleming 1986, 10–11.
182. Fleming 1988, 209. Note, however, that many states in their recent tort reform packages have abrogated or at least modified the collateral source rule.

would result in the plaintiff's tort award being scaled down to take such income-replacement payments into account.[183]

One can begin, then, with the legal point that the milder European version of the collateral source rule renders the rule inapplicable to benefits provided to the victim by social welfare programs. One can then blend in the public policy observation that disability programs in Europe—though of course far less than 100 percent—are much more generous than their American counterparts, and that England, France, Germany, and Japan all operate under systems of socialized medicine (which do cover most of the costs of medical treatment). In a country like England, tort awards include almost nothing for medical costs, and the compensation they provide for income losses is reduced to acknowledge important collateral sources; moreover, as noted, the pain-and-suffering damages that those awards include are measured conservatively. In all, then, it becomes easy to understand why personal injury awards in the United States are so much larger than those in legal systems elsewhere.

Sometimes it is stated that American personal injury victims are more claims conscious—more litigation-minded—than victims elsewhere in the world. "Claims consciousness" or "litigiousness" is here portrayed as an attribute in the psychology of accident victims. Though psychological notions such as claims consciousness are in my view important and intriguing, the evidence offered in support of the particular statement about American plantiffs tends to be anecdotal or circular.[184] The discussion above, however, may provide a somewhat more objective foundation for what may well be a claims-consciousness differential. Consider the personal injury victim who lives in a European country whose public programs provide him with the basic range of medical services and also go a considerable way toward replacing his income losses. If the American victim is more inclined than his European counterpart to consider the idea of filing a tort claim, this may well be the American's predictable

---

183. Fleming 1988, 208–09. In Germany the payment of benefits to the plaintiff by collateral sources tends not to reduce the defendant's liability; but the collateral source then becomes, by way of subrogation or "obligatory assignment," the claimant against the defendant. Fleming 1986, 32–33. In today's Germany, most personal injury suits are initiated by private insurance companies or social security agencies as subrogees. Markesinis 1986, 526.

184. If an American injury victim is psychologically inclined to file suit, that may well be because he is aware of the frequency of suits brought by others in similar circumstances. Hence the victim's mental attitude is clearly one *cause* of his lawsuit—but that attitude is likewise the *result* of what is already a high rate of litigation.

and rational response to the fact that he incurs far larger pre-tort losses on account of his injury and therefore has a much greater need to turn to the tort system as a possible source of compensation.

Conclusion

To summarize, general features of the American legal system seem to be far more influential than actual differences in tort doctrine in explaining the enormous difference between the number and cost of product and malpractice claims in the United States and their number and cost in the other countries here under review. Having said this, I should make clear that my discussion of these features has for the most part tried to be nonjudgmental. To observe, for example, that a limited collateral source rule in conjunction with national health insurance functions to reduce the size of European tort awards tells us almost nothing about the analytically proper scope of the collateral source rule or about the wisdom and feasibility of American national health insurance proposals. Assuming that it is correct to say that the American system of trial by jury results in increases in both the number and the size of plaintiff verdicts, whether this result is a good thing or a bad thing depends on the assumptions that the individual analyst regards as proper. Moreover, the alternative to trial by jury is trial by judge; and in Europe and Japan this alternative may be much more attractive than the same practice would be in the United States. In countries like England and Japan, trial judges are appointed in accordance with highly meritocratic criteria. In the United States, however, these judges are designated by a political appointment process or emerge as winners in local public elections. Accordingly, among American judges there are enormous variations in outlook and ability. These variations would make trial by judge in this country a crapshoot in a way that it isn't in England or Japan.

More generally, to ascertain how extensive and demanding the torts of medical malpractice and product liability should be, one would need to understand to what extent these torts can achieve fairness as between the two parties, how effective they are in achieving socially appropriate deterrence, and what role they might play in advancing society's interests in affording compensation to accident victims. On ultimate questions of this sort, there is now an academic literature that is as voluminous as it is inconclusive. For adequate reason, then, these questions are beyond the scope of this chapter.

References

Albanese, F., and L. Del Duca. 1987. "Developments in European Product Liability." *Dickinson Journal of International Law* 5:193–245.

Atiyah, P. 1987. "Tort Law and Its Alternatives: Some Anglo-American Comparisons." *Duke Law Journal*, 1002–44.

Atiyah, P. S., and P. Cane. 1987. *Accidents, Compensation, and the Law*. 4th ed. London: Weidenfeld and Nicholson.

Bebchuk, L. 1988. "Suing Solely to Extract a Settlement Offer." *Journal of Legal Studies* 17:437–50.

California Medical Association. 1977. *Medical Insurance Feasibility*. San Francisco: Sutter.

Danzon, P. M. 1985. *Medical Malpractice: Theory, Evidence, and Public Policy*. Harvard University Press.

———. 1990. "The 'Crisis' in Medical Malpractice: A Comparison of Trends in the United States, Canada, the United Kingdom and Australia." *Law, Medicine, and Health Care* 18:48–58.

Dungworth, T., and N. M. Pace. 1990. *Statistical Overview of Civil Litigation in the Federal Courts*. R-3835-ICJ. Santa Monica, Calif.: Rand Corporation.

Felstiner, W., and R. Dingwall. 1988. *Asbestos Litigation in the United Kingdom: An Interim Report*. Chicago: American Bar Foundation.

Fleming, J. 1959. "Developments in the English Law of Medical Liability." *Vanderbilt Law Review* 12:633–48.

———. 1982. "Drug Injury Compensation Plans." *American Journal of Comparative Law* 30:297–323.

———. 1986. "Collateral Benefits." In *International Encyclopedia of Comparative Law*, vol. 11, pt. 2. Boston: Martinus Nijhoff.

———. 1987. *Law of Torts*. 7th ed. Sydney: Law Book Company.

———. 1988. *The American Tort Process*. Oxford: Clarendon Press.

———. 1989. "Probabilistic Causation in Tort Law." *Canadian Bar Review* 68:661–81.

Fujita, Y. 1987. "Products Liability: Japan." In *Product Liability: A Manual of Practice*. London: Oceana Publications.

Genn, H. 1987. *Hard Bargaining: Out of Court Settlement in Personal Injury Actions*. Oxford: Clarendon Press.

Giesen, D. 1988. *International Medical Malpractice Law*. Boston: Martinus Nijhoff.

Grossen, J., and O. Guillod. 1983. "Medical Malpractice Law: American Influence in Europe?" *Boston College International and Comparative Law Review* 6:1–27.

Hamada, K., H. Ishida, and M. Murakami. 1986. "The Evolution and Economic Consequences of Product Liability Rules in Japan." In *Law and Trade Issues* of the Japanese Economy: American and Japanese Perspectives, edited by G. R. Saxonhouse and K. Yanamura. Seattle: University of Washington Press.

Harvard Medical Practice Study. 1990. *Patients, Doctors, Lawyers: Medical Injury, Malpractice Litigation and Patient Compensation in New York.* President and Fellows of Harvard College.

Henderson, J., and T. Eisenberg. 1990. "The Quiet Revolution in Products Liability: An Empirical Study of Legal Change." *UCLA Law Review* 37:479–553.

Hensler, D. 1987. "Trends in Tort Litigation: Findings from the Institute for Civil Justice's Research." *Ohio State Law Journal* 48:479–96.

Jolowicz, J. 1986. "Procedural Questions." In *International Encyclopedia of International Law,* vol. 11, pt. 2. Boston: Martinus Nijhoff.

Kaplan, B., A. von Mehren, and R. Schaefer. 1958. "German Civil Procedure." *Harvard Law Review* 71:1193–1268, 1443–85.

Kemp, D. 1990. *The Quantum of Damages in Personal Injury and Fatal Accident Claims.* London: Sweet and Maxwell.

Kojima, T., and Y. Taniguchi. 1978. "Access to Justice in Japan." In *Access to Justice,* edited by M. Cappalletti and B. Garth, vol. 1, bk. 2, 689–761. Milan: Dott. A. Giuffrè.

Langbein, J. 1985. "The German Advantage in Civil Procedure." *University of Chicago Law Review* 52:823–66.

Latin, H. A. 1985. "Problem-Solving Behavior and Theories of Tort Liability." *California Law Review* 73:677–744.

Liebman, S. 1986. "The European Community's Product Liability Directive: Is the U.S. Experience Applicable?" *Law and Policy in International Business* 18:793–814.

Linden, A. M. 1977. *Canadian Tort Law.* Toronto: Butterworths.

Lousanoff, O., and K. Moessle. 1988. "German Products Liability Law and the Impact of the EC Council Directive." *International Lawyer* 22:669–91.

Mann, L. C., and P. R. Rodrigues. 1988. "The European Directive on Products Liability: The Promise of Progress?" *Georgia Journal of International and Comparative Law* 18:391–425.

Markesinis, B. S. 1986. *A Comparative Introduction to the German Law of Tort.* Oxford: Clarendon Press.

Newdick, C. 1988. "The Development Risk Defence of the Consumer Protection Act 1987." *Cambridge Law Journal* 47:455–76.

Orban, F. A. 1978. "Product Liability: A Comparative Legal Restatement—Foreign National Law and the EEC Directive." *Georgia Journal of International and Comparative Law* 8:342–406.

Oldertz, C. 1986. "Social Insurance, Patient Insurance and Pharmaceutical Insurance in Sweden." *American Journal of Comparative Law* 34:635–56.

Ottley, Y., and B. Ottley. 1984. "Product Liability Law in Japan: An Introduction to a Developing Area of Law." *Georgia Journal of International and Comparative Law* 14:29–64.

Peterson, M. A. 1987. *Civil Juries in the 1980s: Trends in Jury Trials and Verdicts in California and Cook County, Illinois.* R-3466-ICJ. Santa Monica, Calif.: Rand Corporation.

Picard, E. I. 1978. *Legal Liability of Doctors and Hospitals in Canada.* Toronto: Carswell.

Ponzanelli, G. [Forthcoming]. "The European Community Directive on Products Liability." In *Tort Law and the Public Interest: Competition, Innovation, and Consumer Welfare,* edited by P. H. Schuck. Norton.

Prichard, J. R. S. 1988. "A Systematic Approach to Comparative Law: The Effect of Cost, Fee, and Financing Rules on the Development of the Substantive Law." *Journal of Legal Studies* 17:451–75.

Priest, G. L. 1985. "The Invention of Enterprise Liability: A Critical History of the Intellectual Foundations of Modern Tort Law." *Journal of Legal Studies* 14:461–527.

Prosser, W. P., and P. Keeton. 1984. *Prosser and Keeton on the Law of Torts.* 5th ed. St. Paul: West Publication.

Quam, L., R. Dingwall, and P. Fenn. 1988. "Medical Malpractice Claims in Obstetrics and Gynaecology: Comparisons Between the United States and Britain." *British Journal of Obstetrics and Gynaecology* 95:454–61.

Ramseyer, J. M., and M. Nakazato. 1989. "The Rational Litigant: Settlement Amounts and Verdict Rates in Japan." *Journal of Legal Studies* 18:263–90.

Ramseyer, M. 1990. "Memorandum on Japanese Products Liability and Medical Malpractice." Unpublished.

Robertson, G. 1981. "*Whitehouse v. Jordan*—Medical Negligence Retried." *Modern Law Review* 44:457–61.

Sarrailhé, P. 1981. "Product Liability: France." In *Product Liability: A Manual of Practice,* vol. 1. London: Oceana Publications.

Schwartz, G. 1979. "Foreword: Understanding Products Liability." *California Law Review* 67:435–96.

———. 1983. "New Products, Old Products, Evolving Law, Retroactive Law." *New York University Law Review* 58:796–852.

———. 1989. "The Character of Early American Tort Law." *UCLA Law Review* 36:641–718.

———. 1990. "The Ethics and the Economics of Tort Liability Insurance." *Cornell Law Review* 75:313–65.

Schwartz, R., and A. Grubb. 1985. "Why Britain Can't Afford Informed Consent," *Hastings Center Report* 15:19–25.

Stoll, H. 1986. "Consequences of Liability: Remedies." In *International Encyclopedia of Comparative Law,* vol. 11, pt. 2. Boston: Martinus Nijhoff.

Tebbens, H. S. 1979. *International Product Liability: A Study of Comparative and International Legal Aspects of Product Liability.* Germantown: Sijthoff and Noordhoff.

"Terms of Settlement: The SMON Litigation." 1979. *Law in Japan* 12:99–117.

Thieffry, P., P. Van Doorn, and S. Lowe. 1989. "Strict Product Liability in the EEC: Implementation, Practice and Impact on U.S. Manufacturers of Directive 85/374." *Tort and Insurance Law Journal* 25:65–91.

Thomas, B. A. 1989. "Canadian and United States Law of Products Liability." *For the Defense* 31:32–35.

Viney, G. 1986. "The Civil Liability of Manufacturers in French Law." In *Comparative Product Liability,* edited by C. J. Miller. London: British Institute of International and Comparative Law.

Wagatsuma, H., and A. Rosett. 1986. "The Implications of Apology: Law and Culture in Japan and the United States." *Law and Society Review* 20:462–98.

Weiler, P. [Forthcoming]. *Medical Malpractice on Trial.* Harvard University Press.

Whitaker, S. 1986. "The EEC Directive on Product Liability." In *Yearbook of European Law 1985.* Oxford: Clarendon Press.

Will, M. 1988. "Liability for Failure to Warn in the European Community." *Boston University International Law Review* 6:125–49.

Wright, C. J. 1989. *Product Liability: The Law and Its Implications for Risk Management.* London: Blackstone Press.

Zepos, P. J., and Ph. Christodoulou. 1983. "Professional Liability." In *International Encyclopedia of Comparative Law,* vol. 11, pt. 1. Boston: Martinus Nijhoff.

CHAPTER THREE

An Industrial Profile of the Links between Product Liability and Innovation

W. Kip Viscusi and Michael J. Moore

ONE OF THE most salient aspects of the impact of product liability has been its effect on innovation.[1] Volumes of anecdotal evidence attest to potential links between the incentives created by product liability and innovation decisions. Pharmaceutical companies report the withdrawal of existing vaccines from the market and the discontinuation of development of other lines of drugs. A National Academy of Sciences panel has called product liability a major source of the lag in developing drugs for contraception.[2]

Although much of the anecdotal evidence has been concentrated in the pharmaceutical industry, the incentive effects of product liability on innovation appear broader. A survey by the Conference Board found a diverse and conflicting set of impacts.[3] As for the negative effects on innovation, 36 percent of all respondents reported that liability costs led them to discontinue product lines, 30 percent reported that product liability costs led to decisions against introducing new products, and 21 percent said that liability costs led to the discontinuation of product research. But the survey also found that product liability affected product quality in a potentially favorable way. For 35 percent of the firms responding, liability costs led to improved safety of particular products; in 33 percent of the cases, they led to an improvement in the safety of the entire product line. Much more broadly affected were hazard warnings, which were added by 47 percent of the firms responding.

Although such surveys do not show the net effect of product liability

---

1. This concern is a central theme of Huber 1988 and a recurring concern in the papers in Litan and Winston 1988. More generally, see Viscusi 1991; Viscusi (forthcoming).

2. Mastroianni, Donaldson, and Kane 1990.

3. McGuire 1988.

innovation, they do suggest the competing economic influences. Ideally, product liability should induce firms to recognize the product safety costs associated with the products they market. That should lead to the development of safer products and, in some cases, the discontinuation of research on very risky new products. There is a potential danger if the courts exhibit a bias against products that introduce new hazards as opposed to products that maintain existing hazards. Such a bias has long been alleged to pertain to government regulation of risk, and if courts also show this tendency, they stymie the innovation which makes possible the economic growth that improves the well-being of us all.[4]

In this chapter we try to quantify the extent of the product liability–innovation linkage. In particular, we explore data pertaining to both product liability costs and innovation to analyze the locus of the distribution of the product liability burden. Among the key questions we address are the following. Which industries bear the greatest share of the product liability burden? Have the firms in the innovative sectors of the economy been most hard hit by product liability, or those in the declining sectors? If manufacturing defects play a dominant role, one would expect the firms in declining industries to bear the greatest share of the product liability burden. But if the innovators are bearing the brunt of the cost for design defect cases, then one would expect the burden to be borne disproportionately by the more progressive segments of the economy responsible for research and new product introductions.

Although the data examined here will not show that the product liability burden is specifically targeted at only one segment of the economy, the broad sweep of the incidence of product liability costs is also of interest. Indeed, the increased share of these costs borne by the innovative segments of the economy may have been the major cause for alarm. In an era when the main source of a firm's liability was manufacturing defects, innovative firms with up-to-date technologies and good quality control practices would be largely free of liability costs. However, once design defect issues introduced the potential of liability for defective product designs, and in particular for innovative designs that often generate new risks, the liability burden would tend to become broader. Recent cries of alarm over the costs imposed by liability may arise not because it is concentrated in only the innovative sectors but rather because those sectors are now bearing a large part of the product liability burden, whereas in earlier decades they were not.

---

4. Huber 1988 notes this pattern with respect to behavior by the courts.

The chapter begins with an overview of the role of liability and innovation throughout the entire economy. We present data for every two-digit manufacturing industry to provide a context for the subsequent discussion. In the sections that follow, we address the nature of liability and innovation in the industries studied in this volume—automobile, aircraft, chemical, and pharmaceutical—plus the machine, tool, and heavy equipment industry. These industries include many leading sectors in which product liability plays an important role. The chapter concludes with an econometric analysis of the determinants of product risks and product innovation.

Many of the patterns yielded by this examination of the links between product liability and innovation are quite striking. Examination of the insurance statistics shows the reason for alarm. In the early 1980s product liability loss ratios for bodily injury coverage averaged 1.2, which implies that losses exceed premiums by 20 percent. Administrative costs are in addition to this amount. In contrast, property damage insurance, which has been less hard hit by the changes in tort liability, had an average loss ratio of 0.8, which reflects the comparatively more profitable nature of this line of insurance. Since a competitive market should equalize loss ratios across different lines of coverage, the continued disparity in these rates reflects the failure of insurance markets to adjust completely to the rise in liability costs that took place in the 1980s. Similarly, one would expect a competitive market to equalize the profitability of liability insurance across industries, so that the ratio of losses to premiums for bodily injury insurance should average about 1.2 for all major industries. What is particularly noteworthy is the wide swing in these loss ratios, ranging from 0.26 to 6.89 for industries defined at the two-digit level, a fairly broad degree of aggregation. Some of the case studies for this volume showed particularly high loss ratios; for example, the chemical industry, which had a loss ratio of 1.49.

The profitability of insurance observed across time also showed wild swings. The performance of liability insurance for product liability coverage is highly volatile. This insurance performance is consistent with a situation in which substantial uncertainty and volatility affect the liability costs for any particular firm.

For many of the industries that have been hard hit by liability costs, innovation is particularly significant. All the pharmaceutical firms in our sample, for instance, indicate that innovation is important in that industry. Moreover, for the other industries in the sample, product and process patents also play a consequential role, as does research and development more generally.

An observed correlation between innovation and liability costs does not necessary imply causality. In an effort to distinguish the relationships at work, we developed an econometric model analyzing the effect of innovation on liability costs as well as the influence of a higher expected liability burden on firms' innovation decisions. We find evidence that each of these links is of consequence. More innovative firms tend to have a higher level of liability insurance costs. There is, however, evidence that these costs have an incentive effect, although we make no judgment here about whether this influence is socially desirable. In particular, what we find is that, for most levels of liability costs, a higher liability burden fosters additional products-related research. However, once these costs become sufficiently large, the effect of product liability is counterproductive, since it dampens innovation. This effect is consistent with firms withdrawing from new product introductions altogether once liability costs become too large.

Overview of Product Liability Costs and Innovation

Before considering the particular case studies highlighted in this book, we present some general statistics pertaining to both liability and innovation for all segments of the manufacturing industry. This breakdown is useful for two reasons. The incidence of product liability costs and innovation is of interest in its own right. And it is useful to ascertain whether the particular target studies examined in this book represent outliers in terms of the product liability costs and their effects or represent broader trends throughout the economy.

Our presentation relies on summary breakdowns of the incidence of product liability costs and the role of innovation in various sectors. This discussion helps to highlight who bears the product liability costs and the relation of these costs to innovation. What it does not do is determine the direction of causality that may be involved. Thus we by no means resolve all the issues pertaining to product liability and innovation. These must be illuminated both by the case studies and subsequent empirical research.

The data base we use for assessing product liability costs consists of the entire ratemaking files of the Insurance Services Office (ISO) for product liability coverage for 1980-84. This data base includes more than 200,000 records, where the unit of observation is the individual policy written for a particular firm's products. For the discussion here, information has been aggregated by industry to calculate a total product liability cost for each industry group. The main purpose of these data is to provide an index of the relative liability cost levels by industry; they do not include all insurance costs and all firms.

Although this data set is fairly comprehensive, it is by no means exhaustive. Most important, firms that choose to self-insure or seek coverage other than through an affiliate of the ISO are not represented in the sample. The pharmaceutical and asbestos products industries, for example, are not well represented. Similarly, extremely large firms, such as General Motors, are also excluded. That the data set does not capture the liability burden for some industry segments particularly hard hit by product liability costs is an important caveat that should be taken into account when considering the subsequent empirical profiles.

A useful starting point for assessing the role of product liability is to consider its price. The main price measure used for insurance is the loss ratio, which is the inverse of the price measured on an ex post basis. The loss ratio is the ratio of losses to premiums for a particular policy. For these data, premiums consist of premiums actually paid, and losses consist of actual losses to date plus all additional losses expected to be incurred.[5] If losses equaled premiums, then the loss ratio would be 1.0. Such insurance would be labeled actuarially fair. There is a lag before the losses must be paid, however, and insurance companies can earn a return on this money during the interim. Thus insurance companies with loss ratios above 1.0 can make a profit if the rate of interest is sufficiently high.

The period covered by the data is the early 1980s, which is known in the insurance industry as a time of heavy price competition.[6] High interest rates enabled firms to maintain low premium levels relative to losses, so that loss ratios in excess of 1.0 should not necessarily be viewed with alarm for this period. Also, this period precedes the emergence of the liability insurance crisis (the rapid escalation of premiums that occurred in 1985–86).

In a competitive market one would expect an insurance firm to equalize the price of insurance across all industries so that the price per dollar of expected losses should be the same. Unfortunately, a firm cannot predict what these loss ratios will be at the time insurance coverage is written. Moreover, loss experiences may be particularly volatile because of the

5. These projections were made by the authors using the Insurance Services Office's loss projection factors.

6. Harrington 1988 and Viscusi 1991 provide a longer-term perspective on liability insurance trends.

Table 3-1. *Product Liability Loss Ratios for Two-Digit Manufacturing Industries, 1980–84*

Standard industrial classification (SIC) code and industry	Loss ratio[a]	
	Bodily injury	Property damage
All manufacturing	1.19	0.76
20 Food and kindred products	0.76	0.85
21 Tobacco products	0.26	0.16
22 Textile mill products	0.92	0.48
23 Apparel and other textile products	0.52	0.33
24 Lumber and wood products	0.75	0.73
25 Furniture and fixtures	0.90	0.64
26 Paper and allied products	6.89	0.82
28 Chemicals and allied products	1.49	1.08
29 Petroleum and coal products	1.05	1.02
30 Rubber and miscellaneous plastics products	0.81	1.08
31 Leather and leather products	0.61	0.26
32 Stone, clay and glass products	1.38	0.97
33 Primary metal products	0.75	0.30
34 Fabricated metal products	0.95	0.47
35 Industrial machinery and equipment	1.32	0.73
36 Electronic and other electrical equipment	1.07	0.50
37 Transportation equipment	1.02	0.45
38 Instruments and related products	0.80	0.26
39 Miscellaneous manufacturing industries	1.36	0.97

Source: Unless otherwise noted, authors' calculations are the source for all the tables.
a. The ratio of losses to insurance policy premiums.

uncertainty of losses and the fact that they may be concentrated in a few large payoff cases.

The statistics in table 3-1 present the loss ratios for bodily injury product liability coverage and property damage property liability coverage for 1980–84. That these statistics represent an averaging of losses and premiums over a five-year period should remove much of the stochastic element of losses, since the averaging process will mute any year-to-year variations.

The patterns in the table are striking in several respects. First, from the standpoint of all manufacturing industries, the loss ratio of 1.19 for bodily injury coverage is well in excess of 1.0 for product liability coverage. Although one would have expected an equalization of loss ratios across lines of insurance, the loss ratio for property damage coverage of 0.76 is considerably lower than that for bodily injury. This pattern is consistent with the rise in product liability lawsuits, particularly those involving bodily injury damage, in the early 1980s.

The enormous range of the loss ratios is also impressive. For bodily injury coverage, the loss ratios range from a low value of 0.26 for tobacco products to a high of 6.89 for paper and allied products. The variation for property damage loss ratios is narrower, but nevertheless considerable. The lowest loss ratio in that instance is 0.16 for tobacco products, and the highest is 1.08 for chemicals and allied products.

Consider the results for the industries that have been targeted for analysis in this book. Although the two-digit level of aggregation includes broad industry groupings that go beyond some of the categories on which the other chapters focus, even at this level of aggregation some of the results are notable. Consider first SIC (standard industrial classification) 28, which comprises chemicals and such products such as pharmaceuticals. The bodily injury line of insurance for that industry experienced a loss ratio of 1.49, and the property damage line a loss ratio of 1.08. Each of these ratios is well above the national average. If losses had been fully anticipated by the insurance company, then much lower loss ratios would have resulted. Thus these statistics do not necessarily denote a high product liability burden, but they do indicate that the level of the product liability losses exceeded the expectations of the insurers during the early 1980s. The likely economic response will be a rise in insurance prices in subsequent years to reflect the changing loss performance of that industry.

The next two-digit case study industry is SIC 35, the industrial machinery and equipment industry. Although the property damage loss ratio is comparable to the national average, for bodily injury coverage the loss ratio of 1.32 is over 10 percent greater than the manufacturing average. As in the chemical industry, losses relative to premiums were quite high, which reflects an emerging problem of product liability costs.

The next target industry for analysis, SIC 37, transportation equipment, has a loss ratio for bodily injury coverage of 1.02 and a loss ratio of 0.45 for property damage coverage. Even lower loss ratios are shown for SIC 38, instruments and related products, which includes medical equipment as a subcategory. Measured in terms of loss ratios at this broad level of aggregation, the chemical industry and the machine, tool, and heavy equipment industry display the highest ratio of losses relative to the premiums charged, so that premiums are likely to rise in the future to reflect the higher loss patterns experienced.

The overall level of liability costs is reflected in the statistics in table 3-2, which present the share of total product liability premiums for various industries and an index of the ratio of product liability premiums to sales. The share values are calculated relative to the total value of product liability premiums for all manufacturing industries. Although miscella-

Table 3-2. *Product Liability Premium Shares for Two-Digit Manufacturing Industries, 1980–84*

SIC code and industry	Premium share[a]		Premiums/sales index	
	Bodily injury	Property damage	Bodily injury	Property damage
All manufacturing	100.00	100.00	0.15	0.08
20 Food and kindred products	5.97	4.93	0.04	0.02
21 Tobacco products	0.03	0.01	0.07	0.01
22 Textile mill products	0.84	0.86	0.24	0.13
23 Apparel and other textile products	2.70	0.68	7.02	0.92
24 Lumber and wood products	1.73	3.00	0.27	0.24
25 Furniture and fixtures	3.32	0.79	3.85	0.47
26 Paper and allied products	0.93	1.48	0.11	0.09
28 Chemicals and allied products	4.81	6.69	0.06	0.04
29 Petroleum and coal products	0.23	0.66	0.01	0.01
30 Rubber and miscellaneous plastics products	3.71	3.66	0.93	0.48
31 Leather and leather products	0.77	0.24	2.24	0.37
32 Stone, clay and glass products	2.02	3.12	0.10	0.08
33 Primary metal products	1.62	3.38	0.10	0.11
34 Fabricated metal products	14.01	15.46	0.38	0.22
35 Industrial machinery and equipment	10.87	9.55	0.14	0.06
36 Electronic and other electrical equipment	5.25	8.25	0.06	0.05
37 Transportation equipment	4.26	3.02	0.05	0.02
38 Instruments and related products	2.76	1.74	0.19	0.06
39 Miscellaneous manufacturing industries	34.17	32.48	6.01	2.95

a. The percent share of total product liability premiums for all manufacturing industries.

neous manufacturing industries constitute by far the largest share, in part because of their broad nature, substantial concentration exists in other industries as well. Among the most notable are fabricated medical products and industrial machinery and equipment, each of which accounts for 10 percent or more of all product liability premiums. Chemicals and allied products also play a large role, since 5 percent of all bodily injury premiums and 7 percent of all property damage premiums are attributed to these products. The total premium share of transportation equipment is a bit less, but this lower value is to be expected insofar as the large automobile companies are not included in the data set.

The values of the index of product liability premiums to sales also vary substantially. Product liability costs for bodily injury are particularly high in miscellaneous manufacturing industries and apparel. Property damage premiums show less variation, although miscellaneous manufacturing industries once again have a high cost of product liability premiums relative to sales. The ratio of premiums to sales may not, however, always be a valid index of the extent of the product liability burden. For example, the chemical industry has a premiums-over-sales index of less than one-half the manufacturing average, which may be only a result of the greater role of self-insurance for some segments of the industry, such as pharmaceuticals. Similarly, transportation equipment has a low ratio of product liability premiums to sales, because the major automobile manufacturers lie outside the scope of the ISO sample. Of much greater interest than the levels in the index of product liability premiums to sales are the trends in the index, which we consider below.

It is useful to explore the degree of innovation that took place in the affected industries and ascertain whether any relation exists between innovation and the product liability cost figures in tables 3-1 and 3-2. The principal data source we rely on to assess innovation is the extensive data set developed by the Strategic Planning Institute at the Harvard Business School. Using survey responses from a sample that consists primarily of larger firms, the institute developed a detailed, firm-specific set of data known as the profit impact of marketing strategies (PIMS) data base. The sample is much larger than that of the Conference Board surveys, as it includes *several thousand* firms. Moreover, the data were not elicited for a specific purpose relating to product liability or product liability reform, so that the potential problem of response bias is less. Nevertheless, the data are not ideal, since the measures of innovation may elicit different responses depending on one's assessment of the particular innovation question. For example, the survey inquires whether product patents are "significant," but standards for significance may vary. Nevertheless, because the survey includes a series of measures of innovation that capture different aspects of the innovation process, it is possible to explore the robustness of the innovation-liability links.

Table 3-3 reports the first set of statistics describing whether the business benefits to a significant degree from product patents or process patents. To the extent that product liability affects products through design defects, one would expect the product patent measure to be directly related to product liability costs. But if manufacturing defects are the main source of the liability problems, then process patents will be relevant, since they influence the way in which products are made and the standards of quality they are likely to meet.

The statistics in the table show that patent innovation is important, but it is by no means the norm. Fewer than one-fifth of manufacturing firms in this survey benefited much from product or process patents. In many cases, including industries like lumber and wood products, the

Table 3-3. *Innovation Rates for Two-Digit Manufacturing Industries, Based on Patents, 1980–84*
Percent of firms

SIC code and industry	Product patents significant	Process patents significant
All manufacturing	18.19	16.25
20 Food and kindred products	14.55	9.09
21 Tobacco products	n.a.	n.a.
22 Textile mill products	19.57	19.57
23 Apparel and other textile products	0.00	0.00
24 Lumber and wood products	n.a.	n.a.
25 Furniture and fixtures	0.00	14.81
26 Paper and allied products	24.00	44.00
28 Chemicals and allied products	14.93	14.93
29 Petroleum and coal products	0.00	0.00
30 Rubber and miscellaneous plastics products	5.88	23.53
31 Leather and leather products	n.a.	n.a.
32 Stone, clay and glass products	50.00	47.22
33 Primary metal products	5.92	2.96
34 Fabricated metal products	21.88	12.50
35 Industrial machinery and equipment	21.88	3.13
36 Electronic and other electrical equipment	20.18	36.70
37 Transportation equipment	0.00	0.00
38 Instruments and related products	33.78	22.97
39 Miscellaneous manufacturing industries	37.50	62.50

n.a. Not available.

firms in the sample did not greatly rely on patents. But as far as the industries examined here are concerned, only the transportation equipment sector makes little use of product or process patents. The other industries largely follow the national patterns. The chemical and allied products industry is somewhat below the national average; the industrial machinery and equipment industry is a bit above the national average for process patents but below it for product patents. The most innovative of the two-digit industries examined here is that of instruments and related products, which includes medical equipment, for which the innovation rates are well above the manufacturing average.

Although table 3-3 captures the role of patents, it does not reflect the extent of their implementation. A better measure of actual implementation of new product attributes is the set of statistics in table 3-4. Four different measures are given. The first three represent each of the possible descriptions the firm could have given to its pattern of product change. The first column shows whether there was no regular or periodic pattern of product change. A higher value for this measure means greater stagnation or less

Table 3-4. *Innovation Rates for Two-Digit Manufacturing Industries, Based on Product Changes, 1980–84*
Percent of firms

SIC code and industry	No regular product changes	Periodic product changes	Regular product changes	No new product development
All manufacturing	76.75	15.82	7.43	24.65
20 Food and kindred products	58.18	14.55	27.27	40.00
21 Tobacco products	n.a.	n.a.	n.a.	n.a.
22 Textile mill products	41.30	36.96	21.74	19.57
23 Apparel and other textile products	100.00	0.00	0.00	0.00
24 Lumber and wood products	n.a.	n.a.	n.a.	n.a.
25 Furniture and fixtures	51.85	3.70	44.44	0.00
26 Paper and allied products	96.00	4.00	0.00	60.00
28 Chemicals and allied products	88.06	11.94	0.00	13.43
29 Petroleum and coal products	100.00	0.00	0.00	0.00
30 Rubber and miscellaneous plastics products	85.29	0.00	14.71	41.18
31 Leather and leather products	n.a.	n.a.	n.a.	n.a.
32 Stone, clay and glass products	88.89	2.78	8.33	33.33
33 Primary metal products	92.31	7.69	0.00	55.62
34 Fabricated metal products	87.50	12.50	0.00	16.41
35 Industrial machinery and equipment	53.91	46.09	0.00	19.53
36 Electronic and other electrical equipment	87.16	4.59	8.26	4.59
37 Transportation equipment	28.57	38.10	33.33	0.00
38 Instruments and related products	85.14	12.16	2.70	4.05
39 Miscellaneous manufacturing industries	12.50	12.50	75.00	0.00

n.a. Not available.

product innovation. The next column pertains to whether the firm introduced product changes periodically, and the third column pertains to whether there are regular product changes. The final column is based on a survey response to a different question, in which the firm indicated whether little or no new product development occurs in its business.

These patterns are similar in many respects to those in table 3-3. The chemical industry, for example, was a bit below the manufacturing average in product patents. In terms of not having product changes it is also above the national average, which is consistent with a lower level of innovation. However, only a small number of firms said they had no new product development, so that products are changed even though the reliance on patents may not be as great as in some other industries.

The industrial machinery and equipment firms are rather evenly divided between those that make no new product changes and those that introduce such changes periodically. This industry's level of product development is somewhat greater than the manufacturing average. As for transportation equipment, we said earlier that patents do not play an important role. This does not mean, however, that there is no innovation. In only a small segment of the industry are there no product changes, since more than a third of the firms introduce product changes periodically and another third introduce regular product changes. Moreover, every respondent said that new product development was important.

The instruments and related-products industry is among the highest in having significant product and process patents; but in making regular or periodic product changes, it is below the national average. The rate of new product development for the industry is, however, quite high.

These statistics suggest that one obtains an incomplete picture of innovation by examining patents or product changes alone. By considering the patent data, one can get a sense of the degree to which the industry is engaging in fundamental research. But one must also investigate the product change data to assess the degree to which this research is transmitted through actual changes in the character of products. Moreover, many product changes may be novel and may fundamentally affect the attributes of a product, but they may not have been patented.

To provide a check on the comparability of these innovation measures with other data series, table 3-5 shows ratios of research and development over sales and R&D over premiums, based on the McGraw-Hill data. Unlike the earlier measures, these R&D indexes take into account the extent of dollar expenditures on research and development. They do not, however, reflect an implementation of these expenditures through product innovations or changes in the riskiness of products.

In general, the McGraw-Hill measures show a reasonable correlation with those just presented. For example, the correlation of R&D sales with the productivity measurement variables is as follows: significant product patents (-0.25), significant process patents (-0.23), no regular product changes (-0.53), periodic product changes (0.42), regular product changes (0.48), and no new product development (-0.54).

The specific patterns in table 3-5 also follow the relationships one would expect given the earlier results. In terms of R&D relative to sales, the most innovative industries are transportation equipment (largely because of the influence of aerospace), instruments and related products, electronic and other electronic equipment, and chemicals and allied products.

The other two columns of the table present evidence on the ratio of R&D expenditures to insurance premiums. A low value for this measure means a high product liability burden relative to the amount of research

Table 3-5. *McGraw-Hill Research and Development Rates for Two-Digit Manufacturing Industries, 1980–84*

SIC code and industry	R&D/ sales	Index R&D/bodily injury premiums	R&D/property damage premiums
All manufacturing	2.75	10.05	13.46
20 Food and kindred products	0.28	0.83	1.80
22 Textile mill products	0.29	1.05	1.79
26 Paper and allied products	0.75	4.32	4.75
28 Chemicals and allied products	3.43	9.08	11.40
29 Petroleum and coal products	1.00	59.04	36.78
30 Rubber and miscellaneous plastics products	1.69	1.54	2.68
32 Stone, clay and glass products	1.09	1.65	1.89
33 Primary metal products	0.83	4.28	3.48
34 Fabricated metal products	0.48	0.28	0.44
35 Industrial machinery and equipment	4.02	4.72	9.37
36 Electronic and other electrical equipment	7.97	14.83	16.47
37 Transportation equipment	23.16[a]	28.98	70.00
38 Instruments and related products	8.63	10.03	27.45
39 Miscellaneous manufacturing industries	n.a.	0.10	0.19

Sources: The R&D/sales values are drawn from McGraw-Hill data, and the authors' calculated R&D/premiums.
n.a. Not available.
a. The figure is 3.68 if the aerospace industry is excluded.

and development undertaken in the industry. Petroleum and coal products and the transportation equipment industry have particularly high levels of research and development relative to the value of liability premiums, whereas miscellaneous manufacturing and fabricated metal products have very low values. The chemical industry, which is a major focus of this chapter, has measures comparable to the manufacturing average.

The Chemical Industry

As our first case study, we consider the whole category SIC 28, chemicals and allied products, as well as its principal components. Since this industry includes both drugs (SIC 283) and such chemical product categories of interest as agricultural chemicals (SIC 287) and miscellaneous chemical products (SIC 289), it offers fairly wide coverage of the key industries analyzed.

The pharmaceutical industry showed considerable growth in the 1980s.[7]

7. U.S. Department of Commerce 1986, 17-2.

The chemical industry also experienced a rise in the value of its shipments, but the level of employment in that industry was declining in the 1980s.[8] The role of agricultural chemicals likewise was stable or somewhat declining in the early 1980s because of the increased competition from foreign imports.[9] In each case, one would therefore expect to see a steady or rising insurance burden.

The figures in table 3-6 summarize the trends in the loss ratios and the premium shares on a yearly basis for 1980–84. This summary is helpful in highlighting the volatility of insurance, particularly within narrow industry categories. Furthermore, by analyzing different segments of the industry, we can explore whether drugs, for example, perform in the same way as other segments of the chemical industry. One would expect large differences, since the nature of firms' liability may be quite different in each case because of the differences in the character of products, in user groups, and in the way products are employed.

The overall cost of insurance for the two-digit chemical industry shows large swings in the loss ratios. In bodily injury coverage, for example, loss ratios hit a high value of 2.45 in 1980, dropping to a low of 0.74 in 1981, with a resurgence to 1.42 in 1984. Losses in this industry are clearly unpredictable and irregular. The premium share for the chemical industry is much steadier, but it showed some decline over the five-year period. Although one would have expected a rise in the insurance price in response to the high bodily injury loss ratios, which would boost the total premium share if quantity were left unchanged, a withdrawal of insurance may also have occurred in that industry. Thus premium share statistics that exhibit a steady pattern or, in this case, a steady decline should not necessarily be regarded as a sign of industry health. Premiums represent the combined influence of price and quantity, where a rise in price may offset the influence of a drop in quantity. The declining value of the premiums-sales ratio is also consistent with the problem of insurance availability.

Of all the industries shown in the table, the drug industry had the most dramatic levels of loss ratios. Bodily injury loss ratios for drugs hit high values of 3.53 in 1982 and 3.20 in 1984. In two years losses were therefore more than three times larger than the total value of premiums—a substantial departure from what one would expect in a well-functioning insurance market. The premium share for bodily injury coverage is declining, but as in chemicals overall, this decline may have been the result

8. Department of Commerce 1986, 11-10.
9. Department of Commerce 1986, 13-2.

Table 3-6. *Product Liability Trends for the Chemical Industry, 1980–84*

Item	1980	1981	1982	1983	1984
	Chemicals and allied products (SIC 28)				
Loss ratio (bodily injury)	2.45	0.74	0.92	1.33	1.42
Loss ratio (property damage)	0.38	1.71	1.73	0.86	0.99
Premium share (bodily injury)	5.87	4.25	4.43	4.78	4.51
Premium share (property damage)	8.18	6.57	6.44	6.43	5.58
Premiums/sales index (bodily injury)	0.08	0.05	0.04	0.05	0.06
Premiums/sales index (property damage)	0.06	0.04	0.04	0.04	0.03
	Drugs (SIC 283)				
Loss ratio (bodily injury)	0.91	1.42	3.53	1.17	3.20
Loss ratio (property damage)	0.11	0.09	0.65	2.56	0.96
Premium share (bodily injury)	0.88	0.33	0.33	0.59	0.52
Premium share (property damage)	0.34	0.26	0.23	0.35	0.32
Premiums/sales index (bodily injury)	0.38	0.15	0.15	0.25	0.26
Premiums/sales index (property damage)	0.07	0.07	0.06	0.08	0.08
	Agricultural chemicals (SIC 287)				
Loss ratio (bodily injury)	0.20	0.08	0.02	1.13	0.00
Loss ratio (property damage)	0.50	0.73	1.93	0.66	1.14
Premium share (bodily injury)	0.55	0.54	0.56	0.47	0.52
Premium share (property damage)	1.13	1.07	1.05	0.96	0.88
Premiums/sales index (bodily injury)	0.44	0.37	0.31	0.27	0.35
Premiums/sales index (property damage)	0.45	0.39	0.32	0.29	0.30
	Miscellaneous chemical products (SIC 289)				
Loss ratio (bodily injury)	5.60	0.85	0.74	0.93	2.24
Loss ratio (property damage)	0.35	1.26	0.78	0.42	1.03
Premium share (bodily injury)	2.17	1.32	1.27	1.42	1.26
Premium share (property damage)	3.43	2.12	2.17	2.29	2.03
Premiums/sales index (bodily injury)	1.35	0.68	0.58	0.64	0.70
Premiums/sales index (property damage)	1.12	0.60	0.55	0.55	0.55

of increased self-insurance by drug firms. Thus the declining premium share should be regarded as a signal of an industry in trouble rather than a sign of economic stability. The premiums-to-sales index exhibited a similar decline for bodily injury coverage.

In contrast, the results for agricultural chemicals show that these are a much more profitable line of insurance once the losses have been incurred, since the loss ratios for bodily injury coverage are well below 1.0

Table 3-7. *Product Liability and Innovation for the Chemical and Allied Products Industry (SIC 28), 1980–84*

Item	1980–84 average	Percent change 1980–84
Loss ratio (bodily injury)	1.49	−42.04
Loss ratio (property damage)	1.08	160.53
Premium share (bodily injury)	4.81	−23.17
Premium share (property damage)	6.69	−31.78
Premiums/sales index (bodily injury)	0.06	−25.00
Premiums/sales index (property damage)	0.04	−50.00
Product patents significant (percent of firms)	14.93	. . .
Process patents signficant (percent of firms)	14.93	. . .
No regular product changes (percent of firms)	88.06	. . .
Periodic product changes (percent of firms)	11.94	. . .
Regular product changes (percent of firms)	0.00	. . .
No new product development (percent of firms)	13.43	. . .

in four of the five years. The results from miscellaneous chemical products are similar, but it is noteworthy that the loss ratio for bodily injury coverage was 2.24 in 1984—down from the high value of 5.60 in 1980. What these results suggest is that even when the loss ratios are not consistently high, they are occasionally quite high and fluctuate widely.

Table 3-7 summarizes the average performance of insurance over the 1980–84 period, the percent changes in the insurance variables, and the innovation values for the whole chemical industry. No trends in innovation appear because firms in this sample usually reported their innovation practices in the initial year of the survey and did not change their responses. The declining premium share and the declining premiums-to-sales index in the industry suggest an insurance market in retreat rather than a situation in which declining prices have led to a drop in the role of premiums.

The specific results for the drug industry in table 3-8 show large jumps in the loss ratio, accompanied by very substantial, but somewhat less dramatic, declines in premiums and in the premiums-to-sales index. As the insurance industry has raised the price of insurance to reflect the high cost imposed by coverage, the market for insurance has shrunk. The role of innovation in this industry as measured by patents is substantial, because product patents are significant for almost half the firms in the

Table 3-8. *Product Liability and Innovation for the Drug Industry (SIC 283), 1980–84*

Item	1980–84 average	Percent change 1980–84
Loss ratio (bodily injury)	1.77	251.65
Loss ratio (property damage)	0.89	772.73
Premium share (bodily injury)	0.54	−40.91
Premium share (property damage)	0.30	−5.88
Premiums/sales index (bodily injury)	0.24	−31.58
Premiums/sales index (property damage)	0.07	14.29
Product patents significant (percent of firms)	42.86	. . .
Process patents significant (percent of firms)	28.57	. . .
No regular product changes (percent of firms)	100.00	. . .
Periodic product changes (percent of firms)	0.00	. . .
Regular product changes (percent of firms)	0.00	. . .
No new product development (percent of firms)	0.00	. . .

Table 3-9. *Product Liability and Innovation for the Agricultural Chemical Industry (SIC 287), 1980–84*

Item	1980–84 average	Percent change 1980–84
Loss ratio (bodily injury)	0.25	−100.00
Loss ratio (property damage)	0.96	128.00
Premium share (bodily injury)	0.53	−5.45
Premium share (property damage)	1.02	−22.12
Premiums/sales index (bodily injury)	0.35	−20.45
Premiums/sales index (physical damage)	0.35	−33.33
Product patents significant (percent of firms)	100.00	. . .
Process patents significant (percent of firms)	50.00	. . .
No regular product changes (percent of firms)	0.00	. . .
Periodic product changes (percent of firms)	100.00	. . .
Regular product changes (percent of firms)	0.00	. . .
No new product development (percent of firms)	0.00	. . .

Table 3-10. *Product Liability and Innovation for the Miscellaneous Chemical Products Industry (SIC 289), 1980–84*

Item	1980–84 average	Percent change 1980–84
Loss ratio (bodily injury)	2.66	−60.00
Loss ratio (property damage)	0.71	194.29
Premium share (bodily injury)	1.51	−41.94
Premium share (property damage)	2.44	−40.82
Premiums/sales index (bodily injury)	0.78	−48.15
Premiums/sales index (property damage)	0.67	−50.89
Product patents significant (percent of firms)	12.50	. . .
Process patents significant (percent of firms)	12.50	. . .
No regular product changes (percent of firms)	100.00	. . .
Periodic product changes (percent of firms)	0.00	. . .
Regular product changes (percent of firms)	0.00	. . .
No new product development (percent of firms)	13.04	. . .

sample, and process patents are significant for almost a third. In each case the role of patents is much greater than in the total chemical industry as well as in manufacturing as a whole. Although regular and periodic product changes are not very important, this result may largely reflect a measurement problem. Most noteworthy is the fact that every firm in this industry responding to the survey said that new product development was important.

The agricultural chemicals industry, whose performance is summarized in table 3-9, is even more innovative. All the sample firms in the industry regard product patents as significant and introduce periodic product changes. In addition, every firm engages in new product development and half of them regard process patents as important. The loss ratios for product liability and bodily injury each average 1.0, but as we noted in discussing table 3-6, these rates fluctuate a great deal. Nevertheless, the agricultural chemicals industry appears to be highly innovative and less hard hit by liability than some of the other industries considered earlier. The declining share of premiums and the declining value of the premiums-to-sales index for that industry may, however, suggest a situation in which the pricing of insurance has led to a shrinking of the market.

Much the same is true for the miscellaneous chemical products industry (SIC 289), summarized in table 3-10. The loss ratio for bodily injury coverage averages 2.66, which is quite large. As expected, the higher price of insurance has led to a declining insurance market. The premium share for this industry dropped by 40 percent during 1980–84. The index of product liability premiums over sales also dropped by roughly 50 percent for both bodily injury and property damage coverage.

Although the chemical products industry has been hard hit by product liability, it cannot be characterized as among the most innovative. The significance of product patents and process patents is below the manufacturing average, and none of the firms in the sample make regular or periodic product changes. New product development is, however, substantial.

The Industrial Machinery Industry

Table 3-11 summarizes the product liability trends for the industrial and commercial machinery and computer equipment industry, as well as for four of the three-digit groups within that industry. The loss ratios for bodily damage in the whole industrial machinery category show losses higher than premiums for all years except 1984, where there is rough comparability. In construction and related machinery, particularly for bodily injury, loss ratios are out of line with what one would expect in a smoothly functioning insurance market. Throughout 1980–84, loss ratios were more than 2.0 each year. The results for metalworking machinery (SIC 354) and general industrial machinery (SIC 356) are somewhat less extreme, but here some years show high loss ratios. In the miscellaneous industrial and commercial machinery and equipment category (SIC 359), the loss ratio exceeds 1.0 in two years. One would expect a situation of comparatively high loss ratios to lead to a rise in insurance price that in turn would cause the market to shrink. The evidence of the shrinking market is strongest for construction and related machinery and metalworking machinery, where the premium share for bodily injury coverage declined substantially in both industries. The comparable results for the period 1980–84 for the industry subgroups in appendix tables 3A-1, 3A-2, and 3A-3 all show a decline in premium share over that period, whereas in table 3A-4 the miscellaneous subgroup shows no growth. For the two-digit industrial category (SIC 35), there is evidence of a decline in premium share from 1980 through 1984 (table 3-11).

Table 3-11. *Product Liability Trends for the Industrial and Commercial Machinery and Computer Equipment Industry, 1980–84*

Item	1980	1981	1982	1983	1984
	Industrial and commercial machinery and computer equipment (SIC 35)				
Loss ratio (bodily injury)	1.03	1.25	1.71	1.83	0.96
Loss ratio (property damage)	0.39	0.72	0.97	0.79	0.93
Premium share (bodily injury)	11.26	11.23	10.59	10.43	10.68
Premium share (property damage)	10.35	9.69	9.44	9.22	8.91
Premiums/sales index (bodily injury)	0.17	0.14	0.11	0.12	0.14
Premiums/sales index (property damage)	0.08	0.07	0.06	0.05	0.06
	Construction and related machinery (SIC 353)				
Loss ratio (bodily injury)	0.56	2.52	3.07	4.26	2.03
Loss ratio (property damage)	0.08	0.90	3.22	1.96	0.00
Premium share (bodily injury)	0.51	0.56	0.51	0.46	0.29
Premium share (property damage)	0.34	0.42	0.37	0.28	0.28
Premiums/sales index (bodily injury)	0.33	0.30	0.25	0.26	0.19
Premiums/sales index (property damage)	0.13	0.13	0.10	0.08	0.09
	Metalworking machinery (SIC 354)				
Loss ratio (bodily injury)	0.22	0.92	0.65	1.18	0.77
Loss ratio (property damage)	0.00	0.00	0.36	0.03	0.32
Premium share (bodily injury)	1.61	1.40	1.08	1.03	1.12
Premium share (property damage)	1.33	1.39	1.13	0.95	0.77
Premiums/sales index (bodily injury)	1.53	1.05	0.76	0.73	0.92
Premiums/sales index (property damage)	0.66	0.56	0.43	0.36	0.32
	General industrial machinery (SIC 356)				
Loss ratio (bodily injury)	3.06	0.61	0.04	1.03	0.91
Loss ratio (property damage)	0.03	0.08	0.00	0.00	0.38
Premium share (bodily injury)	0.09	0.09	0.05	1.03	0.05
Premium share (property damage)	0.28	0.22	0.12	0.10	0.08
Premiums/sales index (bodily injury)	0.24	0.19	0.10	0.06	0.13
Premiums/sales index (property damage)	0.42	0.29	0.13	0.13	0.11
	Miscellaneous industrial and commercial machinery and equipment (SIC 359)				
Loss ratio (bodily injury)	1.29	1.72	1.98	1.92	0.56
Loss ratio (property damage)	0.61	0.29	0.40	0.43	0.73
Premium share (bodily injury)	3.17	2.93	3.44	3.62	3.17
Premium share (property damage)	2.04	1.74	2.24	2.42	2.17
Premiums/sales index (bodily injury)	n.a.	n.a.	n.a.	n.a.	n.a.
Premiums/sales index (property damage)	n.a.	n.a.	n.a.	n.a.	n.a.

n.a. Not available.

The overall premium share results are also influenced by the general economic health of the industry. Declining industries, for example, purchase a diminishing amount of insurance. Real output levels in the industrial machinery industry were increasing in the early 1980s, though the patterns were uneven. For example, there was a decline in construction machinery equipment from 1980 to 1983, and a reversal in this decline thereafter.[10]

Even under relatively stable real growth, the nominal growth level in the segments of this industry rose over that period, so that the total value of the insurance coverage also should have risen. The decline in the premium share in the commercial machinery and equipment industry is suggestive of a rise in the insurance price. Because of loss ratios well above 1.0 in some cases, one would have expected an increase in insurance prices to bring the cost of insurance more in line with the losses experienced. Indeed, the decline in the loss ratios exhibited for the industry groups in table 3-11 is consistent with this changing price story. For the major outlier—construction and related machinery—premium levels remained too low even after the escalation in costs beginning in 1981.

Although detailed innovation data are not available for the three-digit category of industrial and commercial machinery, at the two-digit industry level product patents are important for one-fifth of the firms (table 3-12). Moreover, almost half the firms in the industry make periodic product changes. The frequency of product changes is much more rapid than in manufacturing industries generally. Indeed, whereas just over half of the commercial machinery industry makes no product changes, over three-fourths of all manufacturing firms made no product changes. More than 80 percent of the firms engage in new product development. Thus this is a fairly innovative industry compared with the typical manufacturing industry.

The components for the industrial and commercial machinery industry also display high rates of innovation. The construction-related machinery industry relies on product patents in more than one-third of the cases, although process patents do not play an important role (table 3A-1). In addition, almost three-fourths of the firms make periodic product changes, and over 80 percent of the firms engage in new product development. The metalworking machinery industry relies very little on patents, and the extent of product change and new product development is also well below the national average (table 3A-2). It should also be noted that this

10. Department of Commerce 1986, 22-1–22-2.

Table 3-12. *Product Liability and Innovation for the Industrial and Commercial Machinery and Computer Equipment Industry (SIC 35), 1980–84*

Item	1980–84 average	Percent change 1980–84
Loss ratio (bodily injury)	1.31	−6.80
Loss ratio (property damage)	0.73	138.46
Premium share (bodily injury)	10.87	−5.15
Premium share (property damage)	9.55	−13.91
Product patents significant (percent of firms)	21.86	. . .
Process patents significant (percent of firms)	3.13	. . .
No regular product changes (percent of firms)	53.91	. . .
Periodic product changes (percent of firms)	46.09	. . .
Regular product changes (percent of firms)	0.00	. . .
No new product development (percent of firms)	19.53	. . .

relatively noninnovative segment of the industry exhibited lower loss ratios than did the more innovative construction and related machinery group. The general industrial machinery category included very few firms that relied significantly on patents of any kind (table 3A-3). Moreover, there is no regular pattern to product change in that industry, although roughly two-thirds of the firms did engage in new product development. The high but declining loss ratios and the shrinking premium share are consistent with the problem of insurance availability, but it is unlikely that innovation through new patentable technologies is the cause.

Overall, industrial and commercial machinery and computer equipment is an innovative industry. The insurance market for those firms was in some disarray in the early 1980s, particularly as regards bodily injury coverage. With losses much higher than premiums, there was a need to bring the pricing structure more in line with its costs. These adjustments in turn led to a shrinking role of product liability insurance for this industry.

Transportation Equipment Industry

Insurance trends for the transportation equipment industry follow patterns not unlike those in the other industries discussed. In particular,

Table 3-13. *Product Liability Trends for the Transportation Equipment Industry, 1980–84*

Item	1980	1981	1982	1983	1984
	Transportation equipment (SIC 37)				
Loss ratio (bodily injury)	1.15	0.59	1.61	1.09	0.74
Loss ratio (property damage)	0.32	0.53	0.60	0.32	0.48
Premium share (bodily injury)	4.28	4.39	4.29	4.06	4.25
Premium share (property damage)	2.66	3.23	3.14	3.06	3.09
Premiums/sales index (bodily injury)	0.06	0.05	0.05	0.04	0.05
Premiums/sales index (property damage)	0.02	0.02	0.02	0.02	0.02
	Motor vehicles and motor vehicle equipment (SIC 371)				
Loss ratio (bodily injury)	1.48	0.90	2.10	0.96	0.93
Loss ratio (property damage)	0.27	0.57	0.85	0.30	0.35
Premium share (bodily injury)	2.76	2.51	2.34	2.88	2.80
Premium share (property damage)	1.61	1.77	1.81	2.21	2.22
Premiums/sales index (bodily injury)	0.10	0.08	0.06	0.08	0.09
Premiums/sales index (property damage)	0.03	0.03	0.03	0.03	0.03
	Aircraft and parts (SIC 372)				
Loss ratio (bodily injury)	0.56	0.00	20.46	0.00	0.00
Loss ratio (property damage)	0.00	0.54	0.00	0.00	0.00
Premium share (bodily injury)	0.01	0.02	0.02	0.01	0.00
Premium share (property damage)	0.01	0.01	0.02	0.00	0.01
Premiums/sales index (bodily injury)	0.02	0.04	0.02	0.01	0.01
Premiums/sales index (property damage)	0.01	0.01	0.02	0.01	0.01

there seems to be a consistently higher level of bodily injury loss ratios than property damage loss ratios. Because of the escalating role of product liability lawsuits involving bodily injury, one would expect insurance companies to fail to equalize the loss ratios across the two types of coverage in the short run, but to move toward equality in the longer run.

This pattern is reflected in table 3-13. Although the year-to-year patterns are uneven, over the entire period there was a movement toward declining loss ratios for bodily injury and rising loss ratios for property damage.

Results for the aircraft and parts industry (SIC 372) are particularly intriguing because of their unevenness. While many of the firms most affected by product liability lie outside the scope of the sample, even for the firms included in the data the potential problems arising from an uncertain product liability environment are apparent. Loss ratios in some years are zero, but they escalate to levels as high as 20 and above (in 1982) and make insurers reluctant to write coverage. As the premium share statistics in the table show, the role of product liability in insurance coverage for the aircraft and parts industry had been all but eliminated

Table 3-14. *Product Liability and Innovation for the Transportation Equipment Industry (SIC 37), 1980–84*

Item	1980–84 average	Percent change 1980–84
Loss ratio (bodily injury)	1.02	−35.65
Loss ratio (property damage)	0.45	50.00
Premium share (bodily injury)	4.26	−0.70
Premium share (property damage)	3.02	16.17
Premiums/sales index (bodily injury)	0.05	−16.67
Premiums/sales index (property damage)	0.02	0.00
Product patents signficant (percent of firms)	0.00	. . .
Process patents significant (percent of firms)	0.00	. . .
No regular product changes (percent of firms)	28.57	. . .
Periodic product changes (percent of firms)	38.10	. . .
Regular product changes (percent of firms)	33.33	. . .
No new product development (percent of firms)	0.00	. . .

by the mid-1980s. In effect, this industry lies outside the scope of conventional insurance markets. This result is not due to a low level of liability that makes insurance unattractive. Rather, liability costs are so excessive that these firms have been led to make alternative arrangements. The extremely low index of product liability premiums to sales for this industry reflects its reliance on alternative insurance arrangements.

Table 3-14 summarizes the results for the whole transportation equipment industry. The performance of insurance for this two-digit category is similar to that of the components analyzed below. In the motor vehicle segment of the industry (371), the loss ratio is somewhat higher than the industry average (table 3A-5). However, since motor vehicles comprise over half of all product liability insurance premiums written to the two-digit industrial group, the main industry trends are similar to those for this three-digit industry component. In particular, the loss ratio for bodily injury coverage declined over the five-year period considered, and the premium share was relatively constant for both industry segments. Table 3A-6 highlights the results for the aircraft and parts industry, which experienced a vanishing product liability coverage.

Innovation within the two components of the transportation equipment industry discussed here depends in part on the measure of innovation used. Consider first that of product and process patents. In each case there is no evidence of significant reliance on either class of patents. That, however, does not mean there is no innovation. In the motor vehicle component, for example, all the respondents said that periodic changes in the product took place. Although there were no regular product changes indicated for aircraft and parts, this does not mean that no product changes occurred, only that they did not occur regularly. Indeed, all the firms in the aircraft and parts industry said they engaged in new product development, as did all the respondents in the motor vehicle and motor vehicle equipment industry. In this whole transportation equipment industry, the main source of product change is through product development as opposed to new patentable innovations. Although the aircraft and parts component of the industry seems to be the most hard hit by product liability, there is no apparent correlation of this effect with the innovation measures included here. These, however, do not capture the inherently more novel nature of this product as opposed to forms of transportation developed in earlier years.

The Medical Equipment Industry

Table 3-15 summarizes the product liability and innovation results for the industry groups that include medical and optical goods. The two-digit category exhibits comparatively low loss ratios for both bodily injury and property damage coverage, and even the three-digit category of surgical, medical, and dental instruments and supplies has only one year in which the loss ratio exceeded 1.0. The premium share also shows a much different pattern from that found in the earlier tables, since there is evidence of a growing insurance market. Whereas in the earlier cases product liability insurance premiums were vanishing altogether, in the instrument and medical equipment market there is no such difficulty. This comparative health, as reflected in the growth in premium share is also mirrored in the loss ratios, which have none of the excesses displayed in the industries discussed earlier. Moreover, the value of the index of product liability premiums to sales is also stable.

Table 3A-7 provides the insurance and innovation measures for the two-digit industry category, and table 3A-8 provides those measures for the medical component of this industry. Although the two-digit industry is fairly innovative in that product and process patents are extensive, the surgical, medical, and dental instrument segment is less innovative whether one examines the role of patents or regular product changes. From the

Table 3-15. *Product Liability Trends for the Measuring, Analyzing, and Controlling Instruments; Photographic, Medical and Optical Goods; Watches and Clocks Industry, 1980–84*

Item	1980	1981	1982	1983	1984
	Whole industry (SIC 38)				
Loss ratio (bodily injury)	0.80	1.00	0.49	1.13	0.61
Loss ratio (property damage)	0.18	0.30	0.26	0.34	0.22
Premium share (bodily injury)	2.60	2.65	2.72	2.76	3.09
Premium share (property damage)	1.42	1.54	1.61	1.92	2.26
Premiums/sales index (bodily injury)	0.21	0.19	0.16	0.17	0.21
Premiums/sales index (property damage)	0.06	0.06	0.05	0.06	0.08
	Surgical, medical, and dental instruments and supplies (SIC 384)				
Loss ratio (bodily injury)	0.64	1.08	0.48	0.85	0.51
Loss ratio (property damage)	0.15	0.11	0.03	0.06	0.18
Premium share (bodily injury)	1.39	1.37	1.55	1.54	1.72
Premium share (property damage)	0.21	0.30	0.35	0.50	0.45
Premiums/sales index (bodily injury)	1.01	0.85	0.82	0.80	1.01
Premiums/sales index (property damage)	0.08	0.10	0.10	0.13	0.13

standpoint of new product development, however, the medical instrument component varies greatly.

In each case there is a decline in the loss ratios over the 1980–84 period. Moreover, even in the initial part of the 1980s the loss ratios were at relatively modest levels compared with the extreme values found earlier. The comparatively profitable loss ratios are coupled with a continued growth in premiums, the pattern one expects in a reasonably well functioning insurance market.

A Model of the Product Liability–Innovation Link

To provide a more precise assessment of the product liability–innovation link, one must use an econometric model. An important consideration is the disentangling of the causal link between innovation and risk. In particular, is it possible to separate out the effects of liability costs on innovation? This mechanism operates through an experience rating of individual policies based on accident histories. In addition, can one also determine the effects of innovation on liability costs? Safer product and process designs will reduce the expected liability burden.

We postulate the simple recursive model of the product liability–

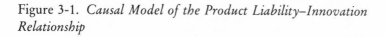

Figure 3-1. *Causal Model of the Product Liability–Innovation Relationship*

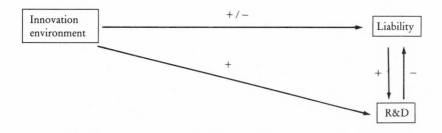

innovation relationship shown in figure 3-1.[11] In this model the innovation environment before the emergence of product liability risks is taken as the basic causal element. An innovative industry can be more or less risky than a less innovative industry, depending on the nature of the innovation. If new products are inherently safer, because of improved processes or advances in technology, then more innovative industries will be less risky. However, if new products incorporate risky designs whose adverse consequences may not be immediately apparent, more innovative industries will have higher liability insurance levels. The direction of causality from the innovation environment to the costs of liability is theoretically ambiguous.

The second link in the model relates the cost of liability to the incentive to invest in research and development. Again, the direction of this relationship is ambiguous. Higher liability costs create incentives for safety that will stimulate efforts to improve product safety, provided the costs are not so great that the products are withdrawn from the market. The firm could eliminate risky product designs from the product mix and return to an earlier model. In this case liability would not have a positive effect on research or product innovations. If the costs of removing or bearing the risk are so high that the firm withdraws the product from the market altogether, increases in liability will lead to decreases in R&D expenditures.

The final link in our model leads directly from the innovation envi-

11. To distinguish these effects, we exploit the longitudinal nature of the PIMS data and the fact that liability costs did not become large until the late 1970s and early 1980s. Measures of innovation before this time provide an index of an industry's innovative activity that is exogenous with respect to the product liability risk. These innovation variables can then be used both as predictors of the risk and as instruments in equations relating risk levels to R&D intensity, which we take as our measure of current innovative activity.

Table 3-16. *Profit Impact of Marketing Strategies (PIMS) Innovation Variables and Insurance Services Office Risk Variables*

Item	Chemicals (1)	Machinery and equipment (2)	Transportation equipment (3)	Instruments (4)	All manufacturing (5)
Product R&D/sales (PIMS)	1.65	2.79	1.71	2.97	1.49
Product R&D/sales (McGraw-Hill data)	3.43	4.02	3.68	8.63	2.75
Technological change (dummy variable, DV)	0.134	0.32	0.53	0.36	0.27
Product patents important (DV)	0.15	0.22	0.0	0.34	0.18
Process patents important (DV)	0.15	0.03	0.0	0.23	0.16
Premiums/firm	7,758	15,890	8,259	9,139	15,832
Losses/firm	18,062	15,640	6,697	8,973	15,910
Sample sizes	67	128	21	74	928

ronment to R&D expenditures. Industries with highly innovative technologies tend to spend more on R&D. Thus we expect a positive relationship between the innovativeness of the firm's environment and expenditures by the firm on R&D.

The variables measuring the innovation environment include three firm-level measures. Two of these indicate the significance of product and process patents, and the third indicates whether the firm has any products it considers new. The innovation variables also include an industry-level measure of the importance of technological change. These have been described in detail earlier, and broken down by industry. For the purposes of our empirical model, we need only note here that each of these variables is time invariant, and each was measured well before the product liability crisis emerged in the mid-1980s. We therefore take each of these variables as exogenous indicators of the prior extent of innovative activity, at the levels of both the firm and the industry.

Product liability risk is proxied in the empirical analysis by losses and premiums for bodily injury, relative to sales. These risk measures are computed on a per firm basis at the four-digit SIC level, and matched to the PIMS firms on that basis wherever possible. If a four-digit matchup is not possible, liability costs are matched to firms at the three-digit level, and so forth. Sales data are drawn from several sources, primarily the *Survey of Current Business* and the *Statistical Abstract of the United States*.

The measure of endogenous innovation activity used in the empirical analysis is a firm-specific, time-varying measure of R&D intensity: product R&D expenditures relative to sales. As noted, R&D intensity should increase with the risk if the safety incentive effect dominates, while it should decrease with the risk if the dampening effect on innovation dominates.

Table 3-16 presents sample statistics describing the principal characteristics of our sample of firms. Columns 1–4 show results for the two-digit SIC categories corresponding to chemicals, machinery and equipment, transportation equipment, and instruments and related machinery. Column 5 shows statistics for all manufacturing firms (SIC categories 20–39) included in our sample. The full sample of 928 PIMS lines of business is used in the empirical analysis reported below.

As the results in table 3-16 indicate, each of the four industries conducts more product R&D relative to sales than do all firms in the PIMS-ISO sample, particularly in the machinery and equipment and in the instruments industries. The pace of technological change in these industries and in the transportation industry is also more rapid. The instrument industry is well above average on almost every R&D measure, and the chemical industry is at least slightly below average on each measure. The other industries are neither consistently above nor below the manufacturing averages.

Table 3-16 also shows the average losses and premiums per firm for bodily injury. The high-R&D instrument industry is well below average on each of these measures. Likewise, the transportation industry, which is typified by average or above-average levels of innovative activity in terms of expenditures and technological advance but which exhibits no patenting activity, is also below the manufacturing average in product liability insurance costs. These results would seem to suggest a negative relationship between risk and innovation. However, the same pattern does not hold for the machinery and equipment industry, where higher than average R&D is associated with average risk levels.

The exact nature of the relationship cannot be determined by using these simple descriptive results. To disentangle the causal relationship among the prior measures of innovation, the liability risk level, and current R&D expenditures, we estimated a regression model based on figure 3-1. This simple model, a prototype for our related research,[12] contains two equations in a recursive formulation. The first equation models the firm's liability cost risk as a linear function of the prior innovation in-variables indicating the importance of product and process patents, the presence of new products in the product line, and the importance of technological change in the industry. This equation can be expressed as

$$(1) \quad \text{Cost risk} = \alpha_0 + \alpha_1 \text{ technical change} + \alpha_2 \text{ product patents}$$
$$+ \alpha_3 \text{ process patents} + \alpha_4 \text{ no new products} + \epsilon_1.$$

The second equation in our empirical model describes the relationship between the current level of R&D activity, as measured by product R&D intensity, the product liability cost risk, and the prior innovation variables. To capture the potential nonlinearities in the relationship, whereby the safety incentive effect may dominate at low liability cost levels and the product withdrawal effect may dominate at high liability cost levels, we model this relationship as a quadratic. This second equation can be expressed as

12. Viscusi and Moore 1989.

Table 3-17. *Bodily Injury Loss Estimated Coefficients*[a]

Item	Bodily injury losses/sales	In (bodily injury losses/sales)
Technological changes	2,961*	. . .***
	(1,901)	(0.08)
Product patents important (DV)	7,077**	0.03
	(2,411)	(0.10)
Process patents important (DV)	784	0.27***
	(2,436)	(0.11)
No new products (DV)	1,054	−0.77***
	(1,914)	(0.08)

a. The numbers in parentheses are standard errors.
*** Statistically significant at the 0.01 confidence level.
** Statistically significant at the 0.05 confidence level.
* Statistically significant at the 0.10 confidence level.

$$(2) \quad RD \text{ intensity} = \beta_0 + \beta_1 \text{ cost risk} + \beta_2 \text{ cost risk}^2$$
$$+ \beta_3 \text{ technical change}$$
$$+ \beta_4 \text{ product patents} + \beta_5 \text{ process patents}$$
$$+ \beta_6 \text{ no new products} + \epsilon_2.$$

The hypothesis developed earlier can be expressed in terms of the coefficients of equations 1 and 2 as follows. In equation 1 the effect of prior innovation on product liability risk will be positive if new products are generally riskier than older products. Therefore, we expect each of the coefficients in equation 1 to be positive if that is true. In equation 2, we expect the coefficient on the linear risk term to be positive, since safety effects should dominate at low risk levels. We further expect the second coefficient, β_2, to be negative if the costs of safety are increasing, which would lead to product withdrawals for very dangerous products. Finally, we expect a positive association between each of the measures of prior innovation and the R&D intensity variable.

Table 3-17 presents estimates of equation 1, where bodily injury losses relative to sales and its natural logarithm are used as dependent variables. In each case there is fairly strong evidence that more innovative industries have higher product liability losses. In the first column, both the technological change and the product patent variables are positive and statistically significant, and the other two coefficients are insignificant. In the second column, where the natural logarithm of bodily injury losses relative to sales is used as the dependent variable, three of the four coefficients are right-signed and significant while the fourth, the product patents

Table 3-18. *Product R&D Intensity Equations Estimated Coefficients*[a]

Item	Product R&D/Sales			
	(1)	*(2)*	*(3)*	*(4)*
Bodily injury losses/sales	0.99E-5 (0.27E-5)	0.80E-5*** 0.26E-5	0.20E-4*** (0.05E-4)	0.21E-4*** (0.05E-4)
(Bodily injury losses/sales)^2	. . .	. . .	−0.6E-10*** (0.27E-10)	−0.82E-10*** (.26E-10)
Technological change (DV)	. . .	0.875*** (0.15)	. . .	0.90*** (0.15)
Product patents important (DV)	. . .	0.089 (0.176)	. . .	0.11 (0.64)
Process patents important (DV)	. . .	. . .	. . .	. . .
No new products	. . .	−1.26*** (0.15)	. . .	−1.27*** (0.15)
R^2	0.013	0.14	0.190	0.15

a. Numbers in parentheses are standard errors.
*** Statistically significant at the 0.01 confidence level.

variable, is positive. The results of the estimation of an equation using bodily injury premiums as the dependent variable were not as strong, although all the significant coefficients were in the expected direction. Thus it appears empirically that the liability cost risk embodied in new products offsets any gains from technological advances and new processes.

Table 3-18 gives estimates of the second equation of our model, which describes the determination of R&D intensity. Four versions of equation 2 are shown in the table. In the first two columns, product R&D relative to sales is regressed on a linear risk term measuring bodily injury losses, and on the linear risk term plus the prior innovation variables. The process patent dummy variable is not included in these regressions, since it was never close to significance in any of the product R&D equations. The results in columns 1 and 2 are consistent with the hypotheses developed above. Increases in risk lead to increases in R&D intensity, suggesting that the safety incentive effect of liability costs is dominant. Firms in more innovative industries and firms that consistently produce new products are also more likely to invest in R&D relative to sales.

The third and fourth columns of table 3-18 add the quadratic risk term to determinate the importance of any nonlinearities in the effect. As the results show, there are important nonlinear effects in each specification of the model. Both the linear and quadratic risk terms are highly significant determinants of product R&D intensity. Their estimated effects indicate that the incentives for safety provided at low-risk levels are more than offset at high-risk levels, leading to reductions in R&D activity beyond some threshold.

Results similar to those in columns 1 and 2 of the table were estimated using bodily injury premiums as the risk measure. However, the nonlinearities in the risk effects were not as strong in this specification. Elsewhere we analyze these and alternative specifications in more complex empirical models, where the nonlinear effect is found to be quite robust.[13]

The results in table 3-18 suggest that there is some threshold beyond which increases in liability losses lead to reductions in R&D intensity. This threshold is of interest as a reference point and is easily computed. However, the risk threshold has no optimality implications whatsoever. It is simply the point at which the net effect on innovation of the existing liability regime switches from being positive to negative.

Computing the partial effect of bodily injury losses on R&D intensity using the results in table 3-18 and solving for the risk level at which the effect on R&D intensity becomes zero yields a liability costs relative to sales of about 1 percent. Of the firms in our sample, only the aircraft and parts industry lies above that threshold. This result is consistent with anecdotal evidence on the problems facing the small aircraft industry and also with the history of catastrophic losses surrounding major air crashes. It also suggests that for most industries the costs of product liability provide safety incentive effects that more than offset the product withdrawal effects.

One cannot conclude from these results that product liability costs will adversely affect sales for every firm for which the ratio of these costs to sales exceeds 1 percent. Our results pertain to the overall industry level of costs in the ISO sample. This value provides an index of relative insurance costs by industry. The actual total level of insurance costs for any given industry will exceed the value used as the liability cost measure here, so that the liability cost share value for which a particular firm will reduce its innovation efforts will exceed 1 percent.

Conclusion

Even in the time period examined in this chapter, which precedes the emergence of the liability premium crisis in 1985 and 1986, there is evidence of liability insurance markets in disarray. Whereas one would have

13. Viscusi and Moore 1989.

expected to find a smoothly functioning insurance market with stable loss ratios equalized across industries and across insurance lines, we found quite a different situation: a substantial disparity in loss ratios that persisted over time. For the period 1980–84 loss ratios for bodily injury coverage were considerably higher than those for property damage coverage, as one would expect in an era in which product liability losses for bodily injury were escalating at a much greater rate.

The main difficulty is that insurance companies are not able to raise premiums sufficiently to reflect the change in their loss experience. With loss ratios of 1.19 for all manufacturing industries and much higher for many industries examined, insurance firms needed to realign the premium structure to better reflect their cost structure. In many of the cases considered, this alignment occurred through the decline in the loss ratios over time, as firms in effect raised the price of insurance. In several instances loss ratios declined to better reflect the rising costs, resulting in an accompanying decline in the premium share for that industry.

Whereas the typical view is that the crisis in product liability did not emerge until 1985, we find the roots of an emerging crisis in the early 1980s. Examining premium trends alone disguises much of the crisis because it misses the fact that industries may be denied insurance coverage or may leave the market altogether. Thus the issue of the availability of insurance is central to any assessment of whether a product liability crisis did indeed occur in the affected industries.

Examination of our sample industries shows that the loss ratios were often quite high or that there was a large drop in insurance premiums reflecting a decline in availability. The aircraft industry is perhaps the greatest outlier, since these firms are primarily outside the scope of the Insurance Services Office data base. The most notable other industry categories are in the chemical and the industrial machinery industries. Each of these industry groups experienced declining loss ratios over 1980–84, accompanied by declining premium shares and declining ratios of premiums to sales. This combination is expected, since a market with rising prices should be accompanied by declining quantity purchased.

An econometric analysis suggests that many of these links are of general consequence. More innovative industries tend to have a higher liability burden, which is consistent with much evidence on the pattern of liability costs. Tort liability does, however, have safety incentive effects. Higher levels of liability costs usually increase product-related research and development. However, extremely high levels of liability dampen innovation as firms reduce their focus on new product development.

Table 3A-1. *Product Liability and Innovation for the Construction and Related Machinery Industry (SIC 353), 1980–84*

Item	1980–84 average	Percent change 1980–84
Loss ratio (bodily injuty)	2.37	262.50
Loss ratio (property damage)	1.18	−100.00
Premium share (bodily injury)	0.47	−43.14
Premium share (property damage)	0.34	−17.65
Product patents significant (percent of firms)	35.29	. . .
Process patents significant (percent of firms)	0.00	. . .
No regular product changes (percent of firms)	26.47	. . .
Periodic product changes (percent of firms)	73.53	. . .
Regular product changes (percent of firms)	0.00	. . .
No new product development (percent of firms)	17.65	. . .

Table 3A-2. *Product Liability and Innovation for the Metalworking Machinery Industry (SIC 354), 1980–84*

Item	1980–84 average	Percent change 1980–84
Loss ratio (bodily injury)	0.68	250.00
Loss ratio (property damage)	0.12	0.00
Premium share (bodily injury)	1.27	−30.43
Premium share (property damage)	1.12	−42.11
Product patents significant (percent of firms)	5.00	. . .
Process patents significant (percent of firms)	0.00	. . .
No regular product changes (percent of firms)	70.00	. . .
Periodic product changes (percent of firms)	30.00	. . .
Regular product changes (percent of firms)	0.00	. . .
No new product development (percent of firms)	50.00	. . .

Table 3A-3. *Product Liability and Innovation for the General Industrial Machinery Industry (SIC 356), 1980–84*

Item	1980–84 average	Percent change 1980–84
Loss ratio (bodily injury)	1.42	−70.26
Loss ratio (property damage)	0.07	1,166.67
Premium share (bodily injury)	0.06	−44.44
Premium share (property damage)	1.16	−71.43
Product patents significant (percent of firms)	0.00	. . .
Process patents significant (percent of firms)	4.17	. . .
No regular product changes (percent of firms)	100.00	. . .
Periodic product changes (percent of firms)	0.00	. . .
Regular product changes (percent of firms)	0.00	. . .
No new product development (percent of firms)	33.33	. . .

Table 3A-4. *Product Liability and Innovation for the Miscellaneous Industrial and Commercial Machinery and Equipment Industry (SIC 359), 1980–84*

Item	1980–84 average	Percent change 1980–84
Loss ratio (bodily injury)	1.47	−56.59
Loss ratio (property damage)	0.50	19.67
Premium share (bodily injury)	3.25	0.00
Premium share (property damage)	2.11	6.37
Product patents significant (percent of firms)	n.a.	. . .
Process patents significant (percent of firms)	n.a.	. . .
No regular product changes (percent of firms)	n.a.	. . .
Periodic product changes (percent of firms)	n.a.	. . .
Regular product changes (percent of firms)	n.a.	. . .
No new product development (percent of firms)	n.a.	. . .

n.a. not available.

Table **3A-5.** *Product Liability and Innovation for the Motor Vehicle and Equipment Industry (SIC 371), 1980–84*

Item	1980–84 average	Percent change 1980–84
Loss ratio (bodily injury)	1.24	−37.16
Loss ratio (property damage)	0.45	29.63
Premium share (bodily injury)	2.67	1.45
Premium share (property damage)	1.91	37.88
Premiums/sales index (bodily injury)	0.08	−10.00
Premiums/sales index (property damage)	0.03	0.00
Product patents significant (percent of firms)	0.00	. . .
Process patents significant (percent of firms)	0.00	. . .
No regular product changes (percent of firms)	0.00	. . .
Periodic product changes (percent of firms)	100.00	. . .
Regular product changes (percent of firms)	0.00	. . .
No new product development (percent of firms)	0.00	. . .

Table **3A-6.** *Product Liability and Innovation for the Aircraft and Parts Industry (SIC 372), 1980–84*

Item	1980–84 average	Percent change 1980–84
Loss ratio (bodily injury)	5.34	−100.00
Loss ratio (property damage)	0.13	0.00
Premium share (bodily injury)	0.01	−100.00
Premium share (property damage)	0.01	0.00
Premiums/sales index (bodily injury)	0.02	−50.00
Premiums/sales index (property damage)	0.01	0.00
Product patents significant (percent of firms)	0.00	. . .
Process patents significant (percent of firms)	0.00	. . .
No regular product changes (percent of firms)	100.00	. . .
Periodic product changes (percent of firms)	0.00	. . .
Regular product changes (percent of firms)	0.00	. . .
No new product development (percent of firms)	0.00	. . .

Table 3A-7. *Product Liability and Innovation for the Measuring, Analyzing, and Controlling Instruments; Photographic, Medical and Optical Goods; Watches and Clocks Industry (SIC 38), 1980–84*

Item	1980–84 average	Percent change 1980–84
Loss ratio (bodily injury)	0.80	−23.75
Loss ratio (property damage)	0.26	22.22
Premium share (bodily injury)	2.76	18.85
Premium share (property damage)	1.74	59.15
Premiums/sales index (bodily injury)	0.19	0.00
Premiums/sales index (property damage)	0.06	33.33
Product patents significant (percent of firms)	33.78	. . .
Process patents significant (percent of firms)	22.97	. . .
No product changes (percent of firms)	85.14	. . .
Periodic product changes (percent of firms)	12.16	. . .
Regular product changes (percent of firms)	2.70	. . .

Table 3A-8. *Product Liability and Innovation for the Surgical, Medical, and Dental Instruments and Supplies Industry (SIC 384), 1980–84*

Item	1980–84 average	Percent change 1980–84
Loss ratio (bodily injury)	0.70	−20.31
Loss ratio (property damage)	0.10	20.00
Premium share (bodily injury)	1.51	23.74
Premium share (property damage)	0.35	114.29
Premiums/sales index (bodily injury)	0.90	0.00
Premiums/sales index (property damage)	0.11	62.50
Product patents significant (percent of firms)	5.26	. . .
Process patents significant (percent of firms)	0.00	. . .
No product changes (percent of firms)	89.47	. . .
Periodic product changes (percent of firms)	5.26	. . .
Regular product changes (percent of firms)	5.26	. . .

References

Harrington, S. 1988. "Prices and Profits in the Liability Insurance Market." In *Liability: Perspectives and Policy,* edited by R. E. Litan and C. Winston, 42–127. Brookings.

Huber, P. W. 1988. *Liability: The Legal Revolution and Its Consequences.* Basic Books.

Insurance Information Institute. 1989. *1990 Property/Casualty Insurance Facts.* New York.

Litan, R. E., and C. Winston. 1988. *Liability: Perspectives and Policy.* Brookings.

Mastroianni, L., P. J. Donaldson, and T. Kane, eds. *Developing New Contraceptives: Obstacles and Opportunities.* Washington: National Academy Press.

McGuire, E. P. 1988. *The Impact of Product Liability.* Report 908. New York: The Conference Board.

U.S. Department of Commerce. 1986. *U.S. Industrial Outlook.*

Viscusi, W. K. 1991. *Reforming the Products Liability System.* Harvard University Press.

———. [Forthcoming.] "Product and Occupational Liability." *Journal of Economic Perspectives.*

Viscusi, W. K., and M. J. Moore. 1989. "The Effect of Product Liability on Innovation." NBER Seminar Notes. Duke University.

CHAPTER FOUR

Product Liability and Motor Vehicle Safety

John D. Graham

T HE LIBERALIZATION of product liability law in the United States has strongly affected the motor vehicle manufacturing industry. In 1950 the typical product liability lawsuit against a vehicle manufacturer alleged that a manufacturing defect was responsible for a crash and associated injuries; in 1990 the typical lawsuit alleged a design defect. Now the plaintiff often claims that the design defect aggravated the severity of occupant injury even if the defect did not cause the crash.[1]

There are no national data to quantify the growth in vehicle-related product liability litigation. As a crude indication of the volume of litigation, in 1950 the industry's largest vehicle manufacturer assigned one full-time in-house attorney to product liability cases; in 1990 the comparable number was about twenty.

The growth in litigation has been accompanied and stimulated by the increasing success of plaintiffs. The Rand Corporation studied product liability cases in Cook County and San Francisco for the years 1960–64 and 1980–84. The percentage of tried cases won by plaintiffs has grown. The average (inflation-adjusted) jury award to successful plaintiffs in auto-related product liability cases rose about 150 percent over the same period. Although punitive damage awards are still infrequent in product liability cases, the Rand study found that the frequency and average size of punitive damage awards have also increased.[2]

Profound changes in legal doctrines and practices are responsible for the growth in product liability risk. Like many industries, the vehicle industry has felt the impact of the transition from the negligence standard

1. Mashaw and Harfst 1990, 274.
2. Peterson 1987.

to various notions of strict liability, the gradual erosion of contributory negligence and the emergence of comparative negligence (which allows plaintiffs to win some compensation even if they were partly responsible for their injuries), the liberalized discovery practices that increase the plaintiff attorney's access to design and economic information, joint and several liability that can cause one of several responsible defendants to incur the entire cost of an adverse verdict, and the growing willingness of judges to allow juries to consider punitive damages against manufacturers. In recent years, however, some states have chosen to limit the manufacturer's liability in certain cases.

Besides these general trends, there are two crucial facets of product liability law in the auto industry. First, the landmark 1968 *Larsen* case opened the door to "second collision" litigation. In this case, which involved the design of General Motors' steering column, the court held that the manufacturer of the vehicle has a duty to design it to protect the occupant in a crash, even though it is not produced with the intended purpose of crashing. Although the *Larsen* viewpoint was not immediately adopted in many jurisdictions, its influence extended throughout the country in the 1970s.[3] Second, in 1966 Congress created federal regulatory authority to set minimum vehicle safety standards but did not permit manufacturers to use compliance with regulation as a general defense in liability lawsuits. The manufacturer must still design the vehicle to satisfy the common laws of the fifty states.

The liberalization of product liability law has been defended on the grounds that it encourages manufacturers to promote injury prevention.[4] This chapter examines that hypothesis, which has become a critical empirical question in public debates about how liability law should be changed. The first section presents a framework for thinking about the elements that induce manufacturers to design and market safer vehicles. Next this framework is used by my associates and me to analyze five case studies of motor vehicle safety. Each case study examines whether liability considerations were responsible for either a pro-safety design change or some other pro-safety development. The concluding section examines whether liability exerts a pro-safety effect in a national time-series model, presents our findings about the role of tort liability as an injury prevention tool, and discusses the legislative implications of these findings.

3. *Larsen* v. *General Motors*, 391 F.2d 495 (8th Cir. 1986).
4. Teret 1981.

Figure 4-1. *Pro-Safety Factors Affecting Vehicle Design Choices*[a]

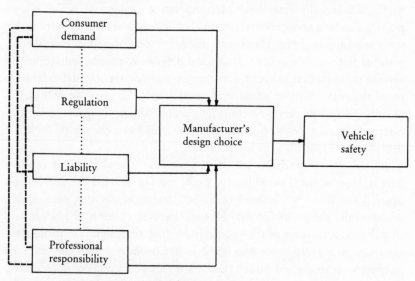

a. Dashed lines show indirect influences on design decisions.

Conceptual Framework

Why would a vehicle manufacturer pay any attention to the safety characteristics of its product? Four possible answers to this question are proposed: (1) consumer demand for safety per se, and/or for a product, and/or for a manufacturer that has a good reputation; (2) regulations that compel vehicle manufacturers to produce vehicles that meet minimum safety standards or to recall defective vehicles for repair; (3) common laws that impose duties on manufacturers to design safe vehicles; and (4) self-imposed standards of professional responsibility that cause manufacturers to design and produce a safe product.

In figure 4-1 these four factors are portrayed as the main pro-safety influences in the design choices of vehicle manufacturers. Note that these factors may influence design decisions directly or they may operate indirectly (as shown by the dashed lines). For example, regulators may release adverse safety information about a vehicle that hurts consumer demand for the vehicle or stimulates costly product liability lawsuits against the manufacturer. Likewise, regulators may pursue mandatory vehicle recalls or new vehicle safety standards on the basis of information generated by plaintiff attorneys in liability litigation. Such indirect forces can create incentives for pro-safety design decisions by manufacturers.

Consumer Demand

Vehicle manufacturers have many incentives not to market a plainly hazardous product. If word gets out, sales of the product will be adversely affected and the manufacturer's ability to develop customer loyalty will be undermined. Moreover, the same executives and design engineers who make the ultimate design decisions are also potential consumers of these vehicles. Since they are concerned about their own safety and the safety of their families and friends, they are unlikely to knowingly design a hazardous product. But do consumers reward those manufacturers who invest in safety innovation and implement incremental safety improvements?

The conventional wisdom in the auto industry that "safety doesn't sell" arose from the Ford Motor Company's experience with an optional safety package on its 1956 models. Ford invested millions of dollars in an advertising campaign to sell a package comprising lap belts, safety door latches, sun visors, crash padding, and a deep-dish steering wheel. The campaign was aborted when Chevrolet, Ford's arch rival, widened its sales lead from 70,000 cars in 1955 to 200,000 cars in 1956 by advertising high-powered V-8 engines and jazzy wheels.[5] Although orders for some of the individual safety features were larger than expected, industry leaders drew the conclusion that safety is a poor marketing device.[6]

The inability of vehicle manufacturers to sell optional safety features should not be surprising. Recent psychological research suggests that people tend to ignore events with low probabilities, regardless of the consequences. The average driver's annual probability of death in a car crash is about 0.00014; the corresponding probability of nonfatal injury is about 0.0025.[7] Even when people know the aggregate risk statistics, they may tend to discount their personal vulnerability ("it won't happen to me"). As my 1984 paper pointed out, drivers are notoriously confident about their own abilities as drivers. Hence safety has historically been a minor consideration in consumer choices compared with more salient product attributes such as vehicle appearance, ride, performance, price, fuel economy, and maintenance record.

There has always been a small segment of the new car market that is highly sensitive to safety. The Volvo, for example, is targeted at the safety-conscious buyer. Moreover, some large luxury models are marketed to

5. Eastman 1984, 228–33; Zola 1986.
6. O'Neill 1986, 4–5.
7. Graham 1984, 41.

safety-oriented, high-income buyers. When safety features are introduced as added-cost options, they are usually first introduced on luxury lines.

The growing population of young, well-educated buyers may be more conscious about safety than their parents were.[8] Domestic manufacturers have tried to capitalize on the new safety concerns of buyers by highlighting the alleged safety problems of Japanese cars. Moreover, a recent survey of new car dealers by the Insurance Institute for Highway Safety indicated that "safety" is second only to "quality" among the attributes sought by consumers.[9] General Motors, for example, has incorporated favorable data on insurance claim frequencies for GM cars into its marketing campaigns since the early 1980s. Manufacturers point to internal surveys showing that safety has become more of a sales factor.[10]

Safety may be a secondary product attribute, but manufacturers are aware that consumers take into account the reputation of a product and manufacturer when making their decisions. For example, Ralph Nader's campaign against the Corvair may have dissuaded some prospective buyers who became worried about safety. More important, the adverse publicity may have damaged the Corvair's reputation as a quality product in the eyes of the consumer.

Safety also may act as a surrogate for the consumer's broader concerns about a manufacturer's ability to produce a quality product. Adverse publicity about the safety of a specific product may damage the manufacturer's general reputation. Audi, for example, recently launched an extensive advertising campaign to boost its safety image in light of the damaging publicity the firm suffered over the "sudden acceleration" controversy.[11] Since consumer loyalty to a manufacturer is an important aspect of new car choices, manufacturers are very sensitive about adverse publicity.

Regulation

In 1966 Congress provided the National Highway Traffic Safety Administration (NHTSA) with two types of regulatory powers: recall authority and standard-setting authority. Although the standard-setting authority applies only to the production and sale of new vehicles, the recall authority enables the government to issue consumer advisories and take corrective action when defective vehicles are already on the road.

8. Sawyers 1990, 3.

9. Letter from Brian O'Neill, president, Insurance Institute for Highway Safety, to John D. Graham, July 18, 1990.

10. Graham 1990, 155; letter from Diane Steed to John D. Graham, Aug. 28, 1990.

11. Sawyers 1990, 24.

In its early years the NHTSA issued dozens of federal motor vehicle safety standards (FMVSSs) that codified industry practice or forced industry to apply new safety technologies. Some of these standards were designed to promote crash avoidance, the more innovative ones to promote "crashworthiness." The early wave of safety standards caused the death rate of passenger car occupants to decline more than it would have done without the standards.[12]

By the early 1970s the rate of standard setting at the NHTSA had slowed considerably. As it slowed, more agency resources were devoted to defect investigations. Considering the agency's twenty-five-year history, some observers have suggested that recall activities diverted resources from standard-setting activities.[13] The NHTSA has recently become more aggressive in standard setting, particularly in the areas of side impact protection and the safety of light trucks and minivans.

The regulatory process at the NHTSA has become highly formalized in part because final standards are subject to litigation and judicial review.[14] Standard setting and enforcement require a great deal of technical evidence to survive judicial challenges. Although some consumer advocates, insurance industry leaders, and legislators are frustrated with the slow pace of standard setting at the NHTSA, Congress has not yet attempted to resolve the issue with new legislation.

Despite the agency's limitations, the NHTSA can use performance rules to compel vehicle manufacturers to incorporate safety into their design decisions. Rather than wait for standards to be issued, manufacturers will sometimes make design changes in advance of standards to influence standard setting or obtain favorable media publicity. In particular, one manufacturer may try to exploit the government's regulatory powers to obtain a competitive advantage over other manufacturers.[15] The case study of air bags, discussed later, shows that GM and Ford have sought to work with the NHTSA at various times to gain a competitive edge.

Liability

Product liability considerations can encourage safety directly by imposing financial burdens on manufacturers that sell unsafe vehicle designs. The resulting crash-related injuries may lead to lawsuits, litigation costs,

12. Crandall and Graham 1984.
13. Mashaw and Harfst 1987.
14. Mashaw and Harfst 1987.
15. Graham 1989, 37–91.

settlements, jury awards, and the possibility of punitive damages. Besides these direct costs, lawsuits may contribute to adverse publicity about the vehicle in question and the manufacturer. Sometimes the reputational damage of publicized liability suits can be more important to manufacturers than the expected financial costs of liability. Although precise information is not publicly available, one analyst has estimated that direct liability costs amount to no more than 0.2 percent of the annual revenues of domestic auto manufacturers.[16]

Liability considerations do not always operate to encourage safer vehicle designs. Some safety features (such as the air bag) may increase the manufacturer's exposure to certain kinds of liability claims (such as failure to deploy, inadvertent deployment, and bag-induced injury). Indeed, one court recently suggested that air bags may increase a car manufacturer's liability if faith in the device causes occupants to stop wearing safety belts. Moreover, liability considerations may discourage a manufacturer from making safety improvements if it is feared that juries will use such improvements as evidence that the manufacturer's previous designs were defective. Admission of such evidence for jury consideration, though historically forbidden, has become increasingly common under the strict liability doctrine.[17]

The liberalization of product liability law has caused increased communication between design engineers and the lawyers responsible for defending companies in lawsuits. According to one large vehicle manufacturer, in 1960 the typical in-house liability attorney spent 5 percent of his time working with design engineers. Today such an attorney spends 40 to 50 percent of his time working directly with design engineers. When a lawsuit persuades engineers and lawyers that a particular design choice has led to poor safety outcomes, the incentives for design improvement can be powerful. Although this phenomenon might seem to be a good sign for vehicle safety, the actual signals sent to design engineers are often confusing.

Liability lawyers settle some cases that design engineers believe are preposterous because it is too risky to put the injured plaintiff before a jury. Even when the plaintiff's allegations against a specific manufacturer are tenuous, defense attorneys may be reluctant to take a case to trial and risk the penalty of joint and several liability. Lawyers also consider the

16. Wells 1986, 17.
17. *Ault* v. *International Harvester Co.* 13 Cal 3d 113; 528 P.2d 1148; 117 Cal Reptr. 812 (1976).

unfavorable publicity during trial and the adverse reputational implications of a large award to the plaintiff. In some situations, engineers employed by a manufacturer are baffled about why a jury would find an older vehicle defective on the basis of contemporary design standards. In light of the unpredictabilities in the liability process, many auto engineers in the industry believe the legal process offers them limited information about how to improve the safety of their products.[18]

Professional Responsibility

Manufacturers may choose safer vehicle designs because of various standards of professional responsibility that are independent of consumer demand, regulation, and liability considerations. Top management may interpret enhanced vehicle safety as part of its social responsibility. More important, design engineers may have stronger loyalties to their technical disciplines than to the profitability of their employer. It is not uncommon for design engineers to argue for a feasible safety improvement even if it is difficult to justify on strictly economic grounds. Moreover, safety professionals within a firm promote their own professional status by advocating design decisions that give weight to safety considerations. Of course, there are plenty of examples of shoddy design practice in the history of the motor vehicle industry to show the gaps in adherence to standards of professional responsibility.

Summary

Vehicle safety is promoted by consumer demand, regulation, liability, and professional responsibility. These factors rarely work in isolation; they typically interact with one another to influence design choices.

Publicity through the mass media can play a powerful role by amplifying each of these forces. Consumer demand for safety may be stimulated by safety-related information conveyed through television or newspapers. Political pressure for regulation may be enhanced when a safety issue receives widespread coverage in the mass media. Publicity about an alleged defect may cause more injured motorists to investigate whether their vehicle was defective and seek compensation from manufacturers. And professional standards of responsibility may be sensitized when safety concerns are widely publicized. The auto industry is an attractive target

18. Eads and Reuter 1983.

for the media because a few huge companies control much of the market. In the case studies that follow, my colleagues and I emphasize the role of the mass media as an institution that magnifies pro-safety forces on the manufacturer.

Case Studies

To determine the interplay of the pro-safety forces described above, we analyzed several case studies of safety-related design choice. These studies were not selected randomly but were chosen in part because advocates of liberalized liability law have cited them as examples of how liability works to promote injury prevention.[19]

The information in the case studies was taken from published sources and interviews with people from government, consumer groups, industry, and other organizations. Interview sources are acknowledged at the start of each case study, but since we wished to encourage frank discussion, we do not attribute specific remarks to specific sources.

Fuel Tank Placement

With the possible exception of GM's Corvair, the Ford Pinto is the most widely known example of a popular car that was redesigned and ultimately discontinued in part because of safety concerns. Despite these concerns, the Pinto had a fairly long product life cycle (a full decade), longer than its competitors had except for the Volkswagen Beetle. This case traces the story of the Pinto and the factors that led to its demise.[20]

Lee Iacocca was a powerful advocate of the Pinto. He argued that the Ford Motor Company needed a subcompact because the Volkswagen Beetle and other imports threatened to undermine Ford's traditionally strong position in the passenger car market. Shortly after becoming president of Ford, Iacocca announced that the Pinto would be made available to consumers beginning with model year 1971.

The idea behind the Pinto was to build a sporty, good-looking economy car that would seat four persons and capture America's imagination.

19. Teret and Jacobs 1989; Teret 1986.
20. This case was written by Douglas Weil. We thank the following persons for providing useful information: Richard Manetta (Ford), James Durkin (GM), John Moorhouse (Wake Forest University).

Table 4-1. *Production Numbers for Pre-1977 Ford Pintos*
Thousands

Model year	Two-door sedan	Three-door sedan	Station wagon	Total
1971	268	59	0	327
1972	172	188	96	454
1973	109	141	205	455
1974	121	160	217	498
1975	59	63	83	205
1976	87	87	99	273
1971–76	816	698	700	2,212

Source: Figures supplied by the Ford Motor Company and rounded to the nearest thousand.

The Pinto was "not to weigh an ounce over 2,000 pounds and not to cost a cent over $2,000."[21] The car was hyped in the popular press as a celebrity and warrior.[22]

Car buyers were soon hooked. In 1973 the Pinto was the top-selling subcompact car in the United States. It accounted for 24.4 percent of the small-car market and 4.2 percent of the entire industry. By 1976 the market had matured and Pinto's share of the small-car segment had fallen to 11.8 percent (13.7 percent when combined with the Mercury Bobcat), but it was still the top-selling small car in America. Pinto sales in its first six years of production were above 2 million cars (see table 4-1).

To meet Iacocca's 1971 deadline, design and development of the Pinto were accelerated beyond industry norms. The California Court of Appeals later alleged that the Pinto was a "rush project," and that "styling preceded, and to a greater degree than usual, dictated engineering."[23]

Among the engineering decisions was the location of the fuel tank. It was placed behind the axle and below the floor pan of the trunk. Some Ford engineers believed it was safer to place the tank there than over the rear axle, as had been recommended by another Ford engineer and as placed in Ford's European-produced subcompact, the Capri. By putting the fuel tank behind the rear axle, Ford was able to keep the tank outside the passenger compartment (thereby preventing gasoline vapors from

21. See "Managing Product Safety: The Ford Pinto," Harvard Business School Case 383-129; "Ford Ignored Pinto Fire Peril, Secret Memos Show," *Chicago Tribune*, Oct. 13, 1979, 80.

22. "Clever Cars, These Pintos," *Motor Trend*, Sept. 1970, 52; "Ford's Top Brass Talks about Pinto Power," *Popular Science*, Sept. 1970, 54–55; "Micro Muscle; Vega and Pinto," *Motor Trend*, Nov. 1970, 73–74; "Beleaguered Detroit Fights Back: Sub-compacts," *Newsweek*, Apr. 7, 1970, 73–77; "Detroit's First Midget Joins the Fight on Foreigners," *Business Week*, Feb. 14, 1970, 23–24.

23. *Grimshaw* v. *Ford Motor Company*, 119 Cal. App. 3d 757, 774 (1981).

entering it), protect the tank from being punctured in a crash by whatever was stored inside the trunk, and avoid placing the fuel filler close to the car's windows (again preventing the possibility of gasoline vapors entering the passenger compartment).

Safety was not the only factor that influenced the placement of the Pinto fuel tank. Placement behind the rear axle was necessary if Ford was to add a hatchback and station wagon to the Pinto line. It also was important so as to maintain luggage space in the trunk.

The trade-off being made to keep these options was to reduce the crush space available in the rear end of the car, which increased the exposure of the fuel tank to the forces of a rear-end collision. The placement of the tank also left it exposed to eight bolts that protruded out from the differential housing. In the course of a rear-end collision, the fuel tank could be driven into the bolts. If so, the tank might rupture, allowing gasoline to spill out.

The Pinto had less crush space than any other American-made car (except the American Motors Corporation's Gremlin) and less than the Capri. The limited amount of crush space in the Pinto was made more hazardous by the lack of any strong reinforcement in the rear of the car. The Pinto's bumper in 1971 and 1972 was essentially ornamental, and unlike Ford cars produced overseas, the Pinto was not reinforced behind with baffling known as hat sections.

Ford made significant changes to the Pinto over its ten-year life. By 1974 structural members were integrated into both sides of the car, and a lateral cross-member was placed both in front of and behind the fuel tank. The original bumper was replaced by a 5 mile per hour (mph) energy-absorbing bumper. The fuel supply hose was lengthened from six to eight inches, and the brake line was rerouted to reduce the likelihood of a fuel tank puncture in an accident. These and other changes enabled the 1974 Pinto to pass a 20 mph rear moving-barrier crash test with little or no damage to the fuel system.

At the time Ford designed the Pinto, the industry standard for fuel tank design in the United States was different from that in Europe and Japan.[24] The fuel tank on most American-made automobiles was behind the axle. In Europe and Japan the preferred placement of the fuel tank

24. Ford Motor Company compiled a summary and description of changes made to the 1971–77 Pinto related to the physical design, materials composition, and metal gauge in the underbody structure on all sides of the fuel tank, which was sent to Lynn Bradford, acting director, Office of Defects Investigation, National Highway Traffic Safety Administration, on Oct. 11, 1977.

in subcompacts was above the axle in order to increase the crush space between the bumper and rear axle.

Six months before introduction, Ford began crash tests on Pinto prototypes. As a result of these tests, Ford changed the shape of the fuel tank and moved the filler pipe, believing it had designed a car that could withstand a 20 mph moving-barrier crash test. The 1971 model year Pinto, as was later revealed, could not in fact consistently pass such a test.

In January 1969 the NHTSA proposed the first of a series of rear-end fuel system integrity standards. According to the 1969 proposed standard, no more than one ounce of gasoline should leak out of the fuel system after a stationary car is hit from the rear at 20 mph by a 4,000-pound moving barrier.

In August 1970, days after the initiation of Pinto production, the NHTSA proposed a tougher set of rear-end standards. Within eighteen months all new cars were to be able to withstand a rear-end collision at 20 mph with a fixed barrier so that gasoline leakage would be less than one ounce in one minute and less than five ounces in five minutes. The following year, the standard would be raised to 30 mph. Ford and the other automobile manufacturers balked, insisting that it would not be possible to meet the new standards. Although GM did not insist that it could not meet the 30 mph standard, it did recommend using a moving barrier instead of one that was fixed. Ford officials had supported the original 20 mph moving barrier standard, adopting it as an internal corporate objective for all their 1973 models. The NHTSA's proposed standard was delayed, in part because of the intensity of industry's objections to its strictness and short lead time.

After the introduction of the Pinto, Ford continued a program of rear barrier crash tests to assess the impact of the proposed new crash standard on its cars. Ford conducted fifty-five tests in all and determined that none of its cars would probably meet the fixed-barrier standards without major modification. Concurrently, Ford continued to ready its fleet to meet the company's internal 20 mph moving-barrier standard.

Ford's crash test program included experimentation with various modifications to the fuel system. Among the modifications were using a reinforced rubber bladder inside the tank, shielding the tank with rubber or steel, and increasing tank toughness by placing a tank inside a second tank. None of these modifications were incorporated into the manufacture of the Pinto. Ford reasoned, for example, that the bladder, while successful in preventing leaks in moderate weather, became brittle and caused refueling problems in very cold or hot climates.

In 1973, three years after the 20 mph and 30 mph fixed-barrier standards were proposed, the NHTSA applied a 30 mph moving-barrier standard to all 1977 and later models (FMVSS 301-75). In response to this standard, Ford made changes in the design of post-1976 Pintos and Bobcats. Most important, a plastic shield was placed in front of the fuel tank, and the rear-end structure was modified to control the crush so that the fuel tank rose over the axle in the course of a crash.[25]

In response to concerns raised by the safety activist Byron Bloch and Ralph Nader's Center for Auto Safety, the NHTSA in 1974 made a preliminary inquiry into the fuel tanks of the Pintos and GM Vegas in widespread use. The agency did not find enough evidence to justify a defect investigation.

On August 10, 1977, the media once again took notice of the popular Pinto, but this time the publicity was negative. *Mother Jones* published "Pinto Madness," an article by Mark Dowie that accused the car of being a "firetrap." Dowie alleged that the Ford Motor Company knew the Pinto fuel system was likely to rupture when hit from behind at low to moderate speeds, yet waited years to modify the car because "it wasn't profitable to make the changes sooner."[26]

Shortly after the *Mother Jones* article was published, the media began to follow the story of the now famous Grimshaw trial. The facts of the case were spectacular.[27] A 1972 Ford Pinto hatchback stalled on the highway and burst into flames when hit from behind. The driver of the car, Lilly Gray, suffered fatal burns and thirteen-year-old Richard Grimshaw, a passenger in the Pinto, suffered severe and permanently disfiguring burns over his face and entire body. The television shows "60 Minutes" and "20/20" ran segments on the Pinto in June 1978 that brought the Grimshaw tragedy into millions of American homes. For the first time, the safety reputation of the Pinto had been tarnished.

On September 13, 1977, responding in part to the allegations in the *Mother Jones* article, the NHTSA initiated a formal defect investigation. The allegations stated that "the design and location of the fuel tank in the Ford Pinto (model years 1971–76) make it highly susceptible to dam-

25. A subsequent evaluation of FVMSS (Federal Motor Vehicle Safety Standard) 301-75 for passenger cars concluded that each year there are 400 fewer fatalities, 520 fewer serious injuries, 110 fewer moderate injuries, and 6,500 fewer passenger car crash fires. The total cost of implementing the standard is estimated at $8.50 per car or $85 million annually. Parsons 1983, 103.

26. Dowie 1977, 20.

27. Taken from the appellate court opinion, *Grimshaw* v. *Ford Motor Company*, 119 Cal. App. 3d 757 (1981).

age on rear impact at low to moderate speeds."[28] As part of the investigation, NHTSA contractors tested eleven 1971–76 Pintos in rear-end crashes under various conditions. Several Vegas were also crash tested under similar conditions. Two of the Pintos that were struck by an Impala at 35 mph caught fire. Two others used in 30 mph crash tests suffered significant leakage. In all the tests the Vegas performed better than the Pintos with respect to fuel system integrity.[29]

In February 1978 a jury awarded Grimshaw $125 million in punitive damages in the midst of the NHTSA's defect investigation. Although the award was reduced by the trial judge to $3.5 million, the case received widespread media publicity and became a landmark event in the history of the auto industry.

During its defect investigation, the NHTSA identified thirty-eight instances of rear-end collisions of Pintos with fuel tank damage, fuel system leakage, and/or ensuing fire. There were twenty-seven associated Pinto-occupant fatalities and twenty-four nonfatal burn injuries (one fatality was attributed to impact injuries). The number of fatalities cited in the NHTSA report is far below the number given by Dowie in the *Mother Jones* article. He claimed that by conservative estimates Pinto crashes caused 500 burn deaths to people who would not have been seriously injured if the cars had not burst into flames.

The NHTSA completed its investigation in May 1978 and determined that "low to moderate speed rear-end collisions of the Pintos produce massive fuel leaks due to puncture or tearing of the fuel tank and separation of the filler pipe from the tank."[30] Specifically, the NHTSA found that the length of the fuel filler pipe and exposure of the front of the fuel tank to rear underbody components created an unreasonable risk to safety. The NHTSA's determination of the defect was highly publicized. Since it applied to approximately 1.5 million 1971–76 Pintos and 1975–76 Mercury Bobcats, the issue had serious consequences for the Ford Motor Company.

Ford officials disagreed with the NHTSA's defect determination. The company believed the actual performance of the Pinto and Bobcat was

28. National Highway Traffic Safety Administration 1978.

29. Memorandum from the acting chief, Defects Evaluation Division, Office of Defects Investigation, Enforcement, to the Director, Office of Defects Investigation, Enforcement, April 19, 1979, "Fuel System Integrity in Rear Impact Collision *1971–1979 Chevrolet Vega.*" ODI Case Number C7-38. See attachment II, "Fuel Tank Integrity Collision Test Results" for Pinto and Vega test conditions and results.

30. "DOT Announces Recall of Pintos and Bobcats," U.S. Department of Transportation, Office of Public Affairs, June 9, 1978.

comparable to that of other subcompact and compact cars manufactured during the same periods. Ford based its claim, in part, on data from the NHTSA's new fatal accident reporting system (FARS), which was designed as an annual census of all motor vehicle fatalities in the United States. The 1975–77 FARS data indicate that the rate of rear-impact fatal accidents per million units in operation was 12.7 for the Pinto, 15.2 for the Gremlin, and 8.2 for the Vega. The rate of fires per fatal rear impact was 21.0 for the Pinto, 34.8 for the Gremlin, and 20.5 for the Vega.[31]

NHTSA officials were not persuaded by Ford's analysis of the FARS data. Fire and explosion were not part of the standard data elements on most of the police reports that supported FARS. Therefore, the NHTSA believed that the FARS data understated the situation. However, if the NHTSA is correct, the understatement would have affected all cars, so that the performance of the Pinto relative to that of other models would still be valid.

Despite Ford's contention about the relative safety of the Pinto and Bobcat, the company reluctantly agreed to recall and modify the cars without charge to the owners. In a letter informing the NHTSA administrator, Joan Claybrook, of the recall, Ford emphasized that attacks on the safety of the fuel systems of the Pinto and Bobcat had resulted in public concern that Ford wished to put to rest.

The corrective modifications reduced the risk of crash-related fires but did not enable the 1971–76 Pintos and Bobcats to meet the 30 mph impact requirements, which were beginning to be applied to 1977 models.[32] The older cars were modified with longer filler pipes and plastic shields similar to those installed in 1977 and later-model cars.

The prolonged period of adverse publicity about the Pinto contributed to product liability litigation. Ford reported to the NHTSA on September 29, 1977, that twenty-nine lawsuits or liability claims had been filed against the company that were allegedly related to the design of the Pinto's fuel tank. Eight of these cases had been settled, or judgment rendered for the plaintiff; two cases had been decided in favor of Ford; the other nineteen cases were pending at the time of the defect investigation.

In September 1978 Ford's legal problem was compounded when the company was indicted on criminal charges related to the Pinto in Indiana. Although Ford was found innocent of the charges in March 1980, the

31. Letter from Herbert L. Misch, Ford Motor Company, to Joan Claybrook, NHTSA Administration, June 8, 1978 (attachment).
32. FVMSS 301-75.

Table 4-2. *The Decline in Pinto's Share of the Small-Car Market,*
1973–79

	Percentage of U.S. small-car sales		
Year	Pinto	Other domestic	Imported
1973	24.4	35.7	39.9
1974	24.4	37.0	38.6
1975	19.7[a]	37.0	43.3
1976	17.1[a]	35.2	47.7
1977	13.7[a]	35.1	51.2
1978	10.9[a]	35.5	53.6
1979	9.9[a]	33.5	56.6

Source: Ford Motor Company data.
a. Bobcat sales are included with Pinto sales.

possibility of criminal action against it for a design decision received widespread publicly throughout the industry.

The decision to discontinue the Pinto in 1980 reflected a long-term decline in the Pinto's ability to hold its share of the small-car market. As table 4-2 shows, the Pinto was effectively attacked in the marketplace by both foreign and domestic competition. Note that the deterioration in the Pinto's market share began before the fuel tank issue was widely publicized. Some analysts have speculated, however, that sales of all Ford models may have been adversely affected by the Pinto fuel tank controversy.[33]

Ford had also appealed the Grimshaw verdict but did not find a receptive judicial ear. In 1981 the $3.5 million award was upheld, in part because the court found that "Ford's conduct constituted 'conscious disregard' of the probability of injury to members of the consuming public," and because "an award which is so small that it can be simply written off as a part of the cost of doing business . . . would have no deterrent effect."[34] Interestingly, this judicial opinion is read in some tort classes by Harvard Law School students and is sometimes cited as an opinion that emphasizes the potential safety benefits of liability law.

The case history of the Pinto shows that consumer demand, competitive forces, regulation, and liability need to be considered in any safety analysis. Adverse media publicity may have played an important role in putting several of these factors to work.

Ford's decision to recall and modify the 1971–76 cars was voluntary, but the NHTSA may well have acted if Ford had not done so. The adverse

33. Wells 1986, 27.
34. *Grimshaw* v. *Ford*, note 19.

publicity provided Ford some reason to take corrective actions, but the step may have been taken in spite of liability risks. Ford officials had good reason to fear that a recall might be characterized as an admission of guilt.

The NHTSA's 1977 fuel tank standard was certainly a sufficient cause of the modifications to the fuel tank made for the 1977 Pinto and Bobcat. Liability considerations may have induced Ford to go beyond the minimum requirements of the standard. Government testing of the Pinto and other small Ford cars showed that these automobiles, for model years 1977–81, exceeded the 30 mph moving-barrier standard by at least 5 mph.[35] Because of the public's reaction to the Pinto scare, Ford may have concluded that the company's reputation could not afford more publicized fire-related injuries and fatalities.

In the absence of the NHTSA standard, liability pressures—acting indirectly through consumer demand and reputational effects—may also have been sufficient to induce the design changes. The direct costs of tort liability per se would not have been a key factor. The small number of fire-related cases would not have generated enough projected financial liability to affect design decisions. On the other hand, fuel tank liability cases act as a catalyst for media coverage that can in turn hurt the manufacturer and its product. Burns are a very infrequent cause of crash-related injury, but they are a spectacular event that makes for great television coverage.

Tort suits may not have been necessary to spur media interest. It is possible that a program like "60 Minutes" would run a show about Ford Pintos without having heard about the Grimshaw case. It is clear, however, that many such shows (including that one) are caused by the enterprising activities of plaintiff lawyers.

Keeping this analysis in mind, it is easy to understand at least one reason why Ford did not move earlier to improve the Pinto's fuel tank. Specifically, before August 10, 1977, and the publication of "Pinto Madness," there simply was not enough bad press about the product to worry Ford.

A similar analysis may also explain why the Mustang II was not recalled along with the Pinto and Bobcat, or redesigned in a similar fashion. The Thirteenth Circuit Court of Appeals alleged that the three cars were

---

35. It is difficult to consider the design of the Escort's fuel tank in the same context as the Pinto. The Escort is a front wheel drive car. Consequently, the fuel tank can be, and is, located under the back seat so that it has been moved away from the rear of the car.

treated as essentially the same vehicle as regards fuel system integrity, yet Ford and the NHTSA did not take any steps to correct potential problems on the Mustang IIs already on the road.[36] A possible explanation is that the public had not discovered any problem. Ford, however, asserts that the Mustang II and Pinto are not equivalent for rear-crash integrity. Specifically, Ford notes that the rear-end crush strength of the Mustang II is almost twice that of the Pinto, in part because of the involvement of the roof of the Mustang II with the rear structure. Furthermore, fuel leaks in the Mustang II are not usually the result of fill pipe pull-out or axle puncture as they are in the Pinto.

Finally, the principal causes of Pinto's declining sales and ultimate discontinuation by Ford are probably not related to safety. The 1973–75 recession depressed car sales. There was also a period in the 1970s when gas prices were artificially frozen by government policy, which further undercut the demand for smaller cars. Moreover, the market share analysis indicated that Pinto was losing its hold on the market before the adverse safety publicity in 1977. Consumers found the new imported and domestic small cars more attractive than the Pinto, though safety concerns about the Pinto may have accentuated this trend during 1977–79. Ford officials contend that the life of the Pinto was actually extended by a year or two through price discounts to help Ford satisfy the government's fuel economy requirements.

Inadvertent Vehicle Movement

Automatic transmission–equipped vehicles produced by all manufacturers have been reported to show inadvertent movement.[37] For example, in September 1987 twenty-two-year-old Kimberly Isaac of Baton Rouge, Louisiana, was badly scraped when a 1977 Ford LTD she had just parked in a grocery store lot backed up, knocking her over and dragging her in circles. More recently, Steven Masaki, a twenty-eight-year-old mechanic, was repairing a 1976 Chevrolet van in Hawaii when it suddenly went into reverse and ran over him. He was left a quadriplegic.

The Ford Motor Company received a small number of complaints about the "park-to-reverse" problem in the early 1970s. From an engi-

36. *Ford Motor Company* v. *Mr. and Mrs. William R. Durrill*, 74 S.W. 2d 329 (Tex. App.—Corpus Christi, 1986).

37. I thank the following persons for providing useful information: Clarence Ditlow (Center for Auto Safety), Richard Manetta (Ford), and James Durkin (GM).

neering perspective, a properly maintained vehicle—regardless of the manufacturer—cannot simply jump from park to reverse. In 1971 there were 4.6 million Ford vehicles in use with automatic transmissions that generated nine park-to-reverse complaints. A routine investigation was undertaken. Ford engineers identified a total of forty such complaints from 1968 to 1971, including several accidents.

In early 1972 the internal Ford investigation was intensified, but Ford engineers concluded there was no discernible defect. They suspected that complaints arose when drivers mispositioned the select lever between park and reverse before leaving the vehicle. Although Ford engineers investigated some technical strategies to reduce the problem of mispositioning, they concluded that none were promising. Ford decided instead to make the parking instructions in owners manuals more explicit and remove the letters "ark" from the word "Park" to encourage drivers to push the shift lever all the way to the left into park.

On October 18, 1977, the NHTSA opened an investigation of selected Ford vehicles equipped with automatic transmissions to determine whether a defect was present. The investigation was based on thirty-one reports of inadvertent vehicle movement in Ford vehicles. Clarence Ditlow, executive director of the Nader-founded Center for Auto Safety, played an important role in stimulating this investigation by drawing the NHTSA's attention to a park-to-reverse accident experienced by Constance Bartholomew of Falls Church, Virginia. Bartholomew's 1976 park-to-reverse complaint had fallen on deaf ears at both Ford and the NHTSA. Although NHTSA officials and Ditlow were aware of park-to-reverse complaints and accidents involving non-Ford vehicles, they believed such incidents were more common in Fords.

In November 1977 and again in August 1978 Joan Claybrook issued consumer advisories warning Ford owners of a possible transmission problem and requesting information about any incidents. These consumer advisories received massive publicity. Consider this segment from ABC News, on August 29, 1978:

Max Robinson: While the airline industry seems to be pleasing its customers, the nation's automakers aren't having things so easy. Recalls have become all too common. The Ford Motor Company, already plagued by the Pinto's accident record, has yet another headache. Jules Bergman reports:

Jules Bergman: Here is the problem. You start the car, move into the driveway, get out to close the garage door after putting it into park and frequently the slamming of the car door alone is enough to pop it into reverse, as it did here. The difference is—I was prepared for the emergency. The 24 people killed and the hundreds injured obviously were not.

Later Ford officials discovered that the NHTSA had supplied a vehicle to Bergman for the show that had several anomalies that made it unrepresentative of the vehicles under investigation by the agency.[38] Nevertheless, Ford was soon receiving hundreds of complaints a month about the transmissions in Ford vehicles. Much to the dismay of Ford officials, the NHTSA's advisories did not ask for reports of park-to-reverse problems in non-Ford vehicles. As a result, the NHTSA's data base on complaints became biased toward finding more cases of inadvertent movement in Fords than in non-Fords. Yet Ford's engineers were not convinced that the park-to-reverse problem was any worse in Ford vehicles than it was in non-Ford vehicles.

The complaints, accidents, injuries, and deaths led to lawsuits. Publicity helped fuel the litigation, especially against Ford.

As the NHTSA's investigation was expanded to include all Ford vehicles produced with automatic transmissions after 1970, Ford's top management began to sense the potential dimensions of this problem. The NHTSA was seriously considering the largest recall action in history (more than 10 million vehicles), an action that could cripple the Ford Motor Company. In August 1978, at the request of Chairman Henry Ford II, Vice Chairman Philip Caldwell convened a meeting of twenty executives and ordered a stepped-up investigation with an assurance that the transmissions in future models would be improved.[39]

On the heels of this meeting, the *Detroit Free Press* ran a story, based on internal Ford memoranda that were submitted to the NHTSA, that Ford knew of the transmission problem in 1972. For example, the *Minneapolis Tribune* of September 4, 1978, ran the headline "Report Says Ford Firm Knew of Car Flaw in '72."[40] As similar stories were run in newspapers throughout the country, the liability implications for Ford mushroomed. Within eighteen months an estimated 1,000 transmission lawsuits were reportedly pending against Ford.[41]

38. Interoffice Memorandum, to R. H. Birney, from Office of the General Counsel, Ford Motor Company, Oct. 2, 1978.

39. Emshwiller and Camp 1988, 1.

40. "Report Says Ford Firm Knew of Car Flaw in 1972," *Minneapolis Tribune*, Sept. 4, 1978, 10A.

41. Emshwiller and Camp 1988, 20.

In response to Caldwell's directive, Ford established a five-city consumer hot line that was designed to encourage consumers who believed they had experienced a park-to-reverse incident to call in so that the complaint vehicle could be inspected promptly. Four independent engineering groups within Ford reevaluated the design of Ford's transmission park system and compared it with competitive designs. In the final analysis, Ford's engineers could not find a defect, and though several design alternatives were evaluated that might prevent or reduce the frequency of driver error, the conclusion was that none of these designs would be effective. The engineers were convinced that most complaints occurred after drivers had mispositioned the shift lever between park and reverse while thinking the vehicle was in the park position. When the driver left the vehicle with the shift lever mispositioned, the lever would sometimes move into park, sometimes remain mispositioned, and sometimes slide into reverse.

Caldwell became convinced there was no defect, but the pressure he exerted on this issue caused Ford to attempt a design modification. A subtle refinement was made in the transmission design for 1980 and later models that might reduce the incidence of operator error. The refinement was intended to make shift-lever movement more pronounced so as to help drivers notice when they had failed to complete a shift into park. The design modification was made in the middle of the 1980 model year (February 1979) and generated widespread media coverage. At this point, the NHTSA officials were reporting that post-1970 Ford transmissions had been linked to 777 accidents, 259 injuries, and 23 deaths.[42]

Meanwhile the defect investigation at the NHTSA languished because the agency's engineers and contractors could not identify a specific defect. Many NHTSA officials were uncomfortable about making a formal defect determination if they could not explain to Ford's engineers or the public what the alleged problem was.

Clarence Ditlow was frustrated by the protracted delays and pressured the NHTSA's leadership to get moving. After the intensive participation of Joan Claybrook, the NHTSA made an initial determination in June 1980 that a safety defect existed involving five specific automatic transmission types in post-1970 Fords. The agency issued a report describing what it believed were the causes of the defect. Claybrook went on national television and explained that she was convinced the design of the Ford

---

42. "Ford Motor Company Changing Shifty Car Transmissions," *Boston Globe*, Feb. 2, 1979, 11.

transmission was defective. The Claybrook decision differed from that of Transport Canada, which found no defect present in the Ford transmissions.

At an August 1980 public meeting called by the NHTSA, Ford officials vigorously contested the preliminary defect finding. They were appalled at the quality of the NHTSA's statistical and engineering arguments, especially the various defect theories. Ford sued the NHTSA, seeking preenforcement review of the administrative proceedings.

Normally, the NHTSA administrator makes a final defect determination. In this case, however, Secretary of Transportation Neil Goldschmidt withdrew the delegation of authority from Claybrook. Nevertheless, in a memorandum from Claybrook to Goldschmidt dated October 3, 1980, she recommended a final defect determination, a recall of three of the five transmission types, and a negotiation of a settlement on the other two transmissions, which she believed might be corrected with a warning device. She was concerned about the mounting number of complaints and the 100 fatalities from unexpected vehicle movement that had been reported to the NHTSA as of June 1980.[43]

Goldschmidt was reportedly "underwhelmed" by the case the NHTSA had made against the Ford transmissions.[44] After the November elections he ordered his attorneys to settle the issue with Ford. No final defect finding was ever made.

Under the terms of an agreement signed on December 30, 1980, the Department of Transportation and Ford agreed that Ford would send a letter and an adhesive label to 22 million vehicle owners. The letter urged owners to place the label on a conspicuous place in the vehicle, such as on the dashboard or sun visor. The letter and label reminded owners of three safety precautions to be followed before leaving the vehicle: put the vehicle in park, set the parking brake fully, and shut off the ignition. The Transportation Department indicated that this action by Ford would adequately address the safety concerns that had been raised.

After Ford began to send the letters in April 1981, the department closed the case on May 3, 1981. Although the Center for Auto Safety challenged the department's decision not to find a defect, its decision was ultimately upheld by the federal courts.[45]

In 1985 the NHTSA also rejected a petition by the Center for Auto

43. Claybrook 1985, 40.
44. Emshwiller and Camp 1988.
45. *Center for Auto Safety, Inc.* v. *Lewis,* 685 F.2d 656 (D.C. Cir. 1982).

Safety to reopen the issue and recall the 1970–79 Fords. The NHTSA's 1985 report argued that a further investigation was unlikely to lead to a defect finding and that the 1981 letters and labels had been effective in reducing the problem of unexpected vehicle movement. The NHTSA had studied information submitted by Ford of 19,445 alleged incidents of inadvertent vehicle movement from 1970 to 1984 and found that the reported rate of incidents in 1970–79 Ford vehicles had declined since the settlement.

In a June 1986 report the General Accounting Office found flaws in the NHTSA's analysis of the effects of the letters and labels. Although the raw number of incidents and the rate of incident reports per 100,000 vehicles on the road steadily declined from 1980 through 1984, the NHTSA did not take into account the effect of publicity on these trends. The GAO also noted that no such obvious decline was apparent in the fatality data, although the NHTSA's analysis showed some indication of reduced fatalities. The GAO concluded that the small number of fatalities and the possibility of reporting biases preclude confident interpretation of the trends in fatality rates.

GAO investigators were convinced that a real problem existed and that the NHTSA needed to take further educational measures to reduce the problem of inadvertent vehicle movement. The GAO noted that while unexpected vehicle movement fatalities are not limited to Ford vehicles, the reported fatality rate in 1970–79 Fords exceeded those reported by other domestic manufacturers by factors ranging from 2.5 to 4.5.[46] The excess may be accounted for in whole or in part by the adverse publicity about Ford vehicles.

Did the model year 1980 design modifications reduce the problem of unexpected movement? Ford officials are skeptical because the rate of consumer complaints for post-1980 models was no less than the rate of complaints for the suspect models sold in the pre-1977 period (before the NHTSA and Ford's publicity campaigns).[47] The GAO has pointed out that the reported fatality rate in 1981–84 models appears to be much less than that in 1970–79 models, despite the difficulty with inferring a causal relationship. Although the persistent decline in reported fatality rates is consistent with the "safety improvement" hypothesis, the numbers of reported fatalities are too small for one to make statistically confident statements.

46. General Accounting Office 1986.
47. Letter from Helen O. Petrauskas (Ford) to Congressman Timothy E. Wirth, July 20, 1983.

The 1980 design modifications and the 1981 letters and labels did not immediately end Ford's legal problems. The *Wall Street Journal* reported in April 1988 that "a trickle of lawsuits in the 1970s became a torrent in the 1980s."[48] After leaving the NHTSA, Claybrook helped organize a 1981 conference to train attorneys on how to win transmission cases against Ford. She believed, the article said, that some big damage awards against Ford might cause the company to recall the pre-1980 vehicles.

Ford mounted a vigorous legal defense of its automatic transmission–equipped vehicles. The *Wall Street Journal* article reported that among the cases that had gone to trial, Ford had won 22 out of 27 as of April 1988. Hundreds more have reportedly been settled, usually for undisclosed amounts of money. The Center for Auto Safety studied about 200 suits and calculated that Ford paid an average of $175,000 each in settlements or jury awards, a total of about $35 million for those cases.[49]

On occasion Ford loses a big case. A jury in Texas assessed $4.4 million in damages in one case involving a fatality—$4.0 million out of the $4.4 million was in punitive damages. A state appeals court upheld the award, stating that Ford knew of the dangerous condition but failed to correct it. Yet Ford triumphed in March 1990 when a federal judge dismissed a class action suit by plaintiffs who alleged they were damaged by the loss in value of their vehicles and were seeking a recall of the pre-1980 Fords.

The number of pending transmission cases against Ford is declining as cases are resolved, publicity about the issue subsides, and more 1970–79 vehicles are retired from the fleet. In early 1990 Ford reported to the Securities and Exchange Commission that the aggregate amount of pending claims in transmission cases was approximately $386 million.[50] Ford's favorable track record in these lawsuits suggests that only a small fraction of the claims reported to the SEC are genuine liability.

Ford is not the only manufacturer to face continued liability in transmission design cases. In February 1988 a jury in Honolulu awarded $16.5 million ($11 million punitive) to the mechanic who was paralyzed by his 1976 Chevrolet van, even though the jury found the plaintiff 40 percent responsible for the mishap. The Hawaii Supreme Court later vacated the punitive damage award and affirmed the economic damage award, while calling for a new trial on the issue of punitive damages only. The case was subsequently settled for an undisclosed amount.

48. Emshwiller and Camp 1988, 20.
49. "Ford Wins Suit's Dismissal in Case of Alleged Defect," *Wall Street Journal*, Mar. 30, 1990, A18.
50. Clark 1990, 6.

In summary, the long, costly, and complicated inadvertent vehicle movement case achieved two outcomes that may have improved safety: the settlement agreement calling for the 1981 letters and labels and the 1980 design modifications. The former were clearly induced by regulatory power, although their ultimate effectiveness is questionable. The motivations behind Ford's design change are more complex and difficult to assess.

The following factors may have been important: the extent of customer complaints and the damage to Ford's reputation as a manufacturer, the likelihood of protracted litigation with the NHTSA and the possibility of a massive NHTSA recall order, a large liability risk of unknown magnitude, and Caldwell's determination to improve the design (even though no defect may have been present). It seems doubtful that any of these factors by themselves were necessary to cause the design modification, and several of the factors may have been sufficient.

Some liability and regulatory considerations actually operated to discourage design modification. Ford recognized that some people might characterize the design modification as signaling the existence of a prior defect. Anytime a manufacturer improves its product, it is subject to the risk that the improvement will be admissible, directly or indirectly, in a product liability suit. Further, since Ford officials were determined to block the NHTSA's defect investigation, they were also worried that any design modification would provide ammunition to their critics within the NHTSA. Ford's decision to make design refinements before the NHTSA's initial defect determination may be an indication that the agency's investigation and recall authority were not the driving factors behind Ford's action.

The Jeep CJ

The Jeep CJ (for "Civilian Jeep") was produced for more than forty years. In 1983 the American Motors Corporation (which purchased the Jeep operations from Kaiser in 1970) discontinued production of the CJ-5. The CJ-7, a slightly longer sister vehicle that was introduced in 1976, was discontinued in 1986, marking the end of the Jeep CJ line. When the Chrysler Corporation purchased AMC in 1987, it assumed much of AMC's liability for the Jeep. The Jeep CJ's replacement was the Jeep Wrangler, a more comfortable, "upscale" vehicle designed for a more urbane consumer. This case examines the demise of the CJ.[51]

51. This case was written by Emily Schifrin. We thank the following persons for providing helpful information: Brian O'Neill (IIHS), Michael Finkelstein (NHTSA), Barry

The NHTSA became involved in the question of Jeep safety in 1971, when it recommended that the Department of Defense not sell surplus M-151 "jeep-type vehicles" to the general public, claiming that drivers required special training to meet the Jeep's unique handling requirements. The department subsequently banned the sale of M-151s to the public. (The military precursor of the CJ was the M-38, which was not banned for public sale.)

Critics of the CJ argued that the vehicle's propensity to roll over arose from a high center of gravity, caused by its high rise off the ground (necessary for accommodating rough terrain), its narrow track width (essential for negotiating narrow trails), and its short wheelbases. Throughout the 1970s an optional roll bar, a critical means of occupant protection in a rollover accident, was soft-mounted to the sheet metal of the wheel housing. As early as 1973 doubts about the efficacy of the roll bars were being raised within AMC.

The concern about rollovers was by no means unique to the CJ series. In 1973 the NHTSA issued two advance notices proposing rulemaking to limit rollover tendencies in vehicles; one a standard on rollover resistance and the other on steering control while braking and turning. The NHTSA commissioned three vehicle-handling studies to gather more information on rollovers but dropped the proposed rulemaking in 1978. Researchers in one study said they were unable to develop repeatable test procedures corresponding to real-world driving.[52]

In 1978 Jeanne Leichtamer and her brother Carl sued AMC for damages from injuries they received in a 1976 rollover accident involving a CJ-7 Jeep. Jeanne was paralyzed from the waist down, and Carl suffered a fractured skull. Their attorney claimed that a defective roll bar had "enhanced" the Leichtamers' injuries.

An Ohio jury awarded compensatory damages of $1 million to Jeanne and $100,000 to Carl. Each received a matching amount in punitive damages. A series of Jeep commercials, which the plaintiffs' lawyer argued constituted an "implied warranty" that the Jeep would withstand rugged terrain, were apparently instrumental in the jury's decision. The case was later appealed to the Ohio Supreme Court, which upheld the awards.

Felrice (NHTSA), Carl Nash (NHTSA), Joan Claybrook (Public Citizen), Benjamin Kelley (Institute for Injury Reduction), Diane Steed (American Coalition for Traffic Safety), William Kittle (Chrysler), Kent Joscelyn (Joscelyn and Treat, P.C.), Tom Walton (GM), Jim Boehm (GM), Fred Gade (Ford), and Allan Maness (U.S. Senate).

52. Insurance Institute for Highway Safety (IIHS) 1980, 4.

Claims have been made that the Leichtamer lawsuit caused an improved Jeep roll bar design.[53] During the trial the Leichtamers' lawyer had called Michael Kaplan, an engineer, as an expert witness. Kaplan testified that while the roll bar itself could withstand 26,000 pounds of pressure, the metal sheeting of the wheel housing to which it was mounted could withstand only 4,000 pounds. He argued that the roll bar could be anchored to the frame at a probable additional cost of about $25 per vehicle. In 1979 AMC made changes in its roll bar support system that Jeanne Leichtamer claimed were in accordance with Kaplan's suggestions.[54] Chrysler officials noted that the roll bar design was reviewed in 1977 and 1978 and that AMC's decision to introduce the new design preceded the trial. In any case, the optional roll bar was made standard equipment on the CJ in the late 1970s.[55]

In 1978 the NHTSA informed AMC that it had received several reports of roll bar failure in Jeep vehicles and asked AMC to provide detailed information on matters such as roll bar construction and installation and lawsuits pertaining to roll bar defects.[56] In its reply, AMC identified twelve such lawsuits but maintained that they occurred because of "the nature of product liability litigation and the broadness of the claims by attorneys for plaintiffs." "We do not believe," they wrote, "that there has been a failure of the roll bar. To the contrary, we believe that the roll bar provides, as it is designed to do, additional protection for occupants. . . . The fact that a roll bar may be deformed during an accident is not a sign of failure; it is rather an indication that it was performing its intended function of absorbing impact energy which otherwise may have been transmitted to the vehicle's occupants."[57]

In 1979, at the request of a man whose fifteen-year-old son was killed in a CJ-5 crash, the NHTSA opened a defect investigation into the stability and crashworthiness of the CJ-5 and CJ-7. A year later, it closed the investigation without taking action, stating that "our analysis indicates that most instances of instability resulting in rollovers occur under instances in which the limits of the vehicle are exceeded."[58] Here the NHTSA concurred with AMC's view that the problem lay in the drivers rather

53. Hogan 1980, 115.
54. Dentzer 1984.
55. Hogan 1980, 105.
56. Letter from Lynn L. Bradford, NHTSA, to George E. Brown, AMC, July 27, 1978.
57. Letter from K. W. Schang, Jeep Corporation, to Lynn L. Bradford, Sept. 11, 1978.
58. IIHS 1980, 10.

than in the vehicles. In the same investigation, the NHTSA found no defect in the optional roll bar.

Critics of the CJ later claimed that AMC knew of the CJ-5's safety shortcomings. In some 1980 maneuvering tests of the CJ-5, AMC acknowledged that it added reinforcements to the roll bar and window frame of the test vehicles. AMC officials claimed that these additions did not indicate a lack of faith in the vehicle's crashworthiness, but rather knowledge that the test drivers were going to be exposed to some "very dangerous situations."[59] They maintained that providing such protection for test drivers is a standard, industrywide practice.

Throughout the 1970s, when the CJ received very little adverse safety publicity, the popularity of the CJ series increased. Figure 4-2 shows that annual sales increased from 9,000 in 1970 to a peak of 90,000 in 1979— three years after the introduction of the CJ-7. Sales of the CJ were quite important to the financial health of AMC, which was suffering from a sharp decline in passenger car sales.

In December 1980 the Insurance Institute for Highway Safety (IIHS) issued a report on "the extremely hazardous tendency of the Jeep CJ utility vehicle to roll over in highway use." The IIHS's preliminary results showed that the CJ-5 had 7.4 fatal rollover crashes for every 10,000 cars registered in 1978 and 1979, and that almost 90 percent of all single vehicle fatal crashes of CJ-5 Jeeps were rollovers. In test situations the CJ-5s overturned performing "J-turns" at 22 mph and during obstacle avoidance maneuvers at 32 mph.[60] AMC stated that the driving in these tests, which was done by computers, was unrealistic because steering was extreme, speed was prolonged, and brakes were not applied. In a 1981 review the NHTSA agreed that Dynamic Science Incorporated, which had done the testing for the IIHS, had used "abnormal test conditions and unrealistic maneuvers . . . generated by an automatic control device which . . . was programmed to provide input not entirely representative of driver input."[61] The IIHS maintained that its tests reflected typical driver behavior.[62]

A 1980 study done by the Highway Safety Research Institute (HSRI) at the University of Michigan concluded that utility vehicles roll over 5 to 11.5 times more often than cars and are involved in fatal crashes 40

59. Emshwiller 1988, 21.
60. IIHS 1980, 3–5.
61. NHTSA internal memorandum from Jonathan D. White, safety defects engineer, to James P. Talentino, chief, Engineering Analysis Division, Nov. 25, 1981.
62. Karr 1982.

Figure 4-2. *Approximate Yearly Sales of Jeep CJs, 1970–86*[a]

Thousands

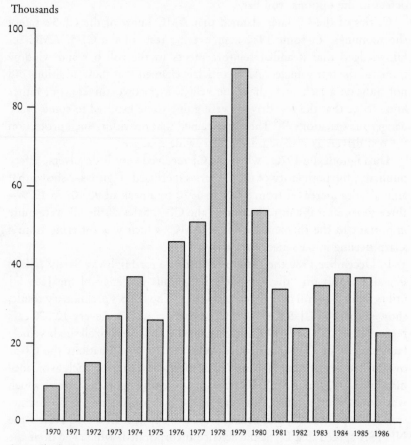

Source: Chrysler Corporation sales figures.
a. 1970: American Motors acquires Kaiser; 1975: CJ-7 introduced; 1981: CJ-5 discontinued; 1986: CJ-7 discontinued.

percent more often. Of the vehicles studied, the Jeep was the most prone to rollovers.[63] AMC criticized the study on many counts, including the use of inadequate exposure measures (that is, vehicle use and driver characteristics were not adequately considered), lack of control for confounding factors, and the use of data that were not necessarily representative of the nationwide situation.[64] The NHTSA also questioned the validity of this study.[65]

63. Snyder and others 1980.
64. American Motors Corporation 1986.
65. NHTSA memo, White to Talentino, Nov. 25, 1981.

Armed with the IIHS and HSRI studies, critics of the CJ reported their study findings to interested media professionals. Benjamin Kelley, a communications expert at the IIHS, played an instrumental role in generating media interest in the CJ story.

On the basis of these studies and information from plaintiff attorneys, "60 Minutes" ran a story in December 1980 that exposed the alleged hazardousness of the CJ series. The *Wall Street Journal* later reported that the bad publicity about safety hurt Jeep sales. In the two months before the "60 Minutes" show aired, CJ-5s were selling at about 50 percent below their 1979 levels; after the show, sales dropped about 65 percent below that rate. AMC's legal problems also mushroomed. In the year before the television exposé, about 50 rollover suits had been filed against the company; the following year brought 200. In acknowledging the impact the show had on AMC, a company official said: "We peg history as 'before 60 Minutes' and 'after 60 Minutes.' "[66]

Adverse publicity was not the only cause of the sharp decline in CJ sales from 1979 to 1982 (when the CJ-5 was discontinued). The total market for utility vehicles plummeted from 372,000 in 1979 to 137,000 in 1981, reflecting rising interest rates, inflation, and diminished consumer confidence in the economy.[67]

The insurance industry continued to question the safety of the CJ. In September 1981 the Highway Loss Data Institute reported that the CJ-5 had the most insurance claims among utility vehicles for the 1977 through 1980 model years, with an overall claim frequency much higher than the average for all 1977–80 vans, pickups, and utility vehicles. The CJ-7 was second.[68] Chrysler officials point to a later HLDI report that combines claims data for passenger cars and utility vehicles. This report shows that the CJ does not have an unusually high crash record.[69]

The questions raised by the IIHS caused some insurers, such as the Nationwide Mutual Insurance Company and the Erie Insurance Group, to refuse policies for new customers who bought Jeeps. Nationwide sent letters to more than 8,000 Jeep owners warning them about the Jeep's "potentially dangerous . . . on-the-road characteristics." The Erie Group sent policyholders a letter calling the Jeep "perhaps the most dangerous

66. "Jeep Defenders Still Bristle Over Old '60 Minutes' Show," *Wall Street Journal*, May 23, 1988, 21.

67. Motor Vehicle Manufacturers Association.

68. Highway Loss Data Institute 1981.

69. "Safe, Safer, Safest," *AIDE: The Insurance Magazine from USAA*, Fall 1984, 26.

vehicle on the road today." AMC demanded a retraction; Erie stopped sending the letter, but retracted nothing.[70] Although some insurers took these steps, most large insurance carriers continued to insure CJ vehicles when the owners met underwriting requirements.

In 1981 Maude Blazejewski, the widow of a man killed in a Jeep CJ-5 rollover accident in 1973, requested that the NHTSA open a defect investigation. The agency rejected this petition in 1982, stating that it did not see "any reasonable possibility" that an investigation could lead to a safety-defect finding.[71]

In 1982 a Nevada state district judge ordered AMC to pay $5.1 million to William C. Buckholt, who suffered permanent brain damage and other serious injuries when his 1975 Jeep CJ-5 overturned. The judge ruled that the design of the Jeep was defective, causing it to have an abnormal propensity to roll over, and that the roll bar was not high enough or strong enough to protect passengers in the event of a rollover. The driver, he determined, was not to blame for this accident, which nullified AMC's main defense. Furthermore, the judge concluded that AMC had suppressed evidence of tests demonstrating this rollover tendency. By continuing to sell the Jeep without correcting these defects or warning drivers, AMC showed "an apparent willingness to injure" Jeep occupants.[72]

Critics of AMC argued that the company knew of the rollover hazard and refused to make design improvements. A 1979 internal AMC memorandum said the Jeep CJ-7 failed to meet the "true safe design limit" against rollovers.[73] CJ critics also claimed AMC tacitly admitted that the CJ was subject to excessive rollovers when it provided retrofit roll cages for celebrities driving CJs in the televised 1978 "Celebrity Challenge" racing events.[74] Chrysler countered that the vehicles were modified in accordance with standards established by SCORE International, an off-road racing organization, and that the CJ modifications were essentially the same as those made to other vehicles used for off-road racing.[75]

AMC consistently maintained that driver behavior and not design was the cause of Jeep CJ rollovers. Although AMC acknowledged that utility

70. Karr 1982a.
71. "Utility Vehicle Warning Rules Proposed by U.S.," *Wall Street Journal*, Dec. 31, 1982, 4.
72. "Judge Says Design of 1975 CJ-5 Jeep Is Defective," *Wall Street Journal*, Apr. 21, 1982, 39; Karr 1982b.
73. Emshwiller 1988, 21.
74. Murphy 1990.
75. Correspondence, Joscelyn to Kittle, Aug. 3, 1990.

vehicles have different handling requirements from passenger cars, it claimed that they were safe when driven intelligently. AMC noted that young drivers often drove the Jeeps recklessly and that alcohol played a role in many of the rollover crashes.

The NHTSA found evidence to partly corroborate AMC's assessment. In its analysis for the Blazejewski petition, the NHTSA noted that in 83 percent of the 409 Jeep CJ-5 rollover accidents studied by its Office of Defects Investigation, excessive speed, reckless driving, alcohol, drugs, and/or sleep had been factors. "The accidents," stated the analysis, "may not have occurred if [these] adverse factors . . . had not been present." Although the NHTSA acknowledged driver fault, it did not completely vindicate the CJ-5. "The Jeep CJ," wrote the agency, "appears to be less forgiving of these factors than are other vehicles."[76]

In late 1982 the Federal Trade Commission issued a complaint against AMC, charging that its advertising campaign misled consumers by portraying the Jeep CJ as safe enough to drive recklessly on off-road terrain, and implying that it handled like a passenger vehicle on the highway. In an unprecedented action, the FTC issued a consent order requiring AMC to send warning stickers to Jeep CJ owners advising them that the vehicles were subject to "loss of control" in sudden turns and abrupt maneuvers and to put a similar warning in the owners' manual. Although it admitted no wrongdoing, AMC stopped making these commercials. The FTC later set aside this consent order with AMC when the NHTSA required all utility vehicles to be sold with a similar warning sticker.

Although all utility vehicles were subject to rollover accidents, the CJ was the major target of product liability litigation. By 1983 an AMC corporate prospectus reported that AMC was facing lawsuits that alleged $2.5 billion in damages stemming from crashes related to the Jeep CJ.[77]

Despite the adverse safety publicity, *Ward's Automotive Yearbook* reported that in 1983 the Jeep CJ was the most popular four-wheel-drive Jeep vehicle. Apparently, many buyers were either unaware of or unaffected by the allegations of danger. Indeed, sales of the CJ-7 recovered from 24,000 in 1982 to a second peak of 38,000 in 1984, though this upsurge was far less than the overall recovery in sales of utility vehicles during this period.

In 1984 a California state court jury awarded over $3.9 million in

76. NHTSA memo, White to Talentino, Nov. 25, 1990.
77. Isikoff 1985.

damages to the estate of Carrie Dustman, an eighteen-year-old killed in
a Jeep CJ-5 rollover accident in 1980. The award against AMC included
$110,000 in compensatory damage and $3.8 million in punitive damages.[78]

AMC lost $125.3 million in 1985, the year of Chrysler's takeover.[79]
By that time, 570 lawsuits involving the CJ were pending against AMC.
This large potential liability played a part in the negotiations between
Chrysler and Renault for Chrysler's purchase of AMC in 1987 (Renault
held 46.1 percent interest in AMC). AMC's July 1986 proxy statement
reported that as of June 30, 1986, the damages specified in these complaints totaled approximately $635 million in compensatory and $1.3
billion in punitive damages. "The company has incurred and expects to
continue incurring heavy expenses in the defense and resolution of such
matters," the proxy statement said.[80] Chrysler ultimately agreed to share
with Renault some portion of this liability, and as of 1988 faced approximately 1,000 such suits.

The NHTSA did take some steps to warn consumers of the general
rollover hazard in utility vehicles. As mentioned earlier, in 1984 the
agency required manufacturers of utility vehicles to place a permanent
sticker on the windshield, dashboard, or other visible location alerting
operators to handling differences between these utility vehicles and passenger cars and warning that sharp turns or abrupt maneuvers could result
in loss of control or rollover, in on-road and off-road situations. The
NHTSA further characterized the utility vehicles targeted by this measure
as having a short wheelbase, narrow track, high ground clearance, stiff
suspension system, and frequently four-wheel drive. The CJ was not
singled out as the principal target of this rulemaking.

In 1986 Representative Timothy E. Wirth of Colorado petitioned the
NHTSA to propose a rulemaking to set a federal motor vehicle safety
performance standard to limit vehicles' rollover propensity, investigate
the safety of utility vehicles, and issue a recall if necessary.[81] In the face
of staff disagreements, Diane Steed, the NHTSA administrator, ultimately denied the congressman's petition. In a December 1988 letter to
Representative John D. Dingell of Michigan explaining her actions, Steed

78. "AMC Unit Ordered to Pay $3.9 Million in Damages in Lawsuit," *Wall Street
Journal*, May 7, 1984, 51.
79. "YC Jeep Tries to Corral Upscale Urban Cowboys," *Advertising Age*, May 19,
1986, 82.
80. "Chrysler's Cost Could Reach $2 Billion, Miller Says," *Automotive News*, Mar.
16, 1987, 57.
81. Letter from Congressman Timothy E. Wirth to Diane K. Steed, NHTSA, Sept.
16, 1986.

acknowledged the need for agency action to address the rollover problem but did not believe that Representative Wirth's proposed stability factor, based on a height-to-track-width ratio, was a sound basis for a standard.[82]

Although Wirth's interest in highway safety declined when he was elected to the Senate in 1988, his campaign for rollover protection was continued by Senator John C. Danforth of Missouri, who looked for legislative avenues to require rollover protection. In 1988 the NHTSA granted a petition filed by the Consumers Union "to establish a minimum standard to protect against unreasonable risk of rollover" in a car, van, light truck, or multipurpose passenger vehicle. The NHTSA cautioned that granting the petition did not necessarily mean a rule would be issued. Since there were no industry-accepted tests for rollover propensity, the NHTSA's work was made both more difficult and more necessary.[83] After conducting several years of research on a rollover standard for utility vehicles, the NHTSA planned to propose a standard by the end of 1990.

The CJ-7 was discontinued in 1987. According to a company official, changing demands of customers, not concerns over safety, prompted the CJ's demise. "The vehicle," the spokesman claimed, "is not being phased out of production because of legal problems, I can assure you of that. . . . Yuppies want a more comfortable vehicle to drive when they have an attache case in the front seat and their Burberry coats folded in the back seat."[84] Market analysis substantiates this explanation. Sales of the more basic, less luxurious utility vehicles (such as the Toyota Land Cruiser, the International Harvester Scout, and the Jeep CJ-5) declined in the early 1980s. In 1983 Jeep introduced the XJ vehicles, smaller versions of the Cherokee and Wagoneer. These XJs, boasting more creature comforts, attracted many customers who visited Jeep showrooms, creating in-house competition for the CJ-7.[85]

The Wrangler (also known as Jeep YJ), a more upscale Jeep, replaced the CJ. A May 1986 headline in *Advertising Age* read: "YJ Jeep tries to corral upscale urban cowboys." The new Jeep was targeted at a more educated, affluent, white-collar, and urban market. Formerly optional equipment was made standard, making the Wrangler's base price about 29 percent higher than the CJ-7's.[86] The Wrangler's premier domestic

82. Letter from Diane Steed, NHTSA, to Congressman John Dingell, Dec. 16, 1988.
83. "Government to Start Work on Rollover Standard," *Consumer Reports*, Nov. 1988, 702.
84. Isikoff 1985.
85. Correspondence, Kent B. Joscelyn to William R. Kittle, Aug. 13, 1990.
86. "YC Jeep Tries to Corral."

Figure 4-3. *Sales Figures for the Jeep CJ-7 and Three Competitive Vehicles, 1983–86*[a]

Thousands

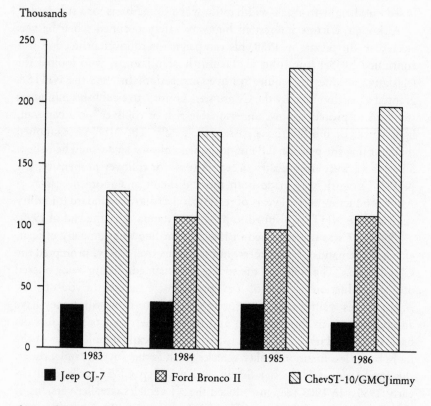

■ Jeep CJ-7   ▨ Ford Bronco II   ◩ ChevST-10/GMCJimmy

Sources: Chrysler Corporation, Ford Motor Company, General Motors Corporation.
a. The Ford Bronco II was introduced in 1984; the Chevy Blazer and GMC Jimmy, "sister vehicles," were introduced in 1983.

competitors were the Chevy S-10 Blazer, the GMC S-15 Jimmy, and the Ford Bronco II, which were scaled-down models of earlier, larger utility vehicles (see figure 4-3). AMC saw the Wrangler as a new strategy to recapture the company's share of the utility vehicle market.

AMC was responding belatedly to a shift in usage patterns that had been noted in surveys of CJ owners. The number of CJ-7 owners who reported regularly using their vehicles for personal transportation rose from 17 percent in 1978 to 95 percent in 1985.[87] Although safety experts applauded the Wrangler's lower and wider design (and resulting lower

87. "YC Jeep Tries to Corral."

center of gravity), the extra resistance to rollovers this change provided may have been incidental. AMC may have been concerned primarily with improving the vehicle's ride. One could also argue that the steel doors that replaced the CJ's canvas ones were a cosmetic change rather than one intended to increase the vehicle's crashworthiness. However, the new, substantial windshield frame tied to the roll bar by steel cross-members can only be viewed as a safety improvement.[88]

Although the Wrangler replaced the CJ series, critics of the CJ continued to press their case. In June 1990 the Public Citizen joined with the Center for Auto Safety in a petition to the NHTSA calling for recall of the 300,000 CJs still on the road.[89] ABC's "20/20" ran a major segment in the summer of 1990 that highlighted the alleged hazards of the CJ, relying primarily on information supplied by plaintiff attorneys, Joan Claybrook, and Ben Kelley. During this period, the Trial Lawyers for Public Justice also filed a class action suit against Chrysler seeking full refunds for the 350,000 CJ owners plus punitive damages against Chrysler. The suit cites the NHTSA's estimate that 150 fatalities occur each year because of rollovers involving CJs.[90]

Considering the entire case history, it is unlikely that the demise of the CJ and the birth of the redesigned Wrangler were caused solely by safety considerations. Changes in consumer tastes and intense competition in this market were the fundamental causes of these outcomes. Adverse safety publicity may have hastened the demise of the CJ and somewhat influenced the design of the Wrangler. Interestingly, while allies of plaintiffs and the Insurance Institute for Highway Safety worked diligently with the media to highlight safety concerns, the NHTSA was never a vocal critic of the CJ.

Occupant-Restraint Design

Over the past five years manufacturers have made three important changes in the design of occupant-restraint systems: the addition of supplemental air bags to conventional front-seat lap-shoulder belt systems in passenger cars, the installation of lap-shoulder belts (rather than lap belts alone) in rear outboard seating positions of passenger cars and certain light trucks, and the removal of belt tension relievers that had been used

88. Hogan 1980, 111.
89. Kurylko 1990, 6.
90. Kahn 1990c, 6.

for more than twelve years to improve the comfort of front-seat shoulder belts.

AIR BAGS.[91] Each year about 25,000 front-seat occupants are killed in motor vehicle crashes. Another 250,000 front-seat occupants suffer serious injuries of varying severity. Many of these injuries could be mitigated or prevented by contemporary air bag technology. Some effectiveness studies suggest that air bags reduce the risk of fatality and serious injury in a crash by 15 to 30 percent among unbelted occupants and by 5 to 10 percent among belted occupants.[92] The wide range of uncertainty in these estimates reflects the limited real-world experience with air bags and variation in the judgments of safety experts.

In the 1990 model year about one-third of new cars sold in the United States were equipped with driver-side air bags. By the 1994 model year, most new cars sold in the United States will be equipped with some type of air bag system. By way of comparison, no new cars were sold with air bags in the United States during the 1977–82 model years. The rapid pace of air bag installation reflects an interesting combination of regulatory and marketplace forces.

Beginning in the early 1970s, the NHTSA permitted manufacturers to install either manual lap-shoulder belts or "passive protection" in new cars. Because of technical and economic considerations, safety belts were the most popular compliance choice. Efforts by the NHTSA to require passive protection in the 1970s were vigorously resisted by Chrysler, Ford, and foreign manufacturers because many safety engineers believed the technology was not yet ready for widespread use.

Under the leadership of its president, Ed Cole, General Motors invested heavily in air bag research and development beginning in the late 1960s and was the first manufacturer to offer air bags for sale on a significant number of new cars. During the 1974–76 model years, GM offered air bags as a $200–$315 option (1974 dollars) on several full-size car lines. Despite a production capacity of 100,000 units in each of the three years, only about 10,000 cars were sold with air bags. The limited consumer interest in the air bag may reflect GM's limited marketing effort and dealer apathy toward the option. Moreover, little was done by the NHTSA during this period to promote consumer interest in the air bag.

91. I thank the following persons for providing useful information: Barry Felrice (NHTSA), Clarence Ditlow (Center for Auto Safety), Stuart Statler (American Trial Lawyers Association), Richard Manetta (Ford), Helen Petrauskas (Ford), and Stephen Teret (Johns Hopkins University). Portions of the case are based on Graham 1989.

92. Graham and Henrion 1984, 27–28.

GM terminated the option in 1977 because of a lack of consumer demand and technological considerations, at about the same time as Cole retired.

On January 18, 1977, the Department of Transportation announced agreements with GM, Ford, and Mercedes to manufacture a "demonstration fleet" of air bag–equipped cars. The agreements were rescinded by the department shortly thereafter, and in July 1977 the NHTSA promulgated a passive-restraint rule. As a result, manufacturers expanded their research and development activities. The NHTSA expected most manufacturers to install air bags. As the September 1981 compliance deadline approached, it became clear to the agency that most manufacturers would choose to install (detachable) automatic belt systems rather than air bags. After the 1980 elections, the agency delayed and then rescinded the passive-restraint rule in 1981. Several manufacturers and suppliers terminated their air bag development programs; Ford was the only domestic manufacturer to retain a program. Although Mercedes-Benz was successful selling air bags in Europe during this period, its air bag offering was not extended to the United States until model year 1984, and then only as an option in the first two years.

Ford's renewed commitment to the air bag in the early 1980s was the key turning point. Several factors led to its new corporate strategy. The retirement of Henry Ford II in 1982 opened the door for air bag advocates such as the auto safety director, Roger Maugh, and Vice President Helen Petrauskas. In December 1982 the NHTSA also played a role by unveiling with the General Services Administration a $35 million program to equip 5,000 government cars with air bags. By March 1983 it was apparent that Ford was the only manufacturer willing to bid on the GSA contract (in part because the government subsidy was not sufficient to cover development and production costs). By the time that the NHTSA and Ford gave final approval to their contract in February 1984, Ford was beginning to work quietly on a plan to offer driver-side air bags as a $815 option on the 1986 Ford Tempo and 1986 Mercury Topaz. The plan was announced in November 1985.

Frustrated with the NHTSA's regulatory process, some activist attorneys advocated the use of tort law to promote air bags. Andrew Hricko of the Insurance Institute for Highway Safety had argued as early as 1977 that the entire auto industry could be held liable for their refusal to market air bags. In May 1982 Joan Claybrook helped organize a meeting of the Trial Lawyers for Public Justice to train plaintiff attorneys on how to make the absence of air bags an issue in product liability suits. In July 1982 Stephen Teret of Johns Hopkins University published an article in

Trial (the magazine of the American Trial Lawyers Association) that induced many plaintiff attorneys to file claims against manufacturers for lack of air bags. As will be seen, the ultimate significance of this litigation is still not apparent.

In contrast, the U.S. Supreme Court dealt the Transportation Department a setback in July 1983 when it ruled unanimously that the passive-restraint rule could not be rescinded lawfully without a careful analysis of air bags. Justice Byron White's opinion for the Court stated that the auto industry "waged the regulatory equivalent of war against the air bag and lost." Although the Court did not compel the department to require air bags, the strong language in White's opinion caused some opponents within industry to acknowledge the inevitability of air bags.

Six months later, the Ford Motor Company broke industry ranks and proposed that all manufacturers be required to install some passive-restraint system in 5 percent of their fleet over a four-year demonstration period. All other manufacturers were opposing passive restraints because of economic and technological concerns and because of the belief that lap-shoulder belts, if worn, could provide the same protection as air bags.

In March 1984 a settlement was reached in *Burgess* v. *Ford* that reportedly provided $1.8 million in compensation to the plaintiff. Front-right passenger Rebecca Burgess, at age eighteen, was rendered a severely brain injured quadriplegic when her Ford Pinto was struck on the passenger side at a 45-degree angle by a Chevrolet Camaro. Although this case was served on Ford on August 30, 1979, and alleged various defects, the plaintiff did not make the lack-of-air-bag claim until November 1983.[93] Joan Claybrook had also signed up as a rebuttal witness for the plaintiff in this case.

A detailed crash investigation would be necessary to determine whether air bags would have deployed and protected Burgess in this particular crash. Air bags are designed to inflate primarily in frontal crashes. Ford officials contend that they settled this case for reasons that have nothing to do with the claim about lack of an air bag.

The Burgess case was highly publicized. The "Today Show" ran a consumer segment that highlighted the Burgess incident. Law and health publications drew attention to the settlement. The historical case information now provided by the American Trial Lawyers Association highlights the lack of an air bag as a claim in this case.

93. Letter from Richard Manetta, Ford, to John D. Graham, Apr. 27, 1990 (attachment dated Feb. 4, 1983, documents Ford's decision to compete for the GSA fleet).

In July 1984 the transportation secretary, Elizabeth Dole, went further and reinstated the passive-restraint standard with a phase-in plan designed to encourage a diversity of passive-restraint offerings such as "friendly interiors" (that is, innovative interior padding schemes) and air bags. Recognizing that the most effective way to save lives was to get people to buckle up, Dole included a provision that would have rescinded the passive-restraint rule if two-thirds of the U.S. population were covered by mandatory use laws by April 1, 1989. Dole made it clear that she was a strong supporter of both mandatory belt use laws and passive restraints.

The new air bag programs at Mercedes-Benz and Ford, combined with the new regulatory pressures, stimulated competitive pressure throughout the industry. In December 1985 and February 1986 the *Wall Street Journal* quoted anonymous sources at Chrysler and General Motors who acknowledged that major air bag programs were under way.

When the NHTSA granted Ford's petition to extend the phase-in period for passenger-side air bags to 1994, Ford announced plans to install driver-side air bags as standard equipment in a majority of its new 1990 and later cars. At a December 1986 public hearing before Senator Danforth, Ford and Chrysler made public promises to provide air bags. The commitment from General Motors was cautious because of lingering concerns about the technology's reliability, especially those concerns about child safety that the NHTSA later used to justify a delay in the passenger-side requirements.

Before long Chrysler became the first domestic manufacturer to commit to offering air bags as standard equipment on all its domestically produced lines. Since 1986 Ford and Chrysler have engaged in vigorous competition to earn the reputation as the manufacturer with the strongest commitment to air bags. GM remains cautious about the air bag even as the company installs the technology in many of its new cars.

Did liability stimulate the availability of air bags? Industry attorneys never regarded the lack-of-air-bag claim as a tenable legal position, and time has proved them to be correct. Hundreds of such claims have been filed against manufacturers. Several federal appeals courts have held that Secretary Dole's 1984 passive-restraint rule preempts the claims of plaintiffs that vehicles without passive restraints are necessarily defective. Because of the industry's success with the preemption defense, only one case—which was won by the defense and appealed—has been tried to a verdict. Since the Dole plan was intended to stimulate a diversity of restraint-system offerings, the courts have ruled that the rule's intent would be frustrated by a common law that requires manufacturers to install air bags or any other specific passive-restraint system. The Supreme Court has refused five times to hear an appeal of the preemption issue, which was a major victory for the defendants in these cases.[94]

Considering the entire case history, liability risk was certainly not necessary to stimulate air bag development. The 1983 Supreme Court decision and the 1984 passive-restraint mandate were sufficient to do so. Moreover, the Ford Motor Company had renewed its commitment to the air bag technology before the air bag claim was ever made in the Burgess case. Indeed, the new corporate strategy at Ford was already hatched before the air bag claim was added to the Burgess case.

Nor does it seem likely that liability risk would have been sufficient by itself to bring air bags to the marketplace. Industry attorneys were confident they would defeat most cases that used lack of an air bag or other passive restraint as the primary defect allegation. In the absence of the regulatory pressures and Ford's new management team, liability considerations would not have been compelling enough to justify the costs of air bag development. Despite the Burgess settlement, manufacturers had little reason to expect that the liability burdens of refusing to install air bags would be any larger than the new liability burdens that might be created by a decision to install air bags.

In summary, liability considerations were probably not a significant pro-safety force in the decisions of manufacturers to offer air bags. Regulation, combined with a new management strategy at Ford, competitive pressures, and improved technology, was the key factor.

REAR-SEAT SHOULDER BELTS.[95] Each year about 2,000 occupants in the rear seats of passenger cars are killed in crashes. Another 28,000 rear-seat occupants suffer serious nonfatal injuries. Many of these injured occupants are children, and most of the injured are unrestrained.[96]

A significant fraction of this trauma may be prevented by the use of lap-shoulder belts. Estimates of (rear-seat) lap belt effectiveness in preventing fatalities range from 24 to 40 percent. Estimates of lap belt effectiveness in preventing serious nonfatal injuries range from 30 to 41 percent. The NHTSA believes the combined lap and shoulder belt can

94. Kahn 1990a, 6.

95. I thank the following persons for providing useful information: Brian O'Neill (IIHS), Benjamin Kelley (Institute for Injury Reduction), Allan Maness (U.S. Senate), Richard Manetta (Ford), Stephen Teret (Johns Hopkins University), James Durkin (GM), Leonard Evans (GM), Joan Claybrook (Public Citizen), Barry Felrice (NHTSA), and Stuart Statler (American Trial Lawyers Association).

96. NHTSA 1988.

augment these effectiveness estimates by up to 8 to 10 percentage points for fatalities and perhaps 15 percentage points for serious nonfatal injuries. The NHTSA's figures have been criticized as too high and too low.

In January 1968 the NHTSA permitted vehicle manufacturers to install either lap belts alone or lap-shoulder belts in the rear-seating positions of passenger cars. The rear seats of most cars sold in the United States for the past twenty years, both foreign and domestic, have been equipped with lap belts alone. Before 1984 only a handful of countries required lap belts in the rear seat of vehicles and only a few of them required lap-shoulder belts. The design practice in America reflected manufacturer confidence in the effectiveness of lap belts, the low rates of rear-seat occupancy, the low rates of lap belt use, fears that shoulder belts might discourage belt use, and concern that shoulder belts would be misused to restrain child seats that required a tether.

In 1982 Kathleen Weber and John Melvin of the University of Michigan petitioned the NHTSA to require manufacturers to install shoulder belts in the rear seats of passenger cars. They argued that the shoulder harness could be used to secure child-restraint systems and to secure older children on booster seats. They also noted that the shoulder belt would provide additional protection to adults.

The NHTSA denied this petition in 1984, citing the superiority of the harness systems already available in child restraints and the potential for misuse of these systems with the shoulder harness. The agency acknowledged that the shoulder belt might offer some added protection to adults but concluded that the extra costs of shoulder belts ($20 per car) could not be justified in light of the low rate of rear-seat lap belt use (about 2 percent in 1982) and the demonstrated effectiveness of lap belts.

The issue went public in a big way in August 1986 when Patricia Goldman of the National Transportation Safety Board released a report criticizing the safety of rear-seat lap belts.[97] On the basis of detailed investigations of twenty-six carefully selected frontal crashes, the NTSB concluded that the lap belt was not providing adequate protection and in some cases was aggravating occupant injury.[98]

The NTSB stressed that it has been known for years that lap-shoulder belts provide better protection in frontal collisions and less inherent hazard than lap belts alone. Although the NTSB study was criticized for

97. Statement by Patricia A. Goldman, acting chair, National Transportation Safety Board, Washington, Aug. 11, 1986.
98. National Transportation Safety Board 1986.

poor methodology and sampling techniques by the NHTSA scientists, the GAO, and independent experts, its conclusions received widespread media publicity.

In August 1986 the NHTSA granted a petition from the Los Angeles Area Child Passenger Safety Association to reconsider the issue. In June 1987 the NHTSA requested public comment on whether rear-seat shoulder belts should be required. A rule was proposed in November 1988 and agreed to in June 1989. The NHTSA expressly stated that its policy change was motivated in large part by the trend toward mandatory seat belt use legislation and the increasing rates of rear-seat-belt use (16 percent in 1987). Although most state laws applied only to front-seat occupants, five states also required rear-seat occupants to buckle up.[99]

In this case manufacturers moved much more quickly than the NHTSA. Before the NTSB study, GM had announced that because of the widespread adoption of mandatory adult-and child-restraint use laws and growing public acceptance of belts, it would phase in rear-seat lap and shoulder belts. GM had also performed its own effectiveness studies and determined that lap belts, though still quite effective, were not performing in crashes as effectively as they (and the NHTSA) had previously thought. In June 1986 GM released an innovative study by Leonard Evans that estimated the effectiveness of rear seat belts in preventing fatalities at about 7 percent (plus or minus 12 percent).[100] A revised analysis by Evans in October 1986 produced an effectiveness estimate of 18 percent (plus or minus 9 percent).[101] By mid-1986 GM was already well down the road toward implementation of its plans to offer rear-seat shoulder belts on certain 1988 vehicles.

At about the same time that the NTSB report was released to the public, lawsuits were being filed against manufacturers for failure to install shoulder belts in the rear seats of vehicles. On March 6, 1986, James Garrett filed suit against the Ford Motor Company on the grounds that his paralysis from the waist down would have been prevented if the lap belts in the rear seat of his Escort had not contained a "tether strap" that allegedly pulled the lap belt off the hips and on to the soft abdomen, and if his Escort had been equipped with a shoulder belt. On June 3, 1986, well before the Garrett case was resolved, Ford approved engineering plans to install rear-seat restraints on the 1988 Taurus-Sable and Lincoln

99. *Federal Register* 54 (1989): 25275.
100. Evans 1986a, 7.
101. Evans 1986b, 7.

Continental.[102] Ford records show that five lawsuits alleging the absence of rear-seat shoulder belts were pending on June 3, 1986.

In September 1986 General Motors paid a $5 million settlement to a nine-year-old girl who alleged she became a quadriplegic because of crash injuries that would have been prevented by a rear-seat shoulder belt. In January 1987 American Motor Honda paid a $2 million settlement to a twenty-two-year-old man who also alleged that his paralysis from the waist down would have been prevented by a rear-seat shoulder belt.

The Garrett case against Ford was one of the first rear-seat lap belt cases to be tried. In December 1987 a federal jury in Baltimore awarded $3.3 million to James Garrett and his family. It should be noted that the Garrett case was not exclusively based on the lack of a shoulder belt; it also included an allegation that the lap belt in the Escort was defective.

Ben Kelley of the Institute for Injury Reduction, working closely with plaintiff attorneys, played a pivotal role in stimulating publicity and litigation on this issue. Manufacturers have settled dozens of additional claims since the Garrett verdict. A recent settlement received front-page coverage in the the *Wall Street Journal.* In April 1990 the Ford Motor Company agreed to pay $6 million to settle the claims made by a California family. Twin boys restrained by lap belts in the rear seat were severely injured in a crash in which their parents were protected by lap-shoulder belts in the front seat. One of the boys was killed and the other was paralyzed. Although the special circumstances of this case led to a huge settlement, the case illustrates the magnitude of manufacturer liability caused by the rapid increase in rear-seat lap belt use.[103]

In February 1988 the NHTSA announced that most manufacturers were installing rear-seat shoulder belts voluntarily. The offerings would increase during the 1988 and 1989 model years and cover virtually all 1990 models. This announcement occurred six months before the NHTSA's proposed rule and more than a year before the final rule.

There is no evidence that consumer demand per se was a significant cause of the new design decisions. Competitive pressure, however, may have played a minor role. Once GM decided to install rear-seat shoulder belts, other manufacturers may have been reluctant to offer cars without them.

Claybrook has expressed the view that "most manufacturers resisted

---

102. Letter from Richard Manetta, Ford, to John D. Graham, Apr. 27, 1990 (attachment dated June 2, 1986, directs installation of rear-seat shoulder belts on 1988 Taurus-Sable and Lincoln Continental; authorization for all car lines was made Oct. 9, 1986).

103. Templin 1990, B1.

installing the harness until pressured by product liability suits from people injured wearing only lap belts."[104] It is worth considering in this case whether liability was a necessary, sufficient, or contributing factor to the design decisions of manufacturers.

Liability was probably not a necessary force since the NHTSA would have regulated sooner or later. Several senators and representatives were pressuring the NHTSA to require rear-seat shoulder belts, and the NHTSA has recently been responsive to congressional pressure. There is certainly no reason to believe that liability was necessary to motivate the NHTSA to mandate rear-seat shoulder belts. However, some factor or factors caused manufacturers to act more quickly than required by regulatory compliance deadlines.

A good case can be made that liability considerations were a sufficient cause of the design change. At 20 percent belt use and 10 percentage points of incremental effectiveness, installation of the shoulder belt might prevent 2 percent of a projected toll of 30,000 fatalities and serious injuries over the life of these vehicles. If the average liability risk associated with these 600 preventable injuries is greater than $400,000 per case, then it is easy to justify the projected expenditure of $200 million ($20 per vehicle times 10 million vehicles). While this calculation does not discount the future liability savings, it also ignores the growing rates of rear-seat-belt use and the adverse reputational effects of liability lawsuits.

Considerations of professional responsibility also appeared to have contributed to the design decisions of manufacturers in this case. Once GM and Ford saw that belt use rates were rising and lap belts were not as effective as previously thought, it was easy for safety professionals within these companies to make the case for shoulder harnesses. Indeed, safety professionals within GM and Ford may have seized on the rear-seat-belt issue to advance their own professional stature. Hence, since the costs of rear-seat shoulder belts are modest, professional responsibility considerations may have played an important role.

BELT TENSION RELIEVERS.[105] The NHTSA defines a tension relief device as "a device permitting the introduction of slack in the webbing of a shoulder belt." In the past this slack was created with a "comfort clip" or a tension relief device such as a "window shade." Comfort clips are

---

104. Claybrook 1989, 12A.

105. I thank the following persons for providing useful information: Brian O'Neill (IIHS), Richard Manetta (Ford), James Durkin (GM), Ralph Hitchcock (NHTSA), Barry Felrice (NHTSA), Roger McCarthy (FAA), John B. Sullivan (Harvard School of Public Health), and Benjamin Kelley (Institute for Injury Reduction).

mechanical clips on the belt webbing operated by the occupant to prevent the belt from retracting. Window shade devices are built into the belt retractor and can be used by the occupant to reduce the amount of tension.

Although the NHTSA briefly considered a prohibition of tension relievers in 1979, the NHTSA administrator, Joan Claybrook, elected to permit the devices in order to improve belt comfort and encourage belt use. The devices can permit the occupant to add some slack if the belt is too tight or relocate the belt away from the neck if necessary. They encourage belt use by improving comfort and allowing each user to adjust the belt to fit personal need. Historically, the instructions for adjusting a manual shoulder belt included a recommendation that no more than a "clenched fist" of slack be used for proper fit.

General Motors first introduced the comfort clip in 1975 and later added the window shade device. Window shade devices have been installed on almost all domestic passenger cars and light trucks for over a decade. Foreign manufacturers have not normally used window shades. The owner manuals for all recent domestically produced cars contain instructions for use of window shades, including a suggested amount of slack (usually one-inch maximum or slack equivalent to a clenched fist) and a warning that excess slack reduces the effectiveness of belts in crashes.

In June 1988 the NHTSA reported that manufacturers were beginning to voluntarily phase out window shade devices. The agency did not require or encourage these actions. Ford and Chrysler did not use window shades on their 1988 cars that had automatic belts and reported plans to phase out window shades on some 1989 models and all 1990 models. General Motors reported that it was reluctant to phase out window shades because it feared a reduction in belt use rates and an increased number of customer complaints. In September 1988 GM informed the NHTSA that it also had decided to phase out window shades on some models during the 1989 and 1990 model years. GM also said it would evaluate the need for tension relief devices on new restraint systems on a design-by-design basis.

The reasons behind the phaseout of window shades are not entirely clear. There is no evidence that consumers were dissatisfied with these features or objected to the very small cost penalty associated with them. The domestic manufacturers were under no great regulatory pressure to phase out window shades. Although consumer advocates, insurers, and some legislators had expressed concern about the diminished effectiveness of belts worn with excessive slack, the issue was not a high priority at the NHTSA in the 1980s.

Although a single jury verdict will rarely cause a manufacturer to make major design changes, liability considerations may have been a factor in this case. *Baird* v. *General Motors Corp.* was decided by a federal jury in Akron, Ohio, on December 15, 1987. The jury awarded $800,000 in damages to a woman who claimed her husband was killed because of a faulty belt design. The case is believed to be the first one challenging the window shade design to go to trial.

According to non-GM sources within the industry, GM had (as of March 1990) lost three out of five "window shade" cases that went to a jury verdict. In one of the two GM victories, the jury found that the belt design, while defective, was not responsible for the occupant's injury. In another case decided in June 1990, a New York jury exonerated GM of charges that window shade devices were responsible for occupant injuries.[106] Ford has recently won two such cases.

With the adoption of mandatory belt use laws, motorists have high expectations for the potential of restraint systems to mitigate injuries. Manufacturers may have reasoned that such expectations cause too much liability risk to justify continued use of window shades.

Professional responsibility considerations may have also played an important role. The design of any restraint system entails a trade-off between comfort and effectiveness. Since front-seat-belt use rates in the United States were quite low (below 15 percent) before 1985, it was reasonable to expect manufacturers to tilt the design trade-off in favor of increased comfort so as to promote use. In recent years usage rates have climbed to about 50 percent owing to the passage of mandatory belt use laws. Manufacturers have responded by paying closer attention to the issue of belt effectiveness. To ease the trade-off between use and effectiveness, manufacturers have also made some improvements in belt geometry and design that may increase occupant comfort without the use of tension eliminators.

To determine whether the use of window shades was a net plus for injury control, one must weigh the diminished belt effectiveness due to increased slack against the possibly higher usage rates that belt comfort may induce. I consider first the available data on the extent of belt slack in actual use and then the consequences for belt effectiveness.

In a study protocol that filmed 1,907 drivers stopped for traffic lights, the Insurance Institute for Highway Safety observed that 27 percent of domestic cars had one to two inches of slack, while 8 percent had three

106. Kahn 1990b, 40.

or more inches of slack. In contrast, only 5 percent of imported cars (which are usually not equipped with window shades) had slack in belts.[107] In the NHTSA's observational study of 200,000 cars in nineteen cities, 3 percent of shoulder belts were coded as "too loose." A belt was coded as too loose if obvious slack was observed in webbing in front of the chest, shoulder belt webbing could be observed on the driver's lap, or obvious slack was observed in webbing between the driver's shoulder and the belt's upper connection to the car.

Crash tests, computer simulations, and logic suggest that introducing slack in belt webbing will increase the amount of crash energy transferred to the occupant.[108] Thirty mph crash tests in 1983 using a Ford window shade on a Mercury Zephyr test car produced the following scores for head injury criteria (where a HIC score of 1,000 + suggests serious head injury): no slack (HIC = 440); one-inch slack (HIC = 640); two-inch slack (HIC = 795); maximum slack of sixteen inches (HIC = 1,800). Computer simulations of crashes at 35 mph suggest HIC scores of 476 with no slack and 1,088 with four inches of slack.

Investigations of real-world crashes, however, have not shown a higher injury or death rate for vehicles equipped with window shades. In a comparison of GM cars with and without window shades, Roger McCarthy of Failure Analysis Associates found no evidence that the cars with window shades experienced a reduction in belt effectiveness.[109]

Very few data have been assembled to assess the impact of tension relievers on belt use rates. Attitude surveys have shown that perceived belt comfort is an important factor in distinguishing belt users from nonusers. Only one study has been performed to assess directly the effect of tension relievers on belt use. McCarthy compared belt use rates during 1984–86 in cars with and without tension relievers. He estimated, using data from the NHTSA's nineteen-city study, that the devices were associated with an increase in belt use of about 5 percentage points (from 7 percent to 12 percent). Analysis of belt use data from accident reports in the states of Michigan and Texas suggests a similar effect, though the effect was somewhat larger when there were mandatory belt use laws.

Taking into account all the evidence in the case study, liability considerations may have been a contributing factor in the decisions of manufacturers to phase out window shades. Whether these design decisions

107. Ciccone and Wells 1988.
108. NHTSA 1988.
109. McCarthy, Padmanaban, and Ray (n.d.).

will lead to fewer injuries is far from clear, since the absence of tension relievers could discourage belt use. It should be noted, however, that European countries have been able to sustain high belt use rates (60–90 percent) without using tension relievers.

If the ultimate effect of the phaseout of tension relievers is to induce manufacturers to devise better belt designs, the outcome may be favorable in the long run. For example, manufacturers are experimenting with alternative belt geometry and design to improve comfort without introducing slack. In the future pyrotechnic pretensioners may be used to detect crash forces and reduce belt slack before the occupant begins to move forward. These devices, while expensive, are available on some Saab and Mercedes-Benz vehicles. Alternatively, manufacturers may move to webb grabbers to reduce belt spool-out. It prevents spool-out of up to 70 millimeters of webbing all within a few milliseconds. As belt use rates increase and customer expectations of crash protection escalate, manufacturers will look for technological improvements. If air bags prove to be successful and are universally implemented, they may make slack in the shoulder belt a less important issue.

The All-Terrain Vehicle

All-terrain vehicles are three- and four-wheeled motorized vehicles with large low-pressure tires, a seat designed to be straddled by the operator, and handlebars for steering. They are intended for off-road use by a single rider on various types of nonpaved terrain. ATVs are usually less than 50 inches in width and weigh 250–400 pounds.[110] This case study examines the safety concerns raised by the increasing popularity of ATVs, including the steps that have been taken to improve ATV safety.[111]

110. This case was written by Marvin Malek. We thank the following persons for providing useful information: Stuart Statler (American Trial Lawyers Association), Mark Berry (Honda North America, Inc.), John Walsh (American Suzuki Motorcycle Company), Charles Baxter (Polaris Company), Roger McCarthy (Failure Analysis Associates), Wade Allen (Systems Technology, Inc.), Nick Spaeth (attorney general, State of North Dakota), Susan Wilson (Specialty Vehicle Institute of America), William Rockwell (American National Standards Institute), Robert Wright (L'Expert Company), Janine Jagger (University of Virginia Medical School), Roy Deppa (Consumer Product Safety Commission), Nick Marchica (CPSC), Gregory Rodgers (CPSC), Carl Blechschmidt (CPSC), John Saar (People Magazine), David Gelber (Columbia Broadcasting System), and Eleanor Prescott (American Broadcasting Company).

111. "All-Terrain Vehicles; Advance Notice of Proposed Rulemaking; Request for Comments and Data," *Federal Register* 50 (1985): 23139–44.

Over 95 percent of ATVs are produced by four Japan-based motor-cycle companies and are now a major product of that industry, since the sale of on-road motorcycles underwent a 67 percent decline between 1980 and 1987.[112] After a decade of slow sales growth, ATV use became wide-spread after a surge in popularity in the 1980s. Figure 4-4 shows that ATV shipments peaked at 650,000 units in 1984 and have since declined,[113] though in 1988 they still accounted for 39 percent of motorcycle industry sales, with more units sold than any other product of the industry, in-cluding on-road motorcycles.[114]

The increasing popularity of ATVs in the 1980s was associated with a surge in the incidence of deaths and injuries among riders. Figure 4-5 in-dicates that the annual number of deaths and injuries increased about tenfold from 1982 to 1985. The annual number of injuries peaked at 86,400 in 1986 and declined to 58,600 in 1989. There has been little change in the number of deaths occurring annually since 1985, when an estimated 295 riders died.[115] As will be seen, both vehicular and behavioral factors contributed to the toll of injuries and deaths associated with the use of ATVs.

The ATV's high center of gravity and unique handling characteristics require a fairly high degree of skill and attentiveness.[116] Safe operation of the vehicle requires precise, simultaneous responses to obstacles, slopes, and unanticipated terrain irregularities. The required motor response is unique because fine adjustments of brakes and steering wheel and shifts in body weight are both critical to the maintenance of vehicle stability. During turns the shift in body weight requires delicate balance: the op-erator is supposed to lean the body into the turn, but shift the body weight away from the turn.[117]

Disregard of safe riding practices has also contributed to injuries as-sociated with ATV use. Over 20 percent of the deaths reported to the Consumer Product Safety Commission (CPSC) have involved people under the influence of alcohol or illicit drugs. In one-third of the fatalities drivers were carrying passengers, in 44 percent occupants were not wear-

---

112. Motorcycle Industry Council 1988, 1–27.

113. 1985 Motocycle Industry data, cited by J. Jones-Smith, chairperson, CPSC, State-ment before the Subcommittee on Commerce, Consumer, and Monetary Affairs of the House Committee on Government Operations, Feb. 28, 1990.

114. "Join a Better Class of Riders." Video. ATV Safety Institute, Specialty Vehicle, Institute of America, Irvine, Calif. 1989.

115. C. Blechschmidt, "Update of All-Terrain Vehicle Deaths and Injuries," CPSC Memorandum, Washington, Dec. 6, 1989.

116. Deppa 1986.

117. Specialty Vehicle Institute of America 1985.

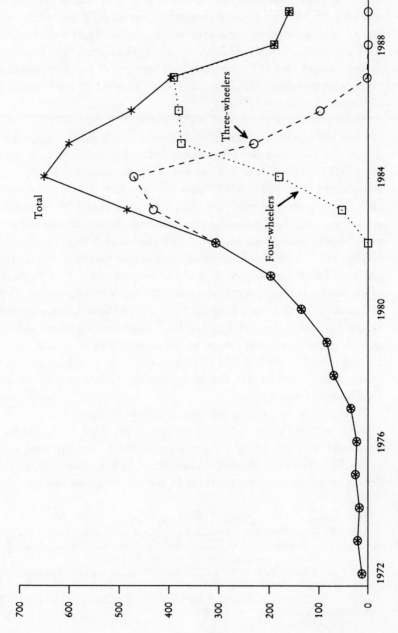

Figure 4-4. *Shipments of All-Terrain Vehicles, 1972–89*

Thousands

Total

Three-wheelers

Four-wheelers

700
600
500
400
300
200
100
0

1972   1976   1980   1984   1988

Source: Motorcycle Industry Council.

Figure 4-5. *ATV-Related Injuries and Deaths, 1982–89*

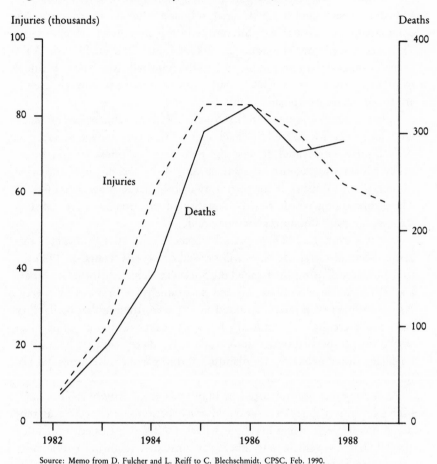

Source: Memo from D. Fulcher and L. Reiff to C. Blechschmidt, CPSC, Feb. 1990.

ing helmets, and in 46 percent the vehicles were being operated on paved roads.[118] It is precisely these kinds of activities that owner manuals and educational materials have warned against.

While riding in ATVs can clearly be risky, proponents and opponents of ATVs have disputed whether the risks are unreasonable. For example, early experience with ATVs suggested that the average person who purchased an ATV might face a one in three chance of receiving emergency room treatment for an injury—a risk of injury that is much larger than

118. E. J. Heiden, Testimony before the Subcommittee on Commerce, Consumer and Monetary Affairs of the House Committee on Government Operations, Feb. 28, 1990 (exhibits).

the unadjusted risks faced by purchasers of trail bikes or snowmobiles.[119] Industry experts and a CPSC analyst made adjustments to such risk comparisons to account for differences in the amount of vehicle usage. They concluded that the adjusted risk of injury and fatality for ATV riders is smaller than or comparable to the adjusted risks faced by riders of other recreational vehicles.[120] Such risk comparisons, though useful, are based on poor exposure data.

Comparisons of injury severity for the different vehicles can be made with more confidence. CPSC data suggest that the average severity of ATV injuries is elevated because the percentage of riders seen in emergency rooms who require hospitalization (13–15 percent) is about twice as high for ATV users as for operators of trail bikes or snowmobiles.[121] The severity comparisons based on fatality information do not reveal such large differences among recreational vehicles.

It was during the 1983–84 period of accelerating sales that safety concerns about all-terrain vehicles were raised on several fronts. In 1983 the four Japanese distributors formed the Specialty Vehicle Institute of America (SVIA) to develop materials and programs to promote ATV safety. As the number of injuries mounted in 1983–84, the number of liability suits also increased. The industry has been successful in defending most of the twenty-odd suits that have gone to verdict,[122] in part because of negligent riding behaviors by plaintiffs and in part because juries did not find the vehicles to be defective.

A major exception occurred in May 1984 in *McKinley* v. *Honda*.[123] McKinley was a thirty-two-year-old construction worker who was rendered quadriplegic when his three-wheeled ATV overturned. McKinley alleged that the vehicle was inherently unstable, requiring subtle rider movements to counterbalance the vehicle's instability, and that the average inexperienced rider lacks the sophistication to properly counterbalance this instability. Honda, the industry leader, paid $2.6 million in damages.

In April 1984 the CPSC first took note of the rising number of injuries

119. Robert Verhalen to Nick Marchika, "ATV Project: Comparative Injury Tables," CPSC Memorandum, June 13, 1986.

120. G. B. Rodgers, "Motorized Vehicle Comparative Safety Data," Memorandum to Terrance Scanlon, chairman, Consumer Product Safety Commission, Mar. 11, 1988; see also Heiden, Testimony before the Subcommittee on Commerce, Feb. 29, 1990.

121. Nick Marchika, "All-Terrain Vehicles (ATV)," Memorandum to the Commission, Consumer Product Safety Commission, July 9, 1984.

122. "Punitive Damages Awarded" 1989.

123. *McKinley* v. *Honda Motor Co. Ltd.*, Ohio, Summit County Court of Common Pleas, 81-CV-10-2674, May 25, 1984, p. 110.

related to the use of all-terrain vehicles and began investigating the product, which stimulated unfavorable publicity. In a number of public appearances, Stuart Statler, one of the CPSC commissioners, emphasized the hazardous nature of ATV operation.

In 1984 a local television station manager in Baton Rouge, Louisiana, contacted the producers of ABC's "20/20" program after his child and a friend were both seriously injured in ATV accidents. A media segment was prepared alleging that ATVs were extremely hazardous. This segment aired in April 1985 on "20/20" and constituted the first national media coverage of the topic.

Also in April 1985 the CPSC decided to make ATV safety a priority project and created the ATV Task Force to coordinate the commission's ATV-related activity. An advanced notice of proposed rulemaking (ANPR) was issued by the CPSC in May 1985.

The first evidence of legislative interest in ATV safety occurred at a congressional hearing in May 1985. Industry experts, representatives of rider associations, and several Republican congressmen defended the vehicles as not posing an unreasonable risk to riders. Testimony from families of injured users, safety advocates, and public health experts alleged that the risks were unreasonable because of the ATV's deceptively safe appearance and the especially great hazard that vehicle operation posed to children. Several Democratic congressmen criticized the CPSC for failing to take stronger actions to mitigate the hazard. The commission later held public hearings in six cities around the country, thus keeping the issue of ATV safety in the limelight.

Industry sources indicate that the series of publicized events in the spring of 1985 had a chilling effect on ATV sales. As shown in figure 4-4, the decline in sales of three-wheeled vehicles was especially pronounced, though a decline in total ATV sales also occurred. While some of this decline in sales may reflect a product's normal life cycle, it is widely believed that heightened consumer concern about safety, sparked by adverse publicity, curtailed consumer demand for all-terrain vehicles.

The ATV Task Force undertook epidemiologic, engineering, human factor, medical, and economic analyses of ATVs. The result was a 14,000-page study, released in September 1986. The key finding was the agreement of both the medical and engineering directorates that ATV operation is extremely hazardous because the vehicle is prone to overturn even under normal operating conditions by unimpaired riders.

The ATV Task Force also monitored industry efforts to educate and train riders and the possible development of a voluntary standard. The

Task Force had strongly encouraged the industry to develop safety standards for ATVs. After two years of such meetings, the CPSC commissioners sent a letter to the SVIA in March 1987 expressing frustration over industry inertia in the standard-setting process.[124] During this period industry experts had voiced strenuous technical objections to the course of the CPSC's investigation.

Despite the absence of new safety standards, ATV manufacturers gradually altered the vehicles' design in many ways. While the original ATV models were suspended only by the seat and the low pressure and large size of the tires, manufacturers began adding front and rear mechanical suspensions to many of the vehicles in the mid-1980s; nearly all vehicles had full mechanical suspensions by 1987.

The marketing of more and more models with four wheels—and marked declines in sales of three-wheeled models—began in 1984. Whereas 473,000 three-wheelers were sold in 1984, only 12,000 were sold in 1987, a decline from 74 percent to only 3 percent of industry sales (see figure 4-4).[125] Industry experts have contended that the switch to four-wheeled vehicles was caused by "market factors" (such as consumer desire for improved ride) and that safety was not a consideration.[126] For example, Suzuki introduced its four-wheeled model well before the alleged safety hazards of ATVs had received national publicity. The addition of mechanical suspensions may also reflect in part consumer demand for an easier ride. The CPSC staff nonetheless regard the introduction of four-wheeled vehicles and the addition of mechanical suspensions among the most important improvements in ATV safety that have so far taken place.[127]

Injury rates are very high among those inexperienced at ATV operation.[128] The CPSC estimated that during the first month of ATV use the new rider is more than ten times more likely to be injured than more experienced riders.[129] To reduce the incidence of injuries among inexperienced riders, the SVIA announced its intention to train 42,000 riders by the end of 1985. By that time, however, it had trained only 4,000–5,000 ATV users. The SVIA found there was a decided lack of interest in hands-on training among ATV users.

124. Commissioners of the Consumer Product Safety Commission, Letter to Alvin Isley, president, Specialty Vehicles Industry Association, Mar. 30, 1987.
125. Jones-Smith, Statement before the Subcommittee on Commerce, Feb. 28, 1990.
126. William Willens, "NBC Nightly News," videotape, Dec. 30, 1986.
127. Personal interviews with Roy Deppa, Nick Marchica, Gregory Rogers, Robert Wright, and Wade Allen.
128. DeLisle, Laberge-Nadeau, and Brown 1988; Adams 1986.
129. Newman 1987.

In December 1986 the commissioners voted to accept the recommendations of the ATV Task Force concerning the need to work with consumer groups, state governments, and the industry to improve safety warnings, promote training, discourage alcohol use and the carrying of passengers, and encourage helmet use. They also accepted the need for a vehicle performance standard, which might compel improved vehicle suspension, and a ban on the sale of three-wheelers. The single Task Force proposal that was not accepted was the recommendation to prohibit ATV use by children under twelve. The commissioners voted to turn the case over to the Department of Justice to explore the possibility of legal action against the ATV distributors.

More bad publicity ensued in the first several months of 1987. *People* magazine published a piece on February 23, 1987, that highlighted the case of Bob Vance, a thirteen-year-old who sustained multiple abdominal injuries when he was operating his new Honda ATV on Christmas Day 1982.[130] The report was prompted by the interest of John Saar, managing editor at the time, who learned of the problem when he read about the accident in a newspaper article. The article noted that the team of attorneys representing the Vances in their liability suit were also involved in approximately 400 other ATV injury cases.

The third significant media piece was "The Most Dangerous Vehicle," which aired on "60 Minutes" on April 12, 1987. A serious injury to the close friend of a CBS cameraman spurred "60 Minutes" to investigate the issue. The *People* and "60 Minutes" staffs both received much assistance from the CPSC and from plaintiff attorneys in developing their pieces.

On December 30, 1987, a preliminary consent decree was announced, and in April 1988 a final consent decree between the ATV distributors and the Justice Department was approved by Judge Gerhard Gesell.[131] Under the terms of these consent decrees, the manufacturers were obligated to

—stop selling three-wheeled ATVs;

—send safety alerts and warnings (but no refunds) to past ATV purchasers;

—place prominent posters at ATV dealers' showrooms and warnings on the vehicles;

130. Plummer 1987.
131. *United States* v. *American Honda Motor Co.*, Preliminary Consent Decree, Dec. 30, 1987; *United States* v. *American Honda Motor Co.*, Final Consent Decree, Apr. 27, 1988.

—provide additional specified safety information at dealerships;

—market only 70–90 cc ATVs to those twelve to fifteen years of age, and only models of less than 70 cc displacement to children under twelve;

—develop improved owner manuals;

—adhere to new CPSC regulations covering distributor advertising practices;

—implement a $8.5 million safety awareness campaign for magazines and television;

—provide free, hands-on training to purchasers and their family members if the ATV was bought after December 1986; and

—develop a voluntary standard for safer vehicle design that would be acceptable to the CPSC.

The failure of the consent decree to provide refunds or require a recall of three-wheelers was sharply criticized,[132] and it prompted the development of legislation requiring refunds.[133] The legislation never came to a vote in either house of Congress.

Over 40 percent of ATV-related deaths and injuries have occurred to children under sixteen. Children—particularly fourteen-to-fifteen-year-olds—have a higher injury rate (per number of vehicles in use) than adults. Many parents have purchased three-wheeled ATVs for their children, possibly deceived by their benign appearance (tricycles with big wheels).[134] ATV industry advertising may have supported this notion by giving the impression that all-terrain vehicles are safe and fun. In response to criticism of their advertising, industry officials have emphasized that ATVs are safe and fun when operated properly—as evidenced by the satisfying experiences of millions of users.

Physicians who care for children and ATV victims, a state attorney general's task force, and consumer groups have argued that elementary school children are not physically mature enough, and adolescents are not emotionally mature enough to operate ATVs safely.[135] While the

132. See testimonies of A. Graham, commissioner, Consumer Product Safety Commission; W. J. M. Cody, attorney general, State of Tennessee; R. M. Narkewicz, president, American Academy of Pediatrics; and S. A. Weiss, legislative representative, Consumer Federation of America, at a hearing on All-Terrain Vehicle Safety before the Subcommittee on Commerce, Consumer Protection, and Competitiveness of the House Committee on Energy and Commerce, Mar. 16, 1988.

133. "The ATV User Safety and Equity Act," H.R. 3991, 100 Cong. 2 sess. (GPO, 1988).

134. Golladay and others 1985.

135. C. Blechschmidt, "Comments on All-Terrain Vehicle Voluntary Standard," CPSC Memorandum, Apr. 11, 1989; Testimony of W. J. M. Cody, attorney general, State of

ATV Task Force recommended prohibiting ATV use by children under twelve,[136] the commissioners did not accept this recommendation. In fact, over 95 percent of ATV-related injuries to children under sixteen have occurred on adult-sized vehicles. Unfortunately, reliable data are not available to demonstrate how the injury rate for children operating small ATVs compares with either the injury rate for children riding adult-sized ATVs or the adult injury rate. The CPSC did accept the recommendation to discourage children from using adult-size vehicles.

Of the five ATV manufacturers, two (Polaris and Kawasaki) never produced the smaller ATVs. Honda and Yamaha ceased marketing the child-sized vehicles in 1988. Suzuki discontinued its 50 cc model (for younger children) in 1987 but still markets the LT80 Quadrunner for the adolescent age group. Thus, by 1988, only one model was still being marketed for adolescents, and no all-terrain vehicles were produced for the under-twelve age group. Unfortunately, there is evidence of poor dealer compliance with the requirement to discourage the purchase of adult-sized ATVs for children.[137] In compliance with the consent decree, the ATV industry has undertaken an ambitious program of driver training through the ATV Safety Institute of the SVIA. This program began in late 1988, and by the latter half of 1989 training was occurring at the rate of 40,000 riders annually. As the consent decree dictates, not only is the training offered free of charge but also riders and their family members are provided with a $50 incentive to undertake the full-day course. This program is likely to cost the industry $10–$20 million a year.

A voluntary standard developed by the industry was approved by a 2 to 1 vote of the CPSC commissioners in December 1988.[138] The standard includes performance requirements for service and parking brakes, front and rear suspension, standardized control locations, handlebar design, operator foot environment, tires, front and rear lighting, and a speed governor for youth vehicles. In fact, the standard provoked little change in vehicle design, since by 1988 nearly all the ATVs were already in compliance with this standard.

Most controversial have been the agreements relating to ATV stability.

Tennessee, and R. M. Narkewicz, president, American Academy of Pediatrics, at a hearing on All-Terrain Vehicle Safety.

136. Consumer Product Safety Commission 1986.

137. G. T. Ford, "Final Report on Undercover Investigation of ATV Dealers," CPSC Memorandum, Nov. 1989.

138. "Four-Wheel All-Terrain Vehicles." ANSI/SVIA-1-1990. Standard for 4-Wheeled All-Terrain Vehicles. American National Standard Institute, Feb. 1, 1990; Approval of Voluntary Standard for All-Terrain Vehicles. *Federal Register* 54 (1989): 1407–28.

Using the static measure of pitch stability, the standard is less stringent than that recommended by the CPSC engineers. In the critical area of lateral stability, no standard was proposed. Instead, the industry offered to spend eighteen months in an effort to develop a "dynamic" measure of lateral stability, arguing that a static standard is not meaningful for a rider-active vehicle. The CPSC's engineering directorate, which preferred a static measure, expressed skepticism about the reliability of any dynamic standard.[139] At the end of the eighteen-month period, no dynamic standard had been proposed. While expressing frustration about the rate of progress, the CPSC chairperson, Jacqueline Jones-Smith, has discouraged consumers from judging vehicle stability with static values, stating that they have not been shown to be correlated with real-world experience of injury.[140]

Important legal ground may be broken with the April 1989 verdict in the case of *Oberg* v. *Honda*.[141] Besides alleging failure of notice and warning of vehicular instability, the plaintiff alleged negligent product development because the usual safety testing done before and after marketing had not been done for ATVs. The plaintiff was awarded $5 million in punitive damages, although the case is now under appeal.

The most recent development in the ATV story is the decision of two of the manufacturers to curtail their roles in the ATV market. In the 1990 model year Kawasaki primarily marketed ATV models for farm, forestry, and work-related purposes, although some models are still appropriate for recreational use. Honda, the originator and dominant producer for nearly two decades, marketed only two models.

In summary, I consider the main forces that may have contributed to the observed decline in ATV-related injuries.

Decline in sales. Much of the decline in ATV sales was provoked by consumer concern about ATV safety. The primary factor was the adverse publicity in large audiences of potential customers that resulted from the national media pieces. The effect of these stories was probably amplified by the common practice of local media to follow up stories that prestigious national media outlets initiate. CPSC regulation and the tort system also

139. R. Deppa, "Report on the Engineering Meetings with Industry to Develop a Voluntary Standard for All-Terrain Vehicles," in C. Blechschmidt, "Voluntary Standards for All-Terrain Vehicles," CPSC Memorandum, Oct. 5, 1988, pp. B-1–10.

140. Letter from J. Jones-Smith, chairperson, CPSC, to Congressman Douglas Barnard, Jr., June 22, 1990.

141. *Oberg* v. *Honda Motor Co.*, Oregon, Multnomah County Circuit Court, A80709-05897, Apr. 28, 1989.

played an important subsidiary role in the adverse publicity. Plaintiff attorneys and their experts provided technical assistance to the media in developing these stories, as did the CPSC staff. Stuart Statler, a CPSC commissioner from 1979 to 1986, made many public statements that attracted media attention. Interestingly, the decline in sales of ATVs has probably cost the industry far more in forgone revenues than the combined costs of product liability suits and safety standards.

Notice and warning of ATV instability. The owner manuals and other industry-sponsored educational materials have always provided instructions on how to operate ATVs safely, including warnings against many unsafe riding practices. They have also warned consumers about the need to wear helmets and refrain from riding when inebriated. Since ATV manufacturers and distributors do not believe the vehicle is unstable, they have not made any specific warnings about vehicular instability. The CPSC did publish a variety of consumer alerts and warnings about ATV safety before the consent decree required more conspicuous warnings. The warnings in the consent decree are especially important because they reach earlier ATV purchasers and provide for highly specific safety information to be displayed prominently by the dealer.

Front and rear suspension. Though the industry has denied that safety was a motivating factor, mechanical suspensions appeared on more and more ATV models through the mid-1980s. It is difficult to isolate a single influence on the industry that motivated this modification. Market factors may have been an influence, since vehicle size and power was increasing through the period and lack of suspension is more uncomfortable for riders on the larger vehicles. It is likely, however, that safety concerns were significant in prompting the change, as suspension of the smaller vehicles also improved. Since the importance of adequate suspension has been emphasized by plaintiff expert witnesses and the CPSC's engineering directorate, it is possible that both liability and regulatory concerns contributed to the change.

Demise of the three-wheeled vehicle. The decline and ultimate discontinuation of the three-wheeled ATV was certainly motivated, at least in part, by the highly publicized safety concerns. Media coverage of ATV safety emphasized this aspect of vehicle design. Fear of liability may have been a minor consideration, since the importance of the fourth wheel was stressed by plaintiff experts. Although the CPSC also emphasized the importance of the fourth wheel to vehicular stability, industry was already well along in the "demarketing" of the three-wheeled model before the ATV Task Force report was published in September 1986. By failing to require refunds for owners of existing three-wheelers, the CPSC chose not to take an action that might have removed many three-wheelers from the vehicle fleet.

Operator training. The CPSC has consistently emphasized operator training as an essential pro-safety activity. Requirements in the consent decree for aggressive follow-up of purchasers—along with financial incentives to appear at training sessions—have been instrumental in overcoming the lack of consumer interest in hands-on training. Whether training will have the desired effect of preventing injuries is currently unknown.

Operator age. The threat of bad publicity and tort liability suits rather than regulatory action prompted the ATV industry to abandon the child and adolescent markets. The CPSC declined to take a leadership role on this issue. Media reports of injuries to children cause much greater outcry from the public than reports of injuries to adults, and the same effect can be expected from juries.

Despite the significant improvements in ATV safety, problems remain. Increasing engine size, which is a strong predictor of injury risk, has not been deterred by any of the pro-safety forces. Many children are still using adult-sized ATVs. There is no national consensus about whether ATVs, after safety improvements, present acceptable risks to users. That debate continues.

Summary of the Case Studies

The case studies establish that vehicle safety is enhanced by the interplay of consumer demand, regulation, liability, and professional responsibility. Each of these forces may be stimulated directly or indirectly by the mass media. To clarify the relative contribution of liability, my colleagues and I considered in each case whether liability was a necessary, sufficient, contributing, or insignificant cause of safety improvements.

The results of the causation analysis are presented in table 4-3. Although our judgment was used to assess the causative roles, we believe the cases have been written in a way that also allows readers to make their own judgments. In a strictly scientific sense, no one knows what factors were decisive because a controlled experiment (natural or otherwise) has not been conducted.

In no case did we conclude that liability considerations were necessary to stimulate a specific safety improvement. In other words, other factors would eventually have led to the safety improvement. A case can be made,

Table 4-3. *The Causes of Auto Safety Improvements as Found in Five Case Studies*[a]

Case study and safety improvement factor	Necessary condition	Sufficient condition	Contributory factor	Insignificant factor
Inadvertent vehicle movement				
1980 Ford design change			C,R,L,P	
1981 mailing to Ford owners	R	R		C,L,P
Fuel tank design				
1977 design change (Pinto)		R,L	C,P	
1977 recall	R	R	L,P	
Pinto sales decline			C,R,L	P
The Jeep CJ				
1979 design change		L	C,P	R
Sales decline			C,L	R,P
Wrangler design			C,L,P	R
Occupant restraint design				
Air bags	R		C,P	L
Rear-seat shoulder belts		R,L	C,P	
Phaseout of window shades			L,P	C,R
All-terrain vehicle				
Sales decline		C	R,L	P
Notice and warnings		R	L,P	C
Vehicle suspension			C,R,L,P	
Four wheels		C	P,L,R	
Operator training	R	R		L,C,P
Less marketing to children		C	L	R,P

a. C = Consumer demand for improved safety
R = Regulation
L = Liability considerations
P = Professional responsibility standards.

however, that liability will sometimes result in more rapid safety improvements than would occur in the absence of liability. For example, the installation of rear-seat shoulder belts and the phaseout of belt tension relievers may have been hastened by liability considerations.

For some safety improvements, we determined that liability considerations were sufficient causes of the safety improvement. In other words, liability risk was enough to cause the safety improvement even if factors such as consumer demand, regulation, and professional responsibility had not been operative.

Our most frequent conclusion was that liability was a contributing factor in achieving safety improvements. By this we mean that liability worked in conjunction with other factors to produce safety improvements. Interestingly, our cases suggest that the indirect effect of liability on consumer demand—operating through adverse publicity about a product's safety and a manufacturer's reputation—is often the most significant contribution of liability to safety. The direct financial costs of liability are usually a relatively minor factor, at least from the perspective of large manufacturers.

The case studies address only the factors that cause safety improvements. We leave it to others to conduct a cost-benefit analysis of the design modifications, declines in product sales, and discontinuation of troubled product lines that may be caused by product liability.

Conclusion

In this final section I assess the impact of product liability on safety, summarize the findings of our analysis of the forces promoting safety in the auto industry, and suggest ways that legislators can improve motor vehicle safety.

Assessing the Overall Effect of Product Liability on Safety

The strength of the case studies is that they allow historical analysis of the factors that contributed to specific safety improvements.[142] Recall that the case studies were selected for examination because advocates of liberalized liability law have suggested that they demonstrate the pro-safety effects of product liability. Although our analysis suggests that liability is sometimes a contributing pro-safety factor, the case studies do not provide any indication of the magnitude of the influence of liability on safety. It would be useful to know, for example, whether the growth of design litigation since the 1968 *Larsen* case contributed to the decline in the death rates of passenger car occupants during the 1970s and 1980s.

To make an overall estimate of the effect of liability on vehicle safety, we estimated a time-series model of passenger car occupant fatalities for the years 1950 to 1988. The multivariate regression equation, summarized in the appendix, extends previous work in the economics literature by adding a surrogate for product liability and extending the time series through the 1980s.[143]

If liability was a major beneficial factor in determining the safety of

142. The analysis in this section was performed with the assistance of Bei Hung-Chang of the Harvard Injury Control Center. We thank Jerry Mashaw for providing us a copy of the student paper written by Bert Wells. We also thank Robert Crandall for providing several useful suggestions.

143. Crandall and others 1986.

passenger cars, we expected the product liability surrogate to be negatively associated with the death rate. In fact, the association was positive and statistically insignificant. Our inference is that any beneficial impact of liability is too small and subtle to be detected in such an aggregate analysis of death rates. It is also possible that the beneficial effects of liability are masked by certain adverse effects of liability that Mackay examines in chapter 5.

The regression analysis suggests that the main factors causing improved passenger safety since World II have been consumer demand (stimulated by rising incomes), construction of the highly safe interstate highway system (where the amount of travel has grown enormously), and vehicle regulation (in the form of the NHTSA safety standards). These trends have more than offset the hazards of rising alcohol consumption, increased truck traffic, faster travel speeds, and the passage of the baby boom generation through the teenage driving years.

In summary, trends in product liability law appear to have had an insignificant influence on passenger car death rates compared with other major forces. Since the surrogate for product liability was constructed without the benefit of precise data, the results should be interpreted with caution.

Findings

Our analysis of pro-safety forces in the motor vehicle industry led us to the following conclusions.

—The expected liability of vehicle manufacturers per injury has grown significantly from 1950 to 1990 because of the liberalization of product liability law, particularly the growth of lawsuits that allege defective vehicle design. The emergence of "second collision" litigation has played an important role in the expanded liability of manufacturers.

—Product liability is one of several forces that induce manufacturers to consider making pro-safety decisions in the marketplace. The others are consumer demand, regulation, and professional responsibility. The interplay among these factors can create powerful incentives for pro-safety decisions, especially when the mass media draw attention to safety concerns.

—The case studies provide little evidence that expanded product liability risk was necessary to achieve the safety improvements that have been made. In the absence of liability risk, the combined effects of consumer demand, regulation, and professional responsibility would have been sufficient to achieve improved safety. In some cases, however, liability seemed to cause safety improvements to occur more quickly than they would have occurred in the absence of liability.

—Although product liability risk is rarely a necessary condition for improved vehicle safety, it is often a sufficient or contributing cause of safety improvements. The direct financial costs of product liability that are borne by manufacturers (that is, litigation costs, settlements, and jury awards) are usually less salient than the potential damages to the product's or manufacturer's reputation. Manufacturers strive to avoid the adverse reputational consequences that highly publicized liability actions can produce. By reducing injuries and the resulting liability actions, manufacturers protect their reputation in the marketplace.

—Although the case studies suggest that product liability considerations are sometimes a pro-safety factor, there is no evidence that expanded liability for design choices has been a significant cause of the passenger safety improvements witnessed since World War II. The chief beneficial forces have been consumer demand stimulated by rising per capita incomes, construction of the modern interstate highway system, and the NHTSA's early wave of motor vehicle safety standards.

—By mobilizing public attention, the mass media magnify the effect of pro-safety forces on vehicle manufacturers. The case studies reveal that the liability system in particular often stimulates media coverage of safety concerns. One limitation of the media's role is that they often highlight relatively infrequent, isolated safety hazards (if they can be portrayed in a compelling fashion) while neglecting widespread safety problems (that may be more difficult to convey through electronic and print media).

—Consumer demand for vehicle safety has historically been latent or sluggish, but the cases show that it can be stimulated through information. The more recent case studies suggest that some consumers are becoming sensitive about safety, and this has caused manufacturers to compete vigorously for a pro-safety reputation.

—The process of vehicle safety regulation by the federal government has weakened over the past twenty years. The case studies indicate that the regulation of vehicle safety problems are often spotty, weak, slow, or nonexistent. At the same time, vehicle safety regulation has proved highly effective in certain circumstances and can provide manufacturers and safety advocates a more predictable and technically sound forum to resolve safety issues.

—The case studies demonstrate that vehicle manufacturers sometimes delayed making seemingly feasible pro-safety design modifications. The liability system may contribute to such delays by creating fears among manufacturing management that design improvements will be used by plaintiff attorneys and juries as evidence that prior designs were defective. Hence the behavioral incentives created by product liability are not always pro-safety.

Implications for Reform Legislation

If legislators are primarily concerned about improving motor vehicle safety, the evidence here suggests that two strategies are particularly promising: provision of better safety information to consumers and a revitalized federal regulatory process. Since consumer demand for vehicle safety appears to be increasing, Congress should take any feasible steps that will provide consumers with more understandable and accurate information about the relative safety of vehicles. Such information, possibly through a new safety-rating system for new cars, could harness competitive forces in the pursuit of safety. Where consumer safety information is difficult to produce or impossible to understand, the National Highway Traffic Safety Administration should be expected to enact prompt and technically sound safety standards. Congress should consider rewarding the NHTSA's recent aggressiveness in standard setting with additional resources to initiate research and standards on a broader array of safety problems.

The NHTSA's standard-setting process is sometimes throttled by intense opposition from individual manufacturers or the entire industry. It is very difficult for the NHTSA to design sound safety standards without the benefit of industry's technical cooperation. One way to discourage industry opposition to standard setting would be to provide limited relief from product liability when design decisions comply with specific federal safety standards. The relief should be limited to punitive damages because it is useful to retain adverse publicity and economic damages as incentives for manufacturers to provide greater safety than is required by minimum federal standards.[144] It may, however, be good for safety in the long run if manufacturers could expect that more federal standards would result in fewer punitive damage awards against manufacturers. The case studies suggest that the application of punitive damage awards is currently unpredictable and may therefore contribute little to improved design.

To promote the safety-enhancing effects of product liability, Congress should investigate the consequences of two reform strategies. First, the

---

144. Jonathan Wiener, special assistant to Richard B. Stewart, assistant attorney general, Land and Natural Resources Division, U.S. Department of Justice, personal communication, Apr. 6, 1990.

power of judges to insist on confidentiality about settlements should be reexamined to determine whether all protected information is relevant to the proprietary interests of businesses or the privacy of plaintiffs.[145] Confidentiality has the potentially perverse effect of limiting the amount of adverse publicity directed at vehicles and manufacturers that are involved in settlements. It is precisely this kind of adverse publicity that can effectively punish firms which have not made the effort to enhance vehicle safety. Second, Congress should take steps to reinvigorate the doctrine of subsequent remedial measures. Tort law should reward, not penalize, those manufacturers that promptly correct design defects and practice safety innovation. The case studies suggest that manufacturers may be inclined to delay design improvements when they fear that improvements will be used against them.

Our analysis of legislative options has considered only the question of how motor vehicle safety might be enhanced through legislation. A complete policy analysis should also examine the potential costs of these suggestions and their ultimate political feasibility.

Appendix: The Multivariate Statistical Model of Passenger Car Occupant Death Rates in the United States, 1950–88

The dependent variable, *CARDEATHS*, is the annual number of passenger car occupant fatalities divided by the estimated number of miles traveled by passenger cars. This death rate has been steadily declining throughout the post–World War II period.

The independent variables include *SPEED* (the average recorded speed on main rural highways), *INTERSTATE* (the proportion of vehicle miles traveled on interstate highways), *TRUCK* (the proportion of miles traveled accounted for by trucks), *REGULATION* (the proportion of vehicles in the fleet that are model year 1968 or later), *UNEMPLOYMENT* (percentage unemployment among working-age adults as a surrogate for the business cycle), *PINCOME* (per capita real consumption expenditures as a surrogate for permanent income), *ALCOHOL* (per capita alcohol consumption), and *LIABILITY* (an index constructed to reflect the penetration of vehicles into the fleet whose design may have been influenced by liability risk).

Since all the variables except *LIABILITY* are explained elsewhere in the economics literature, the focus here is on the liability index. We used information on the annual number of reported crashworthiness cases obtained

---

145. Kolbert 1990; see also Weinstein 1989.

through a LEXIS search by Bert Wells of the Yale Law School.[146] The case counts were then used to construct an annual liability index that reflects product life cycles in the auto industry. For purposes of sensitivity analysis, we estimated the regression equation using three versions of the liability index. *LIABILITY1* is simply an annual count of reported cases. *LIABILITY2* is *LIABILITY1* lagged four years to account for lead time in design decisions. *LIABILITY3* is *LIABILITY2* adjusted for the slow rate at which new vehicles replace old vehicles in the fleet. More detail on the construction of these indexes is available from the author on request.

We used ordinary least squares methods to regress the natural logarithm of *CARDEATHS* on the independent variables. The independent variables are also expressed in logarithmic form unless the small case "l" does not precede the variable descriptor. Results are reported in table 4A-1.

Table 4A-1. *Estimates of the Passenger Car Death Rate Equation*

Independent variable[a]	Estimated coefficients[b]			
	(1)	*(2)*	*(3)*	*(4)*
Intercept	6.97	7.85	9.04	8.32
	(2.21)	(2.42)	(2.80)	(2.45)
lSPEED	0.96	1.11	1.02	1.16
	(2.18)	(2.39)	(2.41)	(2.42)
TRUCK	0.68	0.33	0.50	0.27
	(1.43)	(0.56)	(1.07)	(0.45)
INTERSTATE	−2.26	−2.40	−1.53	−2.08
	(−2.40)	(−2.52)	(−1.54)	(−2.18)
REGULATION	−0.44	−0.43	−0.46	−0.41
	(−2.84)	(−2.73)	(−3.06)	(−2.55)
UNEMPLOYMENT	−0.04	−0.04	−0.04	−0.04
	(−5.91)	(−5.98)	(−6.32)	(−5.88)
lALCOHOL	1.48	1.80	1.23	1.58
	(3.78)	(3.58)	(3.05)	(3.93)
lPINCOME	−0.88	−1.09	−1.15	−1.15
	(−2.78)	(−2.87)	(−3.37)	(−2.83)
LIABILITY1	. . .	0.0014	. . .	. . .
	. . .	(1.008)	. . .	. . .
LIABILITY2	. . .	. . .	0.0048	. . .
	. . .	. . .	(1.793)	. . .
LIABILITY3	. . .	. . .	. . .	0.0048)
	. . .	. . .	. . .	(1.06)
R^2	0.9886	0.9889	0.9897	0.9890

a. The dependent variable is lCARDEATHS.
b. The numbers in parentheses are *t*-statistics.

146. Wells 1986, A4.

References

Adams, B. E. 1986. "Trauma Caused by 3-Wheel Motor Vehicles—An Unrecognized Epidemic?" *Annuals of Emergency Medicine* 15:1288–92.

American Motors Corporation. 1986. "Methodological Problems in Measuring the Rollover Crash Risk."

Ciccone, M. A., and K. J. Wells. 1988. "Improper Shoulder Belt Use by Maryland Drivers." *Human Factors* 30:359–66.

Clark, L. 1990. "Ford 10-K Reveals Legal Headaches." *Automotive News*, Apr. 2.

Claybrook, J. 1985. Internal Memorandum to DOT Secretary Neil Goldschmidt, "Action: Ford Transmission Case," October 3, 1980. In *NHTSA Authorization and Means of Improving Highway Safety.* Hearing before the Senate Committee on Commerce, Science, and Transportation. 99 Cong. 1 sess. Government Printing Office.

———. 1989. "Seat-Belt Laws Help Save Our Lives." *USA Today*, Dec. 11:B11.

Consumer Product Safety Commission. 1986. "Report of the All-Terrain Vehicle Task Force, Regulatory Options for All-Terrain Vehicles." Washington.

Crandall, R. C., and others. 1986. *Regulating the Automobile*. Brookings.

Crandall, R. C., and J. D. Graham. 1984. "Automobile Safety Regulation and Offsetting Behavior: Some New Empirical Estimates." *American Economic Review* 74:328–31.

DeLisle, A., C. Laberge-Nadeau, and B. Brown. 1988. "Characteristics of Three-and Four-Wheeled All-Terrain Vehicle Accidents in Quebec." *Accident Analysis and Prevention* 20:357–66.

Dentzer, S. 1984. "The Product Liability Debate." *Newsweek*, Sept. 10:54–57.

Deppa, R. W. 1986. "Engineering Evaluation of the Safety of All-Terrain Vehicles." In Consumer Product Safety Commission, *All-Terrain Vehicle Task Force Report*, 154–209. Washington.

Dowie, M. 1977. "Pinto Madness." *Mother Jones*, Sept.–Oct.:18–32.

Eads, G., and P. Reuter. 1983. *Designing Safer Products: Corporate Responses to Product Liability Law and Regulation.* R-3022-ICJ. Santa Monica, Calif.: Rand Corporation.

Eastman, J. W. 1984. *The American Automobile Industry and the Development of Automotive Safety, 1900–1966.* University Press of America.

Emshwiller, J. R. 1988. "Rollover Worry Plagues Utility Vehicles." *Wall Street Journal*, May 23.

Emshwiller, J. R., and C. B. Camp. 1988. "Out of Control: On and On Grinds Fight over Old Fords That Slip into Reverse." *Wall Street Journal*, Apr. 14:1.

Evans, L. 1986a. "Rear Seat Restraint System Effectiveness in Preventing Fatalities." GMR-5465. General Motors Research Department. June 24.

———. 1986b. "Rear Compared to Front Seat Restraint System Effectiveness in Preventing Fatalities." GMR-5603. General Motors Research Department. Oct. 30.

General Accounting Office. 1986. *Auto Safety: Effectiveness of Ford Transmission Settlement Still at Issue.* June.

Golladay, E. S., and others. 1985. "The Three Wheeler—A Menace to the Preadolescent Child." *Journal of Trauma* 25:232–33.

Graham, J. D. 1984. "Automobile Crash Protection: Institutional Responses to Self-Hazardous Behavior." In *Risk Analysis, Institutions, and Public Policy,* edited by Susan G. Hadden, 39–58. Port Washington, N.Y.: Associated Faculty Press.

———. 1989. *Auto Safety: Assessing America's Performance.* Dover, Mass.: Auburn House.

Graham, J. D., and M. Henrion. 1984. "A Probabilistic Analysis of the Passive-Restraint Question." *Risk Analysis* 4:25–40.

Highway Loss Data Institute. 1981. *Injury Claim Frequency Results by Size of Claim—Vans, Pickups, and Utility Vehicles, 1977–1980 Models.*

Insurance Institute for Highway Safety. 1980. "NHTSA's '73 Rollover Rulemaking Was Dropped." *The Highway Loss Reduction Status Report,* Dec. 22. Ann Arbor, Mich.

Isikoff, M. 1985. "The Jeep Grinds to a Halt—CJ to Be Phased Out." *Washington Post,* Nov. 28:F1.

Kahn, H. 1990a. "Supreme Court Gives Automakers a Break on Air-Bag Cases." *Automotive News,* Apr. 9:6.

———. 1990b. "Jury Exonerates GM on Window-Shade Belts." *Automotive News,* July 2:40.

———. 1990c. "Class Action Seeks Cash, Removal of Jeep CJs from the Road." *Automotive News,* July 9:6.

Karr, A. R. 1982a. "American Motors Starts a Counterattack on the Studies That Say Jeeps Are Unsafe." *Wall Street Journal,* Feb. 23:37.

———. 1982b. "Driver Not to Blame in Roll-over Wreak of Jeep, Judge Says." *Wall Street Journal,* Apr. 28:12.

Kolbert, E. 1990. "Chief Judge of New York Urges Less Secrecy in Civil Settlements." *New York Times,* June 20:A1.

Kurylko, D. T. 1990. "Three Consumer Groups Ask Recall for Jeep CJ Models." *Automotive News,* July 2:6.

McCarthy, R. L., J. A. Padmanaban, and R. M. Ray. [n.d.] "An Analysis of the Safety-Related Impact of 'Comfort Feature' Introduction in GM Vehicles." Failure Analysis Associates, Palo Alto, Calif.

Mashaw, J. L., and D. L. Harfst. 1987. "Regulation and Legal Culture: The Case of Motor Vehicle Safety." *Yale Journal on Regulation* 4:257–316.

———. 1990. *The Struggle for Auto Safety.* Harvard University Press.

Motorcycle Industry Council. 1988. "Manufacturers Shipment Reporting System, Annual Statistical Report, 1972–1987." Irvine, Calif.

Motor Vehicle Manufacturers Association. Annual. *Motor Vehicle Facts and Figures.* Detroit.

Murphy, J. 1990. "Rolling Over for Detroit." *Public Citizen,* Jan.–Feb:10.

National Highway Traffic Safety Administration, Office of Defects Investigation Enforcement. 1978. "Investigation Report (Phase I)." C7-38. Washington.

———. 1988. "Issue Paper on Tension Relief Devices Used to Provide Seat Belt Slack." June 1.

———. 1989. *Rear Seat Lap Shoulder Belts in Passenger Cars.* Preliminary Regulatory Evaluation. Apr.

National Transportation Safety Board. 1986. *Safety Study: Performance of Lap Belts in 26 Frontal Crashes.* Bureau of Accident Investigation, Washington, July 28.

Newman, R. 1987. "Hazard Analysis: Analysis of All-Terrain Vehicle Related Injuries and Deaths." Consumer Product Safety Commission, Directorate for Epidemiology. Washington.

O'Neill, B. 1986. "The Influence of Regulation, the Marketplace, and Product Liability on New Technologies for Vehicle Safety." Paper presented at the Tort and Insurance Practice Section, American Bar Association. May 8–9.

Parsons, G. G. 1983. *Evaluation of Federal Motor Vehicle Safety Standard 301-75, Fuel System Integrity: Passenger Cars.* National Highway Traffic Safety Administration.

Peterson, M. A. 1987. *Civil Juries in the 1980s: Trends in Jury Trials and Verdicts in California and Cook County, Illinois.* R-3466-ICJ. Santa Monica, Calif.: Rand Corporation.

Plummer, W. 1987. "Trouble on Three Wheels." *People Weekly,* Feb. 23:28–32.

"Punitive Damages Awarded against an All-Terrain Vehicle Manufacturer." 1989. *ATLA Law Report,* Nov. 1989:412–13.

Sawyers, A. 1990. "Changing Tastes: Safety, Once a Pariah, Gains Favor in Ads and With Buyers." *Automotive News,* June 4.

Snyder, R. G., and others. 1980. "On Road Crash Experience of Utility Vehicles: Final Technical Report." Ann Arbor, Mich.: Insurance Institute for Highway Safety.

Specialty Vehicle Institute of America. *Tips for the ATV Rider: An Atventure in Safety.* Costa Mesa, Calif.

Templin, N. 1990. "Ford Settles Big Lap-Belt Injury Suit." *Wall Street Journal,* Apr. 5:B1.

Teret, S. 1981. "Injury Control and Product Liablity," *Journal of Public Health Policy* 2:49–57.

———. 1986. "Litigating for the Public's Health." *American Journal of Public Health* 76:1027–29.

Teret, S. P., and M. Jacobs. 1986. "Prevention and Torts: The Role of Litigation in Injury Control." *Law, Medicine, and Health Care* 17:17–22.

Weinstein, J. B. 1989. "After Fifty Years of the Federal Rules of Civil Procedure: Are the Barriers to Justice Being Raised?" *University of Pennsylvania Law Review* 137:1901–23.

Wells, B. 1986. "The Product Liability System as a Coercive Force for the Production of Safer Automobiles." Yale Law School, Spring 1986.

Zola, D. 1986. "Ford Stresses Safety in New Ad Campaign." *Automotive News,* Dec. 1:14.

CHAPTER FIVE

Liability, Safety, and Innovation in the Automotive Industry

Murray Mackay

THIS CHAPTER explores the relationships that have existed, or are claimed to have existed, among liability, safety, and innovation in the car industry over the last thirty years. To do so requires tracing the evolution of product liability litigation since the 1960s, when new concepts of strict liability were first introduced into traditional tort law. From those early beginnings, cases of liability for claimed defective design have mushroomed into an important industry. That is the first theme.

The second theme is the rise of the regulation of vehicle design. That also began in the 1960s after the National Highway Safety Act of 1966 opened the door to major regulatory activity—turning the car industry from an essentially free market as far as design was concerned into a business in which passing the regulations became a dominant prerequisite.

The third theme is the changing nature of the car industry and how that influences innovation. During the 1960s North America was a self-contained market, dominated by the big-four manufacturers, General Motors, Ford, Chrysler, and American Motors. Apart from that funny little bug, the Volkswagen Beetle, imported cars were for quirky enthusiasts only. In the last twenty years, however, the industry has changed worldwide. It has become internationalized; the rise of Japanese and German products has confounded the traditional relationships; and designs are now conceived for global markets, with joint ventures blurring the traditional rivalries. One-third of the U.S. market now consists of imports or transplants.

These three themes of liability, regulation, and the evolution of the car industry must be considered in turn so as to discover any connections between them and safety and innovation. The task is difficult because innovation itself is hard to assess and impossible to measure. The chairman of Sony, Akio Morita, remarked that anyone can have a good idea. Turning it into a profitable industry is what real engineering is all about. Innovation in engineering is not like discoveries in pure science; it does not consist of sudden flashes of intuition but more often of the clever application of known ideas in a new way. So how innovative designs have been introduced into the business will have to be considered alongside the other evolving characteristics of car design and manufacture.

A word about sources. The background for this chapter, apart from published material, comes from personal contacts and knowledge of the industry for over a quarter-century. Since 1964 I have been conducting research into traffic accidents and injuries and the role of vehicle design in mitigating the frequency and severity of crashes and the subsequent trauma. This research has led to many communications with officials of the National Highway Traffic Safety Administration (NHTSA) and other rule-making bodies, particularly the European Commission and the British government's Department of Transport. And because it has published traffic safety research results for the last twenty-five years, the Birmingham University Accident Research Unit, where I work, has had many contacts with car manufacturers worldwide and has consulted on many safety-related design topics.

In researching this chapter, I used those contacts in government, industry, and litigation. Where possible, I asked for concrete examples to support an opinion, examples to show that, for instance, a particular design choice was made or a new development not used because of considerations of liability or regulation. Most of the people I talked with were open and honest in their opinions and about the facts supporting those opinions, but almost all, and particularly those in industry, stipulated one basic ground rule: no personal attribution.

As a result, I have had to be circumspect in quoting specific cases. And indeed, the nature of the subject precludes the normal specific attribution and quotation of sources. In the course of my research, I talked to senior engineers and directors, both current and retired, from General Motors, Ford, Chrysler, Volvo, Daimler Benz, Volkswagen, Rover, Honda, Toyota, Fiat, Peugeot-Renault, Rolls Royce, and Jaguar. I discussed the issues with suppliers, including Pilkingtons, Corning Glass, Vegla, Romer-Britax, Autoliv, Takata, and TRW. In government I met with past and present officials of the NHTSA, the European Commission, the U.K. Department of Transport, and Transport Canada. When opportunities arose, I examined the views of experienced plaintiff and defense counsel who had a background in trying and settling product liability claims, particularly those relating to safety design. I also obtained much information and help from advocates of consumer issues in the United States and Europe and from television and print journalists. In the following discussion of the issues relating liability to safety and innovation in the car industry, I try to portray objectively the relationships, real and perceived, between those areas.

The Rise of Liability for Defective Design

Many useful, scholarly reviews trace the evolution of strict liability in tort from the traditional negligence concepts of English common law to its current application to vehicle design in the United States.[1] This transition from the *caveat emptor* principles that governed English contract law for centuries toward strict liability, or *caveat vendor,* in the automobile world of today started first with accidents arising from defects in manufacturing. *Vandermark* v. *Maywood Bell* (a Ford dealership) was a case stemming from a 1958 collision in which there was a brake failure caused by the substandard manufacture of certain components. In 1964 the California Supreme Court ruled that Maywood Bell was liable for the accident in spite of a specific agreed warranty that "the dealer's obligation [is] limited to replacement, without charge . . . of such parts . . . acknowledged by Dealer to be defective. This warranty is expressly in lieu of all other warranties express or implied, and of all other obligations on the part of the Dealer."[2]

A similar case was decided in the New Jersey Supreme Court in 1962. In 1955 Helen Henningsen purchased a new Plymouth Plaza car from Bloomfield Motor Company, a dealer in New Jersey. A few days later, according to the driver, a loud noise came from the front of the car, which then veered sharply into a wall. Although no specific evidence was produced that any of the components of the car were defective, the court ruled that there was an implied warranty that an automobile is "reasonably suitable for use": "When a manufacturer puts a new automobile into the stream of trade and promotes its purchase by the public, an implied warranty that it is reasonably suitable for use as such accompanies it into the hands of the ultimate purchaser."[3] Thus, though no part was identified

---

1. Hoenig and Werber 1971; Schmidt and May 1979; Hulsen 1981; Hoenig 1981, 633.
2. Quoted in Huber 1989, 472.
3. Hoenig and Werber 1971, 585.

as defective, the court found against both the manufacturer—Chrysler—and the dealer. So the implied warranty for safety was passed from dealer to manufacturer.

In automobile manufacturing the identification of a defective part should technically be a fairly clear-cut issue. All parts in a mass-produced product are described and specified with great precision. At present, considering the number of vehicles on the roads, catastrophic component failures are extraordinarily rare. When they do occur and lead to a collision, the postcrash investigation may well be complex, but the technical issues are usually apparent. There may be an occlusion in a casting, a fatigue failure in a stressed component, or a missing lock-washer on a crucial bolt.

Thus manufacturing defects are an issue on which the laws in the United States do not greatly differ from those of Europe and the English-speaking world.[4] The introduction of strict liability instead of the higher level of proof required to find negligence coincided in the automobile world with the idea of liability for defective design. In contrast to defective manufacturing, the notion of liability for defective design is much more open-ended. It is this principle that distinguishes litigation in the United States from that of most other countries.[5]

Some early cases attempted to establish the principle of liability for defective design. In a 1964 collision, a Mr. Evans, driving his 1961 Chevrolet, died when he was broadsided by another car. The 1961 Chevrolet had an X-shaped frame in contrast to many other cars of the day that had box or ladder frames for the chassis. The widow brought a claim against General Motors on the theory that the frame of the car provided inadequate protection against a lateral impact. In engineering terms this case introduced much more difficult issues about the relationship of body design to injury potential and about what might constitute adequate as opposed to defective design. In the event, the United States Court of Appeals for the Seventh Circuit in 1966 agreed with the trial court that

> a manufacturer is not under a duty to make his automobile accident-proof or fool-proof, nor must he render the vehicle "more" safe where the danger to be avoided is obvious to all.
>
> Perhaps it would be desirable to require manufacturers to construct automobiles in which it would be safe to collide, but that would be a

4. Wittner 1990.
5. Babcock 1989.

legislation function, not an aspect of judicial interpretation of existing law.[6]

The principle of the duty to provide crashworthy design, however, was established in 1968 in *Larsen* v. *General Motors*, but only in the limited context of enhanced injury, an issue on which technical disagreement is likely. Larsen, the plaintiff, suffered severe injuries in a frontal collision, allegedly because the steering assembly was thrust rearward and upward during the crash to strike him on the head. He was not using a seat belt. He maintained that the rearward displacement of the steering shaft was greater than in other cars that had been designed to protect against such occurrences. It was further alleged that this design caused injuries that otherwise would not have been sustained, or that the design unreasonably exacerbated the severity of the injuries. The defendant, General Motors, argued that the law imposed no duty of care on a manufacturer to design a car that would be safe to occupy in the event of a collision.

In 1968 the Court of Appeals for the Eighth Circuit upheld the plaintiff's allegations. "Noting that 'automobiles are not made for the purpose of colliding with each other,' the *Larsen* court nevertheless recognized that collisions are a 'frequent and inevitable contingency of normal automobile use.' " A manufacturer should be under a duty "to use reasonable care in the design of its vehicle to avoid subjecting the user to an unreasonable risk of injury in the event of a collision."[7]

The court disclaimed any duty to design an accident-proof or foolproof vehicle or even one that floats on water. Liability was to be limited to those injuries that were actually enhanced by the defect:

Any design defect not causing the accident would not subject the manufacturer to liability for the entire damage, but the manufacturer should be liable for that portion of the damage or injury caused by the defective design over and above the damage or injury that probably would have occurred as a result of the impact or collision, absent in the defective design.[8]

Those words introduced the crashworthiness principle into automobile

---

6. Hoenig and Werber, 1971, 580.
7. Hoenig 1981, 637.
8. Hoenig 1981, 637.

design litigation. Among other things, they place an onerous burden on biomechanics and engineering specialists to accurately reconstruct the facts of a collision, the specific causes of the injuries, and the likely consequences of alternative designs on the performance of the car in that kind of collision and in the generality of other collisions.

These early cases have been cited at some length because they ushered in an era of enormous legal activity. Since the late 1960s the United States has witnessed a growth in claims for the consequences of alleged defective design that has no parallel in any other country. The language used in those cases is also of particular interest because it illustrates how general principles can run into difficulties when applied to specific cases. Unlike claims for other products, claims for defective design under strict liability conditions do not condemn the automobile per se, only some aspect of its design.

Now the reality in automotive design is that the final product is a compromise among a host of competing functions. There is normal use: the speed, acceleration, handling, comfort, carrying capacity for people and luggage, and maneuverability considerations. There is styling, appearance, and price. Then there are manufacturing issues of producibility and feasibility, access to raw materials, and reliability in use. And there is crashworthiness, which competes with all these other factors.

And what is adequate crashworthiness? The courts have ruled that meeting the federal regulations is no defense. The state of the art is defined differently in different jurisdictions in the United States.

In many states the burden is on the plaintiff to produce an alternative design that is feasible and economically practical. This can be done by getting an expert for the plaintiff to do original work; more commonly it is done by citing an alternative design used by another manufacturer. Such a technique is powerful and over the years, if liability is having an effect on the design process, must lead toward convergence and uniformity. Any design that is different is open to criticism; from the manufacturer's point of view safety must reside in conformity.

In other states an alternative design is not a legal necessity. Under strict liability doctrine the plaintiff must prove that (1) the product is both defective and unreasonably dangerous, (2) the defective condition was present when the product left the defendant's control, and (3) the defective condition is the proximate cause of the plaintiff's injuries. The standards set by the courts for defect and unreasonableness are shifting sands, varying with time and the specific issues. Two criteria are cited either separately or together: risk-benefit analysis and consumer expectations.

Risk-benefit analysis requires the jury to consider many factors in balancing the harmful characteristics of a design against a range of benefits. These factors are the usefulness and desirability of the product; the availability of other similar products that meet the same need but are safer; the likelihood of injury and its probable seriousness; public knowledge and expectation of danger, especially for established products; the avoidability of injury by careful use of the product (this addresses the effectiveness of instructions and warnings); and the practicality of eliminating the danger without seriously impairing the usefulness of the product or making it unduly expensive.[9] Such considerations place an onerous burden on a jury in technically complex cases.

Consumer expectation, the second criterion of defect or unreasonableness in design, is somewhat simpler. Here a product is defective or unreasonably dangerous if it fails to perform as an ordinary consumer would expect when the product is used in a reasonably foreseeable manner. In practice many states use a mixture of the two criteria in trying to set standards for defective design. A few examples of current issues relating to defining defective design will illustrate some of the difficulties that judges and juries face in arriving at verdicts.

The assumption of risk. No plaintiff's lawyer has claimed that the automobile in principle and as a whole is a defective product. That is not true for some other vehicles, the all-terrain vehicle (ATV) being an example. Three-wheeled ATVs became fashionable in the early 1980s, and millions were sold in the United States. Many accidents, often involving children too young to control a powered vehicle on the highway, occurred; now these vehicles are no longer sold in the United States, undoubtedly because of the aggressive pursuit of product liability claims. In effect, the judicial system was acting as the manager of a piece of social engineering. The courts ruled that the machines were so dangerous that no one should be able to buy one. Here the assumption of risk choice was removed from the individual.

That is not true for motorcycles, though epidemiological considerations suggest that the actual risks run may be as great. Here the rider assumes the risk; consumer expectations are that to ride a motorcycle, especially off road, is a high-risk activity, and hence the rider does not

9. *Byrns* v. *Riddell, Inc.*, 550 Pzd 1065 (Arizona, 1971).

have the right to expect the same level of protection as occurs in an automobile.

But what about subcompact cars? Newton's laws of motion are one set of laws against which there is no appeal. In a two-car collision the forces applied to the small car will inevitably be greater than those acting on the heavier car. How well established is the assumption of risk in this case? To what level of greater risk is it reasonable for a manufacturer to go in offering better utility in other dimensions? To have a car that will park in a twelve-foot space, give forty-five miles to the gallon, and carry two adults and two young children is an attractive proposition. Yet the crashworthiness of such a vehicle in some types of two-car collisions will be less than that of a heavier car. Here the assumption of risk is not nearly so easy to define.

Vans and multipurpose vehicles. The marketplace demands vehicles that have a range of different utilities. Forward-control vehicles, those box-shaped vans of the 1970s, gave an efficient combination of carrying capacity, small overall dimensions, and high sitting position. In terms of crashworthiness, by sitting high up the occupants were well protected against life-threatening injuries to the head, neck, and chest compared with occupants of passenger cars, where the lower sitting position takes the head and chest into the crush zone in severe collisions. But because the occupants of vans sat ahead of the front axle line, their lower limbs were arguably more exposed to the risk of injury. How does one assess the relative merits of such designs in the context of high-speed crashes and severe leg injuries? What are the expectations of the ordinary consumer and what is the assumption of risk?

Multipurpose vehicles represent another technically baffling set of issues for a designer. The American consumer has a great yen to drive off the road over rough terrain, emulating the exploits of that special World War II general-purpose vehicle, the GP, or Jeep. To drive off-road, one needs ground clearance. Higher ground clearance and large tires lead to a higher center of gravity. A high center of gravity can lead to reduced lateral stability and a higher instance of rollover, though many other factors relating to steering and suspension characteristics also have an important bearing on stability. But what are the expectations of the normal consumer? What are the assumptions of risk and how far should a manufacturer go toward warning the rider in such a vehicle about the additional risks to which he or she may or may not be exposed?

The eggshell plaintiff. In litigating crashworthiness there is an implicit, and sometimes explicit, legal assumption that all people are entitled to the same level of protection. The fact is that human tolerance to crash forces varies enormously. Between the healthy twenty-five-year-old football player and the fragile old lady of seventy-five, there is a difference of perhaps a factor of five in terms of tolerable loads applied to the chest by the steering wheel in a collision. How then should a manufacturer optimize his designs for this variation in the population at risk? Superimpose that variation on the skewed population of crashes of which large numbers occur at equivalent speeds of 20 mph compared with a very small number that occur at, say, 35 mph equivalent barrier speed.

The product liability decisions in the courts have so far not addressed this complex design issue. With the tunnel vision that comes from the hindsight of one specific case, it is easy for a plaintiff to point out that a design was not optimal for a particular person in a particular collision. In reality, that is almost never the case almost by definition. But this should not be the design issue. The issue should be whether the designer has incorporated into his design the technical knowledge available at the time to produce a reasonably crashworthy product consistent with the other utilities that the design offers.

What is clear from this short review of the rise of liability of defective design is that claims against manufacturers are commonplace and the standards used to judge defect are variable and in a state of flux. But the broad principle of strict liability for defective design, particularly crashworthiness issues, is well entrenched in the U.S. legal system.

The Effects of Product Liability on the Automobile Industry

In researching this paper, I persistently asked manufacturers what the cost and the consequences of the rise in liability have been. In simple financial terms the answers have varied by a factor of ten, ranging from $50 to $500 per car sold. First, as a matter of principle, it is clear that the customer ultimately pays. He or she pays because the manufacturer has higher costs arising from defending cases in court, from investigating claims in great detail, from making settlements, and from paying fines when found guilty. The manufacturer has increased its overhead because of a legal staff devoted to defending the product and outside lawyers and experts who have to be hired where appropriate. The definition of these costs is difficult. A proportion must be fixed costs that would exist if liability operated only at a much lower level, but the great bulk of the costs of product liability must be directly due to the enormous volume of litigation.

Confusions of definition also arise because warranty claims are included in the activities of legal staff. Although individually small, such claims are numerous, and manufacturers often do not distinguish between the costs of warranty and defect claims. The figure of $50 per car to cover the cost of liability is more typical of an importer of automobiles into the United States. For domestic manufacturers, the total cost of liability runs into hundreds of dollars per car sold, according to the executives of American car companies who were knowledgeable on this subject.

The one effect on which all manufacturers agree, both domestic and importers, is that product liability and its threat has lead to greater uniformity in design. Some engineers spoke nostalgically of the bubble cars of the 1950s as an example of the extremes that would be available to the public if it were not for product liability. A car that weighs 1,200 pounds and is eight feet long, that is capable of normal acceleration and a top speed of 70 mph, and that gets 80 miles to a gallon is entirely feasible and could be made to meet all existing federal safety standards. But such a car would never be made by a major manufacturer because of the risk of suit for defective design.

Undoubtedly product liability has encouraged a convergence toward mainstream conventional design, specific instances of which are discussed later. Here I am concerned only with the overall external effects. All commercial activity costs money and product liability is no exception. Clearly the financial burden is not of the magnitude shown in such industries as general aviation or pharmaceuticals, but at some value up to 5 percent of the price of the product it is a significant amount.

Product Liability in the United States and Other Countries

Among industrialized nations no parallel can be found to the product liability industry of the United States. Many countries have some form of social security or no-fault compensation system in place. Sweden, Australia, New Zealand, and Germany are examples of countries where compensation is paid to the injured victim of a car crash without there having to be recourse to either tort or contract litigation. New Zealand perhaps best represents the traditional common-law doctrine. A suit for personal injury against a manufacturer would be summarily dismissed, because medical care costs are borne by the national compensation scheme for crash victims. A suit for property damage claims against a manufacturer could be pursued, but it would have to be on the basis of negligence, with all the burden of proof which that implies. Rather similar systems operate in the Scandinavian countries.

The twelve countries that constitute the European Community adopted a product liability Directive in 1985, which became effective in 1988.[10] This Directive introduced strict liability into European law, replacing what was generally the practice of the common-law principles of negligence. Under the Directive all a plaintiff has to do is to prove that a defect was present and that it contributed to the injuries.

Within the umbrella of the Directive, member countries have national legislative powers to define certain aspects of the Directive such as having a statute of limitations and a cap on damages. The most important part of the Directive relates to the standard of proof required to establish a defect. It is too early to say whether a state-of-the-art defense or a development-risk defense will be allowed, or indeed whether meeting the regulatory standards required of a product will be sufficient defense against a claim of defect. These precedents need to be established through specific case law; at present those first cases are just beginning to work their way through the judicial system. In talking with lawyers and manufacturers in many countries, I found that four aspects of the American product liability scene are almost unique and are viewed with astonishment by people overseas: the use of juries in civil trials, juries deciding both the verdict and the sentence, the contingency fee structure, and punitive damages paid to the plaintiff and his or her counsel. These are the underlying factors that drive U.S. product liability law and its consequences to what is perceived in other countries as an extreme and inequitable position.

Juries for civil trials are very rare outside the United States, Ireland being one other country that has such a procedure. Most countries hear civil cases before a judge or in some cases a civil tribunal. That method, it is felt, defuses much of the emotional element inherent in presenting personal injury claims. And also the showmanship tactics of some attorneys and experienced experts in the United States would not survive under nonjury proceedings.

That juries decide both sentence and verdict is a unique American procedure. Many countries use juries in criminal matters, but the judge decides on the sentence. It is a common perception that juries in the

10. European Economic Commission 1985.

United States, driven by sympathy for an injured victim weighed against the deep pocket of a large corporation, make awards that are completely out of line with the amounts given for the same injuries in other parts of the world. In most countries judges are guided closely by precedents in making awards. Economic losses are assessed on a strict actuarial basis and awards for grief, pain, and suffering are fairly small. In Britain, for example, there are only two or three awards a year of a million dollars. However, the trend is toward higher awards throughout the whole European Community.

The third aspect of the U.S. system that is perceived overseas as fueling product liability activity is the contingency fee procedure. Charging on a no-win no-fee basis is specifically illegal in many countries, though new legislation to allow contingency fees is being considered in Scotland. Instead of contingency fees, each side usually pays its own costs regardless of verdict; in some instances costs can be assigned at the discretion of the judge against the defendant. Liability for costs is viewed as a significant disincentive against frivolous suits. For the impoverished or poor plaintiff most countries have legal aid schemes that allow cases to be financed from public funds.

The fourth unusual aspect of product liability in the United States is the use of punitive damages by juries in making awards. Punitive damages are almost unknown in other countries and indeed cannot be awarded in Britain or Europe for personal injury cases. If gross negligence by a manufacturer is at issue, then it is more likely that criminal action will be brought against its officers, but in no case would any awards obtained be given to the plaintiff.

These general points are mentioned because they are part of the background thinking of overseas manufacturers when they view the U.S. market. As will be discussed, these views may be inaccurate, but they undoubtedly affect the manufacturer's decision about whether to introduce an innovation into the United States. First, however, it is necessary to review the second major theme of this chapter, the evolution of safety and the role of safety regulations in relation to automotive design.

The Development of Safety and Safety Regulations

Before the mid-1960s automobile design was essentially unregulated. There were certain requirements for lights, glazing, windshield wipers, and other specific features, but beyond those the industry was free to produce whatever combinations of function, style, and safety it considered appropriate.

Safety measures conventionally are classified into primary and secondary ones. Primary safety relates to measures that will prevent collisions, such as brakes, lights, tires, handling, and vision characteristics. These features are part of the normal feedback loop between the driver and the machine and as such they are therefore market-sensitive. A car with poor brakes, bad vision, or unpleasant handling is not going to have success with the customer. As a result, primary safety issues have, generally speaking, been a prime concern for manufacturers since the days of the horse and buggy, and there has been a natural evolution in those items.

The same is not true for secondary safety design. Crashworthiness for the automobile evolved out of aviation experience. Indeed, the very word *crashworthy* was coined by John Lane, the director of aviation medicine in Australia in 1942, when he suggested that aircraft should be certified in two ways: they should be "airworthy" and "crashworthy."[11]

The pioneering work of Hugh De Haven, John Stapp, John Mathewson, and Derwyn Severy generated a body of knowledge indicating that if properly packaged the human frame should be able to survive many of the collisions that were killing more than 50,000 Americans a year. The science of crash protective design and biomechanics was well developed by the early 1960s.[12] A number of secondary safety items were incorporated into cars in the 1950s and 1960s, such as antiburst door locks and lap belts, but at the time the whole thrust of traffic safety activity was largely directed at the road user, the person behind the wheel. The car itself was not viewed as an important mechanism for enhancing safety either by industry or by government.

All that changed after the passage of the 1966 National Highway Safety Act. As director of the National Highway Safety Bureau, William Haddon initiated a set of standards that specified the crashworthiness of cars. The effects of those standards, operative from 1968, have reverberated throughout the automotive world ever since. They have been copied, modified, and adopted by almost every country with a significant car population. The federal motor vehicle safety standards formed the basis for at least thirty safety directives of the European Community, and those standards in some form or another specify safety performance from Aus-

11. Mackay 1983.
12. Arthur D. Little, Inc. 1966.

tralia to Japan, from Germany to Singapore. They changed automotive design from a free-market, styling-dominated activity to one in which certification or passing the standards was of primary importance in the priorities of the manufacturers.

Those first-generation standards covered both primary and secondary safety, the 100 and 200 series, as well as some aspects of postcrash performance relating to fire, the 300 series. But the most important ones for the industry were the crashworthiness requirements of the 200 series.[13]

The first generation of standards took what was good current practice within the industry at the time and made that the required level of performance. Thus the five inches of rearward movement of the steering column of FMVSS 204, the door-latch strength requirements of FMVSS 206, the glass specification of FMVSS 205, the seat strength requirements of FMVSS 207, and the rest, all were fixed relative to good current practice of the 1960s and early 1970s.

The one exception to this process was the occupant protection standard, FMVSS 208. Conceptual work on the air bag is recorded in the patent literature of the 1950s and 1960s, and much development effort was put into refining the technology of sensing, deployment, and crash performance of this type of restraint system.[14] The use of active seat belts was disappointingly low, and the government in particular made a considerable effort to develop the air bag as an alternative to the seat belt.

James Gregory, the administrator of the NHTSA, stated at a House subcommittee hearing in 1974 that "were the standard ultimately to become effective, what you would see in most cars would be an aircushion system with lap belts." In testifying at a Senate committee, however, Robert Carter, the associate administrator of the agency, said, "We know of no necessity or no real reason for the need of the belt."[15] The form of the standard 208, unlike the others in the 200 series, requires a full-scale crash test with an instrumented dummy of established biofidelity. Values for the output signals from the dummy are supposed to correlate with acceptable levels of human tolerance to injury.[16]

The complexity of such a process, together with many genuine scientific difficulties, led to opposition to the proposed passive restraint requirement. Underlying such opposition, however, was undoubtedly a belief within the industry that safety was not a positive marketing att-

13. 49 CFR 49, parts 510–82.
14. Frey 1970.
15. National Transportation Safety Board 1979, 44.
16. Mackay 1983.

ribute. Safety did not sell, according to the engineers and designers of the 1970s. Thus marketing considerations, uncertain technology, and perceived liability risks all combined to produce strong opposition to the proposed timetables for a passive-restraint requirement from the NHTSA in the 1970s.

The politics of rule making appear to require short lead times, which inevitably results in a standard of performance that is already attained by some manufacturers. A current example is the proposed FMVSS 214 side-impact standard, which most manufacturers will be able to comply with in their current models.[17]

The conclusion that must be drawn from the rule-making process is that regulation does not lead to innovation. By its very nature regulation applies known technology; indeed, to be accepted legally in the United States, regulations must be technologically and economically feasible. That is the test on which proposals are judged to be acceptable by the politicians who must approve the rule-making process.

Twenty years after the first generation of federal standards were promulgated, one can look back and see how those standards have worked. They have undoubtedly brought major benefits, but they have brought those benefits by forcing all manufacturers to do what some were doing anyway. Legislation has not, therefore, led to true innovation but has merely enshrined good current practice.

A second factor has influenced safety regulations over the last twenty years. The very quantity of detailed requirements has resulted in true research and development being curtailed in all but the most successful companies. Research departments became in reality compliance-testing departments, the homologation engineer became more important than the research engineer.

From 1974 to 1984 little of major significance changed in the field of vehicle safety regulations aside from some upgrading of existing requirements. The next important regulatory change was the introduction of the passive-restraint requirements of FMVSS 208, phased in between model years 1987 and 1990. Those requirements again reflect known technology, developed within the car industry; the regulations merely specify for everyone what has been available to some for several years.

Regulation of vehicle crashworthiness has lead to two important benefits, but neither of them is innovative. The first way regulations work is to remove current models that do not comply with a new standard.

17. Mackay 1989.

This leveling-up process encourages manufacturers to stop outmoded designs, but it is a one-time process unless the regulations are continually upgraded, which they are not. The second way regulations work is to force a common standard onto all manufacturers. That is more a leveling-down process, because unless a large body of technical knowledge has been ignored by the rule-making procedure, the manufacturer has no incentive to go beyond the minimum required if significant cost and weight penalties are involved, as there usually are.

Substantial bureaucratic inertia exists in the rule-making process. Nowhere is this clearer than in the drafting of regulations within the European Community. The debate on a proposed standard among the twelve member nations, each having a technical or commercial self-interest, caused a time lag of between five and ten years from first discussions to final agreement. This walking-in-treacle procedure ensures that in Europe the regulations cannot hope to reflect the current state of the art.[18] The procedures in the United States are not so cumbersome, but they are nevertheless time consuming and bureaucratic, necessarily so since they address the interests of all parties. Such procedures will not by their very nature be innovative. Innovation lies within the engineering community and with the entrepreneur. Although regulation has had a profound effect on automotive design and practice for the benefit of the driving public, that does not help the process of innovation.

The previous discussion has emphasized the role of regulation on the automotive industry. In considering the wider safety dimensions, it is clear that vehicle design has improved greatly since the late 1960s. Overall traffic safety has improved so that death rates per 100 million miles traveled have declined from 5.4 in 1968 to 2.25 in 1989. Personal safety in terms of motor vehicle deaths per 100,000 population has also declined, from 27.5 in 1968 to 18.9 in 1989.[19] Improved crashworthiness seems to have greatly contributed to that reduction, though many other factors are also operating, such as improved highways, better driving behavior (particularly the control of drinking and driving), and improved emergency medical care. Because of this last factor, fatalities are an increasingly unsatisfactory measure of traffic safety. Seriously injured survivors are a large and increasing burden on the community, and historical comparisons of deaths and death rates alone do not address that aspect of traffic injury. Overall, however, crashworthiness and vehicle safety design have

18. Mackay 1983.
19. National Safety Council 1990, 1, 51.

changed greatly in the last twenty years. This change has occurred because of the initial step taken by the first generation of regulations in 1968, coupled with an increasing recognition of the importance of safety and crashworthy design by the industry and the public in general.

The Changing Structure of the Automotive Industry

It is important to outline the changing shape of the automotive industry worldwide so as to pinpoint some aspects of innovation within the industry. In the 1960s the U.S. market was dominated by the four domestic manufacturers: General Motors, Ford, Chrysler, and American Motors. General Motors enjoyed about 50 percent of the market and was concerned about government antitrust activity: it even supported American Motors to ensure that its own dominance did not stir a trust-busting government into breaking up the corporation. Imported cars had a small niche outside the mainstream of American automotive design, but markets were predominantly national.

But by the late 1960s and early 1970s, the car market in the United States was changing, showing a preference for small, compact, utilitarian cars. The styling excesses of the 1950s—Harley Earl designs, such as the Chevrolet Bel-Air, and the Ford equivalent, Roy Brown's Edsel, which was to prove to be the greatest marketing disaster in modern history— were giving way to more practical vehicles; the commuter preferred function to symbolism.

At that time, Europe had at least twenty-six separate car manufacturers producing cars in significant volumes, though major consolidations were already under way. In Britain, for example, in the space of ten years Austin-Morris, MG, Rover, Jaguar, Standard-Triumph, and Leyland Trucks all became one company. In 1990 Europe had only eight major manufacturers, producing 13 million passenger cars annually.[20]

In Japan in 1967 total vehicle production was about 3 million vehicles, of which 50 percent were trucks. The ratio of carownership to population was 1 to 26. In 1989 Japan produced more than 9 million cars, substantially exceeding the U.S. car production of 7 million.[21]

But national boundaries are now no longer useful in defining automotive design and production. All the top manufacturers are in reality

---

20. Motor Vehicle Manufacturers Association 1990.
21. *The World in Figures* 1990.

multinational corporations. The ten largest companies accounted for 85 percent of the 35 million cars manufactured in 1989. Those cars are designed by a small number of people in Detroit, Tokyo, Turin, Paris, Wolfsburg, Los Angeles, and Stuttgart. They are manufactured through a range of joint ventures and suppliers often operating across national boundaries. Design is more and more assigned to specialized suppliers of subsystems, so that the design process is a complex kaleidoscope of in-house and outside activity. Design engineers still exist, but their function is much more integrated into the production and manufacturing aspects than it used to be.

This internationalization of the car industry in both design and production, and increasingly markets, has a bearing on innovation. The investment in a new model is so enormous that uncertainty must be reduced to a minimum. The car is a mature product, and therefore innovation is unlikely to be radical. At the same time, cars are growing increasingly complex and expensive. The recent success of German manufacturers is acknowledged to be due to both the structural quality of the product and the introduction of advanced technology, with excellence in ride, handling, performance, comfort, and reliability being uppermost.

Part of the trend toward advanced technology relates to safety. The conventional wisdom of most American companies has been that safety does not sell cars. That attitude has now changed, pioneered by Volvo, and both active safety characteristics and crash performance are now entering mainstream marketing. Proponents of this approach are Volvo, Mercedes, Volkswagen-Audi, and BMW, but it is increasingly a general trend for all manufacturers.[22]

My discussions with executives in the industry show a clearly changing attitude to safety issues and crash performance in particular. Instead of having the negative attribute of needing to pass the regulations, safety is increasingly perceived as a positive marketing feature, an added-value item to the product, and hence an area in which research and development leading to innovation can be a positive benefit to a corporation. That is a recent trend being followed most obviously by German and Japanese companies.

Against this background of liability, regulation, and the changing nature of the automobile industry over the last thirty years, I now consider what safety-related innovations have actually occurred and how product liability has influenced those changes.

22. Auto Motor Sport 1990, 127–50.

Safety, Innovation, and Liability

Knowledge acquired through research leads to a better understanding of a problem. It may lead to technological innovation in the form of new devices, or it may lead to better design in which traditional materials and construction are used but configured in a more appropriate or optimal manner. In safety-related design, I use the term *innovation* to cover both types of advances.

Active Safety

Ultimately the control of a car depends on the tire-road interface, those four footprints each about the size of a hand that are the link between the car and the road. In the last thirty years tire technology has greatly changed through the introduction of new, complex materials, radial and belted construction, and advanced tread patterns to cope with wet roads. The wear quality of tires improved so much that large manufacturers went out of business in the 1970s because of reduced demand. On an international scale, tire manufacturing is intensely competitive. As regards product liability, tires are often involved in claims of defective manufacture. Goodyear, for example, had a major recall of the F500 tire. In terms of design, however, tire development does not appear to have been influenced at all by product liability claims, either positively or negatively.

Along with tires, braking is fundamental to vehicle control. In the last twenty years the advent of disc brakes has made brake fade a thing of the past. More recently antilock brakes make brake-induced skidding less likely and provide shorter stopping distances on wet roads while steering control is maintained. These antilock braking systems (ABS) are either mechanical or electronic and were first introduced into production cars in high volume in Europe, most notably by Ford. As volume rises prices fall, and the prediction is that most new cars in Europe, except the cheaper models, will have ABS by 1998. In the United States ABS is still fairly uncommon and limited to top-of-the-range cars.[23]

Four-wheel steering is alleged by some engineers to have safety benefits, but intrinsically such an advance is going to influence only the very small number of crashes that occur right at the margin of cornering

23. Italian Automobile Club 1990.

stability. Although technologically complex and innovative, the safety benefits are negligible according to most people in the industry.

Vehicle lighting has improved significantly with the advent of quartz halogen bulbs and multireflector, homofocal designs. These innovations allow the pattern and intensity of lighting to be controlled very precisely by the designer, improving night visibility and reducing glare. Product liability appears to have had no influence at all on lighting.

A notable safety gain has come from centrally mounted high brake lights. That innovation was driven largely by the NHTSA as a result of university research findings. Product liability played no role in the change.

The next important advance in crash avoidance will come from applying electronics and information technology to the vehicle-highway system. The Prometheus project in Europe is aimed at changing the relationship of the driver to the outside world by providing early warning of congestion, route guidance, and collision-, fog-, and ice-alert systems. Such electronic networking could greatly reduce the opportunities for conflict. Similar smaller-scale projects are under way in the United States and Japan.

The removal of some aspects of the driving function from the driver is now possible. The most obvious safety-related one is radar-controlled proximity braking. Demonstration systems are on test, but their general adoption will depend more on the response of government and the consumer than on the technology. Fear of product liability suits is mentioned frequently in the context of all these electronic advances to explain why manufacturers will not first introduce the systems in the United States. According to all the car and system manufacturers I talked with, Europe and Japan will be the places where these advances will be used initially, because of less exposure to product liability risk.

In the active safety area good ergonomics, seating, comfort, and climate control inside the car have obvious if unquantified benefits. Such advances are largely market driven as engineers have treated the driving environment more objectively and less as a styling exercise. Uniformity of driving controls, for example, is now established worldwide, apparently as part of the internationalization of design and safety standards. Product liability has played no part in that except, according to some engineers, to encourage uniformity of both controls and instrumentation.

One active safety area in which product liability has had a big effect is "unintended acceleration." The Audi 5000 was subject to many suits, but other manufacturers have also been sued extensively. The Audi case is of particular interest because it illustrates the power of the media and a well-organized plaintiffs' bar in generating litigation.[24] By wide publicity of initial claims, numerous new suits were generated. The sales of the Audi 5000 plummeted by over 30 percent in a year. Subsequent technical investigations by the NHTSA and others showed there was no technical justification for these claims; the problems arose from drivers erroneously pressing the wrong pedal.[25] Ergonomic studies illustrated minor differences in pedal geometry across all cars, but the main technical claim of "unintended acceleration" was shown to be without foundation. Those technical conclusions, however, were drawn far too late to save the Audi 5000 model from being a financial disaster for the manufacturer.

Innovation, Safety, and Crashworthiness

Secondary, or passive, safety has changed greatly in the last two decades. Innovation has come from scientists and engineers investing research and development resources in finding solutions to perceived problems.

As with all research, recognizing and describing the problems are the hardest parts of the research process. In the automobile industry, research and development funding is a management decision; resources applied to crashworthiness research reflect the perceptions of management about the importance of the topic and the likelihood that R&D expenditure will result primarily in benefits for the company, with the secondary consideration that fundamental, precompetitive research may generate new knowledge useful to everyone.

In the 1960s and early 1970s, the recognition of the power of good crashworthiness design to diminish vehicle-related death and morbidity spread throughout the industry, driven largely at that time by an activist policy at the NHTSA. Regulatory action then declined, in part because of U.S. domestic politics and in part because of concerned and sustained opposition to new regulation by the automobile industry. Thus little changed in the regulatory area between 1974 and 1985. During that period, however, crashworthiness was becoming institutionalized within the industry. As a consequence, R&D funding was devoted not just to discovering more efficient ways of meeting the regulations but toward understanding the fundamentals of vehicle-related trauma. This focus has led to better science: to new insights into the epidemiology of trauma

24. Tomerlin 1988.
25. U.S. Department of Transportation 1989.

and greater biomechanical knowledge on injury mechanisms, on human tolerance to the force of different impacts, and on variations in that human tolerance; to more realistic anthropomorphic test dummies and instrumentation for better assessing the injury risk in collisions; and to complex computer modeling of the interaction of the car and the occupant under crash conditions.[26]

The motivation of corporations in assigning resources is a complex matter for an outsider to assess. But from many conversations with U.S. and European executives I found that support for crashworthiness research and development is driven by four considerations. First, regulations must be met; second, the marketplace is asking for improved crashworthiness; third, that subject now profoundly affects the design of the vehicle; and fourth, knowledge of the subject is evolving quickly.

What is striking in assessing crashworthiness innovation is that much of it has come from European manufacturers. Any innovation of course is more likely to be applied to a more expensive car than to a cheaper high-volume production unit. The risks are less, the effect on the price to the customer is less, and the first-time buyer of an expensive car is more likely to be willing to pay extra for perceived enhanced crash protection. But that is not the whole story. Crash protective design sells better in parts of Europe than in the United States, perhaps because of the different perceptions and values that buyers have in different countries. Scandinavian countries, particularly Sweden, have a highly educated and informed first-time buyer, and information on crashworthiness from government and consumer organizations strongly influences the market.[27] The same is true to a lesser degree in Germany, the Netherlands, and Britain—and to some extent in France. In the other Mediterranean countries crashworthiness as a public perception hardly exists. Germany is of particular interest because the first-time buyer is probably the most technologically literate consumer in the world and is willing (and able) to pay for high levels of technology in his or her car. For these reasons much of the innovation in crashworthiness design has come from Germany and Sweden, where, too, the most successful international, up-market car manufacturers are based.

A characteristic of the 1980s was the rise of the Japanese motor industry. From producing cheap, somewhat imitative, cars in the 1970s, the multinational companies of Toyota, Nissan, and Honda have revo-

26. Viano 1988.
27. Folksam Insurance AB 1990.

lutionized the production process by widespread use of robots, just-in-time techniques, and computer-aided design and control of the manufacturing process. Productivity levels in the factories of those companies have led the rest of the industry, and their products have been gaining in all markets, particularly those in North America.

More recently, the policies of Toyota, Nissan, and Honda have focused on the up-market, high-technology segments of the business and introduced new models to rival Mercedes, BMW, Volvo, and Jaguar. Honda and Rover collaborate with the Legend and the Sterling, sharing much common design and many components. In entering that segment of the market, those corporations have recognized that safety design is a significant aspect of a successful product. Having a good rating in the different crashworthiness comparisons administered in countries is important.[28] Hence the stated policies of those corporations is to conduct more safety research and to innovate particularly in the area of crashworthiness.[29] That approach coincides with the stated policy of the Japanese government to introduce safer vehicles domestically.[30] In the near term, therefore, innovative safety engineering will probably become a feature of Japanese cars as they compete increasingly in that dimension against their European rivals.

Over the last decade innovation in crashworthiness relates to two general areas, structural design and occupant restraint systems. Some examples will illustrate the point that innovation has come not from the big-three U.S. domestic manufacturers but from the smaller volume, up-market importers who, coincidentally, are less exposed to product liability risk.

Vehicle structural developments have been the subject of much research and development, with Volkswagen-Audi, Volvo, and Daimler Benz incorporating many innovative designs. Daimler Benz has made a marketing success of structural design that is optimized for several crash conditions well beyond the regulatory requirements, as has Volkswagen with its work on compatibility in different crash configurations. Volvo and Opel have successfully marketed cars with high levels of crash performance based on detailed field crash investigations.

In occupant restraints European technology has led to pretensioning seat belts, load limiters, web locks, and antisubmarining seats. These

---

28. Motor Vehicle Manufacturers Association 1990; Folksam Insurance AB 1990.
29. Personal communication with N. Kawamoto and A. Kumura, 1990.
30. International Association of Traffic and Safety Sciences 1981.

innovations can enhance seat-belt performance in the limiting condition. Adjustable seat-belt anchorages illustrate the conundrum of innovation versus liability. The upper anchorage of a seat belt is located on the door pillar, and there is no one fixed position that is satisfactorily comfortable for the range of sizes of occupants in most cars. It is fairly easy to have the mounting point adjustable so that the occupant can set the position to suit himself and the seat position. That type of design was first introduced by Saab in the early 1980s and is now commonplace throughout Europe and Japan. It has been deliberately not introduced into the United States market by several manufacturers with whom I have consulted because of the risk of product liability suits. Among nonspecialists, there is a general feeling that seat belts should prevent all injuries, even in severe collisions. That view has been encouraged by overenthusiastic promotion of seat belts and seat-belt laws by some advocate groups in the United States. Hence if someone is injured wearing a seat belt, the presumption is that something is wrong with the belt system. If the upper anchorage, being adjustable, is incorrectly positioned, then the manufacturer fears it will be liable for defective design, inadequate warnings, and lack of crashworthiness.

The air bag deserves some special discussion because it is poorly understood by many nonspecialists. The air bag is an American invention. It developed from the research stage in the mid-1960s to a viable commercial product in 1970 and was offered on some 11,000 cars by General Motors in 1974–76. At that time seat-belt use was at less than 10 percent, mandatory seat-belt laws were unthinkable politically, and many consumer advocates such as William Haddon, then president of the Insurance Institute for Highway Safety, and Ralph Nader of the Center for Auto Safety were vocal in calling for "passive restraint," meaning an air-bag-only standard. The epidemiology of the real world of crashes was poorly researched and understood, and the air bag was promoted by its supporters as a stand-alone device capable of preventing most vehicle occupant deaths.[31] The limitations and side effects of the air bag were not well documented nor agreed on, and for those reasons, and others, an adversarial relationship developed between government and industry that colored traffic safety issues for more than a decade.[32]

Part of the reluctance of the industry to accept the air bag was due to the technological uncertainties of such a device. It requires the use of

31. National Transportation Safety Board 1979.
32. U.S. Office of Science and Technology 1972.

explosive, complex sensors and electronics, and its benefits, though potentially great, are difficult to assess. The limits of protection are still being evaluated, and issues concerning the out-of-position occupant, the child standing against the dashboard on the passenger side, noise, overpressure, inadvertent firing, the threshold of activation, and the disposal of a system that contains toxic chemicals are all still issues of debate.

One other reason that U.S. carmakers did not accept the air bag in the early 1970s was the threat of product liability. At one stage in discussions with the NHTSA, a deal was proposed that the industry should get immunity from air bag claims in exchange for fitting the system.[33] Another proposal was that the U.S. Department of Transportation should assume the liability for the consequences of passive restraint. Neither proposal was accepted by the government.

The executives and engineers of the early 1970s with whom I have discussed their direct involvement in the negotiations with the government often made a further point: the phase-in period for air bags would have to be long. A large industry would need to be established, developing the necessary technology and volume capabilities to supply 10 million units annually. Offering a safety system on only some of the cars manufactured was viewed at that time as increasing a corporation's exposure to product liability suits. That was subsequently recognized when the passive-restraint requirement was phased in between 1987 and 1990.

The perceived threat of product liability suits appears to have contributed to the industry's opposition to air bags. Such fears are still present today and indeed are being borne out by an increasing number of law suits relating to two issues. The first one is the claim that greater injury occurred because an air bag was not fitted to a model of car built at a time when an air bag was technologically and economically feasible. This issue is currently being judged on a state-by-state basis, and a number of rulings have diminished this risk for the manufacturer. This is the "preemption" decision, in which courts have ruled that the absence of an air bag is not a defect.

The second kind of suit is now gathering speed.[34] In such cases an air bag is fitted but does not fire because the collision did not have a velocity change parallel to the long axis of the car greater than the firing threshold of 10 mph. All side impacts, rear impacts, most rollovers, and about half of injury-producing frontal collisions fall into this category. Air bags can

33. Toms 1970, 141–42.
34. Waters 1986.

provide only supplemental protection in a minority of serious injury crashes, by design. Yet the nonspecialist's perception is that the air bag should be a panacea. A recent ruling by a New York court suggests that a manufacturer misled a driver into not using her seat belt by offering a car with an air bag. She was involved in a side impact, was unrestrained, and the air bag did not deploy.[35]

A further kind of suit, just developing, involves an air bag that is fitted and that inflated, yet the occupant was injured anyway. The perception here is that the design must be defective because it did not live up to the expectations of the consumer.

Considerations such as these affected the thinking of U.S. manufacturers during the 1970s in their opposition to passive restraint. Here clearly liability concerns led the industry into a defensive position, which delayed innovation and halted development of the air bag domestically. In 1981 Daimler Benz in Europe offered a driver's-side supplementary air bag. It is supplementary to an active three-point seat belt and addresses the fact that a driver in a severe frontal collision, correctly restrained by a seat belt, can still strike the steering wheel with his face. Injuries from the arcing forward and downward of the head are one of the most frequent limitations to protection with current seat-belt systems.[36] In 1983 Mercedes offered the system in the United States, and since then most manufacturers have started to offer driver-side air bags as a way of meeting the passive-restraint requirements of FMVSS 208 phased in between 1987 and 1990.

An alternative way of meeting the passive-restraint requirements is with a passive seat belt. That system was pioneered by Volkswagen in 1974, when the company first offered a VW Rabbit with a passive belt and knee bolster. The effect of that innovation was to raise belt use from about 25 percent to about 80 percent.[37] It was one of the most important safety-related innovations of the 1970s in the United States. It undoubtedly protected thousands of occupants who would otherwise has been unrestrained in their collisions. It was the precursor of the Toyota passive-restraint system introduced in 1979 and the other passive belt systems of the late 1980s used by Chrysler, General Motors, Saab, Jaguar, and many other manufacturers.

Its introduction by Volkswagen in 1974 was the subject of intense debate within the company, and the long lead time for it to be adopted

---

35. *Orlich* v. *Helm Brothers Inc.*, Justice C. E. Ramos, Supreme Court New York County, IA, part 7.
36. Mackay 1990.
37. States 1977.

by other manufacturers reflects concern over the product liability implications of passive belt design. The main argument put to me by engineers
in other companies was that Volkswagen would have greatly increased
liability exposure just because the system was different from conventional
active belts. Their arguments, at least in part, for not following the innovation offered by Volkswagen until forced to by the FMVSS 208 requirements of 1987 were based on the perceived threat of liability for
enhanced injury. Other considerations of course apply, notably the technological changes necessary and the different characteristics of the buyers
of VW Rabbits compared with those of other makes and models of automobile.

Other safety-related innovations deserve a mention. Side-impact air
bags are under development by Autoliv in Sweden, a subsidiary of Elec-
trolux AB.[38] These are fired by a simple mechanical sensor in the door
and may provide a new solution to the problem of enhanced protection
in lateral collisions with significant loss of interior space. It is too early
to say how this will enter the marketplace.

Child restraints represent an interesting technological issue in which
the exposure to liability is great. In the emotionally charged atmosphere
of the courtroom, nothing is as compelling as a seriously injured child,
and the size of awards made against child-seat manufacturers reflects this
characteristic of the U.S. legal system. In most other countries awards
made to the parents of seriously injured children are at the level of a few
thousand dollars. In the United States the awards are often measured in
millions of dollars. This risk and exposure has forced several child-seat
manufacturers to withdraw from the market;[39] it has also discouraged car
manufacturers in the United States from addressing the particular needs
of children in cars. One-third of rear-seat occupants are less than ten
years old and less than four feet, seven inches high. For that age group
conventional lap-shoulder belts are not necessarily acceptable, and in the
United States the problem is left for the aftermarket. In Europe and Japan
rear-seat designs are evolving to provide integrated child seats in the
original vehicles.[40] It remains to be seen if a major car manufacturer will
begin to offer integrated child seats in the United States. For example,
the new integrated booster seat in the rear of the 900 series Volvo is not
available in North America.

38. Olsson 1989.
39. Personal communication with A. Starkey, director of Britax Limited, 1989.
40. Tingvall 1987.

Sometimes a new development occurs and fails in the marketplace, passing completely unnoticed by the world of liability. One such example is antilacerative windshields. Various companies, notably Corning Glass and LOF in the United States, Pilkington in Britain, and Saint-Gobain in France, have developed windshields that will cause less laceration to the face than conventional laminated glass. Although not normally life-threatening, facial lacerations to unrestrained occupants are frequent in car crashes. The best of the advanced windshields offer almost total protection against such injuries. Such windshields, however, are more expensive than conventional ones and present several in-service problems because of the inner coating on the glass. So far, such products have been a commercial failure not influenced by the possible litigation consequences, perhaps because the financial exposure from any single case is small, even though the aggregate costs of facial lacerations are substantial.

The world of motorcycle design needs comment because crashworthiness issues over the last ten years have been the subject of much litigation. At the same time, the motorcycle has not been subjected to the same amount of safety-related regulation as the car. As regards crashworthiness, apart from fuel tank design, motorcycles have no secondary safety requirements.

Thus the issue of innovation versus liability for the motorcycle is not clouded by the third dimension of regulations. Innovation in motorcycle crash protection began in the 1960s with work by Bothwell.[41] It centered on the provision of energy-absorbing fairings to protect the legs. The rationale for them is that 80 percent of seriously injured motorcyclists get bad leg injuries, often of outstanding severity.[42] Because most motorcyclists are young men the economic costs are high. Research has progressed in Europe to the stage that a draft European directive was proposed in 1988.[43] As a regulation, the current proposal is easy to criticize on scientific and procedural grounds, but it is backed by substantial research at the British government's laboratory, the Transport and Road Research Laboratory, which at a minimum demonstrates technologically feasible, economically practical designs that offer increased leg protection in a large range of collision types. Prototype trials are under way, and the proposed regulation, downgraded to an EC recommendation, is under detailed debate. In short, an alternative design is

41. Bothwell 1973.
42. Mackay 1985.
43. European Economic Commission 1989.

in the offing that would give the motorcyclist better protection under some circumstances.

The reaction of the motorcycle industry has been to challenge the technical validity of the European work. Within that industry the reasons given are twofold. First, such energy-absorbing fairings will diminish the appeal of the motorcycle in the marketplace. Riding a motorcycle is perceived by many people as one of those free-choice, high-risk activities that should be exempt from the type of safety-related regulation governing other modes of travel. It's fun, not transportation. Second, and more important, if the energy-absorbing fairing gains credence by being specified through an EC recommendation, then motorcycle manufacturers in the United States will be liable for larger injury claims if leg protection is not fitted. That is the clearest example in the crashworthiness area of actual litigation and the threat of further suit holding back the development of an optional safety measure by the industry.

Conclusion

In this chapter I have tried to explore some possible relationships between strict liability, safety, and innovation within the automobile industry. One of the first observations is that the automobile generates more death and injury by far than any other industry. Between 40,000 and 50,000 deaths in the United States annually for the last three decades adds up to more than a million deaths since the 1960s, when strict liability doctrines were first introduced. For every death there are at least ten casualties requiring hospital admission. Worldwide, road vehicles kill at least 500,000 people annually, and that number will rise to more than a million by the year 2000.[44] With trauma on such a scale a visiting Martian might well assume that the epidemiology of such a disease would be well documented. In reality the disease of traffic injury is not well researched. Data bases are inadequate, the evaluation of countermeasures fragmentary, and the resources devoted to genuine scientific understanding of the problems are far fewer than those provided for research into other causes of death and morbidity.

Apart from the absence of good epidemiological data, there have been other major forces acting on the automobile industry since strict liability doctrines were first introduced. Federal regulation of design is the most

44. Trinca and others 1988, chap. 2.

important, and I have traced here some of the effects of regulation on the industry. Regulation undoubtedly has had two main effects. The first is a leveling-up process, in that a new regulation, if based on current state of the art, forces all manufacturers toward a common standard. That has the initial effect of removing old-fashioned designs and encouraging all manufacturers to meet "good current practice." By their very nature regulations cannot innovate; they merely enshrine current practice. If the same regulations remain in force for a long time, and many of the first-generation FMVSS rules of 1968 remain operable in 1990, then regulation has a second, leveling-down effect. If a regulation is in place, a manufacturer has a strong disincentive to offer anything better unless it perceives that a benefit would result.

These effects of federal regulation of automotive design confound any simple epidemiological analysis of collision and injury data since product liability began. It is therefore impossible to see any simple causal link between liability and high-cost verdicts and the changing epidemiology of traffic injury. The one exception is the virtual disappearance from the United States of three-wheeled all-terrain vehicles. In this instance product liability undoubtedly removed a whole class of vehicle from the marketplace. But that has nothing to do with innovation, though it undoubtedly increased safety by removing a high-risk activity from society.

Besides liability and regulation, the third main force acting on the automobile industry has been the internationalization of both design and production; now 85 percent of cars are manufactured by ten multinational corporations. The U.S. market in particular has changed, so that 25 percent of cars are now imported, and the lines between domestic and foreign manufacture have become blurred because of myriad suppliers in different countries and cross-border joint ventures in both manufacture and marketing.

Against these trends, what role has the rise of liability doctrines had on design and innovation in the United States? Specific discussions and evidence from executives and engineers within the industry point to the conclusion that strict liability has had a negative influence on innovation. It has held back new designs, consumed resources that might otherwise have been directed at design improvement, and added on costs to the consumer. Engineers are the people who innovate, not regulators and not lawyers. But engineers can innovate successfully only if encouraged and strengthened by management, and that happens only if the marketplace is receptive to new designs. If management perceives that liability in the marketplace is increased because of innovation, then engineers are not encouraged in that direction. This situation contrasts with that in Western European countries, where liability risks are low and the marketplace pays a premium for innovative technology in safety as well as in other areas. As a result, most safety-related advances in recent years have come from European manufacturers and, more recently, from the Japanese.

However, the relationships are not as simple as that conclusion implies. Relatively small-volume up-market manufacturers are intrinsically better placed because they are making a high-technology product that is purchased by a well-informed first-time buyer. One characteristic of the American car industry is that there are no such manufacturers domestically. Consolidation of the industry into the big three occurred well before the risk of regulation and liability in the 1960s. That has not been true of Europe, where consolidation is still under way, and many specialized, high-quality manufacturers are operating successfully in sectors of the market. It may thus be an accident of history that has placed the Europeans in a better position to react to the growing demands of safety-related innovation.

Perhaps the most obvious test is to reverse the argument. If there were a positive effect of strict liability on innovation, then surely those companies most exposed to liability verdicts would be the most innovative. But no evidence for that exists at all. Ford, General Motors, and Chrysler have the biggest exposure to litigation for alleged product defects. Those companies devote most resources to defending their current product designs; they are also the most cautious about their new products. It must follow that the product liability doctrine has had a negative influence on innovation in the car industry.

References

Auto Motor Sport. 1990. *Crash Test Report*. Frankfurt.

Babcock, C. W. 1989. "Could We Alone Have This? Comparative Analysis of Product Liability Law and the Case for Modest Reform." *Loyola of Los Angeles International and Comparative Law Journal* 10:321–59.

Bothwell, P. W. 1973. "Safety Technical Design of the Motor-cycle." In *Proceedings of an International Congress on Automotive Safety*, vol. 2:1–29. National Highway Traffic Safety Administration.

European Economic Commission. 1985. "Product Liability Directive 85/374." *Official Journal of the European Commission* L210:29.

———. 1989. *Proposed Directive on Leg Protection for Motor-cyclists*. Brussels.

Folksam Insurance AB. 1990. *The Sum of 700,000 Car Accidents: A Report on Car Safety.* Stockholm, Sweden.

Frey, S. M. 1970. "History of Airbag Development." In *International Conference on Passive Restraints,* sponsored by NATO/NHSB, 21–32. Milford, Mich.

Hoenig, M. 1981. "Resolution of Crashworthiness Design Claims." *St. John's Law Review* 55:633–727.

Hoenig, M., and S. J. Werber. 1971. "Automobile Crashworthiness: An Untenable Doctrine." *Cleveland State Law Review* 20:578–96.

Huber, P. W. 1989. "Consent and Coercion in the Law of Accidents." *The World and I,* Feb., 470–81.

Hulsen, H. V. 1981. "Design Liability and the State of the Art: The United States and Europe at a Crossroads." *St. John's Law Review* 55:450–90.

International Association of Traffic and Safety Sciences. 1981. "Japanese Government White Paper on Transportation Safety." Prime Minister's Office, Tokyo.

Italian Automobile Club. 1990. *World Cars.* Turin, Italy.

Arthur D. Little, Inc. 1966. *The State of the Art of Traffic Safety: A Critical Review and Analysis of the Technical Information on Factors Affecting Traffic Safety.* Cambridge, Mass.

Mackay, G. M. 1983. "Reducing Car Crash Injuries: Folklore, Science and Promise." *Journal of the American Association of Automotive Medicine* 5:27–32.

———. 1985. "Leg Injuries to Motorcyclists and Motorcycle Design." In *Proceedings of a Conference AAAM,* 169–80. Washington.

———. 1989. "The Characteristics of Lateral Collisions and Injuries." Institution of Mechanical Engineers, London.

———. 1990. "Kinematics of Vehicle Crashes." In *Trauma,* edited by S. Westerby. New York: Heinemann Limited.

Motor Vehicle Manufacturers Association. 1990. *World Motor Vehicle Data.* Detroit.

National Safety Council. 1990. *Accident Facts.* Chicago.

National Transportation Safety Board. 1979. *Case History of the FMVSS 208: Occupant Crash Protection.* NTSB-SEE-79-5. Washington.

Olsson, J. A., and others. 1989. "Airbag Systems for Side Impact Protection." In *Twelfth International Technical Conference on Experimental Safety Vehicles,* sponsored by the National Highway Traffic Safety Administration, hosted by the Swedish Government. Götteborg, Sweden.

Schmidt, M. A., and May, W. W. 1979. "Beyond Products Liability: The Legal, Social and Ethical Problems Facing the Automobile Industry in Producing Safe Products." *University of Detroit Journal of Urban Law* 56:1021–49.

States, J. D., and others. 1977. "The Volkswagen Passive Restraint System." In *Stapp Conference,* 861–910. Warrendale, Pa.: Society of Automotive Engineers.

Tingvall, C. 1987. "Children in Cars: Some Aspects of the Safety of Children as

Car Passengers in Road Traffic Accidents." *Acta Paediatrica, Scandinavica Supplementum* 339:1–35.

Tomerlin, J. 1988. "The Riddle of Unintended Acceleration." *Road and Track*, Feb.:52–59.

Toms, D. 1970. "Panel Question and Answer Session." In *International Conference on Passive Restraints*, sponsored by NATO/NHSB, 142–52. Milford, Mich.

Trinca, G. W., and others. 1988. *Traffic Injury: A Global Challenge*. Melbourne, Victoria: Royal Australasian College of Surgeons.

U.S. Department of Transportation. 1989. "NHTSA Announces Results of 'Sudden Acceleration' Study." Press Release. NHTSA03-89. March.

U.S. Office of Science and Technology. 1972. "The Cumulative Regulatory Effects on the Cost of Automotive Transportation." National Technical Information Service.

Viano, D. 1988. "Cause and Control of Automotive Trauma." *Bulletin of New York Academy of Medicine* 64:376–421.

Waters, F. 1986. "Air Bag Litigation: Plaintiffs, Start Your Engines." *Pepperdine Law Review* 13:1063–81.

Wittner, N. J. 1990. *Crashworthiness Litigation: Principles and Proofs*. Society of Automotive Engineers Technical Paper Series 900371. Warrendale, Pa.

The World in Figures. 1990. London: Economist Publications.

Comments on Chapters Four and Five

Robert W. Crandall

JOHN GRAHAM and Murray Mackay investigate the effects of U.S. liability law on innovation and product safety in the automobile industry. Mackay relies exclusively on interviews with engineers and his "experience" in the automotive sector; hence his analysis may be thought of as a distillation of the conventional wisdom among automotive engineers. Graham, on the contrary, draws his conclusions from a limited set of case studies involving product liability suits or recalls. Neither method is likely to be convincing to the social scientist, who would prefer to see empirical measures of innovation or safety related to different liability regimes and to other variables. Unfortunately, such tests are difficult to carry out because of the problems in constructing measures of economic agents' expectations of liability exposure.

Mackay

Mackay's thesis and conclusion is that liability law not only punishes general product innovation but reduces innovation in product safety. The combination of strict liability and safety regulation results in a freezing of safety innovation. Regulators simply set their standards at the current best engineering practice and the producers merely comply with these standards, since they are afraid of the liability exposure from untried but potentially safer technologies.

Mackay's only empirical support for his thesis is the observation that the European luxury-car producers have been the innovators in product safety. U.S. firms, fearful of tort suits, have merely copied innovations from Europe. I do not know if this conclusion is generally correct, but even if true, it does not necessarily support Mackay's thesis about the effects of U.S. liability law. European luxury-car producers may be leaders in safety innovation simply because the buyers of their cars are far more exposed to the risk of death than their U.S. counterparts. Vehicle fatality rates have always been much higher in Europe than in the United States.

It is my impression that several of the Japanese producers have also been leaders in crash-safety engineering, yet Mackay does not mention them. If true, this fact may lend more support to Mackay's thesis than his observation on Europe.

At best, Mackay provides some industry insights into the role of tort liability in automotive safety. His technique is useful for formulating hypotheses, not for testing them.

Graham

Although it represents a more thoroughly documented research effort, Graham's chapter also fails to provide a convincing test of the role of product liability in automobile safety. The author reviews five recent episodes of alleged safety defects in vehicles sold in the United States. In each of these episodes, the manufacturers encountered adverse publicity, regulatory investigations, and product liability suits. He concludes that the publicity surrounding each episode and the consequent regulatory pressures did force the companies to make changes in product design, but that the fear of liability suits was only a minor consideration in the manufacturers' decisions to improve the safety of their vehicles.

Graham's conclusions are necessarily subjective. How can he know whether the companies would have responded in the same way if they had had nothing to fear from liability suits? Moreover, much of the adverse publicity derived from the court proceedings themselves. Without the tort system, the next of kin or the injured victims might not have had as much public exposure.

But are new products safer today because of these episodes? Or, as Mackay believes, have these episodes simply frozen safety innovation? How do we know?

Graham makes a valiant effort in a concluding section to incorporate changes in the tort system into a statistical analysis of the overall highway death rate. His conclusion, presented in his appendix, is that there is no significant correlation between any of his measures of potential liability exposure and fatality rates. Unfortunately, his regression analysis is not able to pick up the effects of tort cases on safety *design*, because he uses the overall highway death rate as the dependent variable. Surely the fear of tort suits cannot affect the accident rate for drivers of those vehicles that were produced before the rise in tort suits. Since a large share of accidents are accounted for by older cars and by unregulated trucks, buses, and other vehicles, the regression analysis is not likely to be sensitive to the effects of changes in tort liability regimes.

Conclusion

Both papers provide valuable new insights into the relationships among regulation, product liability, and highway safety. But neither paper provides dispositive evidence on whether tort liability has helped, hindered, or been irrelevant to automobile safety.

CHAPTER SIX

Malpractice, Patient Safety, and the Ethical and Scientific Foundations of Medicine

Stanley Joel Reiser

L IABILITY suits represent threats, the avoidance of which influences medical behavior. In this chapter I use a review of the medical literature and interviews with physicians and medical administrators to determine behaviors adopted in response to the current climate of malpractice. These responses are then described and evaluated. But to determine whether litigation for medical malpractice in the United States enhances the safety of people as patients in our health care system, one must consider how the attitudes and actions produced by liability law influence the foundational safeguards of patient security.

Foundational Safeguards

Two key factors create security for the person who seeks medical attention. One is an ethical commitment by the practitioner to seek the good of the patient. The other is the use of the technological agents of medicine in accordance with the best scientific knowledge of the time. Public policies that reinforce these actions best serve the safety of patients; policies that subvert them create risks and harm.

Ethical Commitment

The ethical commitment of the physician to the patient is essential because of the great burden that being ill places on us. When sick we are no longer our ordinary selves; we are vulnerable. Our anxiety about possible physical suffering and loss of function, and the influence of these disturbances on our role in family life and work, combine to make the experience of illness a difficult passage in life.

It is this vulnerability that has been the chief reason for the growth of the ethical traditions of medicine. Nowhere in the medical literature is this illustrated better than in the document that has greatly influenced ethical conduct in Western medicine—the Hippocratic oath. That crucial section where the oath specifies what the person who is a physician must do in treating a patient begins with the passage: "I will use treatment to help the sick according to my ability and judgment, but never with a view to injury and wrong-doing."[1] This general commitment to protect and never to harm is reinforced in the oath by particular ethical injunctions that follow. The doctor, for example, who will learn secrets and become privy to behaviors the patient has perhaps revealed to no one else, promises to embrace the value of confidentiality. For doctors to help, they must be able to learn about the patient's actions and wishes that may account for symptoms, and the patient must feel secure in disclosing them. Indeed, the patient's act of unburdening is in itself therapeutic. Apart from the confessional booth, the medical relationship remains the principal oasis in society where one can reveal self without the threat of judgment.

To tell another about one's life, to uncover the physical self, to permit intervention of prodding, sticking, and even cutting into the body—to be in such a relationship requires a mutual commitment to work together in an atmosphere of trust toward the end of combatting the illness.

Appropriate Use of Technology

To serve this ethical goal of helping and not harming, physicians seek mastery of medical science and technology. Before approaching patients, doctors must learn all there is to know about the nature of disease and the capabilities and proper application of the medical technologies of their time. To do less is to risk harm to the patient.

Since the beginning of commentaries on the appropriate use of medical technology, many have voiced concern about how to apply therapy to take into account its rational limits. The demand to use medical technologies rightly is raised to the level of an ethical injunction in an eloquent passage from the brief Hippocratic essay on the nature of medicine, "The Art": "For if a man demand from an art a power over what does not

1. Hippocrates 1977, 5.

belong to that art, or from nature a power over what does not belong to nature, his ignorance is more allied to madness than to lack of knowledge. For in cases where we may have the mastery through the means afforded by a natural constitution or by an art, there we may be craftsmen, but nowhere else."[2] The inappropriate use of technology is seen to harm not only the body of the patient but also the fabric of medicine. Thus an environment in which scientific criteria, bolstered by ethical precept, determine how medical technology and technique are applied provides the greatest benefit to patients.

Uncertainty and Liability

Another issue is critical here. Since the time of the earliest records of medicine, uncertainty has been recognized as the companion of medical art. To combat this flaw, doctors have striven to introduce into practice forms of data to increase the accuracy of their judgments. In the twentieth century they have accomplished much toward that end. They continue to replace qualitatively stated evidence with quantitative data in the hope that a precise statement of fact given by a number will lead to greater accuracy. And at times that is true. However, medicine is not yet at the stage, and may never be, where 100 percent accuracy in diagnosis or prognosis is possible. There exist in current practice domains of uncertainty, where all one can ask is that judgments reflect the standards of the day and that incentives to improve exist.

It is in relation to certainty and standards that some of the main problems created by the liability system in the United States arise. Stories of the success of modern medicine in the post–World War II era, from penicillin to organ transplantation, have created a popular view that medicine is capable of staunching virtually any physical breach caused by illness or injury. When patients bring these high expectations into the emergency and consulting rooms, they must be met by the medical staff in a way that sustains hope but reflects the reality of uncertainty that still burdens medical therapy. How to balance hope and technical capability in dealing with patients and family is a continuing problem of medical life.

Physicians among themselves face a similar burden in deciding to what standard of care they should act. For all illnesses that are diagnosable—

2. Hippocrates 1977, 6.

that is, can be placed into recognized categories—literature exists describing what to do. But this literature rarely speaks in one voice. Controversy surrounds virtually all therapy, even therapy done on millions each year, such as prostatectomy and hysterectomy.

Practitioners must judge which of the possible approaches to therapy are generally best and then decide whether variations of this therapy are required to meet the needs of a particular patient. Medicine remains a discipline in which subjective judgment reigns. Thus therapy is best approached if uncertainty, and with it the possibility of error, is acknowledged by patient and physician as an inevitable component of their common actions.

If patients basically perceive error as malpractice and not as sometimes reflecting technical limits of the art, and if the result of either type of error is a lawsuit that endangers the livelihood, reputation, and self-esteem of the practitioner, then patients become potential threats to doctors, and medical encounters become for doctors rife with the possibility of harm. The circumstance of the helped turning on the helper has become a disturbing image for practitioners.

Practitioners recognize that the art and science of medicine have limits and that therefore misjudgment and error are inevitable. They also recognize that in the present climate of liability patients and their families may not distinguish between error that is the result of limits of medical knowledge and error that is the result of negligent behavior. Fearing as a consequence lawsuits and large judgments, doctors have manifested two types of behavior directed at reducing their exposure to this threat: expanding actions to increase the evidence that all conceivable steps have been taken to meet a given clinical problem; and contracting actions to remove the doctor from important sources of legal threat.

Expanding Actions

The most important expanding action is making more intensive use of medical technology. But there are also several other ways in which physicians enlarge their activities to protect themselves against potential lawsuits: increasing documentation in clinical records to justify actions taken, enhancing the level of communication and information given to patients, and developing risk management programs.

Using Technology to Deter Suit: "Defensive Medicine"

The intensified use of technology to deter suit or, in the event of a suit, to substantiate the doctor's case, rather than to improve diagnosis or therapy, is pervasive, as suggested in the medical literature and by my experiences at medical centers around the country. This was remarked on by each physician and administrator interviewed (see the appendix for the questions asked).

In medical encounters technology is increasingly used to reassure the patient that there is no likelihood of disease and the physician that there is no likelihood of a suit. The demand for technology by patients, which they press on doctors for such reassurance, is fueled by a belief that medicine is a science and certitude is possible if only enough technology is brought to bear on a problem. "People expect everything to be perfect," said one interviewed doctor, "but it remains an art."[3] "You can do all the tests and still miss the lesion," noted another clinician. In this context, the worried well generate enormous expenses; for example, such common symptoms as dizziness are often treated with high-technology responses because of the threat of suits. This phenomenon is especially evident in major referral centers where high-technology medicine is offered and practiced.

Enhanced technological capabilities for evaluating symptoms also have contributed to the increase in defensive medicine. Some clinicians interviewed speculated that if they evaluated diagnostic procedures to determine how often their use was followed by resultant therapy, the payoff would be small. One doctor noted, "The law forces you to treat to a level of 100 percent certainty, but this is beyond the capability of medicine." And another said, "If we have a test available, we do it. We must do it." Some clinicians believe that the excessive resources expended on the worried well diminish the nation's ability to pay for the really sick.

An obstetrician described how medical tests have become routinely applied not for the information they might offer to increase the safety of the patient but for the protection of the practitioner. The clinician reported, "Several years ago obstetric patients did not get ultrasound— now they almost all get it." Such defensive testing pervades practice, and patients, in the view of this clinician and others, are not helped by that. "Medicine takes judgment," he went on to say. "Ideally one should ask

3. All interviews cited in this paper were conducted by me between January 25 and March 1, 1990. Six physicians and two medical administrators were interviewed.

of each test, 'What does this show about handling a patient?' But we don't look at tests from this perspective. We stop using tests creatively because of malpractice. We are excessively cautious. We overdo testing before beginning a procedure, producing more work and more cost. This is no substitute for medical judgment. Why do we need a running EKG if you can feel a pulse? We don't really listen."

The clinician then expanded on how defensive medicine has changed his practice:

> Defensive medicine is a given. It's used extensively. Unlike in the past, if there is a slight suspicion I order tests. I obtain blood samples on all babies after delivery, no matter what the Apgar score. Cerebral palsy detected later can lead to a suit. The cost of these blood tests, $180. Some hospitals do it for less but increase the delivery room fee. Thus the cost is passed on to the insurer knowing lawyers can create an image of faulty judgment without such a test ordered. Even with a reasonable case a jury can find you liable. The threat of suit is constantly on the minds of doctors. This is emotionally debilitating. At every meeting I am told, "I'm in private practice. I have to think about malpractice all the time." If you're sued everyone knows. Your professional integrity is damaged—win or lose. And you don't win sometimes, even if you're right. . . . If you see enough patients— you'll get sued.

Studies in the literature cite the fact that, to prevent suit, a doctor must order more diagnostic tests than he judges are needed.[4] One of the best analyses is a 1989 report, *Medical Professional Liability and the Delivery of Obstetrical Care,* based on a two-year study by the Institute of Medicine. The report concluded that among the causes of the growing rate of cesarean section for childbirth in the United States was a concern for malpractice suits and an excessive reliance on the use of the electronic fetal monitor to deter them. The institute's committee study director wrote:

> Routine electronic monitoring in normal as well as high-risk pregnancies and deliveries is now the standard; providers who do not use it flirt with the danger of a major suit should an infant be brain damaged, despite the growing body of evidence that such unfortunate outcomes

4. Charles, Wilbert, and Frank 1985; Hatlie 1990.

are seldom linked to birth events. Not only has medical science failed to determine the cause of cerebral palsy, but studies to date do not support the view that electronic fetal monitoring is effective in identifying or preventing it. Thus, the committee concluded that Americans have adopted electronic monitoring as standard practice . . . despite the failure of scientific evidence to support its use.[5]

Indeed, of the 4 million births in the United States each year about three-fourths are monitored electronically.[6]

Residency training programs also are being influenced by the liability ethos to produce suit-avoiding behavior. One interviewed physician, the chief of a clinical service, concluded:

We're teaching students to be defensive, to use an increased number of tests. The standard of care is being influenced. Lawyers now participate in education programs about charting and incidence reports on how to word forms. This results in overkill and hampers an expeditious way of getting things done. Medical residents order all tests. They don't target—they just order and sort. They won't learn how to care for patients this way.[7]

Liability and the Special Case of Life Support

Using technology to shield the medical staff from the risks of liability has been particularly conspicuous in cases surrounding the withdrawal of the technology of life support. This dilemma began in the late 1950s when the technology of artificial respiration appeared. What seemed to clinicians at first to be a technique that produced unalloyed advantage became a source of difficult ethical choices. Some patients who had been brought to the hospital in a state of physiological collapse, and whose lives the respirator was maintaining, remained in coma. As days, weeks, and months passed families and staff were faced with the problem of finding moral guidance to cope with the dilemma of what to do.

Over the past three decades, through public and medical discussion, books and articles, legislative actions, and court decisions, a consensus has emerged. Those patients whose underlying medical condition could

---

5. Rostow, Osterweis, and Bulger 1989, 1058. See also Institute of Medicine 1989; Lewin 1988, 24.

6. Altman 1990, B19.

7. See Bowman and Murray 1989.

not be reversed by the technology of intense technological intervention, and for whom the prognosis of continued coma or terminal illness was as secure as the medical knowledge and judgment of the time permitted, could have this technology removed through personal declarations or instruments like living wills. This unavailing, unbeneficial care could be replaced by an appropriate level of care directed at comfort and support. In reaching this consensus, the various voices came into harmony with a crucial foundational ethic of medicine—the "do no harm" principle. The idea that health care professionals should not provide therapy without benefit is a critical ethic. Its preservation at the same time sustains humane and cost-effective medical practice.

In Texas the Natural Death Act passed by its legislature gives broad authority to practitioners to withdraw technology that is not beneficial, once the patient is qualified under the act, through simple and reversible living wills that the patient or the family may develop. Under this act medical staff are held immune from suit if acting under the living will directives. To further help physicians to practice the best medicine they can, with their decisions strictly based on the medical needs of the patient, the teaching hospital where I work has developed guidelines that reaffirm and legitimate the ability of physicians to give or withdraw any technology in accordance with its ability to benefit the patient. In addition to the synergistic effects of the Texas Natural Death Act and these hospital guidelines, a supportive and active hospital Ethics Committee, the hospital attorney, and I as the medical ethicist all repeat in our many encounters with staff the basic legal and ethical rightness of the policy of treating only in a manner that confers benefit on the patient. We have gone as far as any hospital I know of in attempting to give our staff the confidence to practice medicine in the way they think is clinically best and directed only to the needs of the patient.

And yet, despite all this, many clinicians suffer a pervasive anxiety of vulnerability to suit, which creates resistance to withdrawing life-supporting technology that cannot benefit the patient, particularly when families insist on it. The present social climate hinders staff in this and other hospitals I have visited in sorting out and acting on the difficult ethical issues of therapy on ethical grounds; decisions instead are often motivated by legal fears. The result is the continued undermining of important principles of ethics crucial to a medicine that must both protect patients and husband scarce resources. In addition, an environment has been created in which patients are less protected by the important ethical principle of "do no harm." In this situation physicians share with patients the need for unattainable certainty from threats they deeply fear—for the patient the pain and suffering of illness, for the doctor the pain and suffering of suit. By thus inducing patients and practitioners to aspire to greater, unrealistic levels of certainty, liability tends to create a medical system that outstrips its economic capacity and subjects the individual patient to greater potential risk.

It is important in medicine that social rules promote an environment that encourages actions based on fundamental concern for and use of ethical principles and traditions in making choices at the bedside. By creating anxieties that serve to diminish the use of ethical reasoning, the current system of liability endangers patients, for it deprives them of having their care dictated by the most humane elements of medical tradition. This same anxiety also challenges adherence by clinicians to a scientific basis for action—by causing technology to be used in a way that thwarts the opportunity for benefit.

Some have argued that despite its origin in defense against liability, information generated by the technology that the ethos of defensive medicine has promoted may improve the quality of patient care.[8] This viewpoint is flawed. The current legal climate, rather than creating a helpful prudence toward others that makes doctors mindful of their responsibilities toward patients (which law at its best induces), has instead become intimidating and encourages a damaging self-protective response by physicians. Any action taken in medicine that uses its techniques in the service of ends not specifically directed to benefiting the patient, such as the legal security of the provider, has many negative results. It exposes the patient to unnecessary risks, demoralizes and makes less effective the physician who knows its true purpose yet orders the test, over time distorts clinical judgment and increases the possibility of error, and diminishes the credibility of the whole medical enterprise for allowing its technologies to be widely misused.

The baneful influence of these practices on clinical judgment is shown in a remark made by an interviewed clinician: "There is increased defensive medicine, testing, and use of X-rays. We exhaust all diagnostic possibilities. We do about twenty-five percent too much. The patient is not better off."[9] If a technology is not thought needed from the considered viewpoint of the clinical circumstances of a case, what credible justification can there be in getting it?

8. U.S. Department of Health and Human Services (DHHS) 1987.
9. See also Shapiro and others 1989.

Using the Medical Record to Deter Suit

Another clinical action caused by the current ethos of liability, frequently noted in the literature and by those interviewed,[10] relates to the excessive use of documentation: the increased effort by doctors to report actions taken in the medical record. Physicians have greatly increased the documentation of what they do so that they have data to use should they need to defend themselves legally. To be sure, this has a beneficial side. As one hospital administrator observed: "Liability got the doctors to record histories, findings, and conclusions. They are no longer devoid of scrutiny, especially in small communities. This has made the job of running hospitals easier."

But this stimulus for documentation, on top of that increasingly required by accrediting organizations like the Joint Commission of the Accreditation of Health Care Organizations, can become draining on the staff. "There's endless paperwork," reports one interviewed chief of a hospital department, "and more worrying about what to document than its therapeutic goal." The documentation required by an accrediting agency can also be threatening to physicians. One noted: "The more HCFA [the Health Care Financing Administration] wants me to document, the more the lawyer has a way of finding a mistake. The document has become confused with reality: that which isn't there wasn't done. This is a source of mischief." Thus the very documentation used to defend doctors against a suit can produce one. Put another way, doctors are caught in a dilemma: whatever they do—documenting too much or too little—can get them into legal trouble.

Self-justifying documentation in the medical record also diminishes the authenticity of that record. It is not sufficiently appreciated that the medical record is virtually the only synthetic agent in health care that brings together the actions of its parts. Into this record come the reports of tests, the views of consultants, the notes of nurses, the work of the house staff, the views of the attending physician, and the numerical, visual, verbal, subjective and objective data that make up the observations of any or all of the some 225 specializations that are part of modern health care.[11] It is troublesome enough that these data are often entered in excessively random order, and sometimes barely legible. Distorting the train of events or judgments to create a literary barrier to suits substan-

10. DHHS 1987.
11. Wilson and Neuhauser 1982, 61.

tially wounds an already weakened document. It diminishes trust in the authenticity of what is written, harms the credibility of the entire document, weakens the principal synthetic foundation of medical practice, and therefore diminishes the security of the patient, whose medical past may be altered.

Informed Consent as Legal Protection

One by-product of the liability system for malpractice has been an increase in communication and information given to patients, a trend cited in the literature and by those interviewed. Indeed, one study of 642 sued physicians, nonsued physicians, and suing patients reported that almost two-thirds of all subjects view better doctor-patient communication as the best means of preventing malpractice claims.[12]

The increased attention doctors give to inform the patient of the prospects ahead and of the benefits and burdens of possible alternative actions—a development that began in the mid-1960s—is one of the most significant and beneficial movements of this century. It changed medical behavior toward the disclosure of bad news or threatening events and away from a policy of concealment that had been set at least 2,500 years before and epitomized in statements like the following from the Hippocratic writing "The Decorum": "Perform all this [medical actions] calmly and adroitly, concealing most things from the patient while you are attending him. . . . [C]omfort with solicitude and attention, revealing nothing of the patient's future or present condition. For many patients through this cause have taken a turn for the worse."[13]

This belief, that giving knowledge of what was to come to the patient was harmful to the patient, remained in place until the civil rights and medical ethics movements in the United States of the 1960s showed that self-determination and the information needed to gain it were overriding necessities and benefits in medical practice. Informed consent became the key event in the passage of such knowledge from physician to patient. This change has been good for patients, and to the extent that the legal process has encouraged its pursuit it has increased the security of patients and better enabled them to make medical choices.

At the same time, however, the threat of suit can also distort the communication process, turning the good of information toward the

12. Shapiro and others 1989, 2193. See also Bartlett 1988.
13. Hippocrates 1977, 8.

benefit of the provider rather than the patient. This was reflected in several of the comments of the physicians interviewed. Noted one, "The tort system has probably helped to inform patients better, but sometimes we go to such an extreme (to protect against suit) that it confuses or frightens them." One administrator observed, "Much information but little explanation is given—we're only reading to patients. We meet legal and not patient needs." One clinician worried about the effect of the liability ethos on the way in which information is transmitted: "The information given to patients is more extensive than ever. This is good. But patients are told things in a hard, unpleasant, cold, factual manner to cover one's backside. We lay it all out: to hell with the human aspects." Another clinician saw the situation less bleakly: "Initially we went to an exaggerated informed consent. Now it has leveled off."

In medicine, words are like scalpels. What is said by a doctor to a patient can inflict great harm if not done properly. It was fear of the power of words that led to the historical restraints on explanation to patients previously noted. In giving information to patients, the physician must strike a delicate balance between saying too much or too little, in using indirect or explicit language. It is a great clinical skill to be able to transmit threatening news in a manner that provides truth and also hope, that balances the possibilities for damage with those for recovery. It is a skill whose cultivation is desperately needed as more is learned about human illness and more information must be passed on to patients and families.

Any event or motive that distorts this significant and exceedingly delicate process of communication introduces decided harms. The distortions of the liability ethos do this. The authenticity and content of the communication and consent process are undermined as their purpose of total concern for the welfare of the patient is altered to incorporate an additional motive—the protection from suit of the professional.

Risk Management Programs and Liability

The liability ethos has helped to spur growth in another area, risk management programs. These are activities in which health care organizations gather data to develop risk-reducing actions.[14] As with the greater use of technology, increased record keeping, and more information passed

14. DHHS 1987.

to patients, risk management activities can be beneficial to patients.[15] But the clinicians and administrators interviewed were concerned that risk management has become focused on activities that present high liability exposure rather than on quality of care, and that it is being spurred by malpractice. There is also a concern that it diverts staff from care-taking to form-filling activities. As one chief of a clinical department said:

> There are now many more programs for risk management. They are redundant and impede good medicine. They complicate care by pulling productive nurses into administrative tasks and nonproductive medical personnel into clinical relationships. This is costly and very aggravating. There are reams of paperwork. Malpractice concerns and hospital certifying agencies constantly demand forms. All of this is just to be legal. It doesn't mean a thing.

Once again the liability ethos diverts a significant activity, risk management, away from its proper focus on the patient's welfare to a concern with professional and institutional liability protection.

Liability and Medical Costs

The various responses to liability have increased health care costs. One influence is the actual cost of insurance to protect doctors from suit. For example, in Florida, such insurance adds $1,119 to the delivery of a baby, in New York $607, and in Arizona $447.[16] The enhanced use of technology to avoid liability also adds cost. In 1985 the American Medical Association estimated that defensive practices added $11.7 billion a year to the cost of doctors' services.[17] Comparing our health care system to that of other Western countries, Humphrey Taylor, president of Louis Harris and Associates, recently wrote: "Nowhere else is the cost of malpractice insurance, and the additional costs of unnecessary defensive medicine aimed at frustrating lawsuits, nearly as high as here."[18] The costs of care at the end of life, which are greater here than in other Western countries, are also linked partly to liability. A health care administrator interviewed expressed concern over the greater costs associated with pro-

15. See Teret and Jacobs 1989.
16. American College of Obstetricians 1989.
17. Hatlie 1990, 584.
18. Taylor 1990, A25.

longing end-of-life care because of fear of suits, and observed: "Every-where I go this issue is discussed."

Studies of the cost effects of the liability ethos remain inadequate: better ones are critically needed. Only then can the country address the effect of this cost on patient welfare, as it is expressed in the comment of an interviewed doctor who sees the issue in terms of allocation of resources: "I sit here and worry how I can get enough money to pay for really sick people, when we waste so much on treating the worried well" with high-technology approaches to prevent suit.

Contracting Actions

Thus far I have examined activities that have increased as a result of malpractice concerns. However, in several areas the threat of liability has diminished medical activity.

Reducing Legally Risky Practice Situations

Physicians have avoided specialties, procedures, and patients perceived to be associated with risk of possible suit. A 1987 study of Maryland doctors found that 17 percent of internists, 32 percent of general practitioners, and 38 percent of gynecologists engaged in such risk-adversive behavior.[19]

The malpractice environment even influences the care of children. A clinician told me: "One of the best children's surgeons I know has quit doing babies because in complex, open-heart procedures about 1 in 100 get brain damage and for it he might be paying the rest of his days. He can't afford the malpractice risk. Congenital heart surgeons all over America are affected. Many don't have good insurance."

The study on medical liability and malpractice issued by the DHHS in 1987 reported more than 150 impairments to medical care access, involving twenty-six states, that were related to malpractice premiums.[20] This practice has been most prominent in the specialty of obstetrics and gynecology. As of 1987, 12.4 percent of U.S. OB-GYN physicians had given up obstetrics because of liability concerns, and 27 percent had

19. Weisman 1989, 21; Wilson and Neuhauser 1982; "Liability Reshapes" 1987; Black 1990.
20. DHHS 1987, 5.

decreased doing high-risk obstetric care. Large numbers of family doctors have given up obstetric practice; for example, in Utah, Alabama, and Nevada more than half have done so. As a result, many pregnant women in these areas must travel some distance for obstetric care.[21] The reason for this particular problem in obstetric services is their great liability risk: obstetric claims make up about 10 percent of all national malpractice claims and nearly half of all indemnity payments.[22]

In part because of this exposure the Institute of Medicine undertook its study of the relation of professional liability to obstetric care.[23] This two-volume report found that rising insurance premiums (annual ones in some large cities are over $100,000, the national average being $37,015) and the risk of suit seriously threatened the delivery of obstetric services in the United States, particularly to women who are disadvantaged, have high-risk pregnancies, and live in rural areas. It further concluded that liability problems compromised the therapeutic value of the provider-patient relationship, changed without medical rationale the type of care given, and increased the costs of obstetric care.

This situation particularly affects low-income patients. Surveys conducted by the National Governors Association in all fifty states showed that 60 percent of medicaid programs and almost 90 percent of maternal and child health programs have difficulty obtaining adequate numbers of maternal care providers. Nine out of ten of these programs said that growing malpractice costs contribute to these problems and influence the practices of nurse-midwives as well as physicians.[24] This view was reaffirmed in interviews conducted with clinicians and administrators. They noted that the threat of malpractice has increased the costs associated with treating the poor: physicians feel increasingly uneasy about taking care of those who present the double problem of liability risk and inability to pay for services. Another factor in this situation is the widespread belief, for which the Institute of Medicine committee found no evidence, that the poor are more litigious than the middle class or wealthy.

Decreased Discussion of Unfavorable Outcomes

Risk avoidance among practitioners from fear of litigation involves not only service delivery but also the discussion and recording of clinical

21. Hatlie 1990, 584.
22. Rostow, Osterweis, and Bulger 1989, 1057.
23. Institute of Medicine 1989.
24. Rostow, Osterweis, and Bulger 1989, 1057–58.

events. While some studies show that litigation encourages doctors to review the quality of the work and improve it,[25] others find this fear discourages the collection and recording of some clinical events, decreases autopsy requests, and diminishes audit of their work. One of the interviewed health care administrators observed: "Physicians don't discuss much about what went wrong and what happened. There is a climate of fear." In the province of Ontario, Canada, a clinical audit came to a complete halt when physicians became certain that its findings could be used in litigation.[26] An article in the *Quality Review Bulletin* reported that "the current malpractice issue and the large sums of money awarded in many lawsuits have caused a tremendous amount of caution within the medical community. This situation may actually interfere with a hospital's ability to assist physicians in learning from their errors and to introduce corrective action when problems exist."[27]

This view was affirmed in a study at the Brigham and Women's Hospital in Boston of adverse outcomes in colon surgery and its implications for cost. The authors argued that a significant but usually neglected aspect of cost-benefit analysis in medicine was the study of the origin and cost of errors. However, they concluded that "it is a paradox that cost-error analysis surveys, in the contemporary world, are inhibited by anxieties over litigation. For example, the critical incident reportage of the National Surgical Study was crippled in several hospitals because of a reluctance to disclose adverse results. . . . It would be a tragic irony if the current epidemic of malpractice lawsuits brought quiet concealment of unfavorable results, so that medical progress is impeded rather than promoted."[28] In fact, in their own report, the authors acknowledged such inhibitions, for they did not supply "data which confer veracity," such as dates of events, because of concern for litigation.

A very important ethical value in medicine is that of disclosure and discussion of error. This was documented exceedingly well in a 1979 study of the clinical and ethical development of surgical residents by the medical sociologist Charles Bosk. The title of his book, *Forgive and Remember*, speaks to the key finding of the study. The learning of surgery, like that of any complicated discipline, will mean making errors. The ethical ethos on the surgical service Bosk studied allowed and tolerated reasonable error-making as part of the learning process *so long as*

25. Black 1990; Weisman and others 1989.
26. Black 1990.
27. Jacoby 1983, 85.
28. Couch, Tilney, and Moore 1978, 645–46.

the resident immediately owned up and called for help from superiors. The worst offense was concealment, attempting to make up for the error and possibly endangering the patient.

The tradition of openness about error, so that one can learn from it and not make it again, is the foundation of such critical activities in hospitals as mortality and morbidity committees, and clinico-pathologic conferences, where the clinical record of a case (usually a difficult one) of a patient who has died is meticulously analyzed before a hospital audience of peers by physicians who did not take part in the therapy. Such candid discussion of clinical judgment, in multiple hospital forums devoted to finding out what happened in the care of a patient, is effective if conducted without fear of blame or retribution. Once again, litigation fears can diminish the candor about mistakes that are essential for a medical staff to learn of and from, thus making medical care less safe and effective.

The Effect of Liability on the Physician's Relationships

I now turn to the effect of the liability ethos in medicine on the physician's significant relationships—with hospitals, society, and patients—and explore how they influence the safety of patients.

Liability and the Physician's Relation with Hospitals

Hospitals are now legally responsible for the actions of doctors practicing within their walls. The heightened anxiety over the possibility of suit has caused them to improve the process of evaluating and following staff—factors that promote the safety of being a patient. Thus hospitals are giving increased scrutiny to the process of granting and reviewing staff privileges, verifying physician credentials, checking the doctor's malpractice claims history more carefully, and continually assessing their staff's competence.[29] Hospitals are also increasing their watchfulness in providing safe and appropriate technology and recognizing the limitation of the facility, and they are strengthening guidelines to guarantee the safe transfer of patients from one facility to another.[30] One of the interviewed administrators noted that liability concerns got physicians "more involved

29. "Liability Reshapes" 1987; Charles, Wilbert, and Frank 1985.
30. Peters 1988.

in hospital relationships. Because of fear they have to work together with us, become more partners."

Liability, however, also has had adverse effects on the environment of hospital practice. As mentioned, peer review activities, though appropriate from the viewpoint of protecting patients and improving quality of care, elicit negative attitudes, even "paranoia," as one chief of staff in a Chicago Hospital described it. He noted that doctors feared that the confidentiality of peer review proceedings could be breached, allowing plaintiffs' attorneys access to the data and hindering the review process. The president of Northwestern Memorial Hospital in Chicago observed: "Peer review activity is increasing. And physicians are willing to participate. But convincing them to put things in writing is a constant process."[31]

Thus, here as in other issues affected by the liability ethos, concerns about liability influence the values underlying medical actions and their justifications. Hospital administrators point to increasing use of liability and malpractice possibilities to justify decisions to staff, rather than state the true and more complicated causes of actions. "We sometimes use malpractice," one administrator told me, "to make doctors do things rather than give them legitimate medical reasons. We scare them. We continually call in our hospital attorney before doing things. We think legally rather than clinically."

Liability and the Doctor's Relation to Society

The relationship of physicians to society and the policy it creates concerning medical issues is also influenced by the liability ethos. The physician is trapped between antagonistic forces. On one side are social policies designed to decrease the costs of health care. Diagnosis related groups (DRGs), into which all in-patient admissions are classified for hospital payment from the medicare fund, and health maintenance organizations (HMOs) that operate from a fixed budget of regular payments by enrollees are examples of a prospective payment approach to health care, which requires doctors to introduce considerations of economic costs into clinical decisions. In an age in which there is the scientific knowledge to generate new technologies to help patients, but inadequate resources to distribute the benefits to all who need them, it is rational

31. "Liability Reshapes" 1987, 56.

and humane to focus attention on costs. Health care providers should learn to balance needs against resources as they craft clinical choices.

However, their ability to do so is thwarted by another social policy that is antithetical to such cost-controlling actions—liability and malpractice law. These create incentives to do more than is needed clinically and to worry about balancing needs and resources because of the grave consequences of suit. As one of the interviewed physicians put it: "DRGs create a conflict. There is an increased anxiety in the doctor to get the patient discharged expeditiously, but he can be liable if he does." An interviewed hospital administrator said, invoking a culinary metaphor: "The physician is in a sandwich. The HMO and PPO [preferred provider organization] environment of managed care presses him to decrease services, and the malpractice environment to increase them."

This problem was demonstrated graphically in the *Wickline* v. *California* case. In its opinion, the court asserted that physicians are responsible for deciding when a patient should be discharged from a hospital even if the third party insurer will not cover the expense of the length of stay the doctor determines is best.[32]

Physicians thus are whipsawed between two conflicting social policies, which leads on their part to consternation, perplexity, and ambiguity about how to treat patients.

Liability and the Doctor-Patient Relationship

This chapter has discussed many behaviors that the threat of malpractice induces in providers of care. In effect, each encounter by a doctor with a patient constitutes a potential threat to the professional, social, and financial life of the doctor. In the words of one physician: "When you hear of a suit settled for millions, you think every patient represents such a risk."[33] An interviewed physician commented: "Liability produces a more cautious practice. The doctor is in a difficult position with the patient, who may take away his livelihood. Doctor and patient are suspicious of each other."

The essence of the medical relationship is a trust, which can produce the openness, dialogue, and mutual nurture that allows two people (initially strangers) to work toward a return of the patient to health. Such

32. 228 Cal RPTR. 661 (Cal App. 2d. 1986).
33. West Virginia obstetrician interviewed on "Nightline," ABC News, April 12, 1990.

a relationship is difficult in a liability ethos, and inevitably patient care suffers.

Quantitative Studies of the Tort System

Several major quantitative studies of the past two decades dealt with the question whether the tort system has prevented injury to patients by inducing better medical practices. The first study, by Don Harper Mills and colleagues, reviewed almost 21,000 in-hospital patient charts from twenty-three California hospitals for 1974 admissions to determine the number of potentially compensable events (disabilities caused by the medical care given). It found them in 970 records—4.65 percent of the entire sample. Only 0.79 percent of the charts contained evidence indicating probable negligence as a cause of disability.[34]

A recent Harvard study, which examined 30,121 medical records of patients hospitalized in New York State in 1984, showed things had not changed much.[35] It found that 3.7 percent of those patients suffered injuries caused by medical care, of which 1 percent involved doctor-or hospital-related negligence.

Extrapolating from these data, the Harvard investigators estimated that of the 2.7 million people hospitalized during the year of the study, about 27,000 sustained injuries involving negligence. However, they estimated that of this 27,000 only 1 in 10 sued, and 1 in 16 received a settlement. Further, many claims were brought by patients whose records did not contain evidence either of negligence or medical injury. In sum, a good deal of negligence behavior never reaches the courts, many such claims that do reach them do not lead to awards, and many other claims are made that are not based on documented evidence of adverse incidents. Over the past two decades there has been no basic change in the level of adverse events, and larger numbers of patients injured through negligence have been uncompensated, all despite the increase in the number of suits, awards, and premium payments. Neither the prevention of adverse outcomes nor payment to those injured by them seems furthered by the present system.

This view is also stated in another recent major study of the influence

34. Mills 1978, 361–63.
35. Harvard Medical Practice Study 1990, 3,6.

of liability on practice by the Institute of Medicine, which, as mentioned, focuses on obstetrics. It concludes:

> There is a crisis in medical professional liability. . . . Compensation is provided to victims only after considerable delay; the threat of liability has far-reaching and severe effects on the availability of obstetrical care and access to it; medically inadvisable procedures are overused, largely because of the threat of liability if they are not; and health care providers, traditionally ambivalent about medical liability, now believe the body of law concerning it to be arbitrary and unfair. It is time for federal and state governments, lawyers, doctors, insurance companies, and patients to work together to resolve the problem of medical professional liability in obstetrics. The stakes are no less than the well-being of mothers and infants.[36]

Conclusion

The conclusion of my study is that the liability ethos does not secure the safety of patients because it damages foundational aspects of medical practice.[37] The greatest security for patients exists when those who care for them are able to follow basic ethical precepts and scientific standards of medicine. This prerogative is undermined by the current way in which this country determines malpractice and compensates its victims. Harm caused to patients by malpracticing doctors must be redressed. But our society should find an alternative way of doing this, one that does not compromise the knowledge and values of health care and deprive patients of the best possible exercise of technique, humaneness, and judgment when they enter into a medical relationship.

36. Rostow, Osterweis, and Bulger 1989, 1060.
37. A widely cited book on medical malpractice written by the economist Patricia M. Danzon in 1985 does not examine this issue but focuses instead on cost-effectiveness in interpreting the current medical tort system, which she believes is "potentially a valuable system of quality control" (p. 227). Further, her evaluation of medical injury is based on the 1978 study by Don Harper Mills and lacks the advantage of the knowledge gained from the 1990 Harvard Medical Practice Study, which shows that little change in injury avoidance has occurred in the interim between the two studies.

Appendix: Questions Asked during Each Interview

1. What overall impact has medical malpractice had on practice of medicine in hospitals?
   a. For example, risk management and quality control programs.
   b. Changes in the information provided to patients and families.
   c. Changes in communication of medical injuries among physicians (such as committees on adverse events).
   d. Development of data systems for assessing risks and injuries.
   e. Use of diagnostic procedures for defensive medicine purposes. Use of innovative (invasive) diagnostic or therapeutic procedures where there may be possibilities of injury.
   f. Changes in the use and allocation of medical personnel in institutions—nurses, physician's assistants, and so on. The issue here entails the expanding of the roles of nonphysicians. For example, having specialized nurses actually monitor and treat patients in specialized services. It also could involve the delegation of responsibilities by physicians to residents, interns, and possibly medical students working on the units.
   g. Have there been any changes or developments in medical education—for example, in academic centers in training of medical students and residents? Also in specialized educational programs for staff? Are hospitals hiring lawyers for the purposes of educating staff and students? Is this a response to malpractice or to more general ethical concerns?
2. When were these changes implemented? Did they reflect the initial malpractice crisis in the early 1970s or the second wave of increased law suits and awards during the early 1980s? Were there differences in the responses during these two periods?
3. Have these changes had any discernible effect on safety? How have you evaluated the impact of these developments? How would one go about assessing the effect of these changes on safety?
4. How does malpractice affect the provision of care for the poor? (For example, does it create disincentives for applying technology in this group?)

References

Altman, L. K. 1990. "Electronic Monitoring Doesn't Help in Premature Births, A Study Finds." *New York Times*, March 1: B10.

American College of Obstetricians and Gynecology, 1989. "Medical Liability: Its Impact on Woman's Health." Washington.

Bartlett, E. E. 1988. "Reducing Malpractice Threat through Patient Communications." *Health Progress,* May, 63–66.

Black, N. 1990. "Medical Litigation and the Quality of Care." *Lancet* 335:35–37.

Bosk, C. 1979. *Forgive and Remember: Managing Medical Failure.* University of Chicago Press.

Bowman, M. A., and J. L. Murray. 1989. "Cost, Correlates and Effects of Malpractice Litigation in Family Practice Residency Programmes in the United States." *Family Practice* 6:146–50.

Charles, S. C., J. R. Wilbert, and K. J. Frank. 1985. "Sued and Nonsued Physicians' Self-Reported Reactions to Malpractice Litigation." *American Journal of Psychiatry* 142:437–40.

Couch, N. P., N. L. Tilney, and F. D. Moore. 1978. "The Cost of Misadventures in Colonic Surgery: A Model for the Analysis of Adverse Outcomes in Standard Procedures." *American Journal of Surgery* 135:641–46.

Danzon, P. M. 1985. *Medical Malpractice: Theory, Evidence and Public Policy.* Harvard University Press.

Harvard Medical Practice Study. 1990. *Patients, Doctors, Lawyers: Medical Injury, Malpractice Litigation, and Patient Compensation in New York.* President and Fellows of Harvard College.

Hatlie, M. J. 1990. Professional Liability: The Case for Federal Reform." *Journal of the American Medical Association* 263:585–86.

Hippocrates. 1977. "Selections." In *Ethics in Medicine: Historical Perspectives and Contemporary Concerns,* edited by S. J. Reiser, A. J. Dyck, and W. J. Curran, 5–7. MIT Press.

Institute of Medicine. 1989. *Medical Professional Liability and the Delivery of Obstetrical Care,* vol. 1. Washington: National Academy Press.

Jacoby, J. E. 1983. "Risk Management Rounds: Promoting Quality Care." *Quality Review Bulletin,* Mar., 85–86.

Lewin, T. 1988. "Despite Criticism, Fetal Monitors Likely to Remain in Wide Use." *New York Times,* Mar. 27:24.

"Liability Reshapes Hospital/Physician Reltionships." 1987. *Hospitals,* Apr., 57–60.

Mills, D. H. 1978. "Medical Insurance Feasibility Study: A Technical Summary." *Western Journal of Medicine* 128:360–65.

Peters, J. D. 1988. "Hospital Malpractice: Eleven Theories of Direct Liability." *Trial,* Nov., 82–90.

Rostow, V. P., M. Osterweis, and R. J. Bulger. 1989. "Medical Professional Liability and the Delivery of Obstetrical Care." *New England Journal of Medicine* 321:1057–60.

Shapiro, R. S., and others. 1989. "A Survey of Sued and Nonsued Physicians and Suing Patients." *Archives of Internal Medicine* 149:2190–96.

Taylor, H. 1990. "U.S. Health Care: Built for Waste." *New York Times*, Apr. 17: A15.

Teret, S. P., and M. Jacobs. 1989. "Prevention and Torts: The Role of Litigation in Injury Control." *Law, Medicine and Health Care* 17:17–22.

U. S. Department of Health and Human Services. 1987. "Report of the Task Force on Medical Liability and Malpractice."

Weisman, C. S., and others. 1989. "Practice Changes in Response to the Malpractice Litigation Climate: Results of a Maryland Physician Study." *Medical Care* 27:16–24.

Wilson, F. A., and D. Neuhauser, eds. 1982. *Health Services in the United States.* Ballinger.

CHAPTER SEVEN

Medical Malpractice and Its Effect on Innovation

Laurence Tancredi and Dorothy Nelkin

Most discussions of medical malpractice focus on the effect of lawsuits on medical injuries, on hospital and physician expenses, and on the relationship between physician and patient. The detrimental effects on physicians have been dramatic over the past ten to fifteen years. In the mid-1970s, for example, 2.5 claims were brought annually per 100 physicians. By 1984 the annual claims rate was 16 per 100 physicians. Similarly, the figures between 1982 and 1985 show an extraordinary increase in medical liability premiums. The average amount of money spent by physicians for medical liability insurance had increased from $5,800 to $10,500 by 1985.[1]

The increase in malpractice claims has been especially costly for hospitals. Between 1983 and 1985 alone, the cost of professional liability insurance premiums for hospitals rose from $800 million to $1.3 billion.[2] The effect has been to increase scrutiny over physicians and to establish means of controlling risks, especially through control over procedural and organizational innovation. Fear of litigation may bear on the willingness of physicians to use new procedures or products. And it may also affect the development of innovative social arrangements in areas of medical care that sorely need reform. Yet few studies explore whether or not malpractice affects medical innovation.

Innovation is an ambiguous concept. Technological procedures and products range from the ones that are clinically acceptable as part of the routine practice to ones that are clearly experimental. Between these points lie many technologies with a less clearly defined status. Good

1. Shapiro and others 1989, 2190.
2. Jones 1990, 1.

medical practice clearly mandates the use of clinically acceptable technologies when appropriate. Innovation in medicine, however, means the use of new technology not yet fully accepted by the medical community. These technologies are the most subject to litigation and are the focus of this analysis.

This chapter is based partly on a review of the literature on malpractice, but such literature has dealt only obliquely with the effect of malpractice litigation on innovation. No good epidemiological information exists on the rate of medical malpractice cases involving innovative technologies. Thus, to enable us to extend the interpretation of the existing studies, we have interviewed clinicians, directors of health care organizations, executives of pharmaceutical and medical equipment firms, legal counsel, and officers in medical associations (see the appendix). Although we find that malpractice creates some disincentives for technological innovation in medical practice, the effect is tempered by consumer demands and expectations as well as by legal pressure encouraging the use of technology. The balance of these countervailing forces is not clear.

Our analysis is necessarily tentative; paucity of material has only allowed us to suggest the relevant arguments concerning litigation's potential effect on innovation and to propose questions for further research.

To establish a context for our analysis we first examine the general link between negligence and technology innovation as it has been expressed in the courts. Second, we address three areas in which malpractice can influence medical innovation: the use of procedures, the willingness of physicians and medical drug and equipment companies to develop and use innovative products, and social innovation in medical practice patterns. Finally, we point to some critical issues to consider in developing further understanding.

Technology and Negligence

By definition, the underpinnings of malpractice law, particularly the standards for determining negligence, discourage innovation in the use of new technologies. For malpractice decisions are nearly always based on the comparison of the questionable practice with standard practice within the specialty.[3] There are, however, revealing exceptions to this conservative

3. Morreim 1989.

posture. Some jurisdictions use the "respectable minority" rule as a defense of malpractice. If a respectable minority of practitioners use a diagnostic or treatment technique, a claim of negligence, even if it defies existing specialty standards, may be counteracted. In addition, in *Helling* v. *Carey*, a trial court held that comporting with customary practice in the use of tonometry in the diagnosis of glaucoma is not conclusive evidence that no negligence occurred.[4] The Supreme Court of Washington subsequently concluded that the jury could find defendant physicians liable for negligence even though they complied with established professional customs.[5] Instead, the Court created "reasonable prudence" as the standard of care.[6] These examples, however, are exceptions, and, for the most part, conservative rules apply. And the effect of conservative standards is augmented by the litigious climate of today's medico-legal realities.

Several factors complicate the relationship between technological innovation and negligence in the present litigious environment. At first glance, medical technologies that enhance the ability of the clinician to diagnose and treat patients should reduce bad outcomes and negligent practices. However, advances in technology can increase negligence claims.[7] To begin with, computers and related electronic information and processing devices are providing more and more information to the public and to injured patients to justify a medical malpractice or product liability suit.[8] In addition, expectations about the effectiveness of a new medical technology open the door to liability claims. A clinician who fails to use an available procedure and thereby misdiagnoses a patient's condition can be accused of negligence if the oversight results in harm. For example, he might neglect to order a CAT scan of a patient's lung and thereby miss a very small tumor that, if it had been discovered, could have been removed to prevent the development of life-threatening metastatic cancer.

4. *Helling* v. *Carey*, 83 Wash. 2d 514, 519 P.2d 981 (1974).

5. *Gates* v. *Jensen*, 92 Wash. 2d 246, 595 P.2d 919 (1974), rev'g 20 Wash. App. 81, 83, 579 P.2d 3–14, 376 (1978).

6. Kibble-Smith and Hafner 1986. The authors point out that information retrieval systems are blurring the line between negligence (medical malpractice) and strict liability.

7. Grady 1988. This article points out some suits involving the dialysis machine. On page 300 Grady points out that new technologies frequently result in increasing the scale of risky activity. He cites the addition of air brakes to trains, which has resulted in an increase in negligence claims. Although the air brakes were certainly an important contribution to minimizing accidents, their presence increased the opportunities for negligence in several ways, for example, failing to inspect or repair the air brakes, not providing proper lookout, and so on.

8. Kibble-Smith and Hafner 1986.

The physician would be essentially liable for "depriv[ing] the patient of what is now a substantial benefit."[9]

The unfamiliarity and complexity of new technologies may open opportunities for error. For example, applying the Byrd respirator introduces several possibilities of negligence. The clinician might improperly intubate the patient by entering the gastrointestinal tract instead of the respiratory system. The machine itself may be incorrectly attached to the airway, thereby compromising the free flow of oxygen. Or possibly, the machine may be inappropriately connected to the wrong gas outlet, thereby seriously injuring if not killing the patient.[10]

New technologies may reduce therapeutic risks and increase precision, but, paradoxically, they may also transfer certain risks from the patient to the physician. Recall the introduction of the dialysis machine. Without this artificial kidney, many patients suffering from end-stage renal diseases had few options for survival. Most of them died from the condition. Before the dialysis machine was developed they did not sue their physicians. Subsequently there have been many suits. In effect, the machine converted the natural risk of death from renal failure into a set of new potential liabilities: negligence in attaching the shunt to the machine, in monitoring the electrolyte content of the perfusing fluid, in preventing failures in the operation of the machine, and even in improperly excluding a patient from the benefits of dialysis. The increased litigation in this area suggests how new technologies can increase clinician involvement, and therefore the possibilities of negligence—in effect, shifting the burden of risk.

The potential for adverse outcomes and possibly negligence in the use of new technologies may decrease over time. When a technology is first introduced and risks are unfamiliar, a lag time occurs before measures are added to reduce risk.[11] Studying the evolutionary phases of technologies, Bonacheck found that a technology may initially produce serious negative results (some of which may occur because of negligence) that may be greatly modified with the introduction of technical improvements. For example, when mitral-commissurotomies were first used to treat

---

9. Grady 1988, 294.

10. Malpractice cases involving improper or inappropriate use of medical technologies are as follows: *Wilkenson v. Harrington*, 243 A.2d 745 (R.I. 1968); *Waddle v. Sutherland*, 126 So. 201 (Miss. 1930); *Dunwood v. Trapnell*, 120 Cal. Rptr. 859 (Cal. 1975); *McKinney v. Tromly* 386 S.W.2d 564 (Tex. 1964); and *Ball Memorial Hosp. v. Freeman*, 196 N.E.2d 274 (Ind. 1964).

11. Danzon 1985, 74. See also Robinson 1986.

mitral valve insufficiency they were nearly universally fatal. The first mitral valve replacements had a mortality as high as 20 percent. At this stage, negligence is probably not involved very much because the knowledge did not exist for producing better results. However, the issue of negligence may still arise during this early phase. The mortality rate of both procedures decreased considerably as doctors developed experience with their use.[12] Similarly, in the early days of coronary care units, monitoring a patient required nearly continuous attention by health personnel. Later, devices added to the computerized systems provided early warnings of cardiac irregularities that would allow for necessary intervention to avert serious harm to the patient.[13]

Physicians are torn between the appeal and prestige of advanced technology, often reflected in consumer demands, and the liability risks that may be involved. They perceive court decisions on liability as haphazard, nonscientific, and resulting in open-ended damage. The nexus between technology and negligence may discourage some clinicians from using new and complex devices. The conservative position is to stay with well-tried, conventional techniques where the errors are understood and manageable. In the current atmosphere of litigation, the effort to avoid risk may affect both procedural and product innovations.

Effect on Procedural Innovation

Malpractice may curtail the use of innovative procedures in several ways. Physicians may seek to avoid new risks simply by avoiding medical technologies, especially innovative ones. This response is called negative defensive medicine. Black observes that physicians avoid procedures that carry a high risk of malpractice claims.[14] He points out that 17 percent of specialists in internal medicine, 32 percent of general practitioners, and 38 percent of specialists in obstetrics-gynecology reported they handled malpractice risks by avoiding certain procedures.[15]

Positive defensive medicine, using a diagnostic or treatment measure to minimize risk of legal actions, has also been a major response to malpractice. The American Medical Association in 1984 claimed that at least $15 billion a year is directly related to defensive medical procedures.[16]

12. Bonacheck 1979, 44.
13. Grady 1988, 300.
14. Black 1990, 36.
15. Weisman and others 1989.
16. American Medical Association 1985, Rept. 1, 3.

Surveys suggest that many diagnostic procedures are ordered mainly for defensive medical purposes.[17] The idea is that a record of tests is necessary to shore up the validity of a physician's judgment should the patient initiate a law suit. Besides adding tests or avoiding certain procedures, some physicians also avoid taking on the care of patients perceived as potentially litigious.[18]

The medical profession considers defensive medicine one of the most detrimental consequences of the current tort liability system. Defensive measures increase the cost of medical care, have an adverse impact on access to care, and may in themselves have adverse consequences. For example, cesarean sections have increased partly in response to fear of malpractice.[19] A recent randomly selected study of 500 hospitals conducted by the National Institute of Child Health and Human Development disclosed a rise in cesarean rates from 14.1 percent of births in 1979 to 19 percent of births in 1984.[20]

Although defensive medicine has become a serious concern in assessing the effect of malpractice, in fact it may have quite a beneficial impact in encouraging the use of responsible diagnostic and treatment procedures. Appropriate responses, however, are difficult to define for the standards of care so important in the courts have never been clearly delineated in medical practice. Serious differences in opinion prevail among practitioners about the necessity of various diagnostic and even treatment procedures. One doctor may elect not to routinely do skull X-rays in trauma cases because the very small yield does not justify their extensive use. A second clinician, preferring the greater degree of certainty, may order an X-ray. It is impossible to distinguish those acts motivated by fear of a malpractice suit from those that comport with the physician's perception of quality medical practice or the demands of patients.[21] Though defensive medicine usually relies on widely accepted technologies, the practice has generated debates over standards of care.

17. Shapiro and others 1989, 2193. Forty-seven percent of sued physicians and 67 percent of nonsued physicians in a study of 642 physicians reported ordering more diagnostic tests because of a malpractice claim or threat of a claim.

18. Charles, Wilbert, and Franke 1985, 437–40.

19. Fear of litigation is not the only reason for the increase in cesarean sections. Other factors, such as the clinical acceptance of fetal monitoring and expanded medical indications for cesarean sections (breech presentation and low birth weight), are responsible. However, fetal monitoring enhances the likelihood of claims of negligence and, therefore, may most likely be a factor compounding the fear of litigation in obstetrical care.

20. Burda 1987, 57–60.

21. Tancredi and Barondess 1978, 879. See also Harris 1987.

Judicial evaluation of appropriate standards of care in some cases can encourage the use of new technologies. The court looks for a standard of at least a "uniform minimum standard [quality] of care" as established by professionals through expert testimony.[22] But as medical and scientific advances enter the arena of health care to supplement physicians' skills, the physician may be expected to use them even if appropriate standards are not fully established.[23] Failure to use an available technology could be seen, not as an error of judgment (that would be a defense in malpractice), but as an error in fact, that is, negligence. Many court decisions have found the physician liable for failing to order a wide range of diagnostic tests or to use treatment technologies.

Even when fiscal constraints discourage the use of innovative technologies, they are not recognized by the courts as justification for failure to use an available, clinically acceptable technology.[24] In the *Wickline* case, for example, the court held the physician "ultimately responsible" for determining when a patient is discharged from a hospital, whether or not the third party would reimburse additional care.[25] Thus, by imposing constraints that restrict the use of medical technologies, an institution or prepaid medical plan may create opportunities for negligence and malpractice.[26]

Thus the threat of malpractice can either encourage or discourage the use of innovative technologies, depending on their acceptance by the medical community as standard clinical practice. Courts may hold clinicians liable for not having ordered an IVP (intravenous pyelogram), an X-ray, or a biopsy that would accurately identify tissue pathology.[27] But they are not likely to hold physicians liable for failing to use a new technology that lies in the nebulous zone between experiment and routine

22. Morreim 1989, 357.

23. Morreim 1989.

24. Manning and others 1984. See also Newhouse and others 1985. Studies have found that health maintenance organizations and third-party payment systems may be constraining the use of costly diagnostic procedures. These constraints affect the use of both clinically acceptable and experimental technologies.

25. *Wickline* v. *State of California*, 1983 Cal. App. 3d 1175, 228 Cal. Rptr. 661 (1986). See also Mehlman 1985.

26. Sloan and Bovbjerg 1989.

27. Cases that deal with liability for failure to order a test are as follows: *DeBoer* v. *Brown*, 138 Ariz. 168, 673 P.2d 912 (1983); *Johnson* v. *Mullee*, 385 So.2d 1038 (Fla. App. 1980); *Morgan* v. *Carter*, 157 Ga. App. 218, 276 S.E.2d 889 (1981); *Rio* v. *Edward Hospital*, 104 Ill. 2d 354, 472 Nat.2d 421 (1984); *Bickford* v. *Joson*, 368 Pa. Super. 211, 533 A.2d 1029 (1987); *Clark* v. *United States*, 402 F.2d 950 (4th Cir. 1968); and *Robinson* v. *Gatti*, 115 Ohio App. 173, 184 N.E.2d 509 (1961).

clinical care use. This would be the case, for example, with positron emission tomography (PET), an imagery technique still principally used for research, though slowly gaining clinical acceptance by cardiologists and neurologists.

Defensive medicine discourages the clinical use of new, invasive technologies—those that pierce the skin or enter the blood system—or that include the use of potentially injurious substances such as radioactive materials, drugs, or dyes. But even for a noninvasive procedure, malpractice risks force clinicians to be sensitive to the trade-offs between new technologies and familiar ones.

In the treatment of patients suffering from terminal conditions, however, fewer legal constraints apply. A study of malpractice and heart transplantations conducted in 1984 revealed no allegations of negligence.[28] Yet, as malpractice rates increase, physicians are likely to use more conservative treatments even in last-resort cases when more dramatic innovations might be helpful. The law suggests that whenever a physician stands alone with a new procedure he (or she) does so at his own risk. He has to show that medical justification exists and that the patient is properly informed.[29] The physician may be forced to trade off the potential benefit for the patient in using innovative technology against the potential risk of malpractice should the new technology fail.

Such cautious behavior may, however, be appropriate. Studies of the general effect of innovation on medical care have ambiguous findings. In 1977 a study of surgical innovations showed that half of those tested by randomized clinical trials resulted in improvements for patients.[30] Also 24 percent of such innovations reduced complications for the patient. However, the researchers concluded that individuals receiving the experimental or innovative treatments fared neither better nor worse than those receiving more conventional treatments.

Physician Liability and Product Innovation

If malpractice affects the willingness of physicians to use innovative products, then it will also affect the willingness of firms to be innovative

28. Overcast, Merrikin, and Evans, 1984.

29. *Kaimowitz* v. *Michigan Department of Mental Hygiene,* Unreported, Cir. Ct. Wayne Co. Michigan 1973. Of course in some circumstances the doctrines of informed consent and assumption of risk may be used to support the physicians' decision. But in some cases the basis of informed consent has been likewise questioned on grounds of competency in the use of experimental or innovative procedures.

30. Gilbert, McPeek, and Mosteller 1977, 685, 688.

in developing new devices and drugs. The linkage between physician liability and product liability is strong. As malpractice cases involving drugs or medical equipment increase, so, too, do product liability cases. This relationship has become more pronounced as many jurisdictions limit medical malpractice through legislative protections, such as caps on awards. These protections can shift the spotlight onto the maker of the tools that the physician uses as patients injured by devices gravitate toward the "deep pocket" of the medical product firms.[31] Defense attorneys in malpractice cases are expanding the cast of those responsible for an adverse event by placing all or some of the blame on the drug or device included in the patient's treatment. The plaintiff then claims that the manufacturer of a drug or device used in the patient's treatment knew or should have known of a defect or potential adverse reaction and failed to warn the clinician or user of this danger.[32]

The last fourteen years have seen an extraordinary increase in product liability cases. In the federal courts alone such cases have been increasing at an annual rate of over 17 percent. And from 1974 to 1985 average jury awards climbed from just under $500 thousand to more than $1.8 million.[33]

Accordingly, companies often hesitate to engage in the development of new technologies. Take, for example, the much-debated issue of new vaccines. Unquestionably valuable, one of the principal success stories of modern medicine, vaccines are not without some risk for the patient. As such risks become the focus of litigation, companies are backing away from work on new vaccines. Recently Genentech announced publicly that it terminated development of an AIDS vaccine because of fear of liability, although the company claimed to be at the edge of developing potential antigens.[34] Other companies have expressed similar economic concerns about product liability, claiming that medical malpractice and product liability suits are influencing their production decisions.[35]

The research and product development of contraceptive agents has a similar history. At least thirteen American pharmaceutical companies engaged in research in contraception and fertility in the early 1970s. By 1988 only one remained.[36] A recent report by a National Research Council

31. Touby 1988, 56.
32. Touby 1988.
33. Weaver 1988, 1.
34. Personal communication from Steve Jualsgaard, Genentech Corp, 1990.
35. Personal communication from Timothy D. Proctor, Merck, Sharp, and Dohme, 1990.
36. Weaver 1988, 9.

Committee on the development of new contraceptives found two features of the current litigation climate particularly problematic: the unpredictable nature of litigation, and the fact that corporate compliance with the regulations of the Food and Drug Administration (FDA) seems to have no special status in the courts.[37]

Similarly, medical equipment companies are increasingly reluctant to innovate because of concern about suits with large numbers of claimants and extraordinary awards. Companies worry that the possibility of negative outcomes will affect the physician's willingness to use certain products or devices. They believe these factors will have a direct and potentially devastating economic effect.[38]

The recent case of the Bjork-Shiley Convexo-Concave heart valve illustrates the effect of liability on the decisionmaking of a company. This di-strut valve has been used in many patients in the United States and abroad, nearly eliminating the risk of fatal blood clots, which is a significant side effect of other heart valves. However, in at least 389 recipients, the valve fractured, and in some cases, parts of it dislodged and moved into the bloodstream. About two-thirds of these patients died. Since the introduction of this valve in the mid-1970s, over 200 law suits and claims have been settled by the producer of the valve. The Food and Drug Administration took the valve off the market in 1986.[39] However, 81,000 patients have di-strut valves, and more legal claims are probable in the future. A case recently brought in California, *Khan* v. *Shiley, Inc.,* adds a new wrinkle to the type of litigation brought against the company for fractured valves.[40] A patient with a functioning heart valve brought a suit alleging fraud and misrepresentation of the valve's possibility for failure. The patient argued that information she received about the risk of death from the fracture of these valves created serious mental and emotional stress, even though her risk after the sixth postoperative year had declined from 1.1 percent a year to about 0.22 percent a year. Her allegation of misrepresentation was found sufficient to support the claim of fraud.[41] This result introduces a new dimension to the potential liability of the manufacturer, extending beyond direct injury to the effect of fear

37. Mastroianni, Donaldson, and Kane 1990, 141–46.
38. A conspicuous example is the effect of the Dalkon Shield cases on the A. H. Robins Company. It stopped selling this product in 1975, and after more than 4,000 law suits concerning the intrauterine device, filed for bankruptcy ten years later.
39. Meier 1990.
40. *Khan* v. *Shiley, Inc.,* 266 Cal. Rptr. 106 (Cal. App. 4 Dist. 1990).
41. *Khan* v. *Shiley Inc.,* 107–08.

on a patient's emotional and mental stability. Given the many patients with di-strut valves, the number of claims on such grounds could be extraordinary.

The effect of this case is all the more poignant because the company has developed a new mono-strut valve, which has had extraordinary success with more than 70,000 recipients overseas since 1983. This valve has some of the same benefits as the di-strut valve. It prevents blood clots without the use of continuous medication and has no history of fracturing or breakage. The FDA has not yet approved the mono-strut valve, and given its history with the di-strut valve, the manufacturer hesitates to market the valve in the United States, partly because of the fear of malpractice and other legal actions in the event of some adverse outcome.[42]

Effect on Social Innovation

Besides constraining procedural and product innovation, the fear of malpractice litigation is also restricting innovation in the social configuration of medicine, the impulse to innovate in the use of health professionals, such as nurses, midwives, and family practitioners, who have been increasingly taking on tasks traditionally assumed by physicians or specialists. The situation of nurse-midwives is a case in point.[43] Their growing responsibilities over the past decade have been a useful social innovation, especially in rural areas with inadequate medical care. Malpractice suits are threatening their role. Nurse-midwives have assumed responsibility for many nonproblematic pregnancies and births, passing patients on to physicians only when unusual difficulties occur. However, the definition of "difficulties" is necessarily vague. When does a condition change from normal to difficult, from healthy to risky, and require specialty care? Although relatively few nurse-midwives are ever sued, the high rate of malpractice in the field of obstetrics is affecting their ambiguous relationship to the profession.[44] In the context of high liability, physicians are reluctant to take on problematic cases, especially when the patients are not their own.

42. Personal communication from legal staff, Pfizer Corporation, 1990.

43. Institute of Medicine 1989. As noted on page 5 of this report there are currently approximately 2,000 to 2,500 practicing certified nurse-midwives. More than one-third of them practice in areas consisting mostly of poor patients. On page 104 it is noted that only 6 percent of certified nurse-midwives have ever been named in malpractice suits up to this time.

44. Institute of Medicine 1989, 104.

Midwives have had problems in maintaining malpractice insurance. The American College of Nurse Midwives lost its blanket insurance coverage in 1985.[45] Though some coverage has been provided through other arrangements, the certified nurse-midwives have had to contend with the difficulties of affording malpractice insurance. The cost of premiums increased by at least 900 percent from 1970 to 1986, when the annual cost was nearly $4,000 a year. Those certified nurse-midwives who manage births in hospitals, but are, in fact, in private practice have been most adversely affected by the problems of malpractice insurance coverage. Most hospitals require them to have coverage for at least $1 million per claim.[46] Though it may be beneficial to deter midwives from attempting to handle complex obstetrical problems beyond their competence, the profession of midwifery has been a critical innovation for obstetric services, especially in rural areas. It is now in jeopardy.

Similarly, medical malpractice has threatened the introduction of family practitioners into community service. Family practitioners have a practice that cuts across surgery, obstetrics, internal medicine, and pediatrics. They have played an innovative and increasingly important role in many communities that lack specialists. A 1987 survey by the American Academy of Family Physicians found that 19 percent of those practitioners who had engaged in obstetrics in their family practices had discontinued obstetrical care. Another 9 percent altered the type of obstetrical procedures they followed because of the cost of liability insurance.[47]

Critical Issues

Three questions bear on the effect of medical malpractice on innovation in the health care system. What forces in society determine whether a diagnostic or treatment protocol is experimental or clinically acceptable?

45. Langton and Kammerer 1985. Certified nurse-midwives have been faced with these kinds of insurance problems over the past seventeen years. Though the coverage provided by Mutual Fire Marine and Island Insurance Company of Philadelphia was terminated in 1985, in 1986 the problem was temporarily alleviated by the formation of CNA, a newly constructed consortium of ten insurance companies that was later approved in forty-nine states.

46. Langton and Kammerer 1985, 150–51.

47. Bowman and Murray 1989, 146. In this article the authors conducted a survey of family practice residency directors and showed that the areas that were of most concern to residents included obstetrics, cost of malpractice insurance, difficulty obtaining coverage, and general anxiety created by malpractice litigation.

What is the relationship between a provider's medical malpractice or negligence and the liability of the producer of the goods that the provider uses? And what are the relationships among the court rulings on malpractice, product liability actions, and regulatory institutions?

From Experimental Procedure to Acceptable Practice

The increasing number of lawsuits, the high cost of malpractice premiums, and large awards have changed the demarcation between experimental treatment and clinically acceptable care. Determining what is experimental and what is clinically acceptable is difficult. There is no clear-cut threshold that defines when a new diagnostic or treatment method becomes clinically acceptable. Some treatment and diagnostic measures are clearly experimental: we are still in the early stages of developing a totally implantable artificial heart and do not fully understand the benefits and risks involved. At the other extreme, many treatments are unambiguously acceptable by clinicians. But a wide range of innovations are in a transition zone between experiment and clinically acceptable practice. These innovations, providing difficult conceptual problems, are the ones most likely to be affected by medical malpractice and product liability.

If the tort system affects innovation, it would impede the movement of such transitional innovations from experiments to clinically acceptable practice. Only a few studies exist that could corroborate this theory. A Harris survey completed in 1982 examined the impact, if any, of the passage of the Medical Device Amendments of 1976, which gave the FDA broad administrative discretion over regulation of medical devices. That survey found that industry had been "largely unaffected" by these amendments.[48] Subsequent studies confirmed these findings.[49] For example, industry sales increased sixfold between 1958 and 1983. Furthermore, studies of patent activity, an important measure of technological advance in the medical device industry, show no decline since the passage of the regulation.[50]

Understanding the shift from experimental to clinically acceptable care raises important conceptual concerns. What is clinically "acceptable?" No social, legal, or professional litmus test can be applied to make the distinction. Yet the distinction between experimental and clinically ac-

48. Louis Harris and Associates 1982. See also Foote 1986.
49. Office of Technology Assessment 1984, 17.
50. Foote 1986, 503.

ceptable is particularly important to insurers making decisions about innovative technology. If new procedures are considered experimental, third-party payers will not cover them. Insurers will cover only those technologies widely accepted in the medical community in conventional therapeutic practice. Denial of third-party coverage will inevitably discourage innovation. Similarly, if insurers charge higher rates for certain procedures with high liability, their use will be discouraged. In this way the relationship between negligence and technological innovation is mediated by third-party payers.

Analysts are only beginning to assess the parameters bearing on the success of various services or procedures. For example, an important parameter is volume. Frequently employed procedures show fewer adverse effects and better results. A seminal study in this area focused on four procedures: open heart surgery, vascular surgery, transurethral resection of the prostate, and coronary bypass.[51] In a subsequent study, Luft discovered that variables, such as the teaching status of the hospital and its geographical location and size, have an impact on mortality, but the relationship between volume and mortality remains most important.[52] Other researchers, studying different patient populations and medical interventions, confirm these findings.[53]

These findings do not suggest that the tort system is responsible for the relationship between volume and quality, but they may have implications for the tort system in the future. For example, the informed consent procedure may require that patients be informed of the morbidity and mortality rates for certain procedures in different hospitals. Indeed, the correlation between volume of services and quality of care suggests the desirability of policies to concentrate patients in specialized hospitals. Epidemiological data supporting the correlation for various surgical and nonsurgical procedures may eventually become a basis for a useful model to represent the transition from the experimental to the clinically acceptable.[54] Such data could link clinical acceptability to specific facilities with the volume of services and the professional and institutional specialization that ensures quality care.

The relationship between experimental procedures and clinically accepted practice will vary depending on the institutional arrangements for providing health services. These arrangements include fee-for-service

51. Luft, Bunker, and Enthoven 1979, 1364–69.
52. Luft 1980.
53. Flood, Scott, and Ewy 1984. See also Hemenway and others 1986.
54. Maerki, Luft, and Hunt 1986.

practice, health maintenance organizations (HMOs), and preferred provider organizations (PPOs). The economic motivations built into these arrangements affect the services provided, and indirectly, the definition of clinically acceptable standards of care because desire to cut costs will foster a conservative stance toward innovation.

Medical Malpractice and Product Liability

The impact of malpractice on technological innovation also depends on how it affects product liability. Medical malpractice and product liability are two separate bodies of tort law. In determining physician liability, the key issue is one of negligence: did the physician deflect from customary standards of care and in doing so injure the patient? In the case of product liability, the test is one of strict liability for defective products.[55] The plaintiff need only establish the causal connection between the product defect and the injury sustained. There is no need to establish a deviation from customary standards, for proof of negligence is essentially irrelevant in strict liability.[56] But, Epstein points out, the differences between medical malpractice and product liability may obscure the important ways in which these two bodies of tort law are similar.[57]

The critical issue to Epstein is not whether the defendant provides a medical service or medical product, but the types of risks assumed by the defendant. Epstein would argue that similar liability rules should operate to control how goods are produced and services are rendered. Appropriate balance between the two would minimize distortions in which products (drugs, medical equipment and devices) are withheld even when useful for the care of the patient.

Medical malpractice suits may directly affect drug and medical equipment producers in several ways to create disincentives for technological development.[58] We have alluded to how efforts to protect the practitioner from risk can shift vulnerability to the producer of goods. Defense attorneys representing physicians often attempt to expand the cast of defendants by shifting some of the blame for injury to the drug or device

55. Kibble-Smith and Hafner 1986, 75–79. For an example, see the case of *Mahar* v. *G.D. Searle and Co.*, 72 Ill. App. 3d 540, 390 N.E. 2d 1214 (1979).
56. Epstein 1987.
57. Epstein 1987, 1141–42.
58. Many of those interviewed through our structured questionnaires spelled out the relationship between medical malpractice and product liability.

used in the treatment. This practice creates, in effect, an alliance between physicians and lawyers, allowing suits that were traditionally tort actions against physicians to be "converted" into suits based on product liability against the manufacturers of goods.[59] In fact, this alliance can encourage a plaintiff to drop a claim against the physician and, instead, to elicit the physician as a witness against the product's manufacturer.[60] In one documented case the physicians who were defendants in a malpractice suit encouraged the plaintiff to focus his attention on the manufacturer of the equipment as the liable party.[61] In this case the jury awarded not only compensatory damages against both the physician and the manufacturer, but also a $3 million punitive damage against the company, Airco.

This dynamic shift in liability from the physician to the manufacturer, augmented by fear of punitive damages, is resulting in great increases in the cost of liability coverage for producers of medical goods. Increased premiums not only elevate the price of products and influence their diffusion by practitioners, but also discourage other producers from engaging in innovative activities that might cause litigation. Products such as vaccines, contraceptive devices, and even anesthesia equipment are especially sensitive.

In a totally rational system, one could assume that the economic costs of high awards in negligence and product liability cases would be handled by simply increasing the price of pharmaceuticals or devices. And when costs of production, including those generated by liability, exceed gains, the product would disappear from the market. In such a rational world, liability could be handled through the objective calculations of its economic effects.[62]

However, the tort system does not necessarily distribute gains and losses appropriately. Damages rules are vague and open-ended, especially with regard to pain and suffering and punitive awards.[63] Nor do those participating in decisions necessarily behave rationally. Physicians and manufacturers respond as much to the fear of an economic loss as to the loss itself. Furthermore, they are apt to overreact to small risks, especially if those risks are perceived as unpredictable and not amenable to rational calculations about their costs. Hence these responses become motivating

59. Touby 1988, 56–58.

60. Foote 1986, 510.

61. See Foote 1986, 510, 521. See the case of *Airco* v. *Simmons First National Bank*, 276 Ark. 486, 683 S.W. 2d 660 (1982).

62. Epstein 1987, 1154.

63. Bovbjerg, Sloan, and Blumstein 1989, 908–28.

factors for behaviors such as defensive medicine or termination of medical practice. There are cogent arguments suggesting that tort law, though intended to ensure appropriate distribution of gains and loses, may not be working at this time in history, given scientific and medical understanding, material circumstances, and social values.[64]

Legal and Regulation Solutions

Medical practice is controlled by regulatory commissions, hospital accreditation committees, hospital boards, professional standards review organizations, and state and federal laws. Their regulations can affect the development of medical technologies in ways that complement the pressure from malpractice litigation. First, these organizations and laws may directly affect the diffusion and utilization of new technologies either through controls limiting the installation of high-cost technologies or through credentialing and licensing activities that restrict the use of highly sophisticated and expensive technologies to certain professionals. Third-party payment systems are important potential agents of control for they almost always limit reimbursements to conventional treatments. Moreover, hospitals determine the professional competence of physicians on the basis of their competency with specific technologies.[65] This practice is reinforced by the Joint Commission on Accreditation of Hospitals, which has required specification of professional criteria in medical staff bylaws. These criteria must reflect relevant training, experience, and professional licensure. Whenever studies show that inadequately trained internists and radiologists are performing complex and potentially risky diagnostic and treatment procedures with new technologies, regulation is encouraged.[66]

Regulations can influence the relationship of technological innovation to negligence and product liability in contradictory ways. The existence of regulations can prevent abuses, reducing the risk of malpractice, and encouraging responsible innovation. However, regulations can also create a framework for identifying negligence by a practitioner or manufacturer. The more regulations, the greater the opportunities for demonstrating departures from the rules. Regulations may thus enhance the overall effect of the tort system on both practitioners and manufacturers of new prod-

---

64. Weisbard 1987.
65. "Credentialing for Technology Use" 1987.
66. "Credentialing for Technology Use" 1987.

ucts.[67] In such cases, regulations and the tort system act synergistically to discourage innovation and to favor conventional medical practice, which in turn discourages risky innovation.

Conclusion

This preliminary examination suggests the difficulty of assessing the effect of medical and product liability on innovation. In some ways legal practice creates disincentives for innovation in both medical practice and product development. Our structured interviews with medical practitioners, executives of drug and medical equipment companies, and legal counsel clearly establish that many people in the health care field feel strongly that the tort system is having a negative effect on innovation in medical care. Moreover, the tort system does not stand alone in creating a centripetal force for conformity. Other developments in health care such as regulations and increasing surveillance of medical practice combine with the tort system to discourage departures from customary practice. Yet consumer demands and expectations, as well as pressure from the courts, encourage the use of available and even new technologies. The balance of these countervailing forces is not clear. And no good empirical research is currently available to substantiate either claim.

What does emerge from our review of the literature and our interviews is a series of potentially researchable questions addressing the impact of the tort system on technological development in health care:

—Under what circumstances are clinicians likely to use more innovative technologies or, conversely, to limit their treatment to more traditional diagnostic and treatment measures? Are doctors more likely to use innovative technologies with the terminally ill when the risk of injury balanced against the likely outcome of the condition is of minimal import? It would be interesting to contrast the adoption of new technology in this context with innovation in obstetrics, where the consequences of injury could result in significant court awards.

—What factors influence the shift from experimental diagnosis and treatment to clinically acceptable modalities? This question could be studied on a specialty by specialty basis. Studies could focus on the effect of

67. Gaumer 1984.

tort law on the procedures set up to monitor the utilization and diffusion of new technologies.

—Are there significant differences nationwide in the incidence of malpractice suits? Some states like Arkansas and North Carolina have relatively few suits compared with Florida, California, and New York. Is there any difference in the use and diffusion of new technologies in these jurisdictions? What about rates of patenting new biomedical innovations? What is the impact of technological innovation and diffusion of "forum shopping" in product liability cases as they contrast with medical malpractice where forum shopping is minimal or nonexistent?

—Because of the limited data on the quality of medical practice, it might be difficult to systematically compare the relative outcomes from the use of new technologies with traditional technologies. However, some comparisons could be developed by focusing on specific medical problems.

—Further work could be done to understand the relationship between medical malpractice and product liability. What are the trends in this relationship, particularly in states where protective legislation minimizes the impact of the tort system on the practitioner? How often are manufacturing companies held responsible for what is predominantly clinical error? What happens to the clinician when the manufacturer is brought into a case? How often is he or she used by the plaintiff as an expert witness?

—How do the guidelines for clinical practice in each specialty affect medical malpractice and, secondarily, technological development? Since practice guidelines are still in the developmental phase, it might be possible to conduct a "before and after" study in a jurisdiction with comparisons to unreformed areas.

—Some jurisdictions, such as New York, are considering the possibilities of a no-fault or other alternative system of compensation for medical injuries, and increased surveillance of practitioners' records. If such a system is put into effect, it could influence innovation. It would be interesting to study the impact of these changes on claims histories before and after the addition of alternative compensation methods. One could then compare these changes with shifts in the rate of FDA approval of devices and patenting rates in various jurisdictions.

Perhaps the most important conclusion of this study is to suggest that the effect of torts on medical innovation cannot be explored without attention to questions of safety and quality of care. Not all innovations are desirable; not all malpractice is unwarranted. It may be that some cautions imposed by malpractice are a benefit to patient care. So-called breakthroughs are often less effective than anticipated.[68] And some innovative procedures can be highly invasive while offering limited gain.[69] Adoptive immunotherapy, an innovative but highly toxic cancer therapy, is an example. Once touted as a panacea, it is now believed to be of limited value.[70] Those concerned about the effect of malpractice on innovation must remember that quality of care, not innovation for its own sake, is the primary goal.

Appendix: Questionnaire on Innovation

1. What overall impact has medical malpractice had on technological innovation? Note: Our interest is in the secondary impact of malpractice on medical innovation industries as they seek to meet the changing needs of practitioners and react to changes in the tort system brought about by the malpractice crises.

2. Has malpractice affected decisions to develop and market drugs or technologies that, though beneficial for patients, may have a high attendant risk that could lead to a suit against the practitioner (for example, vaccines, orphan drug problem)?

3. Has it affected programs for the distribution of drugs or for data collection on safety and adverse outcomes?

4. Has it affected marketing in different states (where specific provisions have been adopted following both the 1970 and 1980 crises that make the industry vulnerable to spillover from malpractice actions)?

5. Are labeling and information disclosure practices influenced by malpractice cases, or are they simply reactions to product liability cases?

6. From the perspective of an innovator, have you perceived changes on physicians' use of innovative technology? The first wave of malpractice (the 1970 crisis) or the more recent increase of cases (the 1980s crisis)?

7. Have the changes made by industry had a discernible effect on safety? Innovation?

8. Have these safety concerns been translated into industry-sponsored educational programs for physicians and other practitioners?

68. Benson and McCallie 1979.
69. Valenstein 1986. See, for example, the case of psychosurgery.
70. Rosenberg 1990.

9. Do you feel the liability system is impacting adversely on our leadership role in health care innovation in the world (for example, comparing pharmaceutical development in countries such as Germany, Switzerland, England, Italy, and Japan)?

References

Adametz, W. B. 1969. "Failure to Make Diagnostic Tests." *Journal of the American Medical Association* 210:213–14.

American Medical Association Special Task Force on Professional Liability and Insurance. 1985. "Professional Liability in the 80s." Report 1, Oct. 1984. Report 2, Nov. 1984. Report 3, Mar. 1985. Chicago.

Benson, H., and D. P. McCallie, Jr. 1979. "Angina Pectoris and the Placebo Effect." *New England Journal of Medicine* 300:1424–29.

Black, N. 1990. "Medical Litigation and the Quality of Care." *Lancet* 335:35–37.

Bonacheck, L. I. 1979. "Are Randomized Trials Appropriate for Evaluating New Operations?" *New England Journal of Medicine* 301:44–45.

Bovbjerg, R. R., F. A. Sloan, and J. F. Blumstein. 1989. "Valuing Life and Limb in Tort: Scheduling 'Pain and Suffering.' " *Northwestern University Law Review* 83:908–76.

Bowman, M. A., and J. L. Murray. 1989. "Cost, Correlates and Effects of Malpractice Litigation in Family Practice Residency Programmes in the United States." *Family Practice* 6:146–50.

Burda, D. 1987. "Liability Reshapes Hospital/Physician Relationships." *Hospitals* 5:56–60.

Charles, S. C., J. R. Wilbert, and K. J. Franke. 1985. "Sued and Nonsued Physicians' Self-Reported Reactions to Malpractice Litigation." *American Journal of Psychiatry* 142:437–40.

"Credentialing for Technology Use: An Important Issue for Hospitals." 1987. *Health Technology* 1:1–9.

Danzon, P. M. 1985. *Medical Malpractice: Theory, Evidence and Public Policy.* Harvard University Press.

Epstein, R. A. 1987. "Legal Liability for Medical Innovation." *Cardozo Law Review* 8:1139–59.

Flood, A. B., W. R. Scott, and W. Ewy. 1984. "Does Practice Make Perfect? Part I: The Relation between Hospital, Volume and Outcomes for Selected Diagnostic Categories." *Medical Care* 22:98–114.

Foote, S. B. 1986. "Coexistence, Conflict, and Cooperation: Public Policies toward Medical Devices." *Journal of Health Politics, Policy and Law* 11:501–23.

Gaumer, G. L. 1984. "Regulating Health Professionals: A Review of the Empirical Literature." *Milbank Memorial Fund Quarterly* 62:380–416.

Gilbert, J. P., B. McPeek, and F. Mosteller. 1977. "Statistics and Ethics in Surgery and Anesthesia." *Science* 198:684–89.

Grady, M. F. 1988. "Why Are People Negligent? Technology Non-Durable Precautions, and the Medical Malpractice Explostion." *Northwestern University Law Review* 82:293–334.

Harris, J. E. 1987. "Defensive Medicine: It Costs but Does It Work?" *Journal of the American Medical Association* 257:2801–02.

Hemenway, D., and others. 1986. "Benefits of Experience: Treating Coronary Artery Disease." *Medical Care* 24:125–33.

Institute of Medicine. 1989. *Medical Professional Liability and the Delivery of Obstetrical Care*, vol. 1. Washington: National Academy Press.

Jones, L. 1990. "Witnesses Agree: Medical Liability System Needs Overhaul." *American Medical News* 11:1.

Kibble-Smith, B., and A. W. Hafner. 1986. "The Effect of the Information Age on Physicians' Professional Liability." *De Paul Law Review* 36:69–94.

Langton, P. A., and D. A. Kammerer. 1985. "The Effects of the Malpractice Crisis on Certified Nurse-Midwives." *Nursing Forum* 22:149–52.

Louis Harris and Associates, Inc. 1982. "A Survey of Medical Device Manufacturers." Study 802005. National Technical Information Service.

Luft, H. S. 1980. "The Relation between Surgical Volume and Mortality: An Exploration of Causal Factors and Alternative Models." *Medical Care* 18:940–59.

Luft, H. S., J. P. Bunker, and A. C. Enthoven. 1979. "Should Operations Be Regionalized? The Empirical Relation between Surgical Volume and Mortality." *New England Journal of Medicine* 301:1364–69.

Maerki, S. C., H. S. Luft, and S. S. Hunt. 1986. "Selecting Categories of Patients for Regionalization. Implications of the Relationship between Volume and Outcome." *Medical Care* 24:148–58.

Manning, W. G., and others. 1984. "A Controlled Trial of the Effect of a Prepaid Group Practice on Use of Services." *New England Journal of Medicine* 310:1505–10.

Mastroianni, L., P. J. Donaldson, and T. T. Kane, eds. 1990. *Developing New Contraceptives: Obstacles and Opportunities*. Washington: National Academy Press.

Mehlman, M. 1985. "Rationing Expensive Lifesaving Medical Treatments." *Wisconsin Law Review* 1985:239–303.

Meier, B. 1990. "Designer of Faulty Heart Valve Seeks Redemption in New Device." *New York Times*, Apr. 17:C1.

Morreim, H. 1989. "Stratified Scarcity: Redefining the Standard of Care." *Law Medicine and Health Care* 17:356–67.

Newhouse, J. P., and others. 1985. "Are Fee-for-Service-Costs Increasing Faster than HMO Costs?" *Medical Care* 23:960–66.

Office of Technology Assessment. 1984. *Federal Policies and the Medical Devices Industry.* Washington.

Overcast, T. D., K. J. Merrikin, and R. W. Evans. 1985. "Malpractice Issues in Heart Transplantation." *American Journal of Law and Medicine* 10:363–95.

Robinson, G. O. 1986. "The Medical Malpractice Crisis of the 1970s: A Retrospective." *Law and Contemporary Problems* 49:5–36.

Rosenberg, S. A. 1990. "Adoptive Immunotherapy for Cancer." *Scientific American* 262:62–69.

Shapiro, R. S., and others. 1989. "A Survey of Sued and Non-Sued Physicians and Suing Patients." *Archives of Internal Medicine* 149:2190–96.

Sloan, F. A., and R. R. Bovbjerg. 1989. "Medical Malpractice: Crises, Response, and Effects." *Health Insurance Association of America Research Bulletin.*

Tancredi, L. R., and J. A. Barondess. 1978. "The Problem of Defensive Medicine." *Science* 200:879–82.

Touby, K. A. 1988. "Products Liability and the Device Industry." *Food Drug Cosmetic Law Journal* 43:55–66.

Valenstein, E. S. 1986. *Great and Desperate Cures: The Rise and Decline of Psychosurgery and Other Radical Technologies for Mental Illness.* Basic Books.

Weaver, R. H. 1988. "Impact of Product Liability on the Development of New Medical Technologies." American Medical Association Proceedings, June 26. Chicago.

Weisbard, A. J. 1987. "On Not Compensating for Bad Outcomes to Biomedical Innovations: A Response and Modest Proposal." *Cardozo Law Review* 8:1161–88.

Weisman, C. S., and others. 1989. "Practice Changes and Response to the Malpractice Litigation Climate: Results of a Maryland Physician's Survey." *Medical Care* 27:16–24.

Problems and Solutions in Medical Malpractice: Comments on Chapters Six and Seven

Randall R. Bovbjerg

How MUCH does the law of medical malpractice affect safety and inno-vation in health care? These are tough questions. Reiser, and Tancredi and Nelkin, have done a fine job in trying to answer them. Given the lack of concrete evidence, they have erected impressive edifices. As the authors recognize, their work is based on a review of the literature and on selective interviews. One might say they have addressed these issues in the old-fashioned way, not with computers and data but by thinking and talking to people.

The Reiser chapter is especially innovative. The author had the task of divining what the law does for safety. Since nobody really knows, he transformed the question. Because one cannot really go forward with evidence, he went backward to first principles of ethics—back to the fifth century B.C., in fact, and Hippocrates. This is a creative approach that merits attention, and Reiser makes some good points. In the chapter he revisits familiar arguments about defensive medicine.[1] But he stresses one thing that is seldom emphasized: defensiveness can lead physicians into hiding information on a particular case or refusing to cooperate in general scientific inquiry. The motivation is to conceal bad outcomes—or at least potentially litigable ones. So long as the resolution of malpractice claims is perceived as unscientific and unfair, such motivation will remain.

The Tancredi and Nelkin chapter is extremely balanced. Their insights suggest effects in all directions. Not only are the vectors multidirectional, but their actual magnitude is also hard to quantify. The chapter is es-pecially impressive for its command of several literatures. The authors do not just cite works on medical effectiveness and malpractice law; they

1. See, for example, Tancredi and Barondess 1977.

have instead pulled together many perspectives, including those of technology assessment, professional regulation, and psychiatry.

The two chapters reinforce each other. Reiser deals with effects on *individual*, clinical decisionmaking, case by case: Dr. Jones taking care of Mrs. Smith. Tancredi and Nelkin emphasize effects on the *general* introduction of technology and on innovations in *patterns* of practice, individual as well as social. Both chapters recognize that bad news and good news arise from this system. All seasoned participant-observers have their horror stories, and the chapters duly repeat some of them. Yet there are bright spots as well, signs of improvements achieved. The authors of both chapters also agree that systematic knowledge is much weaker than one would like, and they specifically call for more information. In this, I sympathize greatly with them.[2]

The two chapters are all the more notable, moreover, because most tort reformers are not interested in objective information. Nor are most defenders of the current system. All broad-based public colloquiums like the one undertaken in this project demonstrate this phenomenon. They attract people who talk past one another. Each orator may wave one bit of information, but it is usually a selective bit. Hence much more can certainly be done. Policymakers are better served by dispassionate, independent analysis than by passionate presentations from the interested parties in reform debates. But of course analysts need to be able to communicate at an accessible level.

Thoughts and Theories

One of the best things about these chapters is that they are thought-provoking. Consider four categories of thoughts they provoked:

—What, precisely, are the problems with the functioning of today's system(s)? Where is the smoking gun? Reformers have an understandable urge to grab for a quick fix—a wholesale redesign—without carefully specifying what is broken.

—What problematic incentives are created for people's behavior? This point has received the most attention in these and other chapters in this volume.

—What conclusions about the system's performance can be drawn? The system should be judged by its role in compensation and in deterrence, its two chief goals.

2. See, for example, Zuckerman, Koller, and Bovbjerg 1986.

—What exactly are the implications for profferred solutions? There are many suggested solutions in quest of a problem. Some of them go forward; many of them would try to turn back the clock.

Problems in Practice

Is malpractice and other litigation "out of control?" "Exploding?" "Skyrocketing?" Such language is common.[3] One often hears that people expect perfection, a risk-free society—that patients want vengeance if they have less than a perfect baby, for instance. Well, that may be true, as a tendency. But as a predictor of actual medical litigation, it is a great exaggeration. The medical system causes far more imperfection and damage than ever gets to a claims adjuster or a courtroom. Negligent bad outcomes exceed claims by a factor of five or ten, according to the best available evidence, not to mention the yet much larger number of non-negligent bad outcomes.[4]

Moreover, one shouldn't forget the plaintiff's lawyers. Despite what one can appropriately say about their being greedy (that is to say, human), they are nonetheless appropriately motivated to screen out low-value and low-merit cases, and they do so.[5] One important difference between malpractice and other areas of liability is that in malpractice it is difficult to tell when adverse events are indeed due to negligence rather than to the underlying condition that brought the patient into the medical system in the first place.[6] So patients, their lawyers, and the courts can all make mistakes (as considered more below). But the biggest problem is the meritorious cases never brought. All in all, malpractice poses rather less of a problem for doctors than product liability does for manufacturers of aircraft, for example, where, as Robert Martin says in chapter 13, crashes seldom occur without a lawsuit.

PSYCHIC COSTS. The first specific problem I want to underline is one evident in Peter Huber's book (1988) but not much noted in the malpractice papers or in any chapters in this volume: the liability system is flat-out obnoxious. Purely and simply, it is agonizingly unpleasant. Reiser referred to the problem of the patient's being vulnerable when she goes

3. Huber 1988; Burger 1982.
4. Danzon 1985, 23, 25, using data from California Medical Association 1977 and National Association of Insurance Commissioners 1980; Harvard Medical Practice Study 1990.
5. Dietz, Baird, and Berul 1973.
6. Keeton 1973.

into medical care. The same psychic phenomenon is what truly annoys doctors and can make them so defensive.

A doctor going into a courtroom is like a patient going into a hospital. Both feel vulnerable. Both know they are at risk. Both have been asked a lot of personal and embarrassing questions in advance. In each case, they are assigned to a room. They are told how to dress. They are confined to one spot in that room and are told when they can leave. They are told to speak when they are spoken to. Then comes more poking and prodding. Throughout, the professionals are clearly in charge. They speak in dense jargon, laced with a lot of Latin. Often they speak only to one another. Periodically, the professional's huddle over in a corner, out of earshot, seemingly settling their client's fate. And the bills in each case can be horrendous, raising fears that the limits of any insurance will be exceeded.

The legal process may take testimony rather than tests. But it is every bit as intrusive as hospitalization. The key psychic fact is that defendant doctors lose control, a commodity they greatly prize. The standard of inquiry is different from their own. The forum is foreign. Physicians must give deference rather than receive it. And, as anyone knows who has sat through a cross-examination, even in practice, it is no fun.

Anxiety over this process is clearly a problem, as shown by the research (cited by Tancredi and Nelkin) into the psychological impact it has on doctors. One suspects that if plaintiffs could interest researchers (and research funders) in exploring their mental states, the findings would be similar. Both sides suffer—at least until one wins. This warping of the psyche under duress is one reason that law students learn that any lawyer who represents himself has a fool for a client and a half-wit for an attorney.

TRANSACTION COSTS. The conventional legal process operates with high cost and long delays. This point is well appreciated,[7] but it bears reiterating that malpractice litigation is among the worst in those regards. Transaction costs are very expensive, far more than for automobile cases or workers' compensation claims.[8]

What else is wrong with how the system works? Well, the system has to do two things: it has to decide liability, and it has to decide damages. There are good theoretical arguments, especially if one doesn't look too hard for empirical evidence, that the system does poorly on both counts. Empiricism yields a mixed picture.

7. See, for example, Kakalik and Pace 1986; General Accounting Office 1987.
8. Bovbjerg and others (forthcoming).

LIABILITY DETERMINATIONS. Liability standards are vague. In their lack of specific guidance, they resemble one of the key FARs (federal aviation regulations) for aviation safety, as Craig describes it in chapter 13. Basically, it says that one should not do anything that is not a good idea or that leads to undue problems. That is typical of the kind of vaguely verbal standard that malpractice law applies. A classic statement runs:

> [Absent] an express agreement, the doctor does not warrant or insure either a correct diagnosis or a successful course of treatment, and the doctor will not be liable for an honest mistake of judgment, where the proper course is open to reasonable doubt. But . . . a doctor will ordinarily be understood to hold himself out as having [and using] the knowledge, skill and care ordinarily possessed and employed by members of the profession in good standing. . . . [I]t is not the middle but the minimum common skill which is to be looked to . . . and . . . the doctor is entitled to be judged according to the tenets of the school the doctor professes to follow.[9]

How does this compare with the standard used in other cases? In most torts, such as auto accidents, the standard is just as vague but apparently more stringent: drivers are judged against the behavior of a "reasonable person" of ordinary prudence. About this hypothetical paragon of virtue, it has been written:

> He is an ideal, a standard, the embodiment of all those qualities which we demand of the good citizen. . . . He is one who invariably looks where he is going, and is careful to examine the immediate foreground before he executes a leap or a bound; who neither stargazes nor is lost in meditation when approaching trapdoors or the margin of a dock; . . . who never mounts a moving omnibus and does not alight from any car while the train is in motion . . . and will inform himself of the history and habits of a dog before administering a caress; . . . who never drives his ball till those in front of him have definitely vacated the putting-green . . . ; who uses nothing except in moderation, and even while he flogs his child is meditating only on the golden mean.[10]

Apparently the law, in textbook theory, expects rather less of a doctor

9. Prosser and Keeton 1984, 186–87.
10. Prosser and Keeton 1984, 174–75, n. 9, quoting Herbert 1930, 12–16.

relative to other doctors than, say, from drivers relative to the hypothetical ideal. As Schwartz explains in his chapter, the "black letter" law in the textbooks looks fairly pro-doctor. But the doctors are convinced, and probably correctly, that it is not applied consistently in every case. In retrospect, of course, and in the calm of a jury room, much common behavior may fall short of the ideal, especially complex decisions taken under stress. And, in practice, the jury in a malpractice case can believe whom it wants. The jury watches the familiar "battle of the experts," which it can resolve however it likes, without having to explain why one expert's opinion was favored over another's.[11]

Using such criteria, it is hard to make such a process predictable. Uncertainty foments disagreement and, hence, litigation. Further, the ultimate legal decisionmaker, the civil jury, is allegedly too inexpert to make complicated judgments about medical negligence and medical causation.[12] Finally, the standard of proof in a civil trial is "more probable than not." So one should expect juries to make mistakes about "objective truth" up to half the time, assuming any process could achieve truth. This 50-50 standard is naturally often a cause for unhappiness on one side or the other. Reform could move the standard one way or the other and make one side or the other happier, but not both.

So much for theorizing. What is known about how well the system actually makes liability determinations? Some evidence suggests that the system works as intended. For one thing, physicians with a history of many malpractice claims tend to have a high-risk future.[13] For another, expert physicians can decide in advance what kinds of bad medical outcomes are moderately or highly avoidable; such avoidable incidents, when litigated, are far more likely than average to be paid.[14] Moreover, there is little statistically significant correlation between paid and unpaid claims, as there would be if settlements were random.[15] This limited empirical evidence does not prove the system is perfect. But it does disprove the common portrayal of random claims and haphazard claims settlement.[16]

11. Kinney and Wilder 1989.
12. American Medical Society 1988.
13. Sloan and others 1989.
14. Bovbjerg, Tancredi, and Gaylin 1990; Sloan and Hsieh (forthcoming).
15. Rolph (forthcoming).
16. Some chart reviews of malpractice cases are also done. See Julian and others 1985, 320–21 (1,001 "risk factors" identified in 220 obstetric claims, only 32 percent correctly managed). But see Cornblath and Clark 1984, 298 (only 31 percent of 250 prenatal brain damage claims deemed preventable, 42 percent nonpreventable, and 27 percent indeterminate).

The system is not *Looney Tunes*, nor even *Roger Rabbit*. As with cartoons, however, production costs are very expensive, and the outcome is unpredictable in any individual case. And Dr. Jones, on trial for his professional reputation and risking a verdict beyond his liability coverage, does not much care about general statistics.

DETERMINING DAMAGES. Here again, the black letter law is vague, but this time no different for doctors than for other defendants. I was astonished when I did some legal research last year—McCormick in 1935 on damages, Dobbs in 1973 on remedies, and recent appellate cases from several jurisdictions. Few standards exist: mainly, the law tells jurors to compute actual losses like medical bills and lost wages, figuring both known past and estimated future losses. The largest cases mostly involve future losses; and here, of course, the discount rate matters greatly (in most jurisdictions), but each jury has to decide it anew. That may be good for economists who want to serve repeatedly as expert witnesses. But for society, it is another recipe for increased disputation, at great expense.

As for nonpecuniary damages, the law is even less precise. Many jurisdictions instruct jurors that there is no standard, there is no market in pain or suffering. So twelve (or six) good people must use their best judgment. That is, they pull a number out of the air, at best from counsel's closing arguments. Any gathering of economists knows that there is a market in risk to life and limb,[17] but the law does not recognize that, and a jury is normally free to do whatever it wants. Moreover, jury decisions can arguably be influenced too greatly by sympathy and other "extra-legal" factors,[18] though sympathy or prejudice may be less influential than defendants think.[19]

Because of the lack of standards and the process of relying on jury discretion, the sky is the limit for damages. Recently, a doctor in Phoenix found liable for a baby's HIV infection from a needed transfusion was facing a $28.7 million verdict.[20] Predictably, the case was settled for far less on appeal (a structured plan with a present value of about $6 million). But meanwhile the verdict convulsed the medical community. The impact of such open-ended, unpredictable potential liability was well captured by one of Reiser's interviewees. A first-rate heart surgeon gave up operating on babies because for one bad case "he might be paying the rest

17. Miller 1989.
18. See, for example, Chin and Peterson 1985.
19. Bovbjerg and others (forthcoming).
20. McGinn 1990.

of his days." That is very scary. And the doctor takes this very personally in an arena where society depends on personal services.[21]

In the aggregate, however, the system performs much better than its reputation. Juries and professional claims adjusters do surprisingly well. Empirical analysis of a large number of closed malpractice claims and of jury verdicts suggests that about 40 percent of the variability in awards or settlements can be explained by only two factors—severity of injury and age of claimant (a proxy for how long permanent injury is going to last).[22] Those are rational factors. If one adds in other logical factors, the proportion of variance explained rises to about 50 percent, and with type of case, to above 60 percent. Furthermore, average damage amounts rise in step with the increasing severity of injury, as they should, until amounts decline for death cases, for which the law has more restrictive standards. The law does not allow damages for loss of the decedent's enjoyment of life; people care about that, but the law does not, largely for historical reasons. So again, there is good news and bad news: more predictability than appreciated but less than desirable, and with open-endedness clearly a problem.

Incentives and Impacts

The main reason for policy concern about malpractice is not its cost in insurance premiums (perhaps 1.5 percent of medical spending), nor the misfunctioning of law per se (considered above). The key is "defensive medicine." Clearly doctors feel threatened and defensive, as Reiser shows. With this much smoke, one must believe there is some fire. But how large is this alleged conflagration?[23] Very high estimates exist. But there are conceptual arguments both ways, and as usual little hard evidence.[24] Estimates of the cost of defensive medicine—positive and negative—vary enormously.

Positive defensiveness means all those extra, "unneeded" tests and procedures, especially so-called high technology. Clearly American medicine does a lot of procedures, leading the world in intensity of care.

21. It is also bad that a company would be lost without sufficient showing of a bad safety record, as occurs in general aviation. See chapter 13.

22. Aggregate results reported in Sloan and Hsieh 1990; Bovbjerg and others (forthcoming), table 3.

23. The traditional estimate is some $15 billion a year (Reynolds, Rizzo, and Gonzalez 1987, 2776). Much higher claims have been made (see note 35).

24. Sloan and Bovbjerg 1989.

Malpractice is often blamed. But there are other explanations than malpractice fears. Doctors are well paid for doing tests and procedures. And, as Reiser notes, patients are very demanding. They want tests. Doctors often explain, "I did not want to give them a drug, I did not want to give them a CAT scan, but I was nervous." They are certainly nervous about liability. But apart from liability, they are nervous about disappointing patients, about living with uncertainty, and about their bottom lines. Going back to first principles, and 500 B.C., one can blame Greek civilization. People in the Western world are not fatalists but activists; they would rather do something than sit still and wait to see what happens. "Watchful waiting" and "accepting the inevitable" are not popular paradigms of behavior, and such attitudes affect patients and doctors alike.[25]

One proof that factors other than malpractice concerns are involved comes from recent health policy research on medical practice patterns. Doctors vary greatly, even within one state, in how much they use tests and procedures.[26] It is far too simple to assert that "doctors do everything possible." They do not. Moreover, practice can be monitored, and education can be put into place. Incentives can be altered. The law is probably less potent than doctors would like to think. It has less basic influence on beliefs and behavior than some other things have.

Positive defensive medicine is bad enough, at whatever level it exists. But at least one can see it, and policymakers can address it. One can talk about what to do about it—how doctors can change practice patterns, the use of low-value procedures, and the like. Negative defensive medicine is more of a problem, for one cannot really see it. That makes difficulties not only for researchers or commentators but also for policymakers. Recall Reiser's observation that doctors fail to enter in-patient information on medical records because they fear possible liability. That is a serious failing that can have adverse effects on patient well-being. Fortunately, doctors have other motives for being complete and accurate.

Most people in the health policy community, however, would be surprised to hear that *innovation* has been stifled by liability litigation. The United States leads the world in high-tech, high-intensity medicine. Americans are quick to adopt new procedures. Drugs may lag but mainly for regulatory reasons. The country is low in physician visits, hospital visits, length of hospital stays, but high in intensity of care and in in-

25. See Katz 1984 on medical fear of uncertainty; Eddy 1984 on the relation of those attitudes to practice patterns.
26. Wennberg and Gittlesohn 1973; Wennberg 1984.

novative, high-tech procedures.[27] Perhaps some of this is positive defensive medicine, but surely negative defensive medicine does not often take the form of avoiding technology, with some exceptions as noted in the Tancredi-Nelkin chapter. The law has not (yet) reached the main engines of medical innovation. The National Institutes of Health cannot be sued for giving the grant that discovered a treatment that hurt a patient. Nor do journal editors or peer reviews have liability fears (although recently a book reviewer was sued for libel).

More credible is the concern that doctors may avoid certain categories of patients and certain types of procedures. Again here, the evidence is not strong, being largely based on physicians' self-reporting about their motives during a period of politicized "crisis." However, particularly in obstetrics, the cumulative effect seems real.[28]

In the end, what ties these strands of concern together? Perhaps the safest conclusion is that the system is simply not credible to the decisionmakers it is trying to affect. So doctors cannot possibly take the rational approach and craft a measured response. They would rather say, "I am out of that kind of surgery." Of course, withdrawal is easier if doctors have options that are economically viable.

Compensation and Deterrence

Compensation and deterrence are the two central goals of tort law. How well does the system achieve them? As a compensation system, malpractice law and insurance perform miserably. They fail to reach most of the injured, take too long to deliver, provide somewhat erratic damages at very high cost, and cause needless anguish in the process. If malpractice law were merely a compensation system, society would have junked it long ago as a woefully inadequate one.[29]

What of deterrence? It is logical that people facing liability, however well insured, should seek to avoid the rigors of the process by being more careful. And that is what the law presumes. But it is mainly a presumption. Even defenders of a fault-based litigation system accept its deterrent value mainly on faith,[30] although they often suggest improvements. Thus far,

27. Rublee 1989; Schieber and Pouiller 1989.
28. Institute of Medicine 1989.
29. Bovbjerg 1986.
30. See, for example, Schwartz and Komesar 1978; Danzon 1985.

even sympathetic empiricists have failed to document that malpractice systematically lowers the rate of bad medical outcomes.[31]

In the battle of anecdotes, supporters of deterrence can cite only a few accomplishments. I have from time to time asked a number of trial lawyers to suggest such beneficial effects, but they are hard pressed to do so. One lawyer once asserted, for instance, that the law deserved credit for medicine's adopting the practice of accounting for each surgical "sponge" used as an operation is concluded. One suspects that right-thinking nurses and surgeons would have begun to do so on their own. More credibly, one may note that organized medicine historically had little interest in improving physician discipline or in promulgating practice standards.[32] The specter of malpractice has certainly changed such attitudes.[33] One can also note that malpractice is not a random event, as some doctors believe, but rather more predictable.[34] So there is at least the potential for a credible deterrent effect.

On the other side of the battlefield, those who would roll back the legal legions also have little more than rhetorical ammunition. Detractors of deterrence, mainly of the medical persuasion, say that the law does nothing to make them more careful or their patients safer. Reiser's interviewees often seemed to take this stance. Yet many of the same people also claim that legal fears prompt them to engage in enormous amounts of wasteful defensive medicine. It is hard to believe that the medical credo is truly "billions for defense; not one red cent for safety."[35] If the medical profession cared so little for patient welfare, that would really be cause for concern.

Perhaps there is only one persuasive conclusion to be drawn about deterrence, or about safety: doctors are the prime decisionmakers in medicine. If physicians firmly believe that legal-insurance decisions are crazy, the system cannot work as intended. And it does seem that doctors do so believe—despite the evidence cited earlier and even though physician-run liability insurers make most payment determinations now. So reform is needed to promote credibility and safety.

31. Harvard Medical Practice Study 1990.
32. Kinney and Wilder 1989.
33. American Medical Society 1988; Eddy 1990.
34. Sloan and others 1989.
35. Estimates of defensive medicine vary by a factor of ten or more. Senator Orrin Hatch went so far in a July 1990 press release as to endorse an estimate that one-quarter of all U.S. health care spending (about $150 billion a year currently) is wasteful defensiveness. Such unsupported estimates do not even merit inclusion in the text.

Selecting among Solutions

What does all this mean for the future, for solutions in particular? Diagnosis always runs ahead of prescription. And society probably does not yet know how best to cope with the issues of medical injury and of creating appropriate incentives for safety and innovation. Historically, liability has been increasing. Without a change in the basic attitudes of judges who make tort law and of citizens who sue and sit on juries, that trend is apt to continue. The end of the 1980s and start of the 1990s have seen downturns in claims and liability premiums.[36] The same occurred after the 1970s era "crisis" as well.[37] But, as before, the traditional continuing rise seems likely to return. And the appropriate solution cannot be more of the same litigiousness and enhanced legal process, despite the trial lawyers' not unreasonable emphasis on how much malpractice exists. The system is too costly to cope with most injuries, especially the smaller ones, and trial dockets are already overburdened.

Nor, however, is less-of-the-same reform the best answer. Less of the same is unfortunately what most reformers have to offer. To date, "conventional" tort reforms have simply tried to reduce medical providers' liability premiums by cutting back on several generations of accumulated pro-plaintiff rules of law. "Capping" damages at some arbitrary level is the strongest single reform of this type.[38] Caps and some other such reforms do work as intended to reduce the frequency and severity of malpractice claims,[39] as well as premiums.[40] But it is unlikely that they can much reduce medical defensiveness, since they do not much change the underlying system or eliminate the fear of unpredictable litigation. Medical providers have complained bitterly about defensive medicine for more than twenty years—since at least two "crises" ago, a time when claims and premiums were relatively low.[41] They also complain in states with and without conventional tort reform. Doctors (like their patients) often seem to want zero risk, as some of them told Reiser. Hence marginal changes in legal exposure are unlikely to have much effect on whatever level of defensive medicine now exists.

36. See, for example, Schiffman 1989; Freudenheim 1989.
37. Danzon 1982; Sloan and Bovbjerg 1989.
38. See, for example, Bovbjerg 1989.
39. Danzon 1986; Sloan, Mergenhagen, and Bovbjerg 1989.
40. Zuckerman, Bovbjerg, and Sloan 1990.
41. U.S. Congress 1969.

More promising are more fundamental reforms of the current system. Anything that could be done to make liability determinations more accurate would be good. What would that be? Perhaps better jury instructions, more careful peer review, more use of voluntary alternative dispute resolution. Another welcome reform would be to improve the consistency and predictability of damage awards, yet without resorting to arbitrary caps. As Schwartz notes in chapter 2, some other countries rely on detailed "tariffs" to compute noneconomic losses.[42] The same could be done in the United States.[43] Similarly, other elements of damages could be made more accurate.[44]

Also promising are major new replacements for today's system. One kind would change the forum in which determinations are made. Such reforms would leave fault-based rules more or less intact, although often changing rules of damages. To its credit, in 1988 the American Medical Association proposed such a plan, one that would help small claimants as well as defendants. The plan could be improved,[45] but at least it is a constructive proposal—and unlike the backward-looking stance of organized medicine in an earlier era. The trial lawyers, in contrast, have come up with virtually no suggestions: they have no plan to help the vast majority of injured patients that they now turn away (or never see to begin with). Nor do they suggest ways to systematically improve the clarity of tort incentives for safety and innovation. Besides the AMA plan, other forum-changing proposals include mandatory, binding arbitration for malpractice claims, for which federal legislation has just been introduced.

The biggest change would be to depart both from the current forum and from the current fault-based approach. Various no-fault ideas exist.[46] One quasi-fault or selective no-fault or selective no-fault possibility is to remove from litigation certain professionally predetermined classes of avoidable bad outcomes. Instead, a simplified insurance process could make such events automatically compensable.[47] Today, the law determines payment responsibility based on after-the-fact, idiosyncratic testimony about allegedly faulty *processes* of care in particular cases. This approach creates all the problems already noted. The selective no-fault

42. Munkman 1989; Viney and Markesinis 1985.
43. Levin 1989; Bovbjerg, Sloan, and Blumstein 1989.
44. Bovbjerg, Sloan, and Blumstein 1990.
45. Bovbjerg 1990.
46. For summaries, see Latz 1989; Physician Insurers Association of America 1989.
47. See, for example, Tancredi 1986; Bovbjerg, Tancredi, and Gaylin 1990.

approach relies on generalized expert judgment applied in advance about statistical *outcomes* of medical care. It holds promise of improving both compensation and deterrence for most economically consequential bad outcomes. Claims of other damage would still have to be resolved case by case, either through tort law or an alternative.

A Final Word

In the end, the United States needs a better system. There is no question about that. But one should not forget that much more bad acting and many more avoidable bad outcomes exist than appear in today's system. We need to find a more active system, a cheaper system. But in that search we should not lose sight of the need for accountability and the social and professional obligation to protect patients.

References

American Medical Society/Specialty Society Medical Liability Project. 1988. *A Proposed Alternative to the Civil Justice System for Resolving Medical Liability Disputes: A Fault-Based, Administrative System.* Chicago.

Blumstein, J. F., R. R. Bovbjerg, and F. A. Sloan. [Forthcoming.] "Beyond Tort Reform: Developing Better Tools for Assessing Damages for Personal Injuries." *Yale Journal on Regulation.*

Bovbjerg, R. R. 1986. "Medical Malpractice on Trial: Quality of Care Is the Important Standard." *Law and Contemporary Problems* 49:321–48.

———. 1989. "Legislation on Medical Malpractice: Further Developments and a Preliminary Report Card." *U.C. Davis Law Review* 22:499–556; reprinted in *National Insurance Law Review* 3:217–71.

———. 1990. "Reforming a Proposed Tort Reform: Improving on the American Medical Association's Proposed Administrative Tribunal for Medical Malpractice." *Courts, Health Science, and the Law* 1:19–28.

Bovbjerg, R. R., F. A. Sloan, and J. F. Blumstein. 1989. "Valuing Life and Limb in Tort: Scheduling Pain and Suffering." *Northwestern University Law Review* 83:908–76.

Bovbjerg, R. R., L. R. Tancredi, and D. S. Gaylin. 1990. "Obstetrics and Malpractice: Evidence on the Performance of a Selective No-Fault System." Working Paper 3733-01. Urban Institute, Washington.

Bovbjerg, R. R., and others. [Forthcoming.] "Juries and Justice: Are Malpractice and Other Personal Injuries Created Equal?" *Law and Contemporary Problems* 53.

Burger, W. E. 1982. "Isn't There a Better Way?" *ABA Journal* 68:274–77.

California Medical Association and California Hospital Association. 1977. *Report on the Medical Insurance Feasibility Study.* San Francisco: Sutter Publications.

Chin A., and M. A. Peterson. 1985. *Deep Pockets, Empty Pockets: Who Wins in Cook County Jury Trials.* R-3249-ICJ. Santa Monica, Calif.: Rand Corporation.

Cornblath, M., and R. L. Clark. 1984. "Neonatal Brain Damage—An Analysis of 250 Claims." *Western Journal of Medicine* 140:298–302.

Danzon, P. M. 1982. *The Frequency and Severity of Medical Malpractice Claims.* R-2870-ICJ/HCFA. Santa Monica, Calif.: Rand Corporation.

———. 1985. *Medical Malpractice: Theory, Evidence, and Public Policy.* Harvard University Press.

———. 1986. "The Frequency and Severity of Medical Malpractice Claims: New Evidence." *Law and Contemporary Problems* 49:57–84.

Dietz, S., C. B. Baird, and L. Berul. 1973. "The Medical Malpractice Legal System. In *Report of the Secretary's Commission on Medical Malpractice,* appendix, 87–167. Department of Health, Education, and Welfare Publication (05) 73-89.

Dobbs, D. B. 1973. *Handbook on the Law of Remedies: Damages—Equity-Restitution.* St. Paul, Minn.: West Publishing.

Eddy, D. M. 1984. "Variations in Physician Practice: The Role of Uncertainty." *Health Affairs* 3:74–89.

———. 1990. "Clinical Decision Making: From Theory to Practice. Practice Policies—What Are They?" *Journal of the American Medical Association* 263:877–80.

Freudenheim, M. 1989. "Costs of Medical Malpractice Drop after an 11-Year Climb." *New York Times,* June 11: A1.

General Accounting Office. 1987. *Medical Malpractice: Characteristics of Claims Closed in 1984.* GAO/HRD-87-55. Washington.

Harvard Medical Practice Study. 1990. *Patients, Doctors, and Lawyers: Medical Injury, Malpractice Litigation, and Patient Compensation in New York.* President and Fellows of Harvard College.

Herbert, A. P. 1930. *Misleading Cases in the Common Law.* Putnam.

Huber, P. W. 1988. *Liability: The Legal Revolution and Its Consequences.* Basic Books.

Institute of Medicine. 1989. *Medical Professional Liability and the Delivery of Obstetrical Care.* 2 vols. Washington: National Academy Press.

Julian, T. M., and others. 1985. "Investigation of Obstetric Malpractice Closed Claims: Profile of Event." *American Journal of Perinatology* 2:320–24.

Kakalik, J. S., and N. M. Pace. 1986. *Costs and Compensation Paid in Tort Litigation.* R-3391-ICJ. Santa Monica, Calif.: Rand Corporation.

Katz, J. 1984. "Acknowledging Uncertainty: The Confrontation of Knowledge, and Ignorance." In *The Silent World of Doctor and Patient*, 165–206. Free Press.

Keeton, R. E. 1973. "Compensation for Medical Accidents." *University of Pennsylvania Law Review* 121:590–605.

Kinney, E. D., and M. M. Wilder. 1989. "Medical Standard Setting in the Current Malpractice Environment: Problems and Possibilities." *U.C. Davis Law Review* 22:421–50.

Latz, R. S. 1989. "No-Fault Liability and Medical Malpractice." *Journal of Legal Medicine* 10:479–525.

Levin, F. S. 1989. "Pain and Suffering Guidelines: A Cure for Damages Measurement 'Anomie.' " *University of Michigan Journal of Law Reform* 22:303–32.

McCormick, C. T. 1935. *Handbook on the Law of Damages*. St. Paul, Minn.: West Publishing.

McGinn, P. R. 1990. "Arizona Doctors Protest Award in AIDS Case." *American Medical News*, June 29:3.

Miller, T. R. 1989. "Willingness to Pay Comes of Age: Will the System Survive?" *Northwestern University Law Review* 83:876–907.

Munkman, J. 1989. *Damages for Personal Injury and Death*. St. Paul, Minn.: Butterworths.

National Association of Insurance Commissioners. 1980. *Medical Malpractice Closed Claims, 1975–1978*. Brookfield, Wis.

Physician Insurers Association of America. 1989. *A Comprehensive Review of Alternatives to the Present System of Resolving Medical Liability Claims*. Lawrenceville, N.J.

Prosser, W. P., and P. Keeton. 1984. *Prosser and Keeton on the Law of Torts*. 5th ed. St. Paul, Minn.: West Publishing.

Reynolds, R. A., J. A. Rizzo, and M. L. Gonzalez. 1987. "The Cost of Medical Professional Liability." *Journal of the American Medical Association* 257:2776–81.

Rolph, J. E. [Forthcoming.] "Merit Rating for Physicians' Malpractice Premiums: Only Modest Deterrent." *Journal of Law and Contemporary Problems* 53.

Rublee, D. A. 1989. "Medical Technology in Canada, Germany, and the United States." *Health Affairs* 8:178–81.

Schieber, G. J., and J. P. Pouiller. 1989. "International Health Care Expenditure Trends, 1987." *Health Affairs* 8:169–78.

Schiffman, J. R. 1989. "Medical Malpractice Insurance Rates Fall: Drop in Number of Claims Cuts Insurers' Costs." *Wall Street Journal*, Apr. 28: B1.

Schwartz, W., and N. Komesar. 1978. "Doctors, Damages, and Deterrence." *New England Journal of Medicine* 298:1282.

Sloan, F. A., and R. R. Bovbjerg. 1989. *Medical Malpractice: Crises, Response and Effects*. Health Insurance Association of America Research Bulletin, May.

Sloan, F. A., and C. R. Hsieh. [Forthcoming.] "Variability in Medical Malpractice Payment: Is the Compensation Fair?" *Law and Society Review*.

Sloan, F. A., P. M. Mergenhagen, and R. R. Bovbjerg. 1989. "Effects of Tort Reforms on the Value of Closed Medical Malpractice Claims: A Microanalysis." *Journal of Health Politics, Policy and Law* 14:663–89.

Sloan, F. A. and others. 1989. "Medical Malpractice Experience of Physicians: Predictable or Haphazard?" *Journal of the American Medical Association* 262:3291–97.

Tancredi, L. R. 1986. "Designing a No-Fault Alternative." *Law and Contemporary Problems* 49:277–86.

Tancredi, L. R., and J. A. Barondess. 1977. "The Problem of Defensive Medicine." *Science* 200:879–82.

U.S. Congress. Senate. 1969. Subcommittee on Nutrition and Human Needs. *Medical Malpractice: The Patient versus the Physician.* Committee Print. 91 Cong., 1 sess. Washington: Government Printing Office.

Viney, G., and B. Markesinis. 1985. *La Réparation du Dommage Corporel: Essai de Comparaison des Droits Anglais et Français.* Paris: Economica.

Wennberg, J. E. 1984. "Dealing with Medical Practice Variations: A Proposal for Action." *Health Affairs* 3:1–32.

Wennberg, J. E., and A. Gittlesohn. 1973. "Small Area Variations in Health Care Delivery." *Science* 182:1102–08.

Zuckerman, S., R. R. Bovbjerg, and F. A. Sloan. 1990. "Effects of Tort Reforms and Other Factors on Medical Malpractice Insurance Premiums." *Inquiry* 27:107–82.

Zuckerman, S., C. F. Koller, and R. R. Bovbjerg. 1986. "Information on Malpractice: A Review of Empirical Research on Major Policy Issues." *Law and Contemporary Problems* 49:85–112.

CHAPTER EIGHT

Prescription Drug Safety and Product Liability

Judith P. Swazey

ASSESSING THE effects of product liability on the safety of prescription drugs is a complex and, in some respects, "mission impossible" task for many reasons.[1] There are, for example, a host of pharmacological and clinical questions, and attendant regulatory, legal, and sociological questions, about what one means by "safety" in the context of drugs and their uses. Given the properties of drugs, to borrow from the late René Dubos's statement about our pursuit of the "mirage of health," the idea of a drug that is both perfectly safe and effective, at least with our present knowledge, "is but a dream remembered from imaginings of a Garden of Eden designed for the welfare of man."[2]

Medically, then, the development, prescribing, and taking of drugs involves the question of "safe in relation to what?"—a calculus that opens onto the more-than-scientific matter of risks and how they are attributed, perceived, assessed, communicated, and managed. The fact that drugs do have adverse effects was legally recognized in 1965, in the American Law Institute's "Restatement (Second) of Torts." Comment k of the "Restatement" holds that prescription drugs belong to a class of "unavoidably unsafe products" because they are "incapable of being made safe for their intended and ordinary use" and therefore should not be viewed as "unreasonably dangerous" per se.[3] However, as will be seen, the varying interpretations of Comment k by courts and legal scholars, including the key question of whether it applies to all prescription drugs (hereafter,

---

1. Except in passing, I do not deal with the bearing of product liability law on the safety of vaccines. For discussions of this topic, see Mariner 1986, 1989; Mariner and Clark 1986; Mariner and Gallo 1987.
2. Dubos 1987, 2.
3. American Law Institute 1965, sect. 402A, Comment k.

drugs), has been one of the main uncertainties besetting attempts to decipher how product liability law and litigation affect drug safety.

A second confounding factor is that pharmaceuticals are one of the most tightly regulated industries in the United States. As a former director of the Food and Drug Administration's (FDA) Bureau of Drugs observed, "The drug industry is unique among American industries in having both its marketed products and its research on new products under federal regulation."[4] Under the authority of the FDA, drugs are subject to detailed regulatory requirements governing virtually every aspect of their testing, formulation, manufacture, marketing, and distribution. Given the pervasiveness of FDA regulations, it is difficult to neatly fence off an arena called "the effects of product liability on drug safety."

Third, there is the problem of data. There are many anecdotes, opinions, claims and counterclaims, and some limited case studies and survey reports about the effects of product liability on prescription drug safety but virtually no solid data. If such data exist—and it is interesting to wonder how policy is made in their absence—they certainly are not accessible to those outside industry.

With these caveats, this chapter deals with four principal topics that together try to provide some understanding of the ways that product liability law, and litigation or the fear of litigation, *may* affect drug safety. These topics have been examined through an extensive search and review of the literature and interviews with a small but highly knowledgeable group of persons involved with drugs and product liability, against a background of prior work I have done on historical, sociological, and policy aspects of pharmaceuticals and the development of patient education materials.

First, given the arguments by the pharmaceutical industry, among others, about the need for product liability tort reforms, I touch on the arguments, opinions, and sparse evidence on the nature and effects of the purported "litigation explosion" and product liability "crisis" for pharmaceutical manufacturers. Second, since drug safety is under the purview of both federal regulation and tort law, I consider the objectives and nature of these two systems of social controls and some of the ways they interact. Third, I examine safety-risk considerations with respect to the *design* of drugs, focusing on scientific and legal issues about what it means to safely design an "unavoidably unsafe" product.

Fourth, I discuss the topic that most experts agree is central to product

4. Crout 1976, 241.

liability and drug safety: labeling, the information about a drug's uses, contraindications, risks, and so on, that is distributed by the manufacturer, subject to FDA requirements and approvals. In part because the "Restatement (Second) of Torts" defines drugs as unavoidably unsafe products, liability law and litigation have focused primarily, though not exclusively, on the adequacy of a manufacturer's *warnings* as conveyed in drug labeling. Traditionally, the question whether a manufacturer has met or breached his duty to warn has been judged by the information provided to physicians, whom the law defines as the "users" of prescription drugs because they are the "learned intermediaries" who dispense these products to patients. In recent years, however, patients or consumers have begun to share the stage with physicians with respect to the duty to warn and labeling, owing to some legally mandated exceptions to the learned intermediary doctrine, expanding sources and types of information geared for consumers, and the controversial matter of direct-to-consumer advertising.

Finally, in a task reminiscent of the four blind men trying to identify the elephant, I try to weave together the strands contained in all the topics mentioned to assess whether, and if so how, product liability has significantly affected the safety of prescription drugs. That assessment, which is tenuous because of the dearth of data, suggests that product liability laws and litigation have had a marginal effect, both positively and negatively, on prescription drug safety, compared with the pervasive influence of FDA regulations and the powerful roles played by pharmaceutical company marketing decisions and by the "learned intermediary" physicians who write more than 2 billion prescriptions a year for their patients.

Prescription Drugs and Product Liability Trends

Advocates of tort reform hold that an "explosive" growth in product liability filings and awards, coupled with the absence of federal product liability standards and the vagaries of state laws and case-by-case decisions, has created a "crisis" that demands state and federal legislative reform. The Pharmaceutical Manufacturers Association (PMA) argues on behalf of its members that the following reforms are needed: enact a government standards provision; eliminate the doctrine of joint and several liability; limit punitive damages and the use of expert testimony; allow payment of large awards by installment; and give courts the authority to reduce an award by the amount a plaintiff is entitled to receive from other sources.[5] These reforms, the PMA maintains, are necessary because

> there has been an explosion in the number and cost of tort cases. . . . If it works properly, the tort law system not only compensates those who are wrongfully injured, but also provides incentives that encourage proper conduct. Today, however, the tort law system has broken down. New theories have created uncertainty about what conduct will result in liability. And—exploiting these expansive theories . . . people are filing suit in record numbers and reaping huge windfalls. A lottery mentality now infects the tort system.
>
> Because of these developments, insurance underwriters have no way to predict the kinds or amounts of claims they may have to pay. The result: broad classes of liability insurance are now unavailable or unaffordable.[6]

Like most controversies, the tort reform debate, which initially focused on liability insurance, has involved deeply entrenched attitudes and beliefs and claims and counterclaims based on "the data." As Hensler and the other authors of a 1987 Rand Corporation report on tort litigation pointed out, the proponents and opponents have "appeared to hold sharply differing views of reality. . . . Each side presented statistical data that appeared to support its position. But the differences in the data cited were puzzling even to those wise in the ways of lying with statistics. Each side claimed to be accurately describing the tort litigation system, yet the two sides seemed to be talking about different worlds."[7]

The studies used to support positions about the effect of product liability on various industries have a major problem: with few exceptions, they used aggregate data for federal and state tort filings, ranges of awards, and so forth. Three studies that provide much needed exceptions to this general pattern were conducted by the General Accounting Office and the Rand Corporation.[8] In general, by disaggregating data on federal product liability filings and, to the extent possible given the nature of state reporting systems, state court filings, all three studies reach comparable conclusions that challenge the specter of a nationwide product

5. Pharmaceutical Manufacturers Association 1989.
6. Pharmaceutical Manufacturers Association (n.d.).
7. Hensler and others 1987, 1–2.
8. General Accounting Office 1988; Hensler and others 1987; Dungworth 1988.

litigation explosion across a range of products. In analyzing the growth in federal product liability filings from 1974 to 1985, for example, the GAO found that only three products were responsible for much of the increase: asbestos for 40 percent, the Dalkon Shield for 12 percent, and Bendectin for 5 percent.

The ways disaggregating data can clarify product liability trends were also demonstrated by Hensler and her Rand colleagues, who, on the basis of their analysis of federal and state filings, showed that "there is no longer, if there ever was, a single tort system. Instead, there are at least three kinds of tort litigation, each with its own distinct class of litigants, attorneys, and legal dynamics."[9] These three "different worlds" are routine personal injury suits; high stakes personal injury suits, including product liability cases; and mass latent injury cases such as the Dalkon Shield, each characterized by a different litigation growth rate, jury verdict trend, and cost profile.

A second Rand study, by Dungworth, reached the same general conclusions as the GAO study with respect to federal product liability trends. But by offering a more detailed analysis than the GAO, it is the most useful study to date for appraising the effect of product liability litigation on the pharmaceutical industry, at least for suits filed in federal district courts. In analyzing the distribution of defendants and cases by industry groups, Dungworth found that 434 companies were named in pharmaceutical suits between 1973 and 1986. Of those suits, however, five companies were the lead defendants in 72 percent, and only two companies—A.H. Robins and Merrell Dow—accounted for 60 percent, owing to the Dalkon Shield and Bendectin litigation. From his analysis Dungworth held that there are at least two main types of product liability litigation, each with a distinctive set of characteristics. The pharmaceutical industry belongs in a "highly concentrated" grouping, which comprises "epidemics" of suits involving a single product, such as the Dalkon Shield, Bendectin, or asbestos. The "dispersed litigation" group, in contrast, has many lead defendants and many cases spread throughout an industry.

Although the GAO and Rand studies have helped to provide a clearer picture of product liability trends, they do not address the effects of actual or potential litigation on manufacturers and their products. For prescription drugs and other products, the publicly extant information is fragmentary and inconclusive at best, because of the general unwillingness of companies to document their claims about a product liability crisis by

9. Hensler and others 1987, 2.

providing data about the actual effects of litigation. Industry surveys, moreover, are so methodologically weak and so generalized regarding categories of industries and products that their applicability to the pharmaceutical industry and drugs is only inferential and suggestive. The type and quality of information available from surveys are illustrated by a 1988 Conference Board report on "the impact of product liability," based on a mailed survey sent to chief executive officers of the country's 2,000 largest manufacturing companies and one sent to a randomly selected group of companies with fewer than 500 employees. Some of the more obvious shortcomings of the study—which was intended and used to bolster the case for tort reform—are the low response rate (270 and 280 usable responses, respectively); the fact that responses from the two groups are merged for most analyses; and the use of very broad categories of manufacturers and product lines—for example, pharmaceutical companies are included under "consumer nondurables." In passing, however, the report does at least note that "even the most vociferous critics of the product liability system concede that, on occasion, the system acts to improve product safety," and it devotes two of its sixty-six tables to these "beneficial effects."[10] According to the responses from 264 companies, *actual* liability experience had led 35 percent to improve the safety of their products, 33 percent to redesign their product lines, and 47 percent to make improvements in product usage and warnings. When asked about the "beneficial impacts" of *anticipated* liability experience, 19 percent of the respondents thought that it would lead to improved product safety, 13 percent to redesigned product lines, and 21 percent to improved product usage and warning.

Another, very small, sampling of the range of opinions, specific to the effects of product liability on pharmaceutical manufacturers and the safety of prescription drugs, is provided by interviews I conducted between January and March 1990:

Health law professor specializing in drug product liability: Liability attorneys for pharmaceutical companies talk and worry about the unpredictability of the courts and juries, and the unpredictability of the law; they're afraid that state laws are changing in ways that will increase

10. McGuire 1988, 1, 20. Similar findings regarding "management action in response to product liability" were reported by risk managers for 232 corporations in a 1987 Conference Board survey report: about one-third said their company had improved the safety design of a product, and over one-third that liability had led to improved product labeling. See Weber 1987, 15.

their company's liability. But it's not clear that liability law is a good deterrent for safety problems, or enhances drug safety, because we just don't have the data.

Attorney in private practice specializing in pharmaceuticals: You will not get hard data on the effects of product liability on drug safety from manufacturers or insurers. But in thirty years of legal practice and government work, with the exception of Bendectin and oral contraceptives, I can't think of an instance where liability or the prospect of liability has affected anything but labeling. Product liability is just not the driving force for the industry. What does worry me, however, is that we seem to be drifting away from a national marketing system for drugs. Because of the effects of state-by-state litigation decisions, and states setting up their own labeling requirements for foods and drugs, we are Balkanizing the system, and I think it will be a disaster.

Senior attorney with a pharmaceutical company: For certain classes of drugs, liability concerns have probably led to safer products, in conjunction with FDA requirements. Companies do worry about liability because of the uncertainty; we understand and can work with the FDA regulations, and the FDA can only disapprove, not sue. I think that liability litigation is always a deep pockets issue for a company. But I personally don't think that the litigation threat is that serious, except for DES-type products where potentially significant risks are discovered well after the drug has been introduced. I believe— though it's heretical—that the liability crisis is largely a myth when one looks at available information such as the actual number of cases. The threat of a runaway jury often makes a company settle before a trial, and most huge jury awards are reduced down the line. The real hassle is the "nuisance money" settlement process. Other than DES-type cases, the tort system for drug product liability "ain't broke," and the tort reform proposals go way beyond what is needed to fix it. Tort law is a law of what ought to be—compensation for injury and, when warranted, punishment.

Product liability litigation attorney with a pharmaceutical company: Overall, I think liability has had a deterrent effect for industry with respect to drug safety; safety has been improved as a result of causes of action under negligence. For example, there has been a decrease in certain manufacturers' excesses, such as not doing an adequate job of reporting and issuing warnings about serious adverse drug reactions. From my experience, though, the vast majority of cases brought against drug manufacturers don't have merit, as seen in the number of claims that actually get to court, and the even smaller number that are decided for the plaintiff. And, it's hard to get a quick and easy out-of-court nuisance suit settlement from a drug company; to settle this way is to condemn your entire product line, and the cost of liability insurance also makes it hard to squeeze a settlement out of a company.

Health care consumer activist: The fact that warnings have been changed and drugs and devices withdrawn from the market suggests that the deterrent effect of liability has been established more clearly for products than for malpractice. But it's hard to tell if companies have really learned yet, because most of the big payouts have just been in the last few years, and the financial costs of irresponsible behavior with respect to warnings and design safety are just coming home to roost. Pharmaceutical companies are really dumb if they haven't learned some lessons, but you also have to recognize that marketing divisions are the tail that wags the company dog.

Controls over Drug Safety: Federal Regulations and Tort Law

From a social controls perspective,[11] efforts to ensure the safety of drugs rely primarily on three entities: the pharmaceutical manufacturer and two external agencies with legal powers over the manufacturer—the FDA through its regulatory authority and the courts through product liability actions under tort law. An understanding of the objectives and powers of these two external control systems, and the ways they interact, is thus an important ingredient in attempting to evaluate the effects of product liability on drug safety.

FDA Regulations: The Government as Guardian

As the FDA's regulatory authority has evolved under congressional legislation, particularly the food and drug acts of 1906, 1938, and 1962, it has had three main objectives concerning the drug industry: "to assure . . . that clinical research on drugs meets appropriate ethical and scientific standards, . . . that all marketed drug products meet certain standards of safety, effectiveness, and quality, and . . . that all marketed drug products

11. For the classic analysis of social controls, see Janowitz 1976.

are labeled accurately and promoted honestly."[12] In the words of the historian J. H. Young, the intent of these regulatory thrusts has been for the government to serve as "guardian" of the public's health by trying to "protect [its] citizens from dangers associated with their . . . drug supplies."[13]

As Young has shown in his studies, the major drug (and food) legislation in the United States has followed a pattern. Six factors have been prominent: "change, complexity, competition, crusading, compromise, and catastrophe," with catastrophe playing an especially critical role.[14] Regulatory controls over the safety of prescription drugs came in the wake of the chemotherapeutic revolution and were triggered by the death of more than 100 people from the diethylene glycol used as a solvent for one of the new wonder drugs, marketed as Elixir Sulfanilimide. Largely because of the outcry over this event, Congress included a "new drug" section in its 1938 Food, Drug, and Cosmetic Act. This provision required, for the first time, that the FDA evaluate a manufacturer's evidence for a new drug's safety before its marketing and approve the drug as "safe for use" for the conditions listed in its labeling.[15]

Safety issues again became prominent in the late 1950s and early 1960s owing to another landmark catastrophe, thalidomide,[16] and have remained in the forefront of industry, legislative and legal, medical, and public-interest concerns about prescription drugs. Attention has centered on such matters as the inherent design safety of drugs, the integrity of drug manufacturers and their willingness to self-regulate, the labeling information provided to physicians and patients, the prescribing habits of physicians, and the adequacy of the FDA's safety-related regulations and decisions. Physicians have received substantial attention regarding their

12. Crout 1976, 241. For accounts of the 1906, 1938, 1962 food and drug acts see Temin 1981 and Young 1982.

13. Young 1982, 11. Young also points out that the United States was the last industrialized country to adopt the guardian role. Currently, under the impetus of federal technology transfer policies, some analysts are concerned that the FDA is becoming a "promoter" of certain drugs and devices rather than a guardian. See Annas 1989.

14. Young writes, "As to catastrophe, in the United States, at least, food and drug bills seem to have required the shock of a major public health crisis to convert them into laws. The crisis atmosphere also influenced provisions in the laws, as well as the psychology of government officials given authority to enforce them" (1982, 11).

15. See Anderson 1946. Under the 1906 Pure Food and Drug Acts, Young points out, "enforcement did not take place until after foods and drugs had been marketed, and the law put the burden of proof upon government officials to show that products were violative" (1982, 12).

16. Kaitin 1988; Witherspoon 1988.

knowledge about drugs and their prescribing practices.[17] But the brunt of the concerns and criticisms that have been raised by academic physicians, conveyed to the lay public by popular articles and books like *The Therapeutic Nightmare*,[18] and investigated by consumer groups and by congressional committees, has been directed at the pharmaceutical industry and at the FDA.[19]

Whatever the shortcomings of the FDA's regulations and actions may be, however, the agency unarguably has authority over almost every aspect of a drug's development, marketing, and manufacturing. In relation to product liability, some features of the chief safety-related FDA requirements that drugs must meet include the following:[20]

The approval process. Two sets of regulations specify the types of research, submissions of data to the FDA, and regulatory reviews and approvals required for a manufacturer to receive permission to market a new drug. These regulations are for the investigational new drug (IND) exemption that allows a sponsor to ship an unapproved drug to investigators and for new drug applications (NDA). Before beginning clinical studies, a manufacturer must submit an IND application that includes safety data on the drug's toxicity from animal tests and any human use data from the United States or abroad. If the agency grants an IND, the sponsor next conducts three phases of clinical testing, which also involve regulations for research with human subjects. Phase I studies, with a small number of human subjects who are usually normal volunteers, are done to establish the safety of the drug at different dosages and to obtain certain basic pharmacologic data; if warranted by phase I results, phase II studies are done with small numbers of patients to test the drug's clinical safety and efficacy. If these initial clinical data indicate that the drug is effective and safe for its intended use, the sponsor then proceeds with phase III trials, involving wider clinical testing with larger numbers of patients.

On completion of phase III testing, the sponsor compiles the data into the voluminous document called an NDA, which the FDA's reviewers evaluate to determine if the manufacturer has provided "substantial ev-

17. Lesar and others 1990; Soumerai, McLaughlin, and Avorn 1989.
18. Mintz 1965. Print and electronic media, both nonfiction and fiction, play an important and often professionally underestimated role in shaping public attitudes, beliefs, and behavior with respect to prescription drugs.
19. Herzog 1977.
20. For discussion of and citations to the FDA regulations dealing with investigational new drugs, new drug applications, postmarketing safety requirements, and good manufacturing practices, see Grabowski and Vernon 1983; Gibbs and Mackler 1987; Walsh and Klein 1986.

idence" of the product's safety and effectiveness through "adequate and well-controlled studies." Of particular relevance to product liability actions, the NDA review includes the drug's proposed *labeling,* which covers all types and forms of information about the product prepared and distributed by the manufacturer. Besides the detailed, technical package insert provided to physicians and pharmacists, labeling information includes the content of press releases, promotional kits, written or verbal advertisements, and material such as pamphlets or brochures prepared for patients.

Before a drug has been approved for marketing, agency regulations sharply restrict promotional claims about its effectiveness or safety. As summarized by a former head of the FDA's Division of Drug Advertising and Labeling, this preapproval constraint

> is related to FDA's mandate to ensure that full information regarding [safety] be presented concurrently and in fair balance with efficacy claims. . . . The sponsor's natural tendency to look on the bright side means that preapproval promotion can be expected to portray a view of the new drug's therapeutic usefulness that is more optimistic than the view that may be finally reflected in the approved labeling [and] without knowledge of an important warning, contraindication, or adverse effect.[21]

Reflecting these concerns, the NDA review of the proposed labeling's format and content has two main foci. First, are the indicated uses for the drug confined to those for which the manufacturer has established substantial evidence of safety and effectiveness? Second, does it meet the agency's specifications for stating the relevant safety information, such as known precautions, warnings, contraindications, and directions for proper use? Failure to conform with the detailed regulations governing labeling can constitute misbranding of the product, on the grounds that its safety and effectiveness have been mischaracterized, a deficiency with potentially severe product liability as well as regulatory consequences.[22]

Postmarketing: adverse drug reaction reports and labeling changes. In relation to safety and product liability, two of the most important sets of FDA regulations governing prescription drugs after they have received marketing approval involve requirements for reporting adverse drug re-

21. Rheinstein 1982, 331.
22. Gibbs and Mackler 1987, 232.

actions (ADRs) to the agency and those dealing with changes in the product's approved labeling. In 1985 and 1987 the FDA issued amendments that strengthened its ADR reporting system. The requirements now include quarterly reports for all drugs during the first three years postmarketing and annually thereafter and an ADR alert report that must be filed within fifteen days after the manufacturer receives information about any "adverse experience" that falls within the agency's definition of "serious." Other aspects of the amendments and related guidelines include the specification of sources that manufacturers are expected to monitor for relevant ADR information, such as a list of "designated journals," and marking a major regulatory shift, requirements for the inclusion of ADR information from foreign sources.[23]

The effects of the new ADR reporting regulations on product liability have yet to be determined. In promulgating the 1985 regulations, Shulman and Ulcickas pointed out, "the FDA specifically repudiated any intent to affect the liability of manufacturers . . . [and] authorized the inclusion of a disclaimer on the ADR report form to the effect that filing the report did not constitute an admission of causality or association between the drug and the adverse event." "However," they reasoned, "it seems fair to say that the increased scope and stringency of the regulations as a whole translate into increased vulnerability to liability claims."[24]

Manufacturers often make labeling changes after a drug has been marketed, primarily to reflect new warning information or new indications for use. New indications must be approved by the FDA before they can be added to the label. But since 1984 the agency has "authorized drug manufacturers to strengthen label warnings, modify dosage in a manner enhancing product safety, and delete unsupported effectiveness claims without prior approval."[25] Indeed, particularly when serious ADRs are recognized, the FDA encourages a manufacturer to issue a warning to physicians as rapidly as possible, although he must advise the agency of an intended labeling change by filing a "supplemental new-drug application providing a full explanation of the basis for the changes."[26] For the most part, however, as Gibbs and Mackler observe, the regulations

---

23. Shulman and Ulcickas 1989; see also Faich 1986. Shulman and Ulcickas note that the FDA's interest in foreign ADR data was due in part to two criminal prosecutions in the United States, against Smithkline Beckman and Eli Lilly, for failing to report foreign information on serious adverse effects (p. 93).

24. Shulman and Ulcickas 1989, 99.

25. Gibbs and Mackler 1987, 233–34. For the labeling regulations see 21 CFR 314.8.

26. Walsh and Klein 1986, 186, n. 71.

"do not specify the circumstances which compel a manufacturer to modify its labeling to reflect . . . increased knowledge [about risk]."[27] This lack of specificity, as will be seen, is a recurrent issue in product liability cases with respect to the timeliness and adequacy of new warning information.

Manufacturing practices. The FDA also has detailed, extensive regulations for good manufacturing practices (GMPs). These regulations "establish minimum criteria for buildings, personnel, equipment, control of components, processing controls, labeling controls, quality controls, and record keeping. . . . [A] sponsor must demonstrate in its NDA . . . that its product will be manufactured in accordance with GMPs. After product marketing begins, noncompliance with GMPs causes the drug . . . to be deemed 'adulterated.' "[28]

New regulatory issues. Two recent aspects of FDA regulation will bear watching by those concerned with the effects of product liability on prescription drug safety. The first is a high-court ruling that makes the FDA, as well as pharmaceutical manufacturers, potentially liable for design or warning defects. In 1988 a unanimous U.S. Supreme Court decided in *Berkovitz* v. *United States* that "the federal government may be held liable under provisions of the Federal Tort Claims Act . . . for failing to study the necessary safety data before issuing a license to market a vaccine. The Court also ruled that the federal government may be liable for licensing the distribution of a vaccine even though the vaccine did not comply with certain government regulatory standards."[29]

A second aspect of FDA regulations that warrants monitoring, for many reasons besides product liability, is its controversial 1987 regulations for the treatment use and sale of investigational new drugs for certain diseases such as AIDs and cancer.[30] In effect, the "treatment IND" provisions have created a parallel track of clinical trials and therapeutic use for some experimental drugs. Arguments abound over whether the benefits of the treatment IND track will outweigh its potential risks to patients, the extent to which standards for ensuring the safety and effectiveness of new drugs will be compromised, and the degree to which the IND

27. Gibbs and Mackler 1987, 232.

28. Gibbs and Mackler 1987, 213, n. 126, 229. The GMP regulations are in 21 CFR 211.

29. Coben, Romney, and Panichelli 1989, 409. Although this is a single decision, involving a vaccine, Coben and others point out its far-reaching liability implications for the FDA. "The cornerstone to liability [in various instances]," these commentators believe, "will be whether or not government employees failed to comport with statutory, regulatory, or agency policy which is both objective and obligatory in nature" (p. 410).

30. 21 CFR 312.34.

track represents a transformation of the FDA from a consumer protection to a drug promotion agency.[31] On the liability front, attorneys are speculating about the ways that "treatment use of investigational drugs under the new regulations may increase product liability exposure for sponsors." These drugs, for example, "may not receive even the limited [tort liability] benefit of whatever protection marketed drugs receive from FDA-approved labeling." Another prospect is tort suits charging manufacturers with "failure to use due care in selecting qualified investigators" who, under the regulations, are also the treating physicians.[32]

Product Liability Law: Objectives and Causes of Action

Both federal regulations and tort doctrine in the United States are concerned with the safety of a drug manufacturer's product. There are some important differences, however, in the social policy objectives of these two systems of control, which bear on the ways they interact and the extent to which one influences the other. As noted, the general role of the FDA can be characterized as guardian of the public's health through detailed regulations intended to ensure the safety and effectiveness of drugs and other products under its purview. As product liability law has evolved as a part of American tort doctrine, it has sought to fulfill a broader range of objectives, but as Mariner noted, "There is little consensus on the specific overall goals of tort law, much less strict liability and negligence. Most commentators refer to the deterrence of harm, corrective justice or retribution, or compensation for injury. A more practical rationale is that of risk spreading, pursuant to which responsibility for injury should be placed on the person who is in the best position to prevent harm or who can best absorb and recoup the cost of injury."[33]

For whichever objective a product liability action is brought, establishing a "defect" is the key factor, and for prescription drugs it can be a thorny matter to define and determine. The law recognizes three types of product defects that can give rise to a liability claim, usually under a

---

31. Annas 1989; Johnstone 1988; Marshall 1989.

32. Johnstone 1988, 539. Although I am far from expert in product liability law, it seems to me that *Berkovitz* suggests scenarios for the potential liability of FDA regarding approvals for sale and use of experimental drugs under the treatment IND regulations, and for NDA approvals based in part on parallel track data.

33. Mariner 1989, 29.

negligence or strict liability cause of action.[34] The first is a *manufacturing* defect that "creates a flaw in the individual product that differentiates it from the normal product produced by the manufacturer."[35] "Historically," Gibbs and Mackler comment, "demonstrating a specific flaw in the manufacturing process in finished goods has been quite difficult for an injured plaintiff."[36] For this reason, coupled with the stringency of the FDA's GMP regulations and the importance that the agency attaches to them for ensuring quality control, manufacturing defect litigation is rare for prescription drugs. As a product liability attorney for a pharmaceutical company commented, "There have been almost no manufacturing defect claims against our company and, I suspect, all other drug companies as well."[37]

The second type is a liability action that can be brought on the grounds that a product has a defective *design*. Many product liability authorities believe that design defect cases will increase for prescription drugs. But to date there have been relatively few such cases, given the Comment k view that these are unavoidably unsafe products and the related fact that "there are considerable uncertainties as to how the concept of design defect ought to be elucidated".[38] The third type, and the most frequently alleged in drug cases, is a *warning* defect. For drugs, such defects involve the content of the label, which, as noted earlier, takes various forms and which is tightly controlled by the FDA.

34. When a product is alleged to be defective, litigation is usually based on one of three main causes of action under common law: negligence, strict liability, and breach of contract. For prescription drugs, litigation has predominantly meant charges of negligence or strict liability. Shulman and Ulcickas provide a concise summary of the differences between these two causes of action: "In a negligence suit, the defendant's conduct is central. To succeed, the plaintiff must establish the following: first, that the manufacturer owed a duty to the plaintiff to act reasonably; second, that the manufacturer breached that duty by acting in a way that falls below the standard of the reasonably prudent manufacturer; third, that the plaintiff has suffered actual harm; and fourth, that the harm was proximately caused by or flowed directly from the breach of the manufacturer's duty. . . . In a strict liability analysis, the initial emphasis is product-oriented, focusing on the safety of the drug rather than the reasonableness of the manufacturer's conduct. Fundamental to a strict liability argument is proof by the plaintiff that the product was defective, that the defect existed when the product left the manufacturer's control, and that the defect caused the plaintiff's injury" (1989, 94). For a review of other liability doctrines, such as market share liability in DES cases, see Goldblatt and others 1989; Wilner and Gayner 1989. See Schwartz 1987 for a concise discussion of contributory and shared negligence in product liability cases.

35. Schwartz 1987, 23.

36. Gibbs and Mackler 1987, 229.

37. Personal interview, Feb. 27, 1990.

38. Schwartz 1987, 25.

Of Floors and Ceilings: Federal Regulations and Product Liability Law

Opinions differ, sometimes sharply, on how the external controls provided by FDA regulations and product liability law interact: which, as a matter of law and social policy, should be determinative when safety is questioned; and how, in fact rather than theory or myth, they individually and jointly affect pharmaceutical manufacturers and their drug products. For this chapter, however, the salient point about the relation between FDA regulations and state tort law is that in drug product liability cases judges and juries have recurrently defined federal drug safety standards as a baseline or floor, not as a ceiling. A finding of *noncompliance* by a manufacturer with an FDA regulation is a "strong sword" for a plaintiff,[39] because it is evidence of negligence or can constitute negligence per se with a presumption of liability. But the converse finding does not apply: *compliance* with the regulations may be accepted as evidence of due care by a manufacturer, but it is at best a "weak shield" in defending against a product liability action.[40] The "judicial response" to a manufacturer's use of what is called the government standards defense—that compliance with the regulations "rebuts allegations of negligence or product defects"—"has been consistent and unresponsive."[41] In short, as Paul Rheingold, a leading authority on drug product liability law, wrote, "While drug statutes and regulations form the everyday basis for the conduct of the drug supplier, they are of little importance when it comes to determining whether liability exists or not in a suit for personal injury."[42]

Prescription Drugs and Design Defects

"The debates and actions about risky drugs," a prominent attorney and former FDA official declared, "involve their labeling, not their [design]

39. The apt images of "strong sword" and "weak shield" are used by Gibbs and Mackler 1987.

40. As Gibbs and Mackler pointed out, the courts "do not . . . explain why noncompliance should always be far more probative than evidence of compliance. Nor do they articulate how much significance a jury should attach to FDA approval relative to other trial evidence" (1987, 223).

41. Shulman and Ulcickas 1989, 98. On this point see, for example, the opinion in *Wells* v. *Ortho Pharmaceutical Corp.* 788 F.2d 741, 745–46 (11th Cir. 1986).

42. Rheingold 1985, 135, n.1.

safety as such. Because, given the molecular nature of drugs, you can't just develop a new widget to make their design safer."[43] This remark underscores an important basic aspect of pharmacology and therapeutics: the indeterminate and probabilistic nature of our knowledge about drugs and their effects. As Mitchell and Link pointed out, "safety" in this context is a problematic term and concept:

> There are . . . legitimate scientific disagreements over the actions of drugs. More and better science can only reduce this range of uncertainty. It cannot eliminate it. Thus, when somebody wants to find some instances of lack of safety or efficacy, he has an uneasy time of it. Unfortunately, as Dr. Wardell put it, "the term 'safety' is giving the public the wrong idea of what is to be expected from drugs." Both regulatory authorities and drug manufacturers agree that there is no such thing as a 100% safe drug, and the public would be better off if this term were abolished and replaced by references to degrees of risk or hazard.[44]

The risk-laden nature of drugs, as noted before, was recognized in the "Restatement (Second) of Torts," which states that certain products like prescription drugs are "unavoidably unsafe" because they are "incapable of being made safe for their intended and ordinary use." Thus, according to Comment k, a prescription drug is neither unreasonably dangerous nor defective under product liability law *if* it was properly designed and is properly labeled.

"If" turns out to be a very big word for drug litigation involving a design defect, for reasons of both fact and law. There are pronounced differences of opinion between courts, litigation attorneys, and legal scholars, for example, on the following points: (1) Should all prescription drugs be legally deemed unavoidably unsafe, or should the applicability of Comment k be determined on a case-by-case basis? (2) For purposes of deciding liability, how should the *proper* design for a drug be determined, and correlatively, (3) what standards and tests should be applied to determine whether a design is defective? (4) Which common law causes of action should be used for a design defect case? And (5) does an inadequate warning constitute a type of design defect?

While a thorough discussion of these product liability law issues is

43. Personal interview, Mar. 7, 1990.
44. Mitchell and Link 1976, xvi.

beyond the scope of this chapter,[45] the ways in which courts deal with them will obviously be very important to both the pharmaceutical industry and litigants. "In recent years," Schwartz pointed out, "increasing numbers of claims have challenged the design of prescription drugs under Section 402A."[46] Thus far only one federal appeals court has upheld a jury's verdict that a prescription drug–in this case, an oral contraceptive—

45. For discussion of product design issues in prescription drug liability cases, including topics such as the Comment k defense, whether "state of the art" should apply to the time of manufacture or the time of use, the risk-utility test, and strict liability or negligence as causes of action, see Birnbaum and Wrubel 1985; Coben, Romney, and Panichelli 1989; Gibbs and Mackler 1987; Mariner 1989; McClellan, Tate, and Eaton 1981; Rheingold 1964; Schwartz 1988a; Twerski and others 1976; Wade 1983.

Although these product liability law questions are largely beyond the scope of this chapter, three points do merit a brief mention. First, understanding, much less adjudicating, the design of a product like a prescription drug—and many other technically complex products—is exceedingly difficult. Since even experts often disagree on what constitutes a "proper design" in relation to the state of the art when a product was developed or used, it is little wonder that there are persisting concerns about the ability of judges or juries to decide whether a product was properly or improperly designed. Second, and not unrelated to the problem of technological complexity, there are legal uncertainties over what standard or test should be applied to determine whether a design is defective. Both the two major standards, the consumer expectation test and the risk-utility or risk-benefit test, have been problematic when applied to drugs and vaccines, as various commentators and courts have noted. Some of the problems that arise with these standards in the case of prescription drugs, for example, were addressed in 1988 by the California Supreme Court in *Brown* v. *Superior Court,* one of the many DES product liability cases (44 Cal. 3d 1049, 245 Cal. Rptr. 412 [1988]). The "consumer expectation" test asks whether a product performed as safely as the ordinary consumer would expect it to when used in its intended manner. But for prescription drugs, the *Brown* court held, this test is inappropriate because, under the learned intermediary doctrine, the prescribing physician is the "consumer," and physicians know that all prescription drugs have inherent risks, both known and unknown. The court also felt that the more widely used risk-utility test is not appropriate for prescription drug cases, because this standard assumes that a safer alternative design is feasible.

Third, a body of court decisions and analyses by legal commentators suggest that distinctions between design defects and warning defects have become vanishingly small, apace with the problems that courts are having in maintaining distinctions between strict liability and negligence in such cases. In 1984, for example, the New Jersey Supreme Court, in *Feldman* v. *Lederle Laboratories,* held that under strict liability an inadequate warning can constitute a design defect, because both types of alleged defects involve the same question: "whether, assuming the manufacturer knew of the defect in the product, he acted in a reasonably prudent manner in marketing the product or in providing the warnings given. Thus, once the defendant's knowledge of the defect is imputed, strict liability analysis becomes almost identical to negligence analysis in its focus on the reasonableness of the defendant's conduct." 97 N.J. 429, 479 A.2d 385 (1984).

The *Feldman* court also took issue with the Comment k position that all prescription drugs, by definition, are unavoidably unsafe. "Drugs, like any other products, may contain defects that could have been avoided by better manufacturing or design. Whether a drug is unavoidably unsafe should be decided on a case-by-case basis." 479 A.2d 383.

46. Schwartz 1988a, 33.

was defective in design.[47] However, the "net effect" of this decision, coupled with the variances in the ways in which other courts have dealt with drug design defect cases, "is that the law governing prescription drug liability is perhaps more unsettled today than it was a decade ago."[48]

For the present and the forseeable future, then, pharmaceutical manufacturers must live not only with the indeterminancy surrounding the pharmacology and therapeutics of their drugs but also with the problems of uncertainty surrounding potential liability for the design of those drugs. Some slight and primarily qualitative evidence suggests that the possibility of design defect liability is affecting manufacturers' decisions about their products in three spheres: the introduction of "me too," or follow-on, drugs, the withdrawal of certain drugs from the market for safety reasons, and the steps being taken to maximize the safest possible use of highly risky drugs that are marketed.

In each of these decisionmaking arenas, manufacturers, much like the FDA and the courts, engage in a risk-benefit or risk-utility analysis that includes economic factors and value judgments as well as technical scientific and medical components.[49] For both regulatory and liability purposes, manufacturers weigh such factors as "the likelihood and severity of the risks created by the design, the benefits of the design, and the feasibility and costs of alternative designs or products that could serve the same purpose but pose fewer risks."[50] Using these types of balancing act assessments, manufacturers, as well as regulators, physicians, and patients, may decide that a greater degree of design-related risk is acceptable for a pioneer or innovator drug (the first of its kind that is effective for a given condition) than for subsequent drugs in the same class: the me-too, or follow-on, drugs with usually minor modifications in chemical structure or in their physiologic effect or mechanism of action.[51]

The knowledgeable people interviewed for this chapter all felt that the

47. *Brochu* v. *Ortho Pharmaceutical Corp.*, 642 F.2d 652 (1st Cir. 1981). In *Brochu* a federal appeals court, applying New Hampshire law, held that strict liability standards should apply to a prescription drug design claim. The plaintiff, who had suffered a paralytic stroke allegedly caused by taking Ortho-Novum 2, claimed that this oral contraceptive was unreasonably dangerous in its design because it had a higher level of estrogen and posed a greater risk of stroke than other equally effective oral contraceptives marketed by the company.

48. Schwartz 1988a, 33.

49. On risk assessment, see Bradbury 1989; Inman 1987b; Nelkin 1983.

50. Schwartz 1988a, 34–35.

51. Wastila, Ulcickas, and Lasagna 1989.

potential of design defect liability is having its greatest effect on the pharmaceutical industry in connection with the risks that seem acceptable for a me-too drug. In the opinion of a product litigation attorney with a leading pharmaceutical company, "If a major opportunity exists for a plaintiff to file a design defect claim, it's with a me-too drug, because a safer alternative design probably was available."[52] Similarly, a senior attorney with another major company believes that "for me-too drugs, the safety profile is more important than the effectiveness profile when the company decides whether to go ahead with testing and marketing. The hook for these drugs is better safety than the predecessor or competitor drugs; a safety profile that looks worse than other drugs in its class will be a me-too drug's death knell."[53] Much the same view was offered by a senior official with the FDA, from his perspective as a regulator and his sense of what manufacturers worry about with respect to drug design liability issues: "Serious risks are what people worry about with a follow-on drug. It's a question of relative economic gain versus economic risk or liability for a company, and that assessment has to include both known hazards with the drug and the odds of someday encountering unexpected problems."[54]

Once drugs have been marketed, different safety-related factors can trigger a decision to withdraw a product. Like a physician's decision to prescribe or a patient's decision to take a drug despite its hazards, a decision by the FDA or a manufacturer to withdraw a drug entails judgments for which, medically, legally, and sociologically, there are no simple guidelines: what constitutes an "acceptable" risk?[55] Because of both the pharmacology and therapeutics of drugs and the relatively small clin-

---

52. Personal interview, Feb. 27, 1990.
53. Personal interview, Jan. 30, 1990.
54. Personal interview, Feb. 21, 1990.
55. In discussing what constitutes an acceptable risk, Dr. W. H. W. Inman, director of England's Drug Safety Research Unit, points out that "a patient may tolerate a reduced quality of life in order to prolong it. . . . [or] [h]e may risk shortening his life in order to improve the quality of what remains. . . . Should the [acceptable] risk of a fatal ADR be more than one in ten thousand, one hundred thousand, or one million? Should it be ten or a thousand times less than the risk of a fatal outcome to the disease? [Take, for example, rheumatoid arthritis.] This horrific, almost malignant disease may shorten life-expectation from the time of diagnosis by at least one third. I know of no drug which is too dangerous to use in rheumatoid arthritis. Several NSAIDs have been removed from the market when the best estimates of annual mortality due to ADRs were between one hundred and ten thousand times less than the annual mortality from the complications of the disease. Certainly it might have been reasonable to curtail their use in lesser illnesses, but not to remove them completely" (1987a, 18).

ical data base on which a marketing approval is based, serious adverse effects may not be identified until a drug has been in use for months or years. In some instances a marketed drug's known risks, even if mild or moderate, may become greater than its benefits if a competitor drug appears with a better safety profile and equivalent efficacy.

The various kinds of risk-benefit factors and decisionmaking processes involved in a manufacturer's decision to remove a drug from the market, however, are seldom fully discoverable by "outsiders." Thus, for example, it can be difficult to determine whether a given drug was withdrawn "only" because it became economically unviable for its manufacturer as newer competitor drugs gained a greater share of the market,[56] rather than because of serious hazards. And when serious adverse effects are the issue, it is not always clear whether a withdrawal is due to impending regulatory action, a regulatory decision, actual litigation, the fear of litigation, or some combination of all of these.[57]

The sparse literature analyzing drug discontinuations does show that only a small percentage of the new chemical entities introduced into the U.S. market are withdrawn for safety reasons. Bakke and his colleagues, for example, examined drug discontinuations for safety reasons in the United Kingdom and the United States for the period 1964–83, with "safety" referring to toxicity problems that caused a drug's risks to outweigh its benefits.[58] For that period they found that a total of twenty-four drugs were discontinued in both countries for safety reasons, amounting to only 2 percent of the new chemical entities that had been introduced. From their data the authors concluded that "drugs that reach the market under the prevailing regulatory systems [of the U.S. and the U.K.] are seldom associated with unacceptable toxicity."[59]

In the absence of solid data on the extent and nature of litigation involving drug design safety issues, apart from decided cases and the GAO and Rand analyses of the "tort epidemic" generated by Bendectin, it is impossible to make even a "best guesstimate" about how that litigation compares with the small percent of drugs withdrawn for safety

56. Weintraub and Northington 1986. As examples in this article show, some drugs that are withdrawn because they are no longer economically beneficial to a company are subsequently reintroduced because of pressure from physicians and patients.

57. The discussion in this section, and in the section on warning defects, does not deal with the separate issue of manufacturers who engage in fraud or the tort of deceit by *knowingly* withholding information about design defects.

58. Bakke, Wardell, and Lasagna 1984. A similar pattern of safety withdrawals was found from 1977 to 1987. See Kaitin and others 1989.

59. Bakke, Wardell, and Lasagna 1984, 559.

reasons. Nor, correspondingly, can one evaluate the extent to which liability concerns per se have led to discontinuations or to efforts to find safer alternative drugs for specified conditions.

However, the sparse evidence available, which includes some case studies, does suggest that product liability law, litigation, and concerns play at least some role in enhancing the design-related safety of drugs. Manufacturers' awareness of or experience with product liability issues can affect the fact that certain drugs never reach the market because of toxicity problems and that others are withdrawn because their medical risks turn out to exceed their benefits. There is, however, a downside element to the role of liability concerns vis-à-vis the basic hazards of drugs. Two examples are discussed by Lasagna in this volume: the first is a uniquely effective drug like Bendectin being withdrawn because of litigation even though no conclusive evidence of serious adverse effects was found; the second is the high probability that several new, uniquely effective uses for thalidomide will never be used outside an IND framework.[60]

To me, however, one of the most interesting facets of design-safety issues does not involve decisions to keep a drug from reaching the market or to discontinue it once marketed. Rather, it is the decisionmaking by the various actors engaged in the marketing and use of drugs that are known to be highly effective but extremely hazardous. These actors comprise the manufacturer, aware of the potential and perhaps likely liability attached to such a marketing decision; the FDA; the physicians and their patients, who, presumptively, are informed about the drug's serious hazards but deem them "acceptable"; and, waiting and watching on the sidelines, consumer activist organizations and litigation attorneys.

Three examples of such drugs are Roche's Accutane (isotretinoin), Sandoz's Clozaril (clozapine), and G. D. Searle's Cytotec (misoprostil). Accutane, prescribed for severe recalcitrant cystic acne, received its NDA approval from the FDA in 1982, with full recognition of the fact that it can cause major fetal abnormalities and thus should not be used by women during or just before pregnancy. "The message to physicians [about the drug's strong teratogenic potential] was and continues to be clear and forceful."[61] But by 1988 severe birth defects in sixty-two infants had been attributed to the use of Accutane during pregnancy, and the FDA's Ep-

60. For more detailed discussions of bendectin and thalidomide, see Barash and Lasagna 1987; Kaitin 1988; Witherspoon 1988.
61. Shulman 1989, 1565.

idemiology Unit estimated that the drug might have caused up to 1,300 birth defects nationwide between 1982 and 1988. Subsequently, on the recommendation of an FDA advisory committee, Roche's physician package insert was supplemented by a pregnancy prevention program kit, containing an instructional videotape for physicians, brochures for patients, an informed consent form, and a true-false test to be completed by the patient so that her doctor can evaluate how well she understands Accutane's risks. The manufacturer is also sponsoring an epidemiological monitoring program.

These steps have been undertaken by the manufacturer in an effort both to avert birth defects and to protect against liability actions. Nonetheless, the liability consequences of Accutane's marketing have been considerable, for, in the wake of thalidomide, the drug has been branded as a "prescription for birth defects."[62] In 1988 the American Trial Lawyers Association formed the Accutane Litigation Group, composed of lawyers representing "victims of Accutane." By that time between ten and twenty lawsuits were pending for birth defects ascribed to the drug, and about the same number of cases alleging serious side effects in adult users such as vision loss and eye, gastrointestinal, cardiac, and central nervous system disorders.[63]

Because of the lasting and powerful memory of thalidomide, many people familiar with Accutane's history are puzzled by the medical and legal risk-benefit calculus in Roche's decision to develop and market a potent teratogen for a disfiguring but not life-threatening condition, and by the FDA's IND and NDA approvals. And given the litigation that has followed its use, many also are puzzled that Roche has not withdrawn Accutane from the market or at least sought FDA permission to restrict its distribution solely to men. Said a former FDA official, "Accutane's marketing and now its litigation illustrates my belief that, although there are some crazy liability decisions, liability has not had a major effect on drug development and marketing."[64]

Clozaril and Cytotec have much shorter development and marketing histories than Accutane but illustrate the same kinds of questions in search of answers about the decisionmaking processes related to the approval, marketing, prescribing, and taking of effective but medically and litigiously risky drugs. Clozaril was approved by the FDA in October 1989

62. Nygaard 1988.
63. Nygaard 1988.
64. Personal interview, Mar. 7, 1990.

for the management of severe schizophrenia in patients unresponsive to standard and less toxic antipsychotic drugs. Before receiving marketing approval in the United States, the drug was available for restricted use in about thirty other countries, because of side effects including seizures and a potentially lethal agranulocytosis, a severe decrease in white blood cells that increases a patient's susceptibility to infection. Owing to these known risks, and clinical data indicating that it was no more effective than already available drugs, the FDA disapproved an initial NDA by Sandoz in 1984. The 1989 approval to market the drug, according to the agency, was based on additional clinical data showing that Clozaril was effective in patients who do not respond to or have intolerable side effects from conventional psychotropic drug treatment. Because of its severe risks and the inability of those taking the drug to understand or consent to those risks, Clozaril's approved labeling makes it available to physicians and their patients on a restricted distribution basis, which includes "a special program that has been developed for safety monitoring. Under the program a home health care company will both deliver the prescribed clozapine tablets and collect blood samples each week to be sent to a national laboratory for analysis. Patients and physicians will be notified of the results. If the results indicate that the patient should stop taking the drug, his or her physician will be notified immediately by telephone."[65] The "Clozaril model," several knowledgeable persons have commented to me, seems like a good idea in terms of restricted distribution and close safety monitoring of a drug with this type of risk-benefit profile. As such, it will be an interesting case to follow, from product liability, regulatory, and clinical perspectives.

G. D. Searle's Cytotec, marketed in 1989, will also be an interesting drug to follow from the same three perspectives, as well as because of its sociopolitically volatile nature. The drug is indicated for the prevention of gastric ulcers induced by the nonsteroidal antiinflammatory drugs (NSAIDs) widely used to treat arthritis. Besides protecting high-risk NSAID users from gastric ulcers and their often serious complications, however, Cytotec is an abortifacient. In seeking approval to market Cytotec, Searle was very aware of the implications of a drug that, while an effective new agent for a prevalent and serious side effect of other widely prescribed compounds, can also induce complete or partial abortions. The company anticipated strenuous opposition from pro-life political groups, the possibility of Accutane-like labeling requirements and "preg-

65. Nightingale 1990.

nancy prevention" strategies being required or "persuasively recommended" by FDA, and the prospect of litigation. Some pro-life opposition to the drug's marketing did develop, but not as much as had been anticipated. As part of its NDA application, the company prepared proposed labeling with contraindications and warning language and formatting that was stronger than the FDA felt it needed to be. Their product liability concerns, however, may be realized, since litigation claims reportedly have been discussed.[66]

These three examples, to which others could be added, suggest the sociological and social policy knowledge that could be gained from in-depth case studies of the "real" decisionmaking factors and processes connected with the marketing and use of drugs that are at once highly effective and highly hazardous. One thing that even a cursory knowledge of such agents does underscore, however, is the importance of labeling, both to protect patients by maximizing the safety of a drug's use, and to serve a "damage control" function that attempts to protect manufacturers against liability.

Read the Label: Liability for Warning Defects

Most prescription drug liability suits against pharmaceutical manufacturers allege negligent failure to warn about risks, rather than negligence or strict liability for design, testing, or manufacturing. In warning defect cases the key issue for plaintiffs and defendants is what constitutes "adequate warning" or "reasonable disclosure" about a drug's risks, including those known at the time the drug was marketed and those discovered through postmarketing use and research.[67] For, as Shulman and Ulcickas wrote, while all drugs may be "unreasonably dangerous" per Comment k, or may be determined to be so on a case-by-case basis, "the protection of Comment k is forfeited . . . if the warnings accompanying the prescription drug are inadequate."[68]

66. Personal communications.

67. Postmarketing research by a manufacturer, initiated by the company or done at the FDA's request, can be undertaken "defensively," to identify toxicity problems, or to study some aspect of a drug's efficacy, including new indications for use. See Medicine in the Public Interest 1985.

68. Shulman and Ulcickas 1989, 95. As this article also points out, the distinction between negligence and strict liability "fades" on the question of what constitutes an adequate warning. "In both causes of action, an examination of the reasonableness of the manufacturer's conduct is required. The language of Comment j of the Restatement, al-

The FDA, as noted, has regulations that strictly control the content and format of the principal source of labeling information, the package insert for physicians and pharmacists that must accompany each drug.[69] Under the regulations labeling is also more broadly defined to include many other forms and types of information conveyed by the manufacturer; for example, replications of the package insert in the form of product cards or sources such as the *Physicians' Desk Reference,* written or verbal advertisements, promotional materials like press releases and promotional kits, "Dear Doctor" letters, and the oral representations made by company detail men.[70]

For product liability purposes, FDA labeling regulations, like other aspects of its public guardian role, set a floor of minimum standards rather than a ceiling. A manufacturer's compliance with labeling regulations does not preempt the holdings of the common law duty to warn, nor, as Gibbs and Mackler pointed out, did the FDA intend it to. "In adopting the [labeling] regulations, the FDA specifically disavowed any intent 'to influence the civil tort liability of the manufacturer or the physician. Rather, it is the agency's intent to ensure that a complete and accurate explanation of the drug is provided to the medical community.' "[71]

What Constitutes an "Adequate" Warning?

Court decisions on alleged warning defects have dealt with the *content* of the physician package insert and other forms of labeling, the *timeliness*

---

though part of strict liability theory, is equally applicable within the context of a negligence action. A manufacturer is required to warn of dangers 'if he has knowledge, or by the application of reasonable, developed human skill and foresight should have knowledge' of the risk" (p. 95).

69. The courts, with one exception, have held that pharmacists do not have a legal duty to warn or counsel patients directly about prescription drugs. See Brushwood and Simonsmeier 1986, 300–25.

70. There are a number of warning defect cases and FDA actions concerning the various forms of labeling other than the physician package insert. In terms of FDA enforcement activity regarding prescription drug advertising, for example, between 1971 and 1983 the agency sent pharmaceutical companies 1,069 letters requesting corrective action, canceled 858 ads and 968 instances of promotional labeling, and held 1,728 advisory conferences. See Fisherow 1987, 231. Consumer activist groups like the Public Citizen Health Research Group play a watchdog role for what they consider misleading advertisements and often petition the FDA to have such ads withdrawn or modified. For discussion of and citations to warning defect cases involving "Dear Doctor" letters sent by manufacturers to physicians about newly identified adverse effects, and liability for detailmen's warnings and overvigorous promotion, see Hirsh 1987, 402–03, and McGarey 1984, 118–19 and note 5.

71. Gibbs and Mackler 1987, 232, quoting from 44 *Federal Register* 37437 (1979).

of warnings, and the question of *to whom* the manufacturer owes a duty to warn. Some of the key points that have emerged in failure-to-warn cases have been the following:

—Pharmaceutical manufacturers have a legal obligation to "utilize methods of warnings which will be reasonably effective, taking into account both the seriousness of the drug's adverse effects and the difficulties inherent in bringing such information [in a timely] manner to the attention of a group as large and diverse as the medical profession."[72]

—The duty to warn is a "continuous one, requiring the manufacturer to keep abreast of the current state of knowledge of its products as gained through research, adverse reaction reports, scientific literature, and other available knowledge."[73]

—The duty to warn "does not arise until the manufacturer knows or should know of the risk."[74]

—A warning must be issued as soon an adverse effect is discovered.[75]

—A drug must not be so overpromoted (for example, by detail men) "that an otherwise adequate warning becomes inadequate."[76]

—Manufacturers can be liable for failing to warn of risks, including rare adverse reactions, associated with but not confirmed to be caused by use of their product.[77]

Two aspects of prescription drug warning defect decisions have been particularly problematic in terms of the regulatory intent and hoped-for effectiveness of labeling information. The first is the extent to which this information should or must incorporate "unsubstantiated" medical evidence about possible hazards. FDA regulations permit manufacturers to issue warnings when new ADRs are documented, without prior approval of such a labeling change. But the agency holds that "the most important feature of the package insert, the one that distinguishes it from other sources of information and makes possible its use as an authoritative reference source, is that its content must be based on substantial evidence.

72. *McEwen* v. *Ortho Pharmaceutical Corp.*, 270 Or. 375, 528. P. 2d 529 (1974).

73. Fern and Sichel 1985, 13, citing *Lindsay* v. *Ortho Pharmaceutical Corp.*, 637 F. 2d 91 (2d Cir. 1980).

74. Fern and Sichel 1985, 13, citing *Ortho Pharmaceutical* v. *Chapman*, 180 Ind. App. 33, 388 N.E. 2d 541 (1979).

75. *Feldman* v. *Lederle Laboratories*, 97 N.J. 429, 479, A. 2d 388–9 (1984).

76. McGarey 1984, 119, citing *Stevens* v. *Parke Davis. & Co.* 9 Cal. 3d 51, 67, 507 P. 2d 653, 662, 107 Cal. Rptr. 45, 54 (1973).

77. *Wooderson* v. *Ortho Pharmaceutical Corp.*, 235 Kan. 387, 681 P. 2d 1038 (1984), *cert. denied*, 105 S. Ct. 365 (1984). In *Wooderson*, the plaintiff was awarded punitive as well as compensatory damages, marking the first punitive damage decision in a pharmaceutical company failure-to-warn case. See Fern and Sichel 1985.

The labeling cannot simultaneously meet this requirement and be fully up to date. It cannot be both authoritative and avant-garde."[78]

A second concern is that product liability decisions, or attempts to ward off litigation, may lead manufacturers to include so much information in the label that it causes a "sensory overload." The potentially detrimental effects of too much warning information has been discussed by some courts as well as by the FDA, legal commentators, and writers concerned with risk-benefit assessments and the expertise and roles of physicians and patients in making such assessments.

A potential but real consequence of imposing liability for failure to warn of all suspected reactions will be to convert the package insert into a cluttered unintelligible list containing virtually every disease which might be suspected to be an adverse reaction to the product. This "overkill" would be the manufacturer's attempt to shield itself from liability. Unfortunately, promiscuous or unwarranted warnings cast doubt upon and undermine those warnings which reflect real potential hazards that the FDA requires to be listed on the label.[79]

The Duty to Warn: Physicians as the Learned Intermediary

A unique legal characteristic of prescription drugs is that, in contrast to over-the-counter (OTC) drugs and other "normal" consumer items, the manufacturer's duty to warn is owed to the physician rather than to the patient who is the drug's end-user. Under 1938 and 1951 regulatory changes intended to protect the public from the potential hazards of uncontrolled access to certain classes of drugs, the FDA required that such drugs could be obtained only through a physician and that adequate information about the use of such drugs needed to be written in medical terms "not likely to be understood by the ordinary individual."[80] With some exceptions, the courts have agreed with this regulatory philosophy,

78. From a 1974 article by Robert Temple, FDA Bureau of Drugs, on "Legal Implications of the Package Insert," quoted in Fern and Sichel 1985, p. 15. FDA labeling regulations also emphasize that the label for a given drug is not intended to be a "dispositive treatise."

79. Fern and Sichel 1985, 16.

80. The FDA first stated this position in 1938 (3 *Federal Register* 3168). Subsequently, in the 1951 Durham-Humphrey Amendment to the Food, Drug and Cosmetic Act, which officially authorized the FDA to establish the prescription or nonprescription status of all drugs, "a practitioner licensed by law" was required to administer prescription drugs (65 Stat. 648 [1951]).

which makes physicians the gatekeepers who control access both to prescription drugs and to information about those drugs. In a term first used in a 1966 judicial opinion, the physician is the "learned intermediary" who stands between the user of a prescription drugs and its manufacturer.[81]

The rationale for the physician's primacy in prescription drug use, as Shulman wrote, "is a familiar one. The physician is considered to be in the best position to weigh the risks and benefits of a specific drug for individual patients. The courts [and regulators] also are persuaded by arguments that direct communications from manufacturer to consumer may be too difficult, could unduly interfere with the doctor-patient relationship, and might frighten or confuse the patient, discouraging compliance with the prescribed therapy."[82]

Under both statutory and common law precepts, then, the effects of product liability law on the safe use of prescription drugs should come about through manufacturers' efforts to better inform physicians about the risks and proper use of their products. Presumptively, physicians will both read and carefully heed the labeling information,[83] and in prescribing a drug they will explain its indications, risks, and proper administration so that the patient can informedly consent to its use. "In practical concept," Rheingold wrote, "a sort of 'Norman Rockwell' practice of medicine was envisioned by [the learned intermediary] decisions—the ignorant, reliant patient, sitting in the presence of the all-knowing doctor."[84]

Erosions of the Learned Intermediary Doctrine

Since the mid-1970s, however, several social currents have been eroding the learned intermediary doctrine and strengthening the position that patients, too, should have access to intelligible information about the

81. *Sterling Drug Inc.* v. *Cornish*, 370 F.2d 82 (8th Cir. 1966). For citations to and discussions of other cases upholding the learned intermediary doctrine, see Brushwood and Simonsmeier 1986; Grant 1988; Rheingold 1964 and 1985.

82. Shulman 1989, 1566.

83. If the labeling is adequate but has not been read or not been heeded by physician before she or he issues a prescription, the physician's failure to follow adequate instructions constitutes misuse that under product liability law, bars a plaintiff's recovery. See Grant 1988. See chapter 7 in this book for a discussion of the relation between malpractice and product liability. As Tancredi and Nelkin suggest, one reason that physicians seldom seem to be defendants in prescription drug product liability cases may be that limitations on malpractice awards in many jurisdictions shift litigation to the "deep pockets" of industry.

84. Rheingold 1985, 136.

safety, effectiveness, and proper use of their prescribed medications. Developments favoring more patient- or consumer-oriented drug information have included a number of court decisions holding, on a case-by-case basis, that there are exceptions to the learned intermediary rule, and some regulatory rulemaking and trends more favorable toward the provision of labeling information to patients. These legal and regulatory moves have been fostered by congressional support for patient or consumer-directed information, questions and concerns about the extent to which physicians approximate the ethical and legal standards for informed, voluntary consent to treatment when they prescribe or administer prescription drugs, and the increasingly active and influential consumer rights movement in the United States. The growing support for and availability of multisource rather than physician-based single-source information, in turn, raises a number of product liability questions, including the viability of the common law position that the pharmaceutical manufacturer's duty to warn is owed only to the physician.

MANDATED EXCEPTIONS. Judicial and regulatory exceptions to the learned intermediary rule have been made for two main categories of prescription products. The first is vaccines used for mass immunizations, which may be dispensed in a setting where no physician provides an individualized balancing and communication of the risks and benefits.[85] The second category includes oral contraceptives, estrogen products, progestational drugs, and intrauterine devices. According to FDA rulemaking and several court cases, the rationales for exempting such products from the learned intermediary rule are that they are used electively by large numbers of healthy women, they are potentially dangerous, and they are prescribed "with no assurance that the users [are] being adequately warned about their dangers."[86]

In 1975 the FDA issued a notice of proposed rulemaking about extending its patient package insert (PPI) program, and then in 1979 issued proposed regulations to require PPIs for all nonelectively used prescription drugs.[87] The history of the proposed PPI program, especially the

85. McGarey 1984, 131.
86. McGarey 1984, 132.
87. The proposed regulations (44 *Federal Register* 40016 [1979]) were based on several considerations. These included studies of the effectiveness of the FDA's four mandated PPIs, a review of the literature on consumer information for prescription drugs, awareness that restricting information solely to physicians did not encourage the safe use of prescription drugs, and a growing political recognition of the consumer rights movement. On the history of the PPI program, see Dorsey 1977; McGarey 1984.

roles played by consumer groups, the medical profession, the pharmaceutical industry, Congress, and the Reagan administration, is a fascinating and instructive sociopolitical study in its own right. Officially, the agency's plans and preparations for instituting a comprehensive program of consumer- or patient-directed information ended in 1982, when final regulations that had been promulgated but not yet implemented were withdrawn as part of the administration's deregulatory thrust.[88]

VOLUNTARY PATIENT EDUCATION AND CONSUMER INFORMATION. For both political and budgetary reasons, it seems unlikely that any type of federally required patient information program will be resurrected. But in the judgment of an FDA official closely involved with the PPI initiative, the "original goal in proposing the program has worked, because a great deal of prescription drug information for patients is now available through many publications and other resources."[89] The 1980s indeed saw a profusion of written and audiovisual materials providing general and specific information about prescription drugs, issued by government agencies, health professional and consumer groups, and industry.[90]

Consumer-directed information about prescription drugs is not intended to *replace* the physician's role in making prescription decisions and discussing them with patients. Rather, its intent is to help remedy long-recognized deficits in the prescribing process and in the use of drugs. The "broader message" of the experience with a drug like Accutane is the need for physicians to give, and patients to receive from their doctor or other sources, better information to help them understand the risks, benefits, and proper use of prescription agents and what steps to take when they experience side effects.[91] The extent to which prescription drug information written for laypersons will accomplish the goals of a multisource rather than single-source drug information system remains to be seen. Studies of PPIs and other printed materials show they can be effective learning tools, especially if used in concert with verbal information or counseling from a health professional.[92] However, their long-

88. Notice of the program's cancellation was published in 47 *Federal Register* 39148 (1982). In December 1982 the FDA was directed by the assistant secretary for health to form a Committee on Patient Education (COPE), to coordinate efforts to educate consumers about prescription drugs and to encourage private sector efforts.

89. Personal interview, Feb. 21, 1990.

90. National Council on Patient Education (n.d.)

91. Shulman 1989.

92. See, for example, Johnson and others 1986; Regner, Herman, and Reid 1987; Sands, Robinson, and Orlando 1984.

term effects on knowledge and actual drug usage, and the degree to which they improve doctor-patient interactions dealing with prescribing, are uncertain.[93]

The bearing of product liability law on consumer-oriented information provided by a pharmaceutical manufacturer is equally uncertain at this juncture. McGarey pointed out in 1984 that "the most serious inadequacy of the case-by-case approach to the single-source [learned intermediary] problem is that it fails to provide a method for improving the safety of prescription drug use."[94] If a prediction made in 1985 by no less an authority than Paul Rheingold proves accurate, however, liability decisions may well be making the learned intermediary an endangered species, at least under product liability law. Rheingold's prediction was that "cases will continue to appear creating what the courts regard as exceptions to the black letter rule [the learned intermediary doctrine]. . . . After that . . . the exceptions will swallow the rule . . . [and] manufacturers will be placed under a general duty to warn the public directly, and that exceptions will relate to those few occasions when such a warning is not due."[95]

At present, product liability concerns seem to be hindering the pharmaceutical industry's voluntary efforts to provide patient-directed information about prescription drugs. Unless required by administrative rulemaking or the courts, manufacturers have no affirmative duty to provide labeling information written for patients, and no regulatory sanctions or product liability is imposed if they do not provide it. Some manufacturers are reluctant to develop prescription drug information for patients because their product liability attorneys fear that any such materials, in lieu of the physician package insert, greatly increase a company's risk of liability. Those manufacturers who have ventured into the patient education arena, in turn, recognize the wisdom of having their literature reviewed and approved by the FDA, which defines it as promotional labeling. And because of concerns about potential liability, companies are extremely conscious of the content and precise wording of patient information materials about specific prescription drugs. In my experience, such concerns can help to ensure the accuracy of the information that is conveyed. But fears of liability can also clutter patient information materials with boilerplate statements and impede the presentation of certain

93. As Tietz (1986) points out, there have been remarkably few informed consent suits involving prescription drugs.
94. McGarey 1984, 139.
95. Rheingold 1985, 144.

types of useful information.[96] One hedge against liability used by industry is to distribute patient-oriented material to the physician, who in turn provides it to his or her patient as part of the prescribing process. But in the opinion of several attorneys, including litigation specialists for industry, there is a question whether a learned intermediary defense would hold up in court in a case involving information written for patients, because the physician could be viewed as just a "pass through" or conduit.[97]

DIRECT-TO-CONSUMER ADVERTISING. Besides industry-sponsored patient information programs, the 1980s saw the beginnings of a more controversial venture by pharmaceutical manufacturers: drug advertising directed to the lay consumer rather than to the physician prescriber and pharmacist dispenser. Beginning with mass media ads for soft contact lenses in 1978, and then advertising campaigns for several prescription drugs in the early 1980s, the industry began to "test the waters" to see if direct-to-the-consumer promotion would be an effective marketing strategy to help them meet "changing market conditions."[98]

Direct-to-consumer advertising promises to be a continuing source of controversy during the 1990s. Opinions differ, often sharply, within and between industry, health professionals, laypersons and consumer organizations, the FDA, and attorneys about the ethical propriety and economic costs and gains of such advertising, its effects on patients and physicians and their interactions, and its product liability implications.

The FDA was given statutory authority in 1963 to regulate prescription drug advertising. These regulations have never prohibited industry from advertising specific prescription drugs to the public once they have received an NDA marketing approval as long as promotional materials include the same "brief summary" labeling information required for

96. This statement is based on my experience preparing prescription drug informational materials for patients for a pharmaceutical company.

97. Personal interviews.

98. Discussing direct-to-consumer advertising at a conference in 1983, Felton Davis, Jr., senior vice president of Government and Public Affairs for Ciba Geigy, stated: "A host of marketing conditions have required a rethinking of our approach. Because the time of patent protection on prescription products has shortened considerably over the last years, market penetration has become even more important. Also, increased restrictions are being placed on prescribers and dispensers, so we thought that we might have a new market by advertising directly to patients. The requirement that we deal only with physicians caused the industry a large problem, because no one knew anything about the industry as an industry. We have always been on the defensive, and we're still defending ourselves against charges. We have never been able to speak directly and positively to the public, and we hope to be able to do so now." Medicine in the Public Interest 1984, 42.

professional advertisements and do not mention an FDA "seal of approval."[99]

Nonetheless, some agency staff, among others, have been concerned about various implications of this marketing approach.[100] Proponents of prescription drug consumer advertising argue that it has an educational as well as a sales function: such ads can provide people with useful information that will make them more informed and compliant users of their medications. Opponents are equally convinced that such advertising will make people "yearn, not learn,"[101] and that industry and its supporters are simply being disingenuous when they argue educational merits. Those concerned about direct-to-consumer advertising worry that it will help "trivialize" prescription drugs, drive up their cost, pressure people to ask their physicians for drugs they do not need, undermine the physician-patient relationship, and confuse laypeople because of the inherent oversimplification in ad messages.[102]

Because it is a relatively new and evolving venture, the effects of consumer advertising on the industry's risks for product liability actions, and, conversely, the effects of liability on such advertising, remain speculative. In 1985 Rheingold predicted that litigation involving consumer advertising will be another area where "the courts may fashion an exception to the black letter [learned intermediary] rule because the drug company has reached out to the public deliberately."[103] He described two consumer advertising situations that might lead a manufacturer to be held liable. The first is when an affirmative representation has been made in an ad that is found to be negligently or intentionally misleading even if the package insert is accurate. Second, even if manufacturers "make no representations of safety in their public advertising . . . the very act, however, of promoting the drug to the public and creating a demand will probably be used by some courts to impose a duty on the supplier to issue warnings directly to the consumer. . . . The purpose of promotion

---

99. Two types of ads, whether geared for health professionals or laypersons, are not required to include the technical brief summary information: ads that present only price information, with no mention of what the product is used for, or how it is used; and what are termed "institutional ads" that discuss a particular medical condition such as arthritis or diabetes but do not mention a specific product.

100. In 1983 the FDA commissioner, Arthur Hayes, Jr., asked pharmaceutical companies to "observe a voluntary moratorium" on direct-to-consumer advertising other than price comparisons and institutional ads, while the FDA studied various issues such as effects on patient education and on the doctor-patient relationship. See Murphy 1984, 20.

101. Miller 1983.

102. Miller 1983.

103. Rheingold 1985, 139.

is but one, to create demand, and it will be reasoned that even though the doctor had to move his hand in order for the patient to get his drug, the drug supplier departed from his reclusive role of dealing with doctors only and therefore must suffer its own adverse consequences."[104]

Whether the prospect of the kinds of liability Rheingold envisioned will act as a brake on the volume of direct-to-consumer advertising, or moderate its tone and content, is an open question. Two knowledgeable attorneys whom I interviewed were not sanguine about such effects, given the counterforce of potential profits from consumer marketing. One attorney, formerly with the FDA, commented that direct-to-consumer advertising is increasing rapidly "and is one more example of the fact that pharmaceutical companies pay more attention to marketing than liability." Another attorney, working for a pharmaceutical company, had a similar opinion, believing that consumer advertising may increase liability risks for the industry but that "such risks will be balanced by the fact that advertising pays off from a marketing vantage point."[105]

Blind Men, Elephants, and the Safety of Prescription Drugs

In the familiar oriental fable, the blind men who feel different parts of an unknown object identify them as a rope, a spear, and so forth. Each was a fair inference from the "facts" they could discern, but these did not enable them to identify the object as an elephant. Assessing the effects of product liability on the safety of prescription drugs is analogous to the blind men's task, except that there are at least two elephants we are groping to recognize. One elephant can be called "safe" prescription drugs. For, as discussed earlier, what one means by safety in the context of these pharmaceutical products, and how it is assessed, are questions that may be answered very differently by pharmacologists, physicians, patients, manufacturers, regulators, judges, and juries. The second elephant has a more unwieldy name, "the effects of various social control agents—industry, the medical profession, patients and consumer groups, regulations, product liability law, and so forth—on the safety of prescription drugs." I am not ashamed to admit that I am like one of those legendary blind men with respect to both these elephants, because I know I am in some very good company. And having failed to identify the

104. Rheingold 1985, 141.
105. Personal interviews.

elephants with any great precision or clarity, I must make my final remarks comparably tentative.

Given the pharmacological and clinical evidence that there is no such thing as a 100 percent safe prescription (or other) drug, the question is how the risks of these unavoidably unsafe products can be contained and their *safer* (as opposed to perfectly safe) use be maximized. Measures to contain the risks and enhance the safest possible use of prescription drugs fall into two broad categories. First, as a drug is developed and tested and, if approved, marketed, many types of evidence and decisionmaking processes are involved in determining its risks and in balancing those risks against its clinical benefits. Second, given the available body of indeterminate knowledge about a drug's risks and benefits, how safely and effectively it is used depends partly on the caliber of the labeling information about its indicated uses, contraindications, risks, dosage and administration, and so on. However, while proper labeling information is necessary to safe and effective prescription drug use, it is not sufficient. For such information must be read and understood by physicians, factored into their prescribing decisions, and adequately conveyed to and comprehended by patients. And once a prescription is written, the medication must be dispensed properly and used "as directed" by the patient. There can be, in short, many a slip between the cup and the lip, and however excellent the whole process is, adverse reactions or "bad outcomes" will still occur.

More than 8,000 prescription drugs (including drug combinations) are marketed in the United States, and physicians write well over 2.3 billion inpatient and outpatient prescriptions each year. Given this huge volume in relation to the number of serious adverse reactions that are known or estimated to occur—some 60,000 "adverse events" associated with drugs and biologics are reported to the FDA annually—the United States seems, on balance, to do a credible job of dealing with the risks of these basically risky products.[106] But given the imperfections and fallibilities of people and the social organizations they invent and manage, the conclusion that we could do a better job of containing the risks and maximizing the safer use of prescription drugs should be self-evident.

106. Ackerman 1988; Faich, Dreis, and Tomita 1988; Myer 1988. Most analysts feel that ADRs are underreported, largely because of the failure of physicians to report adverse effects to a drug's manufacturer or the FDA, and their unawareness of the FDA reporting system. However, the fact that nearly 24 percent of the reports received are for "severe" reactions, involving death or hospitalization, led the FDA to believe they are being notified about "grave clinical outcomes." Faich, Dreis, and Tomita 1988, 786.

Physicians do not always live up to the Norman Rockwell image of the learned intermediary described by Rheingold: they are not omniscient about diseases and treatments, including clinical pharmacology; they usually do not do a very good job of communicating with their patients; and they do misprescribe. Patients, in turn, even if knowledgeable about their illnesses and medications, do not always heed the oral or written information they receive, follow their medication regimen, tell their doctor about other drugs they are taking, and report adverse reactions.

Pharmaceutical manufacturers and their regulators, the FDA, also could do a better job in dealing with prescription drug safety. Their deficiencies, and the many reasons for them, are engraved in legal cases, congressional hearings and reports, press accounts, and so forth. Manufacturers, for example, have been known to let economic benefits outweigh risks to patients in marketing decisions, to be negligently slow to issue warnings when new adverse reactions are identified, and to engage in fraudulent misrepresentation by deliberately withholding information about a drug's hazards from the FDA or physicians or both.[107] The FDA, in its turn, has been subject to recurrent criticisms about matters such as the quality of its staff, the timeliness and the competence of its premarketing and postmarketing reviews and actions, its failures to act on ADR information, and labeling requirements that sometimes stifle manufacturers' attempts to issue warnings. Some more recent regulatory issues, as mentioned, concern the effects of the agency's 1987 IND treatment provisions on safety and effectiveness assessments of new drugs, including potential sources of liability for treatment IND sponsors.[108]

Finally, I respond to the central question I was asked to address: to what extent have product liability doctrines, verdicts, and concerns promoted drug safety? Of all the questions a blind man might be asked about any part of the two elephants, that one seems hardest to answer. For, as repeatedly noted about prescription drug design and warnings, evidence, more weighty than single cases, anecdotes and opinions, and poorly designed surveys, is either nonexistent or not available. Moreover, as has also been stressed, it is exceedingly difficult to disentangle the effects of FDA regulations and product liability on drug safety, especially given the quality and quantity of information one has to work with.

From the sketchy and insubstantial information that is available, it seems reasonable to conclude that product liability law and litigation have

107. Rheingold 1964; Schwartz 1988b, 1148–49; Weisner and Walsh 1988.
108. See Herzog 1977; Grabowski and Vernon 1983; Schwartz 1988b, 1148–49.

had only a marginal effect on the development of safer drugs. Liability is one of many factors involved in decisions not to bring new agents to the market or to withdraw marketed drugs when their risks are judged to outweigh their benefits, and it does not seem to be a paramount consideration. Design defect cases have been much less common than warning defect cases involving prescription drugs. For with those products, one is dealing with nature's molecular structures or with variations devised by "tinkering" with nature. In this context, the type of "error" that an engineer might make in designing a new widget is not a particularly appropriate construct, nor are the more usual tort law notions of "design defects" as a cause of action.

Because of the inherently hazardous nature of prescription drugs, it seems reasonable to assume that product liability would have its greatest effect on the content and timeliness of information conveyed to physicians, and to patients, through the types of materials that the FDA defines as labeling. That law, verdicts, and fear of litigation involving warning defects have helped to foster more accurate and timely information about prescription drugs, and thus by inference their safer use, was the unanimous judgment of the several experts I interviewed, and it is the "received"—though slimly documented—"wisdom" found in the literature. However, liability fears seem to be impeding the provision of patient-directed educational materials about prescription drugs by manufacturers and, to date, having no discernible effect on direct-to-consumer advertising.

Although studies such as those by the GAO and Rand support the view that the pharmaceutical industry has not suffered a litigation explosion, manufacturers are cognizant of and worried about product liability issues. Those issues include the current and emerging content, objectives, and workings of state and federal tort laws in this country and, given the multinational structure of most pharmaceutical companies, developing international trends in product liability law and no-fault compensation for drug-induced injuries.[109]

When one considers the nature of prescription drugs, the scientific and value issues involved in determining the reasons for "bad outcomes," the multiple objectives of tort law, the variety of reasons that impel patients and their attorneys to litigate, and the frequently arcane reasoning and unpredictability of juries and judges, it is not surprising that one can cite product liability laws and verdicts that seem both "proper and improper"

---

109. For a concise review of these international trends, see Shulman and Lasagna 1990.

for prescription drugs and their manufacturers.[110] The industry is pressing vigorously for tort reforms and often cries out at the "wounds" it receives from the "strong sword" of product liability. At the same time, some of the strategies that companies are developing as "damage control" or "preventive medicine" efforts against liability show that they recognize they *can* take steps to further contain the risks and increase the safer use of their prescription products.[111]

110. The phrase "proper and improper" is used by Epstein in discussing one of the "downside" problems of product liability law with respect to warning defect litigation: "Modern common law creates a serious bias, intensified by the discretion left to juries, toward finding all warnings inadequate when judged by the standards of hindsight. On a selective basis, the theory of improper warnings becomes an elaborate, expensive, and erratic pretext for compensating for bad outcomes alone. As every skillful trial lawyer knows, the question of adequacy of warnings is a form of reverse engineering. First find out what warnings were given, and then tailor the claim on adequacy to render them insufficient." Epstein 1987, 172.

111. Examples of such efforts include the development of "product safety programs" and educational programs for pharmaceutical company employees, designed to teach them about product liability and how to minimize it by compliance with regulations, information flow within a company, communications with physicians and patients, and so forth. See Golden 1986.

References

Ackerman, S. J. 1988. "Watching for Problems that Testing May Have Missed." *FDA Consumer* 22:9–11.

Anderson, C. M. 1946. "The 'New Drug' Section." *Food Drug Cosmetic Law Quarterly* 1:71–85.

Annas, G. J. 1989. "Faith (Healing), Hope, and Charity at the FDA: The Politics of AIDS Drug Trials." *Villanova Law Review* 34:771–97.

American Law Institute. 1965. "Restatement (Second) of Torts." St. Paul, Minn.

Bakke, O. M., W. M. Wardell, and L. Lasagna. 1984. "Drug Discontinuations in the United Kingdom and the United States, 1964 to 1983: Issues of Safety." *Clinical Pharmacology and Therapeutics* 35:559–67.

Barash, C., and L. Lasagna. 1987. "The Bendectin Saga: 'Voluntary' Discontinuation." *Journal of Clinical Research and Drug Development* 1:277–92.

Birnbaum, S. L., and B. Wrubel. 1985. "State of the Art and Strict Products Liability." *Tort and Insurance Law Journal* 21:30–43.

Bradbury, J. A. 1989. "The Policy Implications of Differing Concepts of Risk." *Science, Technology, and Human Values* 14:380–99.

Brushwood, D. B., and L. M. Simonsmeier. 1986. "Drug Information for Patients: Duties of the Manufacturer, Pharmacist, Physician, and Hospital." *Journal of Legal Medicine* 7:279–340.

Coben, L. E., M. C. Romney, and M. J. Panichelli. 1989. "Medicine and Law: Recent Developments." *Tort and Insurance Law Journal* 24:408–19.

Crout, J. R. 1976. "New Drug Regulation and Its Impact on Innovation." In *Impact of Public Policy on Drug Innovation and Pricing*. Proceedings of the Third Seminar on Pharmaceutical Public Policy Issues. Edited by S. A. Mitchell and E. A. Link, chap. 6. American University.

Dorsey, R. 1977. "The Patient Package Insert. Is It Safe and Effective?" *Journal of the American Medical Association* 238:1936–39.

Dubos, R. J. 1987. *Mirage of Health: Utopias, Progress, and Biological Change.* Rutgers University Press.

Dungworth, T. 1988. *Product Liability and the Business Sector: Litigation Trends in Federal Court.* R-3668-ICJ. Santa Monica, Calif.: Rand Corporation.

Epstein, R. A. 1987. "Legal Liability for Medical Innovation." In *Medical Innovation and Bad Outcomes: Legal, Social, and Ethical Responses*, edited by M. Siegler, chap. 11. Ann Arbor, Mich.: Health Administration Press.

Faich, G. 1986. "Adverse Drug Reporting and Product Liability." *Food Drug Cosmetic Law Journal.* 41:444–49.

Faich, G. A., M. Dreis, and D. Tomita. 1988. "National Adverse Drug Reaction Surveillance." *Archives of Internal Medicine* 148:785–87.

Fern, F. H., and W. M. Sichel. 1985. "Failure to Warn in Drug Cases: Are Punitive Damages Justifiable?" *For the Defense* 27:12–20.

Fisherow, W. B. 1987. "The Shape of Prescription Drug Advertising: A Survey of Promotional Techniques and Regulatory Trends." *Food Drug Cosmetic Law Journal* 42:213–36.

General Accounting Office. 1988. *Product Liability. Extent of "Litigation Explosion" in Federal Courts Questioned.* GAO/HRD-88-36 BR. Washington.

Gibbs, J. N., and B. F. Mackler. 1987. "Food and Drug Administration Regulation and Products Liability: Strong Sword, Weak Shield." *Tort and Insurance Law Journal* 22:194–243.

Goldblatt, S., and others. 1989. "Products Liability: Annual Survey of Recent Developments." *Tort and Insurance Law Journal* 24:420–55.

Golden, V. G. 1986. "A Product Safety Program: Preventive Maintenance for Drug Companies." *Food Drug Cosmetic Law Journal* 41:450–57.

Grabowski, H. G., and J. M. Vernon. 1983. *The Regulation of Pharmaceuticals: Balancing the Benefits and Risks.* Washington: American Enterprise Institute for Public Policy Research.

Grant, J. E. 1988. "The 'Misuse Defense' in Drug Products Liability Cases." *Pace Law Review* 8:535–70.

Hensler, D. R., and others. 1987. *Trends in Tort Litigation. The Story Behind the Statistics.* R-3583-ICJ. Santa Monica, Calif.: Rand Corporation.

Herzog, J. 1977. *Recurrent Criticisms: A History of Investigations of the FDA.* PS-7702. Rochester, N.Y.: Center for the Study of Drug Development.

Hirsh, H. L. 1987. "Product Liability: Breach of Warranty/Strict Product Liability." *Medicine and Law* 6:397–406.

Inman, W. H. W. 1987a. "Prescription-Event Monitoring: Its Strategic Role in Post-Marketing Surveillance for Drug Safety." *PEM News* 4:15–29.

———. 1987b. "Requirements for Risk-Benefit Assessments of Drugs Before Withdrawal." *PEM News, Supplement,* Mar., i–xii.

Janowitz, M. W., 1977. *Social Control of the Welfare State.* Phoenix edition. University of Chicago Press.

Johnson, M. W., and others. 1986. "The Impact of a Drug Information Sheet on the Understanding and Attitude of Patients about Drugs." *Journal of the American Medical Association* 256:2722–24.

Johnstone, J. M. 1988. "Treatment IND Safety Assessment: Potential Legal and Regulatory Problems." *Food Drug Cosmetic Law Journal* 43:533–40.

Kaitin, K. I. 1988. "Thalidomide Revisited: New Clinical Uses for an Old Drug." *Pharmaceutical Medicine* 3:203–10.

Kaitin, K., and others. 1989. "The Drug Lag: An Update of New Drug Introductions in the United States and United Kingdom, 1977 through 1987." *Clinical Pharmacology and Therapeutics* 46:121–38.

Lesar, T. S., and others. 1990. "Medication Prescribing Errors in a Teaching Hospital." *Journal of the American Medical Association* 263:2329–34.

McClellan, F. M., T. H. Tate, and A. T. Eaton. 1981. "Strict Liability for Prescription Drug Injuries: The Improper Marketing Theory." *St. Louis University Law Journal* 26:1–38.

McGarey, B. M. 1984. "Pharmaceutical Manufacturers and Consumer-Directed Information—Enhancing the Safety of Prescription Drug Use." *Catholic University Law Review* 34:117–52.

McGuire, E. P. 1988. *The Impact of Product Liability.* Research Report 908. New York: The Conference Board.

Mariner, W. 1986. "Comparison of Compensation Programs for Vaccine Injury." Final Report to the National Center for Health Services Research and Health Care Technology Assessment. Grant No. HS 05106.

———. 1989. "Strict Liability for Defects in Vaccine and Drug Design: Necessity or Nemesis?"

Mariner, W. K., and M. E. Clark. 1986. "Confronting the Immunization Problem: Proposals for Compensation Reform." *American Journal of Public Health* 76:703–08.

Mariner, W. K., and R. C. Gallo. 1987. "Getting to Market: The Scientific and Legal Climate for Developing an AIDS Vaccine." *Law, Medicine and Health Care* 15:17–26.

Marshall, E. 1989. "Quick Release of AIDS Drugs." *Science* 245:345–47.

Medicine in the Public Interest. 1984. *Prescription Drug Information for Patients and Direct-to-Consumer Advertising.* Proceedings of a June 27–29, 1983, conference. Boston.

————. 1985. *Post-Approval Pharmaceutical Research and Development.* Proceedings of a May 16–17, 1984, conference. Boston.

Miller, R. W. 1983. "Would Rx Ads Make People Learn or Yearn?" *FDA Consumer* 17:24–27.

Mintz, M. 1965. *The Therapeutic Nightmare.* Houghton Mifflin.

Mitchell, S., and E. Link. 1976. *Impact of Public Policy on Drug Innovation and Pricing.* Proceedings of the Third Seminar on Pharmaceutical Public Policy Issues. American University.

Murphy, D. H. 1984. "Direct to Consumer Advertising of Prescription Drugs. FDA's First Round of Tests." *American Pharmacy* NS24:20–23.

Myer, B. 1988. "Improving Medical Education in Therapeutics." *Annals of Internal Medicine* 108:145–47.

National Council on Patient Education and Information. [n.d.] *Directory of Prescription Drug Information and Education Programs and Resources.* Washington.

Nelkin, D. 1983. "On the Social and Political Acceptibility of Risks." *Impact of Science on Society* 3:225–31.

Nightingale, S. L. 1990. "Approval of Clozapine for Refractory Schizophrenia." *Journal of the American Medical Association* 263:202.

Nygaard, D. A. 1988. "Accutane: Is the Drug a Prescription for Birth Defects?" *Trial,* Dec.:81–83.

Pharmaceutical Manufacturers Association. 1989. "Product Liability Reform." Tort Reform File. Washington.

————. [n.d.] "Unaffordable and Unavailable: The Crisis in Liability Insurance." Tort Reform File. Washington.

Regner, M. J., F. Hermann, and L. D. Reid. 1987. "Effectiveness of a Printed Leaflet for Enabling Patients to Use Digoxin Side-Effect Information." *Drug Intelligence and Clinical Pharmacology* 21:200–04.

Rheingold, P. 1964. "Products Liability—The Ethical Drug Manufacturer's Liability." *Rutgers Law Review* 18:947–1018.

————. 1985. "The Expanding Liability of the Drug Manufacturer to the Consumer." *Food Drug Cosmetic Law Journal* 40:135–44.

Rheinstein, P. D. 1982. "A Head Start, a Broader Audience, and an Emphasis on Difference: The New Frontiers of Prescription Drug Promotion." *Food Drug Cosmetic Law Journal* 37:330–35.

Sands, S. C. D., J. D. Robinson, and J. B. Orlando. 1984. "The Oral Contraceptive PPI: Its Effect on Patient Knowledge, Feelings, and Behavior." *Drug Intelligence and Clinical Pharmacology* 18:730–35.

Schwartz, G. 1987. "American Tort Doctrine since the 1960s." Unpublished manuscript.

Schwartz, T. M. 1986. "Consumer Warnings for Oral Contraceptives: A New Exception to the Prescription Drug Rule." *Food Drug Cosmetic Law Journal* 41:241–56.

————. 1988a. "Products Liability Law and Pharmaceuticals: New Developments and Divergent Trends." *Food Drug Cosmetic Law Journal* 43:33–53.

————. 1988b. "The Role of Federal Safety Regulations in Products Liability Actions." *Vanderbilt Law Review* 41:1121–69.

Shulman, S. R. 1989. "The Broader Message of Accutane." *American Journal of Public Health* 79:1565–68.

Shulman, S. R., and L. Lasagna, eds. 1990. *Trends in Product Liability Law and No-Fault Compensation for Drug-Induced Injuries*. Boston: Tufts University Center for the Study of Drug Development.

Shulman, S. R., and M. E. Ulcickas. 1989. "Update on ADR Reporting Regulations: Products Liability Implications." *Journal of Clinical Research and Drug Development* 3:91–103.

Soumerai, S. B., T. J. McLaughlin, and J. Avorn. 1989. "Improving Drug Prescribing in Primary Care: A Critical Analysis of the Experimental Literature." *Milbank Quarterly* 67:268–317.

Temin, P. 1981. *Taking Your Medicine: Drug Regulation in the United States.* Harvard University Press.

Tietz, G. F. 1986. "Informed Consent in the Prescription Drug Context: The Special Case." *Washington Law Review* 61:367–417.

Twerski, A., and others. 1976. "The Use and Abuse of Warnings in Products Liability—Design Defect Comes of Age." *Cornell Law Review* 61:495–540.

Wade, J. 1983. "On the Effect in Product Liability of Knowledge Unavailable Prior to Marketing." *New York University Law Review* 58:734–61.

Walsh, C. J., and M. S. Klein. 1986. "The Conflicting Objectives of Federal and State Tort Law Drug Regulation." *Food Drug Cosmetic Law Journal* 41:171–94.

Wastila, L. J., M. E. Ulcickas, and L. Lasagna. 1989. "The World Health Organization's Essential Drug List. The Significance of Me-Too and Follow-on Research." *Journal of Clinical Research and Drug Development* 3:105–15.

Weber, N. 1987. *Product Liability: The Corporate Response*. Research Report 893. New York: The Conference Board.

Weintraub, M., and F. K. Northington. 1986. "Drugs that Wouldn't Die." *Journal of the American Medical Association* 255:2327–28.

Weisner, B., and E. Walsh. 1988. "Drug Firm's Strategy: Avoid Trial, Ask Secrecy." *Washington Post*, Oct. 25:A1.

Wilner, D. S., and L. S. Gayer. 1989. "*Hymowitz* v. *Eli Lilly*: New York Adopts a 'National Risk' Doctrine for DES." *Tort and Insurance Law Journal* 25:150–56.

Witherspoon, E. 1988. "Thalidomide—The Aftermath." *Pharmaceutical Medicine* 3:229–303.

Young, J. H. 1982. "Public Policy and Drug Innovation." *Pharmacy in History* 24:3–31.

CHAPTER NINE

The Chilling Effect of Product Liability on New Drug Development

Louis Lasagna

Few would disagree about the litigiousness of American society. Recourse to litigation and the threat of such recourses are common. With regard to pharmaceutical products, certain law firms specialize in litigation dealing with real or perceived harm from medicines. Advertisements are placed in newspapers and other media by lawyers seeking clients who may have suffered drug-related damages. Class action suits seek redress of such injuries. Drugs and medical devices are taken off the market because of the magnitude of the litigation threat to their manufacturers.

How harmful to society are these events? Is innovation threatened by litigation? How important is the withdrawal from the market of pharmaceutical products for reasons of product liability? What is the effect of litigation on the price of drugs?

Since for every known disease one can say that current drug therapy can be improved on, the pharmaceutical industry's traditional commitment to innovation must not be discouraged. More important, for some diseases no effective therapy now exists or available therapy is limited (for example, AIDS and most cancers).

The case histories described in this chapter clearly indicate that the negative impact of litigation has exacted its toll. While the nausea and vomiting of pregnancy, for instance, is often minor and relatively short-lived, it is never pleasant, and to deprive all pregnant women of effective pharmacotherapy for this complaint is hardly a trivial consequence of the Bendectin saga.

With vaccines, the case can be made even more dramatically. Americans in general need vaccines against such diseases as varicella-zoster, herpes simplex, cytomegalovirus, rotavirus, the gonococcus, and Rocky Mountain spotted fever. The U.S. armed forces need protection against malaria, leishmaniasis, Rift Valley fever, sandfly fever, African trypanosomiasis, Japanese encephalitis, and several viral hemorrhagic fevers, among others. In the event of biological warfare, protection against tularemia, anthrax, and Q fever would be important. A vaccine against AIDS would clearly be a dramatic step forward not only for the United States and Africa but also for Brazil, France, and other countries where the disease occurs.

Although this chapter does not specifically address the issues of birth control or medical devices, it is generally agreed that product liability is a serious disincentive to research and development in these areas as well.

Litigation and Drug Prices

The effect of litigation on the price of drugs is difficult to assess. Certainly, part of the cost of doing business in the pharmaceutical industry is attributable to lawyers' fees and related expenditures. Drug firms spend money for both in-house counsel and outside lawyers. Suits brought against a company mean costs incurred in preparing for trial as well as actual court costs and the need to pay damages in the event of an adverse court decision. Such damages may cover not only medical costs but also loss of job income and future earning power, "pain and suffering," and punitive damages.

None of these points is contested, nor is there any doubt that ultimately such costs will be passed on, in whole or in part, to the consumers of the firm's products. What is impossible to obtain is an accurate quantification of even an individual company's legal costs, let alone those for the entire pharmaceutical industry. One can, to be sure, track court awards and the fate of such awards in the wake of the appeals that are frequently made after such court decisions. But out-of-court settlements are common, and firms are understandably reluctant to discuss the size of such settlements for fear of encouraging new suits or inflating future claims. Even the cost of in-house and outside counsel is not readily obtained, let alone the percentage of such cost attributable to product liability actions as opposed to the many other legal needs included in a firm's routine activities (such as patent filings, union contracts, new drug labeling, and advertising issues).

In the rest of the chapter I assess the negative effect of product liability by discussing the following:

—the several factors involved in drawing up a balance sheet to measure the magnitude of disincentives to pharmaceutical innovation and marketing;

—the history of the antiemetic product Bendectin;

—the relation of litigation to vaccine development and marketing;

—the failure of thalidomide to acquire a commercial sponsor despite the discovery, during the last three decades, of several important new medical uses for the drug;

—the impact of product liability concerns on "orphan drugs";

—national and international attempts to deal with product liability; and

—possible future developments.

In my discussion I hope to show that product liability issues prevent needed pharmaceutical research from being carried out and cause drugs with acknowledged utility to be eliminated from the marketplace.

Incentives and Disincentives to Pharmaceutical Development

The extent to which product liability serves as a disincentive to pharmaceutical research, development, and marketing depends on the balance of several separate but related factors.

The anticipated worldwide size of the market for a given product obviously always plays a role in the decision of a sponsor to pursue research, regardless of liability considerations. Because the process of pharmaceutical development is so long and expensive, products that will ultimately serve a limited target population will inevitably be less attractive than those for which a large body of potential users seems likely. Nevertheless, if to the ordinary costs of research are added significant risks in the courts arising out of damage claims related to the untoward effects of drugs, the balance sheet on cost and return will be to some degree unfavorably affected.

In estimating future income, one cannot ignore the strength and duration of patent exclusivity or the profit margin on sales. Effective patent life has gradually eroded because of the increasing length of the drug development process. Instead of the putative seventeen years of patent exclusivity, the average in the United States is now perhaps half this number.

Drug prices will continue to be the focus of attention in the United States as well as other countries. No nation seems willing or able to spend as much money on health care expenditures as it could spend if no limits existed. Waste in the health care delivery area has been addressed, but there is a limit to the economies that can be achieved by eliminating unnecessary diagnostic procedures, operations, or drugs, whereas the ability of science to create new drugs and medical diagnostic and thera-peutic devices is infinite. Accordingly, third-party payers (national health schemes in most countries) are increasingly demanding justification for suggested prices or indeed for remuneration at any level. The decision to reimburse for a drug's cost is ordinarily much more important than the decision by a regulatory agency to allow marketing.

As for litigation itself, the factors to be considered include the actual costs of legal advice and services, the size of damage awards, and the possibility of punitive damages above and beyond the harm inflicted on the plaintiff. Of growing importance is the question whether a defendant will be able to use a "state of the art" defense; that is, to claim that harm ensued as the result of effects that could not have been predicted or prevented.

Another, fairly new disincentive for defendants is "forum shopping," namely, a search by injured parties for jurisdictions in which to bring charges where the rules of evidence and procedure favor the plaintiff. A pharmaceutical company that markets its products internationally (as most large companies do) can in theory be sued in the home country of the plaintiff or the pharmaceutical sponsor. For U.S. companies, suits may be brought in one or more states depending on the site of the offices, research facilities, or production facilities of the company or the relevant subsidiary thereof.

The cost of liability insurance is another factor, one that is obviously related to some of the factors already mentioned. Companies often have to self-insure for much of the damage awards anticipated because of excessive premiums required by insurance carriers.

Finally, there is an extremely important point that is often unappre-ciated: the unpredictability of litigation. In trying to balance risk against benefit, pharmaceutical executives are faced, in the area of product lia-bility, with present and future risks that are almost impossible to quantify but that may be potentially large enough to include financial catastrophe for the manufacturer.

The Bendectin Story

Bendectin was the only prescription drug ever approved in the United States for the treatment of the nausea and vomiting of pregnancy. "Morning sickness" is a common event in pregnancy, and usually it does not last long and is not a serious treat to the health of mother or child. But sometimes this accompaniment of pregnancy can be severe and prolonged.

In 1956 Bendectin first appeared on the U.S. market, sold by the Wm. S. Merrell Company of Cincinnati. The same manufacturer, a few years later, was planning to introduce into this country the German sedative-hypnotic thalidomide until it was realized that thalidomide could cause drastic congenital defects when taken by women early in their pregnancies.

Bendectin enjoyed considerable marketing success. At the time of its withdrawal it was being sold in twenty-two countries and was prescribed for perhaps 25 percent of pregnant American women. Besides the accusation that Bendectin was a teratogen (as will be discussed), the only challenge to the medication occurred in 1972, as a consequence of the review, under the auspices of the National Academy of Sciences National Research Council, of the claims made for drugs approved by the Food and Drug Administration between the years 1938 and 1962. This review was requested by the FDA Commissioner, James Goddard, in order to respond to a mandate from Congress.

From the time of its introduction, Bendectin had been a three-ingredient mixture, consisting of an antispasmodic, a sedative antihistamine, and a vitamin. When the review and the clinical trials related to it failed to show that the antispasmodic component contributed to the therapeutic benefit of the combination, this ingredient was dropped, and Bendectin became a two-ingredient mixture.

The ultimate demise of Bendectin had nothing to do with its therapeutic claims, however. Rather, its doom was traceable to the flood of legal actions that followed assertions in the scientific literature that Bendectin could produce congenital defects in both animals and humans. This spate of litigation finally led in 1983 to the voluntary withdrawal of the product by the manufacturer.

The first case report appeared in Canada in 1969, with additional case reports in 1977, 1978, 1982, and 1984 from Canada, the United Kingdom, and the United States.[1] All these were based on *post hoc ergo propter hoc* arguments; that is, the mother had taken Bendectin during pregnancy and had then given birth to a deformed child. Was it not possible that Bendectin had caused the anomaly?

---

1. Paterson 1969; Paterson 1977; Donnai and Harris 1978; Menzies 1978; Frith 1978; Mellor 1978; Fisher and others 1982; Grodofsky and Wilmott 1984.

Proving a medicine to be a teratogen (an agent that causes medical defects) is never easy. Congenital anomalies occur in 1 to 7 percent of newborns (depending on the definition of an anomaly, the skill of the diagnosing health professionals, and the time of the evaluation) even in the absence of exposure to specific known teratogens. Robert Brent, in an analysis of the Bendectin allegations, pointed out that some 30 million infants had been exposed in utero to Bendectin, and that with an average "background" incident of 3 percent, chance alone could account for perhaps 900,000 malformed infants in the population.[2]

The traditional way to nail down a cause-and-effect relationship between a drug and an effect in patients is to perform a randomized clinical trial that treats half the population with a drug and half with a placebo. Such a trial of Bendectin, intended to detect a teratogenic effect, would have had to be very large, given the probability that Bendectin was not a potent teratogen and that therefore the percentage of newborns with congenital anomalies attributable to the medicine would be low. Furthermore, the trial would have deprived half its subjects of an effective treatment, an eventuality not likely to meet with favor on the part of either patient or physician. Recourse was therefore taken to an alternative mechanism—epidemiologic studies.

Epidemiologic research is not without its own problems.[3] Women may err, for example, in their recollection of what medicines they took during pregnancy. "Recall bias" is a well-known hazard in all surveys, and there is evidence that mothers of deformed babies are more apt to correctly recall drug products ingested during pregnancy than mothers of normal babies are.[4] Furthermore, if the added risk of a chemical is modest, its teratogenicity can be missed unless very large numbers of subjects are studied. At the same time, repeated "data dredging" of epidemiologic results can turn up spurious correlations as a chance phenomenon.

The epidemiologic studies of Bendectin produced disparate results. A handful of such studies supported the possibility of Bendectin's teratogenicity,[5] but a much longer list of studies failed to do so,[6] although the

2. Brent 1983.
3. Epidemiology is the study of the factors determining the frequency and distribution of disease in a population.
4. Werler and others 1989.
5. Rothman and others 1979; Golding, Vivian, and Baldwin 1983; Eskenazi and Bracken 1982.
6. Elbourne and others 1985; Gibson and others 1981; Jick and others 1981; Smithells and Sheppard 1978; Fleming, Knox, and Crombie 1981; Newman, Correy, and Dudgeon 1977; Milkovich and van der Berg 1976; MacMahon 1981; Shapiro and others 1977.

confidence limits on the risk estimates often encompassed a possible teratogenic effect.

Animal studies were likewise ambiguous. These were performed both with the individual components of Bendectin and with the combination, with several dose levels being explored. Rabbits, rats, and primates were used as experimental subjects. Again, the bulk of the evidence tended to support Bendectin's innocence,[7] but some of the findings did not.[8]

Predictably, those who had a stake in proving Bendectin a teratogen found evidence in the totality of animal and human studies to support their view; their opponents found evidence to the contrary.

The FDA found itself under pressure, at various times, from consumerists or Congress, to justify Bendectin's continued marketing. The agency, on the basis of internal review as well as advice from expert advisory committees, consistently maintained that the medicine deserved to stay on the market, but refrained (quite correctly) from giving Bendectin a complete bill of health, as evidenced in a package insert proposed by the FDA in 1980: "It is not possible to prove that any drug [is] totally free of risk, or absolutely safe, if taken during pregnancy. . . . [T]his drug has been the most carefully studied of all drugs which could be used to treat the nausea and vomiting of pregnancy. There is no evidence that any other drug is safer in treating [this condition]."[9]

So much for the science. What about the litigation? Of the suits that came to trial, the Merrell Company won the great majority, either initially or on appeal. But each new liability claim added to the manufacturer's costs, and there seemed no end in sight. Clearly, experts could always be found by plaintiffs to rebut the testimony of Merrell's witnesses. (In one well-publicized trial, the Mekdeci case, Merrell used as an expert the German physician who had been the one to convince the world's scientific community that thalidomide was a teratogen, and the plaintiff's lawyers used an Australian physician who had been the first in his native country to incriminate thalidomide.)

Eventually, Merrell decided to set a limit to its liability by removing Bendectin from the market, faced as it was with a seemingly endless parade of claims and an unfavorable ratio of profits on the medicine's sales and expenses required to fight the legal battles. In 1983, therefore, pregnant women and their physicians lost a therapeutic option (although recently

7. Gibson and others 1968; Tyl and others 1988; Hendrickx and others 1985a, 1985b.
8. McBride 1984.
9. FDA 1980, 80742.

a Canadian firm has marketed the two-ingredient product). It seems safe to predict that never again will a manufacturer petition the FDA to approve for marketing a new prescription drug for the nausea and vomiting of pregnancy.

Vaccine Development

Vaccination is a time-honored method for preventing infectious disease. Vaccines are effective, relatively cheap, and relatively easy to administer. For childhood diseases, the importance of vaccines is acknowledged by the fact that all fifty U.S. states have laws requiring preschool immunization.

The achievements of vaccination are remarkable. There have been no confirmed cases of smallpox since October 1977; in May 1980 the World Health Organization announced the global eradication of smallpox. (No other medical practice has totally eradicated a disease from our planet.) Paralytic poliomyelitis, which afflicted more than 20,000 U.S. inhabitants in 1952, is today almost unheard of in this country. Americans now have fewer polio cases in a decade than they used to experience during a single day in the early 1950s.

Reported cases in the United States of measles, rubella, and mumps have dropped from many thousands a year (almost 900,000 measles cases, for example, in 1941) to 1,000–3,000 in the 1980s. Diphtheria and tetanus have almost disappeared except for a few cases among the unimmunized or the inadequately immunized. Pertussis deaths in the United States used to number 9,000 to 12,000 annually; in recent years the numbers have been 5 to 20. In addition to all these advances, Americans also have effective vaccines against influenza, pneumococcal infection, hepatitis, and meningococcal disease.

Given all these wondrous achievements, why have most U.S. pharmaceutical firms dropped out of the vaccine business? The reasons are many, but litigation is certainly an important part of the explanation.

Before discussing the role of product liability, I will list the disincentives of another sort. Vaccine sales rarely provide a high return on research and capital investment for the following reasons:

—vaccines require demanding and complex production and quality control processes, with specialized production facilities that can only be used part time;

—the lengthy vaccine production "pipeline" (six to twelve months) leads to inventory and cash flow problems;

—unlike the situation with drugs (especially those targeted for chronic illness), target populations for vaccines do not ordinarily require repeated vaccination during their lifetimes. And if a disease begins to be eradicated, the market for a vaccine can disappear;

—except for pediatric immunizations (helped no little by state laws that mandate them as a prerequisite to school admission), the medical profession is usually not prevention oriented;

—patent protection is less effective for vaccines than for pharmaceuticals;

—foreign markets for U.S. vaccines are unpredictable and subject to discriminatory competition because of foreign subsidies to native companies and less stringent marketing requirements abroad; and

—third world nations, which desperately need both old and new vaccines, can often neither afford to purchase them nor provide the health professional infrastructure for dispensing them.

Given all these disincentives, what additional discouragement is provided by product liability?

One problem is that vaccine manufacturers have been deemed liable, in certain jurisdictions, not only if they produce a defective product—that is, fail to manufacture the vaccine in accordance with approved specifications—or fail to warn the medical profession of the possibility of vaccine-related reactions, but also if they fail to warn vaccine recipients (or their guardians) of such reactions.[10] Some have pointed out that this, in essence, changes the role of the manufacturer from the traditional one of providing needed information to physicians (the "learned intermediaries") to one in which the manufacturer is playing a key role in the actual conduct of public immunization programs.

An extra twist has been added in recent years with the advent of so-called acellular pertussis vaccines. These vaccines are allegedly safer than the older ones (although possibly less effective), and it is now proposed that a vaccine should be considered "defective" if a safer one is available.

While some would argue that the magnitude of vaccine-related litigation has been exaggerated, the damages sought are large relative to the small markets and profits available. The suits pending a few years ago for damages allegedly related to diphtheria-tetanus-pertussis (DTP) vac-

10. *Reyes* v. *Wyeth Laboratories*, 498 F. 2d 1264, *cert. denied*, 419 U.S. 1096.

cine, for example, involved claims that totaled an amount many times the gross annual sales of DTP vaccine.[11]

The reluctance of industry to participate wholeheartedly in vaccine production was well shown by the swine flu experience of a few years ago. The federal government, convinced that a major epidemic of swine flu would strike the country, initiated a national vaccination program. Manufacturers of the flu vaccine agreed to produce the material, but on the proviso that they would be granted immunity from liability in the event of flu-related damage claims unrelated to faulty production. Thousands of claims were filed, with settlements (as of 1984) of close to $40 million and judgments for plaintiffs totaling an additional $33 million.

Vaccine-related liability is complicated by other considerations. As with most drug product liability, insurance premiums are so prohibitively high that companies are forced to self-insure up to a very high amount of damages. Nonmeritorious suits are not uncommon, and require the defendants to spend time and money in dealing with them. Vaccine experts are not numerous and may be difficult to enlist in litigation proceedings in view of the multiplicity of suits and the considerable inconvenience and commitment of time involved. Furthermore, government experts (from the Centers for Disease Control or the FDA, for instance) are not available, since government policy usually prohibits such personnel from offering opinions on disputes between private parties. This difficulty is particularly important when claimants contest governmental requirements or governmental immunization policy.

One of the consequences of pharmaceutical concerns about product liability has been the occurrence of either general nationwide or extreme spot shortages of DTP vaccine, the vaccine that has been the cause of the most medical and legal attention.[12]

In 1984 Wyeth Laboratories stopped selling DTP vaccine to the public. Later in the same year, Connaught Laboratories announced it would stop selling this vaccine after it fulfilled existing contracts. The one remaining manufacturer, Lederle Laboratories, had experienced production difficulties.

On December 13, 1984, the Centers for Disease Control recommended that all doctors stop vaccinating children over one year of age, to save supplies for more vulnerable infants. The CDC officials apparently were

11. Medicine in the Public Interest 1974.
12. Meister 1985.

unaware that Wyeth was still making pertussis vaccine, but selling it only to Lederle, so that the shortage proved to be less serious than anticipated. In time, the shortage was overcome, but the event indicated what possibilities exist for future shortages as producers go out of the vaccine business. "Monomanufacturers" exist now for measles, mumps, rubella, and oral polio, whereas there used to be three to six firms manufacturing these vaccines. When only one producer exists, so does the possibility of a public health crisis, as the result of a strike, fire, accident, or the production of a faulty batch of vaccine.

Another consequence of vaccine litigation has been an increase in the price of certain vaccines. In 1988 the *Journal of the American Medical Association* reported that the price of the DTP vaccine had increased by 25 percent and the cost of the measles-mumps-rubella (MMR) vaccine had increased by 30 percent.[13] Part of the rise was explained by the tax levied on childhood vaccines by the National Childhood Vaccine Injury Act. The DTP vaccine carries a tax of $4.56 per dose (about 40 percent of the per dose price increase); MMR, $4.44 per dose; diphtheria-tetanus, 6 cents per dose; and polio, 29 cents per dose. These amounts were allegedly based on estimates of the risk of a given vaccine.

An analysis of price increases indicated that in some instances the entire tax was passed on to consumer, whereas in other instances only part of the tax was so passed on, or the manufacturer actually absorbed the increased cost due to the tax.

In 1988 a letter was written to the editor of the *New England Journal of Medicine* pointing out another consequence of vaccine litigation fears.[14] The author referred to Japanese encephalitis, a mosquito-borne viral infection that occurs in Asia in both epidemic and endemic forms. A vaccine exists to prevent this disease, but the manufacturer is Japanese and the vaccine is available only through the Centers for Disease Control, which distributed it to physicians who register as collaborative investigators under an IND filed by the Japanese firm Biken.[15] On June 30, 1987, however, the CDC announced that the vaccine was no longer available because Biken did not have appropriate liability insurance and there was no statutory mechanism to absolve the firm of liability.

It is paradoxical that the vaccine which has caused the most controversy in the media and the courts has recently been deemed, on the basis of an

13. Marwick 1988.
14. Marcus 1988.
15. IND stands for investigational new drug application, sometimes called a notice of claimed investigational exemption for a new drug.

epidemiologic study of 38,171 Tennessee medicaid children, to provide no significant risk of harm. The authors concluded that "serious neurological events are rarely, if ever, caused by DTP immunization."[16] An accompanying editorial was entitled "Pertussis Vaccine Encephalopathy: It Is Time to Recognize It as the Myth That It Is."[17]

In the United Kingdom, the High Court in 1988 vindicated pertussis vaccine completely and suggested that the vaccine probably *protects* against encephalopathy.[18] The Canadian immunization guide has been changed, as of its 1989 edition, to read:

> Although there may be an increased risk of acute, severe neurologic illness (including encephalopathy) occurring within 72 hours of the administration of pertussis vaccine to previously healthy infants, the majority of such illnesses observed in the National Childhood Encephalopathy Study (NCES) in the United Kingdom were prolonged and/or complex convulsions. All such children were normal on follow-up 12–18 months later. Reanalysis of the NCES data has failed to confirm that there was an increased risk of permanent brain damage following acute neurologic illness occurring within seven days of pertussis vaccination.[19]

Although work is now going on in a number of biotech companies and academic laboratories on an AIDS vaccine, product liability issues are sure to arise with regard to both the testing of such vaccines and their marketing. Producing a vaccine that protects against HIV infection without risking the production of the disease one is trying to prevent is a major challenge per se, but to this worry will be added the specter of litigation instigated by vaccine recipients (many of whom presumably having had increased exposure to AIDS) who after vaccination claim that the vaccine not only failed to protect but actually caused the disease.

Thalidomide Revisited

Thalidomide has achieved the dubious distinction of being the most maligned drug in the history of pharmaceutical medicine. Introduced in 1957

16. Griffin and others 1990, 1645.
17. Cherry 1990.
18. Bowie 1990.
19. National Advisory Committee on Immunization 1989, cited in Bowie 1990, 399.

as a sedative-hypnotic that had the advantage of a huge safety margin in the event of purposeful or accidental overdosage, it quickly became the most popular sleeping pill in West Germany. It was eventually sold in forty-six countries by fourteen pharmaceutical firms under fifteen different trade names.[20]

The first sign of trouble came from case reports of peripheral neuritis. But in 1961 physicians in Australia and Germany described the association of thalidomide with cases of phocomelia ("seal limbs") and other congenital anomalies. By the end of 1961 the drug had been withdrawn from almost all world markets, and "the thalidomide tragedy" led to the passage in 1962 of the Kefauver-Harris amendments to the U.S. federal Food, Drug, and Cosmetic Act.

Although considerable litigation occurred afterward, the death of the drug was unrelated to product liability issues. Where liability considerations have become exceedingly important, however, is in the potential remarketing of thalidomide today in the light of the fascinating medical uses discovered for the drug in the years since 1961.

In 1965, for example, an Israeli dermatologist stumbled on the fact that thalidomide produced a rapid and dramatic reduction in the signs and symptoms of a phase of leprosy called erythema nodosum leprosum. Trials conducted since have established this use beyond doubt, and the drug is now routinely used in such patients.

Thalidomide has also been reported to be effective in many other medical conditions, including actinic prurigo, discoid lupus erythematosus, Behcet's syndrome, orogenital ulceration, rheumatoid arthritis, prurigo nodularis, pyodermia gangrenosum, Weber-Christian disease, recurrent aphthous stomatitis, erythema multiforme, and acute graft-versus-host disease. While the data on efficacy are not equally convincing for all these disorders, it is generally acknowledged that thalidomide has unique antiinflammatory and immunosuppressant properties that make it valuable in managing lepromatous leprosy, a range of diseases characterized by inflammatory dermatosis, and several rare immunological syndromes. Many of these conditions are debilitating, painful, and recurrent.

In 1985 Chemie Grünenthal, the original West German manufacturer of thalidomide, halted all production and distribution of the drug because of fears of liability. In the past few years supplies have been obtained with difficulty from Champion Pharmaceuticals in Brazil, a company

20. Kaitin 1988.

whose products are not FDA-approved and therefore needed to be checked for quality, a process that took about two months for each batch. A small American firm is interested in manufacturing the drug, but uncertainty about supplies has resulted in the Hansen's Disease Center in Louisiana making its own drug and supplying it to eleven other clinics the center runs. That the drug will ever be marketed is exceedingly problematic, even though it has recently been claimed that a stereoisomer of thalidomide is devoid of teratogenic effect in experimental animals. In view of the Bendectin story and the unsavory reputation of thalidomide as a teratogen, will any company be brave enough to weather both the liability issues and the opprobrium that would result were the drug (even as a "safe" isomer) to be remarketed?

Product Liability and "Orphan Drug" Development

In some respects the Orphan Drug Act of 1983 would appear to have been a large success in finding adoptive parent sponsors of medicines that are useful for patients who have relatively rare diseases (defined as fewer than 200,000 U.S. patients with the ailment). The incentives have been adequate enough to achieve FDA approval of 45 drugs, and 133 additional drugs are currently in clinical trials or awaiting approval from the FDA.

If, however, one reads the February 1989 *Report of the National Commissions on Orphan Diseases,* the picture seems less bright. The commission concluded that concern about liability has led to serious delays in product development and to increased liability insurance costs. "For example, the liability insurer for one approved orphan drug cancelled coverage of it; manufacturers of a number of products have indicated their reluctance to release those products without insurance coverage or explicit agreements by others to indemnify them in the event of liability."[21]

The commission recommended that "Congress and state legislatures should promptly resolve product and professional liability issues" and that "Congress should consider special relief in instances where concerns about liability pose insurmountable obstacles to progress on rare diseases."[22]

At commission hearings, there was testimony about the need for a

21. Public Health Service 1989, 103.
22. Public Health Service 1989, 104.

vaccine to prevent infant botulism, but manufacturers are said to be unwilling to make such a vaccine because of liability risks.

National and International Approaches to Product Liability

Whereas the United States has up until now relied primarily on tort law to deal with compensation for drug-related damages, other countries have been experimenting with other mechanisms. Sweden, for example, has had a pharmaceutical insurance scheme in place since 1978; a parallel scheme has existed in Finland since 1984. New Zealand and Japan also have mechanisms that are in principle "no-fault."[23] In 1985 the European Community (EC) issued a Directive dealing with product liability, which is to be implemented by all its member states during the next few years; the Directive also has implications for nonmember states. Vaccine injuries have been dealt with separately in different countries and are the subject of a special statute in the United States. This section summarizes these approaches and is intended to show the degree to which the various countries are attempting to create better systems for compensating the victims of drug injuries.

Scandinavian Approaches

The Swedish and Finnish schemes are the result of voluntary agreements between the pharmaceutical industry and a consortium of insurance companies. They do not stand alone; instead they complement older patient insurance plans for injuries arising in the course of medical treatment. Both drug injury schemes are funded entirely through levies on manufacturers and are administered by insurance pools.

These plans are intended to indemnify personal damages related to the medical use of a drug. Only about 40 percent of claims are accepted and compensated. Proof of negligence is not required. Most claims are prepared and filed with the help of the prescribing physician. While unexpected drug reactions will usually be compensated, indemnification requires that the injured person have sustained an inability to work or a bodily injury, or death. However, if the costs incurred and the loss of income exceed a certain amount (after deducting compensatory income from other

23. For Sweden, Brahams 1988a; for Finland, New Zealand, and Japan, Brahams 1988b. See also Shulman and Lasagna 1990.

services), indemnity is always paid. Indemnification is not paid if the injury is one that could reasonably be expected as a result of proper use of the drug.

In determining whether indemnification should occur, consideration is given to the nature and severity of the disease being treated, the general health status of the injured party, the severity of the injury, and the predictability of the ill effects. The more serious the medical condition, the greater is the degree of risk that the patient is expected to bear without compensation. No compensation is awarded for lack of therapeutic effect or emotional distress secondary to an injury or if the patient willfully misuses a drug or illegally obtains it. But a state-of-the-art defense may not be used to deny compensation.

In both countries benefits are paid in amounts consistent with what would be paid if the injury had been caused by nondrug experiences, such as traffic accidents, and the amounts are purposely left at a reasonable level, in the Nordic tradition of compensating a victim rather than making him wealthy. There are ceilings on what can be paid for pain and suffering and loss of amenities and on the maximum total benefit that can be paid to one person. Lump-sum payments are rare; most benefits are paid on a monthly annuity basis. These benefits may seem low compared with U.K. or U.S. settlements, but it must be remembered that the drug injury schemes are only one part of the national support system; employer's compensation and national health insurance are available to pay for lost wages, medical treatment, and nursing care.

While a claimant may opt out of the scheme and pursue a remedy through the courts, once he or she accepts indemnification, remedies at tort law cannot be invoked. Decisions can be appealed, and arbitration procedures are available. The injured party bears some of the costs associated with arbitration if the procedure is unreasonably invoked.

Sweden and Finland have thus organized schemes that use levies related to pharmaceutical sales and that, while sometimes described as "no-fault" and "strict product liability," are in fact neither. The schemes do not appear unduly onerous and in general seem to be acceptable to industry, the medical profession, and the public.

The New Zealand Scheme

Since 1974 New Zealand has had a comprehensive compensation scheme in force for all accidents. This date saw the implementation of a 1972 statute intended to correct some of the inadequacies of, and dissatisfaction with, older statutes. "Personal injury by accident" means any form of damage to the human system that is unexpected and not designed by the injured person. Claims for damages arising from such injuries cannot be filed in any New Zealand court, except for exemplary damages.

Adverse drug reactions fall into a subcategory called "medical misadventure." No indemnity is permitted for the known side effects of a drug, since the patient is assumed to have accepted the possibility of the side effect when consenting to the prescribed course of treatment. No compensation is available for lack of therapeutic effect or for misadventure arising from misuse of a drug. Injury may be compensable when the prescribing physician has not completely disclosed the risk, but that point has not yet been settled.

Injuries arising out of clinical research are compensated through insurance carried by individual pharmaceutical companies. Most New Zealand companies assume that coverage for unforseen side effects of a drug seen during chemical trials will be provided by the national accident compensation scheme but that claims of negligence will not fall within this scheme.

The medical profession (physician or hospital) advises patients about lodging claims. Denial of a claim can be appealed.

The scheme is funded by compulsory levies on employers, the self-employed, and motor vehicle owners, and by general taxation funds. Benefits are available to cover lost wages, medical and dental expenses, rehabilitation, and non-work-related pecuniary losses; lump-sum payments are made to dependents and to injured persons for permanent disability and noneconomic damages. Payments are low by U.S. standards, but the scheme is generally well regarded and accepted by New Zealanders, though there have been criticisms about its cost, the escalating levels of compensation, especially for minor injuries, and apparent inequities between victims of disease and victims of accident.

Japanese Approaches

In 1979 the Adverse Drug Reaction Injury Relief and Research Promoting Fund Act was passed, to establish a fund to provide prompt compensation for personal injury or death caused by pharmaceuticals in instances where civil liability could not be proved for lack of an identifiable responsible party. A victim can bring a suit in addition to claiming compensation under the act, but if the suit is successful, any monies paid under the act must be returned. Injury is not compensable when a drug has not been taken for an intended use or there has been improper administration. Injury caused by anticancer agents, immunosuppressant drugs, blood products, or compulsory vaccination is excluded, as is injury from drugs taken before May 1, 1980.

Benefits available include actual cost of medical treatment plus medical expenses up to a monthly maximum, pension for disability, pension for raising an injured child, funeral costs, and pension or lump-sum aware for a survivor.

Funds for the program come from government subsidies and by annual contributions (calculated on gross drug sales by a complex formula) from all manufacturers who make or import drugs. In the eight years since it began, the scheme has approved about two-thirds of all claims. Decisions are made by the Central Pharmaceutical Affairs Council, and no appeals are permitted.

British Proposals

In Great Britain no-fault compensation proposals for drug-related injuries have been discussed, but thus far neither the pharmaceutical industry nor their insurers have expressed support for the concept. The British Medical Association favors a no-fault scheme, running along with access to the courts, that would exclude unexpected side effects from drugs. Any such injuries would be covered by a separate scheme funded by the drug industry.

Activity in the European Community

The EC, on July 25, 1985, issued a Directive concerning liability for defective products. According to the Treaty of Rome, which created the Community in 1957, such a directive, once adopted by the council of ministers, is binding. Member states must implement the directive's provisions within a certain period by passing national legislation.

One key provision of this EC Directive is strict liability for damage caused by a defective product, provided cause-and-effect and defectiveness can be shown. Defectiveness is not, however, defined. It is expected that the adequacy of warning labels will be an important factor. Failure to provide an adequate warning of the risks associated with a drug may constitute a defect and lay the basis for a suit.

"Damage" is restricted to personal injury or death. Lost profit, pain and suffering, and loss of use or enjoyment are not included in the definition of "damage," but individual member states can deem compensation for pain and suffering and other nonmaterial damages to be appropriate. The Directive imposes no ceilings, but individual states can set caps on the potential liability of a manufacturer. A state-of-the-art defense can be allowed or not according to the wishes of a given member state. In view of the intended elimination of barriers between EC states, it is conceivable that claimants may seek redress in jurisdictions with rules most favorable to their claim.

The United Kingdom's response to the EC Directive is contained in the Consumer Protection Act of 1987. Since the adoption of this legislation, someone harmed by a faulty product can bring an action in both negligence (which was already an option) and strict product liability. It is not clear whether unlicensed drugs used in clinical trials are covered by the act. The statute requires that, in assessing the degree of safety provided by a drug, importance be placed on warnings or instructions attached to products in future product liability litigation.

A state-of-the-art defense is both clearly set forth as permissible and defined more broadly than elsewhere. A defense can be based not just on the general state of scientific knowledge at the relevant time but also on the way in which a fellow manufacturer may view that knowledge; to wit, it will be a defense for the producer to show "that the state of scientific and technical knowledge . . . was not such that a producer of products of the same description as the product in question might be expected to have discovered the defect if it had existed in his products while they were under his control."[24]

Germany adopted a statute in 1989 to implement the EC Directive, with the new strict liability for products to apply in tandem with the preexisting law of negligence. The statute, which went into effect on January 1, 1990, imposes a cap for aggregate liability. If losses exceed the cap, the plaintiff can seek the balance under a negligence suit. The same applies to pain and suffering. The statute also allows a state-of-the-art defense.

Licensed drugs are specifically excluded from the statute's provisions, presumably because Germany has had specific strict liability legislation for drug-related injuries since 1976. As the 1976 statute does not permit a state-of-the-art defense, it is not clear whether the new statute will ultimately change that in any way.

Although Sweden is not a member of the European Community, the

24. Brahams 1990, 28.

EC Directive has prodded the Swedes into drafting new product liability legislation that moves toward strict liability on all consumer cases. Whether litigation in Sweden will increase in the future is unknown; Swedish compensation procedures have usually involved measures other than tort law, and the level of compensation for injury tends to be standardized. Hence litigants in Sweden have little hope of achieving large sums by litigation. Very few cases end up in court in Sweden; it may not be irrelevant that the losing party must pay the legal costs for both sides. Whether Swedish manufacturers will face growing litigation problems outside of Sweden, only time will tell.

Finland has as yet no specific law governing product liability, and recourse to litigation is infrequent. Since half Finland's foreign trade is with the Community, the country cannot ignore the EC Directive. Accordingly, a draft law has been proposed incorporating most of the provisions of the Directive. But it does not incorporate the state-of-the-art defense and does not provide for caps.

Austria adopted legislation in July 1988 consistent with the EC Directive, including both state-of-the-art defense and compensation for non-material damages. No caps are imposed. Norway passed legislation in January 1989 consistent with the Directive's provisions. It includes state-of-the-art defense in general, but such defense is specifically excluded for pharmaceutical producers. There is no liability, however, for "unforeseeable misuse," lack of therapeutic effect, or in cases where the risk of the adverse effect was a reasonable one to take.

Denmark, Germany, France, Japan, Switzerland, and the United Kingdom all have compensation programs to deal with vaccine injury. Typically, the vaccines covered are those mandated or optionally recommended by public health law or government authorities. Compensable injuries vary widely from country to country, ranging from any and all damage directly attributable to vaccination to severe disability or death. The amount of compensation is unspecified in some of these statutes but capped or set at some accepted level in others. In general, civil remedies are not excluded. Public funds are normally used to supply compensation.

The American Vaccine Injury Compensation Program

The U.S. National Vaccine Injury Compensation Program went into effect on October 1, 1988, having been enacted into law in 1986 as part of the National Childhood Vaccine Injury Act.

The program creates a "no-fault" compensation scheme for adverse reactions to pediatric vaccines. Compensation is available for any person who has suffered death or a serious injury lasting six months or more. Claimants must exhaust administrative remedies available through the program before commencing a civil action against a manufacturer. The intent of the program is to provide reliable compensation for damaged individuals without the need for (and delays inherent in) tort litigation and to reduce the burden and expense of litigation on vaccine manufacturers and thus encourage vaccine research and production.

The program is administered by the U.S. Claims Court, which receives petitions from persons claiming that they or their children have suffered a compensable injury. Eligibility is determined, as is the amount of the award. A vaccine injury table has been constructed to list the types of adverse reactions that are presumed to be caused by a specific vaccine, provided the first symptoms manifest themselves within a specified time. Escape clauses exist for both claimants and government to allow for exceptions to a strict reading of the table.

The benefits permitted include actual unreimbursed medical and rehabilitation expenses, actual and anticipated loss of earnings, compensation for pain and suffering, and $250,000 in case of death. The benefits are paid out of a trust fund that contains monies of two sorts: congressional appropriations for retrospective cases, and surtaxes on vaccine sales by manufacturers.

Rejection of claims can be appealed, or the claimant may proceed directly to a civil action in tort against the entity believed liable for the injury.

This act preempts state law and prohibits civil action against a manufacturer for failure to directly warn the recipient of risks associated with the vaccine. It also exempts manufacturers from liability for injury that was unavoidable even though the vaccine was properly prepared and administered.

Conclusions

Taking these various national approaches as a whole, it seems evident that drug-related injuries are not being ignored at the political and legal levels, but that important transnational differences exist. Whether, under the pressure of EC actions, more uniformity will be achieved not only in Europe but elsewhere, only time will tell. Nor is it clear as yet whether the disincentives provided by excessive liability risks will be adequately investigated.

Possible Future Developments

Society is ill served at present in the United States by our tort law approach to product liability. Compensation for drug-related injuries is currently capricious, inefficient, and slow. It is at times excessive and at other times inappropriately low. Furthermore, the magnitude and uncertainties involved in product liability litigation serve to discourage certain kinds of pharmaceutical research, development, and marketing. What could be done to improve the situation?

1. Our society needs to decide who shall bear the burden of product-related damage. This is a broad issue that goes far beyond pharmaceuticals. How do we wish to handle product-related injury from automobiles, ladders, children's clothing, airplane crashes, and lead paint? Do we distinguish between negligence and unavoidable harm? Do we distinguish between proper and improper drug prescribing? Do we distinguish harm that results from mandatory vaccination and harm from voluntary immunization?

2. Injury achieved by one route should be compensated to the same degree as injury by another route if fault is not involved. Why should an eye lost in the workplace be compensated at one level and an eye lost in the course of exemplary medical care be compensated at another?

3. The Swedish-type compensation scheme described earlier seems to work reasonably well; why can't the United States adopt a similar plan? When damages for injury in the workplace began to show signs of being inequitably and inefficiently awarded, our society moved to workmen's compensation schemes, where compensation is prompt but not of the magnitude occasionally seen in tort law damages.

4. Unpredictably large awards for product-related injury are a bonanza for some claimants and their lawyers but have a chilling effect on pharmaceutical innovation and manufacturer. Caps should help prevent abuse in this situation.

5. "Forum shopping" for court action will add a further destabilizing force to the product liability scene. Limiting this flexibility should help correct some of the current uncertainty and apprehension on the part of pharmaceutical manufacturers.

6. Unreasonable awards for damages will inevitably raise the cost of

drugs to some extent. The public and politicians need to appreciate this fact. In recent litigation involving a heart valve device, the issue was raised whether a patient with such a device in place could sue for damages on the basis of the anxiety generated by knowledge that there could be serious malfunction of the device but in the absence of actual physical harm. Granting such awards will further perturb the development process.

7. Tort reform at the state or federal level can be encouraged so as to reduce or eliminate litigation excesses, including punitive damages. Laws in seven states have, in a variety of ways, set an outer limit on punitive damage awards. In five other states, full compliance with FDA product approval regulations can be used as a defense against punitive damages. Another technique is to permit the division of trials involving punitive damages into two or more phases. In the first place the jury determines only whether the defendant is liable for the plaintiff's injury and the amount of compensatory damages. If so, in a later phase the jury determines liability for the amount of punitive damages.[25] National legislation is also possible along similar lines.

8. The courts need assistance in dealing with the difficult problem of evaluating epidemiologic evidence. One suggestion has been to create a panel of experts that would examine the evidence submitted by both parties in a systematized critique format, rather than asking a lay jury to resolve controversy.[26] Another suggestion is to adopt a more discrete evidentiary standard that would reflect more accurately the realities of causation. A standard based on proportional liability rather than on the preponderance of the evidence rule would avoid the "all-or-nothing" results associated with the current system.

25. Shulman and Lasagna 1990.
26. Lasagna and Shulman 1990.

References

Bowie, C. 1990. "Lessons from the Pertussis Vaccine Court Trial." *Lancet* 335:397–99.

Brahams, D. 1988a. "The Swedish Medical Insurance Schemes: The Way Ahead for the United Kingdom?" *Lancet* 1:43–47.

———. 1988b. "No Fault Compensation Finnish Style." *Lancet* 2:733–36.

Brahams, M. 1990. "Implementation of the EEC Product Liability Directive in the United Kingdom—The Consumer Protection Act, 1987." In Shulman and Lasagna 1990.

Brent, R. L. 1983. "The Bendectin Saga: Another American Tragedy." *Teratology* 27:283–86.

Cherry, J. D. 1990. "Pertussis Vaccine Encephalopathy: It Is Time to Recognize It as the Myth That It Is." *Journal of the American Medical Association* 263:1679–80.

Donnai, D., and R. Harris. 1978. "Unusual Fetal Malformations after Antiemetics in Early Pregnancy." *British Medical Journal* 1:691–92.

Elbourne, D., and others. 1985. "Debendox Revisted." *British Journal of Obstetrics and Gynaecology* 92:780–86.

Eskenazi, B., and M. B. Bracken. 1982. "Bendectin (Debendox) as a Risk Factor for Pyloric Stenosis." *American Journal of Obstetrics and Gynecology* 144:919–24.

Fisher, J. E., and others. 1982. "Congenital Cystic Adenomatoid Malformation of the Lung: A Unique Variant." *American Journal of Diseases of Childhood* 136:1071–74.

Fleming, D. M., J. D. E. Knox, and D. L. Crombie. 1981. "Debendox in Early Pregnancy and Fetal Malformation." *British Medical Journal* 283:99–101.

Food and Drug Administration. 1980. "Draft Guideline Patient Package Insert; Bendectin and Other Combination Drugs Containing Doxylamine and Vitamin B_6." *Federal Register* 45(236); 80740–43, 12/05/80.

Frith, K. 1978. "Fetal Malformation after Debendox Treatment in Early Pregnancy." *British Medical Journal* 1:925.

Gibson, G. T., and others. 1981. "Congenital Anomalies in Relation to the Use of Doxylamine/Dicyclomine and Other Antenatal Factors: An Ongoing Prospective Study." *Medical Journal of Australia* 1:410–14.

Gibson, J. P., and others. 1968. "Teratology and Reproduction Studies with an Antinauseant." *Toxicology and Applied Pharmacology* 13:439–47.

Golding J., S. Vivian, and J. A. Baldwin. 1983. "Maternal Antinauseants and Clefts of Lip and Palate." *Human Toxicology* 2:63–73.

Griffin, M. R., and others. 1990. "Risk of Seizures and Encephalopathy after Immunization with the Diphtheria-Tetanus-Pertussis Vaccine." *Journal of the American Medical Association* 263:1641–45.

Grodofsky, M. P., and R. W. Wilmott. 1984. "Possible Association of Use of Bendectin during Early Pregnancy and Congenital Lung Hypoplasia." *New England Journal of Medicine* 311:732.

Hendrickx, A. G., and others. 1985a. "Evaluation of Bendectin Embryotoxicity in Nonhuman Primates: I. Ventricular Septal Defects in Prenatal Macaques and Baboon." *Teratology* 32:179–89.

———. 1985b. "Evaluation of Bendectin Embryotoxicity in Nonhuman Primates: II. Double-blind Study in Term Cynomolgus Monkeys." *Teratology* 32:191–94.

Jick, H., and others. 1981. "First-Trimester Drug Use and Congenital Disorders." *Journal of the American Medical Association* 246:343–46.

Kaitin, K. I. 1988 "Thalidomide Revisited: New Clinical Uses for an Old Drug." *Pharmaceutical Medicine* 3:203–10.

Lasagna, L., and S. R. Shulman. 1990. "Bendectin and the Language of Causation." Tufts University Center for the Study of Drug Development, Boston.

McBride, W. G. 1984. "Teratogenic Effect of Doxylamine Succinate in New Zealand White Rabbits." *IRCS Medical Science* 23:536–37.

MacMahon, B. 1981. "More on Bendectin." *Journal of the American Medical Association* 246:371–72.

Marcus, L. C. 1988. "Liability for Vaccine-Related Injuries." *New England Journal of Medicine* 318:191.

Marwick, C. 1988. "Pediatric Vaccine Tax Seeks to Cover Injury; Not all Manufacturers Passing on Increase." *Journal of the American Medical Association* 259:1292.

Medicine in the Public Interest. 1984. "Impediments to Vaccine Research." A Report Based on a Conference, Washington, Jan. 9–10.

Meister, K. A. 1985. "Why Isn't the U.S. Immune to Vaccine Shortages?" *ACSH News and Views*, May–June.

Mellor, S. 1978. "Fetal Malformation after Debendox Treatment in Early Pregnancy." *British Medical Journal* 1:1055.

Menzies, C. J. G. 1978. "Fetal Malformation after Debendox Treatment in Early Pregnancy." *British Medical Journal* 1:925.

Milkovich, L., and B. J. van dan Berg. 1976. "Evaluation of the Teratogenicity of Certain Antinauseant Drugs." *American Journal of Obstetrics and Gynecology* 125:244–48.

National Advisory Committee on Immunization. 1989. *Canadian Immunization Guide*. 3d ed. Canada: Minister of Supply and Services.

Newman, N. M., J. F. Correy, and G. I. Dudgeon. 1977. "A Survey of Congenital Abnormalities and Drugs in a Private Practice." *Australian and New Zealand Journal of Obstetrics and Gynaecology* 17:156–59.

Paterson, D. C. 1969. "Congenital Deformities." *Canadian Medical Association Journal* 101:175–76.

———. 1977. "Congenital Deformities Associated with Bendectin." *Canadian Medical Association Journal* 116:1348.

Public Health Service. 1989. *Report of the National Commission on Orphan Diseases*. U.S. Department of Health and Human Services.

Rothman, K. J., and others. 1979. "Exogenous Hormones and Other Drug Exposures of Children with Congenital Heart Disease." *American Journal of Epidemiology* 109:433–39.

Shapiro, S., and others. 1977. "Antenatal Exposure to Doxylamine Succinate and Dicyclomine Hydrochloride (Bendectin) in Relation to Congenital Malformations, Perinatal Mortality Rate, Birth Weight, and Intelligence Quotient Score." *American Journal of Obstetrics and Gynecology* 128:480–85.

Shulman, S. R., and L. Lasagna, eds. 1990. *Trends in Product Liability Law and*

No-Fault Compensation for Drug-Induced Injuries. Boston: Tufts University Center for the Study of Drug Development.

Smithells, R. W., and S. Sheppard. 1978. "Teratogenicity Testing in Humans: A Method Demonstrating Safety of of Bendectin." *Teratology* 17:31–35.

Tyl, R. W., and others. 1988. "Developmental Toxicity Evaluation of Bendectin in CD Rats." *Teratology* 37:539:52.

Werler, M. M., and others. 1989. "Reporting Accuracy among Mothers of Malformed and Nonmalformed Infants." *American Journal of Epidemiology* 129: 415–21.

Product Liability in Pharmaceuticals: Comments on Chapters Eight and Nine

Henry Grabowski

DESPITE the extensive regulatory controls on pharmaceuticals, it is one of the industries most adversely affected by the product liability system. The evidence is mounting that this situation is growing worse in the United States. Our experience appears to be in sharp contrast to that of most other developed countries.

In chapter 3 Viscusi and Moore show that losses notably exceeded premiums for U.S. insurers of pharmaceuticals during the first half of the 1980s. And apparently insurance is becoming less available to pharmaceutical firms. An earlier study by the Rand Corporation found that pharmaceuticals was a leading industry in federal liability suits, with a strong upward trend in the number of case filings in the 1980s.[1]

There is also evidence that the willingness of pharmaceutical firms to undertake research and development for new products has been adversely affected by product liability concerns in some important therapeutic categories. Vaccines have been shown to be among the most socially beneficial therapies emerging from pharmaceutical R&D. However, the number of U.S. firms undertaking vaccine R&D has declined dramatically. The expected cost from product liability actions is a prime reason for this shift from vaccine R&D.[2] Research on contraceptives has experienced a comparable fate in this country.[3]

---

1. Dungworth 1988. While the distribution of filings tends to be concentrated in certain products, the effect on industry incentives and decisionmaking can be much more general. For lawsuits can occur well into a product's market life, can be triggered by unforeseen circumstances, and can involve damages beyond any reasonable expectation in terms of the product benefit-risk profile.
2. Institute of Medicine 1985, 117–20.
3. See Office of Technology Assessment 1982.

As mentioned, these adverse trends have occurred despite an extensive regulatory umbrella designed to offer strong consumer protection from excessive risk from pharmaceuticals. In particular, all new drug products must receive approval from the Food and Drug Administration before they can be introduced into the marketplace; the clinical research process is subject to direct FDA monitoring; product labeling must be approved by the FDA as part of the new drug application before marketing; and pharmaceutical products can be obtained only by patients through a physician's prescription.

The United States therefore now has two powerful societal institutions, the tort liability system and regulation, whose effects overlap. Yet little attention has been given to their combined influence on the incentives for risk reduction, innovation, or other objectives. This would hardly seem to be a desirable state of affairs. One would think that the extensive premarket regulation would provide a strong presumption against firm liability in pharmaceuticals and thereby reduce the number of product liability suits relative to those in other industries. However, in her chapter Judith Swazey describes the current situation as one in which FDA regulation serves as a floor rather than a ceiling for tort liability actions. The system basically works in an asymmetrical way. As she notes, regulatory compliance is not a strong shield for defendants to use as a defense against tort liability. But noncompliance is a strong sword for the plaintiffs.

Louis Lasagna's survey indicates that most other countries have proceeded very differently from the United States.[4] They have relied more on social insurance schemes to compensate accident victims and on regulation to provide appropriate incentives for risk reduction. Compared with the United States, they have greatly restricted the scope of their product liability system for pharmaceuticals.

In these comments I compare the tort liability system with regulation in various areas, focusing on the role of each of these social institutions in generating desirable incentives for risk reduction. I conclude by considering the appropriate mix of these public policy alternatives.

Incentives for Risk Reduction

The following table outlines some of the basic characteristics of regulation and tort liability relative to the specific objective of risk reduction.

---

4. See Shulman and Lasagna 1990 for further discussion of the practices followed in other countries.

	Regulation	*Tort liability*
Central focus	Risks versus benefits	Causality and liability
Timing	Ex ante	Ex post
Decision process	Probabilistic	Deterministic
Decisionmakers	Regulators and scientific advisory committees	Juries and judges
Administration	Federal	State

The present U.S. regulatory system is designed to evaluate the benefits relative to the risks of a new drug product before it is allowed to enter the marketplace. An elaborate R&D process has evolved for the scientific testing of benefits and risks,[5] so that it takes an average of twelve years for a new drug to go from first synthesis to regulatory approval and costs more than $200 million.[6] New drug candidates have a large attrition rate as they proceed from the laboratory to animal and human testing. In clinical analysis the product is tested in double-blind trials and measured against the performance of a placebo or alternative therapies. A sufficiently large number of patients are enrolled in the final phase of testing in humans to establish statistical significance regarding a product's benefits and risks.

The timing of this regulatory process is ex ante, or prior to, a product being allowed on the marketplace. Of course, certain rare side effects and long-term effects may not become apparent until a drug has been used in the marketplace by many patients or until considerable time has elapsed. For that reason regulatory reporting and monitoring continue into the postmarketing period. However, the emphasis of our current system is clearly on premarket screening of new drug candidates.

Another important point is that the assessment or risks under regulation is probabilistic. No drug is completely safe or devoid of side effects. The issue is the frequency and severity of any side effects. Specifically, is the risk of a particular toxic reaction 1 in 10 or 1 in 1,000, and how do the overall risks compare with the therapeutic benefits of a new drug? That is the basic trade-off the FDA uses in evaluating whether a new compound can be allowed into the marketplace.

As shown in the table, the decisionmaking framework is very different

5. Grabowski and Vernon 1983; DiMasi and others 1990.
6. DiMasi and others 1990, 26.

for tort liability. The process is driven by accident cases that occur after the fact. The focus is on whether the drug caused the adverse event, who is liable, and what damages should be assessed. In contrast to what occurs under regulation, risks are not weighed against benefits in any kind of aggregate social benefit-cost calculus.

Another basic difference is that the decisionmaking process is deterministic for tort liability actions. In particular, courts seek to answer the question whether a preponderance of the evidence supports causality and liability. The courts have been traditionally uncomfortable with probabilistic judgments and assessments of liability on the basis of multiple probable causes even when science leads to such conclusions. Hence tort liability tends to have an "all or nothing" quality in contrast to the probabilistic assessments routinely considered under regulation.

Many drug liability suits are centrally concerned with what warnings about risks were communicated to providers and users. Was a warning of the adverse event included in the product label? If so, was it adequate to properly alert users of the risk? If a warning was not included, should it have been? These questions of course have a large element of subjectivity. One might expect that the FDA-approved warnings would have a strong presumption against liability in an industry like pharmaceuticals, but that is usually not true in tort liability actions.[7]

Regulation and the tort liability system also have different decisionmakers. For regulation the key decisionmakers are trained professionals—regulatory officials and scientific advisory committees. By contrast, the key people in the tort liability system, judges and jurors, are not scientific experts. Scientists do participate in the process as expert witnesses. But in this adversarial process the hired experts often disagree with one another. As a rule, lay persons will have trouble in resolving these scientific disputes objectively. Consequently, many observers have called for a scientific court, or a panel of experts, to assess scientific issues instead of juries. This recommendation, however, has so far received only limited application.

Administration of the tort liability system is also balkanized in the sense that there are fifty separate state systems, each with its own set of higher appellate courts and judges. As a result, inconsistent rulings and different policies may emerge across the various states. That has been true, for example, with respect to long-run latent effects from pharma-

7. See Swazey's chapter.

ceuticals, when identification of the firm supplying the product has become an issue.[8] The highly fractionalized nature of the tort liability system can cause mixed signals and much uncertainty in an industry like pharmaceuticals where the life cycles of R&D investment products usually span several decades.

Choosing the Appropriate Policy Mix

The table strongly supports the proposition that regulation is conceptually better suited to the management of societal risks from pharmaceuticals in almost all the areas considered. The drug regulatory process is designed to undertake ex ante evaluations of benefits versus risks and uses scientific experts to assess the relevant evidence. By contrast, the tort liability system occurs after the fact, focuses only on risks rather than benefits, and has lay persons as the main decisionmakers.

A case for a strong tort liability system in pharmaceuticals might be made if one could show that regulators in practice systematically err on the side of excessive risks in their premarket approval decisions. However, a large academic literature indicates that the opposite is true. In our present system regulators have the incentive to avoid type-two errors (acceptance of nonbeneficial drugs) at the possible expense of type-one errors (rejections or delay of beneficial drugs).[9] Evidence from several academic studies, using different approaches, suggests that the United States has been on the very stringent end of the regulatory spectrum compared with other countries. At the same time FDA regulation has greatly increased R&D costs and lessened the availability of new drug introductions.[10]

Given the extensive role of FDA regulation in protecting consumers from risk, a strong case exists for a regulatory standards defense for tort liability actions in pharmaceuticals.[11] Under this approach firm liability would be restricted to cases of fraud or deception, essentially cases in which firms submitted false information to regulators in their premarket applications or failed to report new information on side effects in the postmarketing period in a timely fashion in accordance with the current

8. States have come up with different approaches for dealing with this problem. These include "market share" liability (the Sindell decision in California) and several variants of that approach. At the same time many states have also retained traditional rules for liability requiring identification before any damages can be assessed. Dorfman 1989.

9. Grabowski and Vernon 1983, 1–13.

10. For a survey of these studies, see Grabowski and Vernon 1983, 29–48.

11. For an analysis of the relationship between product liability and regulation in other industries, see Viscusi 1988.

regulations. Tort liability would then reinforce regulatory incentives for risk reduction but avoid the extra costs and disincentives for drug innovation now present.[12]

Our current liability system is often justified on grounds other than its incentives for risk reduction. In particular, it also serves an insurance function or as a means for the compensation of unexpected product-related injuries. But as a system for compensating drug-related injuries, the tort liability system also exhibits several undesirable properties, including a high variance in outcomes, significant administrative costs, and long delays. These characteristics have caused many other countries to substitute social insurance schemes, often financed from earmarked taxes on the sales of drugs, to provide for compensation of certain drug-related injuries.[13] To the extent that the United States wishes to provide societal insurance for drug-related injuries, this approach is a much more efficient and equitable way to do so than the tort liability system. This country has the beginning of such a program in the area of vaccines: the U.S. national vaccine injury compensation program went into effect in late 1988.[14] Although it is still too early to evaluate this program, it seems worthy of further development and encouragement.

12. Free-market-reform advocates have occasionally advocated that drug regulation be relaxed in favor of the tort liability system as a way of lessening the adverse consequences of regulation on innovation. Such proposals, however, have not received serious consideration in the political arena. It is difficult to conceive of such ideas taking root under the present tort liability system.
13. Shulman and Lasagna 1990.
14. Shulman and Lasagna 1990, 41–45.

References

DiMasi, J. A., and others. 1990. "The Cost of Innovation in the Pharmaceutical Industry." Tufts University Center for the Study of Drug Development, Boston.

Dorfman, H. L. 1989. "The Negative Effect of Punitive Damages on the Development of New Drugs by the Pharmaceutical Industry." ABA National Institute on Drug Litigation.

Dungworth, T. 1988. *Product Liability and the Business Sector: Litigation Trends in Federal Court.* R-3668-ICJ. Santa Monica, Calif.: Rand Corporation.

Grabowski, H. G., and J. M. Vernon. 1983. *The Regulation of Pharmaceuticals: Balancing the Benefits and Risks.* Washington: American Enterprise Institute for Public Policy Research.

Institute of Medicine. 1985. *Vaccine Supply and Innovation*. Washington: National Academy Press.

Office of Technology Assessment. 1982. *World Population and Fertility Planning Technologies: The Next Twenty Years*. Washington.

Shulman, S. R., and L. Lasagna. 1990. *Trends in Product Liability Law and No-Fault Compensation for Drug-Induced Injuries*. Boston: Tufts University Center for the Study of Drug Development.

Viscusi, W. K. 1988. "Product Liability and Regulation: Establishing the Appropriate Institutional Division of Labor." *American Economic Review* 78: 300–04.

CHAPTER TEN

Liability, Innovation, and Safety in the Chemical Industry

Nicholas A. Ashford and Robert F. Stone

CHEMICAL products have assumed a steadily increasing role in the U.S. economy throughout this century, contributing to the improvements in the standard of living and the levels of health and safety that America enjoys. At the same time, the fact that the production and use of some chemicals create hazards in the workplace, at home, and in the environment has caused intensified public and private awareness and concern. One mechanism for addressing chemical hazards in this country is tort liability, which permits private parties who sustain chemical injury to seek recovery for damages from the firm responsible.

The purpose of this chapter is to assess the effects of liability for chemical harm, as deployed under the prevailing tort system. In broadest terms, the appropriate measure of the effects is whether liability provides, in some meaningful sense, a net social benefit. For the analysis here, three questions that are related both in theory and in practice need to be considered. Does tort liability for chemical harm promote safety and health? Does tort liability for chemical harm stimulate or inhibit innovation? In trying to control chemical hazards and foster technological advance, does tort liability for chemical harm impose an unacceptably high cost on consumers and industry? (That is, does tort liability for chemical harm result in overdeterrence of chemical risks? Or conversely, are chemical hazards underdeterred by tort liability?)

In this chapter we analyze economic costs and other incentives arising from tort liability that serve to reduce chemical hazards. Our analysis of incentives is performed in the context of innovation theory, which we examine in some detail. To assess whether the safety incentives resulting from liability are excessive or inadequate, we develop an optimal deterrence benchmark, reflecting the total social costs of chemical harm, and evaluate the liability costs borne by the chemical firm in relation to that benchmark. Chemical harm to workers, consumers, and innocent bystanders are analyzed separately. Despite our general finding of underdeterrence for acute chemical injuries and of gross underdeterrence for chronic diseases from chemical exposure, we provide examples of technological improvements showing that some reduction in chemical hazards is occurring in response to tort liability.

Chemicals and Chemical Activities Covered

Too often, discussions about tort liability consist of little more than sweeping generalizations drawn from anecdotal evidence, even though the effects and effectiveness of tort liability seem to vary dramatically depending on the specific industry involved. Similarly, attempts to introduce global improvements to the tort system are generally ill conceived insofar as the perceived defects or limitations of tort liability arise only in particular markets or under special conditions that can be separately addressed and remedied. An attractive feature of the research for this book, therefore, is its disaggregated nature—the analysis of tort liability conducted by examining specific economic sectors in detail.

The economic sector under consideration here has been officially designated as "chemicals," but the range of chemical products and activities is too broad and contains too many disparate elements to be considered as a whole. Two important chemical areas, in particular, have such distinctive characteristics that they have been omitted from our analysis. The first is pharmaceuticals, which is evaluated by Judith Swazey and Louis Lasagna in chapters 8 and 9. The second is the disposal of hazardous chemical residues or wastes, which has been subject to special liability rules under federal legislation—the Comprehensive Environmental Response, Compensation, and Liability Act (CERCLA, or the Superfund Act)—and to aggressive regulatory management—especially the federal Resource Conservation and Recovery Act (RCRA), to prevent accidental releases.[1]

Except for those two chemical areas, this chapter examines the effects

1. Even for hazardous waste injuries (as opposed to property cleanup costs), which are not covered by CERCLA, chemical manufacturers have not been held liable for chemical waste damages unless it is a chemical manufacturer's own waste. Thus tort liability for hazardous waste damages should have, at most, an indirect influence on chemical innovation. However, such liability has had a dramatic effect on hazardous waste treatment, storage, and disposal. See Ashford, Moran, and Stone 1989, chap. 2.

of liability from all chemical production and use, to include (primary) chemical manufacture, (secondary) production using chemicals as inputs, and consumer use of chemicals or chemical products. The direct release (but not the disposal) of hazardous chemicals, as part of primary and secondary production activities, falls within the purview of our analysis.

The Tort System and Its Social Context

The tort system is not a simple, homogeneous entity. Its functioning relies on a vast array of attributes, including liability rules (such as negligence or strict liability), rules of evidence (such as the admissibility of evidence and the evidentiary standard), and damage rules (such as award limits and the availability of punitive damages). Furthermore, these attributes are unique for each jurisdiction (the fifty states and the federal courts), and the import of the attributes also depends on their interpretation and application by the particular judge and jury hearing a tort suit.

It is therefore exceedingly difficult to make statements about which liability rules are in effect or to isolate the impact of specific tort system attributes on chemical safety and innovation. With rare exception, we do not attempt to do so here. Instead, we take the existing tort system—and whatever intricate and heterogeneous combinations of attributes compose it—as given and try to assess the effect of the aggregate tort system on chemical innovation and safety. One consequence of this approach is to limit somewhat our ability to identify specific tort system flaws or to recommend detailed modifications of the tort system to enhance its performance. Nevertheless, we do make a qualitative evaluation of tort liability for chemical harm and suggest the direction of change in which improvements to the tort system can be found.

THE OBJECTIVES OF THE TORT SYSTEM. The tort system serves many social purposes; among them are deterrence, compensation, punishment, and justice. *Deterrence* concerns incentives that induce the prevention of damage—here, from chemical hazards—by reducing the production and use of hazardous chemicals, by taking safety precautions in the use of hazardous chemicals, by developing or adopting safer products and processes, or by minimizing the harm once a chemical accident or release has occurred. Deterrence is inherently forward-looking, since it is too late to prevent damage that has already taken place. Thus the objective of deterrence is always prevention of future damage. *Compensation* refers to reimbursing the victim for damages sustained from chemical hazards. Unlike deterrence, compensation is inherently retrospective; reimbursement is for losses caused by past activities. *Punishment* is a burden imposed on wrongdoers to reflect society's condemnation of their reprehensible conduct, the degree of the punishment to be in proportion to the moral gravity of the wrongdoing. Theoretically, the only punitive measure within the tort system is punitive damage awards.[2] Note that punishment and deterrence incentives are intertwined, since punishment imposed for past wrongdoing serves to deter future wrongdoing. *Justice* as an objective is concerned with the institutional process itself, and with the social values it represents, as much as with the specific "outcome" of the process. From this perspective, the tort process has symbolic significance, establishing or confirming personal rights and moral standards.[3]

Among the several social objectives of the tort system, deterrence is most relevant here. Analysis of the effects of tort liability for chemical harm is almost exclusively concerned with the effects on incentives for chemical safety and innovation provided by tort liability. Other objectives, such as punishment, are pertinent only insofar as they also provide deterrence incentives or otherwise affect chemical safety and innovation.

REGULATION AND OTHER MECHANISMS TO ACHIEVE SOCIAL OBJECTIVES. The tort system does not operate in a vacuum. Many other social institutions and mechanisms also influence private sector behavior concerning chemical safety and innovation. For example, other (nontort) causes of action within the judicial system, particularly under contract law and criminal law, also serve to deter hazardous conduct.[4] The dominant source of social involvement in the promotion of health and safety, however, is government regulation, in its broadest sense, by federal and state legislatures and by administrative agencies. Regulatory activities affecting chemical hazards include the following: the promulgation of regulatory standards, such as design standards, health and safety standards, and risk communication standards (for example, product labeling requirements);

2. In jurisdictions where punitive awards are technically forbidden, they may sometimes be disguised as part of jury awards for pain and suffering.

3. For an examination of this function of the tort system, see Mashaw 1985, 1395–96; Elliott 1988, 781–83.

4. Of course, tort law has, in many ways, limited the role of contract law in the area of health and safety hazards (Prosser and Keeton 1984). Some commentators, such as Huber (1988), have gone so far as to conclude that tort liability has spelled the death of risk contracts. Others have argued that reliance on contract law to resolve matters of health and safety was never a workable plan, which, to have been effective, would have imposed astronomical transaction costs. See, in particular, Hager 1989, 572–79; Page 1990, 689–96.

Criminal sanctions may be applied both to individuals in the firm and to the firm itself to punish and deter reckless conduct that places other parties at risk. See, for example, Coffee 1981; Wheeler 1984; Cook 1984.

economic incentives, such as taxes, subsidies, fines, and risk-internalizing charges; price regulation, such as the control of liability insurance rates; information generation and dissemination, such as government-conducted or government-sponsored health and safety research, new technology demonstration projects, and training and education; and specially created administrative systems, such as workers' compensation.

The tort system and regulation interact in complex ways. To some extent tort liability can be viewed as an alternative to regulation. This corresponds to the position traditionally taken by political conservatives: the courts, by enforcing contracts and remedying tortious conduct, serve as an adjunct to the market and ensure its efficient operation. According to this argument, tort liability makes regulation redundant.[5] A related view is that tort liability and regulation are substitutes. Workers' compensation, the provision of which normally bars workers from suing their employers for job-related injuries and illnesses, is a case in point. The situation in which compliance with a regulatory standard immunizes the firm against claims of negligence is another.

Conversely, tort liability and regulation may act as complements.[6] For instance, toxicological and epidemiological research by the government in support of regulatory initiatives may provide critical knowledge about chemical hazards that can be used in tort litigation.[7] Similarly, health and safety standards may confirm that a product is indeed hazardous and thereby open the door to tort liability, especially when a manufacturer was not in compliance with applicable standards. In other situations, tort liability and regulation may intersect—for example, if the regulatory authority formally creates or modifies bases for tort liability for use as its deterrence mechanism (which, as mentioned, occurred by legislative mandate under CERCLA for hazardous wastes). (Another example of the intersection of regulation and the courts, but one not involving tort liability, is the judicial review of regulatory decisions.) Finally, tort lia-

5. It is ironic that the same political conservatives who have traditionally opposed regulation on ideological grounds now support so-called tort reform and embrace regulation as the preferred mechanism for controlling social hazards. See, for example, Huber 1985a, 79–82.

6. For a formal analysis of the conditions under which tort liability and safety regulations should be used jointly, see Kolstad, Ulen, and Johnson 1990.

7. As an example (though outside the chemical sector), epidemiological studies conducted by the federal Centers for Disease Control, central to the plaintiffs' cases, have been accepted by the courts as evidence in suits involving toxic shock syndrome. See *Ellis* v. *International Playtex, Inc.*, 745 F.2d 292, 301 (4th Cir. 1984); *Kehm* v. *Proctor & Gamble Mfg. Co.*, 724 F.2d 613, 619 (8th Cir. 1983).

bility might be seen as part of a just process that transcends regulation. According to this view, the tort system is to some extent a court of last resort. Victims of chemical harm not satisfactorily protected by regulation, and not controlled by voluntary market transactions, are nevertheless permitted under tort law to confront those parties responsible in a courtroom before a jury of their peers.

The important point is that the effects of tort liability rely fundamentally on the prevailing regulatory environment. Even more significant is the fact that the effects of changes in the tort system, ostensibly made to improve it, cannot be determined independently of the regulatory response. Therefore, even though our assessment of the effects of the tort system on chemical hazards and innovation takes the current regulatory environment as given, in evaluating the policy implications of our analysis we must consider the regulatory ramifications as well.

Technological Innovation: A Framework for Analyzing the Effects of Liability

In this section we explore the theory of technological change, which is based on models of firm behavior, and develop a framework for analyzing the effects of tort liability on innovation. The effect of tort liability on chemical innovation and safety is seen to depend on the "amount" of tort liability—that is, on the amount of deterrence tort liability provides. We construct the optimal deterrence benchmark at a conceptual level for subsequent use.

Basic Concepts

Innovation is the first commercially successful application of a new technical idea. Innovation should be distinguished from *invention*, which refers to the formulation of the new technical idea itself, and from *diffusion*, which refers to the subsequent widespread adoption of the innovation by those who did not develop it. Differentiating between innovation and diffusion is complicated by the fact that adopters sometimes alter the innovation in minor ways to suit their specific needs. When these modifications become sufficiently extensive, they may properly be considered a separate innovation.

Innovations can be categorized in several ways. For example, they may be classified according to the degree of technological change: major technical breakthroughs are termed *radical* innovations, whereas minor technical adaptations are termed *incremental* innovations. An important, basic distinction is that between product and process innovations, the former being a marketable new end product, and the latter a change in the production process.[8]

That innovations are defined as successful commercial applications does not necessarily mean they are inherently socially desirable. If private markets functioned perfectly, then Adam Smith's invisible hand would ensure that each innovation confers a net social benefit. But because of externalities and other forms of market failure, the social desirability of an innovation cannot be guaranteed. New products or processes imposing social costs not reflected in the market, if in excess of their market gain, are "bad" innovations in the sense that society would be better off without them.

The Innovation Process

To assess the effect of tort liability on innovation requires an understanding of the innovation process, including the sources of innovative opportunities, the incentives motivating private agents to engage in innovative search, and the determinants of technological change. The body of literature in the field is vast and largely unsettled, and well beyond the scope of this chapter to review.[9] However, a brief examination of the two main theoretical strands in the innovation literature—only the second of which we embrace—should permit us to identify the salient characteristics of the innovation process.

ORTHODOX THEORY. Consistent with contemporary microeconomic theory, the orthodox (or neoclassical) theory of technological change is grounded on the premise that firms are motivated by a desire to maximize profits. Firms innovate in response to exogenous forces that create profitable technological opportunities. Demand-pull innovations are driven by shifts in market demand or relative prices. Technology-push innovations are developed to take advantage of advances in scientific knowledge whose market value, in the area for which the innovation is being considered, has not previously been determined.

---

8. A "process innovation" should not be confused with the "innovation process," which is the set of activities by which new products or processes are developed. Innovations, whether of the product or process variety, are the result of the innovation process. See Ashford and Heaton 1983, 110–11.

9. Extensive surveys of the literature on innovation and technical change are provided in Stoneman 1983; National Science Foundation 1983; and Freeman 1982.

Despite its simplicity, profit maximization as an explanation of firm decision rules concerning innovation is a powerful concept. The ability to represent maximization rules using calculus and other mathematical tools has facilitated the construction and testing of sophisticated economic models of technological change. For example, models employing a profit-maximization approach have been widely used to analyze the relation between the resources devoted to innovative endeavors and the rate of innovation, however measured (that is, between the inputs and outputs of innovative activities).

Nevertheless, the orthodox theory of technological change is seriously flawed in its attempt to characterize the innovation process itself. The lack of descriptive realism is obviously part of the problem. Even more important is the inability of orthodox theory to reflect or to address the inherently dynamic quality of the innovation process. Maximization models of firm behavior are static: optimization arises only in equilibrium. The dynamic process through which equilibrium comes about—an essential component of the innovation process—cannot be explained within the context of orthodox theory.[10]

EVOLUTIONARY THEORY. Dissatisfaction with the descriptive and dynamic limitations of orthodox theory stimulated the development of an alternative, evolutionary theory of technological change.[11] According to evolutionary theory, firms are still motivated by profit and will engage in innovative search to exploit perceived profitable opportunities, but profit maximization is not their objective, at least not in any traditional sense. Innovation activities are subject to extreme uncertainty (termed "strong uncertainty"). Besides uncertainty about the precise costs and outcomes of alternatives that might arise in normal economic situations, firms undertaking innovative search are likely to lack knowledge of what the alternatives even are. Maximizing over a set of alternatives loses meaning when the alternatives are not well defined.

Confronted with uncertainty, high transaction costs for acquiring infor-

10. Models of adaptive behavior are an attempt to deal with this problem, but such ad hoc specifications are incompatible with the strict maximization principles of orthodox theory. For further discussion, see Griliches 1967.

11. In reality, what is termed evolutionary theory might more properly be viewed as a collection of related evolutionary theories of innovation (even though Richard Nelson and Sidney Winter have called their research "an evolutionary theory of economic change"). The origins of evolutionary theory probably reside in the work of Schumpeter 1934; 1950. Other, more recent, contributions include Klein 1977, Abernathy and Utterback 1978, and Nelson and Winter 1982. Many of the research developments pertaining to evolutionary theory are discussed in Dosi 1988.

mation, and complex real-world problems, firms develop organizational routines—regular and predictable behavioral patterns based on heuristics rather than optimizing decision rules.[12] Organizational routines guide the efforts of firms as they attempt to improve their products and processes. Since those efforts require addressing (typically ill-structured) technical limitations and economic impediments, innovation activity might be broadly viewed as problem solving under conditions of strong uncertainty.

Firms have nontransferable technology-specific skills and institutional traits, such as internal organizational arrangements or external business relationships. These firm capabilities and organizational routines are modified over time as a result of deliberate problem-solving efforts and the good or bad fortune brought about by random events. Because of their capabilities and routines, certain firms will become successful at exploiting specific technological opportunities and translating them into marketable products and processes. Other firms, whose capabilities and routines are less compatible with their economic and technical environment, will become unprofitable (unless blessed by exceedingly good luck during innovative search) and will tend to be weeded out by a market version of natural selection.

Unlike orthodox theory, evolutionary theory portrays technological change as a dynamic process. Not only is innovative search undertaken in response to exogenous market-pull and technology-push forces, but it is endogenously driven by a competitive process whereby firms are continuously improving their capabilities and their products and processes. Uninnovative firms are confronted with the "hidden foot" of competitors willing to take technological risks.[13] The concept of equilibrium, as a stationary point in the innovation process, does not arise in evolutionary theory.

Related Applications to the Chemical Industry

An indication of how dynamic models of the innovation process, embodying evolutionary theory, can be used to evaluate the effects of tort liability on technological change might be provided by examining analogous applications. Of particular relevance are several studies that, using

12. The concept of organizational routine embodies many of the ideas of the behavioral theorists, who first suggested that firms "satisfice" in response to problems of bounded rationality. See, for example, Simon 1959 and Cyert and March 1963, which spawned much of this literature.

13. Klein (1977) introduced the notion of "the hidden foot" as an integral part of his model of dynamic efficiency.

the dynamic model of innovation developed by Abernathy and Utterback, assess the influence of regulation on innovation in the chemical industry.[14] These studies indicate that the innovative response to chemical regulation depends on (1) the nature of the regulatory stimulus (for example, what is being regulated, the regulatory mechanism, and the stringency of regulation), and (2) the stage of industrial maturation of the regulated sector, its susceptibility to market incursions from unregulated sectors, and the characterization of the technology at the time of the regulation. The essential point is that the rate and type of innovation arising due to an exogenous stimulus—here, the demand-pull force of regulation—is reasonably predictable.

Several specific findings concerning the effects of chemical regulation on innovation should be mentioned here because, as will be shown, they parallel tort liability effects. First, excessive regulation, regulation that is too stringent from a societal perspective, or otherwise inappropriate regulation increases research and development costs and risks, diverts scarce managerial resources, reduces firm profitability, and thereby discourages investments in research and development and causes the rate of innovation to decline.[15] Second, regulation that is too lax also discourages innovation; instead it elicits adoption of on-the-shelf technology (and usually add-on technology, such as an end-of-pipe pollution control device, that minimizes the technological response of the firm).[16] Finally, stringent (technology-forcing) regulation usually has a positive effect on innovative performance. Although such regulation increases research and development costs, the innovative firm's early scrutiny of health, safety, and environmental effects of new technology increases the success rate of new products and processes brought to market.[17] Furthermore, those innovations that stringent regulation causes to fail because they pose unacceptable health, safety, or environmental hazards are "bad" innovations

14. See, for example, Ashford and Heaton 1983 and Ashford, Ayers, and Stone 1985, as well as the related research cited therein. The Abernathy-Utterback model focuses on the process of industrial maturation of the firm (or productive segment) to explain the rate and nature of innovation. In the initial (fluid) stage, the firm tends to create a market niche by introducing new products that are purchased for their superior performance. During the following (transitional) stage, major process changes occur in response to rising sales and the need to compete on price rather than performance. In the final (rigid) stage, the rate of product and process innovation declines significantly. At this point in its life cycle, the technology is subject to invasion by new ideas or disturbance by exogenous forces, causing a reversion to an earlier stage. See Abernathy and Utterback 1978.

15. Ashford, Heaton, and Priest 1979, 172–78.

16. See, in particular, Ashford, Ayers, and Stone 1985, 463–64.

17. Allen and others 1978, 36–39.

whose market failure should be encouraged. Hence regulation increases the likelihood of both successes and failures in different attempts to innovate. Regulation may also benefit some firms and disadvantage others. Ideally structured regulation may thus cause a shift in the nature of an industry or product line that is precisely what is needed and intended from a societal perspective.

Tort Liability as an Exogenous Stimulus

In terms of the innovation process, tort liability, like regulation, creates market-driven, demand-pull opportunities for technological change. Tort liability is also similar to regulation in the sense that either insufficient or excessive amounts of the exogenous stimulus will discourage desirable innovations, while the "correct" amount will foster socially desirable innovations and discourage others. The ensuing discussion will first explore the logic underlying liability-induced innovation, then address what the "correct" amount of tort liability is, and indicate the role of this tort liability benchmark in the ensuing analysis.

LIABILITY-INDUCED INNOVATION. Tort liability forces the firm to pay for the injuries, illnesses, and property damage for which its products and production activities are responsible (and for purposes of consideration here, for which they are correctly held responsible). From a static market perspective, tort liability must obviously increase business costs and risks by the amount of harm the firm's existing products and processes are deemed to have caused. In addition, product prices will adjust upward to reflect tort liability costs.[18] The net result is that relatively unsafe activities will be less profitable (compared with the situation without tort liability), and some will become unprofitable. These the firm will discontinue.

From a dynamic perspective, the costs imposed by tort liability also represent valuable market information that firms take into account in planning their innovation activities. Tort liability, by adding new safety dimensions to previous design considerations, increases the problem space

---

18. The dynamics of the market adjustment may, of course, be much more complicated but similar in effect. Assuming a workably competitive industry, product prices will rise by an appropriately weighted average of tort liability costs. Alternatively, differential product risks may result in price spreads favoring safer products. Note that the availability of liability insurance may have a mitigating effect, depending on the ability of insurers to differentiate among product risks.

of the engineer.[19] Furthermore, firms are prompted to enlist the support of toxicologists, epidemiologists, and environmental scientists in the early stages of innovation to assess the safety risks of potential new products and processes, thereby augmenting the firm's technical expertise in developing profitable technological solutions.[20] The activities associated with enhancing and verifying the safety of new products and processes may make innovation more costly, but they also increase the likelihood that the outcome will be commercially successful or have an additional competitive advantage in the longer term.

Thus, correctly applied and properly understood, tort liability provides incentives that both create and destroy market opportunities, but, in general, it redirects innovation toward the development of less hazardous products and processes.

Two related issues should be clarified here. First, even under ideal circumstances, it is possible for the presence of tort liability to discourage the development of an otherwise successful, safe, and desirable innovation. For example, a firm may decide not to initiate the innovation process for a socially desirable product because, hypothetically, the cost of verifying its (actual, but at that time, uncertain) safety exceeds the product's expected profit. Similarly, the higher costs of research and development occasioned by tort liability concerns may reduce the number of innovation initiatives the firm can fund. But unless the firm is held liable for injuries it did not in fact cause, the likelihood of such "perverse" outcomes, and the associated economic loss, must be minimal.[21] The reasons are that (1) the research and development costs attributable to product hazards are usually fairly small, since in the chemical industry *all* the innovation activities through the applied research stage constitute only 17 percent of the total costs of new product development;[22] and (2) the size of the potential market or the per-unit expected profit in the absence of tort liability, or both, must be negligible to be offset by safety R&D costs.

The second issue concerns the appropriate range of innovation activity

19. Allen and others 1978.

20. Many studies of the chemical industry report the contribution to product and process development made by chemical firms' sophisticated analysis of health and environmental risks. See Ashford and Heaton 1983, 133.

21. We argue later in this chapter that such "false positives" are unlikely to occur for the set of chemical firm activities under consideration.

22. Mansfield and others 1971, 118. Furthermore, from 1960 through 1980 research and development expenditures as a percentage of sales steadily declined in the chemical and allied industries, even during periods of intense regulatory activity. See Ashford and Heaton 1983, 115–17.

to be considered with reference to the effects of tort liability for chemical hazards. Ostensibly, the natural choice is new chemical entities: finished products that constitute or contain new chemical formulations, new intermediate chemicals to be used as inputs by nonchemical (secondary) industries, and new basic chemicals to be used in producing intermediate or finished chemical products. The resulting scope of inquiry, however, would be unnecessarily restrictive. A full and complete evaluation must consider all effects on innovative activity throughout the economy, including product and process innovations that entail either the reduction or the elimination of specific chemicals, substitution of less-toxic chemicals or nonchemicals for presently used chemicals,[23] or a change in the mix or control of (existing) chemicals used. Tort liability for chemical hazards can have a positive effect on innovative performance even if the rate of chemical innovation declines, so long as "nonchemical" innovations are sufficiently stimulated.

THE "CORRECT" AMOUNT OF TORT LIABILITY. The way in which tort liability promotes desirable innovations is by internalizing costs; that is, by confronting the firm with the injury costs its activities (would otherwise) impose on other parties. The "correct" amount of tort liability then is simply that level which promotes optimal deterrence, by making the firm bear the entire social costs of the injuries, illnesses, and property damage it causes.

Several features of the optimal-deterrence level of tort liability merit further explanation. First, the social costs to be internalized include both pecuniary costs, such as medical expenses, forgone earnings, and property damage, and nonpecuniary (but real) costs, such as pain and suffering and loss of life.[24]

Second, the "cause" of the harm can itself be a highly controversial legal and philosophical issue.[25] Just to establish a deterrence standard, we assume here that causation can be reasonably determined if all the

23. An example of a nonchemical substitution is using a mechanical pump to replace the CFC delivery system for aerosol sprays.

24. Some analysts (such as Viscusi 1988, 156–57) have noted that less than full compensation is desirable if the injury or illness decreases the victim's marginal utility of income. Furthermore, full compensation for irreplaceable commodities, such as one's life and health, is inefficient (from an insurance perspective), since monetary compensation is, by definition, an ineffective form of reimbursement for these losses (as originally demonstrated in Cook and Graham 1977). The reasoning is correct as far as it goes; but the analysis refers only to optimal *compensation*, which is irrelevant to the objective here of optimal *deterrence*. On deterrence grounds, as noted above, the firm responsible must bear the entire social costs. For further discussion of this point, see Ashford, Moran, and Stone 1989, I-4, I-5.

25. See, for example, Keeton and others 1984; Wright 1985; Landes and Posner 1987.

facts to the case in question are known.[26] Note, however, that the possibility of multiple causes of the chemical harm is not precluded. (Indeed, it is probable.) In cases of multiple causation, we assume that responsibility can be reasonably allocated or apportioned among the various parties involved. For optimal deterrence, the firm should pay only for that proportion of the damages it has actually caused.

Third, to avoid double counting, the damage costs to be incurred by the firm from tort liability should be calculated as a residual, net of the damage payments the firm makes through other means. For example, the workers' compensation benefits and additional salary for accepting more hazardous employment (the wage premium for risk) that workers receive—which constitute a form of ex ante compensation for expected damages caused by the firm—must be taken into account in determining the optimal-deterrence level of tort liability.

Fourth, the costs the firm bears because of tort liability are not restricted to court awards and settlements.[27] They also include the firm's legal expenses to defend the claims, the costs associated with diversion of scarce management and technical skills to respond to tort claims, the premiums paid to insurers to indemnify the firm against damage claims, and any loss of reputation the firm sustains stemming from the tort suits' connotation of fault or wrongdoing.[28]

Fifth, the only exception to full-cost internalization is punitive damages, when the costs borne by the firm may properly exceed the total costs its actions impose on the other party to a particular legal claim. However, the immediate objective of punitive damages is punishment rather than deterrence, the degree of punishment to be in proportion to the moral gravity of the firm's conduct.[29]

26. This assumption is in no way intended to minimize the scientific uncertainty inherent in many cases involving chemical exposure (see, for example, Abraham and Merrill 1986). Note, furthermore, that this uncertainty is not restricted to the tort system. For example, the regulatory process is confronted with the same scientific uncertainty (Latin 1988), and despite putative procedural advantages and superior scientific expertise (Elliott 1985), it is unclear whether administrative agencies are better equipped to deal with it (Elliott 1988, 791–96).

27. For establishing the optimal deterrence standard, it is not relevant what portion of the court award or settlement is received by the plaintiff and what portion by the plaintiff's attorney. All that matters is the total amount of damages paid by the responsible firm.

28. The costs, and associated deterrence value, of loss of reputation can be substantial. For evidence of its importance in the automobile industry, see the chapter by John Graham in this volume. However, in the chemical industry, which is predominantly a supplier industry to other industries, these reputational concerns may not be as important as they are for companies that market consumer products.

29. Although the intellectual foundations differ from state to state, punitive damages are usually intended to punish and to deter simultaneously that tortfeasor and to deter

Finally, the preceding delineation of the optimal-deterrence level of tort liability is intended only to serve as a benchmark against which to compare the actual costs firms incur under current tort liability conditions; it is not necessarily a policy recommendation for specific tort liability rules. Thus, for example, reliance on full-cost internalization to promote optimal deterrence does not necessarily constitute an endorsement for strict liability.[30] Similarly, the fact that optimal deterrence dictates having a firm incur liability costs only for that portion of the damages it has caused does not necessarily imply support for introducing a proportional liability standard in the courts.

ANALYSIS USING THE OPTIMAL DETERRENCE BENCHMARK. The rest of this chapter examines the actual tort liability costs firms incur—in relation to the optimal deterrence benchmark for chemical hazards—and the likely incentive effects of those costs on firm behavior.

The analysis of tort liability costs focuses on three elements: the extent to which the firms that cause the damage incur the liability costs (termed "true positives") and vice versa (the extent to which firms that do not cause the damage do not incur liability costs, termed "true negatives"); the extent to which the firms that do not cause the damage incur liability costs (termed "false positives") and vice versa (the extent to which firms that cause the damage do not incur liability costs, termed "false negatives"); and the magnitude of tort liability costs borne by the firm in relation to the optimal-deterrence benchmark.[31]

These elements are obviously a major determinant of chemical safety and innovative performance. Even if industry (as an aggregate) pays for the chemical damages it causes, if individual firms are not confronted with the costs their chemical activities impose on others, they will not be motivated to develop less hazardous products and processes. As a result, in aggregate, the frequency and severity of chemical accidents,

---

others from doing likewise in the future. Hence the attendant terminology of "exemplary damages" is used in some states. See Ashford, Moran, and Stone 1987, 28–31.

30. In many situations an irresolvable tension exists between two valid concepts of efficient deterrence. One is the level of care, which concerns the safety precautions taken within the context of a given activity and which traditionally has been evaluated by a negligence standard (though a strict liability rule with contributory negligence would serve equally well). The other is the level of activity, which concerns activity choices that maximize social welfare (requiring social costs to be internalized) and which is evaluated on a strict liability standard. See Shavell 1987.

31. See Ashford, Spadafor, and Caldart 1984, 277–79, for more information about the use of true positives, false positives, true negatives, and false negatives in predictive tests.

releases, injuries, illnesses, and property damage are likely to be socially excessive.

Tort Liability and Acute Injuries from Chemical Production or Use

Much of the public concern about tort liability for chemical hazards, certainly as reflected in academic writings, has been limited, either implicitly or explicitly, to *chronic* illnesses from chemical exposure—that is, where there is a fairly long latency period (perhaps as short as several days to a week and as long as several decades) between chemical exposure and the obvious manifestation of disease. Chronic disease can be caused by continuous or intermittent long-term exposure, such as lead poisoning or solvent-related neuropathy, or by short-term or even one-time exposure, leading to cancer or birth defects. Before investigating chronic diseases from chemical exposure, however, we examine *acute* injuries arising from chemical production or use. These are important in their own right and, furthermore, can supply pertinent cost information, as well as serve as a useful comparison, to the subsequent analysis of chronic diseases.

Acute injuries usually arise from a single, discrete episode or accident in which the initial manifestation of the injury is immediate, or nearly so, and the nexus between accident and injury is readily discernible.[32] Highly publicized examples from chemical production and chemical use in manufacturing include the acute injuries and deaths suffered at the 1984 Bhopal disaster in India from exposure to high concentrations of methyl isocyanate (MIC) and phosgene, both highly toxic chemicals, in a runaway chemical reaction, and those suffered from the chemical explosion at the Phillips Petroleum polyethylene plant in Pasadena, Texas, in 1989. Acute consumer product injuries involving chemicals can also be very severe or fatal—in cases of chemical poisonings or explosions, such as from an oven or drain cleaner. Less dramatic and less severe examples of acute injuries to workers, consumers, or innocent bystanders are minor burns or eye irritation from a chemical exposure. Note that acute injuries

32. Consistent with the preceding definition of chronic injury, we shall assume that for acute injuries the delay in manifestation may, in extreme cases, be as long as several days to a week. Obviously the distinction between acute and chronic injuries is not absolute. In ambiguous cases the ability to connect the ailment to its accident source should be the decisive factor in distinguishing acute from chronic injuries for analytical purposes.

arising from chemical production need not involve chemicals (for instance, workers at a chemical plant may also sustain cuts from sharp objects or be electrocuted);[33] however, for convenience, we use the term *chemical injuries* to refer to all injuries associated with chemical production or use.

Analysis of the effects of tort liability for acute chemical injuries will consist of the following three tasks: calculating the chemical firm's payout for acute injuries (including transaction costs) relative to the social costs imposed by the injury; assessing the amount of deterrence created by the firm's liabilities, as reflected in the magnitude and nature of the firm's payout for acute injuries; and indicating the probable deterrence effects of liability on chemical safety and innovation. Each of these tasks is disaggregated according to the four possible types of claimant: an employee of the chemical firm, a worker employed in another firm that uses the chemical firm's product as an input, a consumer using the chemical firm's product, or an innocent bystander. Of necessity, estimates of the costs and payouts will be gross approximations, and the appraisal of the amount of deterrence created by liability and its effects on chemical safety and innovation will be qualitative.

Chemical Firm Payout Relative to Social Costs

To determine the amount of deterrence provided by liability for acute chemical injuries, we first identify the main social costs associated with the injuries and estimate what proportion of those costs are incurred by the chemical firm as compensatory damages or in some other form. This comparison of the chemical firm's payout to the social costs of acute injuries can be thought of as a two-step process: a comparison in the case of successful claims, and an assessment of the likelihood that, in an appropriate sense, the chemical firm was responsible for, or caused, the injuries for which it incurs costs—that is, to estimate the likelihood of the claims being true positives.

SOCIAL COSTS AND SUCCESSFUL CLAIMS. The social costs arising from human injury are dominated by the following: the victim's *forgone earnings* from lost worktime, the victim's *medical expenses* for treatment and rehabilitation, the victim's physical *impairment* or loss of function in nonwork experiences and activities, the *pain and suffering* of the victim

33. In principle, the tort liability costs of nonchemical injuries at chemical plants could induce process innovations to reduce accidents or cause the firm to cease chemical production altogether.

and the victim's family, and the losses associated with the victim's *death* (forgone earnings, lost lifetime experiences, and the family's pain and suffering).

The portion of the social costs borne *by* the chemical firm exceeds the compensation the victim or the victim's survivors receive directly *from* the firm. It also includes the payments made by the chemical firm to economic agents, typically insurers, who assume some part of or all of the firm's liability in case of claims against the firm. It is logical to assume that the price paid by the chemical firm to transfer its risks exceeds the expected cost of the claims, since the economic agent will charge a fee for providing the service. But because the chemical firm derives value from eliminating the uncertainty of injury costs and voluntarily enters into such insurance arrangements, a reasonable measure of the social costs of injury borne by the chemical firm is the sum of the claims paid by the firm and its insurers. (The subsequent analysis contains a loading for insurance claims-processing costs for lawsuits.)

EMPLOYEES OF THE CHEMICAL FIRM. When the claimant is an employee of the chemical firm and sustains a job-related injury, workers' compensation statutes usually bar workers from seeking recovery from the employer through common law (except in cases of gross negligence or intentional harm). Workers' compensation programs, funded by the employer's workers' compensation premiums, provide compensation for injuries according to scheduled rates, on a showing that the injury arose out of and in the course of employment, regardless of fault.[34] For acute injuries, such a showing is usually effortless and uncontested.

The percentage of the social costs of acute injury recovered from workers' compensation by the successful claimant is summarized, according to cost category, in the first column of table 10-1. State statutes usually limit wage recovery to two-thirds of lost wages[35] (unadjusted for anticipated wage increases over time or for retirement contributions or health insurance and subject to various constraints on minimum and maximum benefits and benefits duration). The net effect is to reduce the average percentage recovered to somewhat below 67 percent. In principle, workers' compensation covers total medical costs associated with an acute

34. Note that employees may also receive private disability insurance and life insurance benefits from their employer, but these can simply be treated as part of the workers' risk premium (as discussed later).

35. Viscusi 1988, 165. These wage benefits are not taxable, which makes their value to the employee approximately equivalent to net income. This fact, however, does not affect the amount paid out by workers' compensation (and funded by employers).

Table 10-1. *Percentage Recovery of Social Costs from Chemical Firms (and Their Compensated Agents) for Acute Injuries*

	Claimant		
Social cost of injury	Employee	Third party	Consumer
Forgone earnings	67 – [a]	100	100
Medical expenses	100 – [b]	100	100
Impairment[c]	0	100(?)	100(?)
Pain and suffering	0	100(?)	100(?)
Death	10 – [d]	10 – [d]	10 – [d]
Addenda:			
Other possible recovery from chemical firms			
Wage premium for risk	Yes		
Punitive damages		Yes	Yes
Tort system transaction costs borne by chemical firms			
Chemical firms' legal costs	0 +	Yes	Yes
Opportunity cost of chemical firms' time	0 +	Yes	Yes

Source: Figures derived by the authors from sources indicated in the text.
a. Actual payments are somewhat below 67 percent.
b. Costs are covered but quality of care tends to be minimal.
c. Other than disability.
d. No more than 10 percent and perhaps less than 1 percent of true social costs.

injury, but in practice the quality and level of care provided tend to be minimal.[36] Workers' compensation provides payment for disability, which reflects the socioeconomic consequences of impairment (a strictly medical concept), but normally only insofar as earning power is affected.[37] In that sense, disability payments actually should be classified as part of forgone earnings that extend into the future. However, workers' compensation does not provide benefits for impairment itself or its nonwork consequences; nor does workers' compensation provide recovery for pain and suffering.[38]

Workers' compensation does award death benefits to the employee's survivors, ranging from $70,000 to about $200,000 in most states,[39] but these benefit levels are a minute fraction of the corresponding social cost. Estimates of the valuation of loss of life, based on individuals' willingness to pay for an incremental reduction in risk—which current economic

36. Viscusi 1988, 172.
37. Barth and Hunt 1980, 125–26.
38. The magnitude of these uncompensated nonpecuniary health impacts is not negligible. Viscusi and Moore (1987, 258) derive willingness-to-pay estimates for pain and suffering and impairment (nonwork disability) that equal 1.1 to 1.5 times the valuation of pecuniary losses associated with job injuries.
39. U.S. Chamber of Commerce 1990.

thinking argues is the appropriate conceptual basis for valuing risks to life—have consistently exceeded $1,000,000; most such estimates place the value of human life at more than $3,000,000; and a few estimates exceed $10,000,000.[40] Recent research using more accurate data on job-related fatalities concludes that workers collectively place a value of from $5,000,000 to $6,500,000 (in 1986 dollars) per "statistical" life saved,[41] and these estimates do not include all aspects of the social cost of premature death. Furthermore, federal agencies concerned with health and safety have typically selected a value per statistical life saved in the millions of dollars as a basis for their regulatory decisions. For instance, the Environmental Protection Agency used a loss-of-life estimate of $3,000,000 in its 1987 regulatory impact analysis of protection of stratospheric ozone—and was then criticized for having selected too low a value.[42] By comparison, death benefits from workers' compensation provides no more than 10 percent, and perhaps less than 1 percent, of the social cost of death.

In sum, chemical firms pay, through workers' compensation premiums, 75 percent or more of the social cost of minor acute injuries (entailing little pain and suffering), and pay approximately 50–67 percent of the social cost of acute injuries of average severity (where there is some pain and suffering but no impairment). Because of limits on awards, workers' compensation pays some 10–50 percent of the social cost of severe acute

40. Viscusi (1986, 201) provides a review of the empirical work in the area and suggests that the estimates under $1,000,000 (conducted in the 1970s) either depend on questionable assumptions or are not representative of the general population. (In addition, even these estimates would exceed $1,000,000 in current dollars.) For a more critical view of the estimation procedures used in deriving a value per statistical life saved, and the assumptions on which they are based, see Ashford and Stone 1988, 2–29. The problems they enumerate include (1) the presence of externalities and imperfect information, which violate the assumption of perfectly functioning markets, and (2) model misspecification, errors in variables, and sample bias, which undermine much of the econometric work. Some of these problems clearly result in an underestimation of the value of loss of life.

41. See Moore and Viscusi 1988b. A "statistical" life is merely a linear extrapolation of an individual's willingness to pay for a small reduction in risk. For example, suppose workers demand an extra $0.01 an hour for more hazardous work, with an increased annual risk of a fatality of 1/200,000. On an annual basis (assuming 2,000 hours of work a year), workers will each receive an extra $20 in return for accepting the risk. If 200,000 workers perform the more hazardous work, they will collectively receive $4 million and, on average, one of these workers will die as a result. Thus, in this example, $4 million is the imputed value of a statistical life, based on individual workers' risk decisions entailing small risks to life.

42. See U.S. Environmental Protection Agency 1987, app. G-9. For criticism of the dollar value, see, for example, Ashford and Stone 1988, 29–38.

injuries (with appreciable pain and suffering and impairment) and from 1–10 percent of the social costs of fatal acute injuries.

Workers' compensation, however, is not the only mechanism through which chemical firms incur costs for their workers' acute injuries. To attract workers to perform work that is more hazardous than the average job, chemical firms must offer higher wages.[43] The risk-compensating wage premium employees receive represents a type of ex ante payment by the firm for expected future injury costs. However, for workers to demand a risk premium to offset otherwise uncompensated job hazards, they must have knowledge of the firm-specific and activity-specific risks that confront them, they must be able to process the risk information in a rational manner, their demands must incorporate the interests of their family and friends (to avoid externalities), and the relevant job market must be competitive (otherwise they will be unable to express their demands effectively). Each of these assumptions is unrealistic to a greater or lesser degree,[44] but at least for *acute* chemical hazards—in which the consequences of accidents are immediate—the employees are likely to be cognizant of many of the more serious risks. As a result, one expects that many, but not all, of the "residual" social costs of acute chemical injuries (that is, those not compensated by workers' compensation) are paid out by the chemical firm in the form of wage premiums for risk.

There are no other costs of any consequence that the chemical firm incurs as the result of its employees' acute injuries. The transaction costs of the workers' compensation system are low in the case of acute chemical injuries because the source of the injury is usually obvious and rarely contested. Chemical firms therefore do not generally bear legal expenses or tie up management or technical staff in resolving these injury claims.

43. See, however, Graham and Shakow (1990), who argue that a dual or segmented labor market exists. According to them, most high-risk jobs are competed for in the secondary labor market, which is characterized by low wages, poor working conditions, and no discernible compensation for risk.

44. Consider, for now, problems with the perfect information assumption. First, even if employees are familiar with the toxicity and reactive properties of the chemicals they work with, they are unlikely to know the hazards associated with the plant design or with plant operations that potentially threaten but do not include them. Second, it is well documented that individuals have serious risk-perception problems. (See, for example, Tversky and Kahneman 1974, 1124–31; Machina 1987, 141–47.) In principle, individuals are just as likely to overreact as underreact to hazard information, but in practice worker risk perception appears to be dominated by an "it-can't-happen-to-me" syndrome, which results in known risks being understated and therefore undervalued. See Ashford 1976a, 357.

Finally, being a no-fault system, workers' compensation does not award punitive damages.

In sum, the chemical firm's total payout for the acute injuries of its employees is less than the social costs arising from those injuries—how much less depends largely on the severity of the injury and on the relative efficiency of the job market in internalizing job hazards through wage premiums for risk.

INNOCENT BYSTANDERS AND CONSUMERS OF CHEMICAL PRODUCTS. The share of the social costs of acute injuries borne by the chemical firm—again, in cases where the claimant is successful—is virtually identical for two types of claimant: an innocent bystander (one who has no pertinent economic or contractual relationship with the chemical firm whose activities or product caused the injury) and a consumer injured by a chemical product.[45] Both types of claimant try to obtain recovery by bringing tort action against the chemical firm.

Successful claimants receive the full compensation to which they are entitled from the chemical firm (and its insurers) for all forgone earnings and medical expenses associated with the acute injury.[46] The 100 percent recovery for these social costs is presented, for innocent bystanders and consumers, respectively, in columns 2 and 3 of table 10-1. However, the average liability awards in death cases—including both court awards and out-of-court-settlements—is under $220,000,[47] which is less than 10 percent of the associated social cost, even assuming a value for a statistical life of only $3,000,000.

Presumably, successful tort claimants are fully compensated by the chemical firm for the social costs of impairment and pain and suffering brought about by the acute injury. Nevertheless, the fact that average liability awards in death cases are more than an order of magnitude below their social cost casts doubt on the comprehensiveness of impairment and pain and suffering awards, which—like the valuation of loss of life—

45. Note that these two types of claimants are not treated as equivalent in subsequent analysis.

46. Both innocent bystanders and consumers may also sustain property damage as the result of an acute chemical accident. We assume claimants receive full recovery for these damages, but, to avoid unnecessary complications, we have not included them in the ensuing analysis.

47. The average awards in death cases were derived from both court awards and out-of-court settlements in product liability suits concluded in 1977. The source of the figure (as reported in Viscusi 1988, 173) is Insurance Services Office 1977, 113, adjusted to reflect price increases to 1985 values using the consumer price index. (Unfortunately, the ISO study has not been updated, and other data sources, such as Jury Verdict Research, Inc., 1991, are biased upward because they do not include out-of-court settlements.)

might be considered somewhat subjective.[48] Thus one might reasonably anticipate that juries which award successful claimants less than 10 percent of the death benefits that economic research suggests they should will correspondingly award less than full impairment and pain and suffering damages, and perhaps substantially less.[49] Because of their subjectivity, we grudgingly retain the 100 percent figures but accompany them in table 10-1 with a question mark to reflect our doubts.

Even assuming 100 percent recovery of impairment and pain and suffering costs, the chemical firm's compensatory payments are less than 40 percent of the social costs arising from acute injuries. The reason is that fatal injuries make up such a large share—at least 70 percent, under conservative assumptions—of the total social costs of acute injuries.[50] If

48. However, as mentioned earlier, Viscusi and Moore (1987) have derived willingness-to-pay estimates for pain and suffering and impairment that exceed the pecuniary losses from injury by 10 to 50 percent.

49. One possibility, admittedly untested, is that juries award damages predominantly on the basis of pecuniary losses. That would explain the considerable undercompensation—relative to social cost—in death awards: juries are basing damages primarily on the casualty's discounted future earnings. If that is so, juries are likely to seriously undercompensate impairment losses as well, by treating them as workers' compensation does, as disability benefits for future loss of earning capacity. In that case, the impairment itself and its nonwork consequences would go largely uncompensated. Evidence concerning the magnitude of compensation payments for disability and impairment, being developed by Hensler, promises to shed some light on this matter. Telephone conversation on August 14, 1990, with D. Hensler, Rand Corporation.

50. Data from the Insurance Services Office 1977, 113, indicate that fatal injuries, while comprising only 3.6 percent of the death award cases, account for 18.8 percent of total liability award payments. But, as previously shown, those death awards represent less than 10 percent of the corresponding social cost. Even taking an upper bound of 10 percent, implying the value of a statistical life of $2,200,000, fatal injuries constitute 70 percent of total social injury costs, of which the chemical firm's compensatory payments make up less than 40 percent. For a value of loss of life of $3,000,000, fatal injuries' share of total social injury costs rises to above 75 percent, and the chemical firm's compensatory payments falls to below 30 percent of total social costs. For a value of a statistical life of $5,000,000—a recent lower-bound estimate derived from significantly improved fatality statistics (Moore and Viscusi 1988b)—fatal injuries account for 84 percent of total social injury costs, and the chemical firm's compensatory payments cover less than 20 percent of total social injury costs.

Two possible qualifications in the use of the Insurance Services Office data come to mind. First, the data were derived from product liability cases of all types. Possibly the composition of tort suits involving acute injuries from chemical products and those involving innocent bystanders will be significantly different, but we have no reason to believe that is the case. Of course, insofar as tort suits for acute chemical injuries consist of a larger percentage of fatalities, the share of total injury costs covered by the chemical firm's compensatory payments will decline even further. The second qualification is that liability awards have increased since 1977. (For example, Jury Verdict Research, Inc., 1991, found that the average jury award for a wrongful death of an adult male in 1989 was $1,057,612, but that

impairment and pain and suffering costs are, in fact, incomplete, then the chemical firm's compensatory payments constitute an even smaller share of the social costs of acute injuries.

Compensatory damages are not the only tort costs borne by the chemical firm. Successful claimants may be awarded punitive damages from the firm.[51] On average, trial awards for punitive damages are equal to approximately 25 percent of compensatory damages.[52] But on the basis of very rough estimates, post-trial appeals and settlements reduce punitive damage awards to from 8 to 19 percent of compensatory damages.[53] Using the larger figure of 19 percent and recalling that compensatory damages paid by the chemical firm constitute only 40 percent of acute injury costs, we gauge that punitive damages paid by the firm are equal to approximately 8 percent of acute injury costs.

Chemical firms also incur transaction costs to defend against tort claims. Here we include transaction costs for all claims filed against the chemical firm, both successful and unsuccessful (from the view of the claimant).

---

figure is not representative of all classes of fatality or all liability cases, since settlements are not included. Moreover, the figure will usually include medical expenses incurred by the victim before death. All these factors will tend to bias the reported figure upward relative to the true average.) However, even if awards for fatal injuries were to rise to $1,000,000, assuming the value of a statistical life is $5,000,000, the chemical firm's compensatory payments would still constitute less than 40 percent of total injury costs. To offset the possibility of this effect, we have used a very low value of loss of life in the text.

The reader can verify the preceding results by applying these two formulas: (1) $C = P_I + mP_D$, and (2) $S = (P_I + P_D)/C$, where P_I is total nondeath compensation; P_D is total death compensation; m is the ratio of the true social cost of statistical deaths to death compensation; C is the total social cost of acute injuries (fatalities included); and S is the share of social injury costs covered by the chemical firm's compensatory payments.

51. Recall, however, that punitive damages are, strictly speaking, not intended as an offset to the social costs of injury, but as a punishment for the firm's outrageous conduct.

52. This estimate was reported in U.S. General Accounting Office 1989, 29, based on the GAO's study of product liability lawsuits. Punitive damages are rarely awarded. A Rand Corporation study concluded, "Punitive damages continue to be rarely assessed in personal injury cases, and most frequently are assessed against defendants who were found to have intentionally harmed plaintiffs. In most of these cases the damages were modest." Peterson, Sarma, and Shanley 1987.

53. U.S. General Accounting Office 1989, 45–47, indicates that after appeal the defendant's damages were reduced to 76 percent of the trial award in cases without punitive damages and to 40 percent of the trial award in cases with punitive damages. Furthermore, in the second instance, almost all of the reduction came from punitive damages. From this information alone, we can calculate, crudely, that punitive damages amount to only 12 percent of compensatory damages after appeal. However, the relative size of the appealed to the not-appealed cases and of the appealed punitive damage cases to those without (information not fully obtainable from the data) could alter the percentage somewhat in either direction.

Legal fees and expenses have been estimated to equal about 30 percent of compensatory damages, which translates to about 12 percent of acute injury costs.[54] The chemical firm also bears the opportunity cost of management and staff time spent in contesting claims, other nonlegal expenses, and claims-processing costs (including insurance claims-processing costs) for lawsuits. These have been estimated to be 22 percent of compensatory damages, which is equivalent to about 9 percent of the social cost of acute chemical injuries.[55]

Taking into account compensatory damages, punitive damages, and all transaction costs associated with defending against tort claims, the total costs borne by the chemical firm—for claims filed by innocent bystanders and for product liability claims—constitute just below 70 percent of the social cost of acute chemical injuries. Even this estimate may be too high. It depends on a fairly low value of loss of life and full recovery by the claimant for impairment and pain and suffering. And it ignores the effects of statutory caps on awards and award exclusions (such as punitive damages), which serve to limit the chemical firm's payout even further.[56]

EMPLOYEES OF OTHER FIRMS. Finally, the claimant may be a worker employed by another firm (a firm other than the chemical firm) that uses the chemical firm's product in its business activities. If so, the percentage of the social costs of acute injuries incurred by the chemical firm depends on which of three actions the claimant takes.

First, the worker may file a workers' compensation claim. In that event, the costs borne by the employer are identical to those calculated

54. Kakalik and Pace (1986, 115) calculate that the defendant's ratio of average legal fees and expenses to average compensation, for organizations in nonautomobile tort litigation, is 32 percent in state courts and 18 percent in federal courts. Since most litigation takes place in state courts, a composite 30 percent ratio seems appropriate. Data in U. S. General Accounting Office 1989, 53, suggest a ratio of about 33 percent for product liability cases settled by trial verdicts. Since most product liability claims were reported as being resolved in pretrial settlements, which required much lower legal fees and expenses, an adjustment to 30 percent is not unwarranted. Third-party claims by innocent bystanders might have lower legal fees because the question of comparative negligence is not at issue; however, that effect is largely negated by the fact that the purchase of the chemical product comes with an implied warranty, breach of which gives rise to a cause of action.

55. See Kakalik and Pace 1986, 74, for summary data from nonautomobile tort suits.

56. The effect of caps and exclusions for particular award categories, however, is surely diminished somewhat by the ability of the jury to shift benefits it feels are justified (but statutorily barred) to another award category. Thus, for example, the statutory exclusion of punitive damages may in some cases simply result in inflated pain and suffering awards. Furthermore, some juries may increase the size of the award to offset (their expectation of) the legal fees a sympathetic plaintiff must pay.

earlier for chemical firms whose employees file workers' compensation claims. The only difference is that the employer of the injured worker, rather than the chemical firm, bears those costs.

Second, the worker may file both a workers' compensation claim through his employer and a product liability suit against the chemical firm whose product caused the job-related injury. (Although workers' compensation statutes prohibit workers from filing tort claims against their employers, they are not barred from bringing a tort action against a "third party," such as the chemical firm.) The situation regarding the chemical firm is no different from the product liability claims just analyzed. The total burden on the chemical firm and the employer, however, is normally less than the sum of its parts. Under typical workers' compensation arrangements, a worker who recovers in full from a third party and also receives workers' compensation awards must reimburse the employer for associated payments made by the employer into workers' compensation.[57] Nevertheless, both the employer and the chemical firm bear part of the social cost associated with the worker's acute injury. The employer still pays the worker a risk premium to perform more hazardous work, while the chemical firm incurs product liability costs constituting about 70 percent of the social costs of the acute injury.

Third, the worker may file only a product liability suit against the chemical firm whose product caused the job-related injury. However, this situation leads to the same shared burden between the chemical firm and the employer as when the worker files both for workers' compensation and tort damages. The employer still pays ex ante expected injury damages in the form of wage risk premiums, and the chemical firm incurs liability costs amounting to about 70 percent of the social costs of acute injuries.

We note, for subsequent analysis of deterrence effects, that while the chemical firm's liability burden is less than the total social costs arising from the acute injury, the costs incurred by industry as a whole theoretically could exceed total injury costs when the worker collects from third parties. That outcome, however, is subject to the earlier qualifications about whether tort liability actually supplies complete compensation for impairment and pain and suffering and whether wage premiums provide full reimbursement for residual risk.

---

57. In addition, a few states allow third parties successfully sued by workers under product liability to seek proportionate reimbursement from a *negligent* employer. The effect of this legal option is clearly to reduce the chemical firm's burden. But because this situation is the exception rather than the rule, we do not include it in the subsequent analysis.

TRUE AND FALSE POSITIVES; TRUE AND FALSE NEGATIVES. Up to this point, analysis of the burden of acute chemical injuries borne by the chemical firm has assumed that the firm's payout was purely for the acute injuries it caused. We now examine that assumption.

For employees of the chemical firm or employees of other firms seeking recovery for job-related acute chemical injuries, one can argue that workers' compensation awards are almost always based on valid claims. Acute chemical injuries immediately manifest themselves, and the links from the acute injury to the workplace chemical product or activity to the *employer* are apparent. Some workers may exaggerate the effects of an injury, but that possibility is offset by the fact that others choose not to or are encouraged by their employers not to file a claim at all.

For reasons similar to those just mentioned, tort claims seeking recovery for acute chemical injuries filed by innocent bystanders are generally meritorious, though here the patent connections are from the acute injury to the injury-causing product or activity to the *chemical firm* responsible. The same logic applies with almost equal force to product liability suits filed by employees of other firms or consumers claiming acute chemical injuries. The main complicating factor in a product liability action is the need to determine which liability criteria are relevant to the specific facts in the case and then to apply those criteria judiciously. But we know of no evidence to suggest that the courts have failed in carrying out this charge in cases involving acute chemical injuries or, more generally, that meritless claims for acute chemical injuries are a problem.

Two elements of chemical firm costs arising out of tort liability also need to be addressed within the context of meritorious claims. The first is punitive damages. On the surface, it is difficult not to acknowledge that the magnitude of jury awards for punitive damages is often unpredictable and perhaps occasionally inconsistent from case to case. At the same time, evidence exists that appellate courts have been generally successful in correcting the errors made in the lower court and in narrowing the degree of unpredictability in punitive damages.[58] Moreover, one must remember that the immediate objective of punitive damages is common justice, including punishment for socially reprehensible conduct. Ques-

---

58. See, for example, U.S. General Accounting Office 1989, 47. However, the subjective nature of what constitutes socially unacceptable conduct and what punishment is appropriate in response makes an objective benchmark difficult to define, much less apply. Therefore, what may be characterized as an "error" on appeal might, on occasion, be more accurately described as substituting the appellate court's values and preferences for the jury's.

tions of efficient deterrence are, at best, of secondary importance where punitive damages are concerned.[59]

The second cost element to be addressed is transaction costs. It is possible, though inaccurate, to argue that having the chemical firm (the defendant) bear its own legal costs and other tort-related expenses for the cases it wins represents a type of false positive.[60] The flaw in this reasoning is that before the verdict by the court, the success or failure of the plaintiff's claim is not certain or known by the parties to the suit.[61] Transaction costs are merely the price one pays to obtain social justice: they are the costs of using the tort system to obtain a just decision rather than costs to be decided through the tort process.

The Degree of Deterrence

As mentioned earlier, of the several objectives of the liability system, deterrence is the most relevant to concerns about stimulating the adoption or development of safer products and processes. The liability costs stemming from chemical harm provide a signal to the chemical firm and to other private actors to engage in hazard prevention activities.[62]

The deterrence effects of the liability system need to be examined with great care. From an economic perspective, optimal deterrence is achieved by the internalization of all social costs of chemical production and use. In general, overdeterrence may arise if costs that exceed or are unrelated to the social costs are imposed on private actors. However, we argue that

59. By analogy, one would not excuse convicted criminals from imprisonment just because they would be more productive out of jail.

60. A parallel argument for the successful defendant would be equally wrong. In principle, however, one might argue somewhat differently: that the high transaction costs deter injury victims from filing valid tort claims and result in false negatives. In the case of acute chemical injuries, for which establishing causation is usually not an issue, such arguments would appear to be groundless.

61. By analogy, the risk premium workers receive for undertaking a hazardous job is an ex ante mechanism for reducing uncertainty. If analyzed only after the job is done, however, one might conclude, again incorrectly, that the injured workers were undercompensated and the uninjured workers overcompensated. The point is that at the time the risk premium was paid, it was not known which of the workers would be injured.

62. This is one of the essential lessons to be derived from the earlier examination of the innovation process. Acquiring information and engaging in innovative search are costly to the firm. The uncertainty of liability costs attracts the attention of management and redirects its activities to exploit profitable safety opportunities that arise from the avoidance of these tort system costs. Liability awards not only bring to the attention of industry the advantages of minimizing the hazardous effects of technology but also raise the importance of safety in technological planning in general.

the imposition of punitive damages should not be confused with over-deterrence, because those damages serve a moral and symbolic function, satisfying a need for just punishment of wrongdoers. Good-faith and knowledgeable chemical firms have little to fear from punitive damages, because it is highly unlikely that such damages would be imposed on them. Nevertheless, the specter of punitive damages not only encourages good-faith industrial activity but also prods the firm to gain the knowledge required to assess the risks of its technology.

Many factors influence the firm's response to the expected value of economic costs associated with chemical harm, such as the role of insurance, the extent to which the firm produces a diversified mix of products, and the desire of the firm to maintain its reputation as a good corporate citizen.[63] Table 10-2 presents some possible scenarios for the firm under which it feels varying degrees of motivation to engage in hazard-reducing activity, including the search for safer products and processes.

Firms that are fully insured for worker injuries through workers' compensation have little incentive to engage in preventive activities, beyond an interest in reducing the wage premium for risk that workers demand; the only exceptions are those rare cases where compensation premiums are a high percentage of the cost of doing business and the firm is merit-rated.[64] The same is true for injuries to consumers for chemical firms insured by product liability insurance,[65] and for injuries to others for chemical firms insured through enterprise liability insurance. Through its risk-spreading properties, insurance shifts the total social costs of chemical damage away from the firm, causing underdeterrence. As regards

63. One important factor, not usually relevant for *acute* chemical injuries (except perhaps in Bhopal-sized accidents), is the size of the chemical firm's assets in relation to the magnitude of its tort liability burden and the ease with which the firm can evade that burden by seeking bankruptcy protection.

64. Only the very largest firms, representing about 15 percent of employees, are self-insured. (However, many of the larger chemical firms fall into this category.) The remaining firms are either class rated, based on industrywide safety and health performance, or experience rated, which is a class rating adjusted by the individual firm's safety and health record. Payments by these firms into workers' compensation are only loosely related to the costs their employees' injuries and illnesses impose on the system. See Ashford and Caldart 1991, 228.

65. However, the fact that product liability insurance has become exceedingly expensive in recent years, and often become unavailable, has forced many firms to self-insure. These consequences of the insurance "crisis" have generally served to stimulate risk-prevention incentives (though they may be accompanied by some efficiency losses as well). See, for example, Abraham 1986, 14–16, and Ashford, Moran, and Stone 1989, V-6.

Table 10-2. *Motivation for Developing or Adopting Safer Products and Processes*[a]

| | Economic costs from compensating damage awards | | | | |
| | Expected losses | | Reasonably likely upper bound to losses for self-insured firms with few products or hazards (risk averse) | Punitive damages | Likely overall incentives |
Item	All firms	Self-insured firms with many products or hazards		Reputation	
Under insurance						
Workers' compensation (workers)	--		$(+)$[b]	+	−
Product liability (consumers)	$(-)$[c]			+	+	+
Enterprise (others)	$(-)$[d]			+	+	+
Without insurance						
Workers	+	+ +	+	+	+ +
Consumers	+	+ +	+	+	+ +
Others	+	+ +	+	+	+ +

a. -- denotes great underdeterrence; −denotes some underdeterrence; + denotes slight deterrence; + + denotes modest deterrence, but still less than optimal.
b. Available as a surcharge in a minority of jurisdictions.
c. Possibly unavailable or very expensive.
d. Possibly available for injuries; unavailable for chronic disease.

worker injuries or enterprise liability, the incentives that do exist for insured firms are probably directed to limiting the effects of an accident once it occurs (such as providing fire extinguishers) rather than to preventing it in the first place.[66] Furthermore, minimal loss prevention advice originates with the insurance carriers, who usually lack the requisite technical and scientific expertise to suggest technological changes

66. However, some, though incomplete, deterrence is provided even if the chemical firm has product liability insurance, since many consumers recognize and value safety features and are willing to pay extra for them. Similarly, chemical firms with workers' compensation and enterprise insurance are still motivated to prevent safety hazards that threaten to damage or destroy their own property (though that is usually insured as well). Finally, the terms of most insurance policies contain some deterrence features of their own, such as coinsurance and deductibles, but these clearly are of secondary importance.

Figure 10-1. *Probability of Court Awards and Resources Devoted to Prevention by the Risk-Averse Firm*

Probability of expenditures

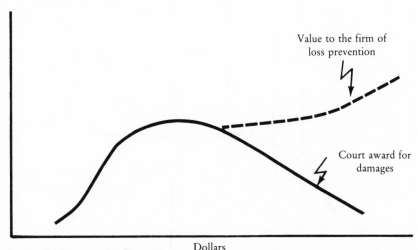

Value to the firm of loss prevention

Court award for damages

Dollars

in chemical products and processes.[67]

As for chemical firms that manufacture many chemical products, the expected value of economic losses due to chemical harm to workers, consumers, and bystanders provides a degree of deterrence, at least insofar as the firms are not insured and must self-insure. For the uninsured chemical firm that manufactures few products, it is the reasonably likely upper bound of a loss, rather than the expected value of the loss, that drives the firm's preventive activities. This extra incentive reflects the risk averseness of those firms against business disruption and sudden catastrophic economic loss. Such firms will go an extra measure to prevent chemical harm, but that should not be confused with overdeterrence. Rather, when firms are insured, there is underdeterrence.

In figure 10-1, the smooth curve depicts the *hypothetical* probability

67. "Insurers have little knowledge of the loss-prevention or loss-protection technologies available to the insured chemical handlers. Interviews with underwriters reveal little interest in developing their own knowledge base about either technologies or losses." (Katzman 1988, 86.) But the recent development of risk retention groups, group captives, and other user-financed insurance mechanisms promises to improve risk management skills and to provide a payoff for the firms that participate. See Ashford, Moran, and Stone 1989, V-5, V-6.

Figure 10-2. *Probability of Court Awards and Resources Devoted to Prevention by the Risk-Averse Firm (Illustrating the Effects of Insurance and Caps on Awards)*

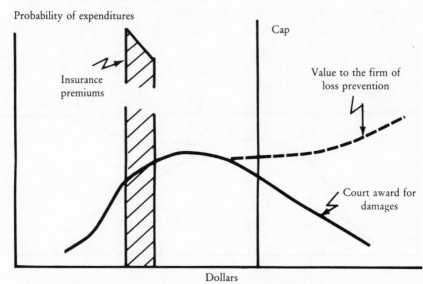

of an award as a function of its size. The value to the firm of avoiding damage is identical with this curve for small awards. As awards increase in size, the risk-averse firm will increasingly value risk reduction and will spend increasing amounts to avoid liability, as shown in the dashed curve.[68] The capping of awards (shown as a solid vertical line in figure 10-2) or risk spreading through insurance (where premiums are collected, as shown by the hatched area) decreases the risk averseness of the firm and, hence, expenditures for developing or adopting safer products and processes.

Attempts to avoid liability claims (with or without the possibility of punitive damages) may drive either an uninsured or an insured firm to take special efforts for prevention. If so, the firm is responding not only to its expected economic losses but also to the value *it* places on maintaining a good reputation. Poor corporate images are avoided by good corporate citizens. Expenditures incurred by firms to develop safer products or processes may exceed the expected value of losses for not doing

---

68. One possible functional relationship is:

$$V = px \, (d + k_1 d^2 + \ldots + k_n d^{n+1}),$$

where V is the value to the firm of avoiding damage costs; p is the probability of damage; and d is the severity of damage. The firm's risk averseness is reflected in the higher-order terms of this expression.

so or even the reasonably likely upper bound of a loss. That too should not be attributed to overdeterrence, since the firm *values* the avoidance of liability beyond the immediate or monetizable economic costs. Similarly, risk-averse firms that decide not to market or use unsafe products or processes may do so because they value the avoidance of liability risk more than the net profits that might have been enjoyed. If the firms that decide not to market unsafe products or to use unsafe processes do not have the intellectual resources to develop new technology, they may suffer economically. However, other firms—notably new entrants—may develop new technologies and profit from them.

As we determined in the previous analysis, the liability system does not impose on the chemical firm even the expected value of the social costs of acute chemical injuries. Rather, it provides an underdeterrence for the development of safer products and processes. But though there is underdeterrence from an economic perspective, the deterrence that does occur because of prospective liability tends to promote safer technologies for those firms that value "doing the right thing."[69] Ensuring that the economic costs associated with acute chemical hazards are fully internalized would create even greater incentives.

Safety and Innovative Performance Related to Tort Liability

Although, as we have just concluded, tort liability provides inadequate deterrence in the area of acute chemical injuries, the tort system—in many cases, in combination with regulation—has stimulated the development of safer products and processes. For example, consumer products with potentially explosive containers (such as some former drain cleaners) have been removed from the market and replaced by safer alternatives, and almost all chemical products contain detailed warnings and instructions about their safe use so as to inform and protect the consumer.

The evidence of liability-induced chemical innovations is probably greatest in the area of process technology, but most of those innovations are incremental (though valuable) ones, and because of underdeterrence

69. For these firms, liability operates much like regulation, in the sense that factors beyond economic considerations stimulate them to engage in a search for better products or processes. For example, an impending ban on a product encourages certain firms to develop substitute products. In the context of tort suits, the possibility of punitive damages or a damage to reputation also stimulates the search for new products and processes, even though the economic factors associated with those damages might not in and of themselves stimulate a search for new products.

many have not been widely adopted as yet. Examples of incremental process innovations include the removal or reduction of toxic chemicals used in the manufacturing process, improved chemical containment technology, and the development of user-friendly technology that can tolerate less than ideal human performance without initiating a chemical accident.

Partly in response to the Bhopal disaster—both because of the risk of massive tort liability and because of the regulatory activities that were themselves initiated partly in response to what happened in Bhopal[70]— chemical firms and secondary manufacturers have reduced the amount of hazardous chemicals they store on site and, in some instances, the amounts they use. For example, at a plant in Texas that makes methylene di-paraphenylene isocyanate, Dow Chemical Company has reduced by 95 percent its inventory of phosgene, one of the deadly gases released in Bhopal. At its New Jersey facility, Hoffmann–La Roche has totally eliminated the use of phosgene by switching to ethyl chloroformate, which reacts similarly but is not as toxic, and PPG Industries has recently developed carbonyldiimidazole, a benign phosgene substitute that can be used in the synthesis of pharmaceutical products. Similarly, Monsanto modified an acrylonitrile process to remove hydrogen cyanide storage (in tanks with a capacity of 375,000 pounds); now the hydrogen cyanide is consumed as feedstock by units that produce lactonitrile and other materials. Monsanto also substituted the less-volatile aqueous ammonia at atmospheric pressure for pressurized anhydrous ammonia at its plant in Dalton, Georgia. As a final example, Dupont removed several chlorine-filled rail cars formerly parked at a siding at its plant in Edgemoor, Delaware; chlorine is brought in only when it is needed.[71]

An example of improved chemical-containment technology is the use, by Monsanto and Hercules, Inc., of 150-pound and 300-pound cylinders to store chlorine rather than the conventional 10,000-pound tanks. Similarly, Hoffmann–La Roche shifted from 12,000–15,000 gallon tanks to 2,000 gallon tanks.[72] Also, there have been significant innovations involving chlorine valves on chlorine railcars—such as corrosion resistance and a pneumatically operated, automatic-shutoff mechanism—but these

70. The most prominent example is title III (the Emergency Planning and Community Right to Know Act of 1986) of the Superfund Amendments and Reauthorization Act of 1986 (SARA), which has imposed significant reporting requirements on industry concerning the identity and amounts of hazardous materials stored, used, and released and has created several emergency planning mechanisms as well.

71. For further discussion about the preceding examples, see Zanetti 1986.

72. Zanetti 1986, 27–28.

valve design improvements have only rarely been adopted in the United States.[73] Examples of user-friendly technological developments include spiral-wound gaskets (to replace fiber gaskets), expansion loops (to replace bellows), articulated arms (to replace hoses), and bolted joints (to replace quick-release couplings).[74] Finally, an example of a radical process innovation is Union Carbide's development in 1977 of a safer technology for manufacturing linear, low-density polyethylene. The Union Carbide technology is capable of functioning as a "swing" reactor, shifting to the manufacture of high-density polyethylene—the product being manufactured at the Phillips Petroleum plant in Pasadena, Texas, at the time of the 1989 explosion. The Phillips technology is a low-pressure, slurry-phase polyolefin process; the Union Carbide technology is a low-pressure, gas-phase fluidized-bed process that does not contain polymer settling legs, which were the site of and a necessary condition for the Phillips explosion.[75] Again, the issue is the rate of adoption of these technological improvements in safety, which greater deterrence would promote.

Tort Liability and Chronic Chemical Illnesses

Our analysis of the effects of tort liability for chronic chemical diseases parallels the tasks performed in the preceding analysis: an estimation of the chemical firm's payout for chronic diseases relative to the social costs of those diseases; an assessment of the amount of deterrence created by these chemical firm liabilities; and an evaluation of the deterrence effects of liability for chronic chemical diseases on chemical safety and innovation. Because much of the groundwork was provided in the evaluation of liability for acute injuries, the following analysis is greatly simplified.

Recall that chronic disease may develop weeks to years after initial exposure to a toxic chemical. Examples of chemical-caused disease are cancer of all organ systems; respiratory diseases including emphysema; reproductive system damage including sterility, impotence, miscarriages, and birth defects; heart disease; and neurotoxicity. Many of these chronic

73. Hunter 1988.
74. See Kletz 1989, 18.
75. Several other factors have been suggested as probable causes of the Phillips explosion, including the use of inexperienced subcontractors, faulty maintenance procedures, and defective mitigation equipment. Nevertheless, that type of explosion would not have been possible in the Union Carbide reactor. See Mark 1986, 425–54; U.S. Department of Labor 1990; MacKerron 1989.

diseases caused by chemical exposures are considered "ordinary diseases of life." Hence, unless there is strong epidemiologic evidence linking exposure with excess incidence of these diseases in the workplace, in a specific geographic area, or associated with a particular consumer use, causation is extremely difficult to establish in either the tort or administrative compensation systems now in operation.

Sometimes chronic diseases constitute so-called signature diseases, which are so rare that, as a practical matter, their incidence can be explained only by exposure to a specific chemical. Examples are angiosarcoma (liver cancer), associated with vinyl chloride exposure, and mesothelioma, associated with asbestos exposure. In some instances the presence of the chemical causing an ordinary disease of life can be ascertained, for example lead in blood and other tissues, or DNA-adduct formation that is chemically specific.[76] In these cases chemical causation may be unequivocally established as a result of biological monitoring.

Chemical Firm Payout Relative to Social Costs

Consistent with the preceding analysis of acute chemical injuries, we evaluate the chemical firm's payout relative to the social costs of chronic diseases in two steps: we first estimate the firm's payout relative to social cost for successful claims and then assess whether, in an appropriate sense, the chemical firm was responsible for, or caused, the diseases for which it incurs costs (and conversely, whether the firm did not cause diseases for which it does not incur costs).

SOCIAL COSTS AND SUCCESSFUL CLAIMS. The portion of the social costs of chronic chemical injuries borne by the chemical firm can be most easily evaluated when compared with the firm's payout for acute chemical injuries. Subject to three important qualifications, the costs incurred by the chemical firm *in cases where the claimant is successful* are approximately the same for acute chemical injuries and chronic chemical diseases (of a given severity).[77]

76. Ashford and others 1990.
77. We are able to dismiss a potential fourth qualification. Because chronic diseases typically arise years or decades after the chemical exposure, it seems appropriate to discount the associated damages to their present value. For example, Moore and Viscusi perform this procedure in calculating the value of life for long-term risks (Moore and Viscusi 1988a; Viscusi and Moore 1989). But since chemical firms are able to defer payment of damages until after the disease manifests itself, these costs must also be discounted by a similar amount. Therefore, for purposes of evaluating deterrence effects, the two discounting procedures cancel each other and need not be performed.

The first qualification is that, because of the difficulty of establishing causation, chronic disease claims are much more likely to be contested and the legal effort required during litigation will usually be much greater than for acute injury claims. As a result, the chemical firm's transaction costs related to chronic disease claims will be larger, even for signature disease claims, which usually have the best chance of establishing causation. For example, legal expenses in workers' compensation death claims based on exposure to asbestos have been estimated as 14 percent of compensation payments, and defendants' legal costs in asbestos product liability suits have been estimated as 58 percent of payments to plaintiffs.[78] Although we do not have comparable data for the average disease claim, evidence from workers' compensation gives some indication of the associated transaction costs. Employers are six times as likely to contest a disease-related claim as they are an injury-related one. Those disease-related claims in which compensation is eventually paid are often hotly contested; indeed, 60 percent of such awards were initially denied.[79]

The second qualification applies only to disease-related cases in which the claimant is a worker. The risk-compensating wage premium that workers receive will typically be smaller for chronic chemical hazards than for acute chemical hazards for several reasons: the etiology of many chemically related diseases is still unknown or not well understood; many of these chronic hazards are not widely publicized in the workplace;[80] and the chronic disease consequences of chemical exposure are normally not obvious, because they are not immediate (since the latency period between chemical exposure and manifestation of disease may last decades). Presumably for these reasons econometric estimates of risk-compensating wage differentials are invariably based exclusively on acute-injury data. Some, albeit imperfect, evidence of the small risk premium workers receive for chronic chemical hazards exists for one class of asbestos victims, asbestos insulators, for whom 44 percent of deaths during 1967–76 were due to asbestos-related disease. The premium for risk they received was estimated as approximately 4.5 percent of their wages, which over their lifetime had a

78. Boden and Jones 1987, 339; Kakalik and others 1983, viii. Note that most of these asbestos claims involve non-signature diseases, such as lung cancer.

79. Viscusi 1988, 169.

80. However, Viscusi and O'Connor (1984) suggest that, on the basis of survey evidence measuring the effectiveness of chemical hazard labeling, workers have a widespread awareness of many of the chemical risks confronting them.

present value of under $10,000 (about $15,000 in 1985 dollars).[81] These figures suggest that the total risk-compensating wage differential received by asbestos insulators per statistical life was only $34,000 (in 1985 dollars).

The third qualification concerns the possibility that the chemical firm will be unable to pay disease-related damages—a situation that normally does not arise for acute chemical injuries. Two characteristics of chronic diseases from chemical exposure account for the difference. First, the potentially lengthy latency period between chemical exposure and manifestation of the disease raises the prospect that the chemical firm will no longer be in business by the time a claim is filed. Second, chronic chemical hazards are capable of affecting a very large number of people. Even if the chemical firm is still in business, it may not have set aside sufficient funds, purchased sufficient insurance coverage, or have sufficient assets to cover the flood of tort claims, possibly totaling billions of dollars. The ease with which firms can seek protection from tort claims through reorganization under federal bankruptcy laws further diminishes the damages that claimants are able to collect.[82]

What is the net effect of these qualifications on the share of chronic injury costs borne by the chemical firm in cases where the claimant receives compensation? First consider employee claims through workers' compensation. Even among those cases of occupational disease in the United States for which workers' compensation is provided, the average award is only an estimated 13 percent of the average wage loss caused by occupational disease.[83] After increasing this amount by an additional 14 percent to reflect the cost of contesting claims, the chemical firm's total costs incurred through workers' compensation for chronic disease are still only 15 percent of the associated wage loss, and therefore no more than approximately 1 to 2 percent of the total social costs of those diseases.

81. See Barth 1983. However, Boden and Jones (1987, 337) suggest that Barth's estimates may not be representative of the wage premium for chronic chemical hazards. They propose that the low figure was not due to complete lack of knowledge about asbestos risks, since the workers in question were part of active health studies. They argue, rather, that the cause was imperfect competition in the industry. The market power of the insulators' union raised wages (ignoring risk) 15 to 30 percent above those for comparable workers. The resulting lack of comparable job opportunities at an elevated wage level induced the insulators to work with asbestos without receiving a significant risk premium.

82. When questions of insolvency arise, so that the firm's available assets must be apportioned among existing and potential claimants, one consequence, of course, is to drive up transaction costs. The bankruptcy filings of several major asbestos manufacturers is one reason the transaction costs for asbestos-related claims are so large.

83. U.S. Department of Labor 1980, 4.

For tort claims, evidence from asbestos cases, though not conclusive, suggests the costs borne by the chemical firm due to chronic disease. For product liability claims involving asbestos worker deaths, the average mean payment for worker deaths during 1967–76 was approximately $100,000 (in 1985 dollars); the payment level increased dramatically during that period, reaching a peak for 1975–76 deaths of approximately $125,000 (in 1985 dollars).[84] If we use the peak figure, and increase it by 58 percent to reflect the defendant's legal costs and by another 22 percent to reflect other transaction costs,[85] the total tort costs borne by the chemical firm in asbestos-related deaths is $225,000, or no more than 10 percent of the corresponding social cost.

Finally, suppose that both a workers' compensation claim and a tort claim are filed for an asbestos-related death and that, in addition, the chemical company bears the cost of the risk-compensating wage differential received, ex ante, by the worker. The average discounted value of workers' compensation payments involving asbestos worker deaths was $47,000 (in 1985 dollars);[86] increasing that amount by 14 percent for legal costs yields a total payout of $54,000 per claim. Adding the $225,000 per tort claim, the $54,000 per workers' compensation claim, and the $34,000 of risk premium received per asbestos worker (insulator) death yields a total cost of $313,000 borne by the chemical firm per *compensated* asbestos worker death, a sum that is no more than 5 to 15 percent of the corresponding social cost.

TRUE AND FALSE POSITIVES; TRUE AND FALSE NEGATIVES. The chief difference between chronic diseases and acute injuries, as reflected in the portion of total social costs borne by the chemical firm, resides not in the smaller average payout to successful claimants in chronic disease cases but in the the fact that most chronic diseases from chemical exposure are false negatives: the chemical firm responsible does not incur any liability costs at all.

Both direct and indirect evidence shows that the number of illnesses associated with chemical exposure is significant. In the early 1970s the

84. These figures are provided in Boden and Jones 1987, 334–35, in 1982 dollars; they were converted into 1985 dollars using the consumer price index. The Rand Corporation study of compensation received by asbestos victims in product liability claims reports that the average recovery for all such claims of asbestos-related disease and death is approximately $37,000, in 1985 dollars (Kakalik and others 1983). However, the composition of the health effects associated with this estimate is not known.

85. Kakalik and Pace 1986, 73.

86. These figures are provided in Boden and Jones 1987, 339, in 1982 dollars; they were adjusted to reflect price increases to 1985 values using the consumer price index.

Figure 10-3. *Indoor-Outdoor Cancer Risks*[a]

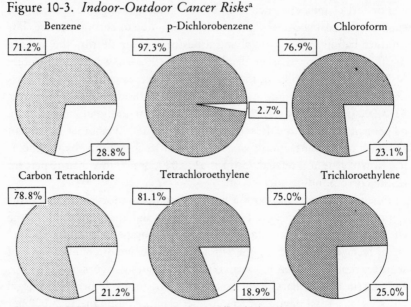

Source: Lance Wallace, Environmental Protection Agency, Office of Indoor Air.
a. The white area in each circle represents outdoor cancer risks; the darker area represents indoor cancer risks.

public health service estimated that there were as many as 100,000 deaths due to occupational disease and 390,000 cases of new occupational illnesses annually.[87] Although these figures were initially contested, independent evidence shows that the figures are essentially correct. In 1965, 27,000 cases of occupational disease were reported in California.[88] Extrapolated to the nation, this implies 336,000 cases of occupational disease annually. A recent study of occupational disease in New York state estimates conservatively that there are 5,000–7,000 deaths each year and at least 35,000 new cases of occupational disease.[89] Extrapolation to national figures yields a tenfold increase that, again, is in line with the estimates twenty years earlier.

Clearly occupational exposure is the greatest source of risk from exposure to chemicals. Lower-level exposures, but equally serious in terms of the number of people affected, are indoor exposures to chemicals in the home and office from consumer and industrial products and building materials. Figure 10-3 presents the relative percentages of the risk of cancer for six commonly found carcinogens, demonstrating that nonindustrial indoor air exposure is a greater risk than outdoor air exposure.

87. Pollack and Keimig 1987, 79.
88. Ashford 1976b, 3.
89. Markowitz and Landrigan 1989, 10.

Figure 10-4. *Synthetic Organic Chemical Production in the United States, 1945–85*

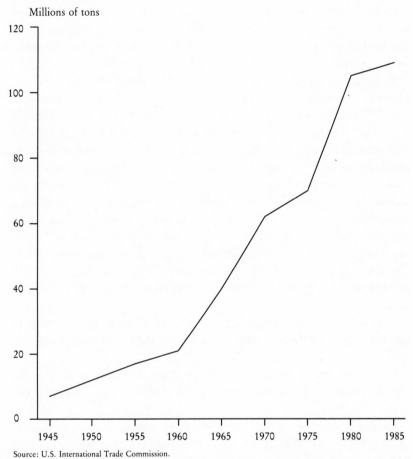

Millions of tons

Source: U.S. International Trade Commission.

Given that the production of synthetic organic chemicals has risen dramatically since World War II (see figure 10-4), it is no surprise that the number of chemically related chronic diseases has grown. For example, cancers of organ systems that can clearly be related to chemical exposure are on the rise.[90] Similarly, cases of asthma have experienced a sharp, unexplained growth in number. Finally, new problems related to multiple chemical sensitivities have been increasingly noted.[91] In sum, though the actual magnitude of occupationally and environmentally caused chronic disease is debatable, the problem is clearly significant.

90. See Schneiderman, Davis, and Wagener 1989; Vineas and Simonato 1991.
91. See, for example, Ashford and Miller 1991.

The requirement in both the workers' compensation system and in the courts—that it be more likely than not that a particular disease of a particular worker was caused by an exposure to a particular hazard—leaves most occupational and environmental disease uncompensated.[92] Of the 300,000 to 400,000 cases of new occupational diseases annually, only 3 percent are reported in workers' compensation records.[93] The Department of Labor concluded that only 5 percent of *serious* occupational disease received benefits through the workers' compensation system.[94] Cancer associated with occupational exposure is of special concern to workers. Table 10-3 lists the industrial processes causally associated with human cancer, and table 10-4 those cancers associated with occupational exposure. Conservative estimates attribute 4 percent of all cancer deaths in the United States to workplace exposures.[95] Using this figure, Caldart has estimated, however, that only one out of every seventy-nine occupational cancer victims in the United States receives workers' compensation, which represents a compensation rate of 1.3 percent.[96] Even in the case of asbestos—the most celebrated and obvious source of occupational disease—workers' compensation claims were filed for only 36 percent of asbestos-related deaths, and tort claims were filed for only 16 percent of those deaths.[97]

Combined with the preceding estimates of chemical firm payouts in successful chronic disease cases, these figures show that even for highly publicized signature diseases the firm incurs no more than 5 percent of the corresponding social cost. For the average non-signature disease, the chemical firm burden is less than 0.1 percent of the corresponding social cost.

Before examining the associated safety incentives, we need to dispose of one additional issue: false positives. Does the chemical firm incur nonnegligible liability costs for meritless cases—in which the claimant's chronic disease is unrelated to the chemical firm's products or activities? A review of successful claims—involving asbestos or Agent Orange primarily, or in rare instances industrial emissions (recall, not including hazardous wastes)—suggests not.

92. See, for example, Caldart 1985, 94–96.
93. Ashford 1976b, 11.
94. U. S. Department of Labor 1980, 3.
95. Doll and Peto 1981, 1194. Many researchers, however, have criticized the 4 percent figure for occupational cancer as being greatly underestimated. See, for example, Schmahl, Preussman, and Berger 1989; Axelson and Forrestiere 1989.
96. Caldart 1985, 94.
97. Boden and Jones 1987, 335–38.

Table 10-3. *Industrial Processes Causally Associated with Human Cancer*

| | Target organ | |
Exposure	Human[a]	Animal
Aluminum production	Lung, bladder (lymphoma, esophagus, stomach)	No relevant data
Auramine, manufacture of	Bladder	Mouse, rat: liver (auramine, technical grade)
Boot and shoe manufacture and repair	Leukemia, nasal sinus (bladder, digestive tract)	No relevant data
Coal gasification	Skin, lung, bladder	No relevant data
Coke production	Skin, lung, kidney	No relevant data
Furniture and cabinet making	Nasal sinus	Inadequate evidence (wood dust)
Hematite mining, underground, with exposure to radon	Lung	Inadequate evidence (hematite); rat, dog: lung (radon)
Iron and steel founding	Lung (digestive tract, genitourinary tract, leukemia	No relevant data
Isopropyl alcohol manufacture, strong-acid process	Nasal sinus (larynx)	Inadequate evidence (isopropyl oils)
Magenta, manufacture of	Bladder	Inadequate evidence (magenta)
Painters (occupational exposure as)	Lung (esophagus, stomach, bladder)	No relevant data
Rubber industry	Bladder, leukemia (lymphoma, lung, renal tract, digestive tract, skin, liver, larynx, brain, stomach)	Inadequate evidence

Source: Tomatis and others 1989, 796.
a. Suspected target organs in parentheses.

Table 10-4. *Chemicals and Groups of Chemicals Causally Associated with Human Cancer for Which Exposure Has Been Mostly Occupational*

	Target organ	
Exposure	Human[a]	Animal[a]
4-Aminobiphenyl	Bladder	Mouse: liver, bladder; rat: mammary gland, intestinal tract; rabbit, dog: bladder
Arsenic and arsenic compounds[b]	Skin, lung, (liver, hematopoietic system, gastrointestinal tract, kidney)	Mouse, hamster: (lung, respiratory tract)
Asbestos	lung, pleura, peritoneum, gastrointestinal tract, larynx	Rat: Lung, pleura, peritoneum (mesothelioma); mouse: peritoneum; hamster: pleura, peritoneum
Benzene	Leukemia	Mouse: lymphoma, lung, zymbal gland; rat: various sites, including zymbal gland, oral cavity
Benzidine	Bladder	Mouse: liver; rat: zymbal gland, mammary gland; hamster: liver; dog: bladder
Bis(chloromethyl) ether and chloromethyl methyl ether (technical grade)	Lung	Mouse: lung, local, skin; rat: lung, nasal cavity; hamster: (respiratory tract)

Chemical	Target organs (humans)	Animal evidence
Chromium compounds, hexavalent[b]	Lung (gastrointestinal tract)	Mouse: local; rat: lung
Coal-tars	Skin, lung (bladder)	Mouse: lung, skin, local; rat: lung; rabbit: skin
Coal-tar pitches	Skin, lung, bladder (gastrointestinal tract, leukemia)	Mouse: skin
Mineral oils, untreated and mildly treated	Skin (respiratory tract, bladder, gastrointestinal tract)	Mouse, rabbit, monkey: skin
Mustard gas (sulfur mustard)	Lung, larynx, pharynx	Mouse: (lung, local)
2-Naphthylamine	Bladder (liver)	Mouse: liver, lung; rat, hamster, dog, primates: bladder
Nickel and nickel compounds[b]	Nasal sinus, lung (larynx)	Mouse, rat, hamster, rabbit: local; rat: lung
Shale-oils	Skin (colon)	Mouse: lung, local; rabbit: local
Soots	Skin, lung	Mouse: skin, local; rat: lung
Talc containing asbestiform fibres	Lung (pleura)	Inadequate evidence
Vinyl chloride	Liver, lung, brain, lymphatic and hematopoietic system (gastrointestinal tract)	Mouse: liver, mammary gland, lung; rat: liver, zymbal gland; hamster: liver, skin, forestomach; rabbit: lung, skin

Source: Tomatis and others 1989, 797.
a. Suspected target organs in parentheses.
b. The evaluation of carcinogenicity to humans applies to the group of chemicals as a whole and not necessarily to all individual chemicals within the group.

Consider claims related to asbestos exposure, for example. Criticism of asbestos awards have been raised on two fronts. First, in *Beshada* v. *Johns-Manville Corporation*,[98] the New Jersey Supreme Court, adopting a strict liability standard, refused to consider the "state-of-the-art" defense raised by the defendant—that the defendant was not capable of warning the plaintiffs of the dangers of asbestos because those dangers could not have been known at the time of the plaintiffs' exposure. Holding the chemical firm liable for hazards that were truly unknowable fails to promote deterrence, since, as a matter of logic, the firm could not reasonably take precautions against unforeseen harm. However, evidence from other asbestos suits demonstrated that asbestos suppliers not only knew of the risks of asbestos but acted to suppress information about those risks.[99] Therefore, the state-of-the-art defense would properly have been rejected under a negligence standard.[100] The second criticism is that most smokers harmed by asbestos could have prevented the harm by not smoking.[101] One might therefore infer that smoking, not asbestos, was the likely cause of their subsequent disease. But such an inference would be unwarranted. With lung cancer, for example, the risks relative to a nonsmoker not exposed to asbestos (whose risk is normalized at 1) are 5 for a nonsmoking asbestos worker, approximately 10 for a smoker not exposed to asbestos, and approximately 50 for a smoking asbestos worker.[102] Therefore, for nonsmokers, asbestos exposure raises their risk of lung cancer fivefold (from 1 to 5); for smokers, asbestos exposure also raises their risk of lung cancer fivefold (from 10 to 50). Thus both smoking and nonsmoking asbestos workers can attribute 83 percent of their lung cancer cases to asbestos exposure.[103]

The Agent Orange case was a class action suit filed by U.S. soldiers exposed to the herbicide Agent Orange, which contains minute traces of the deadly poison dioxin. Hours before the trial was to begin, the claims against the seven chemical company defendants were settled for $180

98. *Beshada* v. *Johns-Manville Prods. Corp.*, 90 N.J. 191, 202, 447 A.2d 539, 545 (1982).

99. See, in particular, Brodeur 1985 and Page 1987, 1331–36, for a review of the evidence.

100. Furthermore, the New Jersey Supreme Court's holding that a defendant could be liable for failing to warn of an unknowable risk has been limited to asbestos cases and has not been adopted in other jurisdictions. Page 1990, 668.

101. Huber 1985b, 300.

102. Selikoff 1981, 23.

103. Note, therefore, that in terms of the optimal deterrence benchmark, only 83 percent of the associated harm should be borne by the chemical firm.

million.[104] Some have criticized the Agent Orange suit as meritless, arguing that there was no association between the plaintiffs' diseases and exposure to the herbicide. In fact, in approving the settlement, Judge Jack Weinstein candidly admitted that the plaintiffs probably could not have provided sufficient proof of causation to win their case in court.[105] Nevertheless, for two persuasive reasons the costs incurred by chemical firms in the Agent Orange case do not qualify as a false positive. First, the issue, in terms of the optimal-deterrence benchmark, is not whether the association between exposure to Agent Orange and a subsequent disease is sufficient to sustain a more-likely-than-not evidentiary standard, but whether any association exists at all. The degree of association determines the share of the social costs that the chemical firms should bear. Second, new scientific evidence has demonstrated a significant statistical association between exposure to Agent Orange and non-Hodgkin's lymphoma, soft tissue sarcoma, skin disorders, subclinical hepatotoxic effects, and porphyria cutanea tarda, as well as some statistical association between exposure to Agent Orange and Hodgkin's disease, neurologic effects, and reproductive and developmental effects.[106] From this evidence, the chemical firm payout for Agent Orange claims is only a minute fraction of the corresponding social costs, not an instance of a false positive.[107]

Finally, the chemical firm occasionally incurs liability costs for claims of bodily harm associated with its industrial emissions. However, most of these successful claims are for signature diseases in which traces of the toxic chemical were found in the claimant's blood or other tissue,[108] and therefore are not false positives. The chemical firm may also receive an isolated product liability claim, alleging a chronic hazard associated with the chemical product. We do not know whether some of these are nuisance

104. Huber 1988, 62.
105. In re *Agent Orange Product Liability Litigation*, 597 F. Supp. 740,755 (E.D.N.Y. 1984).
106. Agent Orange Scientific Task Force 1990.
107. Another issue, not considered here, is whether the federal government should have been immune from liability claims involving Agent Orange. We note, however, that at the time of this writing, the Veterans Administration has sued the federal government for the first time in its history, for the government's failure to acknowledge and compensate the victims of Agent Orange exposure adequately.
108. An example is the case against Gulf Resources and Chemical Corporation in which the plaintiffs alleged that emissions from the firm's smelter had caused high levels of lead in their bloodstreams. The claims were settled out of court. See BNA, "Environmental Reporter," April 15, 1983, p. 2321 (computer file, Bureau of National Affairs, Washington).

suits without merit, but they are only infrequently, if ever, successful. Indeed, for the chemical products and activities covered, what we found remarkable about the associated liability claims was the absence of industry "horror stories."

The Degree of Deterrence

That the total liability costs borne by the chemical firm for chronic diseases from chemical exposure represent no more than 5 percent, and often less than 0.1 percent, of the corresponding social costs suggests that the liability system provides gross underdeterrence, even before the dampening effects of insurance are factored in.

The sources of this extreme underdeterrence include difficulties in verifying chemical exposures, difficulties in demonstrating an association between exposure and subsequent disease by a preponderance of evidence, and difficulties in identifying the responsible firm or industry. The often lengthy latency period between exposure and manifestation of disease exacerbates these difficulties and introduces other problems as well, including legal obstacles, such as statutes of limitation, and the prospect that the firm responsible will have ceased operation before a claim is filed or, if still in business, will have insufficient assets to cover incoming claims. Another problem related to the long latency between exposure and manifestation of disease concerns management incentives. Insofar as management performance is judged by its short-run contributions to corporate profitability,[109] safety investments will appear uneconomic, since the firm's investment costs arise immediately but the benefits from chronic disease reduction may not appear for decades. In effect, corporate management, as a result of its myopic incentives, may try to externalize the costs of chronic health hazards to its successors.

Even for signature diseases, many of these same difficulties apply if the latency period between chemical exposure and manifestation of disease is long. Therefore, there is significant underdeterrence for those diseases as well. However, when subclinical effects of exposure to chemicals give rise to a cause of action (or when the presence of the toxin in the body unequivocally establishes exposure to a specific chemical), liability in the tort system may be pursued before the manifestation of disease and may be successfully established. The opening up of tort liability for subclinical effects and exposure per se has generated some degree of risk averseness

109. Siliciano 1987, 1844–46; Ashford and Caldart 1991, 230.

in many firms, gradually leading them to substitute less toxic chemicals or to change chemical processes.

For non-signature diseases, however, when clearly no opportunity for a successful tort action (or for workers' compensation awards) will arise,[110] very little deterrence exists at all. The one promising source of deterrence for non-signature diseases is the chemical firm's concern that future scientific advances will establish unique links between its products or activities and chronic diseases, effectively transforming what were formerly considered to be ordinary diseases of life into signature diseases.

Causation remains a major problem in establishing the connection between exposure and disease in the context of worker exposure, but even more so in the context of consumer exposure, particularly to common chemical substances such as benzene. A worker might possibly establish a claim for benzene-related leukemia, for example, in the context of industrial exposure, but the consumer is exposed to benzene in so many different ways—in filling his automobile with gasoline and in using consumer products and solvents—that it would be extremely difficult to establish that his leukemia was related to a particular chemical firm's product.

Safety and Innovative Performance Related to Tort Liability

Because the tort system normally provides gross underdeterrence in the area of chronic disease from chemical exposure, liability plays only a minor role in stimulating the development of less chronically hazardous chemical products and processes. Examples of process safety improvements are the replacement of organic solvents—such as trichloroethylene, a possible human carcinogen—with water-based cleaners and the use of less toxic material, or smaller quantities of toxic material, in electroplating activities.[111] But these changes in technology are probably stimulated more by regulatory prodding, particularly restrictions on the disposal of hazardous wastes, than by liability concerns. Furthermore, the adoption of these technological improvements is still not widespread.

A well-known furniture polish is an example of a chemical product whose safety improvement might properly be attributed to liability concerns. The original formulation of the polish contained 97 percent nitro-

110. Indeed, the high transaction costs and poor chances of success confronting potential plaintiffs usually discourage them from even filing valid claims.

111. See, for example, Ashford and others 1988.

benzene. Possibly, if a significant excess of cancer were found in consumers of that product, the manufacturer might be swamped with liability suits that the claimants stood a good chance of winning. Whatever the motivation, the product was quietly reformulated without regulatory action or attention.

Obviously when the safety of a chemical is called into question by either regulation or litigation, the firm has every incentive to retain its market by modifying the final product or changing the inputs and process used to manufacture a final product. The widely publicized assertions of the Monsanto Company—that it was unwilling to market calcium sodium metaphosphate, a substitute for asbestos as a reinforcing fiber and as a friction material, for fear of liability—must be viewed in the proper context.[112] First, there *is* evidence that the material might be carcinogenic,[113] and second, the substitute would be used by workers who had previous exposure to asbestos and who are at a much higher risk of developing cancer already. It is both logical and expected that Monsanto would not be willing to manufacture and market that product.[114] At the same time, it seems unreasonable to view Monsanto's withdrawal of this product as a "failure" of the liability system, if only because there would be no market for asbestos substitutes in the first place were it not for liability (and subsequently regulation).[115] Furthermore, tort liability for chronic disease should be expected to stimulate innovation of *significantly* safer products and discourage the development of products which may

112. See Mahoney and Littlejohn 1989, 1395. Even Vice President Quayle (1990, 1223) has alluded to the product as a victim of tort liability.

113. In fact, the Environmental Protection Agency concluded that the evidence obtained from Monsanto's two-year intrapleural implantation study in rats offered reasonable support for the conclusion that calcium sodium metaphosphate fibers can cause cancer. The agency argued that Monsanto was unable to refute "the low but essentially equal incidences of malignant pleural tumors observed in the calcium sodium metaphosphate and asbestos exposed rats but not in the concurrent control rats." U.S. Environmental Protection Agency 1986 (Status Report of August 19, 1986), 6.

114. While Monsanto may well believe that the product is safe (see U.S. Environmental Protection Agency 1986, submission dated May 15, 1986), the EPA does not, and the workers who are exposed to the new product might develop cancers indistinguishable from cancer caused by asbestos. That must be viewed as a unique situation in the context of product liability. Even if the product were to be used by an entirely different work force, it is not clear that the product would have been marketed when there was a serious disagreement between the regulatory agency and the marketing firm over the safety of the product.

115. Moreover, other Monsanto products, such as its herbicide Roundup, have enjoyed enormous market success. At least part of that success stems from the fact that some competitors' products, containing probable human carcinogens, have been withdrawn from the market, presumably because of liability risks.

present hazards that are only *slightly* less than the materials for which they might be substituted.[116] Thus innovation will be both enhanced and discouraged—and in precisely the socially desirable way—if there is adequate deterrence.

Conclusions and Policy Implications

In discussing acute chemical hazards, we concluded that the chemical firm's total liability costs represent no more than 70 percent of the corresponding social costs and that the liability system provides few-to-modest incentives to engage in preventive activities (see table 10-2). Then, addressing chronic chemical hazards, we noted that for signature diseases the chemical firm bears no more than 5 percent of the associated social costs and that the liability system creates some, but limited, deterrence; for non-signature diseases the chemical firm incurs liability costs of less than 0.1 percent of the associated social costs, and there is even less deterrence that would lead firms to develop safer products and processes. Insofar as positive deterrence exists, the present economic costs associated with liability can play a lesser or greater role. The concern of the firm to guard its reputation or to avoid punitive damages often plays a larger role, especially with regard to acute chemical hazards and signature diseases for which the firm may be clearly associated. That we have observed the development of both new products and processes when there is small or modest economic deterrence leads us to believe that increasing the economic costs associated with liability by more fully internalizing the social costs of chemical production would stimulate new technologies.

As we said in the beginning of the chapter, the effects of liability must be assessed in the context of other governmental interventions concerned with the safety of chemicals. When the inherent safety of a product or process is called into question, by a stringent regulation or ban or as a result of litigation, strong evidence exists that either the regulated firm or a new entrant will seize the opportunity to develop or adopt safer products or processes. Sometimes the regulated firm may simply abandon

116. A huge variety of asbestos substitutes already exist in the market (see, for example, Hodgson 1985). Monsanto's Phosphate Fiber (calcium sodium metaphosphate fiber) was expected to be "competitive" with other asbestos substitutes, but it was not a radical breakthrough with significant advantages over other asbestos substitutes already on the market. (Information obtained during a conversation on May 11, 1990, with James H. Senger, vice president, Environmental Policy, the Monsanto Company.)

the hazardous technology because it is unable to develop a safer substitute, while new entrants with different technological visions may be successful in developing a replacement.[117] An example from the regulatory arena is the development of a substitute transformer fluid by Dow-Silicone for Monsanto's PCBs.[118]

Since regulatory attention yields evidence that can be used in litigation, it is often difficult to apportion the source of the motivation for a firm's development of new technologies. Figure 10-5 shows the numbers of substances that have been designated as carcinogens. As the figure shows, many more substances might be candidates for regulation than have actually been regulated. But the mere fact that the substances have been signaled, tested, or studied epidemiologically makes them candidates for substitution. Conversely, for the many substances that have neither been targeted, tested, nor regulated, very little deterrence exists that might stimulate substitution. However, if the culture of the firm in its development of technology is changed by some examples of liability (perhaps falling on others), the firm may begin to develop safer products and processes across the board.[119] Changing attitudes of industry toward pollution prevention provides evidence of this cultural shift.

Uncertainty plays a large role in causing the firm to develop new technologies. Uncertainty about the possibility of regulation, once a substance has been designated a suspect hazard, drives many firms to develop substitutes so as not to be faced with a short time period in which they would be expected to respond. Uncertainty regarding the likelihood of tort action may likewise stimulate risk-averse firms, or firms guided by organizational routine rather than profit maximization (as discussed earlier), to search for or to develop substitutes.[120]

117. The same situation may arise when liability is the stimulus. Whatever characteristics of the chemical firm make it susceptible to litigation exposure in the first place are likely to impair its ability to develop safer products and processes in response. As a result, safety innovations frequently originate elsewhere in the market. This essential point is missed by those (such as Murray Mackay, in chapter 5 of this volume) who argue simplistically that the effectiveness of liability can be determined by observing whether those companies most exposed to litigation are the most innovative.

118. Ashford, Ayers, and Stone 1985, 432–33.

119. A survey of risk managers of 232 major U.S. corporations found that "where product liability has had a notable impact—where it has most significantly affected management decision making—has been in the quality of the products themselves. Managers say products have become safer, manufacturing procedures have been improved, and labels and use instructions have become more explicit." Weber 1987, 2.

120. Of course, too much uncertainty can have a paralyzing rather than a stimulative effect on the firm. For instance, truly unstable and unpredictable legal doctrine obviously

Because of the gross underdeterrence in the context of chronic chemical hazards and the major underdeterrence in the context of acute chemical hazards, we suggest several changes in policy: an increased governmental role in developing and disseminating information about chemical hazards (beyond SARA title III and the OSHA hazard communication standard); increased regulation and economic charges for toxic and dangerous chemicals; increases in workers' compensation death benefits (particularly for scheduled diseases that are signature diseases or for diseases that clearly have a chemical etiology); and a limitation of access to bankruptcy protection that curtails the responsibility of the firm and removes any incentives to deal with the economic consequences of significant health hazards.

These observations and conclusions indicate that the recent demands for widespread tort reform, while directing attention to dissatisfaction with the tort system, tend to miss their mark, since significant underdeterrence in the system already exists. Thus proposals that damage awards be capped, that limitations be placed on pain and suffering and punitive damages, and that stricter evidence be required for recovery should be rejected. On the contrary, the revisions of the tort system should include relaxing the evidentiary requirements for recovery, shifting the basis of recovery to subclinical effects of chemicals, and establishing clear causes of action where evidence of exposure exists in the absence of manifest disease. Other tort remedies may also be entertained, but they must increase the amount of deterrence in the system, not further weaken the signals sent to the firm.

---

undercuts the firm's ability to make optimal investments in safety. See, for example, Siliciano 1987. However, some uncertainty about having to pay for the damages it causes may stimulate the firm to undertake preventive action. By analogy, some randomness in income tax auditing has been shown to reduce taxpayer underreporting. See, for example, Scotchmer and Slemrod 1989.

	FDA				OSHA		
	Foods, colors, cosmetics	Animal drugs	Human drugs	NIOSH recommendations	Cancer and non-cancer standard	Cancer standard	CPSC banned/ voluntary control

Annual Report chemicals

	Foods, colors, cosmetics	Animal drugs	Human drugs	NIOSH recommendations	Cancer and non-cancer standard	Cancer standard	CPSC banned/ voluntary control
Action	46	2	26	59	52	17	18
No action	6	4	5	53	58	93	6

NCI/NTP chemicals: one or more positive experiments

	Foods, colors, cosmetics	Animal drugs	Human drugs	NIOSH recommendations	Cancer and non-cancer standard	Cancer standard	CPSC banned/ voluntary control
Action	17	4	6	31	29	2	8
No action	31	1	6	31	24	51	6

NCI/NTP chemicals: three or four positive experiments

	Foods, colors, cosmetics	Animal drugs	Human drugs	NIOSH recommendations	Cancer and non-cancer standard	Cancer standard	CPSC banned/ voluntary control
Action	7	1	5	13	16	1	4
No action	12	0	1	26	13	29	3

Source: U.S. Office of Technology Assessment 1987, 20.

a. For each agency or program, OTA included only chemicals in the OTA-defined jurisdiction for that agency or program. Agency decisions that regulation is not necessary or appropriate were included in the no action groups. Because of overlap between the three lists of chemicals, it is not appropriate to add them together.

Key to acronyms: CAA—Clean Air Act; CAG—Carcinogen Assessment Group; CERCLA—Comprehensive Environmental Response, Compensation, and Liability Act; CHIPs—Chemical Hazard Information Profiles; CPSC—

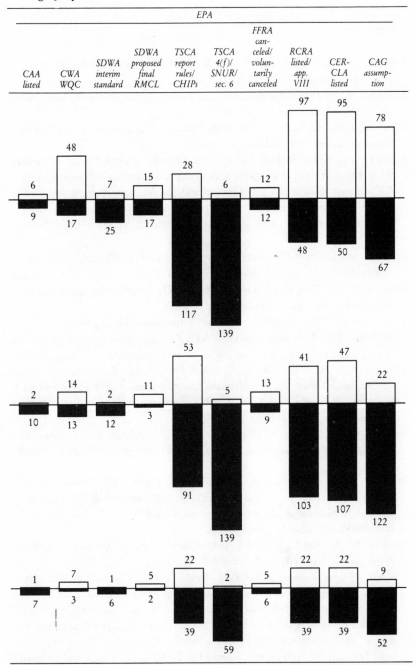

						FFRA			
			SDWA	TSCA	TSCA	can-celed/	RCRA		
		SDWA	proposed	report	4(f)/	volun-	listed/	CER-	CAG
CAA	CWA	interim	final	rules/	SNUR/	tarily	app.	CLA	assump-
listed	WQC	standard	RMCL	CHIPs	sec. 6	canceled	VIII	listed	tion

Consumer Product Safety Commission; EPA—Environmental Protection Agency; FDA—Food and Drug Administration; FIFRA—Federal Insecticide, Fungicide, and Rodenticide Act; NCI—National Cancer Institute; NIOSH—National Institute for Occupational Safety and Health; NTP—National Toxicology Program; OSHA—Occupational Safety and Health Administration; RCRA—Resource Conservation and Recovery Act; RMCL—recommended maximum contaminant level; SDWA—Safe Drinking Water Act; SNUR—Significant New Use Rule; TSCA—Toxic Substance Control Act; WQC—Water Quality Criteria.

References

Abernathy, W. J., and J. M. Utterback. 1978. "Patterns of Industrial Innovation." *Technology Review* 80:41.

Abraham, K. S. 1986. *Distributing Risk: Insurance, Legal Theory, and Public Policy.* Yale University Press.

Abraham, K. S., nd R. A. Merrill. 1986. "Scientific Uncertainty in the Courts." *Issues in Science and Technology* 2:93–107.

Agent Orange Scientific Task Force. 1990. "Human Health Effects Associated with Exposure to Herbicides and/or Their Associated Contaminants—Chlorinated Dioxins: Agent Orange and the Vietnam Veteran, A Review of the Scientific Literature." Report prepared with the American Legion, Vietnam Veterans of America, and the National Veterans Legal Services Project.

Allen, T., and others. 1978. "Government Influence on the Process of Innovation in Europe and Japan." *Research Policy* 7:124–49.

Ashford, N. A. 1976a. *Crisis in the Workplace: Occupational Disease and Injury.* A Report to the Ford Foundation. MIT Press.

———. 1976b. "The Magnitude of the Occupational Health Problem." Proceedings of the Interdepartmental Workers' Compensation Task Force, Conference on Occupational Diseases and Workers' Compensation, Chicago, Illinois.

Ashford, N. A., C. Ayers, and R. F. Stone. 1985. "Using Regulation to Change the Market for Innovation." *Harvard Environmental Law Review* 9:419–65.

Ashford, N. A., and C. C. Caldart. 1991. *Technology, Law and the Working Environment.* Van Nostrand Reinhold.

Ashford, N. A., and G. R. Heaton, Jr. 1983. "Regulation and Technological Innovation in the Chemical Industry." *Law and Contemporary Problems* 46:109–57.

Ashford, N. A., G. R. Heaton, Jr., and W. C. Priest. 1979. "Environmental, Health, and Safety Regulation and Technological Innovation." In *Technological Innovation for a Dynamic Economy,* edited by C. T. Hill and J. M. Utterback, 161–221. Pergamon Press.

Ashford, N. A., and C. S. Miller. 1991. *Chemical Exposures: Low Levels and High Stakes.* Van Nostrand Reinhold.

Ashford, N. A., S. Moran, and R. F. Stone. 1987. "The Role of Changes in Statutory/Tort Law and Liability Insurance in Preventing and Compensating Damages from Future Releases of Hazardous Waste." Report to the Special Legislative Commission on Liability for Releases of Oil and Hazardous Materials. The Commonwealth of Massachusetts, Cambridge, Mass.: Massachusetts Institute of Technology, Center for Technology, Policy and Industrial Development.

———. 1989. "The Role of Insurance and Financial Responsibility Requirements in Preventing and Compensating Damage from Environmental Risks." Final

Report to the New Jersey Department of Insurance. Massachusetts Institute of Technology, Center for Technology, Policy and Industrial Development.

Ashford, N. A., and others. 1988. "The Design of Demonstration or Experimental Programs to Encourage Waste Reduction: An Incentives Analysis." Final Report to the New Jersey Department of Environmental Protection, Division of Science and Research.

———. 1990. *Monitoring the Worker for Exposure and Disease: Scientific, Legal, and Ethical Considerations in the Use of Biomarkers.* Johns Hopkins University Press.

Ashford, N. A., C. J. Spadafor, and C. C. Caldart. 1984. "Human Monitoring: Scientific, Legal and Ethical Considerations." *Harvard Environmental Law Review* 8:263–363.

Ashford, N. A., and R. F. Stone. 1988. "Cost-Benefit Analysis in Environmental Decision-Making: Theoretical Considerations and Applications to Protection of Stratospheric Ozone." Report to the Office of Policy Analysis and Review in the Office of Air and Radiation, U.S. Environmental Protection Agency, Washington.

Axelson, O., and L. Forrestiere. 1989. "Estimated Increases in Lung Cancer in Non-smokers in Italy." Workshop on Increasing Cancers in Industrial Countries, Collegium Ramazzini, Carpi, Italy, October 20–22.

Barth, P. S. 1981. "Economic Analysis of Asbestos-Associated Disease." In *Disability Compensation for Asbestos-Associated Disease in the United States,* edited by I. J. Selikoff. New York: Mount Sinai School of Medicine.

Barth, P. S., and H. Allan Hunt. 1980. *Workers' Compensation and Work Related Illnesses and Diseases.* MIT Press.

Boden, L. I., and C. A. Jones. 1987. "Occupational Disease Remedies: The Asbestos Experience." In *Public Regulation: New Perspectives on Institutions and Policies,* edited by E. E. Bailey, 312–46. MIT Press.

Brodeur, P. 1985. *Outrageous Misconduct: The Asbestos Industry on Trial.* Pantheon.

Caldart, C. C. 1985. "Are Workers Adequately Compensated for Injury Resulting from Exposure to Toxic Substances? An Overview of Worker Compensation and Suits in Tort." In *Chemical Safety Regulation and Compliance,* edited by F. Homburger and J. K. Marquis, 92–98. Basel: Karger.

Coffee, J. C. 1981. "'No Soul to Damn: No Body to Kick': An Unscandalized Inquiry into the Problem of Corporate Punishment." *Michigan Law Review* 79:386–459.

Cook, P. J. 1984. "The Use of Criminal Statutes to Regulate Product Safety: Comment on Wheeler." *Journal of Legal Studies* 13:619–22.

Cook, P. J., and D. A. Graham. 1977. "The Demand for Insurance and Protection: The Case of Irreplaceable Commodities." *Quarterly Journal of Economics* 91:143–56.

Cyert, R. M., and J. G. March. 1963. *A Behavioral Theory of the Firm*. Prentice-Hall.

Doll, R., and R. Peto. 1981. "The Causes of Cancer: Quantitative Estimates of Avoidable Risks of Cancer in the United States Today." *Journal of the National Cancer Institute* 66:1191–1308.

Dosi, G. 1988. "Sources, Procedures, and Microeconomic Effects of Innovation." *Journal of Economic Literature* 26:1120–71.

Elliott, E. D. 1985. "Goal Analysis Versus Institutional Analysis of Toxic Compensation Systems." *Georgetown Law Journal* 73:1357–76.

———. 1988. "The Future of Toxic Torts: Of Chemophobia, Risk as a Compensable Injury and Hybrid Compensation Systems." *Houston Law Review* 25:781–99.

Freeman, C. 1982. *The Economics of Industrial Innovation*. London: Pinter.

Graham, J., and D. M. Shakow. 1990. "Labor Market Segmentation and Job-Related Risks: Differences in Risks and Compensation between Primary and Secondary Labor Markets." *American Journal of Economics and Sociology* 49:307–24.

Griliches, Z. 1967. "Distributed Lags: A Survey." *Econometrica* 35:16–49.

Hager, M. M. 1989. "Civil Compensation and Its Discontents: A Response to Huber" (review of *Liability: The Legal Revolution and Its Consequences*, by P. W. Huber). *Stanford Law Review* 42:539–76.

Hodgson, A. A. 1985. *Alternatives to Asbestos and Asbestos Products*. Crowthorne, U.K.: Anjalena Publications.

Huber, P. W. 1985a. "The Bhopalization of U.S. Tort Law." *Issues in Science and Technology* 2:73–82.

———. 1985b. "Safety and the Second Best: The Hazards of Public Risk Management in the Courts." *Columbia Law Review* 85:277–337.

———. 1988. *Liability: The Legal Revolution and Its Consequences*. Basic Books.

Hunter, D. 1988. "New Valves Promise Safer, Cheaper Chlorine Shipping." *Chemical Engineering* 55:27–28.

Insurance Services Office. 1977. *Product Liability Closed Claim Survey: A Technical Analysis of Survey Results*. New York.

Jury Verdict Research, Inc. 1991. "Injury Valuation: Current Award Trends." *Jury Verdict Research*.

Kakalik, J. S., and others. 1983. *Costs of Asbestos Litigation*. R-3042-ICJ. Santa Monica, Calif.: Rand Corporation.

Kakalik, J. S., and N. M. Pace. 1986. *Costs and Compensation Paid in Tort Litigation*. R-3391-ICJ. Santa Monica, Calif.: Rand Corporation.

Katzman, M. T. 1988. "Pollution Liability Insurance and Catastrophic Environmental Risk." *Journal of Risk and Insurance* 55:75–100.

Klein, B. H. 1977. *Dynamic Economics*. Harvard University Press.

Kletz, T. A. 1989. "Friendly Plants." *Chemical Engineering Progress* 85:18–26.

Kolstad, C. D., T. S. Ulen, and G. V. Johnson. 1990. "Ex Post Liability for Harm vs. Ex Ante Regulation: Substitutes or Complements." *American Economic Review* 80:888–901.

Landes, W. M., and R. A. Posner. 1987. *The Economic Structure of Tort Law.* Harvard University Press.

Latin, H. 1988. "Good Science, Bad Regulation and Toxic Risk Assessment." *Yale Journal on Regulation* 5:89–148.

Machina, M. J. 1987. "Choice under Uncertainty: Problems Solved and Unsolved." *Journal of Economic Perspectives* 1:121–54.

MacKerron, C. B. 1989. "Congress Looks at What Went Wrong in Pasadena." *Chemicalweek*, Nov. 15: 8–9.

Mahoney, R. J., and S. E. Littlejohn. 1989. "Innovation on Trial: Punitive Damages versus New Products." *Science* 246:1395–99.

Mansfield, E., and others. 1972. *Research and Innovation in the Modern Corporation.* Norton.

Mark, H. F. 1986. *Encyclopedia of Polymer Science and Engineering*, vol. 6. 2d ed. John Wiley and Sons.

Markowitz, S., and P. Landrigan. 1989. "The Magnitude of the Occupational Disease Problem: An Investigation in New York State." *Toxicology and Industrial Health* 5:9–30.

Mashaw, J. L. 1985. "A Comment on Causation, Law Reform, and Guerrilla Warfare." *Georgetown Law Journal* 73:1393–97.

Moore, M. J., and W. K. Viscusi. 1988a. "The Quantity-adjusted Value of Life." *Economic Inquiry* 26:369–88.

————. 1988b. "Doubling the Estimated Value of Life: Results Using New Occupational Fatality Data." *Journal of Policy Analysis and Management* 7:476–90.

National Science Foundation. 1983. *The Process of Technological Innovation: Reviewing the Literature.* Washington.

Nelson, R. R., and S. G. Winter. 1982. *An Evolutionary Theory of Economic Change.* Belknap Press of Harvard University Press.

Page, J. A. 1987. "Asbestos and the Dalkon Shield: Corporate America on Trial" (review of *Outrageous Misconduct: The Asbestos Industry on Trial*). *Michigan Law Review* 85:1324–40.

————. 1990. "Deforming Tort Reform" (book review of *Liability: The Legal Revolution and Its Consequences*, by P. W. Huber). *Georgetown Law Journal* 78:649–97.

Peterson, M. A., S. Sarma, and M. Shanley. 1987. *Punitive Damages: Empirical Findings.* R-3311-ICJ. Santa Monica, Calif.: Rand Corporation.

Pollack, E. S., and D. G. Keimig, eds. 1987. *Counting Injuries and Illnesses in* the Workplace: Proposals for a Better System. Washington: National Academy Press.

Prosser, W. P., and P. Keeton. 1984. Prosser and Keeton on the Law of Torts. 5th ed. St. Paul: West Publications.

Quayle, D. 1990. "Now Is the Time for Product Liability Reform." Toxics Law Reporter, Mar. 28: 1221–24.

Schmahl, D., R. Preussman, and M. R. Berger. 1989. "Causes of Cancers—An Alternative View to Doll and Peto." Klinische Wochenschrift 67:1169–73.

Schneiderman, M. A., D. L. Davis, and D. K. Wagener. 1989. "Lung Cancer That Is Not Attributable to Smoking" (letter). Journal of the American Medical Association 262:904.

Schumpeter, J. A. 1934. The Theory of Economic Development: An Inquiry into Profits, Capital, Credit, Interest, and the Business Cycle. Harvard University Press.

———. 1950. Capitalism, Socialism, and Democracy. Harper.

Scotchmer, S., and J. Slemrod. 1989. "Randomness in Tax Enforcement." Journal of Public Economics 38:17–32.

Selikoff, I. J. 1981. "Disability Compensation for Asbestos-Associated Disease in the United States." Mount Sinai School of Medicine, Environmental Science Laboratory, New York.

Shavell, S. 1987. Economic Analysis of Accident Law. Harvard University Press.

Siliciano, J. A. 1987. "Corporate Behavior and the Social Efficiency of Tort Law." Michigan Law Review 85:1820–64.

Simon, H. A. 1959. "Theories of Decision Making in Economics and Behavioral Science." American Economic Review 49:253–83.

Stoneman, P. 1983. The Economic Analysis of Technological Change. Oxford University Press.

Tomatis, L., and others. 1989. "Human Carcinogens So Far Identified." Japan Journal of Cancer Research 80:795–807.

Tversky, A., and D. Kahneman. 1974. "Judgment under Uncertainty: Heuristics and Biases." Science 185:1124–31.

U.S. Chamber of Commerce. 1990. Analysis of Workers' Compensation Laws, 1990.

U.S. Department of Labor. 1980. An Interim Report to Congress on Occupational Diseases.

———. 1990. The Phillips 66 Company Houston Chemical Complex Explosion and Fire.

U.S. Environmental Protection Agency. 1986. "Monsanto Company 'For Your Information' Notices Concerning Calcium Sodium Metaphosphate." TSCA Public Docket 8E Submission 619.

———. 1987. "Regulatory Impact Analysis: Protection of Stratospheric Ozone."

U.S. General Accounting Office. 1989. Product Liability: Verdicts and Case Resolution in Five States. GAO/HRD-90-99.

U.S. Office of Technology Assessment. 1987. *Identifying and Regulating Carcinogens*. OTA-BP-H-42.

Vineas, P., and L. Simonato. 1991. "Proportion of Lung and Bladder Cancers in Males Due to Occupation: A Systematic Approach." *Archives of Environmental Health* 46: 6–15.

Viscusi, W. K. 1986. "The Valuation of Risks to Life and Health: Guidelines for Policy Analysis." In *Benefits Assessment: The State of the Art*, edited by J. D. Benitkove, V. T. Corello, and J. Mumpower, 193–210. Dordrecht: D. Reidel Publishing.

———. 1988. "Liability for Occupational Accidents and Illnesses." In *Liability: Perspectives and Policy*, edited by R. E. Litan and C. Winston, 155–83. Brookings.

Viscusi, W. K., and M. J. Moore. 1987. "Workers' Compensation: Wage Effects, Benefit Inadequacies, and the Value of Health Losses." *Review of Economics and Statistics* 69:249–61.

———. 1989. "Rates of Time Preference and Valuations of the Duration of Life." *Journal of Public Economics* 38:297–317.

Viscusi, W. K., and C. J. O'Connor. 1984. "Adaptive Responses to Chemical Labeling: Are Workers Bayesian Decision Makers?" *American Economic Review* 74:942–56.

Weber, N. 1987. *Product Liability: The Corporate Response*. New York: The Conference Board.

Wheeler, M. E. 1984. "The Use of Criminal Statutes to Regulate Product Safety." *Journal of Legal Studies* 13:593–618.

Wright, R. W. 1985. "Causation in Tort Law." *California Law Review*, 73:1735–1828.

Zanetti, R. 1986. "CPI Alter Their Ways of Dealing with Toxics." *Chemical Engineering* 99:27–30.

CHAPTER ELEVEN

The Impact of Liability on Innovation in the Chemical Industry

Rollin B. Johnson

DESPITE many attempts to evaluate the impact of the liability system on American industry and the economy as a whole, the answer remains elusive. More recently, the question has been recast in terms of the global economy: what is the impact of liability on America's industrial competitiveness?

Most studies have considered this problem for industry overall or for broad categories of industry. Of course, American industry is not as homogeneous as such broad-based studies inevitably imply. Using an industry-by-industry approach can reveal important trends within particular sectors that may not be apparent in a general assessment. With that in mind, in this chapter I take a closer look primarily at the effects of product liability and secondarily at the effects of environmental (Superfund) liability on the chemical industry.

This chapter does not present new data on product liability trends or costs, nor is it a collection of anecdotal stories of products that have been withdrawn from R&D or from the marketplace because of unwarranted product liability suits. Rather, it attempts to critically examine the following claims: unwarranted product lawsuits are a pivotal concern for chemical manufacturers; this makes U.S. chemical companies less willing to innovate; as a result the U.S. chemical industry is at a competitive disadvantage with foreign companies.

The information presented here is based on industry data, published analyses of the tort system and industry, and interviews with corporate counsels, R&D directors, chief executive officers (CEOs), directors of public affairs, insurers, chemical association officials, policy analysts, and others associated with the chemical industry.

The findings of the chapter are that, though frivolous product liability suits may be a consideration in the research, development, and marketing of many, if not all, chemical products, there is little evidence that it is a pivotal concern, has compromised the willingness of chemical companies to innovate to any great degree, or has hindered the competitiveness of the industry significantly. Environmental liability, however, has gradually shifted from users, conveyors, and disposers of hazardous chemicals to the "deep pocket" manufacturers. Depending on how the responsibility for cleanup is distributed, that may become a severe economic drain on the industry and could depress new product innovation by reducing the funds available for R&D, or reduce competitiveness by increasing product pricing, or both.

Even though the evidence on the effect of unwarranted lawsuits on the chemical industry does not justify widespread reform of the tort system, two recommendations seem reasonable. First, limiting liability to those cases in which companies have not complied with the letter and spirit of the regulatory requirements in force at the time of manufacture, and second, ensuring a better hearing for scientific evidence presented by defendants in the courtroom.

The State of the Chemical Industry

Chemical production is one of the nation's largest industries. The U.S. chemical industry makes more than 50,000 chemicals in over 12,000 plants employing about one million people.[1] The classification of the chemical industry by three-digit standard industrial classification (SIC) codes assigned by the Office of Management and Budget illustrates the range of products:

SIC code	Description
28X	Chemicals and allied products
281	Industrial inorganic chemicals
282	Plastics and synthetic materials
283	Drugs
284	Soaps, cleansers, toilet goods
285	Paints and allied products
286	Industrial organic chemicals
287	Agricultural chemicals
289	Miscellaneous chemical products (adhesives, sealants, inks, and so on)

1. U.S. Department of Commerce 1990, 12-1.

The chemical industry is exceptional in many ways, some of which have a bearing on liability. The number of products of this industry, as mentioned, is vast. Unlike the other industries discussed in this study, the chemical industry provides materials essential for the manufacture of products in almost every other industry. For example, the housing-supplies industry and the automobile industry are such large consumers of chemicals that housing starts and automobile sales are frequently used as indicators of the changing market for chemical products.[2] The chemical industry also produces and markets reagents for research and many finished consumer goods, such as soaps, paints, pesticides, fertilizers, and drugs.[3] Thus the prosperity of the industry depends on commodities as well as consumer goods.

While some sectors of the industry do not engage in innovation, others are very innovative; about 1,000 new chemicals are proposed for manufacture each year.[4] The industry trend is toward even greater innovation as companies producing basic chemicals turn increasingly to specialty chemicals and biotechnology products and processes.

The chemical industry is also highly international. Many of the largest American chemical companies report over half of their manufacturing and exports by foreign affiliates. Conversely, many foreign chemical companies have divisions or subsidiaries in the United States. Through such product diversification mentioned above and global distribution mentioned here, many chemical companies have successfully spread their economic risk. However, such breadth may increase exposure to liability.

Statistics for chemical production in the United States show that, except for a slowdown in the mid-1970s and early 1980s, the industry has shown strong growth since 1970.[5] Record industry sales have meant that, since 1983, the inventory-to-sales ratio in the industry was the lowest of the period 1972–87. Operating rates were at higher levels in the late 1980s than at any time since 1974, with record production in many product lines. In September 1987 the industry was operating at 84 percent of capacity according to the Federal Reserve Board, with some sectors over 95 percent.[6] Capital spending on new plants and renovations increased

2. See the annual *Chemical and Enginering News Facts and Figures* and the issues of *Chemical Outlook* over the past thirty years.

3. See Louis Lasagna's chapter in this volume for a discussion of liability and innovation in the pharmaceutical industry.

4. U.S. General Accounting Office 1984, 1.

5. Organization for Economic Cooperation and Development (OECD) 1979; Standard and Poor's 1987.

6. Standard and Poor's 1987.

after 1983 and was described as "monumental" in 1988, a 31 percent increase over the previous year.[7]

As for international trade, the chemical industry has been a net exporter, and its trade balance was greater in 1988 than at any time in the previous ten years.[8] According to a recent report, "while the U.S. has posted massive overall trade deficits for many years, this country's chemical trade surplus reflects the technology, research, and marketing expertise that give the industry competitive advantages in many higher valued products." The report goes on to say that American chemical companies are very attractive to foreign investment, that foreign purchase of U.S. chemical firms continues at a brisk pace, and that foreign chemical companies view the American market as the biggest and most promising for chemical products.[9]

Recent standard reports on the health of the industry, such as *Current Industrial Reports*, do not cite liability as a major concern. The price of oil, trade tariffs, interest rates, the strength of the dollar, the condition of consumer industries, and other such factors are cited frequently. The liability issue does not seem to have crossed the threshold of significance necessary to be included in those reports.

Indicators of Innovation

Two of the main indicators of innovation are the spending patterns for research and development and the trends in the number of U.S. patents. In chapter 3, Viscusi and Moore have provided some new data on alternative ways of looking at innovation that will also be discussed here.

R&D Spending Patterns

According to the National Science Board, "industrial R&D is the principal source of technological developments that benefit the entire economy."[10] In 1989, 72 percent of all research and development done in the United States was performed in industry, a gradual increase from 69 percent in 1970. In 1989 West Germany had a similar share of R&D performed by industry (72 percent), but it had risen more steeply, from

7. Reisch 1988, 10.
8. Standard and Poor's 1989.
9. Standard and Poor's 1989.
10. National Science Board (NSB) 1990.

62 percent in 1973. The Japanese share of R&D performed by industry was somewhat less (66 percent), up from about 57 percent in 1978.[11]

In constant dollars, U.S. industry-funded research and development increased every year from 1975 to 1989 except for the years 1985–86, when it remained effectively at the same level.[12] When examined by sector, the highest growth in U.S. R&D expenditures from 1980 to 1986 was in the chemical and allied products and electrical equipment industries,[13] suggesting that those have been the most innovative of all main industry categories, at least in recent years.

Industrial R&D funding (excluding government funding of corporate R&D) is closely tied to net sales. Between 1957 and 1977 it remained relatively constant, at about 2 percent. The chemical industry has consistently been well above this figure, with R&D ranging from 3.0 to 3.5 percent of net sales between 1968 and 1977 and from 2.8 to 4.9 percent for the period 1978–86.[14] In Japan as well, industry figures show R&D spending to sales ratios increasing from 2.6 percent in 1980 to 4.3 percent in 1986, compared to the average change in all industries from 1.5 to 2.6 percent.[15]

This increase in R&D commitment reflects the importance of innovation to the chemical industry. (However, some portion of the increase in R&D spending, in the United States at least, is for meeting new government regulatory requirements.)[16]

Trends in U.S. Patents

As described by the National Science Board, "one of the main benefits of industrial R&D spending is a stream of new technical inventions that may in turn be embodied in innovations—i.e., in new or improved products, processes, and services."[17] These technological developments are commonly reflected in new patents. With the caveat that some industries may prefer to maintain trade secrets rather than apply for patents, one

11. NSB 1989.
12. It is interesting to note that the years 1985–86 were also the years of the "insurance crisis" (Committee for Economic Development 1989), but even then, R&D spending did not decline.
13. NSB 1989.
14. National Science Foundation (NSF) 1979, 5–6; Standard and Poor's 1987; 1989.
15. Takeda Chemical Industries 1989.
16. NSF 1978.
17. NSB 1990, 134.

can use patents and patent trends as an instructive measure of innovation and competitiveness (see chapter 3 for more discussion on this topic).

The importance of industrial R&D is demonstrated by the prevalence of industrial patents. In 1988, 70 percent of the patents granted to Americans were owned by U.S. corporations, 2 percent were owned by American universities and colleges, and 28 percent by individuals. This dominance of industrial patents has remained within the 70–74 percent range since 1970.[18]

Of all the U.S. patents applied for in 1988, American inventors will receive 52 percent and foreign inventors will receive 48 percent. The foreign countries with the highest share of those patents are Japan (22 percent) and Germany (8 percent). The growth in the Japanese and West German share of U.S. patents averaged 13 percent and 6 percent a year, respectively, after 1983. By contrast, the growth in U.S. patents applied for by American inventors has been only 5.4 percent a year (but that is, of course, on a larger base of patents). The National Science Board concluded that "more and more of the new technologies available for commercial exploitation in the United States are owned and controlled by foreign corporations."[19]

It is instructive to examine how those patents are distributed over various industries. Such analysis shows that where patenting is high for Japanese corporations, it is often low for American ones, and vice versa. For example, Japanese patent strength in the United States is shown in electronics, photography and photocopying, and motor vehicles. Patents by U.S. firms, in contrast, stress chemical areas, including biochemistry, petroleum, and pharmaceuticals.

Because of the increase in patents by foreign inventors (96 percent of whose 1988 patents are owned by foreign corporations), the U.S. share of U.S. patents dropped between 1978 and 1988 in most broad SIC categories except drugs and medicines. The actual number of patents per year in each industry group was maintained or increased except for a drop in transportation equipment.[20]

Japanese patent share increased in all sixteen broad product fields used by the National Science Board, with the largest increases in office, computing, and accounting machines, communications equipment, electronic components, textile mill products, and motor vehicles and other trans-

18. NSB 1990.
19. NSB, 1980, 134.
20. Here, transportation equipment excludes aircraft and aircraft parts.

portation equipment. The increase in the Japanese patent share in the chemical industry was relatively small.

The West German share of 1978–88 U.S. patents was modest overall, but the share increased in motor vehicles and other transportation equipment, aircraft and aircraft parts, and nonelectrical machinery. The share of patents in the chemical industry remained about the same, and declines were seen in the West German share of patents for drugs and medicines and textile mill products.

Patent patterns in the United States will increasingly reflect more specialization of effort in certain technologies as it becomes clear that no one country can be the flagship nation in every technical field. For the United States, the chemical industry is identified as an area of particular strength. The traditional indicators do not support the notion that liability is deterring this industry from becoming competitive.

New Data from Viscusi and Moore

Viscusi and Moore provide alternative means of examining innovation (see chapter 3). Their work uses surveys of companies in different industries and industry subsets to assess the perceived importance of patents (both process and product), the prevalence and frequency of product changes, and the presence or absence of new product development in those companies. Since product changes and new product development do not necessarily imply innovative behavior, the data discussed below will focus upon patents as indicators of innovation.

The patent data presented show again that different segments of the chemical and allied products industry manifest different levels of innovation. Overall (SIC 28), product and process patents are deemed significant for only 15 percent of the industry sample. But 43 percent of the companies in the drug sector sample considered product patents significant, and 29 percent called process patents significant. (The responses are not mutually exclusive; there can be significant overlap.) The patenting of chemical products is considered even more important to the agricultural industry, in which 100 percent of the companies sampled called product patents significant and 50 percent called process patents significant. In the miscellaneous chemical products category (SIC 289), which includes adhesives, sealants, explosives, printing ink, carbon black, and chemical preparations not classified elsewhere, product and process patents were considered significant by only 13 percent of the firms sampled.

Thus the chemical industry has some sectors that are highly innovative by the standards of patent significance, and other sectors that show low innovation by this measure. If the data were available, it would be possible to test for linkage between this measure (and others) of innovation and the number of liability claims or the total product liability litigation expense for companies within each sector since the germination of tort liability in the early 1960s.

Product Liability and the Chemical Industry

According to Mary Heaton of the Chemical Manufacturers Association, whose membership comprises 90 percent of American chemical production, product liability was a prime issue in 1986 and 1987. Today it ranks about fifth in priority out of the eight or so principal issues with which the CMA is concerned.[21] Heaton feels that the level of product liability litigation experienced several years ago by the chemical industry will not be seen again but that current levels of litigation will continue at a steady rate for the foreseeable future.

A main concern for the chemical industry, according to many chemical industry representatives, is that companies are forced to deal with unpredictable risk. Although they normally like to operate with no risk, the next best situation is to work with well-defined risk. In the chemical industry many of the risks are not well defined. For example, one respondent cited new concern over the influence of products on human reproductive health, because these risks have not been well characterized and there are no standard tests on which manufacturers can rely. In contrast, cancer risks are determined by standard carcinogen testing protocols, and these tests are known hurdles that companies can accommodate in their product development. Thus companies developing new products face the double risk of uncertain regulatory approval and product liability suits for newly discovered effects.

The assessment of risk is at the crux of many of the business decisions affecting chemical companies. The risks and uncertainties of the regulatory process and the risks and uncertainties from liability litigation may be perceived quite differently. One insurance executive expressed the

21. The others include clean air, the transport of hazardous material, and tax issues at the federal level. At the state level, the same issues are important, as well as waste minimization and source reduction, hazardous waste, and worker health and safety.

general view that companies are happier with the regulatory system than with the tort system. "The regulatory system is the devil you know. It tells you what you should do and where safe harbor is. The liability system is the devil you don't know. It tells you what you shouldn't do but only after you've done it."

Another view is that regulatory hurdles—such as those embodied in the Toxic Substances Control Act (TSCA)—have a much greater dampening effect on innovation than liability concerns do because of the uncertainty of product approval and the abundance of red tape. The effect of this regulation may be that companies avoid regulating uncertainty by keeping in circulation many previously approved products that should have been modified or replaced long ago. One executive felt that reasonable regulations based on standards devised jointly by industry and government would go far in stimulating more investment in innovative activity in this country.

Background

Regulatory control of chemical products by federal agencies is also strong, though enforcement is frequently limited by small budgets.[22] Like all other industries in the United States, the chemical industry must meet standards set by the Occupational Safety and Health Administration. According to Standard and Poor's industry surveys, the chemical industry has been rated "at or near the top in safety among all industries surveyed since 1980."[23] Part of its outstanding occupational safety record is based on the observation that many chemical plants are highly automated, exposing workers to fewer dangers than in more labor-intensive industries like steel and lumber.[24]

Regulations are also enforced by the Environmental Protection Agency (EPA), the Food and Drug Administration (FDA), and the U.S. Department of Agriculture (USDA) to protect the general public from harmful products or exposures. For example, in the area of environmental control, the EPA enforces such laws as the Emergency Planning and Community Right-to-Know Act, the Clean Air Act, the Toxic Substances Control Act (TSCA), the Resource Conservation and Recovery Act

22. The federal government's budgetary limitations on enforcing regulatory compliance are a commonly cited justification for the need for a tort liability system.

23. Standard and Poor's 1990.

24. Hicks 1989.

(RCRA), Superfund and the Superfund Amendments and Reauthorization Act (SARA), the Clean Water Act, the Safe Drinking Water Act, and the Chemical Diversion and Trafficking Act. Although meeting these requirements increases the capital expenditures and operating costs of companies, it is generally acknowledged that they significantly improve public safety.

Because the regulatory system cannot guarantee safety, product liability allows injured parties to make claims against chemical manufacturers for compensation for personal injury and property damage associated with the use of or exposure to chemical products. As for tort liability suits, some products may attract litigation from workers in a manufacturing plant, some from individual consumers, and a few from large numbers of similarly injured parties in a class action suit.

The tort system has changed since the early 1960s, as summarized by Huber.[25] Traditionally, each plaintiff had to show injury in tort cases. Today personal anxiety over potential injury can be cause for product liability lawsuits.[26] Whereas previous tort litigation typically concerned private injury, the trend in product liability is to bring suits for widespread public risks such as pollution. And whereas the tort system was designed for "bipolar" controversies and judgments between individuals, multiple plaintiffs and multiple defendants are common in product liability cases. Further, any person belonging to a class of exposed people can have standing in court. Hence the risks associated with a single product can, in theory, bankrupt a company. In practice, however, few companies have filed under Chapter 11 because of product liability.

According to a former chemical industry executive, before the 1960s companies had little or no concern about liability but had a lot of concern about social responsibility. Today the potential for litigation is the first concern, and social responsibility comes later. People are more prone to litigate now than before, and will do so over issues they would have ignored previously, such as allergic reactions to drugs or pesticides.

Even though these perceptions may be true, their effect on innovation in the chemical industry is unknown. It can also be argued that concern about potential litigation holds companies to a more common standard than concern about social responsibility.

25. Huber 1985; 1988b.
26. Huber 1988b; Connolly 1988.

Product Liability Trends

For industry overall, federal product liability suits comprised only 3.8 percent of all suits filed in federal courts between statistical years 1974 and 1986.[27] Furthermore, much of the tort activity is concentrated on a small number of companies and on only a few products—particularly asbestos and certain pharmaceuticals and automobiles. The growth in numbers of liability suits is also greatest for these particular companies and these particular products. The pace of filings outside these industries has been slowing. From 1976 through 1981, the annual increase was 11 percent, but showed a decline to about 4 percent a year from 1981 to 1986.[28] This compares favorably with 3 percent growth a year for non-product-liability torts and 7 percent a year for all other private civil suits.[29] The recent rate of growth in product liability cases, therefore, does not seem alarming.

In his study of the distribution of federal product liability cases among fourteen manufacturing industry groups organized by SIC code, Dungworth showed that chemical companies (not including pharmaceuticals and health products) were named lead defendant in 5.2 percent of all cases in statistical years 1974–86.[30] Similarly, they represented only 5.9 percent of the total number of lead defendants named in all suits in those same years.[31]

Dungworth further reported that there were 1,143 chemical companies named lead defendant in 4,418 federal suits between 1974 and 1986. On average, there were four suits per lead defendant over this thirteen-year period, or about one new suit every three years. That is less than the average number (five) of suits per lead defendant in product liability claims across all industries. The number of "major defendants"—that is, those named lead defendant in 250 or more cases over 1974–86—was only a small fraction of the chemical industry defendants, and the growth rate in suits for this group is lower than the growth for nonmajor defendants. Thus the base of companies named is expanding, though slowly. As

27. Dungworth 1988, 30.
28. Dungworth 1988, ix.
29. Dungworth 1988, x.
30. The industries with more cases in statistical years 1974–86 were tools, machinery, and industrial equipment (16.5 percent), stone, glass, and clay (16.5 percent), pharmaceuticals and health products (13.5 percent), and motor vehicles (8.1 percent).
31. Chemicals ranked behind tools, machinery, and industrial equipment (30.7 percent), electronics and electrical equipment (6.3 percent), and food, beverages, and tobacco (6.2 percent).

Dungworth observed, "More and more companies are being named, but they are not being named very often."[32]

Although there are, as mentioned, more than 12,000 chemical plants in the United States (suggesting a smaller but still large number of chemical companies) and more than 50,000 chemical products in the marketplace, only a small proportion of companies (less than 1 percent) and a negligible number of products (less than 0.25 percent) have been the focus of most of the claims each year. When one takes into account that most claims are settled out of court, the financial burden on the total industry is very small. But the burden on the few individual companies who are named as defendants, while a rare event, can be devastating, especially when class action suits are brought.

Of the wide array of chemical products attracting liability litigation, perhaps the best known are dioxin (including Agent Orange), DDT, lead, benzene, and TCE.[33] Such cases are called toxic torts, which are characterized by the involvement of large numbers of people, long latency periods to injury, controversial causation, and uncertainty about the identity of the responsible party. Further, resolution in court requires the presentation of scientific data, often of a pioneering nature, which can be subject to varying interpretations. Litigation of these substances usually moves in waves, as described by Huber.[34] For example, the first wave of DDT cases in Triana, Alabama, involved 1,100 claimants. A second wave of plaintiffs citing identical injuries but living more distant from the pollution source increased that number by 9,000.

During the Vietnam War thousands of military personnel were exposed to the herbicide-defoliant Agent Orange, which contains dioxin, alleged to have caused health problems in those who were exposed and in their offspring. Agent Orange has been responsible for the largest number of product liability cases in the chemical industry, accounting for up to 14 percent of all product liability cases filed with chemical companies as lead defendants in statistical years 1974–86.[35] Of 600 cases coming to trial in the Eastern District Court in New York, as many as 250,000 claimants were represented, averaging about 400 claimants per case.[36] This further

32. Dungworth 1988, 19.
33. Asbestos is not discussed here, since it is classified as a product of the stone, glass, and clay SIC industry category.
34. Huber 1988a, 137.
35. The number is probably less because the U.S. government may have been named as the lead defendant in a number of these cases.
36. Huber 1988b.

illustrates the point that while product litigation in the chemical industry has been a significant burden to a small number of companies, generally the burden has been spread at a low level across the industry.

Personal Injury versus the Superfund

Unlike products of most other industries, many chemical products are toxic, so that their unsafe storage and disposal makes some companies vulnerable to liability litigation. Chemical companies have been defendants in cases concerning contamination of land, water, and air. And they have borne primary financial responsibility in Superfund cleanup efforts (or litigation over cleanup efforts) at hazardous waste dump sites across the country. As Huber said, "Every one of the several thousand major toxic chemical dump sites scattered across the country can be counted as a potential center of liability litigation."[37] The number of sites requiring cleanup has been estimated at between 10,000 (with total costs of several hundred billion dollars)[38] and 425,000,[39] meaning the problem is probably somewhere between gigantic and gargantuan.

As the environmental counsel for a large chemical company put it, "Liability for environmental cleanup, rather than personal injury, is the primary concern. These costs are orders of magnitude greater than personal injury. [Personal injury costs] are zero; they are insignificant by comparison." Personal injury claims associated with exposures to hazardous waste sites (as opposed to dumping into rivers, for example) have not been frequent, in the view of some interviewees, because waste sites are rarely close enough to where people live to be a health hazard.

It is commonly felt in the chemical industry that no cost-benefit calculation has been done on the Superfund issue—that the standards of cleanup are unreasonable and the value of additional health protection provided has not been weighed against the cost of the cleanup required. The monies needed to restore a site to meet the standards of the Superfund Amendments and Reauthorization Act of 1986, which requires that "no known or anticipated adverse effects on the health of persons can occur," is considered extraordinary and could be better spent on other environmental problems. Estimates for cleanup costs at some sites are over $1 billion, and the estimated cost to clean up all sites in the country ranges

37. Huber 1988a, 138.
38. OTA 1985.
39. GAO 1987.

from $100 billion to over $1 trillion.[40] With strict liability and joint and several liability being applied, the financial health of even the largest chemical companies may be at risk, because these "deep pockets" can be saddled with a disproportionate share of the cleanup costs.

Further, participation in cleanup operations by nonproducers can render them vulnerable to lawsuits in the future. Companies may be unwilling to get involved with hazards whose health and environmental effects may not yet have been determined.

The Chemical Industry and Insurance

Much has been made of the relationship between potential product liability and the ability of companies to acquire reasonable insurance coverage.[41] Like all industries, insurance companies work with known risks defined by previous experience. Unfortunately, most liability risks and court awards for injury compensation and punitive damages are unpredictable, and losses can be extreme. Insurance companies are often unwilling or unable to offer coverage at affordable premiums under such conditions.

According to the analyses by Viscusi and Moore using insurance rate-setting files of the Insurance Services Office for 1980–84 (see chapter 3), insurance companies lost $1.49 for every $1 of premium paid by the chemical industry for bodily injury coverage, and lost $1.08 for every $1 paid for property damage insurance.[42]

When looking at trends in the loss-to-premium ratio over time within the chemical industry, the variability from year to year is striking. This underscores the unpredictable nature of risk in this industry, which may be driving insurers to withdraw coverage or increase premiums, both of which encourage companies to self-insure. As coverage is withdrawn from the riskiest sectors, one might expect loss ratios for the insurance industry to stabilize, but that did not appear to happen between 1980 and 1984.

During the same period, the ratios of total insurance premiums for personal injury and property damage to chemical sales dropped markedly—25 percent and 50 percent, respectively. These figures are not the result of a decline in the price of insurance or of an increase in product

40. CED 1989, 107.
41. See Weber 1987; Calfee and Winston 1988; Harrington 1988; CED 1989, chap. 3.
42. These losses are reduced by the interest earned on premiums. Insurance companies can still be profitable when payments are slightly higher than premiums.

sales by the chemical industry but are due to a rationing of insurance by the insurance industry. Indeed, according to a representative of the Chemical Manufacturers Association, chemical companies have been increasingly self-insured since the early 1980s.

Liability and Decisionmaking

As of today, only a handful of companies have closed down or reorganized because of liability litigation. The Committee for Economic Development cited bankruptcies only over asbestos (Johns Manville Corporation and five other companies) and the Dalkon Shield (A. H. Robins Company) in their 1989 report (note that these products fall under the stone, clay, and glass and the pharmaceuticals industries). Most companies that have failed have done so for more traditional business reasons. Thus the more traditional business concerns have been the focus of attention by trade publications and associations.

Although many chemical industry CEOs are aware of the liability problem, management still has trouble getting this issue on the agenda for discussion in corporate meetings—it still has low priority. Some of the interviewees believe that this is because many industries, particularly the chemical industry, are just beginning to notice the effects of environmental liability and of personal injury claims. One chemical industry insurer predicts that within four or five years more companies will have failed under the fiscal burden of product and environmental liability, and this problem will command more attention.

The Conference Board produced two studies designed to evaluate the corporate response to product liability. One approach was to interview risk managers and others who deal more directly with litigation and liability.[43] The results showed that liability concerns had a small effect on product withdrawals, curtailment of R&D, and other similar business actions. This work was widely criticized on the grounds that the decisionmakers—the CEOs—were not the respondents to the surveys.[44] Another criticism was that risk managers responded in ways that demonstrated they were doing their job—managing risk effectively.

43. Weber 1987.
44. One can also make the case, however, that lower-level managers and counsels are more in touch with the early as well as the later decisions about the pursuit of different products, and that this study could have inflated the impact of product liability concerns on innovation.

A second report of the Conference Board focused solely on CEOs or those appointed by the CEO to represent his or her views.[45] These results did show a widespread effect of liability on company decisionmaking. But this perspective is also suspect. In many companies product managers bear the responsibility for decisions about what potential products to pursue and what to drop. CEOs are less involved in risk-management decisions until catastrophic incidents or the adverse publicity surrounding them occur. These low-probability but high-impact events may induce CEOs to "overestimate the risks and focus on avoiding worst-case scenarios, perhaps to the point of taking risk-avoidance measures that are not justified on an objective cost-benefit basis."[46]

What, then, is the appropriate approach to studying the effect of liability on business activities? As the chief corporate counsel in one prominent chemical company commented, the amount spent on litigation fees is not enough to influence the condition of his company as a whole, but some lines of business within the company may be profoundly affected. Although upper-level management may not be much concerned about liability, product managers responsible for cost centers must make budgetary and other decisions with product liability risks and costs in mind. In other companies, the CEO may be directly involved in product decisions. Thus the impact of liability perceptions on decisionmaking may vary according to the decision structures of different companies, suggesting that some analyses should be done for companies grouped by commercial structure.

As indicated earlier, Superfund liability and product liability may affect chemical industry decisionmaking differently because of differences in the predictability of their outcomes and of the size of compensation. According to one chemical insurer, environmental liability for hazardous waste disposal is such that regulatory compliance affords relatively little protection for associated companies, and joint and several liability means that companies frequently pay an unfair share of the burden. A company rarely has an effective defense, save "an act of God, an act of war, or if the producer had no contractual relationship with the party doing the dumping." By contrast, though product liability rules are less certain and judgments more capricious, showing regulatory compliance can help a defendant company in court, and the penalties are usually lower than for Superfund liabilities.

45. McGuire 1988.
46. CED 1989, 110–11.

Potential Superfund liability is a major deterrent to innovation in the hazardous waste cleanup area, according to several interviewees. They feel the Superfund system is so draconian that it discourages companies which might participate in cleanup operations and innovate new technologies for cleaning. According to this view, an entire field of activity has been stifled. The participants tend to be smaller companies that do little or no R&D on cleanup methods, have less experience, and are not as risk-averse as might be desirable—companies that are "quite willing to disappear" if litigation threatens. Insurers are even less willing to back such companies.

Liability and Reduced Innovation

The regulatory and consumer demands for safer products support the view of some industry experts that the current liability system means higher cost (at least in R&D) to bring individual chemical products to market than previously. Today, besides general design and manufacture, companies must carry out a broad range of tests for toxicity of a product and its by-products and design safe means of disposal. Although these requirements will not deter companies from developing new products, they do present an added burden and an increased economic risk, since fewer products in development will meet all the necessary standards. Furthermore, given the increased R&D cost per product in time and dollars, fewer new products will be produced.

It is difficult to assess whether the implied degree of reduction in numbers of products produced has had a significant effect on the innovativeness of products in the marketplace. A representative of one large chemical company stated that about 200 new products are proposed in his company each year. Of these, about 10 are chosen for development. Liability concerns might cause the company to pull 1 of those out of R&D. As mentioned, about 1,000 new chemical products are proposed to the EPA every year. If liability litigation either directly or indirectly prevents the pursuit of even 10 percent of these, meaning that otherwise 1,100 new chemicals might have been proposed for manufacture, this difference would not necessarily be detectable on the landscape of all chemicals produced.

Further, no benchmark exists for evaluating the significance of the report (in both the Conference Board studies mentioned earlier) that a given percentage of survey respondents claimed that product liability affects development and marketing decisions. If 75 percent of the companies surveyed responded that liability concerns had strongly affected business decisions, would that imply overdeterrence or underdeterrence or an appropriate level? Another problem is that decisionmaking processes and previous experience vary widely from one company to the next, so that a level of liability risk that would deter one company might not deter otherwise similar companies. Furthermore, so many factors impinge on a given decision that it is difficult to know when the fear of product liability was largely responsible for a decision or was just a contributing factor. For liability to be an effective deterrent to unsafe practices or poor product design, should it perhaps always be considered at least a contributing factor? Such questions must be addressed if innovation-driven tort reform can be justified.

Anecdotes and the Dearth of Data

Many feel that liability concerns can affect product development decisions, but few examples are available. One well-publicized instance of a company's decision not to market a product because of fears of liability litigation concerned an asbestos substitute produced by Monsanto.[47] Monsanto developed a phosphate fiber product that showed better heat resistance than asbestos for use in automobile brake linings. In one of a series of animal tests, pleural implants of the fibers in a gelatin matrix correlated with the presence of fibrosarcomas. These results raised concern among EPA scientists; Monsanto scientists, however, claimed that the tests were irrelevant, since the normal route of exposure to the fiber is by inhalation and inhalation tests showed no health risk.[48] Monsanto built a pilot project for $105 million in St. Louis to manufacture the fiber. Three months later, the CEO, Richard Mahoney, decided to scrap the project owing to fears that workers with lung cancers from other causes and trial lawyers expert at asbestos litigation might turn their attention to Monsanto's new product.

Although both the EPA and Monsanto views of the animal test results of this product have merit, the fact that the product was associated with cancer in laboratory animals in any test would make the company vulnerable to liability claims regardless of the actual safety of the product for humans. In any case, the ambiguities in this example and the absence

47. Tarnoff 1987.
48. The justification for doing the test was that not enough material was available at the time to do the more appropriate inhalation studies.

of other examples from the industry further undermine the claim that liability concerns curb the willingness of companies to innovate to a significant degree.

Indeed, many other factors, such as previous experience in the courts, might also affect a company's decision to pursue a product line. On the one hand, companies that have, rightly or wrongly, been the defendant in one or more product liability suits may be less willing to subject themselves to further litigation expense and the inevitable costs to their reputation. On the other hand, companies that have had multiple successful cases in court (and that can afford the legal costs) may not be deterred.

Furthermore, companies that are unwilling to take on the risk have the option of selling or licensing their technology to another firm. Indeed, Monsanto reportedly showed an interest in selling or licensing its asbestos fiber technology after deciding not to pursue the product itself.[49] Thus, even if fears of unjustified lawsuits motivate a company to drop a certain technology, the American consumer will not necessarily be deprived of its benefits.

In an interview with *Business Insurance*, a Monsanto risk manager, Robert E. Toth, said he had no knowledge of any other product that Monsanto had withdrawn from the market or stopped development on because of fears of product liability litigation. According to Toth, "the only other product we seriously questioned based on the litigation potential" was a flame-retardant fiber used in children's clothing because it had been confused by consumers with another manufacturer's product that had been linked to cancer.[50]

Thus, except for phosphate fiber, product liability concerns did not appear to much affect corporate product development and marketing decisions in Monsanto before 1987, at least at the highest levels of decisionmaking. Unfortunately, no data are publicly available to show how representative this attitude toward product liability really is today in Monsanto or the chemical industry in general.

Another example of the effects of product liability concerns on the chemical industry has been cited by Reuter.[51] A chemical manufacturer did not allow the use of its product in aircraft landing gear (even though

49. Tarnoff 1987.
50. Tarnoff 1987, 34.
51. Reuter 1988, 27.

the company believed its product would have enhanced the safety of the gear) because counsel advised that "potential liability costs far outweighed any potential profits."

There are not enough specific examples, and no preponderance of evidence of the effects of liability on the product decisions of chemical companies, to support any meaningful conclusions. If many examples exist, they may be obscured by the proprietary nature of most company information, by the reluctance of companies to have their names associated with product liability issues, and by the company's perception that its suspended product may be of some commercial value in the future—that is, such products may be developed later and marketed by the company or sold or licensed to another company for further development. Alternatively, there may in fact be very few cases in which products were dropped because of fears of unjustified liability claims.

Until more data are forthcoming on actual business decisions and how they were influenced by liability concerns, it is difficult to have confidence in any analysis of the effects of liability on industrial innovation. Although one may assume that innovation is restricted to some extent by regulation and liability, with the present data one cannot measure the degree to which liability may constrain creativity or assess whether the costs in lost innovation and economic opportunity outweigh the benefits of product safety.

Liability as a Spur to Innovation

The litigious climate surrounding Superfund and product liability concerns over new products could make companies that might have expertise in handling toxic substances or developing new products be more conservative. On the other hand, the increased attention that liability suits bring to product design and environmental protection might encourage the perception of market opportunities and a new wave of innovation.

One industry leader who believes that environmental and other concerns will spur a new level of new product and process innovations in the chemical industry is Richard Tucker, vice-chairman of the Mobil Corporation. In a recent editorial in *Scientific American,* he shared a vision of the industry employing "precision-designed catalysts working like chemical assembly lines, manufacturing molecular structures to order, carrying out multiple consecutive reactions at different sites—each site approaching the incredible selectivity of a biological enzyme designed by eons of evolution." He sees the need for industry to innovate through devising "catalysts and processes that fine-tune manufacturing to minimize or eliminate unwanted by-products, computer modeling to optimize every manufacturing or production system, new molecular structures that pass harmlessly through the environment, and recycling of wastes."[52]

One representative of a large chemical company feels that many companies (large and small) are now innovating to deal with the hazardous waste problem. Another chemical industry expert sees a booming industry rising over the cleanup, storage, and testing of hazardous wastes. That presents a big opportunity for chemical companies, which have traditionally had more experience in hazardous waste treatment and containment than any other group. For example, one large chemical company has developed a peroxide treatment of dump site soils to create conditions that promote microbial degradation of hazardous waste.

Censorship of some products may create economic incentives to innovate by developing alternative products. For example, the increasing bans on plastic packaging in local communities and in other countries are prompting the chemical industry to develop "degradable" plastics and other products or processes that minimize waste. With the ban on chlorofluorocarbon (CFC) production agreed to by the United States and the twelve European Community nations to take effect in 1990, many companies (such as International Chemical Industries, Union Carbide, DuPont, and Allied Signal) are producing what are claimed to be environmentally safer alternatives to CFCs. There is good scientific evidence to support the prediction that continued CFC production would induce further ozone layer depletion and increase the amount of ultraviolet radiation reaching the earth. Some in the industry view CFC production as a possible area for class action suits for people with skin cancer and cataracts, which are associated with high ultraviolet exposure. Developing new ozone-safe replacements that act as well as or better than existing CFCs in all of their present applications will require a high level of innovation. But it is difficult to determine to what extent fear of lawsuits on its own (as opposed to an outright ban) might have driven innovation here. One environmental counsel for a large chemical company does stress that liability concerns were a strong factor in the company's decision to curtail CFC production and develop alternative products.

Another example of the corporate response to the risk of environmental liability is the implementation of "cradle to grave" product stewardship

52. Tucker 1990, 128.

for some products sold by chemical manufacturers to their industrial customers. This approach presumably adds significant cost to the company (or to the price of its products) but controls the risks of improper storage, use, and disposal of the product or its by-products by downstream users. One company considered controlling risks by collecting wastes generated from the use of its products by customers—an even more expensive proposition—but was deterred by special licensing requirements, the risk of increased liability for the transport of chemicals, and the like. If trends in liability continue, new ideas for control can be expected.

In the aftermath of Bhopal, many American companies reevaluated their operating risks.[53] Companies worked to reduce their on-site stockpiles of hazardous chemicals and to better monitor the remaining stocks. Hercules Chemical Company, for example, discontinued the manufacture of one hazardous product because reasonable measures could not sufficiently reduce the risk of accidents. Many companies more closely scrutinized the transport of chemicals to and from their plants. Shipments are now more often routed through less-populous areas. To further reduce transport hazards, some companies have created on-site facilities for producing materials they formerly shipped in. Others participate more in community-education programs about the products being made, and many have developed or revised detailed community notification and evacuation plans in the event of a major emergency. Finally, more firms have engaged consultants to study the reduction of risk in the handling of hazardous substances.

Liability and International Competitiveness

For industry in general, issues of tariffs, government subsidies of R&D, the savings rate and the cost of capital, the demographics and training of the work force, the strength of the dollar, the inflation rate, and the price of oil all have a profound impact on American competitiveness. With some striking exceptions (for example, private aircraft and contraceptives), the effects of the American liability system on competitiveness are obscured by the magnitude of these other issues. It is doubtful that tort reform would do much to level the playing field for most industries. Moreover, reform of the tort system might induce more regulatory ac-

53. Hicks 1989; Bowman and Kunreuther 1988.

tivity, which may be more costly and detrimental than the present conditions under which chemical companies operate.

As for environmental protection, many observers, both American and foreign, feel that the burden of environmental regulation is not much different in magnitude for the United States than for the main economic competitors of the United States—Japan, Germany, and the rest of Europe. However, in most other countries business is not burdened with the time and cost demands of product liability litigation seen in the United States. Other countries have fewer lawyers per capita, they have no contingency fees, trials are decided by judges rather than juries, and punitive damages are not awarded. Thus many of the incentives for plaintiffs to file suit do not exist elsewhere. The American tort liability system, in contrast, is designed as a mechanism to compensate victims. Many other countries have reliable compensation schemes for health (such as a national health system) and other losses and therefore have less of a need for a court-based compensation scheme. However, universal health and other benefits put burdens on the economies of our competitors that the United States does not carry and can create demands on the regulatory system to be more efficient.

It would be difficult to argue that the uncertainty and unpredictability of the tort system does not affect business planning to some degree. And some risk-averse companies may decide to abandon certain lines of research and development because of concern over liability, leaving those areas open to foreign competitors. But such actions arguably increase the average safety of products, while preserving opportunities for American competitors willing to assume the risk and creating incentives for producers to innovate to make alternative and even safer products.

On the whole, it is difficult to evaluate the magnitude of the disadvantages of the present system and even more difficult to weigh them against the advantages of the deterrence they provide against the introduction of truly hazardous products. Furthermore, the possibility of an occasional "excessive" award may provide greater deterrent value at lower net cost to society than universally applicable regulations do. Leaving the system as it is (and allowing excessive awards), however, raises the problem of the balance between fairness—in deterrence and compensation—and social efficiency. The liability system might benefit from some fine-tuning to make the system more responsive, less expensive, and more equitable. But such attempts may actually make it less effective.

One recommendation that is supported by chemical manufacturers is to limit liability to those companies that violate the spirit or the letter of regulations in effect at the time of production. This measure would protect manufacturers from suits arising from the discovery in the future of hazardous effects of their products. However, it does not include a compensation mechanism for future injury to consumers. Whether producers should be liable for such compensation is controversial.

Chemical Companies in the Courtroom

A combination of factors makes the liability system particularly unpredictable for the chemical industry. First (and foremost), the public has little understanding of chemical substances and their hazards relative to other risks. Second, mistrust of corporations is growing, and organized activism is more sophisticated. Third, chemical products are pervasive: traces of natural and synthetic toxic and carcinogenic substances exist in all food, air, and water. Fourth, the technology for detection of minute quantities of these substances is advancing. Finally, the long-term effects of exposure to some products frequently cannot be predicted.

One chemical industry official paints a bleak picture. Unlike machine tools, chemicals are not easily understood, explanations of their use and their hazards are not easily accessible to the average jury member, and they instill fear—chemophobia—in most of the public. The lack of public understanding of scientific arguments is particularly important in the courtroom, where the data that defendants are obliged to present are typically not appreciated or understood by judge or jury and are often viewed as a smokescreen. That is compounded by the existing general mistrust of large corporations, generated by relatively few legitimate claims which are given high profile by the media. This situation means there is no assurance, no matter how frivolous or dubious the suit or how solid the scientific defense, that a jury will decide in favor of the defendant. There is also no certainty, owing to assessments of awards and punitive damages assessment by juries, about how costly judgments may be.

This surely biased view is not altogether inaccurate. But whether the present situation in the courts is simply a nuisance to chemical companies or something that compromises their willingness to produce innovative products should be determined. Presumably the perception that a bias against a factual defense exists in the courtroom makes the possibility of being a defendant even less palatable and may cause some companies to be more conservative in their choice of products to pursue. However, the probability of being named in a suit in the first place is very low.

Though tort reform cannot be justified by the evidence currently available in the chemical industry, the smaller and more tractable problem of ensuring a proper and thoughtful hearing for scientific and technical evidence in product liability cases in the courtroom deserves significant attention.

Conclusions

The claim that the product liability system unduly compromises the chemical industry is not well supported by the evidence. In fact, the dearth of product liability cases in the chemical sector relative to those in other sectors, the lack of a large body of data—or even a set of unimpeachable anecdotes—and the relative inattention to this issue compared with other concerns such as regulation are notable. Combined with the enviable statistics on the growth of the chemical industry and its innovativeness, as shown by patent data, these observations lead to the conclusion that tort liability is a manageable problem for this industry.

However, environmental liability, and particularly Superfund liability, has the potential to become a major problem. The combination of political attention to the environment, low tolerance for hazardous waste, and high standards for cleanup generate high expectations of chemical companies. Though this scenario is not much different from that in competing countries, the number of sites for cleanup and the application of strict (if not absolute) and joint and several liability mean that American companies may shoulder a much heavier responsibility than their foreign competitors will. The projected expenditures would surely affect the operations of American chemical firms. The expense of cleanup may result in increased prices for products, or it may divert funds away from the R&D necessary to fund the innovations for new products. Either effect could compromise the ability of American firms to be competitive. The cleanup of old dump sites, however, is more of a historical problem, and companies like Monsanto are now innovating to minimize waste and ensure its proper disposal.

But the general economic burden of Superfund liability has little bearing on the finding here that there is no compelling body of evidence that product liability has significant, observable, negative effects on innovativeness in the chemical industry. This state of affairs begs three points. First, more data (coming principally from manufacturing and insurance companies) are needed if the claim that our liability system deters innovation is to be supported. Second, though the chemical industry data do not now support it, the data from other industries may justify tort reform. Third, there may be appropriate marginal reforms that are currently justifiable, such as reforms in the courts for dealing with scientific evidence.

As a caveat, the current situation does not preclude the possibility that product liability suits will be a more important problem in the future for the chemical industry. However, the present data from the chemical industry do not support the notion that it is a significant problem now, nor that tort reform will stimulate innovation—the fundamental assumption behind this initiative.

Does the U.S. product liability system affect the competitiveness of U.S. firms in global markets? Currently not enough evidence is available to determine whether there is a significant effect. Gathering such evidence would require a widespread sea change in the attitudes of American companies toward the release of proprietary information that may be useful and necessary to such an analysis. Presumably, the private sector might be more willing to release such information when and if it perceives that the liability problem is worsening.

Since the current state of product liability presents some risk to industry, however low, how might one expect industry to respond to it? Companies that are most risk-averse may engage in product withdrawal or reduction in new product R&D. Companies that do not perceive liability issues as a serious concern may continue their current practices and policies. Companies that are more comfortable with risk may see market opportunities created by the liability system and may step in to fill the breach.

The questions of how these are balanced in an economy and what factors affect that balance are of key concern to overall safety and competitiveness. Would reform of tort liability change the balance of innovators to conservative producers? If so, would the new balance be appropriate to meet the joint goals of public safety, economic well-being, and competitiveness?

References

Bowman, E., and H. Kunreuther. 1988. "Post-Bhopal Behavior at a Chemical Company." *Journal of Management Studies* 25:386–402.

Calfee, J. E., and C. Winston. 1988. "Economic Aspects of Liability Rules and

Liability Insurance." In *Liability: Perspectives and Policy,* edited by R. E. Litan and C. Winston, 16–41. Brookings.

Committee for Economic Development. 1989. *Who Should Be Liable? A Guide to Policy for Dealing with Risk.* New York.

Connolly, D. R. 1988. "Toxics: Too Risky to Insure?—Yes, No, Maybe So." Paper prepared for the American Bar Association Institute on Pollution Liability: Strategies for Managing the Combined Challenges of Superfund and Toxic Tort Claims. American Bar Association, Washington.

Dungworth, T. 1988. *Product Liability and the Business Sector: Litigation Trends in Federal Courts.* R-3668-ICJ. Santa Monica, Calif.: Rand Corporation.

Harrington, S. E. 1988. "Prices and Profits in the Liability Insurance Market." In *Liability: Perspectives and Policy,* edited by R. E. Litan and C. Winston, 42–100. Brookings.

Hicks, J. P. 1989. "An Industry Revamped by Disaster: Chemical Companies Have Been Applying the Lessons of Bhopal." *New York Times,* Feb. 16:D6.

Huber, P. W. 1985. "The Bhopalization of U.S. Tort Law." *Issues in Science and Technology* 2:73–82.

———. 1988a. "Environmental Hazards and Liability Law." In *Liability: Perspectives and Policy,* edited by R. E. Litan and C. Winston, 128–54. Brookings.

———. 1988b. *Liability: The Legal Revolution and Its Consequences.* Basic Books.

McGuire, E. P. 1988. *The Impact of Product Liability.* Report 908. New York: The Conference Board.

National Science Board. 1990. *The State of U.S. Science and Engineering.* Washington: National Science Foundation.

National Science Foundation. 1979. *Research and Development in Industry, 1977.* NSF 79-32. Washington.

Office of Technology Assessment. 1985. *Superfund Strategy.* Washington.

Organization for Economic Cooperation and Development. 1979. *The Chemical Industry, 1979.* Paris.

Reisch, M. S. 1988. "Chemical Capital Spending to Continue Increasing." *Chemical and Engineering News,* Dec. 19:9–11.

Reuter, P. 1988. *The Economic Consequences of Expanded Corporate Liability: An Exploratory Study.* R-2807-ICJ. Santa Monica, Calif.: Rand Corporation.

Standard and Poor's. 1987. *Industry Surveys: Chemicals, Basic Analysis* 155: 15–48.

———. 1989. *Industry Surveys: Chemicals, Basic Analysis* 157:5–58.

———. 1990. *Industry Surveys: Chemicals, Basic Analysis* 158:1–3.

Takeda Chemical Industries. 1989. *Annual Report.* Tokyo.

Tarnoff, S. 1987. "Fear of Suits Kills 'Safe' Monsanto Fiber." *Business Insurance,* July 20:3.

Tucker, R. F. 1990. "Essay: 'Holographic' Science to Meet Energy Needs." *Science* 262:128.

U.S. Department of Commerce. 1990. *1990 U.S. Industrial Outlook*, 12-1–13-7.

U.S. General Accounting Office. 1984. *EPA's Efforts to Identify and Control Harmful Chemicals in Use.* GAO/RCED-84-100.

———. 1987. *Superfund: Extent of the Nation's Potential Hazardous Waste Problem Still Unknown.* GAO/RCED-88-44.

———. 1988. *Product Liability: Extent of "Litigation Explosion" in Federal Courts Questioned.* GAO/HRD-88-36BR.

Weber, N. 1987. *Product Liability: The Corporate Response.* Report 893. New York: The Conference Board.

CHAPTER TWELVE

Product Liability and Safety
in General Aviation

Andrew Craig

G ENERAL aviation—that segment of flying which comprises private, business, and corporate aircraft—differs in several important respects from the other industries whose liability effects are examined in this book. The population of potential victims is limited, aware, and willing to accept some risk. In addition, owning and operating aircraft is expensive. Accordingly, unlike motorcycles, most aircraft are owned or operated by fairly wealthy people, and each crash results in considerable losses and damages to the insurance underwriter.

General aviation has become safer over time. At the end of World War II, fatal accidents occurred at the rate of 7 per 100,000 hours of flying and total accidents at 78 per 100,000 hours.[1] By 1960 fatal and total accident rates had dropped to about half the earlier values, or 3.3 and 36, respectively. At the same time the general aviation class of airplanes flew a larger number of hours, increasing from 9.8 million hours in 1946 to 13.1 million in 1960. Significantly, even though flight time increased, the number of deaths went down from 1,009 to 787 during this period.[2]

As the risks and costs of flying declined, the demand for private aircraft grew, accelerating sharply after 1960. And as the numbers of private aircraft increased, so did the number of product liability lawsuits (see chapter 13). Up until this time, litigation over defective products in general aviation was not significant.

This chapter explores whether and to what extent the increase in product liability litigation since 1960 has appreciably affected the safety of

1. Data compiled in 1966 by the Civil Aeronautics Board (CAB) and supplied to author by the National Transportation Safety Board (NTSB).
2. Data compiled by NTSB, Jan. 4, 1971, and supplied to author; data compiled in 1966 by the CAB.

private aircraft. In examining the evidence, I draw heavily on a series of cases for which I served as an expert witness for either the plaintiffs or defendants.

At the outset, several important features of product liability litigation in general aviation should be noted. First, every accident is investigated by the National Transportation Safety Board (NTSB) to determine the facts of the crash and to suggest the cause. As a result, an excellent record of the safety of a particular design is available to all constituencies, including potential litigants. Second, crashes lead to claims of product defective design much more often than to claims of defective manufacture. Third, about one-third to one-half of all crashes end up in litigation, the ratio depending on which airplane manufacturer is involved. Finally, the alleged cause of most airplane crashes includes very technical matters, and persuading a lay jury—or dissuading it—can be challenging. Frequently, the outcome in such cases turns on a combination of small risks, such as low fuel, icing conditions, and modest airplane performance, that produce a fatal accident or on an incident in which a catastrophic defect lurking in a particular regime of flight leads to the loss of life. The litigation process leaves some doubt, on occasion, whether the case was decided on technical matters or not.

Taking account of all the evidence I review, I conclude that no definite correlation between improved aircraft safety and product liability could be found. Nor does the evidence support a negative correlation: if there had not been litigation, aircraft safety would have been much worse. Finally, although the links between product liability and aircraft safety are uncertain at best, some evidence suggests that liability litigation has improved the dissemination of information about flight safety, and that, arguably, has encouraged pilots to fly their airplanes more safely.

As shown in figure 12-1, the total general aviation accident rate steadily declined from 1962 to 1986. The fatality accident rate, however, remained roughly constant. From 1979 through 1988, the fatality rate per 100,000 hours of flying averaged 1.67.[3] In contrast, the costs of product liability litigation affecting general aviation jumped sharply in recent years, from $24 million in 1977 to $210 million in 1985. Per fatality, the costs rose from about $17,000 to $223,600.[4] Clearly, therefore, the aggregate accident and liability cost data do not support the view that liability litigation has enhanced safety in this industry. The total accident rate has declined

3. NTSB 1986, table 6.
4. Sontag 1987, 550.

Figure 12-1. *Airplane Accident Rates, 1962–86*

Rate per 100,000 hours flown

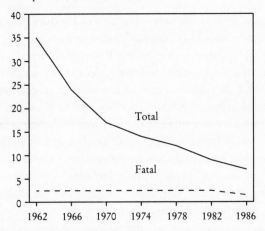

no faster since the explosive increase in liability costs than it did in the earlier period. The fatality rate has remained unchanged. The critical question I examine in the rest of the chapter is whether a link between liability trends and safety can be established at a much more disaggregated level—in the context of specific cases and aircraft designs.

The System of General Aviation

It is essential first to understand the "system" of general aviation safety. In diagram form, the system looks like figure 12-2.

For my purposes here, the two main components are the liability block and the regulation block, each of which has internal elements. Each block has an input and an output to show cause and effect for that component, and the lines interconnecting the blocks show how information, quantities, or actions flow through the system. The output of one block acts as the input to the subsequent member downstream. When a path ends up back at the block where it started, a feedback loop is in place. Feedback makes the system capable of self-correcting behavior; in this case that means alteration to improve safety.

On the left side of the diagram, the block flight operations indicates as its output the accident statistics of general aviation, the measurement of safety. Three inputs into this block are also shown: weather, pilots, and aircraft design. There is no input loop to the weather block, since this function is taken to be outside the control of anything known. Inputs to the pilots and the aircraft design elements are dealt with later.

From here, the system splits into two parallel paths through the large liability and regulation blocks. Both paths then meet as two inputs acting on aircraft manufacturers. The decision of manufacturers to change or not to change the design of their product influences the accident record and thus is of central interest in the debate over product liability.

In short, the task at hand is to discover any interaction between the liability block and the accident record. As shown in the figure, liability and regulation are separate: one or both of them might change safety, but neither can act on the other. This "independence" assumption is discussed later.

The interaction between liability and the safety of general aviation could be tested easily if an example could be found in which the liability pathway was "open," or was not functioning as an input on the aircraft manufacturers. But for the period of time under study, no interval could be found when this part of the system was inoperative. In other words, there were no crashes without subsequent litigation, or certainly not enough instances to be significant.

Alternately, the regulation path might have been "open" and inoperative during the years examined, in which case it could be determined if liability produced safety in a self-corrective manner. Of course that did not happen, since the Federal Aviation Administration (FAA) and the National Transportation Safety Board were active continuously since their inception with the stated goal of promoting (but not ensuring) safety.

In sum, both liability and regulation have potentially acted to influence safety. However, there are important differences between these two blocks in the system.

For liability, the primary purpose is to compensate the victims of an accident. Aviation underwriters facilitate this objective, as shown in figure 12-2, as a dollar outflow to the victims. For the overall liability block, therefore, accidents come in either as awards to the victims or costs to the aircraft manufacturers and aircraft owners. The internal workings within the block, such as insurance costs as a function of accident rates, the number of decisions favoring the plaintiff or the defendant, and the action of aircraft owners in choosing which airplane to operate, will govern the magnitude of this monetary input to the manufacturers. The manufacturers then decide on the basis of costs whether to change the

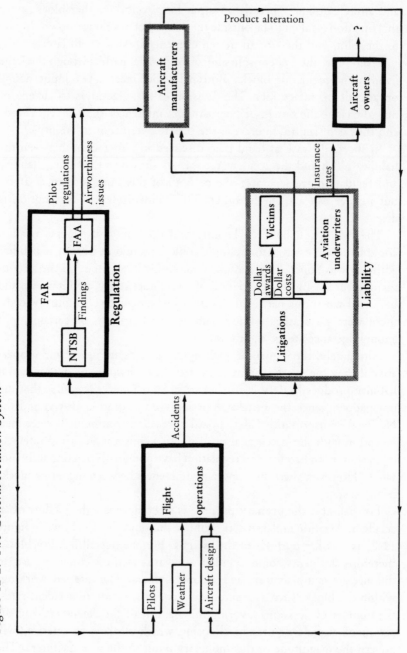

Figure 12-2. *The General Aviation System*

airplane design or not. To this degree, therefore, the compensation provided by the liability system should in principle also affect safety.

In contrast, the sole purpose of regulation is to ensure a given level of safety. In the words of John S. Yodice, general counsel for the Aircraft Owners and Pilots Association, "General aviation, at the federal level, is probably the most intensely regulated of any private activity in this country. Every aircraft is certificated, maintained, and operated to federal standards. Every pilot is trained, certificated, and operates to federal standards." (Hence the input from the FAA to the pilots block.) Yodice goes on to say, "The federal government regulates the navigable airspace and operates the air traffic control system. The federal government investigates aircraft accidents, determines their causes, and makes safety recommendations based on these investigations."[5] (This is shown by the NTSB and FAA blocks.)

Given this regulatory structure, it is certainly conceivable that safety could be produced without the liability block functioning at all. Thus one can imagine that if an airplane is certified by the FAA as complying with the federal aviation regulations, or FAR (shown as input to the FAA block in the figure), safety might be "insured" or "guaranteed" to the aircraft operator. Accordingly, compliance with applicable safety regulations could serve as an absolute defense against claims of product defects.

In fact, however, current liability law regards the federal aviation regulations as *minimum* safety standards and thus compliance with them as *not* providing a defense in liability cases. While such a rule clearly makes sense for an airplane manufactured defectively, aircraft firms are subjected to considerable uncertainty when certification of the *designs* of their aircraft is not held to excuse them from subsequent liability claims. This is especially true since certification of a design to FAR specifications is a lengthy and costly procedure that often culminates in extensive flight testing of the new design to see if it meets the requirements. Nevertheless, one reason that tort law imposes a higher standard for the aircraft context in particular may be that the FAA permits self-certification by manufacturers. Accordingly, even though an airplane is said to be "airworthy" by the FAA, it may later be found to be "unairworthy" in litigation.

In my case studies, one issue I explore is whether the regulation and liability blocks are in fact independent components or whether they are

5. Yodice 1990, 4–5; NTSB 1989, table 6; data complied by NTSB, Sept. 6, 1978, and supplied to author.

interconnected in some way. In addition, an open question in figure 12-2, next to the aircraft owners block, is whether owners affect aircraft safety by reducing their demand for relatively "unsafe" models. Although evidence on this issue is scarce, conventional wisdom suggests that few prospective purchasers of airplanes investigate the safety record of the models they are considering purchasing or examine the history of mandatory changes the airplane has undergone in the interests of safety. If the contrary were true, a connection between safety and airplane sales—that is, demand for the product—could be included in the figure.

Some Case Studies

As already indicated, to find evidence of possible links between litigation and aircraft safety, I examine a number of case histories involving particular features of general aviation aircraft. All the cases draw on the system diagram shown in figure 12-2 and serve to show both workings of blocks within each side of the system diagram and single-instance modifications and interconnections of the system.

A Stall-Spin Case

One large group of fatal aircraft accidents is linked to stall-spin behavior. This condition, which typically occurs at low speed in takeoffs and landings, refers to a loss of normal lifting forces on the airplane, causing uncontrollable departure from level flight into a twisting, helical flight path, called a "tailspin," often seen in many early movies about flying. In most such cases the airplane continues this spin until it strikes the earth, usually killing the occupants.

An FAA investigation of the accidents from 1964 through 1972 showed that, while stall-spin accidents accounted for only 8 percent of all accidents, they represented 24 percent of all fatalities.[6] One particular airplane in this study—a twin-engine, low-wing model—had an incidence of stall-spin accidents (per 100,000 hours flight time) of more than twice the average of the planes in its peer group and almost twice that of the nearest other design. This model was introduced in 1963 as a twin-engine version of the manufacturer's current single-engine model, and more than 400 were sold in 1964. The first stall-spin accident involving that plane oc-

6. Shrager 1977, 1.

curred in April 1964, with a litigation action filed shortly after. By 1970, when the model was discontinued, more than 2,000 such planes had been sold. Thus the FAA investigation covered the production lifespan of this particular airplane almost exactly.

The National Aeronautics and Space Administration (NASA) also examined the stall-spin characteristics of this particular aircraft. The first of these investigations in 1966 led to a series of full-scale wind tunnel tests aimed at discovering the source of the stall-spin difficulties of the design.[7] The initial wind tunnel investigations showed that if the twin-engine airplane stalled when only one engine was working, the tendencies of the airplane to roll inverted and enter a spin were three times greater than the control authority the pilot had available to recover.[8] Stalling after losing an engine was a risk partly because the *Pilots Operating Handbook* or the *Airplane Flight Manual* at the time did not contain information describing at what speed such a stall might occur. A specific technical reason for the accident record of this design had therefore been discovered.

After the original wind tunnel test results were published in 1969, NASA performed four more full-scale wind tunnel tests in an effort to evaluate various "fixes" for the conditions deadly to this design. These were issued as NASA technical notes, from 1972 to 1974.[9] One test showed the benefits of making the two engines on the airplane turn the propellers in opposite directions, "counterrotating" as it was called. The manufacturer took this suggestion to heart by discontinuing the previous twin-engine design and introducing a new model that featured the counterrotating propellers.

Significantly, the design defect largely responsible for spin-stall behavior was not discovered either by regulators or by experts retained in the course of litigation. Nevertheless, the research results were used in court, since litigation stemming from stall-spin accidents in this airplane continued throughout the nine-year period later studied by the FAA. Although the design had some certification difficulties in Great Britain, the type certificate was not withdrawn by the FAA, nor was the airplane modified during that period with regard to its stall-spin characteristics. Indeed, during the production life of this aircraft, the accident record remained the same, and neither the regulation block nor the liability block caused a change in the design.

Interestingly, the pertinent regulation governing spin-stall behavior

7. Fink and others 1972.
8. Lockwood 1972.
9. See, in particular, Verstynen and Andrisani 1973.

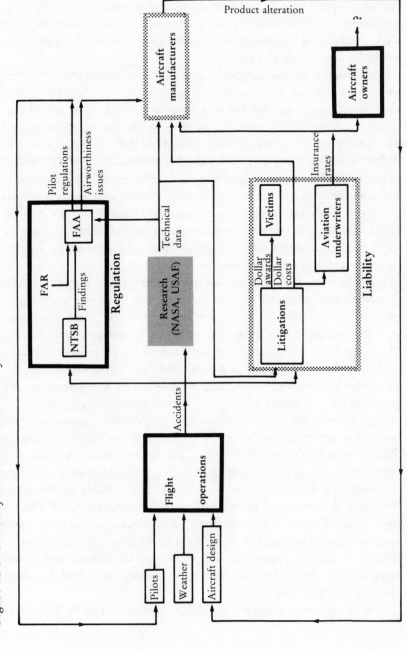

Figure 12-3. A Modified General Aviation System

(FAR 23.205 and its predecessor CAR3.123) was vague and unhelpful: "there shall be no undue spinning tendency." The manufacturer contended it had met this requirement and obtained certification for the airplane. As in the case of automobiles described in chapter 5, the manufacturer designed "down to" the standard.

In short, in this particular case, research by an organization not normally part of the regulation portion of the system caused a change in the design of an airplane: specifically, a termination of one design in favor of a "new" design that incorporated these changes. Exactly how such information entered into the system was not possible to discover, but a modified block diagram that included this research would look like figure 12-3.

What about spin-stall behavior in other aircraft? It declined steadily and substantially. For a group of thirty-six airplanes, encompassing many types, the total stall-spin accident rate per 100,000 hours of flight was cut in half from 1964 to 1972, and the overall fatal accident rate fell from 3.34 to 2.57.[10] Some of the subject aircraft were not in production, either at the end of the study period or at any time during, and it may be that the extinction of their designs lowered the rate of accidents. It is difficult, however, to find any correlation between the improving safety record for these plans and product liability litigation.

A High-Visibility Accident Case

Sometimes a series of accidents is not necessary to produce research into cause and effect, a single incident being sufficient. In such cases, deaths of prominent persons and the attendant litigation can accelerate efforts to uncover product defects. That is especially true when the aircraft are expensive, because it usually means the victims had substantial earning power. Accordingly, the monetary stakes in such litigation can be very large.

In one such case a turbo-prop twin-engine airplane, operated by a state Department of Transportation, crashed in February 1977. When the NTSB issued a report of the crash, it labeled the cause as pilot error, but the agency also commissioned an investigation by a prominent research organization into the handling qualities of the subject aircraft.

The study concentrated on that part of the FAA's certification which related to the permissible range of loading.[11] At the authorized rearward limit of center of gravity—that is, when the total load on the airplane

---

10. Shrager 1977, 27; data complied by NTSB, Sept. 6, 1978, and supplied to author.
11. Fink, Shrivers, and White 1974.

makes it balance as far back from the nose as authorized—the airplane was difficult to control and potentially dangerous. The British had come to similar and more damning conclusions. The source of the problem was violation of a condition called stick-fixed static stability.

Stability means the tendency to return to equilibrium or balance when the airplane is disturbed. One such action is the desired trait of an airplane to try to come back to level flight if a gust disturbs it into climb or into dive. If the aircraft has that kind of stability, the pilot does not have to devote constant attention to controlling the path of the airplane.

In fact, there are two kinds of static stability: stick fixed and stick free. The first means that if, after a disturbance, the pilot simply holds the control wheel in a fixed position, the aircraft will tend to return to normal. The second means the pilot must let go of the control to see if the airplane tends to restore itself. A parallel might be drawn with automobiles: if a person is driving down the highway and a gust of wind makes the car veer to one side, will the car straighten itself out if the driver lets go of the wheel or if she or he holds it fixed?[12]

In aeronautical engineering, stick-fixed static stability is considered to be the first and most important requirement for an airplane, with stick-free behavior second. Stick-fixed stability is often referred to as inherent stability, since it depends mainly on the design of the horizontal tail (it is the reason that the tail is on the airplane). Stick-free stability, in contrast, can be and often is achieved by adding mechanical devices, like springs and weights, to a design after it is in the air. The important point here is that an airplane can be made to be stick-free stable and possess stick-fixed *instability*. In flight, this would mean that if the pilot got into a disturbance and decided to hold the controls fixed, the airplane would diverge into larger digressions.

Although federal aviation regulations have many criteria, such as military requirements in handling qualities, they have no requirement at all for stick-fixed static or inherent stability. Therefore, manufacturers of general aviation aircraft have no regulatory obligation to provide such characteristics.

After the investigation of the 1977 accident and the attendant research, actions by the FAA led to a restriction on the limits of center-of-gravity travel for this airplane. In effect, that meant the aircraft was prohibited from getting close to the "ledge," the point where stability becomes instability.

12. The tendency of the CJ vehicle not to be stable in rolling over while turning corners, as described by John Graham in chapter 4, is an example of loss of stability.

This required no physical alteration in the airplane, simply a change in the way the vehicle was loaded. The existence of the ledge was not removed.

In short, in this case the system responded to a single accident with a mixture of inputs from the liability and regulation blocks, and produced a compromise change toward improving safety in an aircraft four years after it was first certified. Figure 12-2 correctly represents what was in place in the system, with a possible emphasis on some paths gained from the prominence of the operators of the first airplane to crash. As in the previous case study, a research organization too costly for most plaintiffs to hire led to a safety recommendation—one that did not include a design modification but was simply a different way of loading the airplane.

A Study of In-Flight Structural Failure Accidents

Few thoughts strike greater terror in the hearts of pilots than suffering a fire or a structural failure in flight. Statistical records show that in private flying the airplane that has the highest frequency of in-flight breakups has suffered more than 230 crashes since its introduction in 1947. Such a record has produced much dialogue among owners of the aircraft, the FAA, the manufacturer, and safety groups. The manufacturer felt that the airplane met the regulatory requirements for structural integrity and, therefore, that the crashes were not its fault but rather the result of pilot error coupled with bad weather conditions.

In 1964 the manufacturer introduced two new versions of the design that differed only in the arrangement of the tail surfaces. For the period 1964–77, the original model had an in-flight structural failure record twenty-four times greater than the revised models. Questions thus arose about the relative importance of the design of the airplane and weather and pilot action in causing these accidents. Some owners found the statistics persuasive and sold their original planes to buy the modified ones, and the manufacturer eventually discontinued production of the first version.

Over this period various groups urged the FAA to conduct an in-depth investigation into what might be causing the extraordinary accident rate, but no research was done. No modifications came about from either liability or regulation up to the time production of this model was discontinued.

This example speaks to what systems terminology calls "transport delays." That is, inputs come into a system, and any action gets lost internally for a long time, with no visible output. Here the regulation block had no effect on safety, while fatalities marched steadily along throughout the period, notwithstanding a similar parade of product liability lawsuits. If litigation had any effect here, it was to cause the end of production of a design. Neither litigation nor regulation caused any airplanes already in the field to be modified.

Internal Block Functioning

Sometimes an airplane model may be susceptible to accidents, but none of the components of the aircraft safety system induce a change in design. One example has to do with an exchange between the NTSB and the FAA in 1981. James B. King, chairman of the NTSB, wrote to J. Lynn Helms, administrator of the FAA, enclosing a set of recommendations from the board to take certain actions on a twin-engine design in manufacture that had exhibited a record of flat-spin accidents. (Flat spins are the most difficult kind to recover from.) Mr. Helms responded with counterarguments defending the pertinent FAR requirements and the inaction by the FAA. The manufacturer also responded to the NTSB, citing its cooperation with the FAA in previous investigations. (The airplane characteristics had been questioned before by both the FAA and the U.S. Army.)

Thus the system connections between the NTSB and the FAA were functioning, and another feedback path from the aircraft manufacturer to the NTSB and the FAA was added. The airplane was not altered, however, and accidents continued.

Had the airplane been tested by NASA in a full-scale wind tunnel as was done in the first case study, the issue whether or not a defective design had been certified could have been settled, and litigation would have taken a different path, surely with less costs to all concerned. Had the system structure of figure 12-3 been in existence, a request from either the NTSB or the FAA would have obtained the assistance of NASA, true and unbiased experts in the matter.

An Airplane Changed Quickly for Safety Reasons

In 1983 the FAA formed a multiple expert opinion team (MEOT) to reexamine the stall characteristics on a twin-engine airplane then in production. The airplane, originally certified in 1968, was found to be in violation of the pertinent FAR requirements for controllability near stall.

Before the investigation, the subject aircraft had a fatal accident record of 3.8 per 100,000 flight hours, more than twice as high as a directly comparable twin-engine competitor. An article in a trade magazine featured a discussion of the stall behavior of this airplane.[13] The article was quite critical and had prompted an owner of one of the airplanes to protest. Invited to participate with the authors in a flight demonstration of the behavior, he became a convert to the other side and wrote a letter to the FAA administrator expressing his concern about the safety of his airplane.[14] The letter filtered through the organization until it came to the attention of those in the FAA who were responsible at that time for the safety of this aircraft. Apparently, a request had come to the FAA earlier from an aviation safety institute requesting a review of the stall-spin traits of the subject aircraft.

The FAA responded with a mini audit carried out under the auspices of a regional certification office. The findings of the resulting study led to the issuance of an airworthiness directive mandating alteration to the airplane. The study also recommended that if the design was not changed, the delegation option authorization (DOA) privileges of the manufacturer, the scheme by which the airplane would be certified, should be revoked.[15] Shortly thereafter, design "fixes" were proposed by the aircraft manufacturer and by a firm that implemented airplane modifications; both suggestions were approved by the FAA as satisfactory remedies for the defect and included in the airworthiness directive. Aircraft in the field were then required to comply.

A review of the accident record of this airplane after corrective action by the FAA shows no incident of stall crashes when both engines were operating or both engines were off, which was the specific condition found inadequate before. Most accidents after 1983 involved failure of one of the engines, which happens relatively often in this plane, and possible control difficulties in coping with the engine-out situation.

Again, the role of prior and pending litigation at the time of the change in the airplane is difficult to determine. Apparently, an inquiry to the FAA from an owner and a specific crash caused the mini audit that led

13. *Aviation Consumer* 1985, 12.
14. Noland 1982.
15. The DOA system is one in which the FAA authorizes the manufacturer to designate some of its employees to act in-house for the FAA with regard to certifying its airplanes.

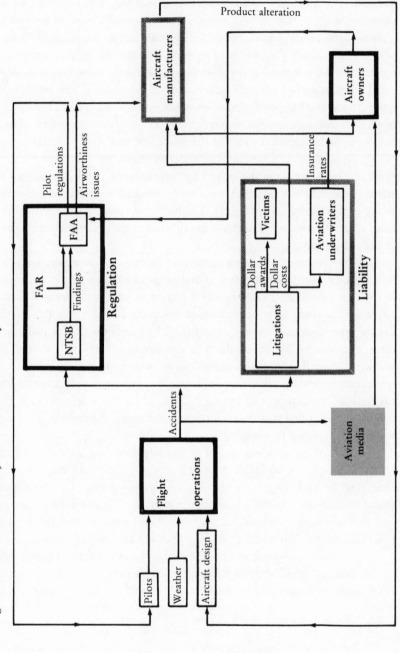

Figure 12-4. *Another Modified General Aviation System*

to a modification. If so, the system block diagram needs a connecting link from the aircraft owners and operators block directly to the FAA block, and a similar block indicating influences of public information channels, such as magazines (see figure 12-4).

What is remarkable in this case study is the very short time interval between the letter of inquiry from an owner (May 1982) until the issuance of the airworthiness directive (AD 83-14-07, July 1983), which shows quick compliance by the system. Shortly thereafter, by October 1983, an FAA-approved modification for relief of the directive was offered.

Comparison of this case study with that of the in-flight structural failure suggests that the regulation block does not have constant or invariant responses. A single accident that prompts a safety action in less than one year is certainly different from no action for a series of accidents over thirty years. Apparently there are some factors not easily determined in how the regulation part of the general aviation safety system works.

Summary of the Case Studies

The case studies just discussed draw on my experience and were chosen because they deal with true technical defects rather than with an accident stemming from a secondary level of risk, as often happens in aircraft crashes. Product liability litigation was associated with each of the case studies. Even so, in only one case was the pertinent airplane design changed. In another, a model was actually terminated.

Thus far, no firm conclusions can be reached about the relative influence of the liability and regulation blocks in improving the safety record of general aviation. At best, the original system diagram might be altered to include a path where litigation produces investigation and research into characteristics of a particular airplane design, and this causes the FAA and the aircraft manufacturer to modify the airplane. In general, it appears that the liability portion of the system, through costs, has acted more as a constraint than as a function for producing safety.

The question mark coming from the aircraft owners block should probably be changed to paths into the aircraft manufacturers, the FAA, and the aviation underwriters, particularly when the owners are bound together into an organization like the Aircraft Owners and Pilots Association. But that still may not connect liability to safety.

So the revised system diagram looks like figure 12-5. The new lines are shown dotted because no specific evidence could be found to verify the importance of their contributions.

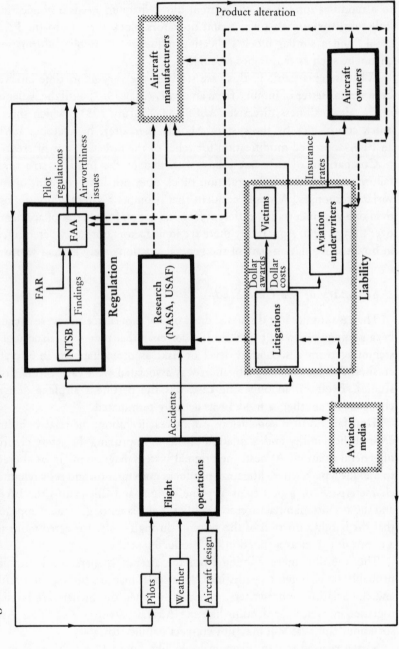

Figure 12-5. *The Final General Aviation System*

One Success Story for Safety

There is some evidence, however, that liability may work indirectly to improve safety by assisting in the dissemination of information through the media and consumer organizations that has enabled *pilots* to fly their aircraft more safely. Indeed, as liability activity increased, airplane manufacturers began to publish and distribute safety-related material to known owners of their aircraft. In lawsuits, failure to warn is frequently claimed by the plaintiff, citing shortcomings in the *Airplane Flight Manual* or the *Pilots Operating Handbook* that may inadvertently lead to dangerous flight behavior. Typically, early versions of these publications—which are required by the FAA for every airplane—spoke more to performance and operational subjects than to safety and the particular handling characteristics of specific airplanes. As verdicts supported the failure-to-warn claims, and as manufacturers developed better policies regardless of litigation outcomes, these manuals grew in sophistication and utility to pilots, helping them to fly more safely.

An example of this improvement to a manual is found in the case study called "Internal Block Functioning." As noted, the subject airplane, a light twin-engine vehicle, had this characteristic: the failure of one engine could lead to a rapid rolling maneuver that left the airplane upside down. In trial testimony an expert witness concluded that the pilot should at least be warned about this possibility; thereafter the manual contained such a warning. The manufacturer, of course, did not describe the behavior at issue as a defect in design but simply as a possible consequence of encountering a stall in that condition.

In conjunction with this action, the General Aviation Manufacturers Association promoted the use of a new criterion for dealing with an engine failure in a twin-engine airplane. A speed called VSSE (safe single-engine velocity) was determined for each airplane design and recommended to the pilot as a better value to use in critical conditions than the previous speed specified by the FAA (minimum control velocity, which is as slow as one can go and still not turn uncontrollably). The intent was to keep the pilot away from critical regimes of speed if they could be avoided. It was hoped that use of the new speed would help prevent crashes in the most hazardous aspect of twin-engine flying. Incorporation of this concept was motivated primarily by product liability litigation.

Better manuals were supplemented by periodic publications from the manufacturer, such as safety communiqués, and disseminated to airplane owners of record. They dealt with safety subjects such as fuel management, icing encounters, and pilot techniques that were based on field experiences with the various airplane designs.

During the period of growth in litigation, the magazine *Aviation Consumer* came into being, the publication mentioned earlier in the case study *An Airplane Changed Quickly for Safety Reasons*.[16] This magazine has often been cited as a source of information about problems encountered with various airplanes and usually offered strong opinions. The general tone of its articles was one of consumer advocacy and safety. It provided a very visible public forum, connecting the elements of the system in a manner not present previously. Comparative accident records of various models of airplanes were often presented and evaluated, and some issues were given over completely to the subject of safety.[17]

Many law firms involved in aviation litigation joined the subscriber list, as did many airplane owners. Since the magazine was mostly critical about safety matters in design, it was championed and quoted more by the plaintiff bar than by the defense. By linking parts of the general aviation system in information exchange or prodding for action, it had a greater influence on owners than the accident reports of the NTSB or the requirements of the FAR. More owners could quote articles from *Aviation Consumer* than could recite accident statistics or certification.[18]

System Changes Now Being Considered

Recent efforts have been put forth to have federal law control litigation costs by statute, which effectively would put the liability block within the regulation block. General aviation, then, would become a completely regulated activity at the federal level, and that system would have only a single element between accidents and the aircraft manufacturers. Feedback in that system would then depend solely on the action of federal agencies.

To provide more technical information when an accident or series of accidents suggests a design defect, the use of independent or neutral experts (responsible to the court and not to either plaintiff or defendant)

16. Noland 1982.

17. See *Aviation Consumer* 1985.

18. For some time before *Aviation Consumer* was published, another voice speaking for general aviation was the Aircraft Owners and Pilots Association. The association's concerns included safety, the costs of flying, and various regulatory rulings that affected its membership.

has been proposed. Experts would undertake research on a scale less than but similar to what happens in a schedule-carrier accident, much like what actually occurred in the case study on stall spin after engine failure. Participation by established government facilities like NASA and Edwards Air Force Base Flight Test would be typical, with their results available to all participants in litigation. That sort of activity would be a positive and potentially decisive link between liability and regulation.

Finally, some have suggested that the constant rate of accidents for the past decade means the system has brought that figure down to a residual rate that reflects the "hazard" aspect of private flying, and thus the system works. If so, it still does not speak to the role of liability in achieving that goal, and of course that subject is hotly disputed.

Conclusion

More insight into the questions raised in this chapter would have been gained if some of the internal elements of the system had been defined by the groups they represent rather than to have been assumed to function a certain way. For example, no definite relationship was shown between the functioning of the aviation underwriters and the improvement of safety in the system, except for the assumed one of basing insurance rates on the accident history of a particular airplane design. A better understanding of this linkage could have been achieved had the two main underwriters contacted in connection with this study responded with useful information.

No consensus was reached by asking attorneys on both sides of the litigation process. The litigation block was simply assumed to be "something everybody knows" in this analysis, slightly modified by the author's experiences with lawsuits. A generalization about the position of both sides might be stated—with some exaggeration—as "plaintiff attorneys believe their actions act as feedback to correct for shortcomings in the system and to recompense the victims" and "defense attorneys feel they must protect the manufacturers from feeding frenzies of voracious attackers." Explicit revelation by the legal profession of exactly how they think they function in product liability litigation would certainly help refine the workings of the system.

It may be that litigation results influence parts of the regulation process. That is, it may be that consistent verdicts favoring the plaintiff tend to persuade elements of the regulation block to change the certification requirements (the FAR) or the way they are applied or to reexamine the pertinent aircraft. But I could not find sufficient evidence in this study to document such a connection.

The question of the effect of litigation on safety remains unresolved. What is undeniably true is that safety, as measured by the fatal accident rate, is not reduced by the costs of litigation, since for the past decade fatal accident rates have remained essentially constant while liability costs have increased tenfold.[19] Although total accident rates for the period of investigation have come down with almost a constant slope, the connection of that result with the increase in litigation is tenuous. Other factors, like the change in the nature of the pilot population and the disappearance of older models of airplanes, add uncertainty to any conclusion.

Any hope to make the system work better will require three things for all blocks within the system structure:

—definition of function, so that each block has a known role to perform;

—specification of criteria, so that each block can measure how well it satisfies its function; and

—recognition of constraints, so that each block knows what the limits are on its participation.

Given those actions, appropriate changes can make product liability serve the cause of safety in aviation.

19. NTSB 1978.

References

Aviation Consumer. 1985. Special Safety Issue. Dec. 1.

Fink, M. P., and others. 1972. "The Effects of Configuration Changes on the Aerodynamic Characteristics of a Full-Scale Mockup of a Light Twin-Engine Airplane." NASA TN D-6896. National Aeronautics and Space Administration.

Fink, M. P., J. P. Shrivers, and L. C. White. 1974. "Wind-Tunnel Tests of a Full-Scale Model of a Light Twin-Engine Airplane with a Fixed Auxiliary Airfoil or a Leading Edge Slot." NASA TN D-7474. National Aeronautics and Space Administration.

Lockwood, V. E. 1972. "Effect of Reynolds Number and Engine Nacelles on the Stalling Characteristics of a Model of Light Twin-Engine Airplane." NASA TN D-7109. National Aeronautics and Space Administration.

National Transportation Safety Board. 1978. "Aircraft Accident Report." NTSB-AAR-78-1. Washington.

————.1989. "Aviation Accident Statistics, 1978–1988." Accident Data Division.

Noland, D. 1982. "Aerostar Stalls: Put to the Test." *Aviation Consumer,* July 6:10.

Shrager, J. 1977. "Analysis of Selected General Aviation Stall/Spin Accidents." FAA-RD-77-41. Federal Aviation Administration.

Sontag, F. B. 1987. Testimony in *A Bill to Amend the Federal Aviation Act of 1958 Relating to General Aviation Accidents.* Hearings before the Subcommittee on Commerce, Consumer Protection and Competitiveness of the House Committee on Energy and Commerce. 100 Cong. 1 sess. Government Printing Office.

Verstynen, H. A., Jr., and D. Andrisani. 1973. "Full-Scale Wind Tunnel Investigation of Effects of Slot Spoilers on the Aerodynamics Characteristics of a Light Twin-Engine Airplane." NASA TN D-7315. National Aeronautics and Space Administration.

Yodice, J. S. 1990. Testimony at "Hearing on S. 60, General Aviation Accident Liability Standards Act of 1989." Subcommittee on Courts and Administrative Practice of the Senate Judiciary Committee. 101 Cong. 2 sess. Mar. 9.

CHAPTER THIRTEEN

General Aviation Manufacturing: An Industry under Siege

Robert Martin

T HE EXPONENTIAL growth of product liability claims and litigations over the last two decades has produced some extreme results. Although it has had a modest effect on some industries, it threatens the very existence of others. Manufacturers of corporate and private airplanes are among those hardest hit.

In this chapter I trace the devastating impact of product liability claims and litigations on three large manufacturers of general aviation airplanes and examine the adverse relationship between high liability exposure and enhanced safety through innovation and the development of new products. I also examine the root causes for the severe, cumulative effect of product liability on this industry and others similarly situated and discuss some of the abuses embedded in the liability system that should be addressed. Unless that is done, the extravagance of the liability system may destroy important segments of the U.S. industrial economy.

The Industry

General aviation can be defined as every form of civil aviation except that directly related to scheduled domestic and international airline operations. Typically, general aviation airplanes are designed to carry fewer than twenty persons and may be fixed-wing or rotary-wing airplanes, powered by piston-driven or turbine engines. Most general aviation airplanes are used for personal transportation, but the industry also produces special mission aircraft, such as military trainers, cargo carriers, agricultural application airplanes, working helicopters, and commuter airliners.

At present, approximately 210,000 active general aviation aircraft are in U.S. registry.[1] This fleet can be divided by service category, as follows:

Category	Units	Percent of fleet
Executive transport	11,000	5
Business aircraft	35,000	17
Personal transportation	123,000	58
Instructional	17,000	8
Aerial application, observation, and other work	14,000	7
Air taxi and commuter airline	11,000	5

More than 80 percent of this fleet consists of true "small airplanes"—single-engine and light twin-engine aircraft capable of carrying two to six persons; 78 percent of the fleet is made up of single-engine small airplanes.

Most of the executive transports, about one-half of the business aircraft, most of the industrial and special-use fixed-wing and rotary-wing aircraft, and virtually all the air taxi and commuter airplanes are flown by professional pilots. Professionally flown airplanes seem to account for less than one-fourth of the units in the general aviation fleet. The rest of the units in service, largely piston-powered single-engine and light-twin airplanes, are flown by private pilots.

In 1988 (the last full year for which Federal Aviation Administration data are available), all U.S. general aviation aircraft combined flew 33.6 million hours. From the same FAA flight data, sorted by type and use, one can calculate that approximately 50 percent of the total hours flown in 1988 by general aviation aircraft were flown with a professional pilot in command. The remaining one-half, or 16.8 million flight hours, were logged by private pilots. Analysis of fatal accident data collected by the National Transportation Safety Board (NTSB) shows that private, or nonprofessional, pilots accounted for over 80 percent of the accidents in

1. Figures on aircraft population, classification, use, and hours flown are compiled from Federal Aviation Administration statistics and published in General Aviation Manufacturers Association (GAMA) 1989a.

general aviation airplanes that resulted in one or more fatalities or serious injuries. A similar statistical value is produced by classifying fatal accidents by airplane category: single-engine and light-twin piston-driven airplanes, which are predominantly flown by their owners, account for over 80 percent of all general aviation fatal and serious injury accidents. The flying skill of private pilots can vary between two extremes: on the one side, the careful, qualified, high-flying-time general aviation pilot who is as capable and as safe as a professional pilot; on the other, the novice pilot, the careless pilot, the reckless daredevil, or the pilot disabled by the use of alcohol or drugs.

Historically, three large general aviation airplane builders have produced about 80 percent of all general aviation airplanes in service in the United States. Cessna Aircraft Company and Piper Aircraft Corporation have become the dominant builders of small, single-engine, fixed-gear two-and four-passenger airplanes. Beech Aircraft Corporation has directed its efforts toward the manufacture of somewhat larger and more expensive airplanes for business and private use. At the present time, and for at least the past decade, more than 100,000 general aviation airplanes in U.S. registry were built by Cessna, more than 50,000 were built by Piper, and about 24,000 were built by Beech. Although several other companies build fine general aviation airplanes, those three companies are a representative sample for a study of the effect of the American tort liability system on general aviation and its manufacturers.

The Growing Effect of Strict Liability Litigation

In January 1963 the Supreme Court of California embraced the rule of strict liability, as proposed in the "Restatement (Second) of Torts," 402A. The rule was that the manufacturer and others in the chain of distribution were to be held liable for injury or loss caused by the use of any product found to have been "in a defective condition, unreasonably dangerous to the user or consumer." This was legal terminology for the concept that a manufacturer who produced a product found to be defective or unreasonably dangerous when put to its intended use, and those who distributed and sold that product, should be held liable for the injuries it caused, without proof of any negligence or fault on the part of the manufacturer or the vendors. This landmark ruling was handed down in a 1963 case,

Greenman v. *Yuba Power Products, Inc.*[2] Although the California Court of Appeals declared fifteen years later that *Yuba Power* was a manufacturing defect case and strict liability was first extended to design defects in *Cronin* v. *Olson Corp.*,[3] in truth the *Yuba Power* decision was almost certainly a design error case, as were many other decisions that quickly followed it. Neither the "Restatement of Torts" nor *Yuba Power* articulated a distinction between defects or unreasonably dangerous conditions arising from design as opposed to the manufacturing process. Courts across the country rushed to adopt the rule of strict liability, and over the next few years the products of industry were placed on trial in courtrooms across the land under rules that imposed liability on manufacturers without fault and without a real effort to define an "unreasonably dangerous product" for the guidance of anyone.

During the late 1960s aviation manufacturers came under attack, and many began to be aware that product liability litigation could become a problem. Because airplanes must be designed and built to be very reliable, almost all aviation product liability cases have involved claims of defective design. By the mid-1970s general aviation manufacturers had gained enough experience with strict liability litigation, particularly in the California courts, to recognize that product liability was indeed a serious problem. Then, and now, California, because of its affluence and its geography, held by far the largest population of general aviation airplanes. Almost 15 percent of all general aviation airplanes in U.S. registry are based in California. Only Texas and Florida, probably for similar reasons, even approach California in aircraft population.

Initially at least, product liability litigation for general aviation was perceived as a California problem, but it soon became clear that such litigation was a problem of national scope. Annual insurance premiums and in-house costs for the defense of a rapidly growing book of cases quickly reached proportions of several million dollars for each of the three large airframe builders. Suppliers of power plants, avionics, instruments, subassemblies, and parts also began to feel the burden of escalating insurance costs and direct involvement in litigation.

In testimony before a joint committee of the Kansas legislature considering product liability legislation, Beech and Cessna estimated that in 1975 the combined expenditures of the two companies for insurance and

---

2. 59 Cal. 2d 57, 377 P.2d 897, 27 Cal. Rptr. 697 (1963).
3. 8 Cal. 3d 121, 501 P.2d 1153, 104 Cal. Rptr. 433 (1972). See *McGee* v. *Cessna Aircraft Co.*, 82 Cal. App. 3d 1005, 147 Cal. Rptr. 694 (1978).

product liability defense would exceed $9 million, and that by the end of 1976, they would exceed $10 million.[4] By 1977 Beech, Cessna, and Piper had hundreds of lawsuits pending against them asserting claims for compensatory and punitive damages that, in total, far exceeded the net worth of all three companies combined. Increasingly, and to an extent that interfered with the performance of their primary responsibility of designing and building airplanes, engineers and managers for the three companies found themselves directly involved with the efforts of lawyers and insurers to defend product liability lawsuits.

In 1975 Frank Hedrick, president of Beech Aircraft Corporation, observed: "General aviation manufacturers have the ability and the resources to solve all of the problems they confront except product liability litigation, but that problem could destroy the industry." In that year Beech, along with Marsh and McLennan Risk Management Services, undertook a two-year study to assess the efficiency of the product liability tort litigation system as a risk-spreading device to compensate persons injured or killed in aviation accidents and to explore the feasibility and cost of no-fault award systems.[5] The data collected in this study established that in a fifty-eight-month period between September 1, 1971, and June 30, 1976, Beech spent $18 million insuring and defending against product liability claims. This figure includes insurance premiums, uninsured legal costs, special investigations and testing for the defense of cases, and the time and expense that Beech executives, engineers, and employees invested in the defense of claims and litigations. For the same period, the authors of the study calculated total awards (judgments and settlements), plus loss reserves incurred on the books of Beech and its insurers, and from that total they deducted 40 percent for plaintiffs' contingent attorney fees and other costs of suit, including fees and expenses of expert witnesses, expenses of depositions, other discovery, and other litigation costs. They then calculated the average delay between the occurrence (the aircraft accident) and the date of payment for losses, which proved to be four years. A time value of money factor of 8 percent a year was then applied to the average four-year delay in settlement, to compare the tort litigation system, as it then functioned, to a no-fault reparations plan that would provide immediate payment. The analysis established that of the approximate $18 million Beech Aircraft had invested in the defense of its

4. Approximately 2 percent of airplane sales, but 25 percent of net income, calculated from annual report figures.
5. Beech Aircraft 1977.

products and the settlement of its losses during the fifty-eight-month period, only $3 million, or 16⅔ percent of the total cost to Beech, would end up in the hands of claimants.

The data analyzed also established that despite the changing of laws to favor plaintiffs, manufacturers were able to prove, in more than 80 percent of the cases brought to trial, that there was no defect in design or manufacture which caused the accident. However, the costs in attorneys' fees, technical investigations, and miscellaneous litigation expenses were even then running hundreds of thousands of dollars for each case brought to trial. What the tort litigation system produced in practice was an extravagant award in some aviation cases, a reasonable award in a few cases, and no recovery at all in most cases. As a reparations or risk-spreading device for persons injured or killed in airplane accidents, strict liability litigation proved to be extravagant and inefficient. Only lawyers prospered from the rising tide of litigation.

A steady escalation of loss and defense costs prevailed throughout the 1970s. As insurers incurred mounting underwriting losses, they increased premiums. Manufacturers were forced to divert a greater share of corporate resources, which otherwise could have been devoted to research and engineering to build better airplanes, to insurance premiums and other costs of defending their products. The upward spiral of product liability costs was in place and accelerating. It had to be reflected in increased prices for new general aviation airplanes because manufacturers had no other source of revenues to cover insurance and litigation costs.

The 1980s brought disaster. The price of new airplanes reached the point at which prospective buyers increasingly chose to purchase a used airplane rather than a new one. Margins were cut, manufacturing plants were closed, engineering staffs were trimmed, and factory employees were laid off, but the escalating costs of product liability absorbed all these cuts and more. At a steady pace, sales and shipments of new airplanes by general aviation manufacturers declined from a high of 17,811 units in 1978 to 1,143 units in 1988.[6] In the same period, total employment by general aviation manufacturers declined 65 percent.[7]

In 1985 the world insurance market, led by European reinsurance and excess underwriters, began to withdraw product liability insurance coverage for U.S. general aviation manufacturers. As one prominent Lloyd's

6. GAMA 1989a, 6. The General Aviation Manufacturers Association reported deliveries in 1989 of 1,535 new units.
7. GAMA 1989b.

aviation underwriter put it: "We are quite prepared to insure the risks of aviation, but not the risks of the American legal system." By 1987 Piper was entirely uninsured for its product liability exposure, Cessna was uninsured for the first $100 million annual aggregate loss and defense costs, and Beech was self-insured for losses and defense costs up to $50 million a year. By 1987 the three airframe manufacturers could calculate that their annual costs for product liability ranged from $70,000 to $100,000 per unit built and shipped during the year.[8] This meant that for light airplanes—two- and four-seat trainers and personal use airplanes—the product liability expense exceeded the cost of either raw materials or labor. By the end of 1986 both Beech and Cessna had shut down most of their light airplane production lines and in some cases closed entire plants devoted to the production of light airplanes. The three largest airframe builders and many of their suppliers incurred heavy operating losses in the 1980s.

Historically, U.S. manufacturers supplied most of the general aviation airplanes worldwide; 20 to 30 percent of the units built by U.S. manufacturers each year were delivered for export. By 1981, for the first time in the history of general aviation, imports of general aviation airplanes, including commuter airliners, exceeded the value of general aviation exports by about $200 million. By 1988 the balance of trade deficit had grown to $700 million. While American general aviation manufacturers were struggling with product liability, foreign airplane builders were able to design and build new airplanes for the expanding commuter airline market at costs U.S. manufacturers could not meet. As U.S. manufacturers were forced to give up the manufacture of small trainers and personal airplanes because of product liability costs, foreign manufacturers—with almost no U.S. fleet outstanding and correspondingly small product liability exposure and expense—increasingly supplied the U.S. requirement for new small airplanes.[9]

In 1986 the General Aviation Manufacturers Association engaged the Wyatt Company, insurance and risk analysts headquartered in Chicago, to collect data and determine the industry's total outlay for its product liability exposure. The results of the study confirmed the worst assumptions. Between 1976 and 1986, paid claims and out-of-pocket defense expenses for the entire industry—airframe, power plant, propeller, avion-

8. *General Aviation Accident Liability Standards Act of 1987.*
9. GAMA 1990b.

ics, and other manufacturers of components and parts—had escalated from $24 million a year to $210 million a year.

In 1987, at the request of the House Aviation Subcommittee of the Public Works and Transportation Committee, Beech performed an analysis of 203 litigations and claims for damages pending at any time during the four years January 1, 1983, through December 31, 1986. The data were accounted for on an occurrence basis; that is, one accident was treated as a single occurrence and a single claim or litigation even if the accident in fact resulted in several separate claims or lawsuits. The following data from this study are indicative of the situation faced by general aviation manufacturers:

—There were 599 people on board airplanes involved in 203 accidents, for an average of approximately 3 occupied seats per accident.

—Of the persons on board, 42 percent were the owner-operator or employees of the owner-operator of the airplane; 44 percent were guests of the owner-operator or nonpaying passengers; and only 14 percent were paying passengers.

—All general aviation accidents are investigated by the National Transportation Safety Board or the FAA, or both. These investigations by trained experts, with engineering and laboratory support as required, produced the following determinations of probable cause (if more than one contributing cause was found, all reported causes are tabulated):

Probable cause	Accidents
Pilot error	118
Design or manfacturing defect[10]	0
Maintenance	22
Weather	21
Air traffic control	1
Other	1
Unknown or undetermined	63

—The average amount claimed, per occurrence, was approximately $10 million.

10. Beech investigators reported two accidents involving a product defect; one was an accident on the ground with no fatalities.

—The average cost to the manufacturer (the total of losses and defense expenses paid, plus reserves actually booked by Beech and its insurers) was $530,000 per accident.

Obviously, something is amiss: trained, experienced accident investigators dispatched by the government agency charged by Congress with finding the probable cause of aircraft accidents find that a design or manufacturing defect in the airplanes caused none of the accidents. They also find that pilot error and other factors, not related to the design or manufacture of the aircraft, were the actual cause of 70 percent of the accidents. Yet plaintiffs and their lawyers file lawsuits claiming that design or manufacturing defects caused 100 percent of the same accidents. In these circumstances, no industry should be expected to respond affirmatively, or place any credence in lawyers' claims about design defects in products or in the novel and often bizarre theories of their expert witnesses as to how and why the accidents occurred.

What the Advocates of Modern Tort Law Failed to Consider

The legal scholars and reformers of the social order, the "Founders" of modern tort law, as Peter Huber has named them,[11] may have been scholarly and sincere intellectuals in pursuit of what they perceived as a righteous cause, but they were not industrialists; and industry was their mark. Huber was accurate in describing several consequences of strict liability the Founders failed to foresee; for example, the flight of insurance coverage; the stubborn refusal of industry to play the victim in the new social order; and an overaggressive and rapidly expanding legal profession that quickly transformed the rule of strict liability into a lawyer's full-employment program and, in many jurisdictions, a national lottery at the courthouse.[12] But also other unforeseen aspects of strict liability, as applied to some industrial products, have proved to be devastating to manufacturers of airplanes and of their components.

In formulating the rule of strict liability, which, as Huber pointed out, places the product itself, as distinguished from the conduct of the manufacturer, on trial,[13] no one considered the distinction between products purchased and used as capital items with a long service life and those

11. Huber 1988, 6.
12. Huber 1988, chaps. 9–10.
13. Huber 1988, chap. 3.

purchased as consumables or near-consumables—products with a relatively short service life. General aviation airplanes are prime examples of a capital item that has a long service life. The average age of an active U.S. general aviation airplane is now twenty-four years, and 25 percent of the fleet of 210,000 airplanes is thirty-three or older.[14] Thousands of general aviation airplanes have been in service forty years or more. Airplanes are complex, expensive high-performance machines designed for the markets into which they are sold, which means that the better, more durable, and reliable the design and construction of a plane are, the more likely it will be a success in the marketplace and the longer it will last once it gets there.

Each general aviation airplane in the active U.S. fleet that carries a manufacturer's data plate represents a separate product liability risk to that manufacturer. The cost of that risk, whether self-insured or underwritten, must be paid each year. On the income side of the ledger, the manufacturer's selling price for the airplane is fixed when it is sold, and the books on that transaction are closed. On the expense side, however, the account remains open for the life of the airplane under the rule of strict liability. When one considers that the expense side of the ledger will remain open, on average, for thirty to forty years, and that the risk-cost each year is subject to inflation (which for the past twenty years has been at rates more than double the national rate of inflation), it is not surprising to find that an industry such as the manufacture of small airplanes can become self-liquidating.

With enough units in service in the United States for a sufficient number of years, the annual risk-cost of those units, which can be covered only by additions to the price of new airplanes currently coming down the production line, will at some point put the manufacturer in the position of having to price its products out of the market. The fewer units the manufacturer can sell at product liability–inflated prices, the more it must add to the price of each unit it does sell to cover the risk-cost of the units in service. That is precisely the deadly spiral into which the industry has been thrown over the last twenty years. It is also the reason general aviation manufacturers have shut down small airplane production lines and closed plants.

In effect, manufacturers that have been forced by the costs of product liability exposure to stop building the kinds of airplanes that currently make up more than three-quarters of the units in service cannot realist-

14. GAMA 1990a.

ically, by innovation or any other means, make such airplanes, or general aviation, better, safer, or more efficient.

An equally important element the Founders overlooked, or ignored, is the distinction between the products of manufacturers that are intensely regulated at every stage of design, production, and testing, and the products of manufacturers that function essentially free of oversight and regulation by an agency of the executive branch of government. The design and manufacture of airplanes of all classes—those for general aviation or airline use—are among the most closely regulated of all American industrial products. Government standards are established for design criteria, performance, type and use definition, testing of raw materials, components and systems, testing of prototypes, and conformance of production airplanes to type certification. Manufacturing and quality control procedures are subject to regulation.[15]

Unlike the way other products are regulated, the use of airplanes, as well as their maintenance, repair, and qualification for airworthiness status, is subject to regulation by the same agency, namely, the FAA. Pilots are licensed by the FAA,[16] air traffic is controlled by it, and airport facilities are regulated by it.[17]

What the Founders overlooked is the fact that a large share of the financial burden of FAA oversight and regulation of the design, testing, production, and certification of airplanes is borne by the manufacturers of airplanes; it is not, as most people believe, totally financed by public funds. In practice, if the FAA questions a design or engineering analysis for a new product, or the modification of an existing product, the manufacturer is required to submit additional analysis or test data to support the design or concept for which approval is sought. If questions arise on the compliance of a design, a prototype, or a finished product with FAA regulations or directives, the manufacturer must develop and supply whatever information the FAA requires to support the product and its compliance with FAA standards. Today a general aviation manufacturer proposing to design, build, test, and certify an entirely new four-to-six-passenger single-engine airplane would have to invest about $50 million in engineering research, design, tooling, prototypes, and testing to meet the requirements of the FAA for type certification, and an additional $50 million in production-line setup and inventory. That is a front-end investment, incurred before the first production unit can be built and sold.

15. 49 U.S.C. 1421, et seq.; 14 C.F.R. 23, 33, 35.
16. 49 U.S.C. 1421, 1422.
17. 49 U.S.C. 1348.

A twin-engine cabin-class general aviation airplane would require about twice the initial investment that a light airplane would, or $200 million.

Safety is the primary objective of the FAA regulatory scheme, as mandated by Congress. No regulatory system of any government is perfect, but a strong case can be made for the proposition that, over the years, the FAA has done an outstanding job of regulating the design, manufacture, and testing of airplanes. American-built airplanes are now, and have always been, the safest airplanes in the world and the standard against which all other airplanes are measured. No one within the industry suggests that FAA regulation is inappropriate or should be scrapped; neither is it argued that FAA criteria and regulations set standards for safety and reliability that are too severe.

Nevertheless, manufacturers of airplanes have two serious and legitimate complaints. First, the courts have simply brushed aside manufacturers' compliance with FAA standards and regulations as proof, or even evidence, that products certified as safe and airworthy are not, in fact, poorly designed and dangerous. They have done so by saying that FAA standards and regulations governing the design and manufacture of airplanes are merely minimum safety standards.[18] Plaintiffs' lawyers argue in the trial of aviation products cases that mere compliance with a government standard shows that the manufacturer was deliberately trying to do as little as could be done to make the product safe and reliable. In that way, compliance with FAA regulations is twisted into subtle but persuasive evidence that the design was less than it should have been and the product was somehow dangerous because the manufacturer complied with FAA requirements.

Second, as Peter Huber has pointed out, juries (and judges and lawyers, as well) are well qualified by life experience to assess the behavior of people and determine whether they are careful, negligent, or even reckless,[19] but they are assuredly not as qualified as scientists, engineers, and test pilots employed by the FAA and the manufacturers to determine whether a given aircraft design is safe or unsafe when used for its intended purpose. The truth is that juries, judges, and lawyers can scarcely comprehend, let alone perform or evaluate, the formulaic calculations, engineering analysis, or test flight protocols by which airplanes are designed, certified by the FAA, manufactured, and tested.

18. The language of the Federal Aviation Act is, "Such minimum standards governing the design, materials, workmanship, construction, and performance . . . as may be required in the interest of safety." Federal Aviation Act, 49 U.S.C. 1421(a)(1). This does not mean "minimum safety standards."

19. Huber 1988, chap. 3.

A similar analysis can be applied to the determination of probable cause of airplane accidents. The NTSB has as its exclusive mandate from Congress the determination of the probable cause or causes of transportation accidents and the responsibility to recommend to other government agencies supervising the design, manufacture, or use of transportation equipment, what action, if any, should be taken to improve safety and avoid the reoccurrence of preventable accidents.[20] The field investigators, engineers, and scientists who provide technical support, and the administrators who formulate recommendations, are far better positioned than juries, judges, and lawyers to determine the cause of accidents and what should be done to prevent them. However, their determinations are entirely ignored in the litigation process.

It is clear to industry that the rulings and judgments of courts and juries are impossible to reconcile with the directives, regulations, and pronouncements of agencies and officers of the executive branch of government and, in many cases, are completely detached from scientific reality. The manufacturers of airplanes, components, and parts find themselves in the same position as manufacturers of vaccines and drugs. They invest enormous sums in an effort to design and manufacture new and better products and to comply with the directives, regulations, and objectives of the executive branch of government, only to be told, after the fact, by lawyers and judges, and occasionally by juries, that despite best efforts and faithful compliance, their products were poorly designed and dangerous and their behavior so inappropriate that punitive damages, in the millions of dollars, can be awarded against them.

The managers of industries perpetually trapped between conflicting and expensive governmental authority exercised by the executive and judicial branches of government are compelled to conclude that they cannot safely innovate, change, or improve their products, and they are eventually forced to abandon good products or withdraw them from the market.

New Products: A Forty-Year History

Great advances in aviation and aerospace technology have been made since the end of World War II. We can now build airplanes that will travel faster than the speed of sound; we can design and build instrument landing and avionics systems that will guide an airplane to the airport

20. 49 U.S.C. 1441(a).

and land it on the end of the runway without pilot input to the flight controls; we can design and build two-to-four-passenger airplanes that will fly at speeds approaching 200 miles per hour and consume less fuel per mile traveled than the average automobile; and we can design and manufacture airframe components, and even total airframes, made of composite materials that are lighter, stronger, and more resistant to fatigue than their steel and aluminum counterparts.

The engineers who design new airplanes, their components, and systems try to incorporate the latest proven technology that can be feasibly applied or adapted to the design objectives. Once the design is complete, prototypes are built and tested, and type certification is granted by the FAA, the basic design of the airplane and the technology it incorporates are essentially frozen. Later models of the same basic airplane that, for example, might carry more powerful engines, fly a few knots faster, have more range, accommodate additional passengers, or incorporate advanced instruments or avionics are limited by the basic type design and the technology at the time of type certification.

In aviation, as in many industries, advances in technology represent or lead to advances in safety. New airplanes are safer airplanes, not just because they are not secondhand, worn out, or even abused, but because they are designed and built on more advanced technology. Some have argued, as the justification for the rule of strict liability, that holding manufacturers responsible for injuries caused by the use of their products regardless of fault will stimulate innovation and improve safety through the design and sale of new, more advanced, and better products. If that is true, then one should expect to see a correlation between the effect of strict liability on general aviation and the development and certification of new and more advanced airplanes.

In light of high-dollar awards and their frequency, plaintiffs' lawyers must all subscribe to the rule that if a little is good, more is better, and most is best. Therefore, one should also find some correlation between the annual cost to the industry of its product liability exposure and the determination, if not the passion, to design and introduce new and better airplanes.

The facts are exactly the opposite. When the problems and burdens of expanding strict liability litigation advance, the industry retreats from innovation and produces fewer new airplanes. In summary, the record is as follows:[21]

—Between 1950 and 1960, when strict liability was not yet envisioned

21. New airplane data were obtained from Beech, Cessna, and Piper; follow-on models judged to be derivatives of the original basic airplane were excluded from the tabulation.

for general aviation, Beech, Cessna and Piper, collectively, designed and brought to the market seventeen new airplanes.

—In the ten years between 1960 and 1970, during which strict liability was embraced by the courts of California, but aircraft manufacturers were not seriously affected, the same three companies designed and introduced twenty-two new airplanes.

—Between 1970 and 1980, when the industry was first seriously affected by strict liability and the litigation it produced, Beech, Cessna, and Piper brought to the market fourteen new airplanes. Yet during the same decade, general aviation manufacturers built and shipped more new airplanes than in any previous ten-year period, excluding military aircraft production during World War II.

—Between 1980 and 1990, the decade when product liability became a crisis, Beech, Cessna, and Piper brought out only seven new airplanes.

As Huber has said, "When the sun never sets on the possibility of litigation, each improvement in method, material, or design can establish a new standard against which all of your earlier undertakings, of no matter what vintage, will be judged. Finding a way to do better today immediately invites an indictment of what you did less well yesterday or twenty years ago."[22] In that way innovation and the willingness to develop new and better products is first discouraged and then stifled. The innovation that is encouraged by strict liability is the "inventive" approach of lawyers and their expert witnesses to claims of design defects and product failures as they relentlessly pursue the manufacturers of airplanes.

Strict Liability and Safety

If enforcement of strict liability through civil litigation against the manufacturers of general aviation airplanes will indeed effectively deter "accident-causing behavior," through resort to innovation and product improvement, then it should follow that the last twenty years of vigorous and costly enforcement should demonstrate its benefits in the safety record of general aviation. Once again, the facts do not support an argument that strict liability has enhanced safety.

Again, taking the last forty years of general aviation history, one can look at the safety record of general aviation for twenty years during which

22. Huber 1988, 160.

strict liability and product litigation had no real effect on the industry and twenty years in which they had an increasingly severe impact.

In 1950 there were 5.1 fatal accidents for each 100,000 hours flown by general aviation airplanes. By 1959 the rate of fatal accidents was 3.5, a reduction in ten years of 1.6 accidents per 100,000 hours of flight. By 1969 the general aviation accident rate had declined to 2.55 accidents per 100,000 hours flown, one-half of the accident rate twenty years earlier. By 1979 the accident rate was 1.63 fatal accidents per 100,000 flight hours, an improvement of 0.92 in the rate. In 1989 the accident rate was 1.4 accidents per 100,000 flight hours, an improvement in the last decade of only 0.23.[23]

The broken lines in figure 13-1 show the actual tracks of the accident rate for 1950–69 and 1970–89. The straight line shows the trends of the accident rate calculated separately for each twenty-year period by linear regression analysis.[24] The figure displays a sharp downward trend for the twenty years that were free of the influence of strict liability, in contrast to a significantly flatter downward trend in the accident rate over the twenty years after the intervention of strict liability and the litigation it has spawned.

These data indicate that strict liability has demonstrated no tendency to promote the safety of flight and, indeed, may have retarded it. The data obviously support Priest's conclusion that "data on deaths and injuries cast great doubt on the proposition that the liability crisis derives from an increase in the underlying accident rate."[25]

It is not surprising to find that strict liability litigation against manufacturers has not enhanced the general aviation safety record. It is generally conceded in the aviation community that pilot error is the overwhelming cause of airplane accidents. Various estimates can be obtained, ranging from 80 percent to near 100 percent caused by pilot error. As discussed earlier, of the pending claims and litigations analyzed by

23. GAMA 1989a, 26–27.
24. $y = a_1 x + a_0$, where

$$a_1 = \frac{\Sigma xy - \dfrac{\Sigma x \, \Sigma y}{n}}{\Sigma X^2 - \dfrac{(\Sigma X)^2}{n}}, \text{ and}$$

$$a_0 = \frac{\Sigma y}{n} - a_1 \frac{\Sigma x}{n}.$$

Note: n is the number of observations.
25. Priest 1988b, 203.

Figure 13-1. *Fatal Accident Rates for General Aviation, 1950–89*

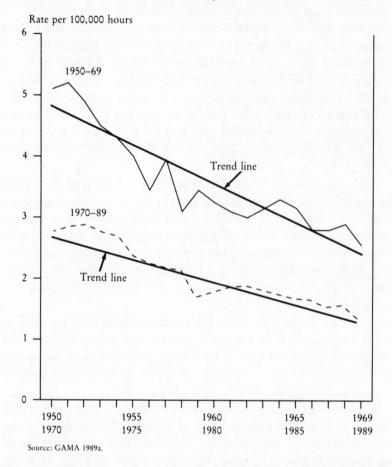

Rate per 100,000 hours

Source: GAMA 1989a.

Beech at the request of a congressional subcommittee, out of 140 accidents for which the probable cause could be determined by NTSB investigators, 118, or 84 percent, were attributed, entirely or in part, to pilot error. That is a biased sampling because it accounts for none of the accidents in which no claim or case was filed against the manufacturer, and those accidents contain a significantly higher proportion of findings of pilot error.

The manufacturer can exercise no control over pilots and weather and very little control over maintenance. Pilot error, combined with weather and maintenance, accounts for at least 98 percent of the probable cause findings. Since, as a practical matter, these causes are beyond the control of manufacturers, the concept embedded in strict liability (now under serious question in many places) that manufacturers can prevent or avoid accidents and injuries more effectively, and at less cost, cannot be valid for general aviation.

A more disturbing conclusion to be drawn from the flattening of the accident rate trend in the last decade is that, almost certainly, it results from an increase in the average age of the general aviation airplanes now in service, coupled with the tendency of strict liability to excuse the failure of owners and pilots to perform their moral and legal responsibilities for both maintenance and safe operation of their airplanes. If thirty- and forty-year-old airplanes continue to be retained in service because new airplanes with advanced technology are too expensive, while owners and pilots are systematically excused by the courts for their negligence and their misuse or abuse of airplanes and the privilege of flying, then obsolete, worn-out airplanes and irresponsible owners and pilots will eventually reverse the downward trend of the accident rate for general aviation.

The Pyramiding Consequences

Airframe manufacturers like Beech, Cessna, and Piper build the fuselage, wings, and empennage of the airplane and, of course, are the final assemblers and vendors of the finished aircraft. Engines are manufactured and supplied to the airframe builder by independent companies that specialize in making power plants. Propellers, radios, avionics, flight instruments, and fuel-handling systems are manufactured by independent companies that specialize in those items. All these products are liability-sensitive, primary components of the finished airplane. When placed in service, each component represents an additional product liability risk and annual risk-cost to each of the manufacturers, as well as to the builder of the finished airplane. Of course, the manufacturers of smaller subassemblies and parts add to the pyramiding of risk-costs.

Because lawyers who file aviation product liability cases frequently have no idea what product or design feature they will ultimately claim was the cause of the accident, manufacturers of most, if not all, of the liability-sensitive components are joined as defendants in product liability cases, and each must bear and pay the risks and costs of defense. The consequences of excessive exposure to product liability litigation, in terms of product costs and constraints on innovation and product improvement, thus affect not only the builder of the finished aircraft but also the manufacturers who supply essential components and parts.

A few examples will demonstrate the adverse deterring effect of strict liability litigation on innovation and product improvement at various levels within the industry.[26]

—A prime manufacturer of aviation ignition systems abandoned the development of a totally new electronic ignition system because of the potential product liability risk and expense of becoming the pioneer of an innovative product.

—Product liability exposure and insurance costs have caused the manufacturer of a "head-up display" for critical flight instruments to decline to market the product for use in light aircraft. The device, originally developed for military and large carrier aircraft, is optically focused to display critical flight instrument data—such as attitude, airspeed, and heading—suspended in space at eye level so the pilot does not have to look down from the windshield to the instrument panel during approach to landing or other flight maneuvers when visual reference to the ground or the horizon is critical.

—A leading U.S. manufacturer of shock-absorbing equipment has ceased to manufacture products for general aviation because of the product liability exposure.

—Various long-term suppliers of proven products to general aviation manufacturers, such as alternators, instrument clusters, switches, control cables, door seals, and fuel system components, have refused to continue selling their products to general aviation manufacturers because of the costs and problems of aviation product liability exposure.

These products either cannot be used in light airplanes or, if essential to the finished airplane, must be procured from a new and less-experienced manufacturing source. Substantial costs are always incurred in developing a new source for parts and components, and sometimes there are adverse effects on quality and reliability resulting from development and production start-up by a less-experienced manufacturer.

Not all new ideas and innovative product improvements originate within the engineering staff of an established and well-financed company. Many bright, ambitious, and technically competent young people have good ideas and new products in mind for aviation. But in the current product liability environment, no young engineer, technician, or businessman with a new and better idea could attract equity capital or borrow money to perfect, manufacture, or market a new or improved design, once prospective investors or bankers analyze the costs and risks of the product liability exposure

26. GAMA 1989b; procurement data, Beech, Cessna, and Piper.

for a new aviation product. The more innovative and advanced the design or proposal, the less likely is the chance that even an established manufacturer would assume the risk of developing and marketing the new product. That is the sad legacy the American tort litigation system has delivered to young engineers, scientists, and businessmen interested in aviation. It is also the legacy for all participants in general aviation—those who build airplanes, those who own airplanes, and those who fly in them.

Conclusion

Strict liability, as applied to general aviation, has proved a dismal failure, both as a reparations system and as a device to encourage innovation, product improvement, and aviation safety. The obvious remedy is to recognize that the concept of judging the product and imposing liability without fault is fundamentally unfair and unworkable (however appealing it may have been as legal theory), scrap the concept, and return to liability based on proof of negligence, at least for capital goods and products manufactured under strict governmental regulation. However, there is no real prospect that such radical change will come about. The intellectual appeal of strict liability in law schools and the halls of justice has left its mark. The plaintiffs' bar has become a powerful lobby, successful in convincing legislators, jurists, and the public that strict liability is an enlightened and necessary approach to the management of an industrialized society.

Other alternatives exist. The fundamental problem with strict liability—allowing courts and juries to judge the product rather than the conduct of persons who may have caused or contributed to causing an accident—is exacerbated by the unrestrained behavior of lawyers in and outside the courtroom. The encouragement of "bounty hunting" by lawyers through advertising and solicitation of cases, unregulated contingent fee and, more recently, contingent litigation expense contracts,[27] and the incessant demand for extravagant awards for emotional injury and punitive damages, with no standards, rules for proof, or limits of liability, are prime examples of abuse. Courts and judges have also abused the system: the creation or manipulation of insurance coverage through product liability litigation is wrong and destructive; redistribution of wealth and income should not be the prerogative of judges; courts ought to

---

27. American Bar Association, "Model Rules of Professional Conduct," rule 1.8(e), adopted August 2, 1983, approving contingent litigation expense agreements.

enforce laws and contracts as written—not as restructured to further socioeconomic objectives. As Priest observed: "If courts want to work seriously to create incentives for accident prevention, they must adopt standards that place liability on manufacturers only when it can be shown that there was some practical method for the manufacturer to have prevented the accident."[28] Unless reform is undertaken, the abuses now embedded in the tort liability system and the absence of continuity and uniformity in the substantive law of strict liability will make it impossible for courts to do what Priest suggests.

The distinction between products with a long service life and products that are consumable or have a short service life must be dealt with realistically through statutes of repose. A "one size fits all" rule will provide no solutions. Airplanes that have flown safely for twenty years or 5,000 hours and have traveled a million miles without crashing ought not to be deemed unreasonably dangerous or defective, but the same standard should not be applied to automobiles. What might be a reasonable useful life standard for automobiles could hardly be applied to farm implements or industrial machines.

The United States should not permit the tort liability system to seek out and punish those manufacturers whose products are so efficient, reliable, and durable that they remain in service for extended periods. If we continue to hold such manufacturers under siege, their products will be lost to the consumer or will have to be imported from behind international boundaries willing to protect industry from the abuses of the American tort liability system.

In time, perhaps many of the middle-ground alternatives for the procedural and substantive reform of strict liability will come about through legislation or judicial decision. If so, the serious question is whether real change, and an adequate measure of uniformity, will arrive before a large part of our industrial complement has been liquidated in our courtrooms, or so disabled that it cannot compete with foreign manufacturers and vendors.

28. Priest 1988b, 221.

References

Beech Aircraft and M&M Risk Management Services. 1977. *Seat Insurance Feasibility Study.* New York.

General Aviation Accident Liability Standards Act of 1987. 1987. Hearing before the Subcommittee on Aviation of the Senate Committee on Commerce, Science, and Transportation. Government Printing Office.

General Aviation Manufacturers Association (GAMA). 1989a. *General Aviation Statistical Databook.* Washington.

————. 1989b. "Product Liability Crisis Threatens General Aviation." Washington.

————. 1990a. "Average Aircraft Age—General Aviation Fleet." Washington.

————. 1990b. *General Aviation Balance of Trade.* Washington.

Huber, P. W. 1988. *Liability : The Legal Revolution and Its Consequences.* Basic Books.

Priest, G. L. 1988a. "Products Liability Law and the Accident Rate." In *Liability: Perspective and Policy,* edited by R. E. Litan and C. Winston, 184–222. Brookings.

————. 1988b. "Understanding the Liability Crisis." In *New Direction in Liability Law,* edited by W. Olson, 196–211. New York: Academy of Political Science.

Comments on Chapters
Twelve and Thirteen

John W. Williams, Jr.

THE CHAPTERS by Andrew Craig and Robert Martin are interesting and important. Both bring out new facts about the connection between liability trends and safety and innovation in the general aviation industry. I will consider each in turn.

Craig on Safety

The charge to Craig was to determine to what extent, if any, recent liability trends have affected safety in the aircraft sector. The author was asked to gather information from relevant technical sources and from interviews with knowledgeable people in that sector. He saw his main task to be to discover any interaction between liability and the accident record. He points out that general aviation accident rates gradually declined until 1979 and that from 1979 through 1986 the rate of both fatal and total accidents remained about the same. During the same period the number of lawsuits per year and the number of accidents stayed nearly constant, but the cost of product liability rose from $24 million in 1977 to $210 million in 1985.

In carrying out his analysis, Craig created an innovative general aviation system diagram that reflects the aircraft accident flow of events as they are related to regulation and liability and the subsequent effect on safety. He found that there appears to be little or no interaction between the liability block and the accident record: liability and regulation take separate routes that might change safety but that do not act on each other. The principal purpose of liability, he says, is to compensate the victims of aircraft accidents. He implies that with all the regulatory agencies (FAA, NTSB, and so on) closely scrutinizing the aviation industry, safety is possible without liability; however, it is reasonable to believe that the fear of liability might promote more concern for safety.

A shortcoming of the chapter is that Craig does not draw international comparisons on the effect of different liability standards and procedures on safety and innovation. Unfortunately, he was also unable to acquire data or even comments from the aviation underwriter companies he solicited. An explanation from them on why they use only the accident history of a particular airplane design to set rates would have been helpful.

In further work Craig should apply his model to commercial aviation as well. He makes a very important point: though it is generally agreed that there should be a federal law controlling litigation to suppress the total costs to general aviation, that will probably never happen because of the strength of the plaintiffs' bar, both in financial backing and political influence. The author's suggestion that product liability lawsuits are highly beneficial to lawyers for the plaintiff, but for few others, is probably correct.

Martin on Innovation

This is the most informative piece I have read on the issue of product liability and the aircraft industry. The author analyzes such data as the number of aircraft in the general aviation fleet, the amount of time flown by professional and private pilots in general aviation aircraft, the percentage of accidents among those two groups, fatal accidents by airplane category, and the number of aircraft built by the different manufacturers, and, most important, he presents a compelling case against the argument that strict liability has enhanced safety.

A major finding is that almost all aviation product liability cases have involved claims of defective design, but in over 80 percent of the cases the manufacturer was able to prove there was no defect or design error. Aircraft are designed and manufactured under such rigorous inspection systems that such an error is exceptional. Martin argues that product liability costs have forced the manufacturers of small airplanes out of business: the manufacturers have been obliged to divert extensive corporate resources to insurance premiums and to costs of defending their products rather than to research and engineering to build better airplanes. The industry suffered disaster when sales of shipments declined from a high of 17,800 units in 1978 to 1,143 units in 1988. Total employment by general aviation manufacturers declined over 65 percent—all because of product liability. The fact that aircraft manufacturers must protect themselves from lawsuits claiming airplane crashes were caused by "defects" has raised the cost of insurance per unit built to more than $70,000, making the cost of a small airplane almost prohibitive. Unless changes are made soon in product liability laws, there will be no small airplanes manufactured in this country.

I am quite familiar with this problem, since I am vice-president of Embry-Riddle Aeronautical University and know how difficult it now is to find small training aircraft. Flight training organizations must look overseas for new aircraft. To solve this problem, the author suggests statutes of repose and limits on punitive damage, some kind of relief from the expectation that aircraft parts last forever, and education of the public about the possible death of an industry.

One minor criticism of the chapter is that Martin does not mention that the liability laws were conceived and developed out of good intentions: that manufacturers are better able to bear losses than injured consumers, and that in many cases losses will be transferred to the buying public in the form of higher prices on products. Having society at large assume the cost of damages suffered by a few is an equitable concept in that it offers relief for those injured by defective products. Moreover, it was originally thought that eliminating the need to prove negligence in a tort action would make manufacturers and sellers more mindful of accident prevention; the system, however, did not work that way. As suggested by Martin and others, strict liability has tended to inhibit the development of new products.

An additional "other side of the coin" issue the author does not address is the fact that the threat of a huge punitive award might cause manufacturers to repair defects. At least, it makes sense to believe manufacturers would not ignore them.

On the whole, however, the chapter is excellent. And one of the most dramatic points it makes is this: of every $6 million paid by the manufacturers for defending the lawsuit and the settlement, only $1 million goes to the claimant! Is it any wonder the American Bar Association resists changes to the product liability laws?

Index

Abel, Richard, 6

Accident rates: connection between liability and, 11; decline in, 5; post-accident findings and, 14; publicity and litigation and, 12–13. *See also* Auto accidents; Aviation accidents

Accident Research Unit (Birmingham University), 192

Accutane (isotretinoin), 312, 313, 321

Adverse drug reaction (ADR), 301–02, 317, 350. *See also* Drugs

Adverse Drug Reaction Injury Relief and Research Promoting Fund Act (Japan), 350–51

Agent Orange, 408, 412–13, 439

Agricultural chemicals, 95–96, 98. *See also* Chemical industry

AIDS, 259; damages in baby's HIV infection case and, 280; vaccines and, 345

Air bags, 125, 126; crashworthiness and innovation and, 214–16; safety analysis and 156–60; safety regulation and, 204; side-impact, 217

Aircraft industry. *See* Aviation manufacturing

Aircraft Owners and Pilots Association, 461, 471

Aircraft and parts industry, 103–04, 105, 113

All-terrain vehicles (ATVs), 13; analysis by "60 minutes," 175; safety and, 168–80, 197

American Academy of Family Physicians, 262

American College of Nurse Midwives, 262

American Medical Association: defensive medical procedures and, 255; innovation and, 7; reforms and, 286

American Motors Corporation, 130; Jeep CJ and, 144, 145, 146–47, 148, 149, 150, 151, 152; Wrangler and, 154

American Trial Lawyers Association, 313

Antilock braking system, 24, 209

Asbestos, 11, 15, 47, 408, 416; bankruptcies over, 442; *Beshada* opinion and, 33, 412; compensation and, 404, 405; English statute concerning, 48; liability burden analysis and, 85; statute

of repose and, 44; warning labels and, 38

Ashford, Nicholas A., 4, 6, 15

Atiyah, P. S., 47, 61, 62

ATVs. *See* All-terrain vehicles

Audi, 124; unintended acceleration and, 210–11

Australia, 19, 61, 200, 346

Austria, 41, 353

Auto accidents: ATVs and, 169–71, 172, 173, 197; car death rate statistical model and, 186–87; crashworthiness and, 203, 206, 219; death of front-seat passengers and, 156; design defects and, 32; FARS and, 134; in Japan, 50; Jeep CJ and, 145–46, 147–48, 150, 151; park-to-reverse, 137, 138, 139, 142; Pinto defect investigation and, 132, 133, 134, 135, 136; probability of death and, 123; underclaiming and, 6. *See also* Accident rates

Auto industry: ATVs and, 13, 168–80; changing structure of, 207–08; liability case example and, 31; Mitsubishi design and, 37; product liability analysis and, 85, 89; product liability in Japan, 37, 50, 51; research and, 24; safety regulation development and, 202–07; specialty sports-car cases and, 48; warnings and, 38. *See also* Motor vehicle safety; *names of specific automobiles*

Automatic transmission, inadvertent movement and, 137–44

Aviation, 278; aircraft as long-lived products and, 14, 487; design and, 16, 17, 463, 465, 467–68, 468–71, 474, 481, 483, 489, 491, 492; disappearance of small aircraft and, 7, 17, 484; foreign manufacturers and, 19, 484; high-visibility accident case and, 465–67; in-flight structural failure and, 467–68; insurance and, 456, 459, 461, 482, 483–84, 496; internal block functioning and, 468–71, 473; Lloyd's and, 17–18; product liability and, 457, 458–62, 471, 473–74, 475, 476, 480–86, 487, 492–95, 501, 502; quick design changes and, 468–71, 474; regulation and, 458–62, 465, 466, 467, 468, 469, 471, 475, 476, 488, 489, 500; rise